ONE NATION UNDER GODS:

A HISTORY OF THE MORMON CHURCH

Also by Richard Abanes

End-Time Visions: The Road to Armageddon?

Cults, New Religious Movements, and Your Family

American Militias: Rebellion, Racism and Religion

Defending the Faith:
A Beginner's Guide to Cults and New Religions

Journey into the Light: Exploring Near-Death Experiences

ONE NATION UNDER GODS:

A HISTORY OF THE MORMON CHURCH

RICHARD ABANES

FOUR WALLS EIGHT WINDOWS
NEW YORK/LONDON

Published in the United States by
Four Walls Eight Windows
39 West 14th Street, room 503
New York, NY 10011
http://www.4w8w.com

More information on cults, the occult, and world religions may be obtained by
contacting Richard Abanes on the Internet through his religious information
website at http://www.abanes.com

Library of Congress Cataloging-in-Publication Data:

Abanes, Richard
   One nation under gods : a history of the Mormon Church / Richard Abanes
      p. cm.
   Includes bibliographical references and index.
   ISBN 1-56858-219-6
   1. Mormon Church—Controversial literature. I. Title.

BX8645 .A23 2002
289.3'09—dc21

                                        2001040430

Printed in the United States

10 9 8 7 6 5 4 3

to
my God, my Rock, my Fortress, my Deliverer;
my family, for their love;
my friends, for their support;
my teachers, for their instruction; and
my mentors, for their wise counsel.

Contents

Mormonism: The Early Years
(1805-1830)

Establishing God's Kingdom
(1831-1844)

Utah: Land of the Prophets
(1845-1901)

Going Mainstream
(1902-2002)

Acknowledgments

This volume could not have been produced without the support, encouragement, and faith of many people. Initial thanks must go to John Oakes of Four Walls Eight Windows, who believed in this project as far back as 1996 and was patient enough to wait for its delivery until I felt ready to tackle the subject. I also must express appreciation to my editor, Rob Grover, whose commitment to completing his tasks in a timely manner has enabled my book to be released on schedule.

I am equally indebted to Lane Thuet, Marian Bodine, and H. Michael Marquardt, who carefully read through the text of *One Nation Under Gods* and provided assistance in making corrections to the original manuscript. Their expertise in Mormonism proved invaluable to me. Another proof-reader of the unedited manuscript was my wife, Bri, whose keen eye for detail and knack for identifying extraneous material helped make this book a more concise and user-friendly volume. I am grateful for her crucial input.

Others who have made this book possible include: Sandra Tanner, who with her husband, Jerald, long ago published *Mormonism: Shadow or Reality?*, which was my introduction to Mormonism more than a dozen years ago; D. Michael Quinn, whose historical studies on Mormonism greatly contributed to my understanding of Mormonism's past; and my good friend, Jerry Bodine, an expert on Mormonism, who before passing away several years ago not only imparted a great deal of his knowledge about Mormonism to me, but also instilled in me the desire to keep exploring the history and beliefs of the Mormon church.

Finally, a word of recognition belongs to all the religion researchers, historians, and journalists before me who have written extensively on Mormonism since its founding in 1830. Their work on the origin, rise, and progress of Mormonism served as groundwork for this book, and their dedication to providing the Mormon church's true history has been nothing short of inspirational for me.

Acknowledgments

Foreword

I was raised in The Church of Jesus Christ of Latter-day Saints (LDS) and am a direct descendent of Brigham Young, the revered second president of the Mormon church, who in 1847 led his followers to Utah's Great Salt Lake Basin. As Young's great-great-granddaughter, I grew up thinking he was one of the finest men who had ever lived. I was trained to believe that the Mormon church and all the LDS prophets were chosen by God. I accepted as true everything I was told about Mormonism and its history by my family, friends and church leaders.

But as I grew older I began having doubts about some of the things I had been taught. Questions filled my mind: Is Mormonism really the only true religion? Why must Mormons keep their temple rituals secret? How can Mormon holy writings be true when they contradict each other? I also began to have misgivings about God's alleged approval of polygamy for Mormons, and found especially disturbing the subtle racism I saw permeating the spiritual belief system.

Such uncertainties only intensified when I attended the LDS Institute of Religion after graduating from high school. I thought I finally would get some answers. However, when I started asking questions during my classes, I was told to stop making inquiries because I was creating doubt in the minds of other students. This unexpected response from Mormon educators caused me to wonder even more about the origins of my faith.

Together with my husband, Jerald, who was also from a fifth generation Mormon family, I sought for answers, researching the history of Mormonism. This led to a completely different perspective of the religion. I reached the painful conclusion that my ancestor, Brigham Young, was not the holy prophet of God I thought he was. Our investigation of Mormon history revealed a dark side to both Brigham Young and Joseph Smith (Mormonism's founder). Their goal was to set up the political kingdom of God at any cost, even to the point of violence. Their practice of polygamy included marrying women who were already married as well as young teenagers.

We discovered, much to our surprise, that the Mormon hierarchy had from its inception been deliberately suppressing this information. Indeed, they had sought to cover-up and whitewash the true history of Mormonism. We also learned that Mormonism, although it uses Christian terminology, actually teaches numerous doctrines about God, man, Jesus, the Bible, salvation, and the afterlife which are radically different from Christianity.

It did not take long for Jerald and I to realize that the historical data we had gleaned from documents existing in church archives, libraries, and private collections needed to be made public. In response to our circulating this information throughout the Mormon community, high-ranking Mormon official LeGrand Richards warned us: "Don't start anything against this church." When I requested that my membership in the LDS church be terminated, my bishop responded by excommunicating me for "Apostasy, and engaging in activities contrary to the best interest of the church."

That was more than forty years ago, when few people were willing to inform the public of Mormonism's true origins and doctrines. Today, however, there are many individuals, like Richard Abanes, who have dedicated the time and energy to not only understand, but also explain, the complex and sometimes confusing history of Mormonism.

Richard Abanes succeeds in detailing not just the LDS church's quest for religious supremacy, but also its desire for economic and political dominance in order to pave the way for the Kingdom of God on Earth. Joseph Smith's occult practices, the creation of the *Book of Mormon*, the mysterious Danite assassins, Joseph Smith's murder, the Mormon move to Utah, blood atonement killings, polygamy, Mormon cover-ups and conspiracies—all are discussed in this volume. *One Nation Under Gods* is a well-written and absorbing book that is ideal for anyone wanting a concise, accurate, and easy-to-understand history of Mormonism from its inception to the present.

Sandra Tanner
great-great-grandchild of Brigham Young

About Mormon History

The tragic reality is that there have been occasions when [Mormon] Church leaders, teachers, and writers have not told the truth they knew about difficulties of the Mormon past, but have offered to the Saints instead a mixture of platitudes, half-truths, omissions, and plausible denials.

D. Michael Quinn[1]
Historian

THE HISTORY OF MORMONISM—The Church of Jesus Christ of Latter-day Saints (LDS)—can only be pieced together using a wide variety of historical sources. It is a complex tale that takes many surprising turns, has numerous divergent paths, and often becomes intertwined with other historical events of the same time period. Unfortunately, some of the least reliable reports on Mormon history, especially with regard to its earliest years, are those that have been produced by the LDS church.[2]

This has been confirmed by numerous historians and scholars, including D. Michael Quinn, one of the most well-known and respected experts in the field of Mormon studies.[3] In his 1981 address to a student history association at Brigham Young University, Quinn revealed that LDS leaders consistently urge historians to conceal "controversies and difficulties of the Mormon past" and to write church history "from a siege mentality to deny any information that enemies of the Church could possibly use to criticize the Church."[4]

According to Mormon scholar Allen Roberts, LDS leaders do indeed "attempt to control depictions of the Mormon past."[5] English professor John E. Hallwas of Western Illinois University and historian Roger D.

Launius agree with Quinn and Roberts, adding that "Mormon scholars too often write history that, if not blatantly, at least tacitly defends the faith." They further observe:

> Their work might be of a scholarly nature, but it strives to reinforce traditional Mormon conceptions about the church rather than to comprehend the full complexity of the past. . . . These historians do not mention Mormon intimidation, deception, repression, theft, and violence, or any other matters that might call into question the sacred nature of the Mormon experience. . . . [T]hey do not make any attempt to portray dissenters or non-Mormon critics of the church as anything but miscreants and troublemakers motivated by religious bigotry.[6]

In response to such criticisms, Mormon leaders have not sought to correct their attitudes, but rather, have resorted to punitive action and intimidation. Quinn, for example, for his written and vocal candor, was excommunicated from the Latter-day Saints church in September 1993. Roberts subsequently observed that Quinn "was not excommunicated because his history writing was inaccurate. He was cut off because his findings did not reinforce pictures the church has painted of its past."[7] Mormons Linda King Newell and Valeen Tippets Avery, co-authors of *Mormon Enigma: Emma Hale Smith*, were temporarily censored and banned from speaking at LDS churches.[8] Other individuals have endured similar treatment (see pp. 414–419).

It is beyond legitimate dispute that the Mormon church has for decades been painting for the general public a decidedly biased picture of the Latter-day Saint faith, especially with regard to the origins of the *Book of Mormon*. Fortunately, a more objective sketch of Mormonism's earliest years can be drawn using non-LDS witnesses, secular media articles, and private journals (Mormon and non-Mormon).

All of these sources will be used in this book to discover how Mormonism's founder—Joseph Smith—formed, controlled, and expanded his church, which today is one of the wealthiest and most influential religions in the world.

A Thread of Prophecy

You will see the constitution of the United States almost destroyed. It will hang like a thread. . . . A terrible revolution will take place in the land of America. . . . [T]he land will be left without a Supreme Government, . . . [Mormonism] will have gathered strength, sending out Elders to gather the honest in heart . . . to stand by the Constitution of the United States. . . . In these days . . . God will set up a Kingdom, never to be thrown down. . . . [T]he whole of America will be made the Zion of God.

Joseph Smith (May, 6, 1843)[1]

Founder, Mormonism

I've never seen it worse than this, where the Constitution literally is hanging by a thread.

Orrin Hatch (November 9, 1999)[2]

Republican Senator, Utah

LISTENERS OF KSL RADIO'S "The Doug Wright Show" were surprised on November 9, 1999 when Wright's guest, Republican Senator Orrin Hatch (a devout Mormon) quoted the infamous "White Horse" prophecy.[3] The prediction by Mormonism's founder, Joseph Smith, contains what has always been the Mormon American dream—i.e., the transformation of the U.S. government into a Mormon-ruled theocracy divinely ordained to "not only direct the political affairs of the Mormon community, but eventually those of the United States and ultimately the world."[4]

This lofty aspiration, which dates back to Mormonism's earliest years, continues to be a dominant element of the faith espoused by

Joseph Smith's followers. Mormon journalist and University of Utah spokesperson, Fred Esplin, candidly explains:

> Mormons believe they have a divine commission to prepare the world for Christ's millennial [i.e., 1000-year] reign in which they will serve as officers and administrators. The faithful Saint believes he is building the Kingdom of God. *This* is what motivates thirty-thousand full-time missionaries [60,000 as of 2002] to preach the gospel, and *this* is what keeps men in their eighties working at a pace that would pitch younger, less-motivated men into their graves.[5]

Non-Mormon pioneers of the early nineteenth century saw Smith's goal as a serious threat to the political stability and social harmony of America's western frontier, where Mormonism took shape. Early Mormons, on the other hand, viewed Joseph's prophetic words as simply a declaration of their spiritual destiny. The divergent opinions not only destroyed any hope of a mutually beneficial relationship between Mormons and their neighbors, but it quickly led to a series of violent conflicts. These ended only after Smith was murdered and his disciples fled to desolate Utah.

Life in the far west, however, only brought a new kind of anxiety to Mormons once they started butting heads with the U.S. government over the legitimacy of polygamy; an indispensable tenet of early Mormonism. Finally, leaders of the Mormon church (i.e., The Church of Jesus Christ of Latter-day Saints) were forced in 1890 to take the politically expedient route and discontinue their sacred practice of taking multiple wives. It was the only way the church would survive into the twentieth century.

This milestone decision initiated a Mormon public relations campaign of unprecedented proportions; one marked by covert doctrinal modifications, deceptive evangelism techniques, media manipulation, and historical revisionism. The successful outcome of these drastic measures has been neatly summarized by historian D. Michael Quinn, a renowned expert in Mormon studies:

Mormons convulsed the social and political order of four states. Mormon leaders fled lawsuits in New York in 1831 and in Ohio in 1837. They were embroiled in civil war twice—in Missouri in 1838 and again at the Mormon capital and second-largest city of Illinois during 1845 and 1846. Mormons then created a metropolis in the high desert of the Far West and launched a half century of conflict with the United States. In 1857 the U.S. president sent federal troops to invade the Mormon capital of Salt Lake City. Congress passed its first anti-Mormon law in 1862. In 1879 Mormonism was the cause for the U.S. Supreme Court's first limitation on the free expression of religion. In 1887 Congress declared Mormonism an organized rebellion, disincorporated the LDS church, and confiscated its assets. By 1890 Congress and the Supreme Court were prepared to deny civil rights to all members of the LDS church. In a stunning turnabout, a century later the LDS church had become the darling of the Republican White House and of such middle-class barometers as *The Reader's Digest*. . . . Mormonism has also altered the landscape of America, becoming the first or second largest religious denomination in nine western states and influencing politics and culture throughout the west . . . [and] has become a player in trade-offs and accommodations of national politics.[6]

Through it all Smith's doomsday predictions against America have continued to resonate in the statements of numerous Mormon leaders. Joseph's successor, Brigham Young, declared: "[W]hen the Constitution of the United States hangs, as it were, upon a single thread, they will have to call for the 'Mormon' Elders to save it from utter destruction."[7] High-ranking Mormon, George Q. Cannon, promised that someday "there would be no stable government outside of the Latter-day Saints; and that it is their destiny as a people, to uphold constitutional government upon this land."[8] Mormon church historian Preston Nibley said "the Prophet Joseph Smith did make the marvelous prediction that it is the destiny of the Latter-day Saints to some day save the Constitution of the United States."[9]

Obviously, when Senator Hatch mentioned the constitution hanging by a thread, he was merely echoing a standard Mormon belief. At the same time, however, his comment stirred long-forgotten memories in non-Mormons of an era when Mormonism existed as a "radical, immoral and un-American band of religious zealots with a charismatic leader—a nineteenth century People's Temple sect characterized by polygamy, theocracy and economic cooperation."[10] Matters were made even worse when Hatch refused to clarify his remark after being asked to do so. Moreover, he quoted Smith's prophecy soon after announcing his bid for the U.S. presidency, a political move consistent with the idea that one day Mormon leaders would rescue America from ruin.[11]

According to talk-show host Doug Wright, also a Mormon, Hatch clearly was "talking to his folks" in the audience. "It just caught me by surprise. It was worded carefully," said Wright. "I'm not sure he saw himself as the one who would fulfill the prophecy, but I thought it walked a fine line. It's such a well-recognized phrase."[12] Jan Shipps, professor emeritus of history and religious studies at Indiana University-Purdue University at Indianapolis observed: "His use of it might indicate a belief that God called him to run. But all it indicates for certain is that, in his understanding, the constitution is threatened."[13] Shipps also noted: "It's a very common belief that the Constitution will hang by a thread and the Church will save it."[14]

Although George W. Bush rather than Orrin Hatch won both the Republican nomination for president and the White House, Hatch's comment remains significant because it brings into focus the prevailing Mormon conviction that America will at some point crumble in the midst of severe political instability and internal strife. The Latter-day Saint (LDS) church will then use its financial wealth and political power base to rebuild the government and restore economic prosperity.

Such an action, it is believed, will precipitate the return of Jesus Christ, who in turn will establish a global theocracy headquartered in, of all places, Jackson County, Missouri.[15] Mormons thereafter will reign with Christ, and every American citizen, along with the rest of the world, will be forced to recognize Mormonism as the one true religion. Orson Hyde, an influential follower of Smith's, put it this way: "What the world calls 'Mormonism' will rule every nation. . . . God has decreed it, and his own right arm will accomplish it. This will make the heathen rage."[16] As for other governments and religions, according to Joseph Smith, they "must eventually be destroyed from the earth."[17]

In the opinion of some religion researchers, LDS leadership has not yet given up on its long-held dream of taking over the U.S. government (and the world) should the opportunity ever present itself. Consider a 1988 statement by the Mormon church's thirteenth president, Ezra Taft Benson, who also served as U.S. Secretary of Agriculture from 1953–1961:

> Joseph Smith predicted that the time would come when the Constitution would hang, as it were, by a thread, and at that time "this people will step forth and save it from the threatened destruction." . . . [Then] the Elders of Israel [i.e., LDS leaders], widely spread over the nation, will at that crucial time successfully rally the righteous of our country and provide the necessary balance of strength to save the institutions of constitutional government.[18]

The significance of Benson's remark becomes immediately apparent when one stops to consider the fact that an impressive number of Mormons have occupied, and continue to occupy, major posts throughout America's governmental system. The Ford, Reagan, and Bush administrations consistently placed Mormons in various key staff positions. President Nixon, too, called upon Mormon politicians. For example, Nixon's Secretary of Housing and Urban Development was George Romney, who clearly shared Ezra Taft Benson's view of Joseph Smith's prophecy. During a 1967 taped interview for *Dialogue: A Journal of Mormon Thought*, Romney, who at that time was Michigan's governor, made a very revealing statement when asked about the U.S. Constitution hanging by a thread:

> Anyone can look at the words of the Prophet Joseph Smith . . . Brigham Young and others. . . . I have always felt that they meant that sometime the question of whether we are going to proceed on the basis of the Constitution would arise and at this point government leaders who were Mormons would be involved in answering that question.[19]

In addition to serving in the Executive Branch, Latter-day Saints have performed in an equally impressive capacity throughout the government's Judicial Branch as court of appeals, district court, and state supreme court judges.[20] Additionally, many Mormons have played major roles in the upper echelons of the military, FBI and CIA, including Lieutenant General Brent Scowcroft, who was National Security Advisor under presidents Gerald Ford and George Bush.[21]

President Reagan seemed especially concerned with finding influential government positions for Mormons. This did not surprise political analysts since Reagan had met privately with eight of the twelve LDS apostles (top leaders) several years before winning the presidency.[22] These LDS officials not only threw their political weight behind Reagan, but encouraged fellow believers to do likewise, which resulted in more than 70% of Utah's ballots favoring Reagan (at that time 70% of Utah was Mormon).[23]

Three years later the Mormon community in Washington, D.C., had grown substantially. And numerous Latter-day Saints suddenly occupied key-level positions in the Reagan administration including the U.S. Treasurer (Angela M. Buchanan), Secretary of Education (Terrel H. Bell), and U.S. Solicitor General (Rex E. Lee). Even Washington columnist Jack Anderson, one of America's most well-known Mormons, noticed that the LDS church had garnered "disproportionate representation under Reagan."[24] President George Bush, like Reagan, also met behind closed doors with "Mormon Church leaders at the Latter-day Saints headquarters" (July 17, 1992).[25]

Mormons continue to fill high-level government positions.[26] In *The Mormon Corporate Empire*, researchers John Heinerman and Anson Shupe speculated that these and other LDS politicians could easily help the Mormon church achieve its various goals by appointing Mormons "to important jobs in the federal government."[27] A staff assistant to Senator Orrin Hatch, for example, has admitted that Hatch "makes at least one visit each year to the [Mormon] First Presidency, reporting on his activities in Washington. . . . On occasion Hatch has done simple favors for Church leaders and consulted with them on legislation."[28] Mormon political scientist J.D. Williams notes:

[T]he practice of Church officials making suggestions to public administrators and lawmakers (since the Church's early days in Missouri and
Illinois) has never died. . . . In the legislative area, relations between
Church officials and lawmakers are still very direct. Some are out-in-
the-open for the public to see; others are behind the scenes.[29]

Heinerman and Shupe further observe: "The U.S. government is, in
their view [i.e., LDS officials], only a temporary convenience until the
Church has established its millennial kingdom. First Amendment free-
doms are divinely provided as fertile soil to allow the seed of Joseph
Smith's revelations to take root and thrive. . . . This was the vision of early
Church leaders, and it is still commonly presented to Mormons today."[30]

In addition to making political preparations for the day when America's constitution hangs by a thread, the LDS church also seems dedicated to making financial preparations. *U.S. News* reported in November
2000 that "[b]y almost any measure, the Church of Jesus Christ of Latter-
day Saints is one of the world's richest" religious movements.[31] The estimated grand total of its business-related assets already has hit the $30
billion mark.[32] In this figure one may include $6 billion in supplemen-
tary income, approximately $5 billion of which is derived from the finan-
cial gifts of church members.

These estimated figures suggest that if the LDS church were a U.S.
corporation, by revenues it would rank 243rd on the *Fortune 500* list,
hovering somewhere near Paine Webber and Union Carbide, and
roughly twice the size of *Reader's Digest*.[33] Such a standing is far beyond
any other religious body of a similar global membership (approximately
11 million). It also is noteworthy that the Mormon church is one of America's largest landowners with property totaling about one million acres
(roughly the size of Delaware). These real estate holdings are valued
well into the billions.[34] Land owned by the LDS church also extends
overseas. In Britain, for instance, as of July 2001, the Mormon church
was *the* largest foreign landowner, and was using "the income from its
vast holdings of prime farmland to spread its teaching in the Third
World."[35] To acquire their 15,000 acres of prime British farmland, the
LDS church has spent $42 million in the last six years.[36]

In short, "[t]he Mormon church wields more economic power more effectively than any other organized religion in the world."[37] Exactly how wealthy is Mormonism? No one outside the church's hierarchy knows because LDS church financial records are held in strict secrecy. News reporter Richard Ostling notes in *Mormon America* (1999) that LDS officials "refuse to divulge routine information that other religions are happy to provide over the phone" and they are forever playing "a cat-and-mouse game with various journalists who have attempted over the years to unveil the vast empire of corporate Mormonism."[38]

The Mormon notion that Latter-day Saints will one day enjoy global domination is predicated, in part, on the LDS belief that Mormons are morally, ethically, and spiritually superior to non-Mormons. Brigham Young remarked: "[T]his people are the best people that ever lived upon the earth."[39] Joseph Fielding Smith, the LDS church's tenth president, wrote that Mormons are "in many ways superior to any other people."[40] This attitude, which also permeated early Mormonism, was actually one of the factors that created problems for Latter-day Saints in the nineteenth century, as historian Dan Erickson has noted: "[I]t was the Saints' self-righteous and implied superiority that raised hatred among non-Mormons."[41]

Even more germane to Mormon end-time beliefs is the LDS doctrine of eternal progression, which teaches that faithful followers of Joseph Smith may eventually become gods. LDS apostle, Bruce McConkie, stated: "That exaltation which the saints of all ages have so devoutly sought is *godhood* itself."[42] This doctrine again originated with Joseph, who proclaimed: "[Y]ou have got to learn how to be Gods yourselves . . . the same as all Gods have done before you."[43] Mormonism's twelfth president, Spencer W. Kimball, similarly preached: "Brethren, 225,000 of you are here. . . . I suppose 225,000 of you may become gods. There seems to be plenty of space out there in the universe."[44]

To these gods in the making, America's day of doom has always been just around the proverbial corner, right along with the realization of their grandiose vision. Celebrated Mormon historian B.H. Roberts put the Latter-day Saint vision of America's future in even starker terms, saying: "[T]he kingdom of God . . . is to be a political institution that shall hold sway over all the earth; to which all other governments will be sub-ordinate and by which they will be dominated."[45] LDS author Duane S. Crowther boldly asserted as much in his 1979 *Prophetic Warnings to Modern America*:

> [T]here will be a complete change of government. Washington, D.C. will cease to be the capital. The present national bureaucracy will have its end. The internal conflict will sweep away the current system of governments and will pave the way for the political kingdom of God and the millennial kingdom through which Jesus Christ will rule and reign. . . . A new government will be established among the saints and that political Kingdom of God will espouse and uphold the principles of Constitutional government.[46]

Who are the Mormons and what do they believe? How did Mormonism begin? Is Mormonism just another Christian denomination seeking the world's betterment, as it claims, or is it an entirely different kind of theological institution? Was Joseph Smith a prophet? *One Nation Under Gods: A History of the Mormon Church* answers these and other questions associated with the origin, rise, and progress of Mormonism in America from its earliest beginnings as a nineteenth century "cult" to its current image as a conservative Christian denomination. *One Nation Under Gods* also documents several of the more fascinating, and rarely discussed, events that shaped Mormonism.

The history of The Church of Jesus Christ of Latter-day Saints is an enthralling saga laced with all the elements of an action-packed Hollywood movie: sex, violence, greed, murder, deceit, betrayal, and spirituality. What remains to be seen is if the story's conclusion will be written as Joseph Smith long ago prophesied: "[T]his nation will be on the very verge of crumbling to pieces and tumbling to the ground and when the Constitution is upon the brink of ruin this people [i.e., the Mormons] will be the staff upon which the nation shall lean."[47]

PART ONE

Mormonism: The Early Years (1805–1830)

THE

BOOK OF MORMON:

AN ACCOUNT WRITTEN BY THE HAND OF MOR-MON, UPON PLATES TAKEN FROM THE PLATES OF NEPHI.

Wherefore it is an abridgment of the Record of the People of Nephi; and also of the Lamanites; written to the Lamanites, which are a remnant of the House of Israel; and also to Jew and Gentile; written by way of commandment, and also by the spirit of Prophesy and of Revelation. Written, and sealed up. and hid up unto the LORD, that they might not be destroyed; to come forth by the gift and power of GOD. unto the interpretation thereof; sealed by the hand of Moroni. and hid up unto the LORD, to come forth in due time by the way of Gentile; the interpretation thereof by the gift of GOD; an abridgment taken from the Book of Ether.

Also, which is a Record of the People of Jared, which were scattered at the time the LORD confounded the language of the people when they were building a tower to get to Heaven; which is to shew unto the remnant of the House of Israel how great things the LORD hath done for their fathers; and that they may know the covenants of the LORD, that they are not cast off forever; and also to the convincing of the Jew and Gentile that JESUS is the CHRIST, the ETERNAL GOD, manifesting Himself unto all nations. And now if there be fault, it be the mistake of men; wherefore condemn not the things of GOD, that ye may be found spotless at the judgment seat of CHRIST.

BY JOSEPH SMITH, JUNIOR,
AUTHOR AND PROPRIETOR.

PALMYRA:
PRINTED BY E. B. GRANDIN, FOR THE AUTHOR.

1830.

Title page from the first edition of the *Book of Mormon*, published the same year Joseph Smith officially organized his Mormon religion as the "Church of Christ" (later changed to "The Church of Jesus Christ of Latter-day Saints"). Notice Smith's original claim to have been the book's "Author." The title page in current editions of the *Book of Mormon* reads: "Translated by Joseph Smith."

ONE

Vagabond Visionaries

Joseph Smith senior, with a family consisting of a wife and eight children, including Joe the Prophet, . . . were an illiterate, shiftless, indolent tribe, without any visible means of a respectable livelihood, nor was it apparent that they earned an honest living—young Joe being the laziest of the crew. The boys, who were frequently seen lounging about the stores and shops in the village, were distinguished only for their vagabondish appearance and loaferly habits. The female portion of the household were pretty much ditto.

Pomeroy Tucker (1802-1870)[1]
Smith family acquaintance

ACCORDING TO JOSEPH FIELDING SMITH, tenth president of the LDS church, Mormonism "must stand or fall on the story of Joseph Smith. He was either a prophet of God, divinely called, properly appointed and commissioned, or he was one of the biggest frauds this world has ever seen."[2] Such an either-or proposition suggests that any study of Mormonism must begin with Joseph Smith, founder of the Latter-day Saint faith. In 1844, however, Joseph claimed "[n]o man knows my history." He added that even he himself would never undertake the task of telling such an amazing narrative, admitting: "I don't blame any one for not believing my history. If I had not experienced what I have, I would not have believed it myself."[3]

Contrary to Joseph's assertion, historians, religion scholars, and other interested parties have for many years known a great deal about the Mormon prophet, his life, family, experiences, and environment. He was born, for instance, in Sharon, Vermont, in 1805, the same year Lewis and Clark reached the Pacific Ocean after trekking across the enormous Louisiana Purchase territory. Thomas Jefferson held the U.S. presidency, westward expansion had begun, and abolition was emerging as a highly significant topic of concern. More importantly to Mormonism, the "Second Great Awakening" was igniting intense religious fervor from New England to as far south as Kentucky.

Unlike the "First Great Awakening" (1730–1742), which stressed the Calvinist doctrine of "divine election," the wave of spiritual excitement that spread across America during the 1800s emphasized the role played by one's own free will in choosing God's gift of salvation (i.e., being born-again).[4] Consequently, itinerate evangelists touring the countryside initiated "new measures" for preaching the Christian message during revival meetings; measures designed to motivate listeners toward a definitive and immediate acceptance of Jesus as their Lord and Savior:

- revival "camp meetings" lasting several days (sometimes weeks);
- extended times of prayer;
- verbal pressure from the pulpit for listeners to make on-the-spot conversions to God;
- the encouragement of lay participation in leadership activities; and
- utilization of the "anxious bench," an area just below the preacher's pulpit where unbelievers prayed and mourned over their sinful condition, and where they were "exhorted to change."[5]

These novel practices and the emotional responses they elicited drew an unprecedented number of lost souls into Christendom's fold. In fact, conversions *en masse* were commonplace. Many revivals were so spiritually arousing that scores of zealous attendees would succumb to fits of ecstatic utterance (i.e., speaking in tongues), wild episodes of "jerking" (i.e., rhythmic back and forth convulsing), and full-blown fainting spells (i.e., getting slain in the spirit).

At one Fairfax County, Virginia, camp meeting in 1809, Methodist organizers went so far as to erect "a boarded enclosure filled with straw, into which the converted were thrown that they might kick about without injuring themselves."[6] Such enthusiasm made for powerful and dramatic scenes. Consider the following account of a Kentucky camp meeting (c. 1810):

> The vast sea of human beings seemed to be agitated as if by a storm. I counted seven ministers, all preaching at one time, some on stumps, others on wagons . . . no sex, nor color, class, nor description, were exempted from the pervading influence of the spirit; even from the age of 8 months to 60 years . . . some of the people were singing, other praying, some crying for mercy . . . some struck with terror . . . trembling, weeping and crying out . . . fainting and swooning away . . . others surrounding them with melodious song. A peculiar sensation came over me. My heart beat tumultuously, my knees trembled, my lips quivered, and I felt as though I must fall to the ground.[7]

Although the War of 1812 caused a brief lull in the country's religious zeal, the post-war years found Americans resuming their quest for spiritual fulfillment—perhaps more energetically than ever before. The period gave rise to some of history's most gifted preachers including Charles Finney (1792–1875) and Alexander Campbell (1788–1866). In addition to a surge in mainstream religious activity (e.g., Presbyterians, Methodists, Baptists), the 1800s also saw "an astonishing degree of religious experimentation and innovation."[8] Dozens of new spiritual movements flourished, including several utopian communities that espoused a wide variety of political and social ideals.

Many of these new cooperatives offered radically different/experimental notions of sexuality and marriage. Consider the Shakers, for example, who experienced spiritual revival from 1837–1847.[9] As early as 1826 these disciples of Ann Lee (who saw herself as a reincarnated Christ) had built community halls near Joseph's hometown. They believed in a total separation of the sexes and celibacy. The Oneida commune, however, based in New York, advocated sexual freedom and practiced "complex marriage" wherein every member was married to each other.[10] This sect also flourished not far from where Joseph grew up. And then there was Isaac Bullard, who wore only a bearskin girdle, promoted

Joseph Smith, Jr. (courtesy of Utah State Historical Society).

communism, taught free love, and regarded washing as a sin. In 1817 his followers gathered in Woodstock, Vermont—only "half a dozen hills away from the old Smith farm."[11]

It is not surprising that the atmosphere of social change and religious intensity that produced the Shakers and the Oneida Community would give birth to Mormonism. Unexpected, however, has been the Mormon church's prosperous survival into the twenty-first century. Odd, too, has been the public's recent perceptions of Mormonism as just another Christian denomination (see Chapter Seventeen), when the Latter-day Saint faith originally was seen by society in general as little more than a dangerous manifestation of one man's lust for power, wealth, and illicit sex.

To most of his contemporaries, Joseph Smith was nothing but a charlatan from a family of illiterate wanderers; a shiftless trouble-maker—albeit a charismatic and imaginative one—with a penchant for superstitions, storytelling, and decision-making based on the occult traditions of nineteenth century rural folk magic. Nathaniel Lewis, for instance, who was the uncle of Smith's wife, Emma, made a telling comment in 1834: "Joseph . . . is not a man of truth and veracity; . . . his general character in this part of the country, is that of an impostor, hypocrite and liar."[12]

Others, however, saw a different side to Smith; one that made him very likable. To these individuals the young would-be prophet was charming, full of humor, and intelligent.[13] He also was a natural speaker. According to Orasmus Turner, Smith was an excellent "exhorter" at Methodist camp meetings.[14] This term, "exhorter," refers to a position created by preachers for youths with public speaking talent. It allowed them to hone their skills in front of a live audience. The experience provided invaluable practice for Smith.

Accentuating Joseph's personality was his physical appearance. At seventeen he was "lank and powerful, six feet tall and moderately handsome. His hair, turning from tow color to light brown, swept back luxuriantly from his forehead. Even at this age there was something compelling in his bearing, and older men listened to his stories half-doubting, half-respectful."[15] Smith's most powerful resource, however, was his clever and facile mind, as one–time follower, C.G. Webb, revealed during an enlightening 1886 interview:

> [Joseph] acquired knowledge very rapidly, and learned with special facility all the tricks of the scoundrels who worked in his company. . . . He learned by heart a number of Latin, Greek and French commonplace phrases, to use them in his speeches and sermons. . . . Joseph kept a learned Jew in his house for a long time for the purpose of studying Hebrew with him. . . . I taught him the first rules of English Grammar in Kirtland in 1834. He learned rapidly.[16]

Despite Joseph's lack of a formal education and his complete disinterest in the more mundane tasks of life (e.g., manual labor), it cannot be denied that he possessed a sharp mind, an indomitable spirit, and a keen wit. He had a highly active imagination and by all accounts was a natural public speaker. Even his most ardent critics have acknowledged his "inventive and fertile genius."[17] It is no wonder that he has been described as "one of the most controversial and enigmatic figures ever to appear in American history."[18]

Smith's story, although not as unbelievable as he suggested in 1844, certainly is one of the most intriguing and colorful in the annals of religious leaders. And his legacy, The Church of Jesus Christ of Latter-day Saints, testifies to his powers of persuasion, political savvy, and religious zeal. Consequently, the story of Mormonism will likely remain a fascinating saga born out of the cultural events that shook America at the turn of the nineteenth century. It all began with an obscure family from New England.

THE SMITHS OF VERMONT

The parents of Joseph Smith, Jr.—Lucy Mack (1775–1856) and Joseph Smith Sr. (1771–1840)—both came from well-established New England families that enjoyed some degree of social status. The Smith line included state and local officials who had acquired a substantial amount of land. The Macks, too, had achieved financial stability and commanded a modest measure of respectability thanks to several professional clergymen in the family.[19] So when Joseph and Lucy married on January 24, 1796, both families were able to help the young couple get started: Joseph received a farm from his father and Lucy's brother gave her $1,000.[20] Their future together as New England farmers could not have held greater promise. But a completely different fate awaited them:

> [O]ne financial disaster followed another. The farm proved barren and rocky; an unscrupulous partner in a ginseng speculation absconded with their substantial investment. Before many years had passed, the Smiths were living an impoverished, nomadic life, endlessly searching for the fresh start that would bring them financial security.[21]

By the time Joseph, Jr. was born on December 23, 1805, the Smith family had grown by four children (including Joseph) and migrated from Tunbridge, Vermont, to nearby Sharon. This was only one of many moves back and forth across parts of Vermont, New Hampshire, and New York. Finally, in 1816, after four more children had been born into the family, all of them settled in Palmyra, New York.[22] Like many of those who moved just north of the Finger Lakes, the Smiths hoped to find better financial times via the thriving commerce flowing from the construction of the new Erie Canal, which would eventually be completed in 1825.

The Smiths unfortunately arrived long after the high-quality tracts

Joseph Smith, Sr. and Lucy Mack Smith, the parents of Mormonism's founder, Joseph Smith, Jr. (Joseph Smith, Sr., courtesy of Utah State Historical Society; Lucy Mack Smith, from Josiah F. Gibbs, *Lights and Shadows of Mormonism,* 1909).

of land had been sold. So to make the best of a very difficult situation, Lucy opened up a "cake and beer shop" where she sold gingerbread, root beer, and oilcloth accessories.[23] Joseph, Sr. hired himself out as a manual laborer until he was able to sign a note for a hundred acres of mediocre terrain near Manchester (a township located just a few miles south of Palmyra).

But even this did not enable the family to make a consistent livelihood from farming. They ended up relying on the common practice of tapping sugar maples for sap to make sugar and syrup. "They made seven thousand pounds in one season and won the fifty-dollar bounty for top production in the county."[24] Such a small accomplishment, however, hardly alleviated their never-ending struggle against the haunting specter of utter destitution.

As a result, Joseph, Jr. received virtually no formal education. He and his siblings, as their age permitted, were forced to join the daily grind of menial labor: building fences, harvesting crops, and assorted odd jobs around town. These hardships continued for many years, until the Smiths finally gave up on finding deliverance from their poverty by any means that might be termed legitimate employment. They turned instead to borrowing, fast-talking, and "money-digging" through occult divination (see p. 28).

Much of the foregoing information appeared in *Mormonism Unvailed* (1834) by E.D. Howe (b. 1798), a book in which nearly one hundred persons acquainted with the Smiths gave statements to Howe's investigator, Philastus Hurlbut. None of the affidavits were favorable toward the family. Joseph Capron, for instance, said "the whole family of Smiths, were notorious for indolence, foolery, and falsehood. Their great object appeared to be, to live without work."[25]

Another neighbor, Roswell Nichols, remembered that "for breach of contracts, the non-payment of debts and borrowed money, and for duplicity with their neighbors, the [Smith] family was notorious."[26] Nichols also recalled that Joseph, Sr. once confessed it was "sometimes necessary for him to tell an honest lie, in order to live."[27] A third individual named Parley Chase (b. 1806) related the following:

> I was acquainted with the family of Joseph Smith, Sen., both before and since they became Mormons, and feel free to state that not one of the male members of the Smith family were entitled to any credit, whatsoever. They were lazy, intemperate and worthless men, very much addicted to lying. In this they frequently boasted of their skill. Digging for money was their principal employment. . . . Joseph Smith Jr. to my knowledge, bore the reputation among his neighbors of being a liar. The foregoing can be corroborated by all his former neighbors.[28]

An additional statement, signed by fifty-one citizens of Palmyra, reads equally as direct:

> We, the undersigned, have been acquainted with the Smith family, for a number of years, while they resided near this place, and we have no hesitation in saying, that we consider them destitute of that moral character, which ought to entitle them to the confidence of any community. They were particularly famous for visionary projects, spent much of their time in digging for money which they pretended was hid in the earth; and to this day, large excavations may be seen in the earth, not far from their residence, where they used to spend their time digging for

hidden treasures. Joseph Smith, Senior, and his son Joseph, were in particular considered entirely destitute of *moral character and addicted to vicious habits.*[29]

For obvious reasons, Mormons have attempted to discredit such statements. Richard L. Anderson, in a 1970 article for *Brigham Young University Studies,* argued that Hurlbut, because he was an apostate Mormon, completely fabricated some of the *Mormonism Unvailed* statements, while inserting into others his own disparaging words.[30] LDS author Milton V. Backman said Hurlbut's affidavits were significant only as evidence of how some suspicious critics will stoop to "manufacturing a variety of preposterous myths" in reaction to Joseph's testimony.[31] But a careful examination of Howe's documents by unbiased scholars and reputable historians has upheld their accuracy. In *Joseph Smith's New York Reputation Reexamined,* nineteenth century religion specialist Rodger I. Anderson lists numerous reasons to trust Howe's published accounts:

> [M]ost scholars outside of Mormonism have tended to accept the non-Mormon side of the issue. The number of witnesses, the unanimity of their testimony, the failure to impeach even a single witness, and the occasional candid reminiscence by Martin Harris, Brigham Young, Joseph Smith, Lucy Mack Smith . . . or other early Mormons have contributed to the conclusion that Hurlbut and his followers were probably reliable reporters.[32]

German historian Eduard Meyer (1855–1930), a non-religious man who was neither hostile nor partial to Mormonism, likewise believed that Hurlbut's reports gave the opinion of Smith's neighbors "in their true, essential form."[33] These same neighbors also knew a great deal about Joseph's storytelling ability, which would play an indispensable role in the founding of his new religion.

INTO THE WOODS

The most important event in Mormon history is undoubtedly Joseph Smith's "First Vision." According to official LDS sources, this event happened in 1820 when Smith was only fourteen years old. A religious revival allegedly was taking place in the Palmyra-Manchester area, which in turn caused the various Christian denominations to compete for members. This left Joseph in a quandary, asking himself: "[W]hat is to be done? Who of all these parties are right; or, are they all wrong together? If any one of them be right, which is it, and how shall I know it?"[34]

While still pondering his spiritual course, as the story goes, Joseph happened upon a startling Bible passage that spoke directly to his situation: "If any of you lack wisdom, let him ask of God, that giveth to all men liberally, and updraideth not; and it shall be given him" (James 1:5). Joseph concluded: "I must either remain in darkness and confusion, or else I must do as James directs, that is, ask of God."[35] So on the morning of a clear day, early in the spring of 1820, Joseph supposedly went into a secluded grove to pray. The official Mormon version of what happened next is nothing less than astonishing:

> I saw a pillar of light exactly over my head, above the brightness of the sun, which descended gradually until it fell, upon me. . . . When the light rested upon me I saw two personages, whose brightness and glory defy all description, standing above me in the air. One of them spake unto me, calling me by name, and said—pointing to the other—"THIS IS MY BELOVED SON, HEAR HIM.". . . I asked the personages who stood above me in the light, which of all the sects was right—and which I should join. I was answered that I must join none of them, for they were all wrong, and the personage who addressed me said that all their creeds were an abomination in His sight: that those professors were all corrupt; that "they draw near to me with their lips, but their hearts are far from me; they teach for doctrines the commandments of men: having a form of godliness, but they deny the power thereof." He again forbade me to join with any of them: and many other things did he say unto me, which I cannot write at this time.[36]

According to LDS historians, the religious leaders and other towns-folk refused to believe Joseph when he tried to tell them about his experience. They even subjected him to great persecution as he became the talk of Palmyra. And although he was just a boy, men of high standing

Late 19th century engraving of Joseph Smith's First Vision (from T.B.H. Stenhouse, *The Rocky Mountain Saints*, 1873). For twenty-five years Stenhouse was a Mormon Elder and missionary. He left Mormonism to became one of its most ardent critics.

actually went so far as to incite the public against him until all the sects
united to oppose him, as he later reflected:

> [H]ow very strange it was that an obscure boy, of a little over fourteen
> years of age, and one, too, who was doomed to the necessity of
> obtaining a scanty maintenance by his daily labor, should be thought
> a character of sufficient importance to attract the attention of the
> great ones of the most popular sects of the day, and in a manner to
> create in them a spirit of the most bitter persecution and reviling. But
> strange or not, so it was, and it was often the cause of great sorrow
> to myself.[37]

This *official* version of Smith's First Vision and its aftermath
appeared in 1842 as installment articles published by the Mormon periodical *Times and Seasons*.[38] David O. McKay, the ninth president of the
LDS church, declared it to be the very foundation of Mormonism.[39] Mormonism's current president, Gordon B. Hinckley (b. 1910), echoed
McKay's sentiment in 1998:

> Our entire case as members of The Church of Jesus Christ of Latter-day
> Saints rests on the validity of this glorious First Vision. . . . Nothing on
> which we base our doctrine, nothing we teach, nothing we live by is of
> greater importance than this initial declaration.[40]

Mormon apostle John A. Widtsoe also emphasized the vital nature of
Smith's reportedly supernatural episode, saying: "The First Vision of
1820 is of first importance in the history of Joseph Smith. Upon its reality rest the truth and value of his subsequent work."[41]

VARIOUS VISION VERSIONS

Although Smith's First Vision is a requisite part of Mormonism's past,
historical documents reveal that it probably never occurred. Details concerning the episode not only evolved over time, but were contradictory
during the religion's earliest years.[42] Oddly, today's currently accepted

official version of the experience did not even exist when Smith organized his church in 1830. James B. Allen, assistant historian for the LDS church, frankly admitted as much in a 1966 article:

> According to Joseph Smith, he told the story of the vision immediately after it happened in the early spring of 1820. . . . There is little if any evidence, however, that by the early 1830's Joseph Smith was telling the story in public. . . . [N]one of the available contemporary writings about Joseph Smith in the 1830's, none of the publications of the Church in that decade, and no contemporary journal or correspondence yet discovered mentions the story of the first vision. . . . [T]he general church membership did not receive information about the first vision until the 1840's. . . . [But] the story of Joseph Smith's first vision was not given general circulation in the 1830's. Neither Mormon nor non-Mormon publications made reference to it, and it is evident that the general membership of the Church knew little, if anything, about it.[43]

The entire premise on which the vision is based (i.e., an 1820 religious revival) disagrees with denominational membership records and newspaper articles from Smith's locality that show no revival occurring in 1820 in Palmyra-Manchester, New York.[44] A revival, however, did affect the region in 1824, which may be the event Smith later incorporated into his story when fashioning it sometime after 1832, the date of the earliest written (but unpublished) version of the First Vision.[45]

This 1832 account, written in Smith's own hand, is quite unlike the official version presented today by the LDS church. It says, for example, that Smith went into the grove to pray when fifteen years old (not fourteen). Moreover, the phrase "This is my beloved Son, hear him" is missing entirely, as is any mention of seeing God the Father (or even a second personage)—i.e., Smith only saw Jesus. Moreover, the main message of the encounter was that Joseph's sins had been forgiven, not that all of the church's were wrong. In fact, the information about God condemning Christian churches as corrupt is nowhere to be found. Instead, the 1832 version says Smith discovered the falsity of Christendom through his own personal Bible studies that began at the age of twelve. Subsequent early accounts of Smith's First Vision (c. 1832–1844) are equally dissimilar to Mormonism's current version (see Tables 1.1 and 1.2).[46]

FIRST VISION VERSION	Date Location	Smith's Age	A Revival?	Personages Appearing	Corrupt Churches Information	Primary Messages
1832[47] by Joseph Smith (Smith's Handwriting) UNPUBLISHED	No Date Specified | No Location Specified	"in the 16th year of my age" (i.e., 15-yrs.-old)	No Revival Mentioned	"the Lord" (i.e., Jesus Christ)	Smith decided for himself that all churches were corrupt and that they all believed incorrect doctrines.	"thy sins are forgiven thee"
Nov. 9,1835[48] by Joseph Smith (Warren Parrish, scribe) UNPUBLISHED	No Date Specified | "silent grove"	"about 14 years old"	No Revival Mentioned	Two unidentified personages and "many angels"	No mention is made of any message received through the vision about all churches being corrupt.	"thy sins are forgiven thee" & Jesus is the "son of God"
Nov.14,1835[49] by Joseph Smith (Warren Parrish, scribe) UNPUBLISHED	No Date Specified | No Location Specified	"about 14 years old"	No Revival Mentioned	"visitation of Angels"	No mention is made of any message received through the vision about all churches being corrupt.	No Messages Specified
Sept. 1840[50] by Orson Pratt (Mormon Apostle) FIRST PUBLISHED VERSION	No Date Specified | "a secret place, in a grove"	"about 14 years old"	No Revival Mentioned	Two unidentified "glorious personages, who exactly resembled each other in their features"	Smith is told by the personages he saw that all churches are believing "incorrect doctrines" and that God acknowledges "none of them."	"his sins were forgiven" Churches In Error Message (ADDED)
June 1841[51] by Orson Hyde (Mormon Apostle) Published in 1842 GERMAN EDITION	No Date Specified | "a small grove of trees"	"his fifteenth year"	No Revival Mentioned	Two unidentified "glorious heavenly personages . . . resembling each other exactly in features"	Smith decided for himself that all churches were corrupt and that they believed incorrect doctrines, and that he lost all hope of finding any sect teaching "unadulterated truth."	Sins Forgiven Message (DELETED) Churches In Error Message (ADDED)

Table 1.1 (Earliest five versions of Smith's First Vision)

Not until the 1870s–80s (half a century after Smith's death) did LDS leaders begin to consistently preach that Smith had seen Jesus and God the Father. Even then, confusion reigned among Mormons, with various church officials contradicting themselves and each other over what happened to Smith in the sacred grove. Mormon leader Orson Pratt, for instance, during a public lecture about Smith's vision (c. 1837/39), said that the two personages "declared themselves to be angels."[52] As late as 1888, LDS church historian, Andrew Jenson, still held to this understanding of the First Vision. In *The Historical Record* he explained, "The angel again forbade Joseph to join any of these churches." Jenson then quoted Smith's *History of the Church* narrative, adding the clarifying word "angel" as follows: "Many other things did he (the angel) say unto me which I cannot write at this time."[53]

FIRST VISION VERSION	Date Location	Smith's Age	A Revival?	Personages Appearing	Corrupt Churches Information	Primary Messages
mid-1842[54] (Times and Seasons) (History of the Church)	early spring 1820 | "the woods"	"a little over 14 years of age"	Religious Revival (ADDED)	Two personages appear and one of them says, "This is my beloved Son, hear him"	Smith is told by the personages that all sects are corrupt. In this account, Smith contradicts his 1832 version by stating, "at this time it had never entered my heart that all were wrong."	Sins Forgiven Message (DELETED) Churches In Error Message (ADDED)
mid-1842[55] (Times and Seasons) (History of the Church)	early spring 1820 | "the woods"	"a little over 14 years of age"	Religious Revival (ADDED)	Two personages appear and one of them says, "This is my beloved Son, hear him"	Smith is told by the personages that all sects are corrupt. In this account, Smith contradicts his 1832 version by stating, "at this time it had never entered my heart that all were wrong."	Sins Forgiven Message (DELETED) Churches In Error Message (ADDED)
July 1843[56] by Joseph Smith (Letter to Daniel Rupp)	No Date Specified | "a secret place in a grove"	"about fourteen years of age"	No Revival Mentioned	Two "personages, who exactly resembled each other in features, and likeness" "Beloved Son" Phrase (DELETED)	Smith is told by the personages that all religious sects and denominations are corrupt	Sins Forgiven Message (DELETED) Churches In Error Message (ADDED)
August 29, 1843[57] by Joseph Smith (David White, journalist)	No Date Specified | "the woods"	"about fourteen years old"	Religious Revival (ADDED)	Two personages appear and one of them says, "Behold my beloved Son, hear him."	Smith is told by the personages that all religious sects and denominations are corrupt.	Sins Forgiven Message (DELETED) Churches In Error Message (ADDED)
May 24, 1844[58] by Joseph Smith (A. Neibaur, diary)	No Date Specified | "the woods"	No Age Specified	Religious Revival (ADDED)	Two personages appear, and the first one has a "light complexion [and] blue eyes." The second one says, "this is my Beloved son harken ye him"	Smith is told by the personages that all religious sects and denominations are corrupt.	Methodist Church Wrong (ADDED) Churches In Error Message (ADDED)

Table 1.2 (1842–1844 evolving versions of Smith's First Vision)

Even Mormons of the highest echelons suffered from uncertainty over their prophet's ever-changing story. In an 1850 letter, for example, John Taylor—third president of the LDS church—made no mention of either the Father or the Son in the First Vision. He merely said "two glorious personages" gave Smith information that answered his questions, making no mention of any "This is my beloved Son, hear Him" comment.[59] Twenty-nine years later, however, Taylor re-told the story very differently. He identified the personages as the Father and the Son, and he included the "This is my beloved Son, hear Him" phrase, which by then had become a standard element of the tale.[60]

Concerning the religious revival that allegedly prompted Joseph to pray in the woods, it already has been noted that such an event never took place. Not yet discussed, however, is how the 1824 Palmyra-Manchester revival actually affected the Smiths. Ironically, it motivated Joseph's mother, one sister, and two brothers to join the Presbyterian church, where they remained members until 1828—long after the supposed 1820 revelation wherein God not only told Joseph that all of the denominations were corrupt, but commanded him to not join any of them.[61]

Significantly, according to Joseph, Sr., it also was in 1824 that Joseph, Jr. "was baptized, becoming thus a member of the Baptist Church."[62] Three years earlier (c. 1821) Joseph apparently had caught a "spark of Methodism" in a camp meeting and at that time became an exhorter for those meetings.[63] Then, as late as June 1828, he sought membership with the Methodist Episcopal Church in Harmony, Pennsylvania, possibly in response to his first child being "still-born and very much deformed."[64] So, not only was there no 1820 revival, but when a revival did hit the Palmyra-Manchester region in 1824, Joseph and his family were drawn into Christendom's churches—in direct opposition to what God had supposedly said to Joseph back in 1820.

Finally, no publications from the Palmyra-Manchester area during 1820–1829 make any references at all to a young Joseph Smith having visions. Neither can any eye-witnesses be found who remember Joseph talking about visions before 1827/28. This complete absence of negative publicity and eye-witness testimony seems to indicate that "no one at that time and for a long time thereafter was aware that he was supposed to have had the vision."[65] In other words, Smith's "persecution" seems to have been non-existent as well, and so was probably added in order to give the event drama and substance when it was invented many years later.

Fawn Brodie, in her definitive work on Smith's life titled *No Man Knows My History,* theorized that the First Vision might have been "the elaboration of some half-remembered dream stimulated by the early revival excitement and reinforced by the rich folklore of visions circulating in his neighborhood."[66] Brodie further speculated that Smith's story could have been "sheer invention, created some time after 1830 when the need arose for a magnificent tradition to cancel out the stories of his fortune-telling and money-digging" (see Chapter Two).[67]

CURIOUS COINCIDENCES

In addition to Brodie's theories, it also is possible that at some point in time Joseph concocted his First Vision by simply stringing together experiences of other visionaries. Consider the tale of Solomon Chamberlain (1788–1862), a disillusioned Methodist, who just happened to visit the Smiths in 1829. Chamberlain had by that time been spreading the news about his own encounter with God that occurred in 1816. He even published a 12-page pamphlet on the experience titled *A Sketch of the experience of Solomon Chamberlin, to Which Is Added a Remarkable Revelation or Trance, of His Father-in-Law, Philip Haskins: How His Soul actually Left His Body and Was Guided by a Holy Angel to Eternal Day.*[68] Solomon's vision bears a striking resemblance to Joseph's eventual First Vision, as the following excerpt from Chamberlain's autobiography (c. 1858) clearly shows:

> [T]he Lord showed me in a vision that there was no people on the earth that was right, and that faith was gone from the earth, excepting a few and that all Churches were corrupt. I further saw in the vision, that he would soon raise up a Church, that would be after the Apostolic Order, that there would be in it the same powers, and gifts that were in the days of Christ, and that I should live to see the day, and that there would a book come forth, like unto the Bible and the people would be guided by

it, as well as the Bible. This was in the year of 1816. I then believed in
gifts and miracles . . . for which I was much persecuted and called
deluded. This vision I received from an Angel or Spirit from the Eternal
World that told me these things.[69]

Chamberlain, who lived only twenty miles from Palmyra-Manchester, actually tracked Smith down after hearing rumors in 1829 about
Joseph finding a Golden Bible (later to become the *Book of Mormon*).
According to Chamberlain's autobiography, he felt as if "the time was
drawing near," and that God would in some way "bring forth his
Church." So he started making inquiries to see if anyone had heard of
"any strange work of God, such as had not been on the earth since the
days of Christ."

He finally learned of Joseph's book after arriving in Palmyra and
feeling "as if some genii or good Spirit" told him to search the town.[70]
Chamberlain's "genii" subsequently guided him to a small farmhouse,
where he spent the night. In the morning, his hosts asked him if he had
heard of the Golden Bible. Chamberlain later recalled: "[W]hen they said
Gold Bible there was a power like electricity went from the top of my
head to the end of my toes, [t]his was the first time I ever heard of the
gold Bible."[71] He immediately set out for the Smith farm in hopes of finding some evidence that God had started to his restoration of divine truth
in the world.

When Chamberlain finally reached his destination, he found
Joseph's brother, Hyrum. He told Hyrum he was a visionary man, and
brought out one of his pamphlets. Hyrum was so impressed that he
called Joseph, Sr. and several others who happened to be on the property. They all sat down and read through the interesting booklet. Hyrum
was so affected he could not even continue reading. The others were
equally impressed. Chamberlain then stood and announced what would
eventually become part of Joseph's vision:

> I then opened my mouth and began to preach to them, in the words that
> the angel had made known to me in the vision, that all Churches and
> Denominations on the earth had become corrupt, and no Church of God

on the Earth but that he would shortly rise up a Church, that would never be confounded nor brought down and be like unto the Apostolic Church.[72]

When Chamberlain was told about the *Book of Mormon* (see Chapter Four), which at that time was only partially completed, he was converted on the spot. Little did he know that details from his vision would ultimately be incorporated into Joseph's story. Visionary tales from other religious zealots may have made a similar contribution to Mormonism. Compare the following accounts with Smith's First Vision, which was not recorded by him until 1832:

- 1816 – A Vermont minister named Elias Smith publishes an account of his vision in the woods, which allegedly occurred when he was sixteen years old: "[I] went into the woods . . . a light appeared to shine from heaven . . . The Lamb [a Christian synonym for Jesus Christ] once slain appeared to my understanding."[73]
- 1823 – Asa Wild, in an article printed by Palmyra's *Wayne Sentinel*, claims to have had a vision through which he received a revelation that would be mirrored many years later in Joseph's vision: "It seemed as if my mind . . . was struck motionless . . . before the awful and glorious majesty of the Great Jehovah . . . He also told me, that every denomination of professing Christians had become extremely corrupt . . . [H]e said that all the different denominations of professing Christians, constituted the New Testament Babylon."[74]
- 1824 – Christian preacher Alexander Campbell speaks out against three unnamed individuals who had announced visions reminiscent of Joseph's First Vision: "This man was regenerated when asleep, by a vision of the night. That man heard a voice in the woods, saying, 'Thy sins be forgiven thee.' A third saw his Saviour descending to the tops of the trees at noon day."[75]
- 1826 – John Samuel Thompson, who taught at the Palmyra Academy in 1825, claims to have had a dream in which he saw Jesus descend from the sky "in a glare of brightness exceeding tenfold the brilliancy of the meridian [i.e., noonday] Sun" and heard him say, "I

commission you to go and tell mankind that I am come; and bid every man to shout victory!"[76]

- 1830 – Stephen Bradley's pamphlet *A sketch of the life of Stephen H. Bradley, from the age of five to twenty-four years, including his remarkable experience of the power of the Holy Spirit on the second evening of November, 1829,* reads: "I saw the Saviour, by faith, in human shape, for about one second in the room, with arms extended." Bradley said he had his vision when he was fourteen years old, the same age Joseph later claimed to be at the time of his first vision of Christ.[77]

Even more complexity is added to Smith's history by his so-called "Second Vision" of 1823, wherein an angel named Moroni supposedly revealed the secret location of ancient golden plates. This "second" vision was for many years the *only* vision that existed.[78] Unlike today's officially recognized 1820 "first" vision, which was rarely, if ever, discussed until the 1840s, Smith's 1823 "second" vision was well-known as early as 1829. In fact, Mormon writers for many years continued to cite Joseph's 1823 vision of Moroni as his very first religious experience, never bothering to mention today's official 1820 First Vision of God the Father and Jesus Christ. Interestingly, Mormonism's earliest years saw the two separate visions actually blended, in many instance, into a single episode.

These additional visionary facets of early Mormonism will be discussed in the next chapter, along with two other sources of inspiration that helped shape the eventual structure of Joseph's new religion: i.e., magic and masonry.

Moroni, Magic, and Masonry

*Untruth was never more picturesque [than in Mormonism]. . . .
From first to last the history of this cult is dramatic and spectacular. One feels that he has stumbled upon a scene in the Ara-
bian Nights, rather than upon a sober chapter of a real religion.*
George Hamilton Combs (1864-1951)[1]
renowned preacher, Disciples of Christ

ALTHOUGH MORMONS HOLD IN HIGH ESTEEM the painstaking process of record-
ing their church's history, LDS documents are strangely silent about their
prophet's activities during the three years immediately following his 1820
First Vision. Not until September 21, 1823, does Smith's remarkable tale
continue in detail.[2] On that night, according to the church's official history,
the second most significant episode in Joseph's life unfolded as he prayed
near his bedside in the dark. A light allegedly filled the room and "continued to increase until the room was lighter than at noonday."[3]

Suddenly, a heavenly personage wearing a white robe appeared:
"[H]is whole person was glorious beyond description, and his countenance truly like lightning."[4] This messenger from the great beyond
declared himself to be Moroni, a resurrected and glorified servant of the
Lord (i.e., an angel).[5] He announced that God had a mission for Joseph;
one involving a book of golden plates that chronicled the history of
America's former inhabitants.[6] The plates—later described as being
about six inches wide by eight inches long, and bound together with
three huge rings—also supposedly contained the fullness of the Gospel
"as delivered by the Savior to the ancient inhabitants."[7]

Early 20th century woodcut of Joseph Smith examining the *Book of Mormon* golden plates under the guidance of the angel Moroni (from M.R. Werner, *Brigham Young*, 1925). This illustration includes the demonic minions, that according to Joseph, attempted to prevent him from retrieving the divine treasure.

In other words, the story engraved on these golden plates included the pure doctrines of Christianity, as opposed to the corrupted dogmas taught by the denominational churches of Joseph's day.[8] According to Moroni, this priceless treasure had been deposited in the earth centuries earlier. Along with the plates were two stones set in silver bows. These stones, called the Urim and Thummim, "were what constituted 'Seers' in ancient or former times; and that God had prepared them for the purpose of translating the [golden] book."[9] Joseph further claimed: "While he [Moroni] was conversing with me about the plates, the vision was opened to my mind that I could see the place where the plates were deposited . . . I knew the place again when I visited it."[10]

That same evening Joseph had two more visions of Moroni, who not only confirmed his original message, but imparted additional information about "great judgments which were coming upon the face of the earth" in the form of famine, wars, and pestilence.[11] These cataclysmic disasters, Moroni said, would afflict the world within a very short time. He also warned that Satan would try to tempt Joseph "to get the plates for the purpose of getting rich."[12] But Moroni's most urgent message, which he repeated during each visit, involved the golden plates buried in the hill called Cumorah, just outside the village of Manchester, about a mile from the Smith residence.

The next day, Joseph supposedly journeyed to the location and found the plates deposited in the earth, in a stone box. Just then the angel again appeared to him, explaining, "the time for bringing them forth had not yet arrived, neither would it, until four years from that time."[13] Moroni then commanded Joseph to return to that location every year at the same time. Smith later reported: "I went at the end of each year, and at each time I found the same messenger there, and received instruction and intelligence from him at each of our interviews, respecting what the Lord was going to do, and how and in what manner His kingdom was to be conducted in the last days."[14]

Finally, on September 22, 1827, the angel allowed Smith to retrieve the plates imprinted with the long lost history of America's ancient inhabitants—i.e., the *Book of Mormon*. Joseph also claimed to have removed from the stone box a breastplate to which were fastened the Urim and Thummim. He now had everything necessary to bring forth the text that would serve as the basis of his new religion.

MORE VISION REVISIONS

Smith's "second" vision (including the 1827 retrieval of his golden plates) is just as rife with internal and external inconsistencies as is his "first" vision. For example, in 1842, when the LDS publication *Times and Seasons*, published a version of the second vision, the angel was named "Nephi" rather than Moroni.[15] Joseph's 1832 account of the "second" vision does not even identify the angel, but instead, refers to the entity as an "angel of the Lord" who told him about plates engraved "by Maroni."[16] Obviously, if the angel in Smith's room spoke *about* Moroni, then he certainly could not have *been* Moroni.[17]

Odder still are the various "second" vision versions that have been infused with elements from Smith's "first" vision. Such accounts effectively eradicate the 1820 encounter with God and Jesus in the woods, thus making Smith's 1823 meeting with Moroni his actual "first" vision. These "blended" stories directly contradict today's LDS-authorized history that presents the 1820 vision in the woods (First Vision) and the 1823 nocturnal appearance by Moroni (Second Vision) as separate events.

One of the most interesting places that such a blending of visions occurred was in the *Latter Day Saints' Messenger and Advocate*, an early Mormon periodical.[18] Part one of the story was printed in the December 1834 issue. Part two was continued in the February 1835 issue. In the second part, author Oliver Cowdery, who was writing under Smith's direct supervision, had to correct previous statements about Joseph's age and the year of his first visionary experience, finally stating that the "first" vision took place *in 1823* when Smith was in his "17th" year (i.e., 16-years-old).[19] But this, too, was a mistake, since 1823 actually would have been Smith's eighteenth year (i.e., 17-years-old).

The *Messenger and Advocate* account mentions no appearance of either Jesus or God the Father, nor does it take place in the woods. And references to Smith being persecuted also are missing. The account, however, does include comments about a religious revival—the same one that allegedly played a major role in the alleged 1820 vision. Cowdery, however, places the revival in 1823, claiming that it motivated Smith to pray *in his bedroom*.[20] Additionally, this version states that Smith resorted to praying in order to find out which church was the correct one amid all the competing denominations—the same reason Smith supposedly went into the woods to pray in 1820.

Another blended account comes from Joseph's own brother, William Smith. Like Cowdery, he places Moroni's visit in 1823 in conjunction with a revival.[21] William, too, makes no mention of God or Jesus appearing, but instead, like Cowdery, has an angel showing up. But William has the "angel" arriving to meet Joseph *in the woods*. This indicates that at some point there may have been a gradual divergence of stories from a single tale. His account reads:

While engaged in prayer a light appeared in the heavens, and descended until it rested upon the trees. . . . An angel then appeared to him and conversed with him upon many things. He told him that none of the sects were right; but that if he was faithful in keeping the command-ments he should receive, the true way should be made known to him; that his sins were forgiven, etc. The next day . . . the angel again appeared to him, and told him to call his father's house together and communicate to them the visions he had received, . . . After we were all gathered, he arose and told us how the angel appeared to him; what he had told him . . . and that the angel had also given him a short account of the inhabitants who formerly resided upon this continent, a full his-tory of whom he said was engraved on some plates which were hidden, and which the angel promised to show him. . . . All of us, therefore, believed him, and anxiously awaited the result of his visit to the hill Cumorah, in search of the plates containing the record of which the angel told him.[22]

Joseph's cousin, George A. Smith, made the same mistake during two sermons he preached. Like William, George merged into one episode the key elements of both visions: 1) the revival; 2) the experience in the woods; 3) the message about all churches being corrupt; and 4) the angel's visit during which information about golden plates was given.[23] Joseph's own mother related an equally confused account in which material from both visions were described as a single 1823 event.[24]

The disparate array of "first" visions, "second" visions, and "first/second" visions may be due to something briefly mentioned at the beginning of this chapter—i.e., the odd silence in official Mormon history covering 1820–1823. LDS documents also are surprisingly quiet about Smith's activities from 1824–1827.[25] Why? It may be due to the fact that during those particular years Joseph regularly engaged in ritual magic and divination, two practices condemned not only by Christians, but also by twenty-first century Mormons.

A COMPANY OF MONEY-DIGGERS

Relatively few Mormons know that at one time Joseph Smith's reputation as an occultist stretched from New York to Northern Pennsylvania. Moreover, the use of occult rituals among his early followers was the norm, rather than the exception (see pp. 87–90). Much of their attachment to occultism centered around the now archaic practice of treasure-hunting via divination—i.e., money-digging. The pursuit held the fascination of countless individuals throughout rural America in the early nineteenth century.[26]

These "money-diggers," as they were called, often spent most of their days and nights trying to "dig up treasure that supposedly had been buried throughout the land by pirates, Spaniards, or ancient inhabitants of the country."[27] The more desperate souls actually formed money-digging companies of like–minded believers dedicated to pursuing a futile search for instant wealth. Their chosen means of locating this elusive treasure was occult divination by magical ceremonies and enchanted tools including "peep-stones" (or seer stones) and divining rods.[28]

Oftentimes money-diggers would hire themselves out to persons who believed that they, too, might profit through occultism. Such activity, however, was illegal because money-diggers habitually defrauded clients out of hard-earned cash by not delivering on their promises to find large caches of buried treasure. Nevertheless, money-diggers rarely found themselves without a roster of gullible customers whose dreams of abundant assets greatly overshadowed any modicum of down-to-earth business sense they may have possessed—and so the profession thrived.

Joseph Smith, Jr., probably gravitated toward money-digging due to his mother and father's predilection for occult ritual, white magic, superstitions, paranormal phenomena, divination, and treasure hunting. An innate interest in such issues seemed to have been very active not only in them, but also in various members of their family lines going back as far the seventeenth century.[29] Neighbor Fayette Lapham learned from Joseph, Sr. that he was "a firm believer in witchcraft and other supernatural things; and had brought up his family in the same belief."[30] Lapham further recalled: "[Smith] also believed that there was a vast amount of money buried somewhere in the country; that it would some day be found; that he himself had spent both time and money searching for it, with divining rods."[31] A similar propensity manifested itself early in the Mack line as well, with family members "into the spiritual realms of visions, healings, and a quest for a new dispensation."[32]

Such inclinations ultimately brought the Smiths in contact with a widespread money-digging network that existed in the Palmyra-Manchester area during the early-mid 1800s.[33] Martin Harris, who financed the first edition of the *Book of Mormon*, explained: "There was a company there in that neighborhood, who were digging for money supposed to have been hidden by the ancients. Of this company were old Mr. Stowel—I think his name was Josiah—also old Mr. Beman, also Samuel Lawrence, George Proper, Joseph Smith, Jr., and his father, and his brother Hiram [Hyrum] Smith. They dug for money in Palmyra, Manchester, also in Pennsylvania, and other places."[34]

According to local rumors, these men encountered "a great many strange sights" including disappearing strongboxes, mysterious horsemen, and nine-foot-tall strangers who beckoned them from afar.[35] The Smiths, who were seen as leaders of the company, seemed particularly interested in telling such tales. Joshua Stafford, for instance, said that shortly after he became acquainted with Joseph's family around 1819/20 "they commenced digging for hidden treasures . . . and told marvelous stories about ghosts, hob-goblins, caverns, and various other mysterious matters."[36]

Most of the residents of Palmyra and Manchester, in fact, knew the Smiths as a close-knit clan of occultists who espoused popular superstitions embraced by nineteenth century practitioners of folk magic. Consider the text from a particularly relevant 1831 *Palmyra Reflector* article:

We are not able to determine whether the elder Smith was ever concerned in money digging transactions previous to his emigration from
Vermont, or not, but it is a well authenticated fact that soon after his
arrival here he evinced a firm belief in the existence of hidden treasures, and that this section of country abounded in them—He also
revived, or in other words propagated the vulgar, yet popular belief that
these treasures were held in charge by some *evil* spirit, which was supposed to be either the DEVIL himself, or some one of his most trusty
favorites.[37]

There is no doubt that Joseph, Jr., was deeply entrenched in occultism
along with the rest of his family. William Stafford, a neighbor and fellow
money-digger, stated that Joseph, Jr., used a seer stone not only to "see all
things within and under the earth," but also to discover "the spirits in
whose charge these treasures were, clothed in ancient dress."[38] According
to Jesse Townsend, Joseph gazed into his stone to "see chests of money
buried in the earth. He was also a fortune-teller, and he claimed to know
where stolen goods went."[39] Joseph Capron had similar recollections:

The family of Smiths held Joseph Jr. in high estimation on account of
some supernatural power, which he was supposed to possess. This
power he pretended to have received through the medium of a stone of
peculiar quality. The stone was placed in a hat, in such a manner as to
exclude all light, except that which emanated from the stone itself. This
light of the stone, he pretended, enabled him to see anything he wished.
Accordingly he discovered ghosts, infernal spirits, mountains of gold and
silver, and many other invaluable treasures deposited in the earth. He
would often tell his neighbors of his wonderful discoveries, and urge
them to embark in the money digging business. Luxury and wealth were
to be given to all who would adhere to his council.[40]

One of the earliest documents referring to Smith's money-digging
reputation is an 1830 letter from Rev. John Sherer to the American Home
Missionary Society. In this communication, Sherer describes Smith as a

person who pretends to look "through a glass, to see money underground." Sherer also labeled Smith a "juggler," a term that used to denote someone who manipulated people for fraudulent purposes—i.e., a con-man.[41]

Additional testimony shows that Joseph, Jr. and his family often engaged in complex rituals based on occult lore generally not known except by avid practitioners of folk magic. For instance, nineteenth century occultists believed there were periods throughout each lunar cycle that corresponded to times when supernatural powers were higher than usual. This is exactly what Joseph believed, according to William Stafford, who noted in his affidavit published by E.D. Howe that when it came to money-digging, Joseph believed there were certain times when the treasures could be obtained more easily than at other times: "The facility of approaching them, depended in a great measure on the state of the moon. New moon and good Friday, I believe, were regarded as the most favorable times for obtaining these treasures."[42]

On some occasions, Smith made animal sacrifices to appease whatever spirits might be guarding the buried treasure. Emily M. Austin recounted one time when Joseph told his money-digging company "there was a charm on the pots of money, and if some animal was killed and the blood sprinkled around the place, then they could get it." Austin remembered: "So they killed a dog and tried this method of obtaining the precious metal. . . . Alas! how vivid was the expectation when the blood of poor Tray [i.e., the dog] was used to take off the charm, and after all to find their mistake . . . and now they were obliged to give up in despair."[43]

Hiel Lewis, a cousin of Joseph's wife, Emma, reported that the sacrifice of white dogs, black cats, and other animals "was an indispensable part or appendage of the art which Smith, the embryo prophet, was then practicing."[44] Sometimes, however, Joseph and his companions relied solely on magical rituals and occult ceremonies. Consider the following incidents, described by two different acquaintances of Joseph, Jr.:

Episode #1	Episode #2
"Joseph, Sen. first made a circle, twelve or fourteen feet in diameter. This circle, said he, contains the treasure. He then stuck in the ground a row of witch hazel sticks, around the said circle, for the purpose of keeping off the evil spirits. Within this circle he made another, of about eight or ten feet in diameter. He walked around three times on the periphery of this last circle, muttering to himself something which I could not understand. He next stuck a steel rod in the centre of the circles, and then enjoined profound silence upon us, lest we should arouse the evil spirit who had the charge of these treasures. After we had dug a trench about five feet in depth around the rod, . . . [Joseph, Sr.] went to the house to inquire of young Joseph the cause of our disappointment. He soon returned and said, that Joseph had remained all this time in the house, looking in his stone and watching the motions of the evil spirit—that he saw the spirit come up to the ring and as soon as it beheld the cone which we had formed around the rod, it caused the money to sink."[45]	"The sapient Joseph discovered, northwest of my house a chest of gold watches; but as they were in the possession of the evil spirit, it required skill and stratagem to obtain them. Accordingly, orders were given to stick a parcel of large stakes in the ground, several rods around, in a circular form. . . . over the spot where the treasures were deposited. . . . Samuel F. Lawrence, with a drawn sword in his hand, marched around to guard any assault which his Satanic majesty might be disposed to make. Meantime, the rest of the company were busily employed in digging for the watches. They worked as usual till quite exhausted. But, in spite of their defender, Lawrence, and their bulwark of stakes, the devil came off victorious, and carried away the watches."[46]

Both of these episodes ended unsuccessfully after the treasure was either stolen away or moved out of reach by demonic forces. Such outcomes were typical in tales circulated by nineteenth-century money-diggers. In *The Refiner's Fire: The Making of Mormon Cosmology, 1644–1844*, history professor John L. Brooke of Tufts University observes: "One of the central themes in the treasure-hunting sagas was the volatility of precious metal: chests of money 'bloom' to the surface of the earth only to fall away when the diggers utter a sound or violate a ritual practice."[47]

Joshua Stafford remembered Smith actually showing him "a piece of wood which he said he took from a box of money" that had mysteriously moved back into the hill.[48] Many years later in Utah, two of Smith's closest associates—Martin Harris and Orrin Porter Rockwell—actually gave recollections of having been present when this corner of a wooden treasure box was broken off before it "slipped back into the hill" under the influence of some unseen power.[49]

MORMONISM MEETS FREEMASONRY

One of the clearest pictures of the Smiths' intricate ties to occultism can be found in the autobiography of his mother, Lucy Mack Smith. In an effort to defend her family against charges of laziness, she wrote the following:

> Let not my reader suppose that . . . we stopt our labor and went at trying to win the faculty of Abrac[,] drawing Magic circles or sooth saying to the neglect of all kinds of buisness[.] We never during our lives suffered one important interest to swallow up every other obligation.[50]

All three practices Lucy mentions are intertwined with ritual magic and occult superstition. Soothsaying is foretelling the future through divination tools such as tarot cards, omens, and crystals/peepstones (a.k.a. "scrying"). Drawing magic circles is an extremely important ritual used by occultists to gain power over evil spirits when they are invoked for a special purpose.[51] *The Ancients Book of Magic* explains that in order to contact spirits, the magician usually draws a circle within a circle, which supposedly forms a barrier impenetrable to demons.[52] This is exactly what Joseph Smith, Sr. did during his money-digging adventure with William Stafford (Episode #1, p. 32).

Finally, Lucy mentions the "faculty of Abrac," which refers to the demon-god Abrac (a.k.a. Abracax or Abraxas), who was viewed by the heretical Basilidians of the second century as "the chief of the 365 genies ruling the days of the year."[53] From his name comes the magical word Abracadabra. Peasants in the Middle Ages believed that this word could guard them from physical injury, danger, evil spirits, diseases, and fevers, especially the plague. To obtain the protective powers (i.e., faculties) of Abrac, Abracadabra was written in a triangle/pyramid form, dropping one letter in each line until only one letter remained. The parchment on which this magical formula had been etched was then worn around the neck by someone who had fallen ill. Afterward, it was "thrown backwards over the shoulder into a stream which runs eastwards."[54] The bearer could only hope that their physical malady or other troubling circumstance would depart as well.

A B R A C A D A B R A
A B R A C A D A B R
A B R A C A D A B
A B R A C A D A
A B R A C A D
A B R A C A
A B R A C
A B R A
A B R
A B
A

The written form of ABRACADABRA, which would have been used by Medieval believers in the powers of the Abrac.

Sketch of Abracax, the demon-god with snakes as feet. The magical word ABRACADABRA comes from his name (from Collin de Plancy's *Dictionaire Infernal*, 1863).

Periodically, various religious bodies have laid claim to the powers of Abrac, one the most notable being Freemasonry of the nineteenth century. The Masonic Lodge is classed among spiritual institutions as a fraternal brotherhood and secret society that predominantly teaches "a system of morality, by the practice of which its members may advance their spiritual interest, and mount by the theological ladder from the Lodge on earth to the Lodge in heaven."[55] In other words, Masonry "is the realization of God by the practice of Brotherhood."[56] Masonic authority Henry Wilson Coil has defined the religion as follows:

> Freemasonry, in its broadest and most comprehensive sense, is a system of morality and social ethics, a primitive religion and a philosophy of life . . . . Incorporating a broad humanitarianism. . . . [I]t is a religion without a creed, being of no sect but finding truth in all. . . . It seeks truth but does not define truth.[57]

Coincidentally, nineteenth century talk of Freemasons knowing how to control the faculty of Abrac circulated primarily throughout Western New York, "specifically in the very neighborhood of the Mormon Prophet Joseph Smith, both in the period he was writing the *Book of Mormon* and in an earlier period of time when he was known to have had magical interests [c. 1818–1830]."[58]

For example, W.W. Phelps wrote an entire article on the connection between Freemasonry and Abrac, and published it an 1830 issue of his *Ontario Phoenix* newspaper, located in Canandaigua, New York (near Palmyra-Manchester). He called Abracadabra a "very Ancient Masonic Charm, or the way of winning the Faculty of Abrac." He also stated: "[T]he magical term—ABRACADABRA, written or repeated in a particular manner . . . is thought to be efficacious in curing agues [i.e., a fever with chills] and preventing FITS and other Masonic diseases."[59] Phelps, interestingly, became a Mormon soon after publishing his article. Joseph became a Freemason in 1842. His brother, Hyrum, coincidentally, already was a Freemason, as were a significant number of other early Mormons.[60]

John E. Thompson, in his thought-provoking article "The Facultie of Abrac: Masonic Claims and Mormon Beginnings," theorized that "the cement which brought some of these early Mormons into New York Masonry may have been the search to "win the faculty of Abrac."[61] It also has been suspected, and with good reason, that Smith borrowed his entire "golden plates" idea from the Royal Arch Freemasonry legend of Enoch, which was popularized in New York state through *The Freemason's Monitor* (1802) by Thomas S. Webb.

This Masonic myth includes many features that parallel Smith's fantastic story: a vision of God by which divine instructions are given; golden plates engraved with "ineffable characters" by a faithful follower of God; an important hilltop/mountain; a holy treasure hidden underground, records preserved for centuries; and servants of God chosen to find the plates.[62] These are but a few of the many similarities between the two tales. Reed C. Durham, a particularly well-known LDS historian (Mormon History Association President), noted in 1974 that virtually all aspects of the Enoch legend "seem transformed into the history of Joseph Smith, so much so that even it appears to be a kind of symbolic acting out of Masonic lore."[63]

Smith eventually would go so far as to adapt some of Masonry's clandestine rituals for use in his temple endowment ceremony.[64] This highly secretive rite continues to be practiced today by faithful Mormons as an indispensable pre-requisite to achieving godhood. Until April 0f 1990, the ceremony actually contained death penalty oaths to keep Mormons from revealing LDS ceremony secrets (similar to the oaths taken by Freemasons against revealing Masonic secrets). These bloody Mormon vows were exposed in 1906 by the *Salt Lake Tribune*, then reprinted by W.M. Paden in *Temple Mormonism* (1931). Consider the following recitation taken from the original Latter-day Saint ritual:

> "We, and each of us, covenant and promise that we will not reveal any of the secrets of this, the first token of the Aaronic priesthood, with its accompanying name, sign or penalty. Should we do so, we agree that our throats be cut from ear to ear and our tongues torn out by their roots." . . . Sign— In executing the sign of the penalty, the right hand, palm down, is drawn sharply across the throat, then dropped from the square to the side.[65]

The above extract mirrors the gory punishment detailed in *Illustrations of Freemasonry* (1827) by William Morgan, who had been a Mason for thirty years. Morgan quoted the Masonic penalty for revealing secrets of the "First Degree" as follows: "[I will] never reveal any part or parts, art or arts, point or points of the secret arts and mysteries of ancient Freemasonry . . . . binding myself under no less penalty than to have my throat cut across, my tongue torn out by the roots."[66] The book also explained that Masons who went through this degree were instructed to make a visible gesture symbolizing the penalty: "[Draw] your right hand across your throat, the thumb next to your throat, your arm as high as the elbow in a horizontal position."[67]

According to Morgan, the "Second or Fellow Craft Degree" demanded that Masons bind themselves "under no less penalty than to have my left breast torn open and my heart and vitals taken from thence and thrown over my left shoulder and carried into the valley of Jehosaphat, there to become a prey to the wild beasts of the field, and vulture of the air. . . . The sign is given by drawing your right hand flat, with the palm of it next to your breast, across your breast from the left to the right side with some quickness, and dropping it down by your side"[68] This oath and its penalty also were incorporated into the Mormon temple endowment as the "Second Token of the Aaronic Priesthood." Paden's *Temple Mormonism* reads as follows:

"We and each of us do covenant and promise that we will not reveal the secrets of this, the Second Token of the Aaronic Priesthood, with its accompanying name, sign, grip or penalty. Should we do so, we agree to have our breasts cut open and our hearts and vitals torn from our bodies and given to the birds of the air and the beasts of the field." . . . The Sign is made by placing the left arm on the square at the level of the shoulder, placing the right hand across the chest with the thumb extended and then drawing it rapidly from left to right and dropping it to the side.[69]

An equally gruesome oath—Masonry's "Third, or Master Mason's Degree"—involved never revealing the Lodge's secrets "under no less penalty than to have my body severed in two in the midst, and divided to the north and south, my bowels burnt to ashes in the center. . . . The Penal Sign is given by putting the right hand to the left side of the bowels, the hand open, with the thumb next to the belly, and drawing it across the belly, and letting it fall; this is done tolerably quick. This alludes to the penalty of the obligation: 'Having my body severed in twain,' etc."[70] This oath, too, along with its penalty, ended up in the LDS temple ceremony as Smith's "First Token of the Melchizedek Priesthood." Mormons swore themselves to secrecy using brutal terminology:

> "[W]e agree that our bodies be cut asunder in the midst and all our bowels gush out." . . . As the last words are spoken the hands are dropped till the thumbs are in the center of the stomach and drawn swiftly across the stomach to the hips, and then dropped to the sides.[71]

By the time Joseph's followers migrated to Utah in 1847, Masonry had become so embedded in Mormonism that Masonic emblems were put on permanent display as part of the architecture in the Salt Lake City temple walls.[72] The many LDS counterparts to facets of nineteenth century Masonry are so unmistakable that even Mormon scholars have been forced to admit the obvious.[73] Reed Durham, for instance, unequivocally stated in 1974 that Masonry greatly influenced Smith's doctrines and the rituals he employed:

> I am convinced that in the study of Masonry lies a pivotal key to further understanding Joseph Smith and the Church. . . . The many parallels found between early Mormonism and the Masonry of that day are substantial. . . . I believe that there are few significant developments in the Church, that occurred after March 15, 1842 [the day Smith became Mason], which did not have some Masonic interdependence. . . . There is absolutely no question in my mind that the Mormon ceremony which came to be known as the Endowment, introduced by Joseph Smith to Mormon Masons, had an immediate inspiration from Masonry. This is not to suggest that no other source of inspiration could have been involved, but the similarities between the two ceremonies are so apparent and overwhelming that some dependent relationship cannot be denied. They are so similar, in fact, that one writer was led to refer to the Endowment as Celestial Masonry.[74]

Penal Sign.
Mason.

Illustrations depicting the grisly Freemason penalties for
revealing Masonic secrets. These "first" *(left)* and "third"
(right) degree penalty oaths, which Joseph Smith took when
he became a Freemason in 1842, were incorporated into the
Mormon Temple endowment ceremony. Although the horrific
verbal vows were removed from the LDS rite sometime in
the early 20th century, the hand gestures depicted above
remained in the ceremony until 1990 (from William Morgan,
Illustrations of Freemasonry, 1827).

Although most twenty-first century Mormons would quickly shy
away from acknowledging any similarities between Masonry and their
sacred doctrines/temple ordinances, nineteenth century Latter-day
Saints had no difficulty with the concept. LDS official Heber C. Kimball,
for instance, remarked in 1858 that Mormons actually practiced "true
Masonry."[75] Kimball, along with other Mormon leaders, believed that
Masonry contained a considerable number of divinely established rites
and rituals, but had lost some of the truths associated with them. Joseph
supposedly recognized the verities and inserted them, along with other
facets of Masonry, into Mormonism. As Kimball plainly stated regarding
the relationship between Freemasonry and Mormonism: "[W]e have the
real thing."[76]

Ironically, the *Book of Mormon* actually denounces Freemasonry via numerous statements against "secret combinations," "secret signs," and "secret oaths" (Alma 37:30; Helaman 3:23; Ether 9:6; Helaman 6:22, 26). These condemnations, although inconsistent with later Mormonism, reflected the anti-Masonic excitement that permeated the culture in which Joseph lived. Smith's insertion of anti-Masonic sentiments into his *Book of Mormon* is only one of many examples of how Joseph's own life contributed to the text that now serves as holy writ for millions of Mormons worldwide (see Chapter Four).[77]

THREE

From Profit to Prophet

Smith went through two critical transformations. He began his engagement with the supernatural as a village conjurer but transformed himself into a prophet of the "Word," announcing the opening of a new dispensation.

John L. Brooke, history professor[1]

Tufts University

JOSEPH USED AT LEAST TWO SEER-STONES during his divining years (c. 1820–1827).[2] He found his first stone, a "whitish opaque stone," in September 1819.[3] Smith supposedly learned of its whereabouts by gazing into a green glass stone he borrowed from his neighbor, friend, and fellow diviner, Sally Chase (Willard Chase's sister). Joseph discovered his favorite stone in 1822, while digging a well for the Chase family. This one would become extremely important in Mormon history (see pp. 55–57). Finally, around 1825 or shortly thereafter, he was given a green stone by Jack Belcher, a diviner and salt digger. This latter piece of divining paraphernalia he rarely, if ever, used.[4]

The year 1825 also witnessed a major turning point in Smith's life thanks to a visit from Josiah Stowell, a farmer from South Bainbridge, New York. Joseph's mother remembered: "A short time before the house was completed [1825], a man, by the name of Josiah Stoal, came from Chenango county, New York, with the view of getting Joseph to assist him in digging for a silver mine. He came for Joseph on account of having heard that he possessed certain keys, by which he could discern things invisible to the natural eye."[5]

Joseph soon moved a hundred miles southeast to the Susquehanna River Valley near Harmony, Pennsylvania, where the lost silver mine was waiting to be found. Although he never located the mine, he did meet the girl of his dreams—Emma Hale. Unfortunately, Emma's father, Isaac Hale, disapproved of Smith because "[h]e was at that time in the employ of a set of men who were called 'money diggers;' and his occupation was that of seeing, or pretending to see by means of a stone placed in his hat, and his hat closed over his face. In this way he pretended to discover minerals and hidden treasure."[6] In 1834, after Mormonism had garnered a considerable amount of media attention, the *Susquehanna Register* published the following statement from Hale:

> [Smith's] appearance at this time, was that of a careless young man—not very well educated, and very saucy and insolent to his father. Smith, and his father, with several other "money-diggers" boarded at my house while they were employed in digging for a mine that they supposed had been opened and worked by the Spaniards, many years since. Young Smith gave the "money-diggers" great encouragement, at first, but when they had arrived in digging, to near the place where he had stated an immense treasure would be found—he said the enchantment was so powerful that he could not see. They then became discouraged, and soon after dispersed.[7]

One aspect of Smith's character that emerged from the Harmony expedition was his apparent unwillingness to help dig. He viewed himself as the group's leader—the one with the "gift." Alva Hale, who would become Joseph's brother-in-law, observed:

> Joe Smith never handled one shovel of earth in those diggings. All that Smith did was to peep with stone and hat, and give directions where and how to dig, and when and where the enchantment moved the treasure. That Smith said if he should work with his hands at digging there, he would lose the power to see with the stone.[8]

The money-digging company under Joseph's guidance eventually left Pennsylvania after failing to find the Spanish silver mine. But rather

Emma Hale, Joseph's wife, also known as the "Elect Lady" (courtesy of RLDS Archives, Independence, Missouri).

than going home, Joseph traveled with Stowell to his Bainbridge, New York, farm where he continued the search for lost treasure. After several months, however, Stowell's sons decided to step in and prevent their father from squandering any more of his money. They, along with Peter Bridgman (Stowell's nephew) brought charges against Joseph and succeeded in having him arrested in March 1826 for being a disorderly person and an impostor.[9]

BOUND IN BAINBRIDGE

The transcript of Smith's appearance in court was first published in 1873 in *Fraser's Magazine* (an English periodical).[10] During this preliminary hearing (then called an "examination"), Joseph admitted that he possessed "a certain stone" that he occasionally used to determine where treasures were hidden in the earth. The court record continued: "[H]e professed to tell in this manner where gold mines were a distance under ground, and had looked for Mr. Stowell several times, and had informed him where he could find these treasures."[11] Stowell attempted to defend Joseph, but ended up doing more harm than good by testifying that he positively knew Smith could "tell, and did possess the art of seeing those valuable treasures through the medium of said stone."[12] He further stated that he had the most implicit faith in Joseph's skills. After others testified that they, too, had witnessed Smith's illegal activities, the court pronounced him guilty.

Joseph escaped jail time, however, when the court subtly suggested he leave town and never return. This common show of mercy, known at that time as "Leg Bail," may have been granted because Smith was only twenty years old. In an 1831 letter to the *Evangelical Magazine and Gospel Advocate*, Bainbridge resident A.W. Benton recounted what he witnessed at Smith's trial: "[C]onsidering his youth, (he then being a minor,) and thinking he might reform his conduct, he was designedly allowed to escape. This was four or five years ago. From this time he absented himself from this place, returning only privately, and holding clandestine intercourse with his credulous dupes, for two or three years."[13] Joel K. Noble, a justice of the peace during that era, corroborated Benton's account, stating: "Jo. was condemned. [The] Whisper came to Jo. 'off, off'—[He] took Leg Bail. . . . Jo was not seen in our town for 2 years or more (except in Dark Corners)."[14]

For many years Mormons steadfastly viewed all such statements, including the court transcript published in 1873, as nothing but anti-Mormon propaganda created to smear the good name of their prophet. In reference to the Bainbridge court record, for example, LDS author Francis Kirkham adamantly declared "no such record was ever made, and therefore, is not in existence."[15] The LDS church-owned *Deseret News* called it a "fabrication of unknown authorship and never in the court records at all."[16] Mormon apostle John Widtsoe stated: "This alleged court record . . . seems to be a literary attempt of an enemy to ridicule Joseph Smith. . . . There is no existing proof that such a trial was ever held."[17] The reason for such ardent denials was articulated well by Dr. Hugh Nibley, one of Mormonism's staunchest defenders. In 1967, he

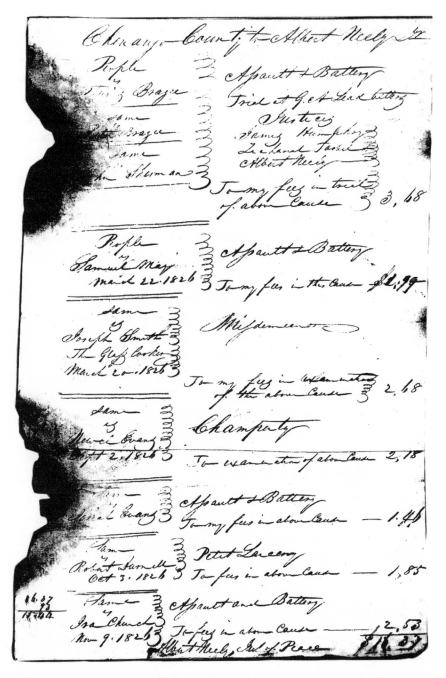

The Justice Neely bill found by Wesley P. Walters in 1971. Midway through the document appears the court's reference to Mormonism's founder. It reads: "Same [i.e., People] V. Joseph Smith The Glass looker March 20, 1826. Misdemeanor—To my fees in examination of the above Cause, 2.68." (In 1826, when the letter "s" was repeated in a word, the two consonants were written similar to a "p.")

wrote: "If this court record is authentic, it is the most damning evidence in existence against Joseph Smith."[18]

Then, in 1971, concrete evidence for the transcript's validity was unearthed by Wesley P. Walters and Fred Poffarl, two religion researchers who had been investigating Mormonism for many years. While searching through court records stored in the basement of an old county jail in New York, they discovered two cardboard boxes shoved against a wall in a darkened corner. They contained bundles of water-damaged court bills dating back to the early 1800s. The 1826 bundle included several bills showing court costs of a Justice Albert Neely. One of his cases referred to none other that "Joseph Smith the Glass Looker." Neely's charges, $2.68, exactly matched the figure given for court costs in *Fraser's Magazine*. The date also was the same—March 20, 1826 (see photo, p. 45).

For many years Mormons tried in vain to cast aspersions on the legitimacy of the Neely document. But finally, in 1992, LDS church historian Leonard J. Arrington conceded that the bill was indeed drawn up by Neely and that it referred to Smith "as a 'glass looker' (one who, by peering through a glass stone, could see things not discernible by the natural eye)."[19]

Interestingly, before Neely's bill had surfaced, Francis Kirkham made a very telling comment based on his complete confidence that no evidence would ever be found to substantiate the 1826 trial: "If any evidence had been in existence that Joseph Smith had used a seer stone for fraud and deception, and especially had he made this confession in a court of law as early as 1826, or four years before the *Book of Mormon* was printed, and this confession was in a court record, it would have been impossible for him to have [legitimately] organized the restored Church."[20]

GOING FOR THE GOLD

After his 1826 brush with the law, Smith temporarily seemed more interested in romance than in money-digging. Even before his arrest, while continuing to hunt treasure for Stowell in New York, Smith often returned to Pennsylvania to see Emma. But when he asked for permission to marry her, it was refused. Her father remembers: "I gave him my reasons for so doing; some of which were, that he was a stranger, and followed a business that I could not approve: he then left the place."[21] Joe, however, would not take no for an answer, and on January 18, 1827, while Isaac was away from home, he took Emma to New York and married her. Smith apparently began pondering his financial situation around this same time, realizing that money-digging alone was bringing in only about $14 a month, which was not nearly enough to support a family.[22]

So, at some point in 1826/27, Smith began telling others, most notably his money-digging friends, about the existence of a golden book he would soon be retrieving from a secret place that had been revealed to him through his seer stone. Smith originally attached no religious significance to the mysterious volume, but instead, touted it as a book that would, according to neighbor Parley Chase (b. 1806), "tell him how to get money that was buried in the ground."[23] In other words, it would compliment to his money-digging activities.

Abner Cole, a former justice of the peace who became editor of the *Palmyra Reflector*, recalled a similar explanation that came directly from young Joseph's father. His account provides invaluable information that suggests how the whole series of stories involving visions probably began:

> [T]he elder Smith declared that his son Jo had seen the spirit, (which he then described as a little old man with a long beard,) and was informed that he (Jo) under certain circumstances, eventually should obtain great treasures, and that in due time he (the spirit) would furnish him (Jo) with a book, which would give an account of the Ancient inhabitants (antideluvians,) of this country, and where they had deposited their substance, consisting of costly furniture, &c. . . . which had ever since that time remained secure in his (the spirit's) charge, in large and spacious chambers, in sundry places in this vicinity.[24]

Eventually, however, Joseph decided that instead of keeping the book as a means of finding more treasure, it would be far more profitable to sell the volume as a speculation about America's ancient inhabitants and their origins.[25] Neighbor Joseph Capron remembered an especially enlightening conversation he had with Joseph, Sr., who never even intimated that the volume would be religious:

> [Joseph, Jr.] pretended to find the Gold Plates. This scheme, he believed, would relieve the family from all pecuniary embarrassment. His father told me, that when the book was published, they would be enabled, from the profits of the work, to carry into successful operation of the money digging business. He gave me no intimation, at that time that the book was to be of a religious character, or that it had any thing to do with revelation. He declared it to be a speculation, and said he, "when it is completed, my family will be placed on a level above the generality of mankind."[26]

But Joseph kept changing his mind again and again, not only about the hidden book's contents, but also about how he discovered its existence, and how he retrieved it. He could not keep his story straight, nor could his siblings, or parents. Parley Chase recalled that when it came to explaining exactly how the plates were found, the Smiths "scarcely ever told two stories alike."[27] In hindsight, some of these accounts sound like a cross between Washington Irving's *The Legend of Sleepy Hollow* (1819–20) and assorted pirate tales featuring the likes of Captain Kidd (1645–1701), whom Joseph, interestingly enough, claimed to have seen "sailing on the Susquehanna River" one day while gazing into his peep-stone. (He also said he saw where Kidd had buried "two pots of gold and silver.")[28]

Long before area residents heard any of the "first" or "second" vision accounts thus far discussed, a number of radically different explanations about the golden plates had been circulated by the Smiths. On one occasion, Joseph, Jr. told his wife's cousin, Hiel Lewis, that he learned about the golden plates *in a dream*, and that on his first attempt to get them in 1823, he was "knocked down" several times by a mysterious power. Joseph then claimed to have seen the ghost of a man "standing over the spot, who, to him appeared *like a Spaniard*, having a long beard coming

Early 20th century woodcut of the angel/ghost giving Joseph Smith the golden plates of the *Book of Mormon*, Urim and Thummim, "Sword of Laban," and an ancient breastplate (from M.R. Werner, *Brigham Young*, 1925).

down over his breast to about here, (*Smith putting his hand to the pit of his stomach*) WITH HIS (the ghost's) THROAT CUT FROM EAR TO EAR, AND THE BLOOD STREAMING DOWN, who told him that he could not get it [the plates] alone; that another person whom he, Smith, would know at first sight, must come with him, and then he could get it" (emphases in original).[29]

Fayette Lapham heard the same scenario from Joseph, Sr.—i.e., that the golden plates had been revealed to young Joseph *via a dream.* And that during this dream "a very large and tall man appeared to him, dressed in an ancient suit of clothes, and the clothes were bloody."[30] The gruesome apparition told Joseph "there was a valuable treasure, buried many years since, and not far from that place . . . [and] he would direct him to the place where it was deposited, in such a manner that he could obtain it."[31]

Lapham was then told the rest of the story just as it had been related to Emma's cousin, including the part about Joseph, Jr. being struck down and seeing the Spaniard appear at the location. According to Joseph, Sr., the macabre ghost had been "sworn to take charge of and protect that property, until the time should arrive for it to be exhibited to the world of mankind; and, in order to prevent his making a improper disclosure, he was murdered or slain on the spot, and the treasure had been under his charge ever since. He said to him [Joseph] that . . . if he would come again one year from that time, he could have them."[32]

The Smiths eventually changed Joseph's "dream" of a ghost to a "vision" of a spirit (but not yet an angel). This version was told to Willard Chase. He recalled that in June of 1827 Joseph Smith, Sr. related an astonishing story that allegedly had been unfolding since 1823 (the same year now accepted by Mormons as the time of Joseph's second vision). According to the elder Smith, a "spirit" had appeared in a vision and communicated to his son that "in a certain place there was a record on plates of gold, and that he was the person that must obtain them."[33] The spirit then instructed young Joseph to go to this location on September 22, 1823, but to do so "dressed in black clothes, and riding a black horse with a switch tail. Joseph was then supposed to demand the book, using a special secret word, and after obtaining plates, "go directly away, and neither lay it down nor look behind him."[34]

Joseph, Sr. informed Chase that his son did in fact dress himself in a suit of black clothes and borrowed a black horse.[35] He journeyed to the hill and briefly retrieved the plates (in 1823) until they supernaturally flew back to where they had been. Apparently, Joseph had placed them down to adjust the positioning of supplies on his horse, which disobeyed the spirit's command to "go directly away." Consequently, the plates slipped back into the hill. One fascinating addition to this particular story involved an as yet unheard of toad-like creature that appeared when Joseph tried to re-obtain the plates after they had deposited themselves back into the hill. This entity "assumed the appearance of a man" and struck Joseph on the side of his head, telling Joseph that it was not yet time to retrieve the plates and that he would have to return in one year.[36]

A subsequent version of Smith's ever-changing tale, one sounding a bit more Christian, was related to Martin Harris, who in turn told it to the *Rochester Gem*, which published a synopsis of it:

> In the autumn of 1827 a man named Joseph Smith of Manchester, in Ontario County, said that he had been visited by the spirit of the Almighty in a dream, and informed that in a certain hill in that town, was deposited a Golden Bible, containing an ancient record of a divine origin. He states that after a third visit from the same spirit in a dream, he proceeded to the spot, removed earth, and there found the bible, together with a huge pair of spectacles.[37]

Over the years these yarns gradually were revised and expanded, eventually becoming today's official account of the 1823 "second" vision featuring the angel Moroni. One element of the earlier stories, however, did not easily give way. Until well into the late 1800s it was widely understood that Smith found the golden plates not by a dream, or a ghost, or a vision—but by looking into his peep-stone and seeing where they had been deposited. Orasmus Turner recalled one day when Joseph was away from home, and his family inadvertently revealed how he actually had found the plates, if indeed, there ever were any:

> [I]n his absence, the rest of the family made a new version of it to one of their neighbors. They shewed him such a pebble as may any day be picked up on the shore of Lake Ontario . . . . They said it was by looking at this stone, in a hat, the light excluded, that Joseph discovered the plates. . . . It was the same stone the Smith's had used in money digging, and in some pretended discoveries of stolen property.[38]

This may have been the most prevalent Mormon understanding of the events leading to the retrieval of Smith's golden plates. Even Brigham Young, Smith's successor to the LDS presidency, knew that Smith used his peep–stone to find the golden plates. In 1856, Mormon pioneer Hosea Stout recorded in his diary that that Young actually "exhibited the Seer's stone with which the Prophet Joseph discovered the plates of the Book of Mormon."[39] Martin Harris, one of Smith's closest allies and a crucial figure in the creation of the *Book of Mormon*, also testified to the peep-stone's use:

> Joseph had a stone which was dug from the well of Mason Chase . . . . It was by means of this stone that he first discovered these plates. . . . [Joseph] had before described the manner of his finding the plates. He found them by looking in the stone. . . . The family had likewise told me the same thing.[40]

No one will probably ever know exactly how these earliest stories developed and merged. But one thing is certain—all of the *religious* aspects of Smith's adventures came much later. Orasmus Turner wrote: "The primitive designs of Mrs. Smith, her husband, Jo, and Cowdery, was money-making; blended with which perhaps, was a desire for notoriety, to be obtained by cheat and fraud. The idea of being the founders of a new sect, was an after thought, in which they were aided by others."[41] In agreement with Turner, Joseph Smith's cousin-in-law, Hiel Lewis, summarized:

> In all this narrative, there was not one word about "visions of God," or of angels or heavenly revelations. All his information was by that dream, and that bleeding ghost. The heavenly visions and messages of angels, etc., contained in Mormon books were after-thoughts, revised to order.[42]

Many of Joseph's doctrines would end up fitting into this category of "afterthoughts"—e.g., his revelations concerning God's nature, inhabitants on the moon,[43] Caucasians advancing to godhood, and the notion that Blacks, Indians, and other people of color are cursed spirits (see Chapter Sixteen). Smith's most significant "afterthought," however, would be his role as a latter-day prophet commissioned to lead humanity into the glorious millennial kingdom of God. But first he would have to decipher the mysterious writing on the *Book of Mormon* plates, and offer his translation to the world.

THE ART OF TRANSLATING

After supposedly retrieving the plates, Smith took extreme measures to avoid at all costs anyone who might want to see them. The angel, according to Joseph, had warned him that he would lose possession of the plates if he let anyone else see them.[44] This certainly convinced his family. But still troublesome to Joseph were the men associated with his money-digging company. They felt that "they had as much right to the plates as Joseph [did]" and that he had "been [a] traitor and had appropriated to himself that which belonged to them."[45]

Smith responded by hiding the plates; first, in the hollow of a tree, then under the hearth of his house, then under an old cooper's shop.[46] As a result, few people, except for Joseph's family and the money-diggers, even believed the golden book truly existed. After all, no one had actually seen the plates, nor would anyone *ever* see them.[47] (After the plates were "translated," they were returned to the angel by Smith, who claimed to have deposited them in a huge cave filled with treasure.)[48]

But unbelievers were the least of Joseph's problems. A far more pressing issue was his lack of funds to carry out the God-given task of translating, then publishing, the *Book of Mormon*. A solution to this problem came in the form of Martin Harris, a prosperous farmer with considerable land. He also happened to be a religious fanatic prone to visions and other supernatural phenomena. Angelic visitations, ghostly encounters, and meetings with Jesus Christ were commonplace in Harris' life.[49]

On one occasion, Harris told Stephen S. Harding that he "saw the devil, in all his hideousness, on the road just before dark, near his farm, a little north of Palmyra."[50] This terrifying encounter began when his horses suddenly stopped: "[Harris] then commenced smelling brimstone, and knew the Devil was in the road, and saw him plainly as he walked up the hill and disappeared. . . . [Satan looked like] 'a greyhound as big as a horse, without any tail, walking upright on his hind legs.'"[51] He told another gentleman in Palmyra that "while the Book of Mormon translation was going on, that on the way [to Pennsylvania] he met the Lord Jesus Christ, who walked along by the side of him in the shape of a deer for two or three miles, talking with him as familiarly as one man talks with another."[52]

Harris believed that the discovery of the *Book of Mormon* went hand in hand with a revelation from God in which he learned that there would be a special work for him to do in the near future.[53] Smith was more than happy to accommodate Harris' impression, and explained to him how by supernatural means he had already seen Harris approaching.[54] God also gave Joseph a special commandment to ask the first man he met in the street to give him fifty dollars. He needed the cash so he could travel to Emma's hometown of Harmony, Pennsylvania, where he would be able to translate the plates in peace and saftey.[55] Harris obeyed; Joseph had found himself a benefactor.

The arduous process of deciphering the unintelligible lettering engraved on the plates of gold would take Smith approximately 1½ years. The characters, he said, were "Reformed Egyptian," a sample copy of which he made in hopes of having their authenticity verified. During the winter of 1828 Harris actually traveled to New York City where he showed the characters to Charles Anthon, professor of Greek and Latin at Columbia College. Anthon was not impressed, labeling the inscription a meaningless batch of crooked characters including "Greek and Hebrew letters, crosses and flourishes, Roman letters inverted or placed sideways."[56]

Upon returning to Harmony, Harris related the whole sad episode to Joseph, even telling him about how Anthon out of curiosity had suggested that Harris bring him the plates. Harris told Anthon that such a thing was forbidden, especially since a part of the ancient record was sealed. Anthon answered: "I cannot read a sealed book."[57] The trip, it seemed, had accomplished little. But this news, rather than discouraging Joseph, excited him. He hurriedly grabbed his Bible and turned to Isaiah 29:11-12: "And the vision of all is become unto you as the words of a book that is sealed, which men deliver to one that is learned, saying, Read this, I pray thee:

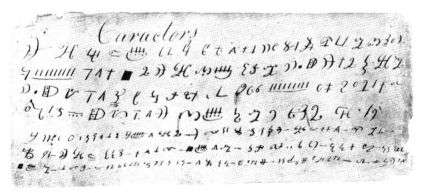

A sample of the "Reformed Egyptian" characters allegedly engraved on Joseph Smith's golden plates. Martin Harris took these "Caractors" to New York City in hopes of having them pronounced authentic by renowned scholar Charles Anthon of Columbia College.

and he saith, I cannot; for it is sealed." Harris was awestruck. God had chosen him to fulfill a biblical prophecy! Finally, every shred of doubt in Harris' mind about Smith or the golden plates immediately disappeared.[58]

The two men subsequently began telling potential converts that renowned scholar Charles Anthon had pronounced the characters authentic, at one point even using Anthon's name to advertise the book. Anthon was incensed when he heard of the deception, and in an 1834 letter to E. D. Howe, wrote: "The whole story about my having pronouncd (sic) the Mormonite inscription to be 'reformed Egyptian hieroglyphics' is *perfectly false.* . . . [T]he paper contained any thing else but 'Egyptian Hieroglyphics.' "[59] Interestingly, Mormons today continue to circulate the false Anthon story even though he and other reputable scholars have for decades declared that there is no such language as "Reformed Egyptian."[60]

But Joseph had little need for scholarly support, nor did he want any assistance translating the mysterious writing into English. Joseph still possessed his seer stone; the very same chocolate-colored, egg-shaped one that he had found in 1822, while digging a well for the Chase family.[61] It had served him well enough for money-digging, and would now come in handy as a translation tool. Emma's cousin, Hiel Lewis, stated that Joseph used this very peep-stone "under the same inspiration that directed his enchantments and dog sacrifices; it was all by the same spirit."[62]

Even Emma, who for a time served as Joseph's scribe, recalled: "In writing for J.S. [Joseph Smith] I frequently wrote day after day, often sitting at the table close to him, he sitting with his face buried in his hat, with the stone in it and dictating [the *Book of Mormon*] hour after hour with nothing between us."[63] The plates themselves were kept "covered with a cloth" on a nearby table.[64] A similar recollection was given by David Whitmer, who would eventually become a key figure in early Mormonism. He described the translation process after an early convert named Oliver Cowdery took over Emma's position as scribe (c. April 1829):

> Smith would put the seer stone into a hat, and put his face in the hat, drawing it closely around his face to exclude the light; and in the darkness the spiritual light would shine. A piece of something resembling parchment would appear, and on that appeared the writing. . . . [U]nder it was the interpretation in English. Brother Joseph would read off the English to Oliver Cowdery, who was his principal scribe, and when it was written down and repeated to Brother Joseph to see if it was correct, then it would disappear, and another character with the interpretation would appear. Thus the Book of Mormon was translated.[65]

Martin Harris agreed with Whitmer, saying: "By aid of the seer stone, sentences would appear and were read by the Prophet. . . . [I]f correctly written, that sentence would disappear and another appear in its place; but if not written correctly it remained until corrected, so that the translation was just as it was engraven on the plates, precisely in the language then used."[66] Mormon historian B.H. Roberts, in his own comprehensive history of the LDS church (1930), wrote that Joseph did indeed have a seer stone that he used to translate the *Book of Mormon* and that the testimonies of Whitmer and Harris regarding this stone's use were accurate.[67] (Joseph would later use his white stone as late as 1835 to receive revelations from God and pronounce words of prophecy to direct his followers.)[68]

Joseph Smith's green seer stone resting on the *Book of Mormon.* Smith used a stone similar to this one to "translate" his golden plates (from D. Michael Quinn, *Early Mormonism and the Magic World View,* 1998; formerly of Princeton University Library).

What happened to Smith's seer stones? They are now in Salt Lake City, in a restricted vault in the president's office of The Church of Jesus Christ of Latter-day Saints. Access to it is denied to all but a few high-ranking Mormons.[69] Whether or not these stones are still being used by today's Mormon president, who like Smith is considered a "Prophet, Seer, and Revelator," remains a mystery.

Smith's Golden Book

Smith hoped to achieve a society led by a modern prophet, prepared for the total, imminent, miraculous transformation of the earth into a millennial kingdom at Christ's coming. . . . One of the Book of Mormon's dominant themes is that only under a theocratic government, ruled by men of God, can a society survive and prosper.

Dan Erickson, adjunct professor of history[1]

Chaffey College

THE INFORMATION PROVIDED THUS FAR has demonstrated that Mormonism emerged from a series of events radically contradicted by the sanitized and streamlined history of Joseph Smith now being proffered by the LDS church. The current version claims that Mormonism sprang from an 1820 vision by Joseph Smith of God and Jesus in the woods; followed by an 1823 visitation from the angel Moroni, which in turn brought about Joseph's retrieval in 1827 of the *Book of Mormon* golden plates, then "translated" with God's help so that by 1830 the volume could be released. Instead, the plausible events leading up to the publication of the *Book of Mormon* were most likely as follows:

c. 1819/20   Joseph Smith, Sr. and his sons—all of whom practice folk magic and embrace beliefs associated with occultism— become involved in money-digging.

1822   Joseph, Jr. discovers a chocolate-colored stone in a well he helps dig for the Chase family. Smith begins using it as a

	"seer stone" to locate buried treasure, stolen goods, and silver/gold deposits. He and his family continue to practice divination and rural folk magic.
1822–24	Joseph's reputation as a money-digger, fortune-teller, and seer spreads throughout New York and Pennsylvania.
1825	Joseph is now being regularly hired by persons who want him to find buried treasure through his occult skills. Josiah Stowell contracts Joseph and his money-digging company to locate a silver mine near Harmony, Pennsylvania.
1826	Joseph continues money-digging in New York until he is arrested, tried, and convicted as a glass-looker.
1826–27	Joseph begins spreading a story about an 1823/24 dream wherein he learned from a bloody ghost about the secret location of some golden plates hidden in a hill. The plates supposedly contain information relating to the location of buried treasure.
1828–30	The bloody ghost dream gradually develops into a vision of a spirit, then into a vision of an angel, then into a vision of an angel named Nephi and/or Moroni. Finally, in September 1827, Joseph allegedly retrieves the plates. He subsequently changes his story, eventually claiming that the plates are actually a theoretical treatise (i.e., a speculation) about America's ancient inhabitants. Joseph soon attributes religious significance to them, which in turn motivates him to use the volume to attract a religious following.

Even before the golden plates had been fully "translated," the Smiths, Martin Harris, the Hale family, and several initial Mormons began hearing the *Book of Mormon* story from Smith. According to him, the plates contained a chronicle of God's dealings with the early inhabitants of the Americas from approximately "2,200 years before the birth of Jesus Christ to 421 years after the death of Jesus Christ."[2] These inhabitants supposedly arrived in the New World by way of three migrations from the Eastern Hemisphere. This story would prove to be one of Smith's best tales.

ALL MANNER OF "ITES"

The first migration spoken of in the *Book of Mormon* is that of the "Jaredites." Smith said it took place soon after humanity's language had been confounded at the Tower of Babel (cf. Gen. 11). According to the *Book of Mormon* (hereafter referred to as the *BOM*), God commanded this group to travel over the "great waters" until they reached the promised land. Under the leadership of righteous Jared and his brother, these people eventually produced a great civilization that lasted nearly two thousand years until it was "destroyed by internal conflicts that ended in brutal and total war."[3]

The second migration took place during the reign of Zedekiah, king of Judah (c. 600 B.C.). At the Lord's command, a prophet allegedly named Lehi and his friend Ishmael led their families out of Jerusalem and into the wilderness. Like the Jaredites before them, this group ended up crossing the ocean to the Americas. They, too, established a great civilization, and were soon joined by a final migratory group from Palestine called the "Mulekites," under the leadership of Mulek—allegedly a son of King Zedekiah.

Unfortunately, all did not go well for the ancient colonizers. A sharp division within the populace created two warring factions: the "Nephites" and the "Lamanites." The Nephites, named after their mightiest prophet, Nephi, were "faithful members of the Church" and "believed the revelations and sought to keep the commandments of God."[4] This group included Nephi's sisters, and the families of Nephi, Sam, Jacob, Joseph, and Zoram.[5] Depending on their lineage, they also were known as "Jacobites," "Josephites," or "Zoramites."

The Lamanites, named after Laman (Nephi's brother), their most powerful leader, "were rebellious . . . [Their] minds were darkened by unbelief . . . [and] were apostates from the Church."[6] This faction included the family of Ishmael, and those of Lehi's two rebellious sons, Laman and Lemuel. Consequently, some Lamanites were also referred to as either "Lemuelites" or "Ishmaelites." (The Mulekites sided with the Nephites.)

After the division occurred, God not only prohibited inter-marriage between the two groups, but reiterated his wishes by pronouncing a terrible curse upon the Lamanites: i.e., "a skin of blackness" so that they "might not be enticing" to the "white, and exceedingly fair and delight-some" Nephites.[7] According to the *BOM*, the appearance of the Laman-ites with their black skin was so repulsive that that they became "loath-some" to look upon.[8] They also became "an idle people, full of mischief and subtlety."[9] Moreover, God warned the Nephites, "[C]ursed shall be the seed of him that mixeth with their seed: for they shall be cursed even with the same cursing."[10] Fortunately, God mercifully declared that repentant Lamanites wanting to join the Nephites could do so, and in so doing, "their curse was taken from them, and their skin became white like unto the Nephites; And their young men and their daughters became exceedingly fair."[11]

For hundreds of years the Lamanites and Nephites lived at enmity with each other, until one day Jesus Christ appeared to all of them, offer-ing his gift of salvation.[12] Jesus further explained about his crucifixion and resurrection in Palestine, and taught them the same things he had taught to those living in Galilee.[13] (Coincidentally, in most instances, Jesus used exactly the same wording found in the 1611 King James Ver-sion of the New Testament, even though the *BOM* was supposedly written more than 1,000 years before the King James Bible was published in Eng-land.) Everyone eventually chose to follow Christ, which brought peace to the New World and unity to all its ancient inhabitants. As the first edition (1830) of the *BOM* stated: "[T]here were no envyings, nor strifes, . . . There were no robbers, nor no murderers, neither were there Lamanites, nor no manner of Ites; but they were in one, the children of Christ."[14]

Soon afterward, however, war again erupted between the Nephite and Lamanite nations. Fierce battles raged as the Lamanites pursued the Nephites further and further north. Millions were killed on both sides, until all the remaining Nephites and Lamanites gathered for one final battle in western New York, near the Hill Cumorah. The Lamanites emerged victorious, allowing only a handful of Nephites to survive. But the fighting did not end. Within a few years the Lamanites became so evil that they began warring among themselves. By the time Columbus found them, these so-called American Indians had become a "filthy, and a loathsome people" (*BOM*, Mormon 5:15) who had lost all memories of their Jewish origins. They also had no idea that their dark-skinned appearance was a curse traceable to their failure to follow God.[15]

Smith's "history" also revealed that the chronicle of America's ancient inhabitants would have been lost if not for faithful prophet-historians like Mormon, who wrote down on golden plates an abridged version of the complex saga. He then delivered these plates to his son, Moroni, who in turn "added a few words of his own," and buried them in the Hill Cumorah.[16] For centuries they remained undisturbed, until Joseph found them in fulfillment *Book of Mormon* prophecies.[17]

INDIAN ORIGINS

Scholarly studies concerning the *BOM* have rightly surmised that its genuineness is "largely dependent upon the veracity of the idea that the Native Americans are descendants of the Israelites."[18] Here it must be noted that no professional non-Mormon anthropologist or archaeologist has ever given any merit to the idea that Native Americans are descended from Israelites. No evidence exists to support such a theory.

So where did Joseph get his inspiration for a lengthy manuscript devoted to the subject of American Indian origins? According to historical documents, speculation concerning Native Americans was a popular topic of conversation in the western New York region. This was due, in part, to the numerous burial mounds dotting the countryside. Curiosity about the nature and origin of these structures "made an amateur antiquarian of almost everyone in the area."[19]

As early as 1819 an article in the *Palmyra Register*, published in Joseph's hometown, theorized that "this country was once inhabited by a race of people, at least partially civilized, & that this race has been exterminated by the forefathers of the present and late tribes of Indians in this country."[20] An equally relevant article appearing in the February 19, 1823, *Palmyra Herald* suggested that the mounds were built by descendents of Noah's sons who had crossed the Pacific Ocean. It concluded:

"What wonderful catastrophe destroyed at once the first inhabitants . . . is beyond the research of the best scholar and greatest antiquarian."[21] Few persons lacked a speculation. Even De Witt Clinton, the famous New York governor, threw his guess into the grab-bag of conjectures by stating that the Moundbuilders "were unquestionably a lost race, which had once been vast in number and greatly superior in civilization to the Iroquois."[22] Fawn Brodie, in *No Man Knows My History*, observed:

> The theory persisted for half a century that the Moundbuilders were a race of peaceful farmers and metalworkers who had been invaded and utterly exterminated by a bloodthirsty race that was ancestor to the modern Indian. William Henry Harrison, shortly before his election to the Presidency, wrote that the last great battle took place on the banks of the Ohio, where "a feeble band was collected, remnant of mighty battles fought in vain, to make a last effort for the country of their birth, the ashes of their ancestors and the altars of their gods."[23]

By 1823/24 the growing number of rural residents whose interest had been piqued by New York's mysterious mounds included young Joe Smith. He loved hearing, as well as telling, tall-tales about American Indians. According to Joseph's mother, her son skillfully composed yarns about Native Americans while still just a teen; long before any golden plates had been found:

> Joseph would occasionally give us some of the most amusing recitals that could be imagined. He would describe the ancient inhabitants of this continent, their dress, mode of travelling, and the animals upon which they rode; their cities, their buildings, with every particular; their mode of warfare; and also their religious worship. This he would do with as much ease, seemingly, as if he had spent his whole life with them.[24]

Even more fascinating to Joseph was the contemporary theory linking Native Americans with Israelites. Such a proposition had been circulating as far back as 1567, when Fredericus Luminius, in *De*

Extremo Dei Judicio et indorum vocatione, put forth his idea that the New World's inhabitants were the lost Ten Tribes of Israel.[25] This legend would play an enormously important role in Joseph's future revelations, his notions about America's apocalyptic demise, and his thoughts on the establishment of God's Mormon-ruled kingdom of righteousness—i.e., Zion.

ISRAEL'S LOST TRIBES

Of all the nineteenth century notions concerning the "red man" of the New World, none was more widely held than the one identifying Native Americans as descendants of the lost Ten Tribes of Israel. The mythology surrounding these tribes sprang from the Bible's historical account of Abraham, who lived in the land of Canaan. Abraham, along with his son Isaac, and Isaac's son, Jacob, were the three Jewish Patriarchs—i.e., the founders the Hebrew nation. Jacob, whose name was eventually changed to Israel, is perhaps the most well-known Patriarch because from his sons (Reuben, Simeon, Levi, Judah, Dan, Naphtali, Gad, Asher, Issachar, Zebulun, Joseph and Benjamin) sprang the mighty Hebrew nation that fell into Egyptian bondage for 430 years (Ex. 1-14).

At the time of their emancipation, these Hebrews were united as twelve distinct tribes distinguished along familial lines stemming from ten of Jacob's sons (Reuben, Simeon, Judah, Dan, Naphtali, Gad, Asher, Issachar, Zebulun and Benjamin) and two of Joseph's sons (Manasseh and Ephraim). The descendants of Levi were put in a separate category because they served as holy priests. These tribes eventually settled in the land of Canaan as a united people—the Israelites.

But by approximately 930 B.C., the tribes had split into two kingdoms: the House of Israel to the North (consisting of ten tribes) and the House of Judah to the South (basically derived from the remaining two tribes). Both of these kingdoms eventually were conquered and exiled. The northern tribes were subjugated by the Assyrians, while the southern tribes fell to the Babylonians. It is at this point that the Ten Tribes legend begins to take shape.

According to historical evidence, the House of Judah returned to their homeland in 539 B.C. Much less, however, is known about the House of Israel—i.e., the ten northern tribes. It is only certain that they were deported to Assyria, and settled in Halah, Habor, and the city of Medes (2 Kings 17:6). Questions concerning the ultimate fate of these tribes have produced numerous tales throughout the centuries, one of the most common being that their descendants are the Caucasians scattered throughout earth.[26]

This concept first gained wide acceptance in Victorian England (1837–1901) when multitudes embraced the notion that they were biologically linked to Israel; a concept known as British-Israelism.[27] It initially gained a degree of recognition through the publications of Scotsman John Wilson (d. 1871). In 1840 he published a series of lectures as *Our Israelitish Origins*, which supposedly gave evidence "as to the peopling of England by the race identified with Israel."[28] Wilson further believed that nearly all Northern Europeans—including the German, French, Swiss and Scandinavian—were the lost tribes of Israel.[29] Another exponent of British-Israelism was Edward Hine (1825–1891), who began looking at the issue in 1840 after hearing a speech by Wilson. Hine disagreed strenuously with Wilson, though, by maintaining that only the British were Israelites. He explained his position in *Forty-Seven Identifications of the British Nation* (1871).[30]

Exactly how British-Israelism was introduced to the United States remains unclear, but by the late 1870s it was firmly established throughout America as a viable alternative to more orthodox views of Jewish history. The related concept suggesting that Israel's ten lost tribes had migrated to the Americas and were the ancestors of Indians enjoyed a similarly popular acceptance among U.S. citizens of the early nineteenth century. Joseph Smith was the first person to blend both theories into one grand scenario that neatly addressed the concerns of his day. As Disciples of Christ founder Alexander Campbell observed in 1830, the *Book of Mormon* commented on nearly "every error and almost every truth discussed in New York for the last ten years."[31] For many religious seekers, the *BOM* would be their long-awaited answer to prayer; a mode of salvation "in the *last days*."[32]

PROPHECY OR PLAGIARISM?

During the 1800s Joseph undoubtedly came into contact with books, newspaper stories, and clergymen, promoting various ideas about Israel's lost Ten Tribes.[33] The *Wayne Sentinel* of Palmyra, for instance, printed a speech by Mordecai Noah in its October 4, 1825 issue. This rabbi, who also served as editor for the *New York Enquirer*, had purchased Grand Island on the Niagara River, and there "dedicated the city of Ararat as a refuge for oppressed Jews around the world."[34] He believed the Indians were "'in all probability the descendants of the lost tribes of Israel,' and invited them to join their brother Jews on the Island."[35] The October 11 *Sentinel* added the following: "Those who are most conversant with the public and private economy of the Indians, are strongly of opinion that they are the lineal descendants of the Israelites."[36] Significantly, Joseph Smith, Sr. subscribed to this newspaper and had even run several advertisements in it, which means Joseph, Jr. certainly would have had access to the publication's contents.[37]

Numerous books also were available for Smith's perusal. There was Thomas Thorowgood's *Jews in America*, which in 1650 "promoted the idea that the Indians were descendants of the lost tribes of Israel."[38] In 1775 James Adair released *The History of the American Indians*. The year 1799 saw Charles Crawford publish his *Essay Upon the Propagation of the Gospel*, in which there are facts to prove that many of the Indians in America are descended from the Ten Tribes. Another work was *A Star in the West; or, a Humble Attempt to Discover the Long Lost Tribes of Israel* (1816) by Elias Boudinot, who wrote: "What could possibly bring greater declarative glory to God, . . . than a full discovery, that these wandering nations of Indians are the long lost tribes of Israel."[39]

All of these pre-dated Smith's *Book of Mormon*, which meant that writing anything more of substance about the Ten Tribes would be extremely problematic, as well as incredibly difficult—and Smith was smart enough to know it. History professor Fawn Brodie explained in *No Man Knows My History* that Joseph instead chose to describe only two Hebrew families, in essence, making his job much easier: "He began the book by focusing upon a single hero, Nephi, who like himself was peculiarly gifted of the Lord. This device launched him smoothly into his narrative and saved him from having bitten off more than he could chew."[40]

In recent years it has come to light that Joseph not only drew inspiration from contemporary works linking Native Americans to Israel, but actually copied portions of them into his *BOM*. For example, Smith almost certainly read Josiah Priest's *The Wonders of Nature and Providence Displayed*, published in 1825 (see Table 4.1).[41]

The Wonders of Nature[42]	Book of Mormon[43]
"a narrow neck of land is interposed betwixt two vast oceans."	"the narrow neck of land, by the place where the sea divides the land."
"From whence no traveller returns."*	"[F]rom whence no traveller can return."*
"Darkness which may be felt. . . . vapours . . . so thick as to prevent the rays of the sun from penetrating . . . an extraordinary thick mist. . . . no artificial light could be procured . . . vapours would prevent lamps, &c. from burning. . . . [T]he darkness lasted for three days."	"[They] could feel the vapour of darkness; and there could be no light . . . neither candles, neither torches; . . . neither the sun . . . for so great were the mists of darkness . . . [I]t did last for the space of three days."

*This phrase is from Shakespeare's Hamlet: ". . . from whose bourn no traveller returns" (Act 3, Scene 1).
Table 4.1

More striking are the parallels between the *BOM* and Ethan Smith's *View of the Hebrews*, published in 1823. Both books share the same basic storyline and premise—i.e., that a large contingency of Israelites arrived in the New World and separated into warring factions, the more savage of which prevailed after annihilating "their more civilized brethren" until all were left in a "savage state."[44] Other instances of *BOM* similarities to Ethan's work are so numerous that only a brief listing of select ones can be presented (see Table 4.2).

View of the Hebrews[47]	*Book of Mormon*[48]
"[T]hose far distant savages have (as have all other tribes) their Great Spirit, who made everything."	"Believest thou that this Great Spirit, which is God, created all things . . . ? And he saith, Yea, I believe that he created all things."
"[T]he places . . . are noted; among which are 'the isles of the sea.'"	"[W]e have been led to a better land, . . . [W]e are upon an isle of the sea."
"*I will hiss for them.*" God is represented as hissing for a people. . . . [To] behold the banner of salvation now erected for his ancient people. . . . This standard of salvation."	"[M]y words shall hiss forth unto the ends of the earth, for a standard unto my people, which are of the House of Israel."
"And it shall come to pass in that day that the Lord shall set his hand again, the second time, to gather the remnant of his people."	"[A]nd the Lord will set his hand again the second time to restore his people from their lost and fallen state."

Table 4.2

Even Joseph's idea about finding a buried book of history written by the ancestors of Native Americans may have been lifted from *View of the Hebrews*, which asked: "If the Indians are of the tribes of Israel, some decisive evidence of the fact will ere long be exhibited. . . . But what kind of evidence shall we expect?" Ethan Smith then provided information about a discovery near Pittsfield, Massachusetts of some parchment that supposedly contained Hebrew characters. These parchments, according to Ethan's story, had been found buried in a place called Indian Hill.[45] Moreover, both the *BOM* and *View of the Hebrews* contain the following similarities:

- begin with frequent references to Jerusalem's destruction;
- tell of inspired prophets among the ancient Americans;
- quote heavily from the biblical book Isaiah;
- describe the ancient Americans as a highly civilized people; and
- declare that it is the mission of the American nation in the last days to gather Native Americans into Christianity, thereby hastening the day of the glorious millennium.[46]

Interestingly, when *View of the Hebrews* was first published in 1823, and then again in 1825, one resident of the same small town in which the book was released (Poultney, Vermont) was a teenager named Oliver Cowdery, Joseph Smith's third cousin and future scribe.[49] The Cowdery family also just happened to be associated with the Poultney Congregational Church, the very same church led by none other than Pastor Ethan Smith, author of *View of the Hebrews*.[50]

Smith's creativity also seems to have been enhanced by his familiarity with the 1611 King James version Bible and the Apocrypha (i.e., a set of religio-historical books not recognized as divinely inspired by Protestants).[51] For example, several Bible stories were blatantly re-worked to fit *BOM* characters, as Fawn Brodie pointed out in her work on Smith's life:

> The daughter of Jared, like Salome, danced before a king and a decapitation followed [cf. Matt. 14:1-12]. Aminadi, like Daniel, deciphered handwriting on a wall [cf. Daniel 5:13-30], and Alma was converted after the exact fashion of St. Paul [cf. Acts 9:1-19]. The daughters of the Lamanites were abducted like the dancing daughters of Shiloh [cf. Judges 21:19-23]; and Amon, the American counterpart of David, for want of a Goliath, slew six sheep-rustlers with his sling [cf. 1 Sam. 17:1-54].[52]

Many names/words in the *BOM* were taken from either the King James Bible or the Apocrypha as well, in some cases, with only a letter or two changed to disguise their origin (see endnote #53 for examples).[53] In other places Smith simply plagiarized portions of text (see Tables 4.3 and 4.4). As a result, his finished manuscript—supposedly a translation of plates written in "Reformed Egyptian" between 600 B.C. and 33 A.D.—

contained non-Hebrew/non-Egyptian words inconsistent with the era and location of the *BOM* saga (e.g., *Greek*: Timothy, Alpha, Omega, Christ, Gentiles). Joseph also ran into other problems in attempting to uniformly use the archaic English of the King James Bible:

[T]here is a continual use of the "thee", "thou" and "ye", as well as the archaic verb endings "est" (second person singular) and "eth" (third person singular). Since the Elizabethan style was not Joseph's natural idiom, he continually slipped out of this King James pattern and repeatedly confused the norms as well. Thus he lapsed from "ye" (subject) to "you" (object) as the subject of sentences (e.g. Mos. 2:19; 3:34; 4:24), jumped from plural ("ye") to singular ("thou") in the same sentence (Mos. 4:22) and moved from verbs without endings to ones with endings (e.g. "yields . . . putteth," 3:19).[54]

Apocrapha[55]	*Book of Mormon*[56]
We will assay to abridge in one volume. . . . labouring to follow the rules of an abridgment. . . . But to use brevity . . . is to be granted to him that will make an abridgment."	"I make an abridgment of the record . . . [A]fter I have abridged the record. . . . I had made an abridgment from the plates of Nephi. . . . I write a small abridgment . . . . [A]fter having made an end of abridging the account of the people."
"[T]hey commanded that this writing should be put in tables of brass, and that they should be set . . . in a conspicuous place; Also that the copies thereof should be laid up in the treasury."	"And I commanded him . . . that he should go with me into the treasury. . . . I also spake unto him that I should carry the engravings, which were upon the plates of brass."
"Then the king, in closing the place, made it holy . . . many men call it Nephi."	"And my people would that we should call the name of the place Nephi; wherefore, we did call it Nephi."
"And it came to pass . . . I dreamed a dream by night."	"And it came to pass . . . Behold, I have dreamed a dream."

Table 4.3

Bible (King James Version)[57]	*Book of Mormon*[58]
"For, behold, the day cometh, that shall burn as an oven; and all the proud, yea, and all that do wickedly, shall be stubble: and the day that cometh shall burn them up."	"For behold, saith the prophet, . . . the day soon cometh that all the proud and they who do wickedly shall be as stubble; and the day cometh that they must be burned."
"[T]he Sun of righteousness arise with healing in his wings."	"[H]e shall rise from the dead, with healing in his wings."
"[T]he axe is laid unto the root of the trees; therefore every tree which bringeth not forth good fruit is hewn down, and cast into the fire."	" [T]he ax is laid at the root of the tree; therefore every tree that bringeth not forth good fruit shall be hewn down and cast into the fire."
"[T]he gall of bitterness, and in the bond of iniquity"	"[T]he gall of bitterness and bonds of iniquity."
"O wretched man that I am!"	"O wretched man that I am!"
"[B]e stedfast and immovable, always abounding in good works."	"[B]e ye steadfast, unmoveable, always abounding in the work of the Lord."
"Stand fast therefore in the liberty wherewith Christ hath made us free."	[S]tand fast in this liberty wherewith ye have been made free."

Table 4.4

HISTORY OR HIS STORY?

Another source of inspiration for the *BOM* may have been Joseph's own life, neighborhood, family, and friends. Joseph's adventures as a money-digger, for example, are described in a section of the *BOM* where one character speaks of hidden treasures in the earth that "have slipped away" back into the ground (cf. pp. 32–33).[59] And then there are the various *BOM* names such as "Lemuel," a wicked character.[60] This may refer to Lemuel Durfee, a neighbor who in 1825 bought the Smith's farm when they could no longer afford it, thus forcing them to live as tenants.[61]

Moroni (the angel) and Cumorah (the hill) may have come from any 1800s map of Africa. On such a map Joseph would have found the "Comoros" Islands off the eastern coast of Mozambique, which prior to its French occupation of the late 1860s, was known by its Arabic name, "Camora." (In the 1830 edition of the *BOM*, Cumorah was consistently spelled "Camorah.")[62] Geographical sources in the 1800s listed the capital of the Camora Islands as "Moroni."[63] The word Moroni, however, might also have been borrowed from the name of an Italian painter (i.e., Moroni), whose portrait of Galileo just happened to be part of the "Sarti Collection" exhibited in Boston in 1829, the same year Joseph was working on his *BOM* "translation."[64] These are but a few of the many *BOM* parallels to Smith's life.[65]

When the original 1830 *BOM* was released, Smith's lack of formal education also could be seen in the atrocious grammar that permeated the work. He consistently inserted an unnecessary "a" before participles, used "no" when he should have used "any" (creating a double negative), formed past participles incorrectly, and often used the incorrect form of the past tense.[66] There exist dozens of these types of errors in the original 1830 edition of the *BOM*, as the following partial listing of them illustrates:

"Moroni was a coming against them" (p. 403).

"As I was a journeying to see a very near kindred. . . . And as I was a going thither" (p. 249).

"[T]hey did not fight against God no more" (p. 290).

"[I] have not sought gold nor silver, nor no manner of riches of you" (p. 156-157).

"[N]o man can look in them . . . lest he should look for that he had not ought" (p. 173).

"[T]his they done throughout all the land" (p. 220).

"[T]his he done that he might subject them" (p. 225).

"[A]nd they had began to possess the land of Amulon, and had began to till the ground" (p. 204).

"[A]nd also of Adam and Eve, which was our first parents" (p. 15).

"[B]oth Alma and Helam was buried in the water" (p. 192).

"[T]hey was angry with me" (p. 248).

"And thus ended the record of Alma, which was wrote upon the plates of Nephi" (p. 347).

"[W]hen they had arriven in the borders of the land" (p. 270).

"[T]he Lamanites did gather themselves together for to sing" (p. 196).

"[T]hey did cast up mighty heaps of earth for to get ore" (p. 560).

"[W]e depend upon them for to teach us the word" (p. 451).

Other facets of the 1830 *BOM* inconsistent with its allegedly divine nature included out-of-place verbiage such as the decidedly American-ized name "Sam" (1 Nephi 2:5, 17) and the French word *adieu* (Jacob 7:27), which is an odd farewell to find in a book originally written in "Reformed Egyptian" centuries before Christ, then translated into Eng-lish in the 1800s.[67] Most of the errors in Joseph's 1830 *BOM* have since been corrected by LDS church leaders. As of 2001, in fact, the book had undergone a textual facelift consisting of nearly 4,000 substantive changes.[68] This despite the fact that Smith declared his original *BOM* to be "the most correct of any book on earth."[69]

Not every error, however, has been removed from the *BOM*. Those that remain involve a wide variety of disciplines: anthropology, history, geography, zoology, and botany. For example, Joseph's Israelites leave Palestine for the New World *before* the Babylonian captivity and proceed to build synagogues in the Americas "after the manner of the Jews."[70] But the Jews in Palestine did not construct synagogues until *after* their Babylonian captivity had begun.[71]

Consider, too, the problem in 1 Nephi 17:5, which describes Arabia as being "bountiful" because of its fruit and wild honey. The fact is that Arabia has never had bountiful supplies of either fruit *or* honey. The *BOM* also speaks of a river in Arabia named Laman continually flowing to the Red Sea (1 Nephi 2:6-9), yet there has never been such river in Ara-bia.[72] And then there is the description in 1 Nephi 18:25 of the New World having cows, oxen, asses, horses, and goats "for the use of man" 600 years before Christ. In reality, there were no such animals in the New World until Europeans brought them to the continent several hundred years later.[73]

THE NEVER ENDING SEARCH

Discrepancies between the *BOM* and historical fact are so numerous that it would require an entire volume to catalog and explain them. But the most damaging strike against the *BOM* is the lack of *any* archeological evidence to support it. In 1973 distinguished anthropologist Michael Coe—Professor Emeritus of Anthropology and Curator Emeritus of Anthropology at the Peabody Museum—unequivocally stated: "The bare facts of the matter are that nothing, absolutely nothing, has ever shown up in any New World excavation which would suggest to a dispassionate observer that the *Book of Mormon*, as claimed by Joseph Smith, is a historical document relating to the history of early migrants to our hemisphere."[74] In 1993, Coe reiterated his position, saying: "I have seen no archaeological evidence . . . which would convince me that it [*Book of Mormon*] is anything but a fanciful creation."[75]

Dr. Bradley Lepper—Curator of Archaeology at the Ohio Historical Society, and Assistant Professor in the Department of Sociology and Anthropology at Denison University (Granville, Ohio)—has extensively researched American Indian history and agrees with Coe: "There is no archaeological evidence for Old World culture in the Americas. Where the *Book of Mormon* makes specific claims around that, it's found wanting."[76] Even the Smithsonian Institution has issued an official statement refuting any claims of *BOM* historicity, explaining: "Smithsonian archeologists see no direct connection between the archeology of the New World and the subject matter of the book."[77] Some Mormon scholars, such as Dee F. Green, have conceded that there exists no such thing as *BOM* archeology.[78]

A similar conclusion forced two of the most prominent LDS scholars, B.H. Roberts (1857–1933) and Thomas Stuart Ferguson (1915–1983), to abandon their faith in the *Book of Mormon*. This shocking turnabout in their perspectives still haunts LDS church officials who adamantly declare that the two icons of Mormon scholarship never repudiated their testimonies. But private letters and various other manuscripts written by Roberts and Ferguson indicate otherwise.[79]

B.H. Roberts, described as "one of the [LDS] church's most valiant writers and speakers in defense of the *Book of Mormon*," began having doubts about the authenticity of the *BOM* after studying Ethan Smith's *View of the Hebrews*. He subsequently wrote two highly sensitive manuscripts that severely challenged the veracity of the *Book of Mormon*.[80] Both of these works were suppressed until long after his death, when they were acquired and published in 1980 by Jerald and Sandra Tanner under the title *Roberts' Secret Manuscripts Revealed*. The manuscripts were eventually published in 1985 by the Illinois of University Press as *Studies of the Book of Mormon*.

In these manuscripts Roberts acknowledges that Joseph Smith could have indeed written the *BOM* using his own talents and creativity.[81] Roberts' writings reveal that he grew especially doubtful about the divine origins of the *BOM* after comparing it to the works of Josiah Priest (*The Wonders of Nature*, 1825) and Ethan Smith (*View of the Hebrews*, 1823). His final conclusion diametrically opposed his former stance as one of Mormonism's staunchest defenders:

> The evidence I sorrowfully submit, points to Joseph Smith as their creator. It is difficult to believe that they are the product of history, that they come upon the scene separated by long periods of time, and among a race which was the ancestral race of the red man of America.[82]

Shortly before his death in 1933, Roberts told Wesley P. Lloyd that he had come to believe the *Book of Mormon* was a non-historical document. Lloyd wrote in his diary that Roberts said the plates "were not objective but subjective with Joseph Smith, that his exceptional imagination qualified him psychologically for the experience which he had in presenting to the world the *Book of Mormon*."[83] Lloyd also recorded: "These are some of the things which has made Bro. Roberts shift his base on the *Book of Mormon*. Instead of regarding it as the strongest evidence we have of Church Divinity, he regards it as the one which needs the most bolstering."[84]

Thomas Stuart Ferguson, even more than B.H. Roberts, dedicated his life to finding objective proof for the *Book of Mormon*. He founded the New World Archaeology Foundation at Brigham Young University, which was established specifically for the purpose of unearthing archeological evidence supporting the *BOM*. In *One Fold and One Shepherd*, he explained his hopes and dreams:

> The important thing now is to continue the digging at an accelerated pace in order to find more inscriptions dating to Book-of-Mormon times. Eventually we should find decipherable inscriptions. . . . referring to some unique person, place or event in the *Book of Mormon*.[85]

In 1962, Ferguson excitedly announced: "Powerful evidences sustaining the book are accumulating."[86] But by 1972, his expectations had been all but utterly destroyed, writing: "Ten years have passed. . . . I sincerely anticipated that Book-of-Mormon cities would be positively identified within 10 years—and time has proved me wrong in my anticipation."[87] In 1975 Ferguson finally prepared a 29-page report in response to papers written by Mormon apologists John Sorenson and Garth Norman, both of whom were claiming that archeological evidence for the *BOM* existed. Ferguson pulled no punches in criticizing his fellow Mormon scholars:

> With all of these great efforts, it cannot be established factually that anyone, from Joseph Smith to the present day, has put his finger on a single point of terrain that was a Book-of-Mormon geographical place. And the hemisphere has been pretty well checked out by competent people. . . . I must agree with Dee Green, who has told us that to date there is no Book-of-Mormon geography. I, for one, would be happy if Dee were wrong.[88]

Furguson, however, explained in a February 20, 1976 letter that he had decided it to keep relatively quiet about his findings because to do otherwise could destroy the faith of others. He suggested that like-minded Mormons do the same thing, noting that "Mormonism is probably the best conceived myth-fraternity to which one can belong" and that Joseph Smith "can be refuted—but why bother. . . . It would be like wiping out placebos in medicine, and that would make no sense when they do lots of good."[89] He further explained :

> Why not say the right things and keep your membership in the great fraternity, enjoying the good things you like and discarding the ones you

can't swallow (and keeping your mouth shut)? . . . [W]hy try to be heroic and fight the myths—the Mormon one or any other that does more good than ill? Perhaps you and I have been spoofed by Joseph Smith. Now that we have the inside dope—why not spoof a little back and stay aboard? Please consider this letter confidential—for obvious reasons. I want to stay aboard the good ship, Mormonism. . . . Kindly do not quote this letter and please do not cite me.[90]

In February 1983, Ferguson told Pierre Agrinier Bach, a longtime friend and archaeologist, that "'he was working on a project, a manuscript which would (according to him) expose Joseph Smith as a fraud.'"[91] Ferguson said that when his manuscript was completed, it would be a real "bombshell" on the *Book of Mormon*, "showing both positive and negative evidence from Mesoamerican archaeology, but concluding that the *Book of Mormon* was produced through Joseph Smith's own creative genius and through his use of contemporary sources, including Ethan Smith's *View of the Hebrews*."[92] Just before publishing his volatile study, Ferguson unexpectedly died in 1983—his manuscript mysteriously disappeared and has never been recovered.

Despite such overwhelming evidence against the veracity of the *BOM*,[93] millions of Mormons worldwide continue to regard it as a miraculous translation of ancient golden plates delivered by the power of God to Joseph Smith. These modern-day followers of Smith, like their early nineteenth century counterparts, see the *Book of Mormon* as a divine revelation designed to re-establish the true church on earth in preparation for Christ's glorious return. Such a perspective has been present since the very genesis of Mormonism in 1830, as history professor Dan Erickson has noted in *As A Thief in the Night*, his insightful study of Mormon end-time beliefs:

Joseph Smith's prophetic calling, supported by sacred scripture in the form of the *Book of Mormon*, provided revelatory answers to religious "seekers." Searching for spiritual authority, social cohesiveness, and divine direction in their lives, these "seekers" hoped to join God's elect saints gathered in the New Jerusalem on American soil. Here they would establish both physical and social boundaries, and consummate their American millennial dream.[94]

Law Office of

Thomas Stuart Ferguson
Robert R. Hall

23 Orinda Way
Orinda, California 94563
254-3930

February 9, 1976

Mr. & Mrs.

Dear Mr. and Mrs.

This is in reply to your letter of February 6, 1976.

In the December issue of Reader's Digest is an article on the importance
of myths to the human family. People must believe in something. (Otherwise
we face the abyss of death and extinction.) Mormonism is probably
the best conceived myth-fraternity to which one can belong. It's
a refinement of Judaism (which would never have sold, had Moses
announced as his own ideas, the ideas he came up with on Sinai) and
a refinement of the Jesus story (which sold because of one supernatural
account after another--written down long after the events--creating
a story difficult to refute -- as in the case of Moses, who was alone).
Joseph Smith tried so hard he put himself out on a limb with the Book
of Abraham, and also with the Book of Mormon. He can be refuted --
but why bother when all religion is based on myth, and when must have
them, and his is one of the very best. It would be like wiping out placebos
in medicine, and that would make no sense when they do lots of good.
(I'm sure placebos and myths can do harm in some instances -- but I
also think, at this point, that they do far more good than harm.)

Why not say the right things and keep your membership in the great
fraternity, enjoying the good things you like and discarding the ones
you can't swallow (and keeping your mouths shut)? Hypocritical? Maybe.
But perhaps a realistic way of dealing with a very difficult problem. There
is lots left in the Church to enjoy-- and thousands of members have done,
and are doing, what I suggest you consider doing. Silence is golden -- etc.
Precious few believers will you change--no matter how the evidence mounts.
They believe because they want to believe -- and don't want to face the
chasm of death and extinction etc. etc. Rulers of the nations have used
religion since the dawn of civilization because of the good things religion
provides -- peace to the person and a measure of orderliness to family and
the nation. (One of the major reasons for the high degree of lawlessness in
the world today is the breakdown of the mythologies we call religions.
People that don't accept "divine law" are prone to make their own rules and
the going can get rough.) So why try to be heroic and fight the myths --
the Mormon one or any other that does more good than ill?

Perhaps you and I have been spoofed by Joseph Smith. Now that we
have the inside dope -- why not spoof a little back and stay aboard?

Page 1 *(above)* and page 2 *(page 80)* of a letter written by Mormon scholar Thomas Stuart Ferguson,
who for many years was a stalwart believer in Joseph Smith. He founded the New World Archeological
Foundation at BYU and for twenty years attempted to locate archeological evidence supporting the
historicity of the *Book of Mormon*. He found no such evidence, concluding in the end, that Smith's
volume was "fiction." He remained a Latter-day Saint in deference to his family and friends.

- 2 -

Please consider this letter confidential -- for obvious reasons.
I want to stay aboard the good ship, Mormonism -- for various reasons
that I think valid. First, several of my dearly loved family members
want desperately to believe it and do believe it and they each need it.
It does them far more good than harm. Belonging, with my eyes wide
open is actually fun, less expensive than formerly, and no strain at all.
I am now very selective in the meetings I attend, the functions I attend,
the amounts I contribute etc. etc. and I have a perfectly happy time.
I never get up and bear testimony -- but I don't mind listening to others
who do. I am much more tolerant of other religions and other thinking
and feel fine about things in general. You might give my suggestions
a trial run -- and if you find you have to burn all the bridges between
yourselves and the Church, then go ahead and ask for excommunication.
(The day will probably come--but it is far off--when the leadership of
the Church will change the excommunication rules and delete as grounds
non-belief in the 2 books mentioned and in Joseph Smith as a prophet etc...
but if you wait for that day, you probably will have died. It is a long way
off--tithing would drop too much for one thing. (And I wouldn't worry
about the tithing people pay -- almost all of it comes back to the people.
The Church is as free of graft and corruption regarding money as any
organization in the world.)

Reading:

> Mormonism, Shadow or Reality?
> Jerald & Sandra Tanner (1972)
>
> The True Believer
> Eric Hoffer (Non-LDS, found in good bookstores as paperback
> at cost of about 95 cents.)
>
> No Man Knows My History (1975 edition)
> Fawn Brodie
>
> The Early Accounts of Joseph Smith's First Vision
> by Dean C. Jesse (He is on the staff of the LDS Church
> Historian's Office, SLC.)
> Article appears in BRIGHAM YOUNG UNIVERSITY STUDIES,
> Vol. Ix, Number 5 (Spring, 1969), pp. 275 ff.

I recently wrote a paper concerning the big weak spots in the Book of Mormon,
from the archeological point of view and for $5 will make a photocopy of
it for you if you wish to read it.

Kindly do not quote this letter and please do not cite me. Your confidence
will be appreciated. I have tried to help you as best I can. If you are
out this way, come and see me. Kind regards.

Sincerely,

Thomas Stuart Ferguson

On this page of Ferguson's letter, he actually recommends the anti-Mormon book *Mormonism: Shadow or Reality?* by Jerald and Sandra Tanner and also asks: "Kindly do not quote this letter and please do not cite me."

PART TWO

Establishing God's Kingdom (1831–1844)

An 1887 drawing of Lieutenant General Joseph Smith rallying his Nauvoo Legion during his last address to the Saints (courtesy of Utah State Historical Society).

FIVE

People of Zion

Soon we shall reach the promis'd land,
With all the ransom'd race
And meet with Enoch's perfect band,
To sing redeeming grace.
There we shall be when Christ appears,
And all his glory see,
And reign with him a thousand years,
When all the world is free.

Mormon Hymn (July 1832)[1]

ON APRIL 6, 1830, THE MORMON CHURCH was formally organized in New York by 24-year-old Joseph Smith, Jr.[2] By the end of that year he and his initial devotees had gathered into their fold 200-500 converts from Pennsylvania, New York, and Ohio.[3] All of them embraced without reservation the authenticity of the *BOM* and implicitly believed the revelations Smith had started issuing; revelations dictated in the first person as if God himself were speaking.[4] As far back as 1829, for example, the Lord had used Smith to promise that a "great and marvelous work" was about to come forth.[5]

The birth of Mormonism and its instant success can be linked directly to the religious climate of Joseph's neighborhood. This locality of western New York, known as the "Burned-Over" district, had been repeatedly scorched by the flames of religious enthusiasm. Consequently, the region became famous "for its history of revivalism, radicalism, utopian experiments. It was fertile ground for new ideas to take root and spread to other parts of the country."[6]

A PREPARED PEOPLE

The spiritual atmosphere of the Palmyra/Manchester vicinity was only one of many factors that helped Smith's religion emerge so rapidly. Early converts themselves seemed psychologically outfitted to receive the teachings specific to Mormonism. In the words of history professor John L. Brooke, the first Mormons were drawn from a "peculiarly prepared people, families that often had long stood outside the mainstream of New England orthodoxy."[7] Moreover, Smith himself could not have been better suited to be their prophet. His family background, spiritual ideals, personality, and superstitious nature seemed tailor-made for those who would eventually follow him.[8]

Disillusioned By Denominationalism

Early Mormon converts shared many attitudes and beliefs that literally drove them into Smith's congregation. A highly negative opinion of nineteenth century Christendom, for example, permeated their thinking, which included the following notions: 1) every denomination had strayed from the pure teachings of Christ; 2) nearly all clergymen were "wicked hirelings," interested in ministering only for financial gain; and 3) the emerging social order represented the resurrection of evil Babylon.[9]

According to LDS history professor Marvin S. Hill, Smith's earliest followers, in addition to being considerably less than middle class economically and poorly educated, "were religiously alienated, either having fled themselves from one of the leading denominations, or else come from parents or grandparents who had taken flight from sectarianism to become religious seekers."[10] These individuals longed for a restoration of "pure" Christianity, having concluded from their own experiences and biblical studies that the faith founded by Christ in the first century had been lost.[11] When Smith came along, they had no problem embracing his new religion, which according to him, was not new at all, but rather, very old—i.e., original Christianity.

Martin Harris, before even hearing about either Joseph's visions or the *Book of Mormon*, allegedly had been told by the Spirit of God to not join any church because they were all wrong.[12] W.W. Phelps had reached the same conclusion, explaining in 1834 that he "never believed that any of the sects of the day, *had it* [right]."[13] Thomas B. Marsh, an 1830 convert, embraced a similar conviction before hearing the Mormon gospel, recalling: "I withdrew from all sects . . . . I expected a new church would arise, which would have the truth in its purity."[14] And long before Joseph was even born [c. 1794], his mother came to the realization that every denomination was "unlike the Church of Christ, as it existed in former days!"[15] His father, too, had dismissed all churches, believing that the "religionists" of his day knew no more about God's kingdom than did secular persons.[16]

Such opinions certainly must have figured into Joseph's decision to start a church based on his new *Book of Mormon* (*BOM*), which coincidentally, stressed that in the last days God would re-establish his true church in opposition to the "defiled" churches of Christianity.[17] Smith himself made numerous references to the apostate condition of other religious bodies, often by revelation. In May 1829, for example, God spoke through him to condemn "those that do wickedly and build up the kingdom of the devil" by building churches "to get gain."[18] Two months earlier, the Lord had used Joseph as a mouthpiece to deliver a parallel message and an assurance: "[I]f the people of this generation harden not their hearts, I will work a reformation among them, and . . . I will establish my church, like unto the church which was taught by my disciples in the days of old."[19]

Smith, of course, claimed that he alone possessed the ability to restore Christianity. Such an assertion would have been difficult for Joseph to prove had it not been for God himself, who backed up the claim via revelation concerning his handpicked servant. It did not seem to bother Smith's followers at all that these revelations about Joseph also happened to come through Joseph:

> I have reserved those things which I have entrusted unto you, my servant Joseph, for a wise purpose in me, and it shall be made known unto future generations; But this generation shall have my word through you.[20] [T]hou wast called and chosen to write the *Book of Mormon*, and to my ministry; and I have lifted thee up out of thine afflictions, and have

counseled thee, that thou hast been delivered from all thine enemies, and thou hast been delivered from the powers of Satan and from darkness![21]

The anti-Christendom perceptions among Smith's converts quickly became a defining feature of Mormonism, which for decades vehemently denounced as satanic all denominational forms of Christianity. Until the mid-twentieth century, in fact, Mormons prided themselves on being radically different from the so-called "Christian" world—i.e., literally, the church of the devil. Consider the following quotations from Smith's two successors:

Brigham Young (2nd LDS President): "I saw that all the so-called Christian world was grovelling in darkness. . . . [T]hey cannot tell you so much as Balaam's ass told him. They are more ignorant than children. . . . The Christian world, so called, are heathens as to their knowledge of the salvation of God. . . . With regard to true theology, a more ignorant people never lived than the present so-called Christian world."[22]

John Taylor (3rd LDS President): "[A]re Christians ignorant? Yes, as ignorant of things of God as the brute beast. . . . [T]he devil could not invent a better engine to spread his work than the Christianity of the nineteenth century. . . . What does the Christian world know about God? Nothing."[23]

The sentiment behind these comments has remained an integral part of modern Mormonism, which officially still teaches that all Christian churches are corrupt. Of course, the harsh rhetoric once used to express this viewpoint has been drastically toned down in a concerted effort by Mormons to infiltrate mainstream religious circles (see Chapter Seventeen). Occasionally, however, the long-held Latter-day Saint opinion of Christianity seeps through the barrier of political correctness. LDS apostle Bruce McConkie (1915–1985), for instance, in his widely read *Mormon Doctrine*, explained how a "perverted Christianity holds sway among the so-called Christians of apostate 'Christendom.'"[24] In 1984, Brigham Young University professor Kent Jackson went even further, stating in the LDS church's official magazine, *Ensign*, that "Satan sits in the place of God in Christianity."[25]

Enthralled With Magic

Smith's long association with occultism also helped draw spiritual "seekers" into Mormonism because his affinity for the paranormal enabled other occultists to easily identify with him. There existed an instant camaraderie between Smith and like-minded practitioners of folk magic. Consequently, Mormonism rapidly became a haven for individuals, who, like Smith, had for many years been steeped in occult tradition.[26] The entire Whitmer family, for instance, several of whom were "witnesses" to the *Book of Mormon*, believed in magic and witchcraft.[27] In *Early Mormonism and the Magic World View*—a highly detailed, 646-page look at Mormonism's occult origins—historian D. Michael Quinn succinctly notes:

> [T]he first generation of Mormons included people with a magic world view that predated Mormonism . . . [namely,] the witnesses to the *Book of Mormon*, nearly half of the original Quorum of the Twelve Apostles, and some of the earliest converts from New York and New England.[28]

In *The Refiner's Fire*, Tufts University history professor John L. Brooke agrees with Quinn, observing that many of Mormonism's initial families were "very much attuned to the supernatural powers of witchcraft."[29] According to Brooke, Mormonism flourished as a direct result of having begun "in a culture of magical practice" prone to witchcraft lore, conjuring, supernaturalism, and superstitions.[30] The sheer number of early converts associated with occultism is highly significant, as is the variety of occult practices they employed.

Many of Smith's followers, for instance, possessed and/or used seer stones (a.k.a. peep stones): e.g., Jacob and David Whitmer, Hiram Page, Philo Dibble, W.W. Phelps, Lucy Mack Smith, and Elizabeth Ann Whitney, to name but a few.[31] The brother of Mormon Bishop Newel K. Whitney recalled how "Mormon elders and women often searched the bed of the river for stones with holes caused by the sand washing out, to peep into."[32] Even Mormon children used such stones.[33] The daughter of Elias Pulsipher, for example, had a peepstone by which she located "drowned persons, lost cattle and other items for people who sought such information."[34]

The widespread use of seer stones among Mormons continued well into the late 1800s, due in part to Smith's failure to condemn them. In fact, on December 27, 1841, he did the very opposite by displaying one of his stones to the Quorum of the Twelve Apostles. Many years later Brigham Young reminisced that during this presentation Smith said "every man who lived on the earth was entitled to a seer stone, and should have one."[35]

Other expressions of occult belief were just as popular. Mormon women, in following the ways of Joseph's mother, Lucy Mack Smith, practiced "palmistry, card-divination, and tea-leaf reading" as late as the 1880s.[36] Mormon males (including Martin Harris, Orrin Porter Rockwell, Josiah Stowell, and many others) tended to participate in money-digging ventures. And Alvah Beaman, one of Smith's money-digging companions, was a rodsman—i.e., someone who used a divining rod to find buried treasure.[37] Joseph and his father also used a divining rod.[38]

William Cowdery, yet another rodsman, spent several years in the Vermont-based New Israelite sect.[39] This group was led by Nathanial Wood, a visionary, who coincidentally, claimed to possess the powers of revelation as a literal descendant of the Lost Tribes of Israel. Wood preached a message filled with doomsday prophecies about a "Destroying Angel" that would bring earthquakes and plagues upon the gentiles on January 14, 1802.[40] His group, he said, would then "inherit that region of the country."[41] When nothing happened on the predicted date many of his followers dispersed westward, carrying their occult superstitions with them.

The New Israelites also advocated magic in connection with hunting for buried treasure by use of divining rods. Methodist preacher Laban Clark of Vermont was told that Wood's followers could find and "raise up from the earth 'vast quantit[ies]' of gold and silver, sufficient to 'pave the streets of the New Jerusalem.'"[42] The gold was said to appear in both "its native state [and] in currency."[43] Upon further inquiry, Clark learned that the cult's adherents included Justis Winchell, who "'understood refining gold' and kept 'himself secreted in the woods.'"[44] This account has led some researchers to theorize that the sect was to some extent an elaborate screen for a counterfeiting operation.[45]

Winchell just happened to board at the home of William Cowdery,[46] whose son, Oliver (Smith's closest ally during Mormonism's formative period), became extremely proficient at using a divining rod. In April 1829, Joseph went so far as to receive a revelation praising this "gift" of Oliver's as something of divine origin. Speaking in the first person for God, Smith declared: "[Y]ou have another gift, which is the gift of working with the rod: behold it has told you things: behold there is no other power save God, that can cause this rod of nature, to work in your hands, for it is the work of God."[47]

Like Cowdery, other prominent members of early Mormonism used divining rods: e.g., Martin Harris, Orrin Porter Rockwell, Joseph and Newel Knight, and Josiah Stowell.[48] Brigham Young and Heber C. Kimball were given their divining rods by Joseph, Jr. himself as a symbol of gratitude for their loyalty.[49] Kimball often received answers to prayer by praying "with the rod in his hand."[50] Brigham used his rod to find "where the Temple should be built" in Salt Lake City.[51] Young also owned two seer stones and a protective "bloodstone" amulet that he carried "on a chain when going into unknown or dangerous places."[52]

The depths to which Joseph and his family were immersed in the world of occultism is perhaps best illustrated by the various magical artifacts they used in conjunction with their beliefs: a magic dagger, three homemade magical parchments, a special pouch to hold the parchments, and a special "Jupiter" talisman (see Figure 5.1), which Smith had with him for protection, ironically, on the day of his murder in 1844. Several interesting bits of information can be gleaned from Smith's occult paraphernalia, especially the parchments, each of which had a direct link to magic used in finding buried treasure:

The "Holiness to the Lord" parchment (see Figure 5.2) was used to procure visits from "good angels," reveals its probable date of creation as September 1823—the very same month Joseph allegedly received his first visit from the angel Moroni.[56] Its many symbols include four penta-grams (necessary for invoking spirits) and the initials I.H.S. (i.e., *In Hoc Signo*, or "In This Sign" [thou shalt conquer]).[57]

The "Jehovah, Jehovah, Jehovah" parchment includes a magical sym-bol for another treasure-seeking angel named "Jubanladace." This entity was supposed to protect individuals from "'putrid infection and sudden death.'"[54] Smith's source for the symbol was Reginald Scot's 1665 *Discourse Concerning Devils and Spirit*, which explained that Juban-ladace also assisted in locating buried treasure.[55]

The "Saint Peter Bind Them" parchment (see Figure 5.3) contains the magical symbol for Pah-li-Pah, the second of seven angels in ceremonial magic. If invoked properly, Pah-li-Pah helped find buried treasure for the parchment's owner. The reverse side contains an inscription for Nal-gah, the third angel in ceremonial magic, "devoted to the protection of those who are assaulted by evil spirits or witches, and those whose mind are sunk in fearful and melancholy apprehensions of the assaults of the Devil."[53]

All of these items, except the pouch, were inscribed with not only magical symbols and incantations, but also with astrological markings. As it turns out, the Smiths, as well as many other early Mormon families, were entrenched in astrology—so much so that Smith chose to organize his church on April 6, 1830, a day known as the beneficial "DAY-FATAL-ITY" in folk belief, which in 1830 coincided with a particularly positive alignment of Jupiter with the Sun.[58]

Fixated On Doomsday

Another force that shaped early Mormonism was millennialism—i.e., the popular belief that Jesus Christ will someday return to set up a 1,000-year kingdom of peace and righteousness.[59] Although ultimately a glorious period of global harmony and godliness, this "millennium," it is believed, will be initiated through global cataclysm: i.e., social/political

Figure 5.1

Both sides of Joseph Smith's magical "Jupiter" talisman. The Jupiter Table *(left)* contains Hebrew letters, each of which has a corresponding numerical value. These numerical values, when added together in any direction, give the same total: 34. The total of the four columns is 136, which according to *Amulets and Superstitions*, written by Egyptologist E. A. Walls Budge, is "the number for the spirit and Demon of the planet" (p. 394). The opposite side *(right)* contains various magical symbols including the astrological sign for the planet Jupiter, a cross for the spirit of Jupiter, and a symbol that stands for the orbital path of Jupiter. Significantly, Smith was born under the governing astrological influence of Jupiter.

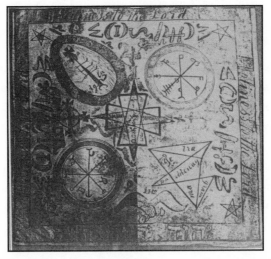

Figure 5.2

Smith's extremely complicated "Holiness to the Lord" (as written in borders) parchment, which contains numerous occult symbols, two of which were taken from Ebenezer Sibley's 1784 volume titled *A New and Complete Illustration of the Occult Sciences*. The explanation for one symbol (upper-right quadrant) reads: "'Whosoever beareth this sign nead [sic] fear no Foe." The stated purpose of the other symbol (lower-left quadrant) reads: "Whosoever beareth this sign all Spirits will do him homage."

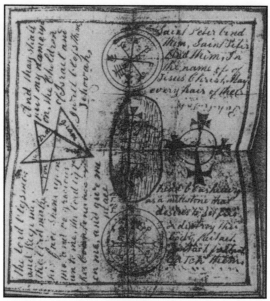

Figure 5.3

Smith's "Saint Peter Bind Them" parchment, used in hopes of warding off evil spirits. The Tetragrammaton symbol at left-center is copied exactly from Ebenezer Sibly's 1784 *A New and Complete Illustration of the Occult Sciences.*

upheavals, unprecedented natural disasters, devastating famines, widespread plagues, and bloody wars culminating in the battle of Armageddon and Jesus' second advent. According to history professor Dan Erickson, millenarian strength often took control of people's lives in rural areas when a prophet like Smith happened to appear on the scene:

> [It] required a prophet to give a millenarian movement meaning and coherence. . . . [T]he poor would seek improved conditions through divine intervention and by receiving prophets or would-be messiahs. They anticipated the final battle between the righteous and the wicked was about to transpire, after which Christ's kingdom would be established.[60]

A better description could not be given of early Mormonism. There is no question that it began as a doomsday sect led by an end-time prophet. Early declarations by Smith were filled with apocalyptic imagery and threatening predictions about the imminent end of the world. The *Book of Mormon* itself issued various warnings to nineteenth century readers. "Behold, the sword of vengeance hangeth over you," read one passage. "[A]nd the time soon cometh that he avengeth the blood of the saints upon you."[61]

Joseph's disciples came to him expecting to see such prophecies fulfilled in their day. Parley P. Pratt, for example, explained in his testimony that he saw Smith's declarations and the *BOM* as "a *new dispensation or commission*, in fulfilment of prophecy . . . to prepare the way before the second coming of the Lord."[62] Phineas Howe Young likewise testified that the *BOM* came forth "to overthrow all false religions, and finally to bring in the peaceful reign of Messiah."[63]

These perceptions were probably inspired to some degree by the many years of end-time speculation preceding Mormonism. As far back as the early 1600s, New England Puritans were extremely confident that the end was near. Cleric Michael Wigglesworth penned an extremely popular poem titled "The Day of Doom" in 1662. Deacon William Aspinwall of the state's General Court predicted the world's demise "no later than 1673."[64] There was also the influential Puritan Cotton Mather (1663–1728), who thought that all the prophecies needing fulfillment before Christ's second coming had occurred. He envisioned the world ending in 1697, but later changed this date to 1716. After that year passed, 1736 became his new deadline.[65]

By the time Mormonism emerged in the early 1800s, decades of doomsday predictions had created a widespread belief that God's era of deliverance had arrived. Smith, along with other nineteenth century Americans were not just living in the "shadow of Christ's second coming more intensely than any generation," but to borrow the words of historian Ernest Sandeen, they were metaphorically "drunk on the millennium."[66] Not surprisingly, in an 1828 letter to his cousin, Joseph Smith warned that "the sword of vengeance of the Almighty" hung over their generation and that it would "fall upon the wicked, and sweep them from the earth" unless they repented, obeyed the Gospel, turned from their wicked ways, "humbling themselves before the Lord."[67]

Joseph was saying nothing new, in essence only repeating what had been appearing in print for many years. An 1823 edition of Palmyra's *Wayne Sentinel*, for example, published a common sentiment that undoubtedly primed the spiritual receptors of early Mormon converts:

> The millennial state of the world is about to take place; that in seven years literally [i.e., 1830], there would scarce a sinner be found on earth; that the earth itself, as well as the souls and bodies of its inhabitants, should be redeemed, as before the fall, and become as the garden of Eden.[68]

Another impetus for the millennial madness of the nineteenth century came in the form of social and cultural pressure. Scholar Norman Cohn's work suggests that end-time obsession increases "when people are being uprooted and their traditional ways of life—however unpleasant they may have been—are being destroyed."[69] This description perfectly fits America's landscape during Mormonism's formative years.

Social oppression, dramatic cultural changes, uncertainty about the future, and economic stresses all contributed to the apocalyptic expectations of those who turned to Mormonism for psychological, emotional, and spiritual relief. Smith's doomsday pronouncements provided a kind of comfort the world could not offer. He relieved their minds of painful realities and filled their hearts with more uplifting subjects upon which they could dwell—e.g., the end of suffering, re-uniting with loved ones who had passed away, vindication of the righteous, punishment for the wicked, a world of perfect peace, true justice for all, and a fulfilling existence.[70]

The Mormons, of course, were only one of many millennial-minded groups that sprang up during the nineteenth century. In fact, the rise and fall of the most notable end-time movement in American history—the Millerites—coincided with the genesis of Mormonism. The Millerites, led by Baptist preacher William Miller, looked forward to the world ending in 1843 with Jesus' return and the establishment of God's millennial kingdom. Miller's views were first presented in several 1832 issues of the *Vermont Telegraph* (barely two years after the *BOM* was released).[71] The dashed hopes of Millers followers would go down in history as "The Great Disappointment."

Like Miller, Smith became a prophet to a special generation of faithful believers concerned with preparing themselves to enter the millennial Kingdom of God.[72] Several crucial differences, however, separated the Millerites from the Mormons; most notably, the Latter-day Saint belief that they were divinely chosen vessels destined to rule the earth *along with Christ*. Martin Harris often called public meetings during which he would address the townspeople, telling them that "God, through the Latter Day Saints, was to rule the world."[73] Albert Chandler, a Palmyra resident who helped bind the first edition of the *BOM*, remembered Harris very clearly:

> I heard him make this statement, that there would never be another President of the United States elected; that soon all temporal and spiritual power would be given over to the prophet Joseph Smith and the Latter Day Saints. His extravagant statements were the laughing stock of the people of Palmyra.[74]

Despite the many threads that tied Joseph to the people of western New York, his pool of converts around Palmyra/Manchester dried up by the end of 1830. Had Smith led a different life before the *Book of Mormon*, he might have gathered even more followers from that region of the country. But too many neighbors knew him as "an idle worthless fellow," a money-digger, and habitual liar.[75] Consequently, neighbors derided his claims and mocked his followers.

This in turn led to even more dire pronouncements; ones specifically directed toward unbelievers. Calvin Stoddard, who had married Joseph's sister, Sophronia, made a typical threat in 1829, saying that if Palmyra did not repent "it would meet the fate of Sodom and Gomorrah."[76] Oliver Cowdery voiced an equally strong position, saying in 1830 that he had been commissioned by an angel "to go out & bear testimony, that God would destroy this generation."[77]

According to the Mormons, perilous times were at hand. The signs were everywhere that global upheaval stood at the doors of history. King

Charles X of France had abdicated and been succeeded by Louis Philippe. Terrible storms had battered the West Indian Islands. Simon Bolivar was leading a bloody civil revolt against the Bogota government of Colombia.[78] "We are the most favored people that ever have been from the foundation of the world, if we remain faithful in keeping the commandments of our God," Smith told his followers. "Behold the prophecies of the *Book of Mormon* are fulfilling as fast as time can bring it about."[79]

But for those who either ignored or rejected this message, the news was not good. In a letter to followers living at Colesville, New York, Smith promised that vengeance would soon be taken upon their enemies:

> [W]oe will be unto them if they do not repent and be baptized [i.e., into Mormonism] . . . for God will not always be mocked, and not pour out his wrath upon those that blaspheme his holy name, for the sword, famine and destruction will soon overtake them in their wild career, for God will avenge and pour out his phials [sic, vials] of wrath and save his elect.[80]

Even on the joyous occasion of the church's formal organization, Joseph took the time to make dire predictions. saying: "Prepare ye, prepare ye for that which is to come, for the Lord is nigh; and the anger of the Lord is kindled, and his sword is bathed in heaven, and it shall fall upon the inhabitants of the earth."[81] And again, less than six months later, Joseph prophesied horrifying death and excruciating torture for the earth's wicked inhabitants (i.e., non-Mormons):

> [T]he hour is nigh, and the day soon at hand, . . . [T]here shall be weeping and wailing among the hosts of men. . . . I will take vengeance upon the wicked, for they will not repent: For the cup of mine indignation is full. . . . I the Lord God will send forth flies upon the face of the earth, which shall take hold of the inhabitants thereof, and shall eat their flesh, and shall cause maggots to come in upon them, and their tongues shall be stayed that they shall not utter against me, and their flesh shall fall from off their bones, and their eyes from their sockets. . . . [T]he beasts

of the forest, and the fowls of the air, shall devour them up: And that great and abominable church, which is the whore of all the earth, shall be cast down by devouring fire.[82]

Smith continued to warn neighbors and other townsfolk about their hellish futures until he realized there simply were no more area residents willing to accept his claims. Finally, in a December 1830 revelation, Smith instructed all Mormons to move westward to Ohio. It was the first time Joseph had given any commandment about a "gathering" together the Saints in one location.[83] Ohio, he had learned, was ripe for harvest thanks to the conversion of Sidney Rigdon, a popular Ohio preacher who had turned to Mormonism through its millennial teachings.[84] He would become Smith's right-hand man and one of Mormonism's most charismatic evangelists.

To facilitate the Ohio migration, Joseph began to stress the fast-approaching destruction of the wicked, making sure his followers knew that their only escape would be to "flee withersoever the Lord will[,] for safety."[85] On January 2, 1831, he warned that only by moving to Ohio would anyone be safe from the angels who were awaiting "the great command, to reap down the earth, to gather the tares that they may be burned."[86] Within days Smith issued another revelation, speaking in the first person, as if it were Christ himself communicating with the people:

[B]ehold the days of thy deliverance are come. . . . [I]nasmuch as my people shall assemble themselves to the Ohio, I have kept in store a blessing such as is not known among the children of men. . . . The kingdom of heaven is at hand. . . . [Prepare] the way before my face, for the time of my coming; for the time is at hand. . . . Behold I come quickly.[87]

Other Mormons gave similar warnings. Martin Harris sauntered into the bar-room of a hotel one day and told curious listeners that "all who believed the new bible would see Christ within fifteen years, and all who did not would absolutely be destroyed and dam'd."[88] LDS Apostle George A. Smith recalled that Mormons in the early 1830s thought "nine or ten years would be sufficient to wind up the whole matter of the warning of the wicked nations and the gathering of the Saints preparatory to the coming of the Messiah."[89] Some of the Saints actually believed they "would never die."[90] Clearly, the Lord was beginning "to build the New Jerusalem, the holy city of Zion in America, where the righteous would flee for safety and security while Christ's cataclysmic return destroyed the wicked and purified the earth."[91]

Smith's admonitions worked. His disciples packed up their belongings and started making their way toward Ohio. This would only be a temporary stop on their way to Zion. Although its exact location had not yet been revealed, the Saints were marching onward in obedience to the words of their prophet, who had at least given them assurances that the New Jerusalem would be established somewhere "on the borders by the Lamanites."[92] The Reverend Jesse Townsend wrote to Phineas Stiles about the their departure:

> The Mormonites have left . . . Joe Smith dare not come to Palmyra, from fear of his creditors; for he ran away to avoid their just demands. . . . We consider the founders and propagators of the Mormon "religion" simply as base impostors, whose sectarian assertions are false and absurd.[93]

By early February 1831, Joseph and Emma also had moved to Ohio, where Mormonism's future began to look very promising. Smith's critics had been left far behind, financial gifts to the church had made Smith's life much more comfortable, and determined missionaries were bringing in converts on an almost weekly basis.

PROPHET, SEER, AND REVELATOR

Having secured his base of power in Ohio, Smith unleashed a flurry of commands from God that he used to direct not only his own affairs, but the affairs of others. For example, on one occasion he commanded, via revelation, one individual to not sell their farm.[94] He also received a revelation wherein God allegedly declared: "[M]y servant Joseph should have a house built, in which to live and translate."[95] Joseph had used such manipulative techniques as far back as 1830, when he commanded

Martin Harris to either part with his money in order to "pay the printer's debt" for the *BOM*, or face God's wrath.[96] Such commands would become commonplace.

Meanwhile, the Mormon church's membership steadily grew, as did its infrastructure, which Smith gradually built using additional revelation, doctrinal modifications, prophecies, and visions whereby heavenly messengers presented him with more authority and/or previously unrevealed "information" about how the church should be run. Joseph even went so far as to begin revising the first few chapters of Genesis. He claimed that his revision (by revelation) not only deleted mistakes in the Bible's first book, but also re-inserted a great deal of material that supposedly had been excised from it by corrupt and evil men.[97]

One of the most important events relating to the church's organization allegedly took place back in 1829, with a visit from John the Baptist, who appeared to both Smith and Oliver Cowdery. During this meeting, John supposedly gave them divine appointments to lead all "true" Christians, as defined by Smith. Additionally, John bestowed upon them the Levitical (i.e., Aaronic) Priesthood, which is currently given to "every worthy male member," starting at the age of twelve.[98]

The more powerful Melchizedek Priesthood (i.e., High Priesthood) was officially established in June 1831. It had been granted to Smith back in 1829 as well. On that particular occasion, Smith supposedly met the apostles Peter, James, and John.[99] He explained the importance of this encounter at the Mormon General Conference of October 1831, declaring the order of the High-priesthood had "the power given to them to seal up the Saints unto eternal Life."[100] In other words, Mormon high priests possessed the authority to bestow salvation. Such authority had always been viewed by Christians as belonging to God alone. Consequently, this new revelation on salvation only served to distance his church even farther from mainstream Christianity.

BUILDING UP THE PROMISED LAND

An unending series of questions filled the minds of Joseph's followers during 1831. Where would God build Zion? When would its location be revealed? What exactly were "the borders of the Lamanites" that Joseph had mentioned? All the while, Smith continued releasing divinely-inspired statements reiterating the end-time horrors God was about to unleash against the world. In February 1831, for instance, he warned that the great day of the Lord was at hand, saying: "[P]repare for the great day of the Lord. . . . [T]he day has come, when the cup of the wrath of mine indignation, is full. . . .[T]he great Millennial [reign], which I have spoken by the mouth of my servants, shall come."[101]

On March 7, 1831, he gave another revelation about Zion (i.e., the New Jerusalem), stressing that only those who obediently migrated there (wherever that was) would find their promised land of inheritance—"a land of peace, a city of refuge, a place of safety" in the midst of global destruction.[102] Finally, the time to reveal Zion's location came on June 7, 1831, just after the church's General Conference: "[Y]e shall assemble yourselves together to rejoice upon the land of Missouri, which is the land of your inheritance."[103]

Missouri was an ideal location to build God's kingdom. The territory's huge parcels of land could easily sustain thousands of Saints. It was remote, undeveloped, expansive, and close to Lamanite (i.e., Indian) territory, which was important because the *Book of Mormon* had prophesied that mass conversions among the Lamanites would immediately precede Christ's second coming. The Saints could live entirely free from the prying eyes of unbelievers; isolated from the wicked world's vicious accusations against God's people and their chosen prophet. Smith also wanted to establish a printing press in the area, construct a magnificent temple, and as he put it, buy up the "whole region of country."[104]

Of course, achieving such a goal would require huge financial resources; resources Smith did not possess. He overcame this obstacle by using the revelation about Missouri to acquire money from his flock, saying that every Saint moving to Missouri would have to give their money to church officials to be used as needed. To illustrate his point, he delivered a revelation calling upon the ever-reliable Martin Harris to give all of his money to the church and move to Independence as an example to others of godly obedience.[105] Smith declared on one occasion that God wanted Isaac Morley (1786–1865) to sell his farm. Then, in September 1831, Smith warned that only those willing to give at least 10% of their income would escape being "burned" in the fiery judgment to come.[106]

Smith's economic arrangement, which he called the "United Order," rested on the idea that the earth belonged only to the Lord and God's servants were merely stewards of His property. Consequently, members were expected to "consecrate" their possessions back to God (i.e., the church), which in turn would allocate land and goods to families based on need. This "Law of Consecration"—delivered through a revelation on February 9, 1831—initially appealed to poor and rich alike. The poor would receive provisions they needed. The rich would enjoy not only the gratitude of less fortunate Saints, but also admiration for their sacrifices. In this way Smith accumulated the necessary funds he needed to build up Zion.[107]

Several months earlier, perhaps in preparation of his coming announcement, Joseph had made it known that hesitation to obey revelations would not be tolerated. In June he thundered: "Wo unto you rich men, that will not give your substance to the poor, for your riches will canker your souls! and this shall be your lamentation in the day of visitation, and of judgment, and of indignation: . . . my soul is not saved!"[108] For any doubters left in the church, he later issued a revelation informing his flock that any of them who received a command with a "doubtful heart" or followed a command "with slothfulness," would be "damned."[109]

The majority of Saints obeyed their prophet and poured their assets into the church's storehouse before flocking to Missouri. Their only hope of survival was to reach the land of safety before God's wrath destroyed the world around them. William McLellin, who later left the church, remembered that he chose to follow Smith in 1831 partly due to the message of destruction preached by two missionaries that came through town: "[T]hey came into the neighbourhood proclaiming that these were the last days, and that God had sent forth the book of Mormon to show the times of the fulfillment of the ancient prophecies when the Saviour shall come to destroy iniquity off the face of the earth, and reign with his saints in Millennial Rest."[110]

Getting the Saints to move to Missouri presented little difficulty. Unfortunately, a great portion of God's promised land was already occupied by pioneers known as Old Settlers. Furthermore, the very epicenter of Zion, where the New Jerusalem was to flourish, had been known for nearly five years as the town of Independence in Jackson County.[111] Joseph intimated that this might cause some problems, saying in his initial revelation about Missouri that the land of inheritance was "now the land of your enemies."[112] According to Joseph, however, God's enemies ultimately would be vanquished and their riches plundered, as Ezra Booth explained in a letter to the *Ohio Star*:

> [The Saints] are to receive an everlasting inheritance in "the land of Missouri," where the Savior will make his second appearance; at which place the foundation of the temple of God, and the City of Zion, have been laid, and are soon to be built. It is also to be a city of Refuge, and a safe asylum when the storms of vengeance shall pour upon the earth, and those who reject the Book of Mormon, shall be swept off as with the besom of destruction. Then shall the riches of the Gentile be consecrated to the Mormonites; they shall have lands and cattle in abundance, and shall possess the gold and silver, and all the treasures of their enemies.[113]

In other words, all pre-Mormon settlements "were merely in the way. It was but a matter of time until all Jackson County would belong to the Saints."[114] The Old Settlers of Missouri, however, would have something entirely different to say on the subject.

SIX

No Rest for the Righteous

Within four years from September 1832, [I testify] there will not be one wicked person left in the United States; that the righteous will be gathered to Zion (Missouri,) and that there will be no President over these United States after that time. . . . I do hereby assert and declare that in four years from the date thereof [1832], every sectarian and religious denomination in the United States, shall be broken down, and every Christian shall be gathered unto the Mormonites, and the rest of the human race shall perish.

Martin Harris (c. 1832)[1]
Witness to the *Book of Mormon*

ALTHOUGH THE SAINTS IMMEDIATELY began gathering to Missouri in 1831, most of their leaders (including several key merchants, landowners, and businessmen) remained in Kirtland. From there, until 1838, the administrative affairs of the church were directed. During these years Smith issued dozens of revelations, had numerous visions, and produced additional holy texts, each of which contained not only important doctrinal modifications, but also several brand new teachings.[2]

Meanwhile, a steady stream of Mormons trekked to Missouri, declaring all along the way that Jackson County would soon be the central hub of God's millennial kingdom.[3] They demonstrated the sincerity of their faith by the sheer industry they displayed in building up Zion. Within two years they had erected numerous homes and started a school. They were farming, raising churches, opening stores, operating a ferry, and publishing *The Evening and the Morning Star*, a monthly newspaper commissioned to announce salvation "before the great and terrible day of the Lord."[4]

But from the moment they arrived in Independence, the Mormons were looked upon as troublemakers. Their new home was a frontier town populated primarily by rough, illiterate, and anti-social hunters, tradesmen, trappers, gamblers, and assorted ruffians. Such individuals did not take kindly to being disdainfully termed "Gentiles" and being told that they would one day have to evacuate the area so God's kingdom of righteousness could be established. Furthermore, Zion had been settled by Southerners, and Mormons were Northerners. As such, they were hated by the Missourians before they had ever done or said anything offensive.

Even the more refined Missourians—doctors, lawyers, clergymen, editors, journalists, etc.—were both irritated and troubled over the unorthodox theology of the Mormons, their unbridled zeal, and radical ideas concerning America's role in prophecy. Consider the following excerpt from a list of Old Settler grievances that would eventually be drawn up against the Mormons:

> We are daily told [by the Mormons] . . . that we, (the Gentiles,) of this county are to be cut off, and our lands appropriated by them for inheritances. Whether this is to be accomplished by the hand of the destroying angel, the judgments of God, or the arm of power, they are not fully agreed among themselves.[5]

Mindless devotion to Smith's teachings also raised the ire of non-Mormons attempting to reason with the Saints about the folly of their beliefs. Reason and logical thinking meant little to Mormons, who commonly rejected analytical thought in favor of supernatural experience. Most claimed to have received "actual knowledge" of their faith's validity from God himself through revelations, visions, or angelic visitations.[6] No amount of argumentation could dissuade them, as one non-Mormon explained in a letter to the *Painesville Telegraph* (Ohio):

> [T]he great mass of the [Mormon] disciples are men of perverted intellect and disordered piety, with no sound principles of religion, with minds unbalanced and unfurnished, but active and devout; inclined to

the mystical and dreary, and ready to believe any extraordinary
announcement as a revelation from God. None of them appear to be
within reach of argument on the subject of religion.[7]

Most of the those who traveled to Missouri also were some of the
church's poorest members. They believed God would provide great
wealth for them in Zion if they faithfully built it up. This, too, angered the
Old Settlers, who viewed their new Mormon neighbors as the very dregs
of society.[8] Even more offensive was how these same Saints had the
temerity to display "a haughty and clannish self-righteousness. . . .
[T]hey knew Jackson, County belonged to them by divine right."[9] The
Mormons, however, were merely living out their revealed future as
found in one of Smith's revelations, in which God had promised to "consecrate the riches of the Gentiles" unto his people in the last days.[10] A
number of Saints actually boasted that they would "claim Jackson
County by force if necessary."[11]

The Evening and the Morning Star did not help matters by haranguing non-Mormons in the region about repenting, going so far as to
threaten them with imminent destruction if they did not do so. One
issue boldly announced: "[I]t is the time when the wicked shall be
destroyed . . . when plagues shall be sent to humble the haughty. . . . [I]t
is a time when the wicked can not expect to see the next generation;
yea, it is that great time."[12] Unfortunately, only fear, suspicion, and
anger would rise in the hearts of neighboring settlers. As for repentance, it would be the last thing on their minds.

CALLING ALL LAMANITES

By September 1832 Smith had officially defined the "wicked" as anyone rejecting Mormon beliefs. "[W]hoso cometh not unto me is under the
bondage of sin," he announced. "[A]nd by this you may know the righteous from the wicked."[13] Everything was defined in black and white
terms. Believers were Saints, Israel, and the elect. Non-believers were
sinners, Gentiles, and the wicked.[14] James West Davidson, in The Logic
of Millennial Thought, described this phenomenon as the "rhetoric of

polarization."[15] In other words, the Mormons had adopted an "us vs. them" mentality. Such an outlook accomplished several things.

First, the polarization enabled Smith's followers to view unbelievers as "part of Satan's forces who would block the kingdom's progress."[16] Second, it caused Saints to view any disagreements with, or criticisms of, their beliefs as nothing more than evil attacks prompted by the devil. Third, it intensified apocalyptic expectations since their prophecies had stated that persecution against God's people would increase as doomsday drew nearer. After all, the ungodly had persecuted Christ, who warned: "If the world hate you, ye know that it hated me before it hated you" (John 15:18).[17] Fourth, it encouraged zealous evangelism efforts that, if successful, would strike a blow against the numerical superiority held by God's "enemies," in whose hands rested the promised land. Fifth, the "us vs. them" mindset motivated many Mormons to respond to criticisms with more doomsday threats, prophetic condemnations, and verbal attacks about the spiritual ignorance and blindness of God's enemies. As historian D. Michael Quinn noted, "Nineteenth century Mormonism was not polite."[18]

Tension between Mormons and non-Mormons also grew out of a basic *BOM* premise: i.e., that Zion would be a gathering place for Native Americans as well as Mormons. This was related to *BOM* prophesies about "lost Israel" (i.e., the Indians, the Lamanites) eventually coming to understand their true identity and joining forces with God's people to build the New Jerusalem. Smith's missionaries, therefore, were instructed to begin seeking converts among the Indians soon after the *BOM* was released, and well before any Missouri migration had been announced.

After the Mormons arrived in Zion, President Andrew Jackson's ongoing Indian relocation policies were considered nothing less than God's hand moving Indians toward the promised land to join their long-lost brethren.[19] Old Settlers watched with great trepidation as waves of Native Americans trudged toward destinations chosen for them by U.S. officials:

> Through Independence trekked Shawnees, Kickapoos, and Pottawattamies. . . . The old settlers counted the Indian guns and listened uneasily to their lamentation and despair, but the Mormons watched the migration with a kind of ecstasy.[20]

Missourians became even more apprehensive upon learning yet another facet of the Mormon plan to establish Zion; one involving the unique role Indians were to play in the unfolding drama. According to Latter-day Saint beliefs, Native Americans would serve as God's arm of destruction. As historian Dan Erickson explains, "If gentiles continued in unrighteousness, these latter-day Lamanites would rise from the dust and begin to destroy them 'as a young lion among the flocks of sheep' (*[BOM]* 3 Ne. 20:16)."[21] The annihilation would be total, swift, and eternal. This apparent Mormon-Indian alliance was viewed as nothing less than a conspiracy to seize the entire western frontier, which made non-Mormon pioneers in and around Independence rather uncomfortable with the rapid influx of Mormons and Indians.[22]

Political fears gripped the Old Settlers as well. In 1830 Jackson County was home to about 2,800 citizens, and surrounding counties were even less populated.[23] The concern was that Mormons, as a single block of voters, would be able to seize political control of the region. Such fears were not unfounded. The Mormon population in Jackson County increased from 300 in May 1832 to 1,200 in 1833. Missourians knew that within another year or two Joseph's followers would be a clear majority and be able to use their combined voting power to affect elections. Furthermore, they would be able to use their collective finances to out-bid non-Mormons for precious land.

Kenneth Winn, resident historian at the Missouri Historical Society and adjunct history professor at Washington University, observes in *Exiles in a Land of Liberty* that the Missourians felt "their very livelihood was at stake." Winn explains:

> If gentiles [Old Settlers] did not wish to live among the Mormons, they would be forced to sell out to them and most likely at a loss. . . . On the other hand, if the gentiles [Old Settlers] attempted to remain in Jackson County, Mormon immigration ensured the Saints would soon make up the majority of the population, which would thereby permit them to oust the old settlers through ostensibly legal methods.[24]

But this seemingly unavoidable destiny would never materialize. Contrary to what God had declared through Smith's revelations, peace would not reign in Zion. In fact, the Saints' land of promise, their land of inheritance, would quickly become anything but a place of safety and refuge. Their determination to go on, however, would be fueled by a new doctrinal concept that seemed to explain everything in the most miraculous of terms—i.e., not only were they God's chosen people, but they were God's chosen people because they were literal descendants of Israel.

THE HOLY ONES OF ISRAEL

During the earliest years of Mormonism, converts to Smith's new faith believed that as God's latter-day Saints they would be "grafted" into the House of Israel. In other words, because none of them were Israelites by birth (i.e., God's chosen people), they would have to *become* Israelites via adoption. In this way, their migration to Zion (i.e., the New Jerusalem) could fulfill biblical prophecies, *Book of Mormon* predictions, and Smith's revelations about God gathering his people, Israel, to the promised land in the last days.[25]

But it soon became apparent to the Mormons that at some point in time they were going to end up second-class Israelites. After all, the gathering to Zion of God's holy servants would ultimately include persons who actually had Israelite blood running through their veins—i.e., Native Americans (Lamanites) and Israel's "lost" tribes. Where would this leave Mormons, who although residents of Zion, would be God's chosen people by adoption only? Smith and his followers apparently did not want to find out the answer to this question, so they began placing an ever-increasing emphasis only on their identity as "Israelites," rarely referring to themselves "as gentiles needing to be adopted into Israel."[26]

The Saints gradually came to embrace the notion that they were true Israelites descended from the biblical Joseph, son of the Hebrew Patriarch, Jacob. Some claimed to have a lineage going back to Joseph's younger son, Ephraim (Tribe of Ephraim), while others thought they had Israelite blood traceable to Joseph's firtsborn son, Manasseh (Tribe of Manasseh). Brigham Young, for example, in a reference to Joseph Smith, said that Mormonism's prophet-founder was a "pure Ephraimite."[27] Young believed that he, too, was an Ephraimite, and that he, like other Mormons were of "the House of Israel, of the royal seed, of the royal blood."[28]

Mormons today continue to maintain that they are literal descendants of Israel. A majority of them, in fact, assert that they, like their beloved prophet, have bloodlines going back to Ephraim. This information usually is imparted to LDS members when they received their "Patriarchal Blessing." Such a claim fits well with an early revelation given by Smith wherein he stated: "[T]he rebellious are not of the blood of Ephraim."[29]

Such a concept was particularly easy to establish in Smith's day when Anglo-Israelism was gaining popularity throughout both England and America (see p. 66). However, unlike classic believers in Anglo-Israelism, who held that nearly all Caucasians were Israelite descendants, the Saints believed that only they were of Israel.

This identification not only increased the Saints' sense of superiority over non-Mormons, but served to further distance them from unbelievers, all of whom were summarily condemned as "Gentiles" (i.e., *not* God's people). Most interesting was the evangelistic safeguard that Mormons built into their belief system for any Gentiles, who for whatever reason, might want to become Mormon without being descended from Israel. For these unfortunate souls, Smith came up with a novel idea that would literally make them Israelites: a heavenly blood transfusion. In his *History of the Church*, Smith explained this miracle by contrasting what happens at conversion to true Israelites, as opposed to those who must be made Israelites:

> "[A]s the Holy Ghost falls upon one of the literal seed of Abraham, it is calm and serene . . . while the effect of the Holy Ghost upon a Gentile, is to purge out the old blood, and make him actually of the seed of Abraham. That man that has none of the blood of Abraham (naturally) must have a new creation by the Holy Ghost. In such a case, there may be more of a powerful effect upon the body, and visible to the eye, than upon an Israelite."[30]

Several years later, Brigham Young clarified these words, recalling how Joseph taught "that the Gentile blood was actually cleansed out of their veins, and the blood of Jacob made to circulate in them; and the revolution and change in the system were so great that it caused the beholder to think they were going into fits."[31] The Saints, of course, did recognize that there existed many other descendants of Israel among the nations of the world—i.e., other Caucasians who had not yet heard the Mormon gospel. Consequently, a huge missionary effort was initiated to reach these lost brethren and convince them to come to Zion.

The most obvious place to start was England, which eventually provided Mormonism with a staggering number of converts. LDS missionaries arrived there for the first time in 1837. "Less than a decade later, one out of every three Latter-day Saints in the world was British, and a vast majority of those were English."[32] This high number of Caucasian converts who viewed themselves as God's chosen people greatly contributed to the ease with which Smith introduced one of his most offensive doctrines—i.e., persons of African descent are cursed by God (see Chapter Sixteen).[33]

SAY GOODBYE TO INDEPENDENCE

Non-Mormon anxieties over the growing population of Smith's followers only increased when *The Evening and the Morning Star* began publishing doomsday rhetoric in June 1832. The newspaper printed not only Smith's revelations, but also his letters to the church in Zion. Its very first issue included an 1831 revelation wherein God commanded that the Saints purchase as much land as possible in Missouri, which would ultimately serve as their "New Jerusalem, a land of peace, a city of refuge, a place of safety for the saints of the most high God."[34]

Smith then commissioned the press to print in book form all of his revelations since 1828—i.e., the *Book of Commandments*. Three thousand copies were to be printed and distributed. This would prove to be a poor decision on Smith's part. Even before the book was finished, his newspaper had been pushing the point that Missouri rightfully belonged to Mormons as "the land where the saints of the living God are to be gathered together and sanctified for the second coming of the Lord

Jesus."[35] To announce the release of a book brimming with such talk only succeeded in making the Missourians even more aggravated.

Additionally, the editor of Smith's paper, veteran journalist W.W. Phelps, seemed oblivious to how some of his articles might be viewed by the surrounding populace. For example, he often printed highly provocative references to Native Americans. "It is not only gratifying, but almost marvelous, to witness the gathering of the Indians," one article stated. "[T]he great purposes of the Lord are fulfilling before our eyes . . . Last week about 400, out of 700 of the Shawnees from Ohio, passed this place for their inheritance a few miles west, and the scene was at once calculated to refer the mind to the prophecies concerning the gathering of Israel in the last days."[36]

Magnifying the fear-inspiring quotient of such articles were subsequent issues of the paper that continued to make reference to the world's destruction. In November 1832, for instance, the following announcement appeared: "I will make mine arrows drunk with blood, and my sword shall devour flesh; and that with the blood of the slain and of the captives from the beginning of revenges upon the enemy."[37] This same issue also printed an alarming prayer: "O that God would arm me for the battle and prepare me for the war;—'For I will fight until I conquer, though I die.'"[38]

Then, in January 1833, Smith himself voiced more end-of-the-world opinions in a letter printed by the *American Revivalist and Rochester Observer*: "I am prepared to say by the authority of Jesus Christ, that not many years shall pass away before the United States shall present such a scene of *bloodshed* as has not a parallel in the history of our nation."[39] Smith also intimated that this bloodshed might occur in or near Missouri. He most certainly fixed the timing of the carnage within the generation of those hearing his words—on this point everyone was agreed:

> The people of the Lord . . . have already commenced to gather together to Zion, which is in the state of Missouri; therefore I declare unto you the warning which the Lord has commanded me to declare unto this generation, ... '[T]he hour of His judgment is come.' . . . [F]lee to Zion, before the overflowing scourge overtake you, for there are those now living

upon the earth whose eyes shall not be closed in death until they see all
these things, which I have spoken, fulfilled.[40]

Doomsday's nearness was apparent to every Mormon. It had
already been a full year since Smith declared: "[T]his generation of Jews
shall not pass away until every desolation which I have told you concerning them shall come to pass."[41] Moreover, the number of signs
heralding Christ's return were mounting quickly. Some of the many
events during the 1830s that seemed to signal an imminent establishment of Zion included: political tensions in Europe; cholera "spreading
over the whole earth;" rebellion in South Carolina (c. 1832); the plague
in India; and various fires in American cities that sent smoke into the
air, which fulfilled biblical prophecies about "signs in the heavens, and
on earth, blood, fire, and pillars of smoke."[42] Only the spiritually blinded
could miss the obvious:

> [O]h! such fearful looking for the wrath of God to be poured out upon
> this generation, together with the evidence of Holy writ, ought to con-
> vince every man in the world, that the end is near; that the harvest is
> ripe, and that the angels are reaping down the earth![43]

As if things were not stressful enough, a rumor began circulating in
early 1832 that the Mormons (Yankees espousing anti-slavery attitudes)
were sowing seeds of dissension among slaves. Church officials promised to look into the matter and censure the offenders, if indeed there
were any. But by that time scattered acts of violence by the Old Settlers
had already begun: "[N]ight-riding gentiles stoned Mormon homes,
broke windows, set hay stacks afire, and discharged random shots into
church settlements."[44]

This type of vandalism and intimidation tactics continued until July
1833, when a handful of free Blacks who had become Latter-day Saints
attempted to emigrate to Independence ("Zion"), just as all faithful Mormons were doing. But Phelps knew that Missouri law forbade the
entrance of free Blacks unless they possessed a certificate of citizenship

from another state, so he published the applicable statute in *The Evening and the Morning Star*, explaining that it was being published "[t]o prevent any misunderstanding among the churches abroad, respecting free people of color, who may think of coming to the western boundaries of Missouri, as members of the Church."[45]

Unfortunately, Phelps's article, which he had unthinkingly titled "FREE PEOPLE OF COLOR," ended with an easily misunderstood statement of caution: "So long as we have no special rule in the Church, as to people of color, let prudence guide . . . [T]hey, as well as we, are in the hands of a merciful God."[46] This same July issue also included a letter from "The Elders Stationed in Zion, to the Churches Abroad," saying: "As to slaves, we have nothing to say; In connection with the wonderful events of this age, much is doing towards abolishing slavery, and colonizing the blacks, in Africa."[47] Phelps seemed to think the articles actually would assuage Old Settler fears.

Instead, the Old Settlers saw the July issue as a thinly-disguised invitation to free Blacks that included instructions on how to legally migrate to Missouri using a citizenship certificate. Residents of Independence no longer had any doubts that the Mormons were intending to incite economic and social upheaval. According to the slaveholders, free Blacks circulating among people of color still in bondage would invariably lead to an uprising. The Old Settlers soon called a town meeting during which they drew up a manifesto demanding that the Mormons immediately leave Jackson County.

It explained that the Missourians had assembled together because the Mormons were threatening their "civil society." Ironically, to save their "civil" society, the Old Settlers had decided to rid themselves of the Mormons "'peaceably if we can, forcibly if we must.'"[48] After referring to Smith's followers as "deluded fanatics" and "knaves," the manifesto repeated the accusation that Mormons had been trying to sow dissension among slaves. It then referred to Phelps' "FREE PEOPLE OF COLOR" article as an invitation for free blacks and mulattoes to settle in Jackson County, and "corrupt our blacks, and instigate them to bloodshed."[49] The hundreds of townsfolk who signed the document included numerous city leaders: the jailor, county clerk, deputy county clerk, postmaster, judge of the court, justice of the peace, constable, deputy constable, and various merchants.[50]

Shock and alarm rippled through the Mormon community as the manifesto began circulating around town. Phelps could not believe his eyes, and as one historian has put it, "somersaulted backwards to undo the mischief."[51] In an attempt to defuse the explosive situation before another anti-Mormon meeting scheduled for July 20, 1833, could take place, Phelps hastily drew up and released an "Extra" edition of *The Evening and the Morning Star* that frantically tried to explain:

> Having learned with extreme regret, that an article entitled, "Free People of Color," in the last number of the *Star*, has been misunderstood, we feel in duty bound to state, in this *Extra*, that our intention was not only to stop free people of color from emigrating to this state, but to prevent them from being admitted as members of the Church.[52]

But in his haste, Phelps foolishly added from his previous issue the statement: "As to slaves, we have nothing to say; in connection with the wonderful events of this age much is doing towards abolishing slavery, and colonizing the blacks in Africa."[53] The Missourians either ignored, or misunderstood, Phelps's recantation. On July 20 five hundred of them gathered at a mass meeting and drew up five demands: 1) Mormon immigration to Jackson County must cease; 2) Mormons already in Missouri must sell their lands and leave; 3) the Mormon press, storehouse, and shops must close immediately; 4) leaders will be responsible for making sure the demands are met; and 5) "those who fail to comply with these requisitions, be referred to those of their brethren who have the gifts of divination, and of unknown tongues, to inform them of the lot that awaits them."[54]

It goes without saying that these demands were illegal and diametrically opposed to the rights and freedoms guaranteed by the Constitution. But the Mormons had no defenders among the Old Settlers, who adjourned for two hours so a delegation could deliver the ultimatum.

Mormon leaders, who were given only fifteen minutes to accept the demands, did not reject the proposal outright, but simply asked for more time to consult with church headquarters in Ohio.

This answer, however, did not satisfy the mob. That afternoon witnessed the beginning of what would be a long series of brutal acts against the Mormons reflective of the barbarism so prevalent on the frontier during the mid-nineteenth century. "[A] large body of Missourians swarmed into the Star office, throwing the press and type out of an upper story window before pulling down the building."[55] The mob then chased W.W. Phelps and his family out into the street and destroyed their home. They also threw unbound pages of Smith's *Book of Commandments* on the ground, while continually shouting insults about Smith and mocking his followers.[56]

The Missourians further satiated their thirst for violence by tarring and feathering Mormons Edward Partridge and Charles Allen. The tar had even been laced with some type of acid solution so it would burn away the flesh. Still not satisfied, the mob drove Mormon men, women, and children from their homes and into nearby cornfields, wooded areas, and thickets. They were able to return only after night had fallen. In one afternoon, the residents of a town named "Independence," had trampled to bits the Saints' freedoms of speech, press, and religion.

Three days later, after receiving no signs of a Mormon exodus, the Old Settlers invaded the Mormon settlement with dirks, pistols, clubs, whips, and rifles. They threatened church officials with hundreds of lashes, which meant certain death, and promised that unless every Saint left the area, slaves would be ordered to destroy all the Mormon crops.[57] The mob then assured Latter-day Saint leaders that "every man, woman, and child would be whipped or scourged until they were driven out of the county."[58] Mormons leaders had no choice but to agree that the entire colony would depart.

Meanwhile, back in Kirtland, word had not yet reached Joseph that his press located nearly 1,000 miles away had been destroyed and his followers abused. He was busy laying the cornerstone of the first Mormon temple. This new venture so aroused his millennial fervor that he received yet another revelation on August 2, 1833, the contents of which seemed to indicate that God also was unaware of the Missouri tragedy: The Lord commanded that a new temple was to be "speedily" built in the land of Zion, and that all the Saints were to give 10% of their assets in order to finance it.[59]

Disobedience to this directive would result in "sore affliction, with pestilence, with plague with sword, with vengeance, with devouring fire."[60] But obedience, God promised, would bring blessings and prosperity to Zion. "And the nations of the earth shall honor her, and shall say: Surely Zion is the city of our God, and surely Zion cannot fall, neither be moved out of her place."[61] Fawn Brodie, in her volume on Smith's life, commented: "No other of all Joseph Smith's revelations was so badly timed."[62]

When Smith finally heard about what had occurred, he issued a revelation telling his followers in Missouri to "renounce war and proclaim peace."[63] At the same time, however, this revelation included a radically new concept that would ultimately affect how Mormons would respond in the future to the American government. Smith, for the first time, defined his church as a religious sovereignty within the civil sovereignty of the United States of America. The revelation "established the primacy of religious law over secular law . . . and not only authorized but commanded Mormons to disobey secular law and civil leaders not conforming to the commandments of God."[64]

Smith then petitioned Missouri's governor, Daniel Dunklin, for justice. Dunklin sympathized with the Mormons, but declined to help unless the Mormons first dealt with the issue in local courts. The Saints in Jackson County, although doubting their chances of receiving fair legal treatment, subsequently retained four attorneys on October 30, which only served to further enrage the Old Settlers. The next day fifty men attacked a small isolated Mormon colony and partially demolished ten cabins, "whipped and stoned the men, and drove the women and children shrieking into the woods."[65] This anti-Mormon violence persisted for several nights in a row, compelling the Saints to organize armed defensive units for patrolling their settlements. Finally, on

November 4, an inevitable clash occurred when a Mormon patrol led by David Whitmer ran into some marauding Missourians. The ensuing "Battle of Blue River" left two Old Settlers and one Mormon dead.[66]

Lieutenant Governor Lilburn Boggs, an Independence resident, realized that things had gotten out of hand and called the militia to restore order. But Boggs, who was anything but impartial, named Thomas Pitcher—a known anti-Mormon—as the militia's head. A few days later, after assembling the militia, both Boggs and Pitcher then ordered the Mormons to surrender their arms, promising that in order to restore peace the Old Settlers would be disarmed as well. The Saints reluctantly obeyed, but Pitcher, predictably, reneged on his pledge to disarm the Missourians.

That night the mob systematically sacked the defenseless Mormon community, beat the men, and "drove the women and children out like cattle. Before morning twelve hundred people had been herded forth in the teeth of a November gale."[67] They had neither provision, nor direction. Some fled to nearby Clay County, but most of those exiled remained huddled in the woodlands by the Missouri River. Their only comfort was the hope that Christ would soon deliver them.

Interestingly, on November 13, 1833, within days of their departure, an apparent answer to their prayers appeared in the heavens in the form of a magnificent meteor shower. One Mormon, Benjamin Johnson, remembered that night well:

[M]y pen is inadequate to give a description of the scene then presented, for the heavens were full of a blazing storm, from zenith to horizon, and a view more sublime and terrible the eyes of man may never have seen. To the fearful it struck terror, and even some of the Saints seemed almost paralyzed with fear, for it appeared for a time that both the heavens and the earth were on fire. I gazed upon the scene with wondering awe, but with full realization of its purport as a sign of the last days.[68]

The nation's presses universally condemned the Jackson County mob, which meant that for the first time in its short history, Mormons had public opinion on their side. But the media's denunciation of the events in Missouri would not be enough to save Zion. By January 1, 1834, nearly every Mormon had left Independence and settled in neighboring Clay County, where the residents were appalled at what had taken place. But there was no consoling the Saints. The greatly prized land of their inheritance "had become the land of empty promise."[69]

ZION'S CAMP

Joseph Smith had put his prophetic reputation on the line by claiming that the Lord himself had named Independence as the "center place" of Zion. Consequently, he was both unwilling and unable to admit defeat. His only choice was to re-establish a Mormon presence in Jackson County; if necessary, by making war on the wicked "Gentiles" who had frustrated his plans. He went so far as to claim on December 16, 1833, that he had received a revelation condoning military intervention. God decreed: "[B]reak down the walls of mine enemies; throw down their tower, and scatter their watchmen. . . . [A]venge me of mine enemies, that by and by I may come with the residue of mine house and possess the land."[70]

But first, Smith took the time to write to president Andrew Jackson, including with his letter, a copy of a 3,000-word revelation that said, among other things, that if something was not done for the Mormons, the Lord would "vex the nation" in fury.[71] Smith must have known that Washington would do very little. Even before receiving a reply, he issued another revelation wherein God stated that "the redemption of Zion must needs come by power." This divine message continued: "Gather yourselves together unto the land of Zion . . . And inasmuch as mine enemies come against you . . . ye shall curse them . . . And my presence will be with you even in avenging me of mine enemies"[72] God also commanded Joseph to raise volunteers for an army to battle the Missourians just as the ancient Israelites had fought against God's enemies in the days of the Old Testament.

The church's high council agreed with Smith's decision and unanimously elected him "commander-in-chief of the armies of Israel." By

April 1834, approximately 200 Saints had come under Smith's command, and were ready to march to Missouri and reclaim Mormon lands. Smith's rallying speech set forth the importance of their mission:

> [W]ithout a Zion, and a place of deliverance, we must fall; because the time is near when the sun will be darkened, the moon turn to blood, the stars fall from heaven, and the earth reel to and fro. Then, if this is the case, and if we are not sanctified and gathered to the places where God has appointed, [despite] with all our former professions and our great love for the Bible, we must fall, we cannot stand; we cannot be saved; for God will gather out his Saints from the gentiles and then comes desolation or destruction and none can escape except the pure in heart who are gathered.[73]

Finally, the response to Smith from America's Secretary of War arrived, but it only confirmed what he knew all along. His proper recourse was to appeal to Missouri authorities—not the president. The reply was inconsequential since Smith had already started toward Missouri with his military contingency, which had come to be known as Zion's Camp.[74]

By the middle of June, Zion's Camp had traveled more than 600 miles, and were encamped just ten miles northeast of Liberty, Missouri, just above the Little and Big Fishing rivers. The Old Settlers were poised to attack on June 19, but on that very night, a fierce rainstorm caused the river to raise 30-40 feet, thereby thwarting the offensive.[77] It was a fortunate turn of events since the Missourians outnumbered Zion's Camp by several hundred and would have certainly slaughtered all of them.

But Smith's luck ran out only a few days later when cholera swept through his rag-tag troops. As the disease spread, Smith released a revelation saying that their undertaking was being endangered because of a lack of righteousness in the camp, and that God was not pleased with the assembly. The cholera eventually infected sixty-eight of Smith's followers, thirteen of whom died, including Smith's cousin, Jessie.[78] By the end of June, Smith realized that the whole mission was futile. He subsequently disbanded God's army, explaining that everyone would have to get back

Late 19th century depiction of "Zion's Camp" as it marches off to war in May 1834. The military campaign to reclaim Mormon lands seized by the mobs in Jackson County, Missouri, was a complete failure. (from T.B.K. Stenhouse, *The Rocky Mountain Saints*, 1873).

to Ohio on their own, "the best way they could."[79] In *The Mormon Hierarchy: Origins of Power*, D. Michael Quinn concisely explains the significance of Zion's Camp, even though it was by all accounts a failure:

> Zion's Camp did not redeem Zion, but it transformed Mormon leadership and culture. . . . This was one of the first acts of the newly organized high council which thus acknowledged Smith's religious right to give God's command to "go out unto battle against any nation, kindred, tongue, or people." Zion's Camp was the first organization established for the external security of Mormonism. A year later, the military experience of Zion's Camp (rather than any ecclesiastical service) was the basis upon which Smith said he was selecting men for the newly organized Quorum of the Twelve Apostles and the Seventy. Unlike other American denominations, "the church militant" was a literal fact in Mormonism, not just a symbolic slogan.[80]

Before leaving Missouri, Smith issued one last revelation to his disheartened soldiers, as explained in a letter by Mormon Reed Peck: "[A]ll hopes were destroyed of 'redeeming Zion' for the present, but to console the Mormons under this disappointment, Joseph Smith, before he returned from the campaign prophesied publicly to them, that 'within three years they should march to Jackson County and there should not be a dog to open his mouth against them.'"[81]

Smith ultimately placed blame for the humiliating venture not on his own shoulders, but upon the sinful conduct, lack of faith, and ungodly attitudes of those traveling with him.[82] As for the 1,000-plus Saints from Independence who had lost their property, and nearly their lives, they were instructed to stay in Clay County, just north of Independence. There they were warmly welcomed as persecuted and misunderstood religious eccentrics. Clay County residents had gone so far as to provide the now poverty-stricken Saints with provisions and shelter. But this situation, too, would gradually change amid more threats, more violence, and more deaths.

A DIVIDED KINGDOM

The failure of Zion's Camp caused a fair amount of dissension back in Kirtland. What had gone wrong? When would Zion be redeemed? Why did the campaign fail?—These were but a few of the questions posed to Joseph by other church leaders. Some of the Saints were decidedly harsher, as Smith would relate in his history:

> I was met in the face and eyes, as soon as I had got home, with a catalogue of charges as black as the author of lies himself; and the cry was Tyrant—Pope—King—Usurper—Abuser of men—Angel—False Prophet—Prophesying lies in the name of the Lord—Taking consecrated monies—and every other lie to fill up and complete the catalogue.[83]

But Joseph rose to the occasion. He had already announced before dispersing his troops that the decision to not fight was based on a revelation wherein God instructed him to acquire the lands of Missouri by purchase rather than violence.[84] In this same revelation God explained that Zion's Camp actually had been a successful venture because it served as "a trial of their faith."[85] The mission had weeded out the wheat from the chaff; the righteous from the sinful. Even the deadly cholera that struck came from the hand of God as a means of chastisement.[86]

Nevertheless, Smith faced a trial before his High Council that lasted upwards of six hours, during which time he argued himself hoarse. His persistence worked. The final judgment came back in his favor. In a fol-low-up letter to his High Council, Smith promised that Zion would indeed be redeemed. God, in fact, had told him that it would occur by September 1836. Presently, however, the Saints needed to be patient and continue following in obedience and faith.[87]

The Zion's Camp debacle, as difficult as it was for Joseph to survive, provided a crucial bit of information that would help Smith increase his authoritative power: i.e., a virtual list of whom he could, and whom he could not, trust. When the time came for him to enlarge his leadership base, he used the roster of Zion's Camp to call forth those who had stood by him. Select participants were rewarded with positions of power as members of either the "Twelve Apostles," or a special "Quorum of Sev-enty."

After appeasing the church's leadership, Smith turned his attention to the more uplifting task of finishing the construction on his new Kirt-land temple. The idea for this edifice had come to him just after Christ-mas in 1832, when he received a revelation commanding the Saints to build a temple of prayer, fasting, faith, learning, glory and order—"a house of God."[88] It ultimately cost his impoverished followers nearly $70,000, but the emotional and spiritual payback would be well-worth their sacrifices of time and money.[89]

Every Saint wanted to be involved in the project. From 1833–1836, the temple "became a symbol of hope and anticipation . . . Those who had property mortgaged it to buy lumber and plaster; the poor gave of their own sweat."[90] Smith told his followers that not until the building was finished would Zion be freed from bondage. Consequently, the sooner the work was done, the sooner the land of promise would be back in Mormon hands, which in turn would open the way for Christ's return.

After the temple's completion, Smith's first order of business was to ready his closest allies to perform the rites and rituals that would be associated with the temple. In hopes of distancing his church meetings from those of corrupt Christendom, Smith initiated the practice of several ceremonies found in both ancient Judaism and early Christianity: i.e., footwashings, anointings with oil, and ceremonial bathing.[91]

On the temple's March 27 dedication day, nearly a thousand people crowded into the structure, while at least another thousand stood outside, "hoping to catch echoes of the Lord's mysteries."[92] The event greatly enhanced the spiritual vigor of the Saints, especially when Smith and other leaders lifted their voices in prayer and praise. Joseph's dedication prayer contained a clear reference to Zion and the Saints' persecution:

> We ask thee, holy Father, to establish the people . . . that no weapon formed against them shall prosper; . . . [A]nd if any people shall rise against this people, that thine anger be kindled against them: and if they shall smite this people, thou wilt smite them—thou wilt fight for thy people as thou didst in the day of battle, that they may be delivered from the hands of all their enemies.[93]

Later that evening the men returned to begin a special two-day marathon of prayer and fasting. The lengthy ceremony inspired the same type of spiritual excesses that had marked old-style religious revival: speaking in tongues, heavenly visions, prophesying, shouts of religious ecstasy, fits of shaking, and miraculous manifestations of God's presence (e.g., strange lights appearing, angels arriving, and supernatural fire in the air). During the event members of the High Council also "commenced to curse their enemies."[94] According to the Mormon publication, *Millennial Star*, these curses were called down "upon the enemies of Christ, who inhabit Jackson county."[95]

By the end of the week, the building's completion had served its purpose. The Saints' faith had been rejuvenated, and Smith's image as a competent, divinely-led prophet had been confirmed. Nevertheless, Joseph knew that nothing short of a spectacular closing to the dedication week would be acceptable to the crowds. So during the final April 3 service, Smith and Oliver Cowdery, with great ceremonial show, disappeared from the congregation behind two special veils that had been lowered in front of them. No one knew what would happen.

The temple, filled to capacity, grew silent as the audience sat in rapt anticipation. After a short period of time the veils were rolled back to reveal both Oliver and Joseph gazing heavenward. "Oliver was deathly pale" and quite incapable of speech.[96] Joseph, however, was able to break away from his trance to tell the audience what had transpired: "We saw the Lord standing upon the breastwork of the pulpit, before us."[97] Such an unexpected miracle certainly meant that the Lord was pleased. Joseph continued:

> His eyes were as a flame of fire; the hair of his head was white like the pure snow; his countenance shone above the brightness of the sun; and his voice was as the sound of the rushing of great waters, even the voice of Jehovah, saying: I am the first and the last; I am he who liveth, I am he who was slain; I am your advocate with the Father. . . . . Let the hearts of your brethren rejoice, and let the hearts of all my people rejoice, who have, with their might, built this house to my name. For behold, I have accepted this house, and my name shall be here; and I will manifest myself to my people in mercy in this house.[98]

Elijah, too, had come into the temple for a brief meeting behind the veil. The highly regarded prophet of the Old Testament delivered a particularly important message: "[T]he keys of this dispensation are committed into your hands," he said to Joseph. "[A]nd by this ye may know that the great and dreadful day of the Lord is near, even at the doors."[99] Moses appeared as well. He gave Joseph "the keys of the gathering of Israel from the four parts of the earth, and the leading of the ten tribes from the land of the north" (i.e., the North Pole). For hundreds of years they had been waiting to be led back home to America at Christ's second coming. And preparing them for their return to civilization was John the apostle, who according to Smith, had never died.[100]

Curiously, Smith also told several followers that the Ten Tribes were located on a planet by the North Star; a planet originally part of the earth. According to Smith, it was broken off and sent hurtling into space. Smith theorized that at Christ's second coming, this planet would return, crash back into earth at the North Pole, and clear a path of land across the North Sea, over which the Ten Tribes would travel on their return to America.[101]

Exactly where the tribes were located, of course, did not matter. What mattered was that Joseph would have the privilege of taking part in the magnificent end-time gathering.[102] Moreover, the heavenly visitations in the temple could only mean one thing: God had accepted the new temple and was pleased not only with Joseph, but also with the many Saints who had helped build the new house of God. "For weeks afterward the Saints spent all their time going from house to house, feasting, prophesying, and pronouncing blessings on one another."[103] The splendor of the time would never be forgotten, nor repeated. Mormon John Corrill, in his work, A *Brief History of the Church of Christ of Latter Day Saints*, recalled: "[O]ne would have supposed that the last days had truly come."[104]

SEVEN

Woe in Ohio

*Some revelations are of God: some revelations are of man: and
some revelations are of the devil.*

Joseph Smith[1]
statement to David Whitmer, c. 1830

AFTER THE KIRTLAND TEMPLE opened in 1836, doomsday rhetoric appeared
frequently in the speeches and writings of Smith and other church officials. For example, "[T]he end of all things is at hand, be ye therefore
sober and watch unto prayer [1 Peter 4:7]" was chosen as the opening
scripture for the *Latter Day Saints' Messenger and Advocate* May issue.[2]
One of its main articles, titled "The Saints Of The Last Days," gave assurances that Mormons, who alone understood the "signs of the times,"
would soon see their millennial expectations realized.[3] In July, the periodical printed "A Prophetic Warning" by Orson Hyde:

> [T]he hour of God's judgment hath come. . . . This is the Lord's recom-
> pense for the controversy of Zion. . . . [F]lies shall go forth among the
> people, and bite them, and cause worms to come in their flesh, and their
> flesh shall fall from their bones; and their eyes shall fall out of their
> sockets; . . . Serious losses will soon be sustained both by sea and land;
> because of whirlwinds and tempests, and devouring fire. . . . [T]he world
> is fast ripening for the judgements [sic] of God.[4]

Hyde's pronouncement came as no surprise. Smith already had predicted in 1835 that the signs of the times indicated "[f]ifty-six years

should wind up the scene."[5] Such apocalyptic forecasts served as necessary reminders that the Saints, if they could just hold on a bit longer, would be relieved of their emotional, physical, and spiritual burdens. After all, as exciting as the temple dedication had been, it did not alleviate numerous hardships the Saints had to endure.

Persecution, for instance, was ongoing in Kirtland, where local residents feared that the Mormons, through numerical superiority, would someday capture political control of the city.[6] At one point, Kirtland's citizens actually tried starving out the Mormons. They collectively bought all the grain in the Kirtland area and subsequently refused to sell any of it to Smith's followers.[7] Fortunately for the Mormons, grain was available in neighboring Portage County. Starvation was averted and the Saints remained.[8]

But poverty, the bane of Mormon life, continued to be a troublesome affliction, especially since 1834. During that fateful year, Smith's revolutionary economic system—the United Firm—proved impractical and was dissolved by Smith's high council. The ensuing deconstruction of the church's financial arrangement meant that all the communal property had to be re-distributed to various church leaders. This, of course, was accomplished by revelation. Rigdon received the tannery, Cowdery got the printing shop, and others were given the lots on which they lived.

To conceal the identities of these recipients, Smith used code-names in the revelations. He called himself Gazalem (or Gazelam), Rigdon was Pelagoram, and Cowdery—Olihah. Others were given similarly foreign-sounding names. Many of the Saints, except for a few top leaders, thought these terms referred to names of people living in the days of Enoch (i.e., several thousand years ago). Smith even used the tactic to obscure property that he dolled out. The printing shop became the Laneshine house, while the Mormon-owned store was called Ozondah.[9]

This period also witnessed significant changes to the governing policies and organizational structure of Joseph's church. The year 1835 additionally saw publication of the *Doctrine and Covenants* (*D&C*), which was a re-publication of Smith's *Book of Commandments*, plus additional revelations. Interestingly, about one third of the revelations from July 1828 to April 23, 1834, were drastically "amended, added to, excised, and in some cases assigned different historical settings" (see pp. 408–411).[10] The emendations "softened language, reinterpreted economic matters, added offices existing at the time of revision, and inserted references to priesthood restoration."[11] These changes either reflected Smith's updated views on various issues, or helped a "revelation" appear more in harmony with events as they actually had transpired after the revelation's original composition.[12]

More importantly, it was during these years that Smith and other church leaders adopted a code of behavior that historian D. Michael Quinn has labeled "theocratic ethics."[13] This philosophy placed Mormon concepts of right and wrong on a level above both civil laws and biblical mandates. Right and wrong became whatever Smith said was right and wrong. Such a method of determining appropriate individual and corporate conduct not only helped solidify Smith's position as an anointed prophet, but also widened the social and cultural chasm between Mormons and non-Mormons.

Furthermore, "theocratic ethics" granted Smith and other church officials the freedom to do as they pleased. For example, when Smith decided that one of his most faithful disciples—widower Newel Knight— deserved to marry whomever he desired, Joseph violated Ohio law by marrying Knight to the undivorced Lydia G. Baily. Quinn notes: "In addition to the bigamous character of this marriage, Smith had no license to perform marriages in Ohio."[14] To justify the union, Smith used his theology, saying: "I have done it by the authority of the holy Priesthood and the Gentile law has no power to call me to an account for it. It is my reliligious priviledge [sic]."[15]

Smith not only continued to perform marriage ceremonies without a license, but did so for participants who had not obtained licenses giving them civil permission to enter into marriage. This became a common practice since "Kirtland was full of converts who had left behind them spouses who could not be persuaded to join the church."[16] Instead of obtaining licenses from the State, these couples received marriage certificates from Smith that were "according to the rules and regulations of the Church of the Latter-day Saints."[17]

Oddly, such actions blatantly contradicted a previous revelation given by Smith wherein God had stated, "Let no man break the laws of the land, for he that keepeth the laws of God hath no need to break the laws of the land."[18] But Joseph's new standard of ethics came forth as a matter of necessity. He needed it in order to introduce one of the most controversial and widely discussed aspects of early Mormonism—polygamy.[19]

HERE COMES THE BRIDE . . . AGAIN

The officially-recognized revelation concerning polygamy that is now contained in modern editions of Mormonism's *Doctrine and Covenants* (section 132) is dated July 12, 1843.[20] But long before this statement was issued, Smith had been sexually active with women other than his wife, some of whom he married in secret ceremonies.[21] In fact, by the time *D&C* 132 was transcribed, Smith had taken at least twelve additional wives. As far back as 1830, Joseph had sought extra-marital relations with an Eliza Winters of Harmony, Pennsylvania. According to Levi Lewis, a cousin of Smith's wife, Emma, Joseph tried to seduce Winters, but failed to do so.[22] A year later, however, Smith would use his clout as the church's prophet to justify infidelity and influence women to accept his sexual advances. Circumstances greatly favored such a move on his part.

First, Smith had positioned himself in Kirtland as a prophet-leader of several hundred followers; a prophet-leader whose word was law. Second, both the Aaronic and Melchizedek priesthoods—spiritually authoritative roles—had been established in the church, which placed Mormon women at the bottom of the church's power structure. Third, the location of Zion had just been announced, which heightened the spiritual fervor of Mormons. Fourth, end-time revelations had been filling the minds of Mormons for nearly two years, which instilled in them an absolute certainty that Christ and all his angels were poised to reap the earth in terrible judgment. Finally, the cursed Lamanites, their continuing state of ignorance, and the mark of their sinful ways (i.e., their dark skin) had become a regular topic of conversation within the Mormon community.

On July 17, 1831, Smith realized that the time had come for him to reveal a new doctrine; one so sensitive and spiritually advanced that only his closest allies could be entrusted with it. W.W. Phelps, in a letter to Brigham Young, revealed that this new doctrine was given in 1831 while Smith was with several other church leaders in Missouri. The revelatory announcement encouraged Mormon males to take Indian women as wives. This was to be done, God said, so Native Americans could start turning white in fulfillment of *BOM* prophecies: "[I]t is my will, that in time, ye should take unto you wives of the Lamanites and Nephites, that their posterity may become white, delightsome and just."[23] W.W. Phelps, who transcribed the revelation, added a short follow-up paragraph, clearly explaining what Joseph also apparently had in mind when making the proclamation:

> I asked brother Joseph, privately, how "we," that were mentioned in the revelation could take wives from the "natives" as we were all married men? He replied, instantly "In the same manner that Abraham took Hagar and Keturah; and Jacob took Rachel . . . by revelation—the saints of the Lord are always directed by revelation."[24]

Smith may have gotten this idea from Martin Harris, whose wife had left him over his *Book of Mormon* dealings in New York. Martin claimed in 1831 to have had a revelation to go to Missouri, and "obtain an Lamanite squaw for a wife to aid them in propagating Mormonism."[25] Soon afterward, Joseph had his own disclosure from the Lord about Indian women. Although Joseph tried to keep the new doctrine a secret because God had forbidden him to "make it public, or to teach it as a doctrine of the Gospel," the teaching leaked out to various followers, who eventually left the church.[26] Ezra Booth, for example, wrote to the *Ohio Star*, saying:

> It has been made known to one, who has left his wife in the state of N.Y., that he is entirely free from his wife, and he is at liberty to take him a wife from among the Lamanites. It was easily perceived that this permission, was perfectly suited to his desires. I have frequently heard him

state, that the Lord had made it known to him, that he is as free from his wife as from any other woman.[27]

Lifelong Mormon Orson Pratt, likewise remembered that as early as 1832 "Joseph told individuals, then in the Church, that he had inquired of the Lord concerning the principle of plurality of wives, and he received for answer that the principle of taking more wives than one is a true principle, but the time had not yet come for it to be practised [sic]."[28] Although Smith never took any Lamanites as wives, he did begin establishing what would gradually become a fairly large harem of young girls and women taken from his flock of "white and delightsome" disciples.

His first polygamous union occurred in 1832/33 with Fanny Alger, the 16-year-old daughter of a neighboring Mormon family.[29] Benjamin Johnson remembered Alger as "verry nice & Comly young woman" whom everyone liked.[30] According to Martin Harris, Smith made "improper proposals to her, which created quite a talk amongst the people."[31] Harris found out about the affair when Smith sought his advice on what to do about the spreading gossip. Martin wanted no part of the controversy, telling Joseph that he would have to find a way out of his troubles "the best way he knew how."[32] Smith's novel solution was to marry Alger in a secret ceremony and have her move into his home in 1835 as a maid-servant and adopted daughter.[33]

Twenty-seven-year-old Joseph acquired his new bride by first approaching her uncle, Levi Hancock, one of his most ardent followers. In the spring of 1832, Smith told Hancock: "[T]he Lord has revealed to me that it is his will that righteous men shall take Righteous women even a plurality of Wives . . . preparatory to the ushering in of the Millenial [sic] Reign of our Redeemer"[34] Smith then proposed a bargain. He said he would permit Hancock and his sweetheart (Clarissa Reed) to marry, if Hancock could convince his niece (Fanny Alger) to become Joseph's second wife.[35]

Hancock agreed and talked to Fanny, saying: "Brother Joseph the Prophet loves you and wished you for a wife will you be his wife?" The young girl agreed and went with her uncle to be given to the prophet. Hancock married them on the spot by simply repeating the words of the marriage ceremony as Joseph himself dictated it. This same scenario would be repeated again and again—i.e., Joseph obtaining a new wife through the use of an intermediary; a male relative of his prospective bride.[36]

Fanny's parents were honored to have their daughter marry the prophet. But others, most notably, Joseph's wife, Emma, felt differently. She responded with shock and outrage after accidentally discovering Joseph and Fanny "in the barn together alone. She looked through a crack and saw the transaction!!!"[37] The scene devastated Emma. Ann Eliza Webb Young, wrote: "She [Emma] was extremely fond of her [Fanny] . . . and their affection for each other was a constant object of remark, so absorbing and genuine did it seem."[38]

But Emma's fondness understandably gave way to other emotions, as Young relates: "[I]t was with a shocked surprise that the people heard that sister Emma had turned Fanny out of the house in the night. . . . [I]t was felt that she [Emma] certainly must have had some very good reason for her action."[39] William McLellin, an early Mormon leader, also remembered the incident, and related it many years later to Joseph's son, Joseph Smith III, telling him in a letter: "He [Smith] found he was caught. He confessed humbly, and begged forgiveness. Emma and all forgave him."[40] But this would not be the last time Smith's affections turned to other young girls, especially those living under his own roof as either adopted wards or maid-servants. Emma's heartbreak had only just begun.

After rumors began circulating about Smith and Alger, other Mormons pursued polygamous relationships, believing they were emulating their prophet. Smith, however, had not officially introduced the doctrine into the church, nor had any high-ranking leaders publicly sanctioned the practice. Nevertheless, several Saints sought multiple partners, which in turn left the Mormons open to outside persecution and internal strife. Church officials decided to stop the licentiousness by reprimanding anyone found indulging in the freedom that Smith had allowed for himself.[41] Then, an attempt to cover-up the Smith-Alger affair appeared in the church's 1835 edition of the *Doctrine and Covenants* (section 101). It denounced polygamy:

Inasmuch as this church of Christ has been reproached with the crime of fornication, and polygamy: we declare that we believe, that one man should have one wife; and one woman, but one husband, except in the case of death, when either is at liberty to marry again."[42]

After Emma's discovery, Fanny was forced to live with neighbors committed to concealing Smith's actions, which were in direct violation of the 1835 *Doctrine and Covenants* anti-polygamy statement. Interestingly, when the *D&C* was re-published in 1876 (several years after polygamy had become an established tenet of the Mormonism), the 1835 statement condemning polygamy was expunged from the text. Fanny ultimately left Kirtland in late 1836, never to see Smith again.

By 1835, then, polygamy had successfully been initiated, albeit secretly. Smith would not take another wife until 1838. Until then, several things would consume his time: e.g. more Missouri problems, dissension among the church's hierarchy, apostasy in his congregation, and lawsuits over unpaid debts. Even more problematic would be the fallout from his illegitimate banking activities.

BANKING BLUNDERS

The construction of the Kirtland temple greatly boosted the city's economy, but after the building's dedication, the town's financial system steadily declined as poor converts arrived in ever increasing numbers.[43] Additionally, Kirtland residents during the 1830s were overcome by a land speculation craze that was sweeping the country. Most speculators would buy land expecting its worth to dramatically rise, and while waiting for this increase, leave it unused. Others would develop the land, hoping that the eventual profit from higher land values would cover their costs. Most of the time, neither scenario panned out, which caused disastrous economic consequences.

Kirtland's land speculation frenzy developed, to some extent, after Mormons began to see speculation as a route to riches. A number of Saints foolishly purchased large amounts of land on credit. Their assumption was that the land's value would rise and they would be able to sell it for a hefty profit before any loans came due. Church leaders, too, indulged in this get-rich-quick scheme. Mormon Ebenezer Robinson recalled the scene many years later:

> A spirit of speculation was poured out, and instead of that meek and lowly spirit which we felt had heretofore prevailed, a spirit of worldly ambition, and grasping after the things of the world took its place. Some farms adjacent to Kirtland were purchased by some of the heads of the church, mostly on credit, and laid out into city lots, until a large city was laid out on paper, and the price of the lots put up to an unreasonable amount, ranging from $100 to $200 each according to location.[44]

The mad rush to acquire land in hopes of cashing in on it at a later date consumed the thoughts of nearly every Saint, including Smith.[45] He owned "one hundred and forty acres of land adjoining the temple besides his four acres of business property."[46] To these holdings he added two more large acquisitions after entering into a partnership with fellow-Mormons: a 240-acre tract of land for $9,777.50 and a small 132-acre plot of real estate for the inflated price of $12,904.[47] Joseph in turn began selling small parcels of his land at exorbitant rates—to his own followers! One trusting Saint bought a tiny, half-acre piece of earth from Smith for the outrageous sum of $800.[48]

But even these types of sales would never have freed Smith from debt. Over the years he had borrowed a considerable amount of cash from creditors (well over $40,000), while other Mormon leaders had secured approximately $60,000 worth of goods for the church on credit.[49] At the same time, a $13,000 bill covering residual costs of his new temple was still outstanding.[50] To pay off some of these loans, he borrowed even more money. And all of their due dates were fast approaching.

So in November 1836, Smith decided to solve his economic dilemma by establishing a bank for the purpose of land speculation. Consequently, Oliver Cowdery went to Philadelphia to have expensive plates made so bank notes could be printed under the auspices of Smith's new Kirtland Safety Society Bank. Orson Hyde, meanwhile, traveled to the legislature in Columbus to petition for a bank license. Cowdery

returned with the plates and the notes began to be printed. Hyde, however, came back empty-handed. The state had denied their request for
a bank charter.

Smith was furious, claiming that God had told him that the bank was
to be opened.[51] Nothing would stop him from obeying the Lord. According to Smith, the license had been denied simply because they were Mormons.[52] So Joseph proceeded to open his institution not as the Kirtland
Safety Society "Bank," but rather, as the Kirtland Safety Society *Anti*-
Bank*ing* Company, complete with currency that had the prefix "anti" and
the suffix "ing" lightly stamped around the bold-typed word "BANK."
Smith actually believed that his debts, along with those of his followers,
could be wiped out by merely printing these notes and using them to pay
creditors.

The bills, however, were practically worthless because Smith had
virtually no silver/gold coinage to back up the paper he issued. His entire
capital stock consisted of nothing but land valued at inflated prices. For
example, he set the value of his own modest land holdings at a staggering $300,000. He pleaded with followers to support the financial associa-
tion, leading them to believe that God had given him the idea and that it
would "become the greatest of all institutions on earth."[53] To augment
their confidence in the organization, Smith resorted to a rather ingen-
ious deception:

> Lining the shelves of the bank vault . . . were many boxes, each marked
> $1,000. Actually these boxes were filled with 'sand, lead, old iron, stone,
> and combustibles' but each had a top layer of bright fifty-cent silver
> coins. Anyone suspicious of the bank's stability was allowed to lift and
> count the boxes. 'The effect of those boxes was like magic;' said C. G.
> Webb. 'They created general confidence in the solidity of the bank and
> that beautiful paper money went like hot cakes. For about a month it
> was the best money in the country.[54]

Smith spread the word that he had $60,000 in hard coinage to back
the paper notes, and could lay his hands on $600,000 more if necessary.

Mormon money produced by Smith's illegal "Anti-Banking" bank.

In reality, he had barely $6,000. He also said that he had only printed up about $10,000 in bills, when at least $150,000 had been distributed.[55] These notes were circulated as legal tender from a joint-stock company. As one historian has commented, "[e]veryone's pockets bulged with bills."[56] Debts were paid off, new merchandise was purchased, prosperity reigned throughout the community, or so it seemed.

Smith opened for business after installing himself and Sidney Rigdon as the institution's main officers, while supporting positions within the Society's corporate structure were filled by most of his twelve apostles. His confidence never wavered during its first few weeks of operation, as evidenced by a January 1837 conversation he had with his inner circle. He told them that while he was alone in a room, God had spoken to him in an audible voice, promising that if the Saints followed his commandments, "all would be well" with the Society.[57]

But after more than $36,000 in notes had been passed in Cleveland, that city's merchants began panicking over rumors that Smith's "Anti-Bank" had been established by a revelation from God. Various businesses then learned that merchants in Buffalo and New York had never even accepted the notes. Soon, nearby shopkeepers began rejecting the paper. The *Painesville Republican* then announced that Smith's notes had been refused by the Bank of Geauga County, adding that for this reason businessmen should not accept them.[58]

Those who were left holding the bogus bills suddenly wanted to get rid of them. Hundreds of notes began flooding back to Kirtland for redemption in hard coinage. It was a disaster. Less than one month after opening, Smith's currency was exchanging at 12 $\frac{1}{2}$ cents on the dollar.[59] The authorities quickly heard about the scandal and on February 1, 1837, a writ was sworn out against Joseph Smith, Jr., and Sidney Rigdon accusing the two men of "illegal banking and issuing unauthorized bank paper."[60] Their trial was scheduled for the court's fall session. Despite these signs of impending calamity, the Society remained open and continued issuing notes, which by March were worth between only 1-10 cents on the dollar.[61]

Lawsuits from creditors then began piling up, dissension within the church started spreading among some its most powerful leaders, and the newspapers proceeded to have a field day at Smith's expense. Joseph knew his bank would not survive for much longer, yet he persisted on a course of ruin, delivering a scathing rebuke to "those characters that professed to be his friends & friends to . . . the 'Kirtland Safety Society' but had turned traitors & opposed the currency & its friends."[62] Such individuals, railed Smith, "have become covenant breakers for which they will feel the wrath of God."[63] By mid-year of 1837, apostasy had infected virtually every corner of the church. Smith's supporters responded with predictions of doomsday, calls for unity, and threats of damnation for those outside Zion:

> The salvation of the saints one and all depends on the building up of Zion; for without this there is no salvation; for deliverance in the last days is found in Zion. . . . [G]ather up your gold and your silver, and all the means you have, and send on to the saints who are engaged in this great work of building the zion of our God, that there may be a place of refuge for you, and for your children in the day of God's vengeance.[64]

At approximately this same time, Parley Pratt published his pamphlet titled *A Voice of Warning*, which would become "perhaps the most widely reprinted piece of LDS literature in history, aside from the Book of Mormon."[65] It served not only as a "proclamation of truth," but also as a defense against "misrepresentations, and lying slanders, of the foulest kind," that had been spread in order to destroy the influence of Mormonism and Joseph Smith.[66]

Such pronouncements, however, could not prevent Smith and Rigdon from facing a trial in October. They were found guilty of violating state banking laws and fined $1,000 each, plus small costs. As Mormon historian B.H. Roberts concisely stated in his history of the church, "The 'Kirtland Safety Society' enterprise ended disastrously."[67] But Smith's woes were not yet over. The trial's judgment unleashed a rash of personal threats against Smith's life and numerous lawsuits from creditors suing for damages.[68]

MEANWHILE, BACK IN MISSOURI

While Smith was handling his troubles in Ohio, the Missouri Saints in Clay County were dealing with their own exigencies. By mid-1836, Clay County residents had grown weary of the Mormons, who had again made themselves onerous to their neighbors. The complaints were the same as those that had been voiced by the mobs in Jackson County. The Mormons were rapidly acquiring lands, haranguing non-Mormons with end-time threats about possessing all of Missouri, fraternizing with Indians, and attempting to form a numerically superior block of voters that would ultimately seize control of Missouri's political system. In a letter dated July 4, 1836, Missourian Anderson Wilson explained: "[The Saints are] flocking here faster than ever."[69]

Wilson's communication also mentioned Mormons paying huge sums of money for lands previously valued at considerably lower prices—a temporary extravagance, they said, which would last only until all non-Mormons moved out in response to their moving in. Wilson's conclusion summarized Clay County citizen feelings: "[W]e must either submit to a Mormon government or trample under foot the laws of our Country."[70] Additionally, Clay County residents had come to believe that the Mormons would have no problem seizing Missouri by force:

According to Joseph Thorp, a Clay County resident, the Mormons told local settlers that "this country was theirs [the Mormons'] by the gift of the Lord, and it was folly for them [the Missourians] to improve their lands, they would not enjoy the fruits of their labor; that it would finally fall into the hands of the saints."[71]

Like the Old Settlers in Jackson County, the citizens of Clay County asked the Mormons to leave. Their June 29, 1836 request, however, was significantly more polite, stating that it had been drafted "in a spirit of frank and friendly kindness."[72] It advised the Saints to "seek a home where they may obtain large and separate bodies of land, and have a community of their own."[73] Unlike Jackson County residents, Clay County folks gave Mormons plenty of time to comply with their courteous appeal. They could depart "when their crops are gathered, their business settled, and they have made every suitable preparation to move."[74] It was not a harsh demand. The Mormons themselves had promised that their presence in the county would be temporary, lasting only as long as they were welcome. Now, according to the Missourians, the Mormons were no longer welcome.

Fortunately, the Saints were able to retain the help of Democratic Representative Alexander Doniphan, who succeeded in guiding a bill through the legislature "incorporating Caldwell County in sparsely settled northwestern Missouri as a Mormon refuge. The new year [i.e., 1837] found the Saints building their third Missouri settlement in six years."[75] The new major city of Mormonism was appropriately named Far West. This location quickly became the new gathering site for the Saints.

In fact, on November 2, 1837, Smith announced the Lord's will for all faithful Mormons to gather at Far West. God had given him yet another revelation, which stated: "[P]eace shall soon be taken from the earth . . . for a lying spirit has gone out upon all the face of the earth. . . . [B]ehold saith the Lord, very fierce and very terrible war is near at hand, even at your doors."[76]

GO WEST, YOUNG MAN

Throughout 1837 Smith seemed both unwilling and unable to cope with his troubles. He intermittently disappeared from Kirtland, and even went on extended "missionary" trips; first to Canada, then to Missouri, where he helped set up the new Mormon settlements of Far West, in Caldwell County. But each time he returned to Kirtland he found that things had only gotten worse. The church in Ohio, in fact, had fallen to pieces in his absence.[77] Several high-ranking leaders left the congregation, and an angry brawl had broken out in the temple between Saints criticizing Smith and those still loyal to him. This fiasco resulted in the arrest of Smith's father and sixteen other supporters.[78]

Upon returning from Missouri, Smith and Rigdon were forced to verbally battle their disillusioned brethren in a vicious ecclesiastical trial held inside the temple. The bitter war of words began with Smith defending himself. Rigdon then addressed the hostile crowd of disaffected members, accusing them of lying, stealing, adultery, counterfeiting and swindling. He finally resorted to shouting, name-calling, and violent words "that stunned the Saints."[79] Smith's dissenters yelled back even louder, until the heated arguing digressed into a near riot. Joseph himself then lost control:

> Shouting above the din, he called for an end to debate and a vote on the excommunications. "Yes," yelled a dissenter, "you would cut a man's head off and hear him afterward!" The meeting finally broke up, and Joseph left the temple conscious that he had lost, probably forever, what had been seven years in building.[80]

Thirty Mormons, including some of the church's most powerful officials, would forsake Smith after hearing the severe criticisms of their prophet. Soon afterward, the final nail in the Kirtland congregation's coffin was procured in the form of an arrest warrant for Smith on the charge of banking fraud, a much more serious offense than the one

for which he and Rigdon had already been convicted (i.e., illegal banking). Smith knew he was guilty, but to be taken back to court could end
his dream of establishing God's kingdom on earth.

So, in the dead of night, January 12, 1838, Smith and Rigdon fled
Kirtland on horseback, in hopes of finding peace and safety in Far West
(Caldwell County), the newly established LDS refuge near Zion. His
hasty departure came about as a result of a revelation he received
wherein God declared him innocent, adding that he could now leave
because his work in Kirtland was over:

> Let the presidency of my Church take their families as soon as it is prac-
> ticable and a door is opened for them and move unto the west as fast as
> the way is made plain. . . . [T]he time has come that your labors are fin-
> ished in this place. . . . You are clean from the blood of this people and
> woe unto them who have become your enemies. . . . [T]heir judgement
> lingereth not and their damnation slumbereth not.[81]

In his history, Smith would write that he was "obliged to flee"
his persecutors, just as the Apostles and Prophets of old were forced
to do. Jesus himself had said, "when they persecute you in one city,
flee to another."[82] Joseph further blamed his troubles on the illegal
activities of his enemies, who wickedly sought to attribute their guilt to
him:

> [W]e left Kirtland . . . to escape mob violence, which was about to burst
> upon us under the color of legal process to cover the hellish designs of
> our enemies, and to save themselves from the just judgment of the law.[83]

The Kirtland temple eventually was seized by the dissenters, and
within its walls, they passed resolutions proclaiming Smith's depravity.[84]
Most of the faithful saints followed Smith, hoping to join him in Far West,
Missouri, and somehow escape the wrath to come by being near Zion.
Thus ended Mormonism's presence in Kirtland as a force with which
Ohioans would have to reckon.

The feelings of disillusioned former members were summed up well by Warren Parrish, Smith's one-time scribe, who in a February 1838 letter to the *Painseville Republican*, reflected on the events with grief and anger, saying: "[Smith and Rigdon] lie by revelation, swindle by revelation, cheat and defraud by revelation, run away by revelation, and if they do not mend their ways, I fear they will be damned by revelation."[85]

EIGHT

Big Trouble in Little Missouri

The plan of said Smith, the Prophet, is to take [over] this State,
and he professes to his people to intend taking the United States
and ultimately the whole world. This is the belief of the Church.
                                        Thomas B. Marsh[1]
                              Mormon Apostle, October 24, 1838

BY THE TIME SMITH REACHED FAR WEST, MISSOURI (Caldwell County), on
March 14, 1838, the Mormon town had become a thriving settlement. It
already consisted of approximately "one hundred fifty log cabins (with
perhaps an equal number under construction), four dry-goods stores,
three family groceries, six blacksmith shops, two hotels, and a large
school." The Mormons also "owned a printing press, which they used to
publish the *Elders' Journal* and miscellaneous pamphlets." Smith's new
home would eventually grow to a population of 2,000, "making it the second-largest town (after Liberty) in western Missouri."[2] More Saints were
on their way, of course, especially after Kirtland fell as a church stronghold. In fact, by the end of 1838 the Mormon population of northwest
Missouri would grow to nearly 10,000.[3]

Much to Smith's delight, he arrived to find virtually no persecution
directed against his people. As Mormon John Corrill noted: "Friendship
began to be restored . . . old prejudices were fast dying away."[4] This
social tranquility resulted from the fact that Caldwell County had been
established for the expressed purpose of being a Mormon refuge; a place
where Smith's faithful followers could finally dwell in unity, undisturbed
by Gentiles. The Missourians had no reason to feel threatened because

they understood that Smith's people would confine themselves to Caldwell County.

Clay County Representative, Alexander Doniphan, who had helped secure Caldwell for the Mormons, understood the agreement in such terms. Missourian Neil Gilliam, who served on the Clay County Committee that assisted in locating the new county, felt the same way. And the Mormons, content with their new haven of refuge, seemed more than content to stay within their allotted territory. Consequently, it came as no surprise that problems had not occurred between the Saints and non-Mormons living in the surrounding counties of Daviess to the North, Ray to the South, Clinton to the West, and Livingston and Carroll to the East. Relations with these Missourians actually had become rather cordial.

But after Smith arrived, the Mormons suddenly could not remember making an agreement to limit their settlements to one county. Even if LDS leaders in Missouri had recalled making such a commitment to the Missourians, it would have meant little to Joseph. He certainly made no agreements about land, nor would he ever dream of confining to one small county the glorious Zion he envisioned as the millennial home for Christ's reigning Saints, many of whom were now streaming into the Promised Land. God would need far more land to set up His kingdom, and Smith was determined to take it. Within days of moving into the region he "set about surveying and laying claim to enormous tracts of territory."[5]

SETTLING ON SACRED GROUND

Only eight weeks after arriving in Far West, Smith decided to expand LDS settlements beyond Caldwell County. His first new town sprang up virtually overnight deep inside Daviess County, at a place he named Adam-ondi-Ahman, commonly called Diahman by the Saints.[6] Joseph discovered this pristine location on one of his expeditions up the Grand River. While on a bluff overlooking the waterway, a member of his party discovered a rocky formation vaguely reminiscent of an ancient altar.[7] Joseph gazed at the rocks, then noticed the lush prairie stretching out before him.

Suddenly, a revelation filled his soul. He announced that the apparent ruins were indeed an altar; one built by none other than Adam, the first man. In fact, the very spot on which they all stood was where Adam and his wife, Eve, had fled after being expelled from the Garden of Eden for disobeying God. The revelation made perfect sense to those with him. Smith already had told them that the Garden of Eden was located in Jackson County.[8] Now, he had discovered where the first human couple had settled after their fall from perfection. It was nothing less than a miracle of divine guidance that had brought them to the spot. Furthermore, Smith revealed, Adam would soon be returning in fulfillment of prophecies relating to Christ's second coming.[9]

Interestingly, Mormonism today still promotes this notion that Jackson County contained the Garden of Eden and that Adam, along with Eve, fled to Daviess County from their paradisiacal locale. Twenty-first century Mormonism also continues to propagate Smith's view that a veritable Who's Who of Old Testament figures lived in Missouri, including: Cain, Abel, Jared, Enoch, Methuselah, and Noah. How did other events in the Old Testament end up taking place throughout the Middle East? According to Brigham Young, we have Noah's Ark to thank for transporting the survivors of the Great Flood across the Atlantic Ocean to those lands more in keeping with biblical narratives.[10]

Predictably, Diahman, Adam's former home, quickly became a popular new gathering place for Mormons migrating to Missouri. By the end of the summer, hundreds of Saints had settled there, "making it by far the largest town in the county."[11] Still not content, Joseph ordered that the sparsely populated village of DeWitt in Carroll County be literally taken over by the Saints, who purchased half the town's lots and began moving into the area in record numbers. At the same time, Mormons began settling farms in Clinton, Chariton, Ray, Livingston, and every other surrounding county. Zion was spreading; and spreading very quickly.

Meanwhile, the Mormons also succeeding in rapidly creating various businesses that reaped significant profits from the garrison stationed at Fort Leavenworth, only thirty miles from Caldwell County. Residents of the fort not only purchased huge amounts of supplies for themselves, but also for the Indians tribes living on nearby reservations.[12] The Saints

The stones that Joseph Smith claimed were remnants of an altar built by Adam at Adam-Ondi-Ahman in Daviess County, Missouri (from Wilford Wood, *Joseph Smith Begins His Work*, vol. 1, 1958).

then began bidding for government contracts, which if obtained, promised to bring incredible wealth to Smith's booming frontier towns. All of these achievements impacted the Missourians of surrounding counties in an extremely negative way. They quickly were losing land, business, income, and political power.

Before 1838 ended, the Mormons had all but taken over the entire region. At least 2,000 of them were in Daviess County, where non-Mormons became outnumbered two to one. The Saints in Caldwell County rose to 5,000, while another 2,500 made their presence felt throughout other counties. Both Smith and Sidney Rigdon (who had also arrived in Far West) were ecstatic over the prospects before them. "Urge all the saints to gather immediately if they possibly can," they wrote in a letter sent to Pennsylvania. "Land is very cheap[,] the old settlers will sell for half the price yes, for quarter price[;] they are determined to get away."[13] A new wave of millennial zeal was sweeping through Zion for the Kingdom of God was fast approaching; Christ would soon return. As one letter in the *Elders' Journal* said, "[T]he Lord our God is about to establish a Kingdom, which cannot be thrown down."[14]

Unfortunately, Smith's long-held dream of establishing Zion in Missouri would be frustrated once more. This time, however, opposition to his plans would not just come from Old Settlers unwilling to give up their lands, rights, and futures. A far greater threat, from a far more potent enemy, was attempting to destroy Smith's church by poisoning the minds and hearts of his faithful followers. This new foe had come to Missouri from Ohio. Zion, Smith discovered, had been polluted by the very spirit of apostasy that had driven him from Kirtland.

THE DISSENTERS

The dissension that fractured the Kirtland congregation did not disappear with Smith's departure for Far West. In fact, by the time Joseph reached Missouri, some of his most ardent critics had journeyed to Zion. Their reason for traveling to Caldwell County, however, was not to build up the kingdom. They had come to tear down Smith. His enemies included a host of influential leaders. Smith's scribe, Warren Parrish, left the church, due in part, to Joseph's affair with Fanny Alger. Parrish and Cowdery knew "that Joseph had Fanny Alger as a wife for [t]hey ware [s]pied upon & found togather [misspelling in original]."[15] Of the twelve apostles chosen in Kirtland, only two—Brigham Young and Heber C. Kimball—had remained faithful to Smith.[16] Other powerful leaders such as John Whitmer, William McLellin, W.W. Phelps, Lyman Johnson, and Frederick G. Williams also would eventually apostatize. Even the three witnesses to the *Book of Mormon*—David Whitmer, Martin Harris, and Oliver Cowdery—condemned Smith.

Harris had been excommunicated as far back as September 1837 along with several other lesser officials. He subsequently went off to join the Shakers, apparently wanting no part of the coming ecclesiastical battle between church leaders. Others, however, most notably Warren Parrish, Oliver Cowdery, and David Whitmer, were not as willing to let Smith escape his misdeeds. These men mounted a very public and very verbal attack against him—in Missouri, of all places. They had arrived in Far West well before Smith, and met with other dissenters in early 1838, at Cowdery's Caldwell County home to discuss their strategy.

This committee of Smith detractors accused their former leader and other Mormon officials of attempting to unite church authority with civil authority, forcing men to use their finances "contrary to their own interest and privilege," and demanding loyalty to leaders who had committed moral indiscretions.[17] January also saw Cowdery and John Whitmer sell their Jackson County property in direct violation of revelations Smith had given to the Saints. Cowdery then went so far as to write a letter denouncing Joseph for "a dirty, nasty, filthy affair" with Fanny Alger.[18] In February, he wrote a second letter, in which he called Smith's newest teachings "disorganized doctrines" and called the prophet's loyalists a bunch of "hot headed power seeking, ignorant men."[19]

That same month church leaders still faithful to Smith met together and stripped David Whitmer, John Whitmer and Phelps of their presidential offices.[20] Weeks later, just after Smith and other leaders "began trickling into Far West," the Missouri High Council charged David and John Whitmer, Oliver Cowdery, and Lyman Johnson "with various counts of dereliction of duty, violation of church policy, and disrespect for the church leadership and cut them off from the church."[21] But this did little to stop their dissension from spreading throughout the Mormon community.

Smith, Rigdon, and their supporters finally launched a counter-offensive of character assassination against the apostates. "Believe not the slangs and foul reports against our beloved brethren, Joseph Smith, Jr., and Sidney Rigdon," read one letter published in the *Elders' Journal*. "They are groundless and as black as the apostate authors."[22] On one occasion Smith attacked several of his detractors by name, declaring: "Such characters as McLellin, John Whitmer, David Whitmer, Oliver Cowdery, and Martin Harris, are too mean to mention; and we had liked to have forgotten them."[23]

Smith additionally would refer to David Whitmer in connection to William McLellin, saying: "I would remember William E. McLellin, . . . [he] has no other dumb ass to ride but David Whitmer . . . he brays out cursings instead of blessings. Poor ass! Whoever lives to see it, will see him and his rider perish."[24] As for Rigdon, he wrote a decidedly hateful article titled "Argument to argument where I find it; Ridicule to ridicule,

and scorn to scorn," which viciously slandered and mocked the dissenters, labeling them drunkards, thieves, beasts, lackeys, and liars—
veritable puppets of Satan.[25]

Threats of legal action by the apostates prompted even harsher
replies from both Rigdon and Smith, who declared that they "had been
harassed to death, as it were, for seven or eight years, and they were
determined to bear it no longer, for they would rather die than suffer
such things."[26] Joseph went so far as to say that "he did not intend in [the]
future to have any process served on him, and the officer who attempted
it should die; that any person who spoke or acted against the presidency
or the church should leave the country or die."[27] As he put it, "any person who said a word against the heads of the Church, should be driven
over these prairies as a chased deer by a pack of hounds."[28]

To back up his threats, Joseph permitted the formation of a secret
group of enforcers to "sustain church leaders without question."[29] More
bluntly, they were organized "for the purpose of plundering and murdering the enemies of the Saints."[30] Smith apparently sanctioned the
brotherhood as a primary weapon "in the hands of God, of bringing forth
the millenial kingdom."[31] But according to Kenneth Winn, adjunct history professor at Washington University, Smith's secret cadre of ruffians
and assassins was little more than "an aggressive, malicious, secret
police force . . . a nineteenth-century version of storm-troopers."[32] They
called themselves "Danites."[33]

SMITH'S DESTROYING ANGELS

In a February 1834 revelation, Joseph likened apostates to salt that
had lost its flavor, adding that such individuals were "good for nothing
but to be cast out and trodden under foot of men."[34] It was this divine
declaration, coupled with a biblical passage from the Gospel of Matthew,
which Sidney Rigdon used to publicly give a nod of approvable to the
Danites in a "rabble-rousing discourse" delivered on June 17, 1838
before a large congregation.[35]

Reed Peck, a witness to the event, recorded in his personal writings
that Rigdon told the audience there were dissenters among them, and

that it was the "duty of the Saints" to trample them under their feet and "into the earth" because the traitors were trying to "destroy the presidency." Rigdon accused Cowdery and the others of lying, cheating, counterfeiting, and other moral failures. He then called for the people "to rise en masse and rid the county of such a nuisance." Another solution suggested was to "erect a gallows on the Square of Far West and hang them." Rigdon thundered, "[T]he angels would smile."[36]

When Smith addressed the seething crowd, he not only endorsed his partner's words, but went on to inform the crowd of a new teaching about Judas, Christ's betrayer. Contrary to the biblical narrative, which reports that Judas hung himself, Smith said Judas was hung by Peter the apostle in retribution for having turned against Jesus. Peck recalled: "[W]ith this hint the subject was dropped for the day having created a great excitement and prepared the people to execute anything that should be proposed."[37]

The Danites, organized as a covert brotherhood that would eventually be known as the church's "Destroying Angels," had been released to do their sacred duty of intimidating dissenters and waging warfare against any who might cause trouble for the Saints. And Joseph undoubtedly approved of them, as D. Michael Quinn concludes: "What the Danites did militarily during the summer and fall of 1838 was by the general oversight and command of Joseph Smith."[38] Joseph's own private journal, transcribed by George W. Robinson, acknowledged the group's purpose:

> [W]e have a company of Danites in these times, to put to right physically that which is not right, and to cleanse the Church of verry [sic] great evils which hath hitherto existed among us inasmuch as they cannot be put to right by teachings & persuasyons [sic].[39]

The direct commander of the Danites was Sampson Avard, a ruthless and ambitious follower of Smith's, who functioned on a single principle—"blind obedience to the prophet."[40] He taught this code of service to initiates using the most unsettling and direct of terms:

[A]s the Lord had raised up a prophet in these last days like unto Moses, it shall be the duty of this band to obey him in all things, and whatever he requires, you shall perform, being ready to give up life and property for the advancement of the cause. When any thing is to be performed no member shall have the privilege of judging whether it would be right or wrong, but shall engage in its accomplishment and trust God for the result.[41]

To dispel any doubt among the troublemakers about the seriousness of their situation, Rigdon drew up "A Note of Warning" threatening the Whitmers, Cowdery, Johnson, and Phelps with violent removal from the county if they did not voluntarily leave.[42] The June 18 letter was signed by eighty-four elders, including Joseph's Brother, Hyrum, and Caldwell County's Mormon Sheriff, George Pitkin. "[O]ut of the county you shall go," it read. "[A]nd no power shall save you."[43] The missive ended: "[T]here is but one decree for you, which is depart, depart, or a more fatal calamity shall befall you. . . . [We] will put you from the county of Caldwell: so help us God."[44]

In hopes of securing legal assistance, some of the dissenters rode to Clay County. The Danites, not wanting to waste time in taking advantage of their absence, systematically went to each of the dissenters' homes, turned their families out into the wilderness, and seized all of their property, including personal possessions, clothing, and furniture.[45] Fortunately, the families reached safety in neighboring counties where they were reunited with their loved ones. But all of them were now virtually destitute. Not everyone, of course, approved of the actions. In fact, a number of prominent Saints (e.g., John Corrill, Thomas Marsh, and others) would in time voice opposition to the tactics Smith and Rigdon had used. They, too, would be dubbed traitors.

According to Reed Peck, Caldwell County quickly fell under the tyrannical rule of a "despotic government where even liberty of speech was denied to those not willing to support the New Order."[46] John Corrill, in his volume *A Brief History of the Church of Christ of Latter Day Saints*, remembered how some individuals "went so far as to state, that they would kill any person, if the presidency would say it was the will of God; for these things were necessary sometimes to save the church from corruption and destruction."[47] The attitude of Smith loyalists was summed up well by Mormon Alexander McRae, who in reference to U.S. president Martin Van Buren, stated: "If Joseph should tell me to kill Van-Buren . . . I would immediately start and do my best to assassinate him [and] let the consequences be as they would."[48]

Zion clearly was controlled by Smith, run by Rigdon, and guarded by the Danites, which quickly swelled in number to between 800 and 1,000.[49] Smith now had a virtual army; one organized into militia units, and commanded by men with military titles of rank: Jared Carter, Captain General of the Lord of Hosts; Sampson Avard, Major General; George W. Robinson, Colonel.[50] Under these men were Lieutenants, Majors, Captains of fifties, Captains of tens, and Privates, all of whom were "under the administration of the presidency of the church and wholly subject to their control."[51] They marched in the streets, drilled openly, and by all accounts, seemed to be preparing for battle.

Although Smith succeeded in driving away the dissenters, he had not fully considered the Missourians, who began feeling uneasy after hearing rumors about the Danites. They also could not help but notice with their own eyes that Smith was never going to be satisfied with one county. The 1838 Missouri Civil War was about to begin.

BEHIND THE BATTLE LINES

Conflict on a large scale between the Mormons and the Missourians around Caldwell County might have been avoided had Smith and his followers not become so militaristic. Anxiety among non-Mormon settlers also increased when they realized that at some point the Saints had decided to no longer subject themselves to civil authority. The Danites led the way by pledging oaths of allegiance and protection to one another no matter what offenses they might commit in the eyes of Gentiles. Lyman Wight, for example, known for his fiery temperament, instructed new Danite recruits as follows:

> [I]f any brother should have stolen a horse, or committed any other
> offence, and is arraigned before a justice of the peace for trial, you must,
> at the risk of your lives, rescue him, and not permit him to be tried by
> the Gentile law.[52]

It is no wonder that relations between the Saints and the Missourians slowly began to strain. Still, no real troubles between the two groups occurred, even after Rigdon's "Salt Sermon."[53] The Missourians actually seemed committed to continuing their pursuit of a peaceful co-existence with the Mormons. No non-Mormon mobs had formed, no complaints had been lodged, and no alarms had been sounded. In fact, most of the non-Mormons living near the Saints were quite unaware that violent conflict was brewing, even though they had indeed heard rumors about various incidents involving strife among the Mormons themselves.

But everything changed on July 4, 1838, when Sidney Rigdon delivered yet another stirring oration that included threats of violence. This time, however, his remarks were not directed toward internal dissenters, but rather, toward those outside the church. "[C]ome on us no more forever . . . we will bear it no more," he shouted. "The man or the set of men, who attempts it, does it at the expense of their lives."[54] Rigdon then made an announcement that surrounding communities took as nothing less than a declaration of war:

> [T]hat mob that comes on us to disturb us; it shall be between us and
> them a war of extermination, for we will follow them, till the last drop of
> their blood is spilled, or else they will have to exterminate us; for we will
> carry the seat of war to their own houses, and their own families, and
> one party or the other shall be utterly destroyed. . . . Neither will we
> indulge any man, or set of men, in instituting vexatious law suits against
> us, to cheat us out of our just rights, if they attempt it we say wo be unto
> them.[55]

The incendiary sermon, published soon afterward as a pamphlet, proved to be "the beginning of the end of the Mormon community in Missouri."[56] Word quickly spread that Rigdon had blatantly challenged the authority of law and order in the territory. A letter printed in the Liberty, Missouri, *Western Star* reported that the inflammatory speech contained "the essence of, if not treason itself."[57] Suddenly, long-buried suspicions were raised and old prejudices renewed. The Mormon settlements outside Caldwell County soon came more into focus. It all seemed to be making sense now to the Missourians—the Mormons had intended to take over all along.

In response to the new threat, citizens in Carroll County overwhelmingly voted in their August election for the Mormons to leave DeWitt. But when a Missouri citizens committee entered the town and demanded that the Mormons return to Caldwell County, their request was met with a firm no. In fact, Mormon leader George Hinkle threatened the committee. About one hundred non-Mormons later responded by riding into DeWitt, shooting up the place, and threatening the Mormons.[58] This only prompted more Mormons to move into the area, which in turn created additional animosity.

Meanwhile in Daviess County, tensions rose sharply as election-day approached. So many Mormons had moved into the sparsely populated region that by August 1838 they "held the balance of power in the Daviess county election."[59] Ballot day would be their day to take over and they knew it. The Missourians were especially agitated because the August 6 state and county elections would be their first opportunity to elect their own county officers. Consequently, some of the Missourians began suggesting that the Mormons not be allowed to vote. Others actually started making plans to insure that they did not vote. Judge Josiah Morin tried to warn the Mormons, telling them that "there would probably be trouble at the polls" specifically at the county seat of Gallatin. But the Saints, believing that Morin was merely "electioneering for the Democrats," ignored the information.[60]

About thirty Mormons were in Gallatin on August 6, just a handful among some one hundred settlers who had come to the little town to vote. Among these citizens were several candidates, including William Peniston, who had attempted to secure the Mormon vote, but failed to do so. In retaliation, he spoke to the voters milling around the polling area, calling their attention to the fact that the Saints were "horse thieves,

Late 19th century depiction of the "Fight at Gallatin" between Mormons and Missourians (from T.B.H. Stenhouse, *The Rocky Mountain Saints*, 1873).

liars, counterfeiters, and dupes."[61] The Mormons looked on, but caused no trouble, even after Peniston ended his speech by calling for a suspension of the Mormon right to vote. The boisterous candidate then invited everyone into the saloon for a drink.

Trouble began when Dick Weldon, a long-time resident of Daviess County, became drunk and accosted a timid and much smaller Mormon named Samuel Brown—a shoemaker. Weldon asked Brown if he was a Mormon preacher, and if he, along with other Mormons, believed in healing the sick, speaking in tongues, and casting out devils. "We do," Brown answered. Weldon replied: "You are a damned liar. Joseph Smith is a damned imposter."[62]

When Weldon began to strike Brown, several Mormons attacked the Missourian; five or six Missourians accosted the Mormons. Then, Mormon John L. Butler, a man of enormous stature, stood and gave the Danite call of distress: "O yes, you Danites, here is a job for us."[63] At least ten Danites joined the tussle, which in turn summoned forty to fifty more Missourians into the now raucous fight. Whips, clubs, rocks, knives, pottery, fists—all were used in the brief, but bloody, melee. Although no one was killed, significant injuries were suffered by combatants on both sides. John McGee, a non-Mormon observer, who wisely stayed out of the battle, later commented: "I had witnessed many knock-downs in my time, but none on so grand a scale."[64]

WAR IN THE WILDERNESS

The Gallatin skirmish put Smith's forces on high alert. The Missourians, too, considered their options as news of the conflict traveled from county to county. Eight weeks of mounting anxiety and displays of aggression followed. Smith, for example, rode through the countryside with at least one hundred Danites, who intimidated several Missourians into signing statements opposing all persecution of the Saints. In response, the settlers from Daviess County traveled to surrounding counties and gave authorities exaggerated accounts about armed Mormons threatening to murder various citizens. Smith, meanwhile, petitioned a judge in Richmond, in Ray County, for his intervention on behalf of the Saints.

Missourian vigilante groups subsequently formed and began harassing Mormon settlers in isolated areas. In one instance, a gang of fifteen men drove Asahel Lathrop from his home, and for over a week held his sick wife and children as hostages. Sadly, one of Lathrop's children died during the extended siege and was buried by the Missourians. His wife and two other children were eventually freed by a company of Mormons, but died soon after their rescue due to lack of medical care. Vigilantes also rode into DeWitt and ordered the Mormons to leave, or else they would be killed. After a lengthy standoff, the Mormons finally surrendered and left the town.[65]

In October, the Mormons retaliated by invading Daviess County with several hundred men. They first marched to Gallatin, frightened away the Missourians, plundered the town of all its merchandise and livestock, then burned it to the ground. They also burned and looted Millport and Grindstone Fork. The Mormons went on to dispatch raiding parties that scoured the countryside for vigilantes, all along the way, ransacking and torching any non-Mormon cabins they happened to find.[66] According to Stephen C. LeSueur's *The 1838 Mormon War in Missouri*, the armed units showed no mercy, even to Missourians who had never been part of the vigilante forces:

> The settlers often fled from their homes with nothing but the clothes they wore, and in some cases fled in their bare feet. After fleeing with

her small children from Millport, Milford Donaho's wife gave birth prematurely to a child who reportedly suffered permanent damage as a result. Another woman with a four-day-old baby also fled from her home. A horrified [non-Mormon] Taylor family watched as Mormon soldiers plundered and burned their home because guns and ammunition were found hidden in the cornfields. The Mormons allowed the Taylors to keep just what they could carry, and only through the forceful intercession of Benjamin F. Johnson, a young Mormon soldier, was Mr. Taylor able to retain a horse for his pregnant wife and children to ride.[67]

Responses to the Mormon pillaging of Daviess County were swift. Non-Mormon Militia companies mobilized in Livingston County harassed Mormon settlers and confiscated their property. Two hundred Missourians marched through both Clinton and Daviess counties, "driving Mormon settlers from their homes, plundering and burning."[68] And from Ray County, fifty to sixty Missourians under the command of Captain Samuel Bogart marched to the Caldwell County line to act as a preventative force against any Mormon invasion. Along the way they succeeded in driving nearly all Mormons from their homes. Bogart then crossed into Caldwell County and began threatening Mormons in their own territory.

The Battle of Crooked River

News of Bogart's incursion quickly reached Far West, along with information about three Mormons who had been taken prisoner by Bogart: William Seeley, Addison Greene, and Nathan Pinkham. It also had been reported, falsely, that these men were scheduled to be executed. Smith was outraged and gathered a formidable force of men to rescue their brethren. With regard to the Ray County Missourians, Smith gave an explicit command: "Go and kill every devil of them."[69] They headed out under the command of Captain David Patten, one of Smith's most trusted apostles, also known as "Captain Fearnought."[70]

By daybreak the Mormon militia unit had crossed into Ray County to reach Crooked River, where Bogart and his men were encamped. Patten led the charge from the woods about eighty yards above the river's bank. "Go ahead, boys; rake them down," he ordered.[71] But the Missourians fired first, cutting down five or six of the Saints with two volleys. But before a third round could be unleashed, the Mormons had drawn their swords and slashed their way into the enemy's ranks, shouting, "God and Liberty!" Bogart's men fled, giving the Mormons a victory. One Saint had been killed, and nine lay injured, including David Patten and Patrick O'Bannion, both of whom would die from their wounds within days. As for the Missourians, one was killed; six were wounded.

Unfortunately, the Mormons had not attacked a vigilante mob, but had unknowingly besieged a state militia unit. In doing so they inadvertently, as Governor Lilburn Boggs would later write, had "made war upon the people of this state."[72] And the Mormons had done so without mercy. One case in point that court officials would later cite involved the vicious hacking of wounded Missourian Samuel Tarwater. As the unconscious militiaman lay severely injured and defenseless, the Danites mutilated his face with their swords, striking him repeatedly in the mouth and face, "cutting off his under teeth, and breaking his jaw." His cheeks were torn off as well.[73] He also received a "terrible gash in the skull, through which his brain was plainly visible."[74] The Mormons left him for dead, never imagining that he would survive to press charges against each of them for attempted murder.

When residents throughout the various counties heard that Mormons actually had attacked state troops, panic gripped the entire region. Hundreds of men enlisted in newly formed militia units, weapons were primed and readied for action, letters were sent to state military personnel, and Governor Lilburn Boggs was notified of the Crooked River skirmish by a number of individuals. Unfortunately, the stories that reached Boggs were exaggerated. He was told, for instance, that the Mormons had killed ten soldiers of a state militia unit, wounded many more, and took the rest prisoner. This particular communiqué from Judge E.M. Ryland of Lexington ended alarmingly:

> [P]ut a stop to the devastation which is menaced by these infuriated
> fanatics. . . . [Those you send] must go prepared and with the full deter-

mination to exterminate or expel them [the Mormons] from the State
enmasse. Nothing but this can give tranquility to the public mind, and
re-establish the supremacy of the laws. . . . The Mormons must leave the
State, or we will—one and all.[75]

Boggs agreed. On October 27, with little regard for the fallout of his
actions, the governor issued to one of his state militia generals an extermination order against the Saints:

> Head Quarters of the Militia
> City of Jefferson, Oct. 27, 1838
>
> [To:] Gen. John B. Clark
>
> I have received . . . information of the most appalling character, which
> entirely changes the face of things, and places the Mormons in the atti-
> tude of an open and avowed defiance of the laws, and of having made
> war upon the people of this State. . . . Your orders are, therefore, to has-
> ten your operations with all possible speed. The Mormons must be
> treated as enemies, and must be exterminated or driven from the State
> if necessary for the public peace—their outrages are beyond all
> description.[76]

Additional orders were sent to Major-General Willock, Brigadier
General Parks, and Generals Doniphan and Lucas, each of whom commanded several hundred state militia troops. Now, under the leadership
of General John Clark, and with directives issued by the governor, all of
them were marching to Far West. Before their arrival, however, one of
the most despicable acts of brutality in Mormon history would be perpetrated by a renegade group of vigilante militiamen determined to resolve
the Mormon situation themselves.

The Haun's Mill Massacre

October 30, 1838, dawned as usual for the Mormon families living at
Haun's Mill, a serene location just inside Caldwell County. These Saints

had not retreated into Far West because of a miscommunication with Smith. Nothing extraordinary marked the early morning hours of the fateful day: children were playing on either side of Shoal Creek, mothers were doing their domestic chores, and the men were either on guard or gathering in crops. According to Joseph Young, who survived the day, "all was tranquil" and uneventful, until a few Mormons looked up to see approximately 250 soldiers emerge from the woods about 100 yards away; some marching, some on horseback.[77]

The Saints had no idea it was an attack. Some of them even thought the troops, who had darkened their faces and attached red-cloths to themselves for identification purposes, were Mormon reinforcements from Far West.[78] The militiamen formed into three companies, under the command of Colonel Thomas Jennings and Captains Nehemiah Comstock and William Mann—well-known anti-Mormon. None of them had received any state orders to assemble, march, or attack. Nevertheless, they formed their own battle plan as a self-appointed vigilante squad.

The baffled Mormons continued looking on in curiosity, until the horror of it all slowly began to dawn on them. These soldiers were not fellow Saints. Those who had been watching the scene unfold shouted the alarm and scrambled to find their "wives, husbands, children, and the nearest shelter."[79] Mormon leader, David Evans raised his hands and frantically gave the signal for peace. Comstock responded by firing one shot into the air, which was followed by about ten seconds of silence. Then, all at once, the soldiers aimed their weapons at the tiny village.

The rolling crack of their first volley sent balls of lead into the Mormon encampment, which consisted of little more than a mass of tents and a few makeshift wooden structures. Amanda Smith, a new arrival, tried to run to the blacksmith's shop and alert the men who had been having a short prayer service there. But before even reaching the door, bullets tore through the shop. Smith grabbed her two little girls, and with Mary Stedwell, fled across the mill-pond as countless shots were fired in their direction. When a rifle ball finally pierced Stedwell's hand, she hid behind a log, enabling Amanda and the children run on. Later, nearly two dozen musket balls would be found in the fallen tree behind which Stedwell had fainted.[80]

Meanwhile, the Missourians raced into the camp, ruthlessly killing men and boys, many of whom had run to the blacksmith's shop, where they "had previously determined to fight if they were attacked."[81] These unfortunate souls were picked off one by one as the Missourians took aim through the "unchinked cracks between the logs of the shop's walls."[82] The vigilantes advanced far enough to where they finally just "shoved their muskets through the logs and fired into the crowd of bodies."[83] After about half the Mormon men had been killed, the others attempted to flee the building, but were butchered as they ran the gauntlet of Missourians outside.

Sixty-two-year-old Thomas McBride, who was running toward the woods, was finally caught and commanded to surrender his gun. After doing so, Missourian Jacob Rogers used it to blow a hole in McBride's chest. The unrestrained militiaman then hacked away at McBride with a scythe until his body was mutilated "from head to foot."[84] Any Mormons found injured by the Missourians were killed, like McBride, in cold-blood. The Missourians then stripped the fallen Mormons of their clothes, weapons, personal affects, and departed. By the time the smoke from the atrocity cleared, more than two-dozen Saints had been wounded; eighteen were dead or dying, including one non-Mormon who happened to being staying with the group.[85]

Shortly after the gunfire ceased, Amanda returned to find battered bodies strewn about the ground. Her husband, Warren, had been killed; his new boots stolen off his feet. Her youngest son, seven-year-old Alma, had been shot in the hip, the entire joint of which had been blown to bits when one of the Missourians placed his gun-barrel to the child's hip, and pulled the trigger. Alma would survive, but barely. The invaders also had discovered Amanda's other son, 10-year-old Sardius, who attempted to hide under the bellows in blacksmith's shop. He was murdered by a Missourian, who put a rifle to the child's head and then, according to eyewitness testimony, "blowed off the upper part of it," splattering his brains

Late 19th century sketch of the Haun's Mill Massacre (from T.B.H. Stenhouse, *The Rocky Mountain Saints*, 1873).

and hair onto the surrounding walls. Another little boy, a 9-year-old, was killed nearby.[86]

Shortly thereafter the bodies were gathered up by the women with the help of those men who had survived by hiding into the woods. Not knowing whether or not their assailants would return, the Mormons were forced to dig no graves, but instead, dump the bodies—some head-first, some feet first—into a well and seal it with earth. The Mormon men then fled back to Far West, while the women gathered as many belongings as possible before leaving. To add insult to injury, before all of the Mormon women departed, the Missourians returned and built a latrine over the make-shift grave, which they used to desecrate the remains of those who had been buried there.[87]

EXPELLED AS EXPECTED

On the same day of the Haun's Mill Massacre, Smith assembled his men and announced to them that his intelligence sources had learned about several large mobs—unusually large mobs—heading toward Far

West. He promised his followers that they would give these vigilantes a fight, no matter how many of them showed up. "God should damn them," he yelled. "We will play hell with their applecart."[88] He also assured them that angels would be fighting on their side.

A few hours before sunset on October 30, the Saints at Far West spotted the Missouri army marching for them. The advancing legions struck terror in the hearts of every citizen. One Mormon guard yelled, "Retreat!" Smith retorted: "Retreat! Where in the name of God shall we retreat to?"[89] He then led three hundred of his men to the edge of Far West and formed as much of a battle line as possible. But instead of attacking, the massive Missourian army set up camp just over a mile south of the town. This apparently was only the first group to arrive. Other soldiers continued pouring into the swelling ranks throughout the night and into the next day, until more than 2,500 of them were poised to crush the Mormon rebellion. The Saints had less than half as many able-bodied warriors.

Almost as soon as the army encamped, Smith sent Reed Peck to them in hopes of negotiating a compromise. Peck returned with good news: the generals would hold off their attack until morning. The next day Peck, John Corrill, George Hinkle, and other representatives returned to the army to negotiate. John Taylor, who would later become Mormonism's third president, recalled in an 1882 sermon that Smith's bravery and stalwart defiance never shined as brightly as on that day:

> [T]he first thing we knew a flag of truce was seen coming towards us .... Joseph Smith, our leader, then sent word back [to the Missourians] ... said he, "Tell your General to withdraw his troops or I will send them to hell." I thought that was a pretty bold stand to take.[90]

The bravado greatly impressed Smith's followers, especially his Danites, who were ready to watch God reap vengeance on his enemies through their muskets. But both Peck and Corrill, to whom Smith spoke privately about the negotiations, remembered Joseph telling them, to "beg like a dog for peace."[91] He commanded Hinkle to secure a treaty "on any terms short of a battle."[92] And that is exactly what happened. The terms of surrender included four demands:

1. Turn over Mormon leaders Joseph Smith, Sidney Rigdon, Parley
   P. Pratt Lyman Wight, and George W. Robinson to be tried and
   punished for their crimes.
2. Financially compensate non-Mormon state citizens for all damages to them or their property; the payments for which should be
   taken from those who took up arms to commit the damage.
3. Leave the state.
4. Give up all arms and weapons of every description.

General Lucas told Hinkle that his prophet had barely one hour to
comply. The conditions were harsh, but Smith had no real choice in the
matter. Not only were the Mormons outnumbered three to one, but General Clark had brought a cannon. Moreover, he seemed anxious to use it.
Clark waited barely thirty minutes before mobilizing his men to march
in full battle array toward Far West. The Mormons would get no time
extension. He stopped six hundred yards from the town, when he saw
Hinkle and Corrill riding madly toward them—Smith and the others
were on their way.

At 8:00 a.m. the following day, Smith, now a prisoner, sent a message
to Far West telling them to surrender. Less than two hours later, the Mormon troops exited Far West and deposited their weapons on the ground
in front of the riotous taunts and jeers of hundreds upon hundreds of
Missouri militiamen, some of whom "attempted to intimidate the Mormons by picking their flints and priming their guns, as if they were making ready to fire."[93] The women were sobbing and screaming, believing
their husbands would be killed. But none were. General Lucas, however,
did march his entire force of 2,500 soldiers through the streets of Far
West. The gloating Missourians continued their mockings, derisively
shouting, "Charge, Danites! Charge!"[94] But none did. The Missouri War
of 1838 was over.

Smith, meanwhile, along with the others who had given themselves
up, were being carted away in prison wagons, bound for Liberty, Missouri.
There they would be tried for numerous crimes including murder and
treason. Behind them remained a defenseless town of men, women, and

children, which would be plundered for many days by the Missouri army.[95] Not until a week later did the torment subside. General Clark at that time ordered every Mormon male into the town square. Conspicuously absent were some sixty men who had been arrested during the preceding days. Like Joseph, they would be hauled away to stand trial. Clark had summoned the remaining men together to receive his departing words. "The orders of the governor to me were, that you should be exterminated, and not allowed to remain in the state," he said. The General continued:

> [Y]ou must not think of staying here another season, or of putting in crops, for the moment you do this the citizens will be upon you. . . . As for your leaders . . . their doom is scaled. . . . You have always been the aggressors, you have brought upon yourselves these difficulties by being disaffected and not being subject to rule—and my advice is, that you become as other citizens, lest by a recurrence of these events you bring upon yourselves irretrievable ruin.[96]

The Saints understood Clark all too well. It was time to leave. So thousands of them packed up what little they had left and eventually migrated to a large tract of land near the "sleepy little Mississippi river village known as Commerce, Illinois."[97] Here the Saints began again to build a gathering place. The beleaguered Mormons called their new home Nauvoo, a term meaning "The Beautiful Place." As for their beloved prophet, Joseph, his fate was in the Lord's hands. All they could do now was pray for him and remain faithful to their God.

DIVINE DELIVERANCE

When Smith and his fellow Mormon leaders finally received their preliminary hearing in Richmond, Missouri, the evidence clearly revealed that Joseph had directed most, if not all, of the illegal activities in which the Saints had been engaged. The prosecution's witnesses included not only long-time accusers such as John Whitmer and W.W. Phelps, but also a several more recently added individuals to the growing list of dissenters from Smith's Mormon ranks (e.g., George Hinkle, John Corrill, and Reed Peck).

Smith bore all of their testimony with stoic defiance. But then into the courtroom walked none other than Sampson Avard; supposedly the most loyal follower of them all. He spilled his proverbial guts, exposing to a Gentile court of law every Danite secret. He even produced a list of Danite officers, which included a Secretary of War.[98] The judge, it seemed, was seeking specific information proving Smith's plans to establish a kingdom within the U.S.—a treasonous offense.

Eventually, after numerous witnesses were produced, the judge ordered all but eleven of the Mormon prisoners to either be released or admitted to bail. Of the eleven, four were committed to the Richmond jail, while six others, including Smith, Rigdon, Pratt, and Smith's brother, Hyrum, were remanded to the Liberty jail in Clay County. All were to be tried for a variety of crimes including murder, arson, and robbery, and treason.[99] Only three LDS leaders eluded the State's dragnet—"the wily Brigham Young, the gentle Edward Partridge, and the clowning Heber Kimball."[100] As for Smith, his hearing would not start for several months. But instead of wasting his time, he used the endless days and nights to write several letters to the Saints at Quincy, Illinois, and elsewhere. In these communications he denied the charges against him, claimed that he was "ignorant as well as innocent" of all the Avard-inspired Danite crimes, renounced polygamy, and promised that Zion would yet thrive.[101]

Finally, six months after being incarcerated, the prisoners were transferred back to Gallatin in Daviess County to stand trial. And given the evidence, it seemed as if Mormonism's primary leaders were doomed to a life of imprisonment. Their future, however, turned in an entirely different direction when Smith's lawyers won a change of venue, which transferred the Mormon captives to Boone County. This was the opportunity for which Smith had been waiting. He and Hyrum bribed the Sheriff with a jug of whiskey and $800.[102]

On April 15, 1839, only about twenty-five miles from Adam-ondi-Ahman, the Sheriff and his men passed out drunk in the dead of night, thus allowing their prisoners to escape.[103] Joseph once again climbed on to the back of a horse and fled, leaving his troubles behind him. They all reached Far West "just in time to join the last group of the Mormons heading for the Mississippi."[104] Smith had no idea that his departure from Missouri would mark the beginning of the last chapter in his life.

NINE

March to Martyrdom

I combat the errors of the ages; . . . I solve mathematical prob-
lems of universities, with truth—diamond truth; and God is my
'right hand man.' . . . [God] will make me be God to you in His
stead, . . . and if you don't like it, you must lump it. . . . I have
more to boast of than ever any man had. . . . I boast that no man
ever did such a work as I.

Joseph Smith[1]
History of the Church, 1844

EVEN WHILE SMITH WAS STILL IN PRISON awaiting trial, his followers began establishing their new Zion in Commerce, Illinois, a tiny village on the banks of the Mississippi River. It was an ideal location for God's kingdom and within three years the industrious Saints would transform Commerce into a boomtown of about 10,000 residents, making it the second largest urban center in Illinois next to Chicago.[2] After having its name changed to Nauvoo in 1840, the town quickly became renowned for its beautiful homes, fine shops, and magnificent Mormon temple on a bluff overlooking the city and the river. Nauvoo even boasted a university and hotel.[3]

Illinois originally gave the Saints a glad welcome. Soon, however, dissention in the church created yet another wave of bad publicity for the Mormons. Antagonism from outside the church then came from those fearing Mormonism's increasing political clout. An atmosphere of extreme tension between the Saints and non-Mormons inevitably resulted, especially in Hancock County, wherein Nauvoo was situated.

Matters were not helped by Nauvoo's city charter, which enabled Smith to establish his "Beautiful Place" as a virtual state within a state.[4] It granted town officials wide judicial privileges, the authority to create a standing army (i.e., the Nauvoo Legion), and the right to enact rather stringent laws governing nearly every facet of city life. Curfews were enforced, non-residents had to register as visitors before walking Nauvoo's streets, and the city council could remove high-ranking city officials from office at their pleasure.[5]

Few Saints would have argued that such measures were unnecessary. Their expulsion from Missouri demolished all hopes of building up Zion in or around Jackson County. Even more problematic, however, were the many statements Smith had made concerning the certainty of God establishing the Saints' land of inheritance in the last days. Fortunately for Joseph, his followers were more than willing to accept any excuse he might give them. After all, they had a great deal at stake—emotionally, psychologically, and spiritually. Moreover, intellectual reasoning and logical thought never had played more than a minor role in their belief system (see pp. 104, 412). So rather than dealing with the numerous false prophecies he had made about Zion being in Missouri, he simply introduced new revelations that canceled out his previous declarations. As Mormon scholar Marvin S. Hill observes, such a change had little effect on the Saints' faith:

> Relatively few Mormons seemed to care whether what had been prophesied was perfectly consistent with what happened afterward. It did not matter how often the prophet altered or expanded theology; the Saints valued the process of revelation more than the product. Although Joseph Smith revised his revelations from time to time, including the Book of Mormon, few elders ever objected.[6]

Joseph first alleviated the incongruity between the Lord's initial command to establish Zion and the Saints' expulsion from Missouri. He explained the disparity through a revelation wherein God said that if a certain task is commanded, but impossible to complete because followers are "hindered by their enemies," then that task will no longer be

An 1840s daguerreotype of Nauvoo, the City of Joseph,
after it had been abandoned. The newly completed
temple sits on the distant horizon overlooking the town
(courtesy of Utah State Historical Society).

required.[7] Although this explanation attributed a surprising lack of vision to the Saints' supposedly omniscient deity, the excuse worked.

Smith then had to identify a "Zion" that could still be built up, or else risk having his entire end-times scenario unravel. As the Mormon First Presidency declared in January 1841, the gathering "must take place before the Lord comes to 'take vengeance upon the ungodly.'"[8] To meet this need, Joseph simply broadened his identification of the promised land to include the whole of North and South America.[9] This explanation, too, was accepted without reservation by most of the Saints. Consequently, raising up Zion during the "last days" continued uninterrupted in Illinois.

The significance of Nauvoo in Mormon history cannot be overstated. According to Ronald K. Esplin of Brigham Young University, "Nauvoo was, and is, and will be important to the Latter-day Saints because it was the City of Joseph. It was the city he built, where he lived and acted, where he died. Above all, it was the city where he fulfilled his religious mission."[10] More than any other Mormon location, Nauvoo provided "the first full-scale model" of the theocratic kingdom Smith had envisioned.[11] Unfortunately, in lieu of Jesus Christ, who would reign supreme at his second coming, Smith installed himself as Zion's dictator. He accomplished this "by holding all the important offices in Nauvoo, controlling the political life of his community, directing the voting behavior of his followers, and planning to establish a political kingdom of God on earth (with himself in charge)."[12]

Although such actions would eventually bring ruin to both Smith and his boomtown on the Mississippi, the initial results were compatible with everything Joseph had ever dreamed of achieving. He had wealth, power, admiration, and authority. The eternal had effectively been blended with the temporal; spirituality with the things of earth; heavenly rule with earthly government. But as the English historian and moralist Lord Acton (1834–1902) so eloquently and insightfully noted: "Power tends to corrupt; absolute power tends to corrupt absolutely."[13]

JOSEPH, JOSEPH, JOSEPH

As far back as the Kirtland days, most of Smith's followers viewed him as a modern day Moses against whom they were "not to murmur."[14] As Heber C. Kimball put it, "It is not for us to reproach the Lord's anointed, nor speak evil of him; all have covenanted not to do it."[15] The idealization of Smith can also be seen in the 1836 statement of Wilford Woodruff, who would become the LDS church's fourth president:

> There is not a greater man than Joseph standing in this generation. The gentiles look upon him & he is to them like bed of gold concealed from human view. [T]hey know not his principle, his spirit, his wisdom, virtue, philanthropy, nor his calling. His mind like Enoch's swells wide as eternity. Nothing short of a God can comprehend his soul.[16]

Others viewed Joseph in a similar light. Brigham Young stated that Smith's character was easily on par with Jesus Christ's and that no person could be found to present "a better character to the world."[17] He also declared that "a better man never lived upon the face of this earth."[18] Heber C. Kimball proclaimed that one day the world would look upon

Joseph "as a God."[19] In truth, comments by early Mormon leaders, especially after Smith's death, indicate that at that time the Saints already viewed their prophet as a god. Brigham Young, for instance, warned that no one would ever get into God's celestial kingdom "without the consent of Joseph Smith. . . . He reigns there as supreme a being in his sphere, capacity, and calling, as God does in heaven."[20]

Such high regard for Smith has not diminished in the least among modern-day Mormons, who tend to view Smith as important to their spirituality as Jesus Christ. For instance, in an April 14, 1961, letter by Levi Edgar Young—an LDS official of notably high rank—the "grandeur of Joseph Smith's life" was noted as the all-important truth that the world needed to hear. Levi's prayer was that thousands would turn not to God, but to Joseph.[21] In 1966, the Mormon writer John J. Stewart expressed the common LDS sentiment that Joseph Smith was "perhaps the most Christ-like man to live upon the earth."[22]

Brigham Young went so far as to twist a well-known biblical passage about Christ in such a way as to make it apply to Joseph. The original verse, First John 4:3, reads: "Every spirit that confesseth that Jesus Christ is come in the flesh is of God: And every spirit that confesseth not that Jesus Christ is come in the flesh is not of God: and this is that spirit of antichrist." Young, however, declared: "'Whosoever confesseth that Joseph Smith was sent of God . . . that spirit is of God; and every spirit that does not confess that God has sent Joseph Smith, and revealed the everlasting Gospel to and through him, is of Antichrist.'"[23]

How did such adulation actually affect Joseph himself? There is every reason to believe that it greatly fed into what contemporary psychiatrist Robert Anderson has labeled Smith's "narcissistic personality," which probably formed early in his childhood due to various traumas he experienced.[24] According to Anderson, who created a psychological profile of Smith based on the prophet's many statements and the *Book of Mormon*, Joseph undoubtedly suffered from the mental pathology associated with narcissism, as outlined in 1980 by the American Psychiatric Association:

A pervasive pattern of grandiosity (in fantasy or behavior), need for admiration, and lack of empathy, beginning by early adulthood and present in a variety of contexts, as indicated by five (or more) of the following:

(1) has a grandiose sense of self-importance (e.g., exaggerates achievements and talents, expects to be recognized as superior without commensurate achievements)

(2) is preoccupied with fantasies of unlimited success, power, brilliance, beauty, or ideal love

(3) believes that he or she is "special" and unique and can only be understood by, or should associate with, other special or high-status people (or institutions)

(4) requires excessive admiration

(5) has a sense of entitlement, i.e., unreasonable expectations of especially favorable treatment or automatic compliance with his or her expectations

(6) is interpersonally exploitative, i.e., takes advantage of others to achieve his or her own ends

(7) lacks empathy: is unwilling to recognize or identify with the feelings and needs of others

(8) is often envious of others or believes that others are envious of him or her

(9) shows arrogant, haughty behavior or attitudes.[25]

An examination of Smith's life reveals that he regularly exhibited all of these characteristics, especially trait #1, which often manifested itself in statements reflecting delusions of grandeur (e.g., see opening quote). Hezekiah McKune, for example, stated that "in conversation with Joseph Smith Jr., he (Smith) said he was nearly equal to Jesus Christ; that he was a prophet sent by God to bring in the Jews, and that he was the greatest prophet that had ever arisen."[26] Sophia Lewis likewise remembered a conversation between Joseph and a Rev. James Roach, in which Smith said he "was as good as Jesus Christ."[27] Levi Lewis heard Joseph say "it was as bad to injure him as it was to injure Jesus Christ."[28] In his own *History of the Church*, Smith declared: "I am the only man that has ever been able to keep a whole church together. . . . Neither Paul, John, Peter, nor Jesus ever did it."[29]

WEBER STAKE WARD TEACHERS' LESSON.

Lesson for January, 1922.

A PARALLEL.

Jesus the Redeemer.	Joseph Smith the Prophet.
The Advent of Christ.	**The Advent of Joseph Smith.**
At the time of the birth of Jesus Christ, the national religion which had satisfied the parents, no longer proves satisfactory to the children.	At the time of the birth of Joseph Smith the world was convulsed with religious discord, and the people were not satisfied with the teaching offered by the churches.
The parents of Jesus were of humble origin.	The parents of Joseph were of humble origin.
The voice of God proclaimed the Christ at his baptism, saying, "This is my beloved Son in whom I am well pleased."	The voice of God spake unto Joseph Smith, saying, "This is my beloved Son—hear him."
Christ presented himself for baptism, and he was baptized by John the Baptist in the river Jordan.	John the Baptist appeared to Joseph Smith and conferred the Aaronic Priesthood upon him, and by the authority of that Priesthood He was baptized.
Christ demonstrated the power of the priesthood by healing the sick, etc., and he bestowed this power upon his disciples.	Joseph Smith by the power of the Priesthood healed the sick, and he conferred this priesthood and power upon his disciples.
Christ was persecuted and the message that He gave to the people was rejected.	Joseph Smith was persecuted and the message that he was sent to deliver to the people was rejected.
Christ sealed his testimony with his blood on Calvary.	Joseph Smith sealed his testimony with his blood at Carthage, Ill.

WHO SHALL DOUBT THE DIVINE MISSION OF THESE SAVIOURS OF MANKIND?

God moves in a mysterious way
His wonders to perform;
He plants his footsteps in the sea,
And rides upon the storm.

A 1922 religious lesson plan that reveals the level of Mormon adoration for Joseph Smith, who has been elevated by his followers to a near god-like status, often in comparison to Jesus Christ (from Weber Stake Ward, 1922, reprinted in "News of Mormonism," *Light On Mormonism*, September 1922, vol. 1, no. 2, 5, published by The Utah Gospel Mission of Cleveland, Ohio).

Others recalled how the Mormon prophet talked incessantly about himself in glowing terms (trait #9). Charlotte Haven, for instance, a young woman who visited her Mormon brother in Nauvoo for a year, perceived Smith as "a great egotist and boaster." She often heard him tell others about how "he was so 'handsome and good looking.'"[30] Haven also heard Smith say that "he had done and could do more than other mortals, and remarked that he was 'a giant, physically and mentally.'"[31]

On one occasion, when the editor of the *Pittsburg Gazette* visited Joseph in Nauvoo, Joseph spent the entire interview boasting. And whenever the journalist tried to turn the conversation in another direction, Smith "would adroitly bring it back to himself. . . . Running on in his voluble style, he said: 'The world persecutes me . . . When I have proved that I am right, and get all the world subdued under me, I think I shall deserve something.'"[32]

AMERICA'S FIGHTING PROPHET

Smith's inflated ego and elevated status in the community of Saints often led to behavior on his part that was fairly inconsistent with a number of Christian virtues: e.g., love, kindness, gentleness, and self-control. One of his most notably negative traits was that of a *fighter*, who thoroughly enjoyed a good brawl, especially since he was a rather large, physically agile, and muscular man. Smith, in fact, was an excellent wrestler, and he often sought to prove it by beating up individuals who had displeased him in some way. In the words of historian D. Michael Quinn, Smith was a "church president who physically assaulted both Mormons and non-Mormons for insulting him."[33] And afterward, in a manner consistent with his narcissism, Smith would boast about his violent deeds.

In the *History of the Church*, for example, under the date of March 13, 1843, we find this entry: "I wrestled with William Wall, the most expert wrestler in Ramus, and threw him."[34] On March 28, Smith wrote: "Josiah Butterfield came to my house and insulted me so outrageously that I kicked him out of the house, across the yard, and into the street."[35]

On June 30, 1843, Smith fought and boasted again of his strength, saying: "I feel as strong as a giant. . . . I pulled up with one hand the strongest man that could be found. Then two men tried, but they could not pull me up."[36] Then, in August, Smith got into a fight with the tax collector:

> [Walter] Bagby called me a liar, and picked up a stone to throw at me, which so enraged me that I followed him a few steps, and struck him two or three times. Esquire Daniel H. Wells stepped between us and succeeded in separating us. . . . I seized him by the throat to choke him off.[37]

Joseph's violent temper was aroused most easily when someone dared criticize or question him. Benjamin F. Johnson, a close associate of Smith's, wrote in a letter to Elder George S. Gibbs about his leader's response to those who did not follow the path of obedience:

> [C]riticism, even by his associates, was rarely acceptable, and contradictions would rouse in him the lion at once. . . . [H]is associates were more than once, for their impudence, helped from the congregation by his (Joseph's) foot. . . . [H]e soundly thrashed his [own] brother William.[38]

Jedediah M. Grant, a high-ranking LDS leader under Brigham Young, recalled that on one occasion Joseph accosted a Baptist minister for simply doubting that Smith had seen Jesus Christ. According to Grant, Smith hit the preacher and threw him to the ground so violently that the minister "whirled round a few times, like a duck shot in the head."[39] LDS apostle Luke S. Johnson remembered a similar instance that took place in Kirtland, when Smith felt slighted by a minister. He "'boxed his ears with both hands, and turning his face towards the door, kicked him into the street.'"[40]

According to D. Michael Quinn, Smith's predilection for violence might actually have manifested itself in a conspiracy to murder anti-Mormon Grandison Newell, who had been causing Joseph a great deal of trouble in Kirtland. Although Smith was acquitted of the charge due to lack of evidence, during the case, testimony from two apostles—both of whom were supposed to have been supporting witnesses for Smith—revealed that he had indeed discussed plans to murder Newell:

> Orson Hyde testified that "Smith seemed much excited and declared that Newell should be put out of the way, or where the crows could not find him; he said destroying Newell would be justifiable in the sight of God, that it was the will of God. . . ." Luke S. Johnson acknowledged to the court that Smith had said "if Newell or any other man should head a mob against him, they ought to be put out of the way, and it would be our duty to do so."[41]

Smith's violent tendencies, along with his habitual use of force to accomplish goals, were most obvious in his raising of an army. The Nauvoo Legion, over which he placed himself as Lieutenant-General, existed as the ultimate symbol of the aggressive personae he presented to the world.

LIEUTENANT-GENERAL SMITH

Smith's role as Nauvoo's undisputed prophet-leader only added to the uneasiness felt by non-Mormons living nearby. Time and again it was demonstrated to observers that Smith's word was law. Former Danite, John D. Lee, confirmed in his 1877 book *Mormonsim Unveiled* that in Nauvoo it was "the duty of all men to obey the leaders of the Church, and that no man could commit sin so long as he acted in the way that he was directed by his Church superiors."[42]

Moreover, it was clear that Joseph's extended jail-time in unsanitary and uncomfortable conditions had embittered him against his enemies: i.e., the federal government, the mobs, the state of Missouri, and all persecutors. He longed to see God pour out vengeance on those who had wronged him and the Saints. He expressed this hope and conviction even before escaping, writing in a letter to his Saints, that "the time shall soon come when the Son of Man shall descend in the clouds of heaven" to destroy the Saints' oppressors.[43]

An 1840s sketch by Sutcliffe Maudsley of Lieutenant General
Joseph Smith in full military regalia (taken from John C. Bennett,
History of the Saints, 1842).

Smith had made similar statements in the past, but now he seemed
determined to establish God's kingdom, even if he had to personally
expedite the process. There would be no more waiting, compromise, or
running from mobs. The formation of the Nauvoo Legion demonstrated
his resolve on these issues.[44] His army, although organized under state
militia laws, included in its articles of formation some rather interesting
provisions. First, its commissioned officers, unlike those of other state

militia units, were given law-making powers. This effectively blended the military with both the legislative and executive branches of government. Second, the legion could be called upon by the mayor to enforce city laws; a radical departure from customary militia practice.

In other words, Smith had formed nothing less than an independent city-state governed by a small body of officials, most of whom were military, under whose command existed an army to enforce civil law. And it was a formidable force that Smith had organized. As of September 1841, the legion consisted of 1,490 men. By mid-1842, the army had twenty-six companies and about 2,000 troops. The state even provided Smith's army with three cannons and about 250 small arms.[45] In some ways the militia was a resurrection of the Missouri Danites, but with far more polish and provision. They were at times even taken through Danite drills during their training.[46] Interestingly, Smith succeeded in not only forming his "own little army," but organized it under a uniquely-worded charter, which allowed it to exist, except under very special circumstances, "independent of and not subject to the military laws of Illinois."[47]

Of course, it did not take long before Illinois residents noticed that Joseph had organized a substantial army. In fact, his Nauvoo Legion would by 1843/44 number approximtely 4,000 soldiers, second in size only to the U.S. Army (8,000–8,500 troops).[48] The *Warsaw Signal* mentioned the large Mormon militia in terms that were critical as well as apprehensive:

> How *military* these people are becoming! Every thing they say or do seems to breathe the spirit of military tactics. Their *prophet* appears, on all great occasions, in his sp[l]endid regimental dress[,] signs his name Lieut. General, and more titles are to be found in the Nauvoo Legion, than any one book on military tactics can produce. . . . Truly *fighting* must, be a part of the creed of these Saints![49]

In his landmark book *Nauvoo: Kingdom on the Mississippi,* Robert Flanders described how militarism quickly engulfed Nauvoo as "'Colonel,' 'Captain,' or 'General' came to replace 'Brother,' 'Elder,' or

'President' in the address of the Saints. Military trappings were for them a particular symbol of status, prestige, and reassurance."[50] Smith preferred to be addressed as either General Smith or Lieutenant-General Smith, a self-appointed title held by no other officer in the United States.[51] In fact, except for George Washington, no other U.S. officer "had held the permanent lineal rank of lieutenant general up to that time."[52] Joseph also enjoyed strutting about in full military regalia. Consequently, he often scheduled militia parades, drills, and sham battles. Fawn Brodie explains:

> His uniform was smartly designed: a blue coat with a plentiful supply of gold braid, buff trousers, high military boots, and a handsome chapeau topped with ostrich feathers. On his hip he carried a sword and two big horse-pistols. Delighting in the pomp and splendor of parades, he called out the Legion on every possible occasion, marching at the head on his magnificent black stallion, Charlie.[53]

The war-mongering spirit so thoroughly pervaded Nauvoo that both Joseph and his brother, Brigadier General Don Carlos Smith, wore military outfits, complete with swords, during the cornerstone laying ceremony for the Nauvoo Temple.[54] But Joseph apparently felt that more had to be done to establish God's kingdom on earth. Even his outlandishly high rank of lieutenant general seemed inadequate for the grand role he felt called to play as God's representative on earth. So in 1844 Smith decided to run for President of the United States.

PRESIDENT SMITH AND HIS COUNCIL OF FIFTY

The Mormons who migrated from Missouri to Nauvoo were incensed over being uprooted from their homes yet again. It seemed that the rights supposedly guaranteed by the American Constitution were non-existent for them. Furthermore, neither state, nor federal authorities, had taken any action against the injustice of it all. Finally, in November 1839, Smith tried to right the wrongs that had been perpetrated against his people by traveling to Washington, D.C., with hundreds of affidavits and petitions from the Saints. His demand for $2 million in damages would be presented to various congressmen, the Senate Judiciary Committee, and U.S. President Martin Van Buren. Unfortunately, Joseph's grievances were directly tied to that highly sensitive political issue of states' rights.

No politician wanted to wrestle with the subject. Southerners already were battling over the issue of slavery with Northerners and Smith's cause was simply another North vs. South hotbed of controversy. Few politicians saw any reason to further antagonize a southern state such as Missouri. In fact, during his meeting with Van Buren in November 1839, the president candidly replied, "'I can do nothing for you. If I do anything, I shall come in contact with the whole state of Missouri.'"[55] Reportedly, Van Buren also said: *"[Y]our cause is just . . . but I can do nothing for you. If I take up for you I shall lose the vote of Missouri."*[56]

Nevertheless, Smith left his petitions with the Senate Judiciary Committee and went to Philadelphia to consult with Parley Pratt. In his absence, Washington politicians contacted Missouri officials (e.g., Governor Boggs), who in turn forwarded to them the damaging testimony against Smith and the Danites that had been given at the preliminary hearing in Richmond, Missouri. Joseph now had no chance of having his petitions granted.

Smith left Washington enraged. The government had become not only *his* enemy, but *God's* enemy. To insure that the world understood the official Latter-day Saint position on the political system that had so cruelly betrayed them, Mormon leaders unleashed a steady stream of anti-government rhetoric, both oral and written. The prophet, for instance, predicted doom for the nation, writing: "I see, by the visions of the Almighty, the end of this nation, if she continues to disregard the cries and petitions of her virtuous citizens."[57]

Parley Pratt had been right, or so thought the Saints, when he warned in 1838 that the *Book of Mormon* had "set the time for the overthrow of our government and all other Gentile governments on the American continent."[58] Pratt made another bold announcement that same year: "I will state as a prophesy, that there will not be an unbelieving Gentile upon this continent 50 years hence; and if they are not greatly scourged, and in a great measure overthrown, within five or ten years from this date [i.e., 1888], then the Book of Mormon will have proved itself false."[59]

America was headed for destruction, of this there was no doubt, as Apostle Wilford Woodruff lamented in 1841:

> O America . . . From this time forth perplexity shall rest upon the nation, confusion reign in thy government wisdom righteousness & truth will depart from thy senator & rulers, Discord & folly shall sit in thy congress & senate. Thy shame shall be known among the nations of the Earth. . . . [Woe] Shall come upon thee by Sword, fire, tempest, Earthquakes, & pestilence from the hand of God. Even these things shall come upon thee untill [sic] thy government is broken up & thou art destroyed as a nation from under Heaven.[60]

It was during these days, immediately after the disappointing trip to Washington, that Smith began to dwell on those ideas that would eventually crystallize into his famous May 1843 "White Horse" Prophecy against America (see Introduction). In July 1840, for example, he announced, "when the Constitution is upon the brink of ruin this people [i.e., the Mormons] will be the staff upon which the nation shall lean."[61] Then, in early 1841, he observed that the U.S. government "is fallen and needs redeeming," adding that it could no longer "stand as it now is but will come so near desolation as to stand as it were by a single hair. . . . [T]his is the redemption of Zion — when the saints shall have redeemed the government and reinstated it in all its purity and glory."[62]

In apparent confirmation of this notion, Smith had a prophetic dream in March 1843 wherein an old man sought his protection from the mobs. By April, Joseph had interpreted the dream to mean that one day the United States (i.e., the old man), would be invaded by a foreign foe, probably England, and that at that time the government would call on Smith "to defend probably all this western territory and offer him any amount of men he shall desire & put them under his command."[63] Clearly, such a calling far exceeded his original calling from God to simply translate the *Book of Mormon*, restore the pure doctrines of Christianity, and gather together the Saints in preparation for the establishment of Jesus' glorious earthly kingdom.

Somewhere along the way, probably during the six months he languished in a Missouri jail awaiting trial, Smith seems to have decided that a *political* kingdom of God (under his rule) would precede the *apocalyptic* kingdom of God (under Christ's rule). The former would be "the kingdom militant, struggling against a hostile world," while the latter would be "the kingdom victorious, having subdued all its enemies."[64] Finally, in December 1843, nearly seven months after delivering his "White Horse" Prophecy, Smith pronounced almost certain destruction upon America due to the government's continued unwillingness to grant reparations for the Saints' losses in Missouri. He prophesied: "[I]f Congress will not hear our petition and grant us protection, they shall be broken up as a government."[65] When Congress ignored him once more, he wrote an angry letter to Senator and former vice-president John C. Calhoun. It was brimming with threats of divine retribution:

> [I]f the Latter Day Saints are not restored to all their rights, and paid for all their losses, according to the known rules of justice and judgment, reciprocation and common honesty among men, that God will come out of his hiding place and vex this nation with a sore vexation—yea, the consuming wrath of an offended God shall smoke through the nation.[66]

But again, Joseph's words had little effect. And so, after careful deliberation, Joseph Smith decided his only recourse was to actually become U.S. president. Moreover, the highest political office in the land certainly would further the establishment of Zion. He chose as his vice-presidential running mate none other than Sidney Rigdon, then ordered the elders of the church to campaign for him. Brigham Young stated: "It is now time to have a President of the United States. Elders will be sent to preach the Gospel and electioneer."[67] In possible preparation for the day when he would be president, Smith actually petitioned Congress in mid-1843 for the right to raise a 100,000-man army![68]

Although the petition was denied, Smith continued pursuing his dream of establishing an earthly kingdom by setting up a shadow-gov-

An 1844 flyer advertising Joseph Smith's bid for the
U.S. presidency.

ernment on March 11, 1844. He called this body of behind-the-scenes
rulers his Council of Fifty, which according to one member was created
as "the Municipal department of the Kingdom of God set up on the Earth,
and from which all Law emanates, for the rule, government & control of
all Nations, Kingdoms & towns, and People under the whole Heavens."[69]
According to Wilford Woodruff, the Council's stated purpose was to
"organize the political kingdom of God in preparation for the second
coming of Christ."[70]

To determine the basic principles and laws by which they would
establish and run their global regime, the council regularly met in Nauvoo. Their first order of business was to spearhead the presidential campaign of Joseph in an effort to begin establishing God's government. During the April 1844 LDS Conference, Rigdon explained that it was a
universal mistake to suppose that "[s]alvation was distinct from govern-

ment." He then affirmed that when "God sets up a system of salvation, he sets up a system of government; . . . a government that shall rule over temporal and spiritual affairs."[71] Furthermore, Rigdon's statements, reprinted soon afterward in the Mormon publication *Times and Seasons*, included the extraordinary assertion that the ultimate goal of Mormonism's system of government was to "set aside at will the laws of the United States and of all other secular governments."[72] The Council of Fifty would serve this purpose.

Significantly, former Danites accounted for one-third of the men Smith admitted to the group.[73] The Danites, it seemed, had been somewhat of a precursor to Nauvoo's Council of Fifty.[74] Members of the Council even took a Danite-like oath of secrecy, under the penalty of death; an oath that was to remain in effect "'until God should reveal to the contrary.'"[75] The Danite oath, as recounted by Sampson Avard, stated: "In the name of Jesus Christ, the Son of God, I do solemnly obligate myself ever to conceal, and never to reveal, the secret purposes of this society . . . Should I ever do the same, I hold my life as the forfeiture."[76]

Within a week of Rigdon's speech, Joseph took his plans a step further by having the Council of Fifty ordain him "a king, to reign over the house of Israel forever."[77] In a later revelation given by John Taylor, Mormonism's third president, God allegedly confirmed that Smith had indeed been divinely installed as "King and Ruler over Israel."[78] Smith no longer had to wait for the results of any kind of earthly presidential election. Mormon leaders already considered him the legitimate, God-ordained ruler over humanity. As Lyman Wight and Heber C. Kimball wrote to Smith in 1844: "[Y]ou are already President Pro tem of the world."[79]

THE BEGINNING OF THE END

According to Mormon scholar Kenneth W. Godfrey, former director of the LDS Institute at Stanford University, "[a]ntagonism toward the Mormon Prophet was further incited when it was correctly rumored, that he had been ordained 'King over the Immediate House of Israel' by the Council of Fifty."[80] But Godfrey's comment only gives a partial picture of the dynamics in Illinois that eventually led to the murders of Joseph and Hyrum Smith, and the expulsion of the Saints from that state. There existed many factors that caused the conflict in and around Nauvoo between Mormons and non-Mormons.

First, the ever-present threat of the political power resident within the sheer number of Saints terrified non-Mormons living in close proximity to them. The Mormons regularly voted as a bloc; a bloc that by the 1840s approached 20,000.[81] Illinois politicians reeled under the growing awareness that the Mormon vote "had become the key to the state's national policies."[82] Most disconcerting was the idea among Mormon leaders that the only acceptable government would be a global theocracy. Hence, Smith's desire to run for president and his coronation as king of the world. As Joseph himself had stated in July 1842: "It has been the design of Jehovah, from the commencement of the world, and is his purpose now, to regulate the affairs of the world . . . to stand as head of the universe, and take the reigns of government into his own hands."[83]

Such a perspective caused great consternation among Illinoians, who began to see the Saints as a major threat to the democratic process. The Mormon vote, for example, had completely changed the face of the 1843 Congressional race between Cyrus Walker and Joseph Hoge. Smith had promised the Mormon vote to Walker, but based on a last minute revelation received by Hyrum, he told the Saints to vote for Hoge. They did and Hoge won.[84]

The political clout wielded by the Mormons was beyond question, and growing ever-stronger as more Saints arrived in Nauvoo. Then, when Smith announced his bid for the presidency, Illinoians trembled at the thought of what might occur, especially when the Mormons were able to mobilize in one day a total of "337 political missionaries to twenty-six states and the territory of Wisconsin."[85] And this was only "part of the total number of LDS missionaries campaigning for Smith's candidacy."[86] As one politician remarked: "Their vote will about turn the Scale in the State."[87] It is no wonder that in 1842 the *Sangamo Journal* noted: "[Smith's] ambition would secure to himself the control of our State elections."[88] The *Quincy Whig* published a similar report:

It is not so much the particular doctrines, which Smith upholds and
practices, however abominable they may be in themselves, that our citizens care about—as it is the anti-republican nature of the organization,
over which he has almost supreme control. . . . The spectacle presented
in Smith's case of a civil, ecclesiastical and military leader, united in one
and the same person, with power over life and liberty, can never find
favor in the minds of sound and thinking Republicans.[89]

Even the Freemasons, who were originally thrilled over Smith's
desire to join their fraternity, became alarmed by the Mormon ten-
dency to overwhelm "existing structures of non-Mormon society."[90]
Additionally, the Mormons usually reacted to situations as a united
front, under the leadership of Smith. So when hundreds of Mormon
males in Nauvoo joined their prophet in Freemasonry and established
a lodge, non-Mormon Masons soon realized the Saints would quickly
capture a majority membership, which in turn would produce some
unsettling results:

Within five months of its establishment in 1842, the Nauvoo lodge conducted "six times as many initiations and elevations as all the other
lodges in the state combined." When Joseph Smith established Nauvoo
there were barely 100 Freemasons in the entire state. By the time he
organized the Council of Fifty, nearly 700 Mormons were Freemasons
. . . . [A]mong local Masons there was "well-founded fear that within a
short time the Mormon Lodges, if allowed to continue, would become
more numerous than all others in the jurisdiction, and thus be able to
control the Grand Lodge [of Illinois]. And that is apparently what Smith
wanted to do."[91]

In addition to fears of a political take-over in Illinois by the Saints,
non-Mormons disliked Smith's ongoing status as a fugitive from justice.
Throughout his years in Nauvoo, Smith circumvented the law and
employed body guards to escape extradition orders delivered by law
enforcement personnel seeking to take him back to Missouri. Smith even
used Nauvoo's broadly-written city charter to pass laws that made it vir-

tually impossible for him to be captured. For example, the city council actually enacted the following "special" ordinance:

> [I]f any person or persons shall come with process, demand, or requisition . . . to arrest said Joseph Smith, he or they so offending shall be subject to be arrested by any officer of the city, with or without process, and tried by the Municipal Court, upon testimony, and, if found guilty, sentenced to imprisonment in the city prison *for life*; which convict or convicts can only be pardoned by the Governor, *with the consent of the Mayor of said city* [Joseph Smith himself was Mayor when this ordinance was passed].[92]

Numerous arrest warrants and various extradition orders against Smith were issued from 1839–1844. But of special significance was the order for him to stand trial as an accessory to the May 6, 1842, attempted murder of former governor Lilburn Boggs in Missouri. Boggs, of course, had issued the infamous extermination order against the Mormons. Joseph, it seems, may have commissioned one of his Danites—Orrin Porter Rockwell—to kill Missouri's ex-governor in retaliation for the Mormons' Missouri troubles and subsequent expulsion from the state.

Killing Boggs would have been consistent not only with Smith's 1833 revelation justifying murder of personal enemies (*D&C* 98:31), but also with an 1839 pledge to Joseph expressed by Danite Alanson Ripley: "I, from this day declare myself the Avenger of the blood of those innocent men [i.e., the Haun's Mill Massacre victims], and the innocent cause of Zion."[93] When Boggs was shot in the neck and head several times through a window, suspicion soon fell on Rockwell, who had been visiting the area at the time. *The Wasp*, a Mormon publication, called the attempted assassination a "noble deed."[94] Smith, understandably, denied all involvement.

But William Law, a prominent Mormon official, who would later leave the church, claimed that in 1842 Smith told him: "I sent Rockwell to kill Boggs, but he missed him, [and] it was a failure; he wounded him instead of sending him to Hell."[95] Joseph allegedly had prophesied to his congregation in 1841, that Boggs "should die by violent hands within one year."[96] Then, when in 1842 Rockwell inexplicably disappeared from Nauvoo, Smith reportedly told John C. Bennett—Nauvoo's mayor and major general of the Nauvoo Legion—that the faithful Danite had "GONE TO FULFILL PROPHECY!"[97] (Rockwell returned one day before word reached Nauvoo that Boggs had been shot.) Years later, Rockwell admitted he was the assassin, saying: "I shot through the window and thought I had killed him, but I had only wounded him; I was damned sorry that I had not killed the son of a bitch!"[98] Smith, although arrested twice for his alleged role in the deed, escaped on both occasions.[99]

Yet another issue that brought Smith trouble were the many new doctrines he introduced to the Latter-day Saint faith during the Nauvoo era. Some were imparted through Smith's new *Book of Abraham* (see Appendix C), which Joseph claimed to have translated from several ancient Egyptian scrolls he had acquired in 1835. Additionally, Smith delivered various revelations that presented a more organized system of beliefs relating to the afterlife (i.e., baptisms for the dead by proxy), temple rituals, the multiplicity of gods, eternal progression (i.e., Mormon deification), the nature of God as man of flesh and bones, and the importance of obedience to church officials.[100] These beliefs only served to distance the Mormons even further from mainstream religious thought. No doctrine, however, would cause Smith as much trouble as that of polygamy, which by the Nauvoo period had come to be commonly known as plural, or celestial marriage.

WOMEN, WIVES, AND WORRIES

After his illicit marriage to Fanny Alger in Kirtland, Smith took Lucinda Pendleton as a wife in 1838/39. Pendleton, coincidentally, was the widow of Captain William Morgan (see pp. 36–37), who was kidnapped and murdered for exposing Freemasonry secrets. Not until 1841 in Nauvoo, however, was Smith's seemingly insatiable lust for women and young girls unleashed. He began cautiously by taking only three plural wives in 1841: Louisa Beaman (26-years-old), Zina Diantha Huntington (20-years-old), and Presendia Lathrop Huntington (31-years-old).[101] After these successful ventures into the forbidden realm of polygamy,

Smith in 1842 married eleven more women. Then, in 1843, he acquired at least another seventeen wives.[102]

These thirty-three marriages are so well-documented that they are beyond legitimate dispute. Other historians—e.g., Fawn Brodie, D. Michael Quinn, and George D. Smith—have identified even more women who were probably married to Joseph. Their research indicates forty-eight, forty-six, and forty-three wives, respectively. Although an examination of each of these cases is far beyond the scope of this book, some interesting facts concerning the best-documented wives can be mentioned.[103]

One rarely discussed aspect of Joseph's polygamy is that many of the women he married were already wed to other men "and cohabitating with them when Smith married them."[104] Smith, then, advocated not only polygyny (i.e., marriage by a man to more than one woman), but also polyandry (i.e., marriage of a woman to more than one man), both of which are subsets of polygamy (i.e, multiple marriages). Interestingly, out of Smith's first dozen marriages to other women, nine of them were already married to some of his closest friends, each of whom were also high-ranking members of his leadership core.[105] Moreover, the wives continued to live with their husbands after marrying Smith, but would have conjugal visits from Joseph whenever it served his needs.

Smith often demanded the wives of his male followers as a test of their devotion to him. Then, when they, after agonizing over the issue, finally offered up their wives, he would tell them they had passed a test of allegiance and would not have to follow through with their decision. For instance, Smith went to John Taylor, who would become the LDS church's third president, and said to him, "'Brother John, I WANT LEONORA.'" Taylor was stunned, "but after walking the floor all night, the obedient Elder said to Smith, 'If GOD wants Leonora He can have her.'" According to Wilford Woodruff: "That was all the prophet was after, to see where President Taylor stood in the matter, and said to him, Brother Taylor, I don't want your wife, I just wanted to know just where you stood."[106]

One of the most obvious examples of this involved Heber C. Kimball, Smith's long-time friend and unwaveringly loyal apostle, who dearly loved his wife Vilate. Heber and Vilate were "intensely devoted to each other," apparently a bit too devoted for Smith. So in early 1842, the prophet made a shocking demand of his devoted disciple to "surrender his wife, his beloved Vilate, and give her to Joseph in marriage!"[107] For three days Kimball anguished over giving his wife to Joseph, until finally he was asked to choose between Mormonism and his wife. He chose Mormonism:

> With a broken and bleeding heart, but with soul self-mastered for the sacrifice, he led his darling wife to the Prophet's house and presented her to Joseph. "Joseph wept at this proof of devotion, and embracing Heber, told him that was all that the Lord required." It had been a test, said Joseph, to see if Heber would give up everything he possessed.[108]

Joseph's wives also included at least one mother/daughter pair (Patty Bartlett and Sylvia Sessions) and three sets of sisters: Delcena and Almera Johnson; Sarah and Maria Lawrence (aged seventeen and nineteen, respectively); and Emily and Eliza Partridge. These marriages are significant because by entering into them Smith blatantly violated God's Old Testament prohibition against marrying either a woman and her mother (Lev. 18:17) or a woman and her sister (Lev. 18:18).

Smith's youngest wife was fourteen-year-old Helen Mar Kimball, the daughter of Heber and Vilate. Helen was first asked by her father to become Joseph's wife. But she refused. Then Smith himself approached Helen, saying to her the same words he had uttered to seventeen-year-old Sarah Ann Whitney: "'If you will take this step, it will ensure your eternal salvation & exaltation and that of your father's household & all your kindred.'"[109] Helen agreed, later recalling: "This promise was so great that I willingly gave myself to purchase so glorious a reward."[110]

Emma, meanwhile, did everything in her power to fight Joseph's polygamous activity. She threatened to leave him, argued with him, denounced him, and refused to accept the new doctrine.[111] In an effort to silence her objections, Joseph issued a revelation wherein God commanded Emma to cease condemning her husband, and accept his divinely-appointed wives—or else be damned.[112] This July 12, 1843, revelation was read to Emma in private and given to several of Smith's most trusted followers, but it would still be kept secret from the vast majority of Saints living in Nauvoo.[113] It would not be publicly released until 1852, and not printed in the *Doctrine and Covenants* until 1876.

In Nauvoo, however, Smith did authorize a few select leaders to begin enjoying the practice after personally teaching them its glorious principles.[114] William Clayton, who served as Joseph's secretary and official "Clerk of the Kingdom," remembered: "From him I learned that the doctrine of plural and celestial marriage is the most holy and important doctrine ever revealed to man on the earth."[115] But history professor Jan Shipps, after examining a number of historical documents relating to the Nauvoo practice, observed that quite soon enough, many of the men "came to resemble children suddenly told that eating candy was good for them."[116]

At the same time, Smith consistently and vehemently denounced polygamy as sinful, maintaining that monogamy was God's perfect design for marital relationships and that it was the only model of marriage he wanted to see practiced by his followers. The level of Joseph's hypocrisy incensed many individuals within Smith's inner circle. For example, on March 4, 1843, he married nineteen-year-old Emily Partridge, after which time he waited only four days before taking to himself her twenty-two year-old sister, Eliza. But then, only one week later, the March 15 issue of Smith's *Times and Seasons* denied polygamy:

> We are charged with advocating a plurality of wives . . . [T]his is as false as the many other ridiculous charges which are brought against us. No sect has a greater reverence for the laws of matrimony or the rights of private property; and we do what others do not, [we] practice what we preach.[117]

Joseph's public pretense at monogamy continued for several years, much to the chagrin and anguish of several high-ranking LDS leaders, each of whom would eventually forsake the church. Their actions, although they did not realize it at the time, set in motion a series of events that would eventually lead to Smith's death.

JOSEPH'S FINAL CONFLICT

Most of the people who lived in Illinois in the 1840s were opposed to both polygamy and adultery. Consequently, a storm of controversy swept through Illinois when word about Smith's secret teachings on wife-sharing, plural wives, and marriage to teenaged girls leaked out to non-Mormons in the Hancock County area. The information had come from Mormon insiders who personally knew Smith and were privy to all of his licentious activities: Robert D. Foster, Francis Higbee, Chauncey Higbee, Charles Ivins, Charles Foster, Wilson Law, John C. Bennett (former mayor of Nauvoo), and most notably, William Law (Smith's counselor and major general of the Nauvoo Legion), who went so far as to establish the Reformed Mormon Church in April 1844.

These and other apostates expounded on Smith's double life to all who would listen, wrote informative letters to newspapers, and preached against the evils thriving in Joseph's city of debauchery and despotism.[119] Then, on May 10, 1844, William Law and others dissidents from the church distributed a prospectus for their new publication, *The Nauvoo Expositor*.[110] In addition to advocating the "unconditional repeal of the Nauvoo city charter," it promised to decry "gross moral imperfections" wherever found and to provide evidence of the "cases of flagrant abuses, or moral delinquencies" abounding in Nauvoo.[120]

Smith did nothing. Bad press had dogged his trail before, and he remained confident that the coming "persecution" would be as ineffective as all other attempts to thwart his plans. Smith, however, did not realize the level of secret information that had been gathered by the dissenters. Only when the newspaper's first issue of June 7, 1844, appeared did he understand what had happened. Resolution 12 in the publication, which read "we will not acknowledge any man as *king or law-giver* to the church; for Christ is our only king and law-giver," indicated that a member of the Council of Fifty had betrayed him.[121]

Joseph knew his ordination as king would not be received well by outsiders. In fact, after bestowing that title unto himself at the council's meeting, the church's clerk, William Clayton, recorded in his diary: "Joseph whispered and told me either to put the r[ecords] of K[ingdom] into the hands of some faithful man and send them away, or burn them, or bury them."[122] But now his entire plan to rule the world was at risk of being exposed. The dissenters declared:

> We are earnestly seeking to explode the vicious principles of Joseph Smith, and those who practice the same abominations and whoredoms . . . . Many of us have sought a reformation in the church, without a public exposition of the enormities of crimes practiced by its leaders, thinking that if they would hearken to counsel, and shew fruit meet for repentance, it would be as acceptable with God. . . . [B]ut our petitions were treated with contempt; and in many cases the petitioner spurned from their presence, and particularly by Joseph, who would state that if he had sinned, and was guilty of the charges we would charge him with, he would not make acknowledgment, but would rather be damned; for it would detract from his dignity, and would consequently ruin and prove the overthrow of the Church.[123]

The Nauvoo Expositor also lodged serious charges against Smith for adultery, fornication, lewd behavior, and abuse of his flock, especially numerous women, who after swearing to never divulge what was revealed to them, under penalty of death, were told that they were to become Smith's spiritual wives.[124] The writers of the *Expositor* lamented: "It is difficult—perhaps impossible—to describe the wretchedness of females in this place, without wounding the feelings of the benevolent, or shocking the delicacy of the refined; but the truth shall come to the world. The remedy can never be applied, unless the disease is known."[125] Additionally, the dissenters accused Smith of holding himself above the law, stealing from non-Mormons, attempting to unite church and state, harboring ungodly resentment against enemies, forcing unjust and unwarranted financial demands upon the Saints, and misappropriation of church funds.[126] To make matters worse, the initial issue promised that future publications would include affidavits "to substantiate the facts alleged."[127]

This time Smith refused to let the abuse go unanswered, nor would he allow any more information to be disseminated to the hostile Gentiles already closing in around him. Furthermore, dissension within the church was again growing and there seemed to be little he could do about it. Joseph saw only one option. He went before the city council, declared the *Expositor* a civic nuisance, and passed a resolution approving its destruction.[128] The order was carried out on June 10, 1844, between 7 p.m. and 10 p.m. by approximately 200–300 members of the Nauvoo Legion armed with muskets, swords, pistols, Bowie knives, and sledge-hammers.[129] They entered the offices of the *Expositor*, demolished the press, destroyed the type, and burned every remaining issue of the publication they could find.

According to LDS writer William E. Berrett, the destruction of the *Nauvoo Expositor* "proved to be the spark which ignited all the smoldering fires of opposition into one great flame. . . . The cry that the 'freedom of the press' was being violated, united the factions seeking the overthrow of the Saints as perhaps nothing else would have done."[130] In response to Smith's actions, those opposing the Mormon prophet filed a complaint against him in Hancock County, Illinois, claiming that Smith had violated the freedom of the press. Smith was arrested, but quickly tried in Nauvoo and released. The opposition immediately accused Smith of manipulating the law. Suddenly, the familiar threat of mob violence surrounded Nauvoo. Smith declared martial law on June 19 and put his troops on full alert.

Illinois Governor Ford then stepped into the situation, demanding that Smith give himself up to be tried in Carthage, Illinois. But Joseph, with his brother, Hyrum, decided instead to flee into Iowa. Once there, however, they began to have misgivings about running from the law. First, they had abandoned their flock, which produced in them a significant degree of guilt. Second, their presence in Iowa did not insure their safety since that territory's governor had never agreed to ignore Missouri's extradition order for Smith on the old charge of treason. Third, Smith's departure had left the Saints with virtually no leadership since many of the loyal apostles were away on missions. Fourth, a messenger informed Smith that the Nauvoo Legion had divided between those who wanted to defend the city and those who wanted to flee. So back across the Mississippi both he and Hyrum journeyed, continuing on to Carthage, where they were placed in the town's jailhouse.

Smith understood all too well the seriousness of his situation. On the morning of June 27, he sent a letter to Emma. He seemed to sense that he had but a few more hours to live. "Dear Emma," he began. "I am very much resigned to my lot, knowing I am justified and have done the best that could be done. Give my love to the children and all my friends, Mr. Brower, and all who inquire after me. . . . May God bless you all. Amen."[131] Soon after finishing this note, Joseph scribbled another message addressed to Jonathan Dunham, telling him to bring the Nauvoo Legion in order to "break the jail, and save him at all costs."[132]

The messengers galloped off with Smith's communiqués. Nauvoo was only fifteen miles away, but Dunham never came. No one really knows why. Perhaps he was secretly dissatisfied with Smith's leadership. Maybe he knew that to make any move with the legion would result in a bloodbath in both Carthage, then in Nauvoo as Illinois militias retaliated. Either way, after receiving the note, Dunham pocketed it, neglected to act, "and no other man in Nauvoo knew of the prophet's peril."[133]

Around five o'clock that afternoon, Joseph, Hyrum, Willard Richards, and John Taylor were quietly talking when they suddenly heard loud noises, shouts, and several shots being fired just outside the door that led into the jailhouse. A lynch mob of about 250 men with their faces blackened to conceal their identities had descended on the prison and were forcing their way inside. Smith and the others quickly threw themselves against the door, but were forced to fall back as musket balls ripped threw the wooden panel. The door flew open and immediately several shots rang out.

Hyrum was struck in the face and stumbled backward, crying out: "I am a dead man!" Just before hitting the floor, several more bullets tore into his already lifeless body. Joseph called to him, "Oh dear! Brother Hyrum!" Then the Mormon prophet, who had been smuggled a six-shooter, fired all of his rounds at the door, severely wounding the man who had just killed his brother.

Another shower of bullets sprayed the room, four of which hit John Taylor, who would miraculously survive. Willard Richards somehow avoided being hit by staying close to the doorway. But Joseph retreated, throwing his gun at the assailants and lunging for the second-story win-

The murder of Joseph Smith on June 27, 1844
(from John D. Lee, *Mormonism Unveiled*, 1877).

THE ASSASSINATION OF JOSEPH SMITH.

dow in a vain effort to escape. Just then, two musket balls hit Smith in the back as he leapt from the window. Another hit him from the outside as shots rang out. He lurched forward, desperately yelling out the first four words of the Masonic call of distress: "Oh, Lord my God."[134]

For a few moments he just swung there helplessly from the sill as the mob watched. Levi Williams shouted, "Shoot him! . . . Shoot the damned rascal!" But before anyone could fire, Smith dropped to the ground, still alive, but not for long:

> He twisted as he fell, landing on his right shoulder and back, and then rolled over on his face. One of the militia, barefooted and bareheaded, grinning through his black paint, leaped forward and dragged him against the well–curb in the yard. The prophet stirred a little and opened his eyes. There was no terror in them, but whether the calmness was from resignation or unconsciousness one cannot know. Colonel Williams now ordered four men to fire at him. As the balls struck he cringed a little and fell forward on his face.[135]

Joseph Smith—Latter-day prophet, candidate for president, Mormonism's king—was dead. The mob, knowing that their task had been completed, quickly scattered. Later that day, the bodies of Joseph and Hyrum were removed back to Nauvoo and the Saints began to grieve. In tribute to the slain brothers, Eliza R. Snow wrote a lengthy and deeply mythic poem, the substance of which would carry Smith's followers into their next adventure as God's chosen people:

> [N]ever since the Son of God was slain
> Has blood so noble flow'd from human vein . . .
> Once-lov'd America! what can atone
> For the pure blood of innocence thou'st sown . . .
> Now Zion mourns—she mourns an earthly head:
> Her Prophet and her Patriarch are dead!
> Ye Saints! be still, and know that God is just—
> With steadfast purpose in His promise trust:
> Girded with sackcloth, own His mighty hand,
> And wait His judgments on this guilty land![136]

PART THREE

Utah:
Land of the Prophets
(1845–1901)

Brigham Young, 2nd LDS prophet-
president, 1847-1877 (from M.R.
Werner, *Brigham Young,* 1925).

John Taylor, 3rd LDS prophet-president, 1880–1887 (from Edgar Folk,
The Mormon Monster, 1901).

Wilford Woodruff, 4th LDS prophet-
president, 1889–1898 (from Edgar
Folk, *The Mormon Monster,* 1901).

Lorenzo Snow, 5th LDS prophet-
president, 1898-1901 (from Edgar
Folk, *The Mormon Monster,* 1901).

Joseph F. Smith, 6th LDS prophet-
president, 1901-1918 (from J.F.
Gibbs, *Lights & Shadows of Mormonism,* 1909).

TEN

A New Beginning

The signs of the times are portentious and clearly indicate the approaching downfall of the nations, and the overturning of kingdoms, empires, and republics, preparatory to the coming of Christ and his personal reign on the earth.

Orson Pratt (1853)[1]
Mormon Apostle

TO THE MORMON DISSENTERS who had been ostracized and declared apostates by their church, Smith's death was a result of his own reckless foray into the world of sin. Unrepentant abandonment to the "lust of the flesh, and the lust of the eyes, and the boastful pride of life" (1 John 2:16) had caused Joseph's ruin; nothing more, nothing less. As William Law wrote in a July 20, 1844, letter: "[T]he wicked slay the wicked . . . I can see the hand of a blasphemed God stretched out in judgment. . . . [H]e has taken sudden vengeance."[2]

But in Nauvoo, "The City of Joseph," shockwaves of anger and anguish reverberated throughout the community's heart and soul.[3] The city's collective spirit of grief demonstrated itself when eight thousand Saints turned out to view the bodies of Joseph and Hyrum, which were returned home in caskets of roughly hewn pine. Most of the onlookers wept openly, while others prayed for divine vengeance. A few men wanted to retaliate by burning Carthage to the ground.[4] Many individuals just stared blankly in disbelief. Some Mormons, like Henry W. Bigler, felt a gamut of emotion. "At first I felt mad and could have fought like a tiger," Bigler wrote in his diary. "[B]ut soon I felt like weeping and a feeling of loneliness came over me."[5]

The bitterness, grief, and trauma of the double murder did not easily fade. As the *Times and Seasons* of December 1844 reported, a kind of
"gloom" engulfed the minds of the Saints. "[T]hey felt that every principle of humanity was violated, and they were among a horde of savage
barbarians."[6] At the same time, Mormons faced the particularly vexing
problem of having to choose a new leader. Who would become their new
Prophet, Seer, and Revelator?

CLAIMING THE PROPHETIC MANTLE

Joseph had never publicly named anyone to take his place. He, in
fact, had not even left a clear directive concerning his desired method for
choosing a successor. This is not to say Smith left no instructions on the
matter. If anything, he left too many instructions. Between 1834 and
1844, Joseph "had by word or action established precedents or authority
for eight possible methods of succession."[7] The various means by which
a replacement could be found left surviving Mormons confused, to say
the least. It also left the door open for several legitimate claims to
Joseph's position.

Making the situation more difficult was the absence from Nauvoo of
three-fourths of the Twelve Apostles and other church authorities. They
were nowhere near the city on the day of the murders, but instead, were
preaching and campaigning for Smith as far away as New York and
Boston. Most of them did not even learn of the killings until several
weeks later, and then, only through newspaper accounts. For many of
these officials, the calamity was too horrible to accept. Only after receiving word from the Saints at Nauvoo near the end of July did they finally
believe the widely circulating stories detailing the deaths of Joseph and
Hyrum.[8] The high-ranking LDS authorities subsequently began making
their way back home as quickly as possible.

Meanwhile, other church leaders—i.e., those who had been in Nauvoo throughout the tragedy—assured their followers that the church's
"onward course" would be plotted as soon the Twelve Apostles and other
authorities were able to reconvene.[9] A crisis in leadership, however, had
already begun, and it would only grow more heated after the apostles

reached Nauvoo in early August 1844. The problem was summed up well in the diary of William Clayton:

> The greatest danger that now threatens us is dissensions and strifes amongst the Church. There are already 4 or 5 men pointed out as successors to the Trustee & President & there is danger of feelings being manifest. All the brethren who stand at the head seem to feel the delicacy of the business.[10]

The first claim to the church's highest leadership position came from Sidney Rigdon, who raced back to Nauvoo from Pittsburgh, ahead of the Twelve Apostles. He immediately announced that he had received a special revelation to be the guardian of the church. Emma, however, along with other church members backed William Marks, a very influential and high-ranking LDS official.[11] Samuel Smith, one of Joseph's brother's, also seemed a reasonable choice to many Saints. In fact, he nearly took control of the church before the Twelve had returned, much to the irritation of Willard Richards, who wanted no leader to be named until all the apostles were present.

Richards may have gone so far as to have Samuel murdered to prevent any succession. Samuel's wife believed this to be the case, naming as her husband's murderer, the Chief of Police—Hosea Stout, a Danite widely known for having a violent streak and a cold-hearted disposition. Everyone knew he was more than capable of homicide. He had already been, and would continue to be, connected with several murders and assaults involving apostates and church critics (see Chapter Eleven). In the case of Samuel Smith, Stout had acted as Samuel's care-giver when he fell ill, and in that capacity had given Samuel "white powder" medicine daily until his death. Samuel's wife, daughter, and brother (i.e., William Smith) all believed the powder to be poison.[12]

Such tension over who would lead the Saints certainly had a great deal to do with everyone's desire to find a competent leader in the midst of tumultuous times. But even more imperative to top LDS leaders was finding a person, or persons, willing to continue Smith's propagation of polygamy, which by 1844 was being enjoyed by select members of the

Twelve Apostles—the church's most powerful men.[13] Unfortunately for these church leaders, two of the primary candidates seeking Joseph's prophetic mantle, Sidney Rigdon and William Marks, stood unalterably opposed to plural marriage. The other serious contender in the fight for leadership, however, was Brigham Young, head of the Twelve Apostles, himself a polygamist. This controversy peaked during the August 1844 Special Conference, as the most powerful claimants to succession—Sidney Rigdon, William Marks, and Brigham Young—made their pleas before the church and the Twelve Apostles.

Rigdon had little chance of swaying his listeners. In fact, his bid to lead the Saints was practically dismissed outright. He was not well-liked by the Twelve, having earned a reputation over the years for being reactionary and unthinking in his conduct. Many LDS leaders believed that the Saints' troubles in Missouri were a direct result of his infamous declaration of July 4, 1838 (see p. 155). They even blamed the oration for their expulsion from the state even though Joseph himself had approved the controversial lecture. More damaging to Rigdon, however, was his church service, which had been unstable at best. Although recently chosen as Joseph's vice-presidential running-mate, Rigdon had fallen out of Joseph's favor a number of times since the early 1830s.[14] And his recent revelation about taking Joseph's place impressed no one. Wilford Woodruff called it a "second class vision."[15]

William Marks had a far greater chance of seizing leadership. Just weeks after Joseph's death, before any of the apostles had returned, Marks was almost installed as church president by several high-ranking leaders, who happened to be in Nauvoo. The appointment, however, was stone-walled at the last minute when Newel K. Whitney—whose daughter was one of Joseph's plural wives—privately informed William Clayton that Marks sided with William Law and Emma on the issue of polygamy. Clayton, who by that time had already taken his own wife's sister as a second wife and impregnated her, wrote in his diary: "[I]f Marks is appointed Trustee our spiritual blessings will be destroyed inasmuch as he is not favorable to the most important matters."[16] In reference to both Clayton and Newell, historian D. Michael Quinn starkly commented: "Neither man wanted a new church president who would brand polygamous wives as whores."[17]

Not surprisingly, Marks had the backing of the prophet's widow, Emma. Moreover, Emma neither trusted, nor liked, Brigham Young. She also may have believed that Marks would ease the monetary straights in which she found herself. A great deal of her financial security had been derived from Joseph's income and his lands, which Brigham and the other LDS leaders now said belonged to the church.

During the conference it soon became apparent that Marks' anti-polygamy stand would indeed prove to be his downfall. His chances completely evaporated when on the very day of the decision, Heber C. Kimball approached Emma during a break between speakers and gave her $1,000 "to show the goodwill of the Quorum of the Twelve."[18] Emma, according to Kimball's diary, immediately responded by becoming "humble and more kind."[19] She then pulled her support from Marks, thus ending his bid for Joseph's job.

In the end, no successor was chosen, but instead, the church voted to place supreme authority in the hands of the Twelve Apostles with Brigham Young at their head. "You are now without a prophet . . . to guide you," Young said in an August 1844 *Times and Seasons* article. "But you are not without apostles, who hold the keys of power to seal on earth that which shall be sealed in heaven, and to preside over all the affairs of the church in all the world."[20] But such an explanation, for all intents and purposes, was a show. Brigham clearly had control of the church, if not in technical terms, then at least in practical terms. This would be confirmed in 1847, when he organized (on a level above the Twelve Apostles) a First Presidency consisting of two counselors and himself as president.

Not everyone accepted the new model of leadership presented by Brigham and the Twelve. Sidney Rigdon refused the judgment and returned to Pittsburgh, where he tried to start his own church, all the while claiming to be Smith's successor. He also continued to verbally attack not only the Twelve Apostles, but also their ongoing acceptance of polygamy.[21] Within a few years, however, his efforts to establish a new church failed miserably. He ended up dying in virtual obscurity, a powerless individual, who never achieved the greatness he had sought for so long.[22]

As for Marks, he seemed to have accepted his lot and caused little trouble for Young, the apostles, or the church. He never seemed all that interested in the presidency to begin with, and more or less fell into the whole situation in deference to those who simply did not want to be led by Brigham. Marks did end up leaving the LDS church, eventually becoming a prominent member of the Reorganized Church of Jesus Christ of Latter-day Saints (RLDS), headed by Joseph's son, Joseph Smith III. This church, founded in Missouri in the 1850s by former Mormons Jason Briggs and Zenos Gurley, would become the most influential and successful faction of early Mormonsim.[23] Emma would belong to the RLDS church for the remainder of her life, after refusing to follow the Saints organized under Young.

Other off-shoots of Mormonism would include a church started by William McLellin and David Whitmer, as well as the reformed church lead by William Law (see p. 196). A third splinter group migrated to Texas under Lyman Wight, a former Danite, member of the Council of Fifty, and a long-time friend of Smith's. Yet another disciple, the youthful and charismatic James Strang, gathered to himself a sizable number of Saints, including some rather prominent LDS leaders.[24] Over the years even more factions would emerge under the leadership of disenfranchised Saints with their own views of what should have occurred at the 1844 conference.

The majority of Mormons, however, remained faithful to the decision of the Twelve Apostles. Brigham Young's era of Mormonism had begun. He and the other LDS officials would take the Saints onward to a new Zion in the far west, outside U.S. boundaries. The prophetic mantle had successfully been transferred. Young himself concisely explained the situation, declaring: "[I]f you don't know whose right it is to give revelations, I will tell you. It is I."[25]

LAWLESS NAUVOO

A halt to the violent conflict between Mormons and anti-Mormons lasted but a brief period of time after Smith was killed. Armed mobs of Illinoians, incited by endless newspaper articles covering Mormon issues, soon began to conduct raids against isolated church settlements. Saints were threatened, LDS homes were burned, rumors about various Mormon atrocities circulated, and militias were called out by the governor. Church dissenters and critics, meanwhile, continued to expose aspects of Mormonism that church leaders did not want revealed. The Saints retaliated with verbal intimidation, religious condemnation, and acts of physical violence. In response to the conflict, the Illinois legislature terminated Nauvoo's city charter in January 1845, effectively ending the legal authority of the Nauvoo Legion, which was forced to disband.[26]

The LDS hierarchy then took drastic security measures that turned Nauvoo into a veritable den of repression. Moreover, the community quickly sunk beneath a standard of lawlessness that could only be seen as "lawful" by men like the Twelve Apostles, who had adopted "theocratic ethics" as their guide of behavior and decision-making (see p. 129). Mormon thieves, who regularly stole from non-Mormons. This had been a long-standing complaint about Saints in the area. In fact, eight out of fourteen issues of the *Warsaw Signal* published between September 18, 1844, and January 1, 1845, included articles titled "Mormon Thieves." And for several weeks beginning on Christmas Day, 1844, the publication ran stories about "Mormon Stealing."[27]

As early as mid-1843 stealing from Gentiles apparently had been approved by Smith, who told Porter Rockwell that "it was right to steal."[28] Other church leaders, such as Apostle Orson Hyde, explained to followers that a Saint actually could "steal & be influenced by the spirit of the Lord to do it," as long as the thievery was committed against non-Mormons.[29] As John Bennion recorded in his journal, "[Hyde] said that he never would institute a trial against a brother for stealing from the Gentiles[,] but stealing from his brethren he was down on it."[30]

More disturbing were the many murders, vicious beatings, and intimidating assaults perpetrated by the Nauvoo police against perceived enemies of the church. Policeman Allen J. Stout summed up the rationale of the Saints on these matters, explaining that to his mind such activity was nothing more than avenging the blood of Joseph and Hyrum. In reference to the Mormon dissenters remaining in Nauvoo, Stout expressed a common sentiment: "I feel like cutting their throats." He additionally vowed to forever seek the destruction of church enemies, especially any persons, or the descendants of persons, involved in the killing Joseph and Hyrum:

I hope to live to avenge their blood; but if I do not I will teach my children to never cease to try to avenge their blood and then teach their children and children's children to the fourth generation as long as there is one descendant of the murderers upon the earth.[31]

The resolve of Allen Stout, however, paled in comparison to that of his brother, Hosea, Chief of Police and one of Brigham Young's many henchmen. Throughout the Saints' final years in Nauvoo, Hosea often met with LDS apostles to discuss, as he put it, ways to "rid ourselves of traitors who are in our midst."[32] One method was frighteningly straightforward—i.e., to "cut him off—behind the ears—according to the law of God."[33] This solution mirrored the suggestion given by Sidney Rigdon, who in 1844 said: "There are men standing in your midst that you can't do anything with them but cut their throat & bury them."[34]

Although the exact number of murders committed by Mormons between 1844 and 1846 remains unknown, it is certain that a majority of them were handled by Danites Porter Rockwell, Hosea Stout, and Allen Stout. Rockwell killed several "anti-Mormons," beginning on September 16, 1845. His first victim was Frank Worrell, a jail guard in Carthage, who had allowed the mob to murder the Smith brothers. Rockwell happened to see Worrell and his men chasing Hancock County Sheriff J.B. Backenstos, a non-Mormon ally of the Saints. When Backenstos asked for help, Porter raised his gun and shot Worrell out of his saddle, killing him with a bullet to the stomach.[35] Later that day, Rockwell murdered four more non-Mormons in Highland Branch, Illinois.[36]

A week later, several Saints captured a young man by the name of McBracking, who apparently had been burning Mormon homes. A non-Mormon citizen of Warsaw named George Rockwell detailed in a letter the atrocity that followed, and the condition of McBracking's body when friends found him the next day:

After shooting him [i.e., McBracking] in two or three places they cut his throat from ear to ear, stabbed him through the heart, cut off one ear & horribly mutilated other parts of his body [i.e., castrated him].[37]

According to Mormon dissidents Jehiel Savage and John E. Page, in the fall of 1845, apostles Heber C. Kimball and Orson Hyde actually ordered Nauvoo's police force to kill apostate Lambert Symes, who subsequently disappeared without a trace.[38] A suspected anti-Mormon spy named Phineas Wilcox also vanished after traveling to Nauvoo. He was last seen being led away to the Nauvoo Masonic temple by three Mormons.[39] Another anti-Mormon, Andrew Daubenheyer, disappeared on September 18, 1845, on the road to Carthage. He eventually was found buried in a shallow grave near a campsite on the Carthage road.[40]

The particularly brutal murder of Mormon dissenter Irvine Hodge, presumably by Nauvoo policemen (Hosea Stout, William Earls, John Scott) occurred at night almost right in front of Brigham Young's house.[41] Hodge had made the mistake of going to Nauvoo and threatening to expose every Mormon who had been involved in stealing from non-Mormons. He then foolishly threatened to physically harm Young and Nauvoo policeman Elbridge Tufts. But on June 23, 1845, it was Hodge who wound up lying on Young's doorstep after being stabbed four times in the back with a bowie knife.[42] The following Sunday, Brigham calmly preached: "I don't know nor care who killed him for if he lived he would add sin to sin. There are other men in Nauvoo, that I pray God they run against the same snag that Irvin[e] Hodge did."[43]

Other homicides were taken care of by members of the Council of Fifty. Lewis Dana, for example, killed his supposed friend Jonathan Dunham, the man who had "ignored the prophet's direct order to lead the Nauvoo Legion in a rescue at Carthage Jail" (see p. 199).[44] And on July 4, 1845, Council member Cyrus Daniels attempted to murder a number of non-Mormons by sabotaging a cannon slated to be used during an Independence Day celebration in LaHarpe, Illinois. When the cannon exploded, no one was killed, but one man was maimed.[45]

All of these instances are not recounted in order to suggest that every dissenter, or unwelcome visitor in Nauvoo, was murdered. There were other forms of punishment meted out by the Saints. On September 14, 1845, for instance, Hosea Stout had three men flogged because they "were not in good fellowship."[46] Then, on January 9, 1846, after spotting an alleged anti-Mormon "spy" named William Hibbard, Stout and John Scott struck Hibbard on the back of the head with a rock, which "came very near taking his life."[47] Stout's diary also includes an account of a temple grounds trespasser being beaten "almost to death" by his men. Young, according to Stout, heartily approved of the brutality.[48]

Those persons fortunate enough to not be either murdered or severely beaten were usually "whittled" out of town by Brigham's "Whistling and Whittling Brigade." This violent gang of Mormons included policemen, deacons, elders, and others in good standing with the church. Armed with ten to fourteen-inch knives, members of this roving band would assemble in groups of a dozen or so and surround a suspected dissenter or suspicious non-Mormon. They would then press in close to him and begin whistling while whittling in a menacing way.

William Pace's autobiography explains: "[W]hittling with those large knives was enough to strike terror to the hearts of the victims and he got out of town as quick as his legs could carry him."[49] On one such occasion witnesses saw a dissenter "going out of town whittled by about twenty men with long bowie knives kicking him down & [pushing] him in the mud &c. for three quarters of a mile."[50] Hosea Stout recorded in his diary that Austin Cowles was similarly whittled out of the city for siding with William Law and his condemnations of the church.[51]

Another intimidation tactic used in Nauvoo to drive away dissenters was introducing them to Queen Peggy, also known as Aunt Peggy, a euphemism for outhouse refuse. In these cases, church enemies were smeared with excrement and latrine mud. The first unfortunate soul to endure Queen Peggy was Washington Peck, described by William Clayton as "'one of those mean traitors who lurks about continually in our midst communicating with our enemies & seeking to have the twelve destroyed.'"[52] Clayton's journal further states: "During the evening some person or persons took Washington Peck and "'bedaubed him all over with privy dirt.'"[53] John Taylor, in the May issue of the *Nauvoo Neighbor*, stated that since Peck had been introduced to "'Queen Peggy's privy cabinet,'" every man minded his own business.[54]

Orrin Porter Rockwell, Danite killer known as
Brigham Young's "Destroying Angel" (from R.N.
Baskin, *Reminiscences of Early Utah*, 1914).

Chief of Police in Nauvoo, Hosea Stout *(left)* and his younger brother, Allen J. Stout, a policeman in
Nauvoo *(right)*. Both of these Danites were responsible for several murders in Illinois (courtesy, Utah
State Historical Society).

MOVING ON AND MOVING OUT

Frank Worrell's murder (see p. 212) ended all hopes of the Mormons staying in Illinois. The *Quincy Signal* read: "MURDER OF ONE OF OUR BEST MEN—TO ARMS! TO ARMS!"[55] A subsequent town meeting in Quincy ended in a vote for the Mormons to leave the state. Then, in Carthage, citizens from several counties demanded that all Mormons resign from their county offices, that no lawsuits be brought against non-Mormons for destruction of LDS property, and that all Mormon "lawlessness" end immediately.[56] A similar gathering had previously been held just a few days after Joseph's death. That gathering concluded only after participants had drafted a letter to Illinois Governor Ford requesting that all Mormons be expelled from the state.[57]

By September 1845, the majority of Illinois residents were weary of the Mormons and wanted them to depart. A group of prominent Quincy, Illinois, residents actually wrote to Young asking him to lead his Saints elsewhere, or suffer the consequences. Young, understanding the situation all too well, released a written declaration to the public, the substance of which read: "[W]e propose to leave this county next spring."[58] The Saints would have to move yet again.

This time, however, they would migrate far beyond U.S. borders, outside the reach of mobs, militias, and meddling politicians. Their exodus would be organized and directed by Smith's Council of Fifty.[59] Brigham Young declared: "We will go to a land where there are at last no old settlers to quarrel with us. . . . [W]e will leave this wicked nation, to themselves, for they have rejected the gospel, and I hope and pray that the wicked will kill one another & save us the trouble of doing it."[60]

The move *en masse* was to begin in the spring of 1846. But then word came from Washington, D.C., about the impending arrival of federal troops. They were to be stationed just west of Nauvoo and demand that the Mormons surrender all of their arms.[61] This action, according to the information received by the Mormons, was in connection to several failed arrest warrants that had been issued against Brigham Young and other church leaders on counterfeiting charges. Government records indeed indicate that Young, along with apostles Willard Richards, John

Taylor, Parley Pratt, Orson Hyde, and others were involved in making counterfeit coinage dubbed "Nauvoo Bogus."[62]

Nauvoo's counterfeiting operation actually may have started under Joseph's leadership, since Edward Bonney and Marinus G. Eaton—two out of the only three non-Mormons on his Council of Fifty—were known counterfeiters.[63] Bogus money also had been passed by Mormons Theodore Turley, Cyrus Chase, Rufus Adams, George Reader, Peter Haws (Council of Fifty), Warren Snow (future bishop in Utah), and Dominicus Carter (future member of Stake Presidency in Utah).[64] Moreover, a number of individuals claimed that Joseph knew about, and approved, the use of bogus presses and money dies in the city.[65]

When U.S. marshals finally reached Nauvoo in December 1845 to arrest Young, he went into hiding in hopes of possibly circumventing the law as Joseph had done so many times. But when faced with the possibility of federal troops showing up, Young decided the exodus west could no longer wait. Young announced his response to the new threat on February 3, 1846, before a crowd of Saints that had gathered in the newly finished temple. He did not try to explain away the counterfeiting charges, nor declare that he would allow the courts to prove his innocence. Instead, Young simply stated that he would be taking his family westward as soon as possible.

The next morning hundreds of wagons filled with Mormon families began their journey to *somewhere* beyond the Rocky Mountains. Wave after wave of Mormon pioneers streamed across the Mississippi for months, leaving Nauvoo to die the death of a ghost town. Young, Taylor, Woodruff, Kimball, Clayton, Hyde, the Pratt brothers, Stout, Rockwell, and every other stalwart of Mormonism had left before the year's end:

> From the Mississippi River to Council Bluffs, Iowa, there were approximately 20,000 Mormons scattered on the prairies in a thin line that stretched more than four hundred miles. They had only what they could load into wagons or carts, along with cattle, pigs, chickens, sheep, and a few horses. Although several temporary settlements were built along the four hundred-mile route, thousands were camped by the road side in wagons, tents, and dugouts.[66]

A Mormon wagon train making its way to Salt Lake City through Echo Canyon, Utah, 1867 (from M.R. Werner, *Brigham Young*, 1925).

Finally, on December 7, 1846, relatively few Mormons were left in the mid-west, prompting Governor Thomas Ford to declare: "[I]t is with much satisfaction that I am enabled to state . . . [that the] people called Mormons have been removed."[67]

KING OF UTAH

After leaving Nauvoo, the first stop for Mormons on their westward journey was Winter Quarters, a make-shift town they established in Indian territory, just west of the Missouri River, in present day Omaha. It was a place of "discipline and preparation," where the Saints made harnesses, readied wagons, and organized supplies.[68] Their stay at the camp dragged on for months, until April 16, 1847, when the church's vanguard—a group of 143 emigrants including Brigham Young, Heber C. Kimball, Wilford Woodruff, Orson Pratt and several other LDS leaders—finally left in search of a new home.

The route traversed by this initial group was harsh and difficult. They followed the Oregon trail at first, on the north side of the Platte River, up to Pueblo, Colorado, then to Sweetwater River and across the

Continental Divide, until they reached the historical trading post of Fort Bridger. From there, the Saints left the Oregon Trail, heading west over the California Trail's Hasting's Cutoff, to find the Donner-Reed wagon tracks of 1846, which led them all the way to Northern Utah.

Their perseverance paid off on July 22, when most of the wagons in Brigham Young's lead company reached the promised land; "a broad open valley about twenty miles wide and thirty long, at the north end of which the waters of the Great Salt Lake glistened in the sunbeams."[69] Young reached the valley two days later and immediately began colonization. Thousands of Saints would make the trek to Mormonism's new place of refuge.[70]

The kingdom of God on earth that Brigham envisioned was vast. So after arriving in the Salt Lake area, he laid claim to all lands stretching west to east from San Diego to the crest of the Rocky Mountains (near present-day Denver), and north to south from the Wind River Mountains of Wyoming to Arizona's Gila River. Zion, as originally staked out by Young, encompassed not only Utah and Nevada, but sections of Idaho, Oregon, Colorado, Wyoming, New Mexico, most of Arizona, and a large portion of California. The expansive region, totaled about 265,000 square miles, or roughly one-sixth of America's current geography.[71]

Beginning in 1846, Young's proposed homeland for the Saints was governed by church courts headed by LDS authorities "aided by appointed or elected marshals who meted out corporal punishment and enforced court decisions, thereby going beyond the spiritual sanctions normally associated with church courts."[72] In other words, church and state were merged into a single ruling body. This form of government, however, gave way in 1849 to a provisional civil administration called the State of Deseret, which LDS leaders formed in lieu of U.S. statehood.[73]

But according to David Bigler, author of *Forgotten Kingdom: The Mormon Theocracy in the American West, 1847–1896*, the constitution adopted by the Mormons in 1849 "was in fact intended as a cover for the theocratic apparatus behind it that truly governed [the people]."[74] Bigler points out, for example, that July 2 witnessed the first meeting of Deseret's General Assembly, which consisted of a Senate and House of Representatives, even though no legitimate elections had been held.

An engraving of Salt Lake City in 1853. The same year this engraving was made, Mormon apostle John Taylor declared: "Let us now notice our political position in the world. What are we going to do? We are going to possess the earth. Why? Because it belongs to Jesus Christ, and he belongs to us, and we to him; we are all one, and will take the kingdom and possess it under the whole heavens, and reign over it for ever and ever" (*Journal of Discourses*, April 8, 1853, vol. 1, 230, photo from M.R. Werner, *Brigham Young*, 1925).

How were these positions filled? To date, no one knows because no records exist pertaining to the formation of this all-Mormon political body. The Assembly simply appeared ready-made, its members having been culled from the church's most prominent authorities.[75]

Unfortunately for the Saints, Utah became a U.S. Territory in 1850, which again placed Mormonism under the watchful eye of Uncle Sam and federal employees appointed to various territorial offices. The arrangement would prove to be problematic, to say the least, especially considering the distance between Salt Lake City and Washington, D.C. As for Brigham Young, he served as Utah's first governor, which for all practical purposes, put ultimate control of the whole region right back in church hands. "As the Lord lives," Young promised during one sermon. "[W]e are bound to become a sovereign State in the Union, or an independent nation by ourselves."[76]

Young, although officially a governor, acted more like a dictator than anything else. He proudly admitted as much during an 1871 sermon, saying: "'I have been your dictator for twenty-seven years—over a quarter of a century I have dictated this people.'"[77] On another occasion, he said: "I present myself before you this morning in the capacity Providence has lead me to occupy, acknowledged and sustained by you as the dictator, counsellor, and adviser of the people of God."[78] Heber C. Kimball plainly preached: "President Young is our governor and our dictator."[79]

According to William Clayton, obedience to Young and "those in authority" was imperative if the Saints were going to be "blessed and prosperous."[80] Consequently, Brigham's wishes were followed without question; at least by persons wanting to stay in the good graces of the church. The Saints were told where to live, how to worship, and even what to wear. During one sermon, for instance, Young declared: "[T]he man whom God calls to dictate affairs in the building of his Zion has the right to dictate about everything connected with the building up of Zion, yes even to the ribbons the women wear; and any person who denies it is ignorant."[81] Regarding economics, the prophet ordered: "[C]ease trading with any man or being in this city or country who does not belong to the church. If you do not, we are going to cut you off from the church."[82]

Those who dared object to these stringent directives were immediately disciplined. Rank-and-file Mormons were not even able to voice opposition about, or make decisions concerning, the land on which they lived. They did not own the land, nor were they permitted to own it. Instead, the Saints were *allowed* to live on whatever tract had been partitioned to them by the church.[83] Church members also were forced to "consecrate" all of their personal property to the church—i.e., deed it over to the church's trustee-in-trust, Brigham Young. Young justified such measures by teaching that since the earth belonged to God, no one could legitimately own any of it. Therefore, the Saints were merely acting as stewards of God's property for the purpose of building up the kingdom under the direction of those whom the Lord had placed at the church's head.[84] As a result, those who apostatized were "obliged to abandon their property, and precluded from selling it."[85]

Smith had been the one to first articulate this concept, saying: "[H]e that sinneth and repenteth not shall be cast out of the church, and shall not receive again that which he has consecrated."[86] This mindset no doubt contributed to the LDS notion that Mormon church leaders would ultimately control every nation. They, after all, were God's representatives to humanity. As such, they were the only ones with a legitimate right to be stewards of the Lord's property—i.e., all creation. Gentiles, on the other hand, because they had no claim to the earth, would have to give up to the Saints what they mistakenly viewed as their property.[87]

Closely associated with this belief was Brigham Young's role as God's chosen sovereign; the one divinely anointed to rule over earth as Christ's latter-day prophet. The idea came directly from Smith. However, unlike Joseph, who taught that the Saints' reign was to begin in the future, Brigham asserted that God's kingdom had already come. "[T]hat Kingdom is actually organized, and the inhabitants of earth do not [even] know it," Young said in 1855.[88] He assured his followers: "[W]e will roll on the Kingdom of our God, gather out the seed of Abraham, build the cities and temples of Zion, and establish the Kingdom of God to bear rule over all the earth."[89]

Given these doctrines, it is no surprise that Young, according to Mormon Bishop Andrew Cahoon, proclaimed himself "king" in Salt Lake City in 1847.[90] As one popular nineteenth century Mormon hymn read: "Hail to Brigham Young, hail to Brigham Young, Praise him every tongue; and sing, God bless our Prophet, Priest and King, our Leader, Brigham Young."[91] Young's sovereign status would be confirmed again and again by Mormons, as well as dissident Saints, who left Utah and told the world their story. An Englishman named William Jarman, for instance, explained in his exposé on Mormonism exactly what British converts to the religion were told:

> [I]t is well understood by British Mormons that the Prophet is "King over all the earth" in this day. I was unmistakably told that the Prophet of Utah is "King," and the only King reigning upon the earth by "Divine authority:" that I must obey him in preference to any king, ruler or potentate on earth.[92]

Eventually Young came to be viewed as practically a god on earth to the Saints; the one through whom the Almighty God in heaven ruled. In the words of Heber C. Kimball, Young was anointed to be "God's agent to us in the flesh," or put another way, "God's representative in the flesh

. . . the mouth-piece of God unto us."[93] Consequently, salvation for the Mormon rested on their obedience to Brigham, just as their salvation previously had rested on obedience to Joseph. In Mary Ettie V. Smith's account of her life as a Mormon in Utah, she recounted one exchange with Young that clearly illustrates Kimball's teachings:

> "Brother Brigham," said I, with a firmness of resistance I had never before felt in his presence, "are you my Saviour?"
>
> "Most assuredly I am," said he. "You cannot enter the Celestial kingdom, except by my consent. Do you doubt it?"[94]

As earthly lord and king over the Mormons, Brigham understandably held in very low regard the nation out of which he and his followers had recently emerged—i.e., the United States. He also believed that one day soon he "would himself become president of the United States, or dictate who should be president."[95] The Mormon kingdom would then swallow up nation after nation until the world had been completely subjected to LDS leadership. Apostle John Taylor saw Young's governmental system with crystal clarity, explaining in 1857: "We used to have a difference between Church and State, but it is all one now. Thank God."[96]

Such a political structure would endure for nearly fifty years and stretch throughout the terms of three Mormon presidents: Brigham Young, John Taylor, and Wilford Woodruff. It finally ended in 1896, the year Utah was granted U.S. statehood. Until then, however, during the region's pre-statehood era, Mormon leaders ruled via a ruthlessly oppressive theocracy wherein they kept followers in line through violence and intimidation, especially during Brigham's reign. Heber C. Kimball warned the Saints in 1853:

> Brother Brigham is his [Joseph's] successor; his word is sacred; and if you do not observe it, it will not be well, and there is where I fear for you, brethren. I do not fear so much for myself as I do for you, because it will go hard with you, if you disobey his advice. . . . I have got my old Gospel preparation [i.e., my pistol] laid up drying, preparing himself for action. Do I fear? No. I do not fear anything that lives on the earth, or that is in

hell; Indians or anything else never will disturb us, the Saints, from this time to all eternity, if we will do precisely as we are told.[97]

It was not that the Saints in Utah lacked faith. Each of them arrived with zeal, commitment, and faith. But these qualities would not be enough to satisfy Young, who like Smith, understood the need for absolute obedience if Zion was successfully going to be built up. To insure the necessary submission to his authority, he implemented Mormonism's infamous "Reformation," one of the most violent periods in LDS history. Far from civilization, both Saint and sinner were forced to live under Brigham's iron-fisted dictatorship that regularly resorted to censorship of church critics, harsh disciplinary actions, and numerous murders committed at the behest of Young and other high-ranking Mormon officials.[98] Most of these homicides were directly related to the Latter-day Saint doctrine known as "Blood Atonement."

ELEVEN

Bloody Brigham

What bloody deeds, what sin and strife,
What sacrifice of human life
What deeds of plunder have been done,
To raise a gory throne for [Brigham] Young.

Aaron Dewitt (1875)[1]
Mormon dissenter, Utah

IN NINETEENTH CENTURY UTAH, any person, or persons, who threatened to pull people's loyalty or trust away from the church were looked upon with misgivings. Physicians, for instance, especially those prescribing "gentile medicines," were highly suspect. Prayer was the most relied upon remedy in the region, followed by "quinine for fever, laudanum for pain and loose bowels, and the 'cure all' of the day, calomel, a mercurial purgative, for just about everything else."[2] To discourage use of other cures, one Utah law forbade doctors from administering any drug or preparation to a patient without first explaining the treatment in "plain, simple, English." Violation of this law was punishable by a fine of $1,000 and a year in jail.[3]

Lawyers, along with their "man-made" ordinances, were particularly reviled by the Saints due to the many legal battles waged against Mormonism in Ohio, Missouri, and Illinois. To curb attorney powers, Young's administration passed some rather unique ordinances. For example, no law could be "read, argued, cited or adopted" in court unless it had been approved of by Young and his Legislative Assembly.

Moreover, "no report, decision, or doings of any court" could be "read, argued, cited, or adopted as precedent in any other trial."[4]

An even greater level of contempt was held in Utah for federal officials, government employees, and Washington, D.C., politicians, all of whom represented the corrupt government of the United States. In the eyes of the Saints, America's doom had been determined the day Joseph died.[5] It would only be a matter of time before the nation's utter destruction. As a result, politicians became a particularly favorite target of Mormon criticism and harassment.

BRIGHAM YOUNG vs. UNCLE SAM

In reference to the U.S. government, Daniel H. Wells, second counselor to Young, said: "I do not think there is a more corrupt government upon the face of the earth."[6] Orson Hyde agreed, saying: "The Constitution now serves but little purpose other than a cloak for political gamblers, merchants, and hucksters."[7] Joseph Young, Brigham's brother, called U.S. government administrators "insane" for not realizing that Mormon leaders held the keys of salvation.[8] Lorenzo D. Young, another of Brigham's bothers, admitted during one lecture: "I have long prayed that the Lord Almighty would destroy the nation that gave me birth, unless the rulers thereof repent."[9]

Brigham himself taught that the U.S. government was controlled "by ignorance, folly, and weakness."[10] He specifically hated a number of U.S. presidents and regularly castigated them during sermons. Young damned Zachary Taylor and James K. Polk to hell, said James Buchanan was not fit for the presidency, and described Abraham Lincoln as having so little strength of character and political resolve that he was "as weak as water."[11] As late as 1869, Young was still ranting:

Who goes to the White House these days? . . . A gambler and a drunkard. And the Vice-President is the same. And no man can get either office unless he is a gambler and a drunkard, or a thief. And who goes to Congress? You may hunt clear through the Senate and House, and if you can find any men that are not liars, thieves, whoremongers, gamblers, and drunkards, I tell you they are mighty few, for no other kind of men can get in there.[12]

Conflict between Mormons and federal appointees to various government posts in Utah was inevitable. These began almost immediately after the region was declared a U.S. Territory in 1850, as federal officers were subjected to threats, harassment, and physical violence at the hands of Young and his security forces. One of the earliest confrontations involved Broughton D. Harris, a non-Mormon appointed to be Secretary of Utah. His responsibilities included certifying that year's elections and overseeing the census, which U.S. law required in order to apportion representatives.

But when Harris finally reached Utah he found that Governor Young had not only taken his own census, but already had used its results to apportion the number of representatives. Moreover, elections already had been carried out, but under the provisional laws of the State of Deseret, rather than the statutes of a U.S. Territory. After some investigation, Harris further discovered that Young's census was "false and exaggerated" in that it contained highly inflated population numbers. Concerning the election, Harris considered it a mockery of political process.[13]

Federally installed judges noticed other governmental oddities. For instance, chief justice Lemuel G. Brandebury was supposed to have sworn in Brigham Young as territorial governor. But upon Brandebury's arrival, it was revealed that high-ranking Mormon Daniel H. Wells—chief justice of Deseret and member of the Council of Fifty—had done the honors months earlier.[14] A third gentile appointee, Justice Perry Brocchus, received his own unique introduction to Utah politics via a July 24, 1851, speech delivered by the aforementioned Daniel Wells. During the sermon Wells denounced the federal government for deliberately trying to exterminate the Saints. Then, Young stood up and railed against President Zachary Taylor, who had died in office a year earlier. "Zachary Taylor is dead, and in hell," Young remarked. "[A]nd I am glad of it."[15]

Before the year ended, these officials fled Utah, believing that to stay would mean certain death. Each one informed U.S. President Millard

Fillmore of their experiences, describing how Mormon leaders were dis-
loyal to the government as well as in complete control of the people. LDS
authorities countered the accusations by charging all three men with
refusing to do their jobs and fleeing for no legitimate reason. Significantly, before a dozen more years had elapsed, a total of sixteen federal
officers would abandon their Utah posts and lodge similar complaints
about Mormon threats, intimidation, and non-compliancy with federal
laws and directives.

Not every federal employee, however, was lucky enough to escape
unscathed. On August 30, 1856, David H. Burr, the Surveyor-General for
Utah, wrote to the General Land Office in Washington with disturbing
news. One of his deputies, a Mr. Troskolowski, had been "assaulted and
severely beaten by three men under the direction of one Hickman, a
noted member of the so-called 'Danite band.'"[16] The beating apparently
had been ordered by LDS leaders, in response to Troskolowski's efforts
to make sure twelve-year-old Emma Wheat escaped her impending marriage to a polygamist. The federal deputy was attacked the very night
after putting Emma on a stagecoach bound for Ohio, where she would be
safe:

> [I]n the Salt Lake City store run by Hooper and Thomas S. Williams he
> [i.e., Troskolowski] met and spoke briefly to Bill Hickman. . . . When
> Troskolowski stepped outside, three other Danites sneaked behind him
> and knocked him down. While one beat him about the head with the
> butt of a whip, the others stamped and kicked him. "Kill the d—d son of
> a b—h," Hickman screamed joining in, "kill him quick, I'll stand the con-
> sequences." Hooper and Williams eventually rescued Troskolowski, who
> by then was choking on his own blood.[17]

When Burr requested local law enforcement authorities to take
action, he was told that Troskolowski probably deserved the punishment
because he had been "talking and railing" against Mormonism.[18] Burr
himself was later threatened by Acting District Attorney Hosea Stout (former Nauvoo Police Chief) and Territorial Marshal Alexander McRae.

They showed him a copy of a letter he had written to Washington, wherein he charged Young with extensive depredations. The two Mormons told Burr that they knew all about his letters to Washington, and that he would have to stop submitting unfavorable reports—or else.[19] Burr recalled:

> They did not deny the truth of the charges I had made, but asserted the right of doing what they did, stating that the country was theirs, that they would not permit this interference with their rights, and this writing letters about them would be put a stop to.[20]

Soon afterward Burr and his men successfully escaped back to Washington. One of them, however, a clerk named C.G. Landon, was able to flee Utah only after being beaten on the night of July 25, 1857. Wearing only a pair of pants and some old socks, Landon was presumed dead until he unexpectedly showed up two months later in Placerville, California. He had walked all the way from Salt Lake City with no provisions, surviving only by his wits and will to live. Just before leaving Mormon territory, Burr expressed his own concerns in a final letter to Washington:

> *[T]hese people repudiate the authority of the United States in this country, and are in open rebellion against the general government.* . . . So strong have been my apprehensions of danger to the surveyors that I scarcely deemed it prudent to send any out. . . . We are by no means sure that we will be permitted to leave, for it is boldly asserted we would not get away alive.[21]

Yet another event that riled Washington officials just month's before Burr's run-in with Stout and McRae involved federal judge George P. Stiles. On December 29, 1856, several Mormon leaders raided his offices, seized his books and various other legal papers, then pretended to burn the documents in a nearby outhouse.[22] This blatant disrespect shown to a federal official, the invasion of a federal site, and the near destruction of federal property suggested that something would have to be done. Utah clearly was "obstinately out of step with the rest of the nation."[23]

The problem, as Washington politicians eventually realized, was Brigham Young's absolute command of every Saint. Federal Agent Major Jacob H. Holeman, in a letter to the Commissioner of Indian Affairs (December 1851), noted: "[Young's] power and influence is so great, that no officer neither of the Territory or the Government, who is Mormon, will dare to disobey his will."[24] Holeman also wrote that he frequently heard Mormons cursing and abusing "not only the government, but all who are American citizens."[25]

Washington officials finally decided that only a military expedition sent to Utah would be able to restore territorial order to the region. This conclusion was partially based on six charges delivered in March 1856 to the United States Attorney General. The list, which certainly suggested that the operation of a free society had been comprised in the area, alleged the following:

1. Mormon allegiance to Brigham Young, an absolute dictator in Utah, has compromised LDS loyalty to the U.S. government and laws enacted by Congress.

2. Through secret oaths to Young, male members of the LDS church have vowed to resist the laws of the country and obey only the law of the Mormon priesthood.

3. A group of men have been "set apart by special order of the church, to take both the lives and property of any person who may question the authority of the church." Moreover, such individuals, with Young's "knowledge and approbation," have destroyed court records.

4. Federal officials have been "insulted, harassed and annoyed by the Mormons."

5. Federal officers have been made to hear the "American government traduced, the chief executive of the nation, both living and dead, slandered and abused from the masses as well as from all the leading members of the church."

6. Laws are administered unfairly against Gentiles, while Mormons are favored in the courts.[26]

On May 28, 1857, marching orders to Utah were given to three full regiments (at least 2,500 men), or one-sixth of the U.S. Army, with a compliment of artillery. President James Buchanan's justification to Congress for the decision came in the form of nearly five dozen letters and reports written over a six-year period, "alleging treason, disloyalty, or other serious offenses," against Mormon leaders.[27] The president's detachment of soldiers, originally under the command of Brig. Gen. William Harney, would eventually be led by Col. Albert Sidney Johnston of the Second U.S. Cavalry, West Point graduate, and a highly capable officer.

Johnston could not have known that the Mormons already knew he was coming, and were more than ready to meet him in battle.[28] They had been preparing not only their Nauvoo Legion for war, but more importantly, their spirits. Utah, unbeknownst to Johnston, was in the midst of Brigham Young's infamous Reformation, a period of religious fanaticism, extreme spiritual subjugation of the masses, and brutal acts of violence to purge the church of its weak, faithless, or sinful members. The hallmark of this era would be the Mormon doctrine of blood atonement.

THE JUDGEMENT OF GOD

Brigham had every reason to believe that the Mormon dream of establishing God's kingdom was near fulfillment. By 1853 approximately 30,000 Mormons had traveled to Utah and thousands more were on their way. The land in which they had settled was large enough to serve as a new gathering place for the Saints, the church had highly capable men at its helm, the Nauvoo Legion had been resurrected, and the Council of Fifty had been reorganized. Moreover, Danite leaders, although no longer functioning in any official capacity, were continuing covert operations against church enemies.

But Young and other LDS leaders were perceptive enough to know by 1856 that the federal government would not put up with their activities for much longer. That same year saw Congress ignore the Mormon bid for statehood. Additionally, the Republican platform of 1856 actually called for a prohibition in U.S. territories of "those twin relics of barbarism—polygamy and slavery."[29] Utah was heading for war with the

U.S. and Mormon leadership understood that if they were going to survive the coming onslaught, the church would have to be purified.

Only the most obedient Saints could go on with Young. As he told his followers, "We need a reformation in the midst of this people; we need a thorough reform, for I know that very many are in a dozy condition with regard to their religion."[30] Leading this movement would be the fiery Jedediah M. Grant, who had dubbed himself "Mormon Thunder" in honor of how well he could preach and move his listeners to a desired response. Others called him "the sledgehammer of Brigham."[31]

This is not to say that Grant was a ruffian. He was more of a verbal combatant seasoned by years of debating with Christendom's ministers. His mission would be to instill fear and terror into the Saints through classic fire and brimstone preaching. Other men, Brigham's enforcers, would see to the more unpleasant tasks of the reformation. This collection of rogues, commonly known as Young's "Destroying Angels," was comprised of long-time Danites, brutal gunslingers, and assorted desperadoes. The most notorious angels of destruction were Porter Rockwell and "Wild" Bill Hickman (a.k.a. the "Danite Chief of Utah").[32]

Young often commented on such individuals, favorably listing their unique qualities and extolling his gratitude for their presence in the territory, boasting: "We have the meanest devils on the earth in our midst, and we intend to keep them, for we have use for them; and if the Devil does not look sharp, we will cheat him out of them at the last, for they will reform and go to heaven with us."[33]

The reformation began on September 14, 1856, with coordinated sermons of condemnation preached at key gatherings throughout the territory. In Salt Lake City, Brigham severely rebuked and chastised his entire congregation for "lying, stealing, swareing [sic], committing Adultery, quarrelling with Husbands [and] wives & children & many other evils."[34] Meanwhile, in Davis County to the north, Grant likewise reproved his listeners and commanded them to "repent and be baptized for the remission of their sins" even though many had already done so years earlier.[35]

A week later Young and Grant shared the church platform in Salt

Lake City to jointly reiterate their counsel and reveal the penalty for sin-
ning against God, his church, and his anointed servants. Brigham's sermon made the entire congregation quake with fear. He spoke primarily
to any individuals present, who were still unsure of their desire to stay in
Utah and still uncertain as to whether or not Mormonism was true. "I
would advise those persons to repent of their sins forthwith," Young
warned. He then delivered his infamous teaching on blood atonement, a
doctrine based on the idea that some sins are so serious that God can
only forgive them if the perpetrator spills their own blood and dies to
atone for the wrong committed:

> There are sins that men commit for which they cannot receive forgive-
> ness in this world, or in that which is to come, and if they had their eyes
> open to see their true condition, they would be perfectly willing to have
> their blood split upon the ground, that the smoke thereof might ascend
> to heaven as an offering for their sins.[36]

Young then confirmed that the term "cutting off" from the church
had previously been used, and would continue to be used, as a euphemism for killing a dissenter. "I know," Young began, "when you hear my
brethren telling about cutting people off from the earth, that you consider it is strong doctrine; but it is to save them, not to destroy them."[37]
He went on to insist that scores of faithful Saints, if they knew that they
had committed a sin unforgivable through repentance, "would beg of
their brethren to shed their blood, that the smoke thereof might ascend
to God as an offering to appease the wrath that is kindled against
them."[38] Young concluded by saying that some men already had come to
him to "offer their lives to atone for their sins."[39]

Grant's words were even more disturbing, if possible. In reference to
those whom he called "old hardened sinners," he revealed: "[M]y prayer
is that God's indignation may rest upon them, and that He will curse
them." Grant then invoked blood atonement imagery, specifically targeting those Saints who had broken their covenants—i.e., rebelled against
the church:

> [T]here are men and women that I would advise to go to the President immediately, and ask him to appoint a committee to attend to their ease; and then let a place be selected, and let that committee shed their blood. . . . I would ask how many covenant breakers there are in this city and in this kingdom. I believe that there are a great many; and if they are covenant breakers we need a place designated, where we can shed their blood. . . . They are a perfect nuisance, and I want them cut off, and the sooner it is done the better. [40]

In the days, weeks, and months that followed, fear swept through Utah. The growing hysteria escalated even further when low to mid-level church leaders viewed as complacent were warned that unless they woke up spiritually and purged their individual flocks of questionable members, they themselves would be "cut off."[41] All powerful LDS authorities called for all Saints to repent, renew their covenants, and be re-baptized as a pledge of loyalty.[42]

To root out the evil in their midst, Grant drew up a list of highly intrusive questions to be used for probing the personal lives of those dwelling within the boundaries of Brigham's empire.[43] Mormon preachers, bishops, and teachers went from house to house in a relentless effort to find sinners. Grant had issued a stern command: "[L]et their names be written down, and let the offence and place of residence be written against the name, that we may know who are living in sin, where they live and what their offences are."[44] This situation evolved into a reign of terror when Young encouraged faithful Saints to murder, out of "love," all unfaithful Mormons so their souls might be saved:

> [T]ake a person in this congregation who has knowledge with regard to being saved in the kingdom of our God . . . and suppose that he is overtaken in a gross fault . . . and that he cannot attain to it without the shedding of his blood, and also knows that by having his blood shed he will atone for that sin. . . . [H]e would be glad to have his blood shed. That would be loving themselves, even unto an eternal exaltation. Will you love your brothers or sisters likewise, when they have committed a sin that cannot be atoned for without the sheding [sic] of their blood? Will

you love that man or woman well enough to shed their blood? . . . This is loving our neighbour [sic] as ourselves; if he needs help, help him; and if he wants salvation and it is necessary to spill his blood on the earth in order that he may be saved, spill it. . . . That is the way to love mankind.[45]

By 1857, Heber C. Kimball was publicly advocating widespread slaughter, declaring: "[W]hen it is necessary that blood should be shed, we should be as ready to do that as to eat an apple. . . . [Y]ou may dig your graves, and we will slay you, and you may crawl into them."[46] Kimball justified his words with the Bible by comparing apostates to Judas, and invoking Joseph Smith's view of the Savior's betrayer: "Judas lost that saving principle, and they [i.e., the eleven apostles] took him and killed him. It is said in the Bible that his bowels gushed out; but they actually kicked him until his bowels came out."[47] Such a concept originated as far back as Nauvoo, where Joseph claimed in one sermon that a man guilty of murder should not be hung, but rather, be shot or have his head cut off, so his blood could spill on the ground and rise to God as a sacrificial offering.[48]

John D. Lee, a Council of Fifty member and influential Danite, recalled: "I knew of many men being killed in Nauvoo by the Danites. It was then the rule that all the enemies of Joseph Smith should be killed, and I know of many a man who was quietly put out of the way by the orders of Joseph and his Apostles."[49] In Utah, being an enemy of the prophet (i.e., Brigham Young) would not be the only sin worthy of death. Adultery, murder, lying, immorality, stealing, apostasy, using God's name in vain, refusing to be converted, inter-racial marriage, attempting to flee Utah, lack of faith, disobedience, and a host of other wrongs meant certain execution.[50]

SACRIFICIAL ACTS

Blood began to flow profusely in Utah not long after the reformation was launched. Indeed, several blood atonement-related murders already had been committed prior to 1856. Young had hinted publicly at the doctrine as far back as 1849, while at the same time explicitly teaching the

The 1862 murder of Joseph Morris and several members of his church by Mormon soldiers. Morris dared challenge Brigham Young's authority by first declaring himself to be a prophet. He then gathered a following of 500-1,000 Morrisites from out of the LDS church. After the killings, Morris' body was put on public display as a warning to others. This crime, although not technically part of the 1856/57 reformation, was consistent with how dissidents were handled in Utah (from T.B.H. Stenhouse, *The Rocky Mountain Saints,* 1873).

doctrine in private to select persons, who could be trusted. To these initiates it was no surprise when in 1856, about a year before the reformation, Young preached the following:

> There is not a man or woman who violates the covenants made with their God [through the endowment ceremony], that will not be required to pay the debt. The blood of Christ will never wipe that out, your own blood must atone for it; and the judgments of the Almighty will come, sooner or later, and every man or woman will have to atone for breaking their covenants.[51]

Heber C. Kimball, always ready to support the teachings of his prophet-leader, added during one of his lectures: "[I]f men turn traitors to God and His servants, their blood will surely be shed, or else they will be damned, and that too according to their covenants"[52] Apostates certainly were viewed as the worst of sinners, although every reprobate received the same penalty. As Brigham instructed his flock: "'If any miserable scoundrels come here, cut their throats.'"[53] To this comment, according to the church printed *Journal of Discourses*, Young's congregation gave a hearty "Amen." Whether or not the outside world knew what was going on in Utah seemed of little consequence to Young, who revealed his thoughts on the issue in 1855:

> What do you suppose they would say in old Massachusetts . . . . What would they say in old Connecticut?" They would raise a universal howl of, "how wicked the Mormons are; they are killing the evil doers who are among them; why I hear that they kill the wicked away up yonder in Utah." . . . What do I care for the wrath of man? No more than I do for the chickens that run in my dooryard.[54]

One of the first "evildoers" to die was Alonzo Bowman, a successful Mexican trader, who was originally from New York. During a chance-meeting with Young in 1853, Bowman made the mistake of innocently asking about LDS beliefs and the facts behind the Saints' troubles. Bowman had no idea that his easy-going, independent manner would leave Young feeling somewhat slighted and fearful that a "spy" had come into his midst. Young ordered him arrested on "suspicion" of various crimes. Several weeks later, Bowman finally was released from confinement, after which time he attempted to leave the area. But Brigham had met with other LDS leaders and passed sentence on him.

"[W]e must make some arrangements as to Bowman at once," Young said. "We must adopt some plan by which to end his existence. It will never do to allow him to leave the territory: for if he is once at liberty again, he will set the Spaniards and Indians against us, if not half the world besides, and that will never do."[55] Daniel Wells then proposed that two men be selected to carry out the Prophet's "counsel." John Norton and James Furguson were chosen, and after waiting in ambush for Bowman, shot him twice, one shot "hit him full in the breast, and the other in the forehead."[56]

A 1904 sketch of Bill Hickman shooting Hartly as he tried to escape Utah (from Bill Hickman, *Brigham's Destroying Angel*, 1904).

In 1854, non-Mormon lawyer, Jesse Hartly, erred by falling in love with, and marrying, a Mormon. Brigham suspiciously eyed this new-comer, until one day during a gathering of Saints he pointed out the gen-tile. "This man, Hartly, is guilty of heresy," Young roared. "He has been writing to his friends in Oregon against the Church, and has attempted to expose us to the world. He should be sent to Hell."[57] When the com-munity shunned Jesse, he knew he had been marked for death, and tried to escape, hoping to return for his wife.[58] But in the canyons, Bill Hick-man, under orders from Orson Hyde, shot and killed Hartly, leaving his body to rot in a creek bed.[59]

In March 1857, 49-year-old William Parrish and his 22-year-old son were murdered as they attempted to leave Utah. According to Parrish's wife, Alvira, William and his son did not believe in "killing to 'save,' as taught by the teachers."[60] LDS leaders also believed that Parrish's depar-ture, if allowed, would set a bad example and tempt others to leave, which was forbidden. According to Aaron DeWitt, who wrote to his sister in 1875, escape from Utah was virtually impossible:

> Dear Sister, . . . I will tell you the reason why we could not leave this blood-stained land, I mean ten or twelve years ago. In the first place, we were a thousand miles from the nearest town East, eight hundred miles to the nearest settlement West, and God only knows how far to any place north and south. On all this vast tract of land no white man dwelt. No civilization was known, none but the red men roamed the dreary solitudes. To travel such a space required considerable food, a good wagon and team, in fact, everything necessary for a three month's pilgrimage. Nor was it safe for a few men to go together, unless they were well-armed. Again, every Bishop knew your business and was always on the lookout. If you started they would send men to drive off your stock, and thus you would be compelled to return. Then if you did not behave and act the hypocrite, the bishop would send the Danites to use you up and send you across lots to that bright brimstone home we read about. Thus you see it was almost impossible to get away.[61]

DeWitt also wrote his sister about the day he witnessed Brigham teach blood atonement and the warning given during the message:

> In the fall of 1857, I heard our Prophet in a congregation of three thousands souls, tell his bishops they were to "counsel" the brethren to do as they were told; and, said he "if they don't do it, lay righteousness to the line and judgment to the pummel. If you don't know what that is, come to me and I will tell you." He then threw back his head and with a revolting grin, drew his finger across his throat.[62]

Persons simply passing through the territory were not even safe, especially if they appeared wealthy. Consider, for example, Richard Yates, another individual killed in obedience to Brigham's orders. Yates was a highly successful trader, whose only sin was trading with government personnel. Young branded him a "spy," which seemed to be a favorite accusation against undesirables. When Yates happened to be

Two 1904 sketches depicting the murder of Richard Yates by Bill Hickman and Hosea Stout and their subsequent delivery of Yates' money to Brigham Young. Hickman claimed he acted on direct orders from Brigham Young and LDS apostle Orson Hyde (from Bill Hickman, *Brigham's Destroying Angel*, 1904).

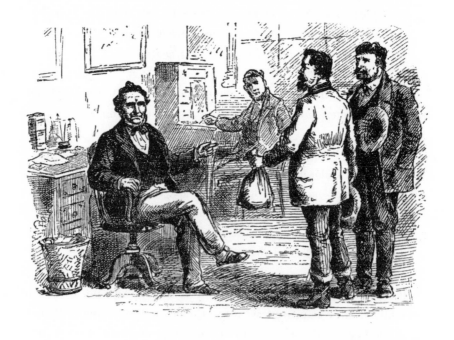

found traveling alone toward Green River, he was arrested and handed over to Bill Hickman. The original plan was to take Yates into Salt Lake City, but on the trail Hickman was met by Joseph A. Young, one of Brigham's sons. According to Hickman: "He hailed me (I being behind) and said his father wanted that man Yates killed, and that I would know all about it when I got to Jones' camp."[63] The murder was committed that night:

> Col. Jones and two others, Hosea Stout and another man whose name I do not recollect, came to my camp-fire and asked if Yates was asleep. I told them he was, upon which his brains were knocked out with an ax. He was covered up with his blankets . . . and a grave dug some three feet deep near the camp by the fire-light, all hands assisting. Flack and Meacham were asleep when the man was killed, but woke up and saw the grave digging. The body was put in and the dirt well packed on it.[64]

In 1858 the particularly gruesome double-murder of Henry Jones and his mother took place. Their fate was sealed when gossip spread about them living in an incestuous relationship. Henry received a warning in February, when several Mormons disguised as Indians dragged him from his bed in the middle of the night. Porter Rockwell then castrated Henry, leaving him to die of exposure. He survived, however, staggering back home to recover.[65] Two months later, according to neighbor Nathaniel Case, a secret meeting was held in the home of a Mormon bishop, who along with other church officials, including Rockwell, committed the murders:

> Henry Jones and his mother had been killed. I went down to the dug-out where they lived. . . . The old woman was laying on the ground in the dugout on a little straw, in the clothes in which she was killed. She had a bullet hole through her head. . . . In about 15 or 20 minutes Henry Jones was brought there and laid by her side; they then threw some old bed clothes over them and an old feather bed. . . . The next Sunday after the murder, in a church meeting in Payson, Charles Hancock, the bishop, said, as to the killing of Jones and his mother he cared nothing

about it, and it would have been done in daylight if circumstances would have permitted it.—This was said from the stand; there were 150 or 200 persons present. He gave no reason for killing them.[66]

Front cover to Bill Hickman's revealing confessional book (1904) detailing the crimes he committed in Utah, many of which were carried out at the request of Brigham Young (portrait is of Hickman).

Many such crimes in compliance with Brigham's blood atonement took place during this era. Bill Hickman, who ultimately left Mormonism and detailed his actions in a book titled *Brigham's Destroying Angel*, confessed to either personal knowledge of, or involvement with, at least thirteen murders, many of which were committed at the orders of Young himself.[67] One such case involved the 1857 slaying of the Aiken party, a company of cattle buyers from California.[68] They had come to Utah intending to meet Johnston's army. Unfortunately, the men drew considerable notice as they traveled through Mormon country: "They were a prosperous looking company, outfitted with pack mules, and well dressed, equipped, and mounted, And at least one wore a money belt full of gold eagles, six coins deep around his whole body.[69]

According to *Brigham's Destroying Angel*, the company of men worth an estimated $25,000, were declared a cadre of spies and arrested just twenty-five miles north of Salt Lake City. All six were then murdered over the course of several days by Hickman, Rockwell and others. The task became a lengthy affair because two of the men temporarily escaped from their captors and had to be hunted down. Some of the victims were buried, while others were weighted down with stones and thrown into "one of those 'bottomless springs'—so called—common in that part of Utah."[70] So many homicides of this type occurred throughout Brigham's term as LDS president that R. N. Baskin, who would serve as a Chief Justice of the Supreme Court of Utah, noted:

> In the excavations made within the limits of Salt Lake City during the time I have resided there, many human skeletons have been exhumed in various parts of the city. . . . I have never heard that it was ever the custom to bury the dead promiscuously throughout the city; and as no coffins were ever found in connection with any of these skeletons, it is evident that the death of the persons to whom they once belonged did not result from natural causes, but from the use of criminal means.[71]

Of all the atrocities committed in Utah, none was more savage than the massacre by the Saints of 120–135 non-Mormon men, women, and children at a place called Mountain Meadows.

VENGEANCE IS OURS

Arguably the most despicable deed in Mormon history happened in September 1857, during a time when tension in Utah had reached an unprecedented high. Barely a year had transpired since the inauguration of Brigham's reformation. Moreover, winter was coming, which always meant additional hardship for the Saints. And Johnston's approaching army was almost within striking distance of the territory. "We are invaded by a hostile force who are evidently assailing us to accomplish our overthrow and destruction," Young announced on August 5.[72] Antic-ipating an attack, he then declared martial law, ordering all his forces to "hold themselves in readiness to march, at a moment's notice, to repel any and all such threatened invasion."[73]

Into this volatile region came the Baker-Fancher wagon train, under the leadership of well-seasoned plainsmen John T. Baker and Alexander Fancher. The group, comprised mostly of farmers headed for what they hoped would be a new life in California, included approximately 120–135 emigrants from Arkansas and Missouri.[74] There were nearly two dozen women, the majority of whom were young mothers, and some sixty young children and babies, twenty of whom were girls between the ages of seven and eighteen. The rest were adult males, mostly heads of fami-lies, along with some teamsters and other hired hands.[75] On August 3 they arrived in Salt Lake City, where they immediately became a marked train.[76] Their presence in Utah would go down in history as a classic tale of being in the wrong place at the wrong time.

First, unlike other caravans that had wheeled through Utah on a westward trek, the Baker-Fancher party of thirty to forty wagons, was comprised of affluent persons. The train held an estimated value into the tens of thousands.[77] Each family also had a good deal of cash on them, costly equipment and livestock. As many as 1,000 cattle were being driven along with the company, as well as work oxen, horses, and mules.[78]

Second, most of the company was from northwest Arkansas, only one county away from where Apostle Parley P. Pratt had recently been murdered. He died at the hands of a jealous husband whose wife had become part of Pratt's polygamous harem.[79]

Third, the wagon-train, after leaving Salt Lake, took the California trail heading through southern Utah, where many of the most fanatical believers in blood atonement lived.[80] As John D. Lee noted about Spring-field, Utah, in the south: "[I]t was one of the hot-beds of fanaticism, and I expect that more men were killed there, in proportion to population, than in any other part of Utah. In that settlement it was certain death to say a word against the authorities, high or low."[81]

Fourth, as the wagon-train traversed the southern route, conflict erupted between the emigrants and the Mormons, who refused to sell badly needed food and supplies to the travelers. Such conduct was unthinkable to the Baker-Fancher company. They had no idea that the refusals were in obedience to Brigham's prohibition on trading with Gentiles (see p. 221).[82]

By the time the unwelcome settlers passed Cedar City to make camp at Mountain Meadows, the entire company already was doomed. Too many tempers had flared along the way and too many arguments had ensued. A few of the men in the party apparently had boasted, foolishly, that they were present with the mob that killed Joseph and Hyrum. One man reportedly went so far as to brag that he possessed the very gun that took the prophet's life.[83] Whether these claims were true or not has never been determined. Either way, the emigrants could not have known that two of the sins worthy of blood atonement were condemning Joseph Smith and/or consenting to his death.

In Cedar City, on September 6, LDS Stake President Isaac Haight, a highly zealous partaker of the reformation, complained angrily to fellow church leaders about the troublesome wagon-train, but did not know precisely what to do.[84] (See Glossary for the definition of "Stake.") As the highest ranking member of the priesthood in Cedar City, Haight's word was law in the area, and his followers would have done anything he requested.[85] But instead of moving on his own initiative, Haight dispatched a messenger to receive instructions from Brigham Young. The prophet, however, already had decided the fate of the Baker-Fancher party a week earlier, at a secret meeting in Salt Lake City with several Indian chiefs.[86] Brigham had promised all the cattle in the wagon-train to the Indians if they would do away with the entire company.[87]

It was the perfect plan. Young's wishes would be fulfilled, the Indians would feel indebted to the Saints, and the LDS church would appear blameless. Journals kept by Mormon pioneers and modern investigations into that era of Utah history have brought to light various pieces of information that indicate Young clearly contracted with the Indians. In addition to Young's promise of cattle, the following also is known:

- During his meeting with Paiute leaders, Young linked the presence of the Baker-Fancher train with the U.S. government and the danger it represented, telling the Indians: "[T]hey have come to fight us and you, for when they kill us they will kill you."

- Young, as superintendent of Indian Affairs in the Utah Territory, ordered the distribution of more than $3,500 in goods to the natives "near Mountain Meadows" less than three weeks after the massacre.
- The patriarchal blessing given to Col. William Dame (commander of the Mormon militia in Beaver, Iron and Washington counties) prophesied that he would one day lead Mormons and Indians "in the redemption of Zion and the avenging of the blood of the prophets."
- In an August 4, 1857 letter to Mormon "Indian missionary" Jacob Hamblin, whose mission was to obtain the Indian trust, Young stated: "[T]hey must learn that they have either got to help us or the United States will kill us both."[88]

So on the morning of September 7, the Mountain Meadows Massacre commenced. This atrocity, which turned into a six-day ordeal, began just before daybreak, perhaps as many as two hundred Indian warriors, along with a very small group of Mormon soldiers dressed up as Indians, crept up to the wagon train camp and opened fire on the unsuspecting emigrants. Although as many as ten men were killed and several others wounded, the company quickly recovered and returned fire, "reportedly killing and wounding several natives."[89]

The Arkansans then proceeded to chain their wagons together, dig rifle pits, and fight back with incredible courage, taking deadly aim at their attackers. What was supposed to have been a speedy massacre unexpectedly turned into a stand-off. Two days later, when Maj. John M. Higbee of the Nauvoo Legion arrived with a select group of his soldiers from Cedar City, the Indians still had not finished the job. The Arkansans could not flee, but neither could the Indians attack. It was clearly a situation that had to be resolved. But by September 10, Higbee knew the Indians were not up to the task. To use John D. Lee's words, Mormons at the scene "were in a sad fix."[90]

At about this time, three of the train's best scouts—Abel Baker, Joseph Miller, and John Milium Jones—somehow managed to slip out of camp in hopes of making it on foot to California. They carried with them an account of the tragedy, the names of those in the party, and a plea for help. But all three were killed, hunted down by Indian trackers, led by 22-year-old Mormon, Ira Hatch.[91]

Meanwhile, back at Mountain Meadows, the Mormons overseeing the assault on the wagon-train—John D. Lee, Isaac Haight, John Higbee, William Dame (Bishop of Parowan), and Philip Klingensmith (Bishop of Cedar City)—conceived of a plan whereby the emigrants could be coaxed out into the open. John D. Lee explained in his first-person account of the event that the original idea was to have the Indians "do all the work, and the whites do nothing, only stay back and plan for them, and encourage them."[92] But the turn of events called for more drastic measures.

So on September 11, John D. Lee and William Bateman approached the wagon-train under a white flag. After entering the camp, they convinced the Arkansans that their only chance was to surrender their arms and exit the area under the protection of the Mormon militia that had arrived and was waiting to serve as an escort. Soon afterward, the men of the Baker-Fancher party gave up their weapons and fell into a processional suggested by their Mormon rescuers.

The first wagon, carrying children under six years old, was driven by Samuel McCurdy. The second wagon, driven by Samuel Knight, carried two or three wounded men and a woman. The remaining women and older children marched at a slight distance. About a quarter of a mile farther back walked the unarmed men, formed in a single line, each one escorted by an armed Mormon guard. Then without warning, the wagons stopped between some hills thick with brush.

Higbee, on horseback at the rear flank of the male emigrants, also halted. "Do your duty," he shouted.[93] With sudden fury, the Mormon soldiers shot and/or knifed the men they were escorting, as the women and children up ahead looked back and began screaming in horror. At that same moment, the gunfire cued Indians hiding in the nearby brush to emerge and begin their attack against the defenseless children and their mothers, all of whom finally understood with terrible clarity what was happening. The Indians, along with several Mormons disguised by native clothes and war-paint, butchered their victims with "bows and arrows and stones and guns and knives."[94]

Two 19th century drawings of the Mountain Meadows Massacre based on eye-witness testimony and
government investigations.

Mothers vainly attempted to fight back or flee with their young ones.
Six-year-old John Calvin Miller could only stand by helplessly as his
mother, Matilda, was repeatedly shot with arrows. He kept pulling them
"from her back until she was dead."[95] The screams and gunshots continued, as the wounded emigrants in the wagons were executed at point blank
range. A few of the Arkansas men, who had managed to avoid the initial

assault by their escorts, desperately tried to run to the aid of their families. But they were cut down by Mormons on horseback almost as soon as they began racing toward the carnage. John D. Lee recalled the following:

> [O]ne little child, about six months old, was carried in its father's arms, and it was killed by the same bullet that entered its father's breast; it was shot through the head. . . . McCurdy went up to Knight's wagon, where the sick and wounded were, and raising his rifle to his shoulder, said: "O Lord, my God, receive their spirits, it is for thy Kingdom that I do this." He then shot a man who was lying with his head on another man's breast; the ball killed both men. . . . Knight then shot a man with his rifle; he shot the man in the head. Knight also brained a boy that was about fourteen years old. The boy came running up to our wagons, and Knight struck him on the head with the butt end of his gun, and crushed his skull. By this time many Indians reached our wagons, and all of the sick and wounded were killed almost instantly. I saw an Indian from Cedar City, called Joe, run up to the wagon and catch a man by the hair, and raise his head up and look into his face; the man shut his eyes, and Joe shot him in the head. The Indians then examined all of the wounded in the wagons, and all of the bodies, to see if any were alive, and all that showed signs of life were at once shot through the head. . . . Just after the wounded were all killed I saw a girl, some ten or eleven years old, running towards us, from the direction where the troops had attacked the main body of emigrants; she was covered with blood. An Indian shot her before she got within sixty yards of us. That was the last person that I saw killed on that occasion.[96]

The brutal assault lasted but a few minutes.[97] The only survivors were seventeen children and infants, all six years old or younger, some of whom had been wounded by the gunfire. They had been spared because their blood, according to the Mormon doctrine, was still innocent. Fifty men, about twenty women, and approximately fifty children between the ages of seven and eighteen, had been slaughtered. Their bodies were left exposed until the next day, when Lee, Haight, and other local church leaders rode back to the location and dumped the corpses into shallow trenches, covered by a thin layer of dirt. Within a few days, however, wolves arrived on the scene, as one Mormon witnessed: "The wolves had dug open the heaps, dragged out the bodies, and were then tearing the flesh from them. I counted 19 wolves at one of these places."[98]

AFTER MOUNTAIN MEADOWS

In the weeks and months following the massacre, Brigham Young and his inner circle hid their culpability behind a veil of recriminations and cover-ups. It is now known that "at least 40, and perhaps close to 60, Mormons participated in the massacre."[99] One of the most important aspects of the crime that needed to be concealed was the fact that "white men did most of the killing."[100] This, according to Mormon Francis Lyman, who received the information in 1895 from Nephi Johnson and Dudley Leavitt (ancestor of Utah's governor Mike Leavitt), two participants in the slayings.[101]

These men, along with the others directly involved, were sworn to never tell Gentiles what had happened. Moreover, LDS church leadership blamed the Indians entirely and investigations made by federal agents were frustrated. But the truth finally came to light after U.S. Army Maj. James H. Carleton traveled to Utah himself in 1859 to investigate the bloodbath. Signs of the nightmarish event still had not completely vanished. Carleton wrote to Washington:

> The scene of the massacre, even at this late day, was horrible to look upon. Women's hair, in detached locks and masses, hung to the sage bushes and was strewn over the ground in many places. Parts of little children's dresses and of female costume dangled from the shrubbery or lay scattered about; and among these, here and there, on every hand, for at least a mile in the direction of the road, by two miles east and west, there gleamed, bleached white by the weather, the skulls and other bones of those who had suffered.[102]

Carleton soon began to notice discrepancies between stories told by Mormons in the area. After talking to various Indians, he finally pieced together what had happened. Carleton was outraged over what he called the "hellish atrocity" perpetrated by Utah's "Latter-Day Devils." He eventually handed his report over to Washington, but before leaving the territory, he and his men of Company K collected as many bones as they could find and buried them in a common grave. Over the remains they placed a conical structure of granite stones and a twelve foot cross, cut from cedar wood. On the cross, as a reminder to those who had committed the crimes, Carleton's men carved: "Vengeance is mine; I will repay, saith the Lord." When Brigham Young visited the site in 1860 and saw the monument, he callously acknowledged Carleton's epitaph, suggesting: "It should be 'Vengenace is mine and I have taken a little.'"[103] With a dismissive hand motion, he ordered the monument and cross torn down. In five minutes, it had been demolished.

Regarding the property taken from the train, it was divided up throughout the various Mormon communities via a public auction at Cedar City. Nothing was discarded. According to Carleton's report, the Mormons even took "[t]he clothing stripped from the corpses, bloody and with bits of flesh upon it, shredded by the bullets."[104] These were either sold or given away after lying in the church's tithing office for about three weeks. As for the seventeen remaining children, they were finally returned in 1859 to Arkansas relatives, after being located and claimed by federal agent Jacob Forney. The Mormons, in turn, actually billed the U.S. government thousands of dollars in reimbursements for boarding, clothing and schooling the children during their time in Utah.[105]

The denials, lies, and legal obstructions would continue for twenty years.[106] Finally, after intense pressure from the government and surviving members of the slain emigrants, the LDS church picked a scapegoat—John D. Lee. Out of all the participants, he alone was convicted for his role in the massacre. Oddly, Mormon witnesses only seemed to remember Lee in connection with the event, perhaps because he had so consistently voiced remorse over his actions, and strenuous objections to what had occurred.[107]

On March 23, 1877, 64-year-old Lee was taken back to Mountain Meadows to be executed by federal authorities. In his final statement, the former Danite said he no longer believed "everything that is now being taught and practiced by Brigham Young" and that he thought Young was "leading the people astray, downward to destruction."[108] Lee then sat calmly down on the edge of his coffin, and there was shot by a firing squad. He fell backward into his final resting place. The epitaph on Lee's grave was the biblical verse: "Know the Truth, and the Truth shall make you free" (John 8:32).

Interestingly, Lee's constant companion throughout his trial and jail time was not a Mormon bishop, elder, apostle, or neighbor. It was a Methodist prison chaplain, George Stokes, who became his friend, confidant, and comforter, even though Lee had been taught all his life that Christendom's minister's were satanically-inspired and corrupt. Lee's great grand-daughter, Thelma Geer, in her fascinating narrative *Mormonism, Mama, and Me* remarked:

> [T]his Methodist minister's friendship and compassion meant much to my forlorn and forsaken forebear. This clergyman must have been a providential blessing, especially sent by a merciful and sympathizing God to accompany and strengthen Great-grandfather Lee as he had returned, for the first time since its perpetration, to the scene of the horrendous crime and its haunting, brutal memories. This Christian minister had pityingly and prayerfully sought every means to assuage the grief and despair of the doomed man, undergirding him every tortuous step of the way.[109]

As for Brigham's other henchmen, most of them remained faithful to Young until their deaths. Orrin Porter Rockwell, for instance, never repudiated Young. He died of natural causes in 1878, while awaiting trial for murder. At the time of his death, the *Salt Lake Tribune* editorialized that he "participated in at least a hundred murders."[110] Others, however, like Bill Hickman, eventually abandoned Mormonism and revealed to the world what had happened under Brigham's rule.

To this day Mormons revere Young's destroying angels as well as the Danites. In February 2000, in fact, residents of Lehi, Utah, honored the villainous Porter Rockwell by unveiling a $60,000, life-size sculpture of the Destroying Angel. Commissioned by Lehi officials and the Lehi His-

EXECUTION OF JOHN D. LEE AT MOUNTAIN MEADOWS (1877)

Lee was taken back to Mountain Meadows to face execution by firing squad. In the top photo, Lee (wearing a scarf) sits on the edge of his coffin, awaiting the firing squad. Once bystanders were cleared away, soldiers masked by a blanket screen near the wagon (right side of photo) shot Lee where he was seated. Spectators on horseback can be seen in the distance. Lower (left): John D. Lee; lower (right), Lee in his coffin after execution (from J.F. Gibbs, *Lights and Shadows of Mormonism*, 1909 and R.N. Baskin, *Reminiscences of Early Utah*, 1914).

torical Preservation Commission, the monument to Rockwell was placed in a new park dedicated to the Mormon pioneers. Eighty-four-year-old John Broadbent, a lifelong resident of Lehi, proudly observed: "It's hard to believe in this little town we can have anything that great as a representative of the early people of this community."[111]

With regard to the Mountain Meadows massacre, the LDS church has continued to vehemently deny Brigham's involvement and any church responsibility. On September 11, 1999, in fact, at the dedication of a new monument to the slain victims, Mormon president Gordon B. Hinckley inserted into his speech a well-crafted statement indicative of the long-standing view held by LDS authorities that rogue individuals were to blame. Hinckley stressed: "That which we have done here must never be construed as an acknowledgment of the part of the church of any complicity in the occurrences of that fateful day."[112]

To date, no general authority of The Church of Jesus Christ of Latter-day Saints has yet made an official apology for the massacre, recognized the church's role in the tragedy, or admitted the significance that Brigham's blood atonement doctrine contributed to the mass murder. And it seems that such a declaration may never come forth. As Brigham Young University President Rex E. Lee (a descendant of John D. Lee) unequivocally stated at a 1990 Mountain Meadows dedication of a memorial marker: "Our task for today is not to look backward, nor rationalize, nor engage in any kind of retroactive analysis nor apology."[113]

TWELVE

Wars and Rumors of Wars

*[Brigham Young] declared that the thread was cut between us
and the U.S. and that the Almighty recognized us as a free and
independent people and that no officer appointed by government should come and rule over us from this time forth.*

Hosea Stout (c. 1857)[1]
Mormon Leader

*The Almighty has established this kingdom with order and laws
and every thing pertaining thereto . . . [so] that when the nations
shall be convulsed, we may stand forth as saviours . . . and
finally redeem a ruined world, not only in a religious but in a
political point of view.*

John Taylor (1862)[2]
Mormon Apostle

ON SEPTEMBER 13, 1857, just two days after the massacre at Mountain
Meadows, Quartermaster Capt. Stewart Van Vliet of the U.S. Army found
himself being warmly introduced by Brigham Young to the Salt Lake City
congregation.[3] Van Vliet had come as an emissary from the U.S. War
Department, slightly ahead of the army making its way toward Utah's
capital. Van Vliet's mission was to let LDS leaders know that Mormons
would have to start obeying American law and that Young would have to
step down as governor. Brigham was supposed to have handed the job
over to someone else when his term expired in 1854, but he decided to
retain the position "on the narrow ground that he had not been properly
notified of his removal from office."[4]

Mormons did not think it unreasonable that Young had remained governor. As king he would continue to be their undisputed ruler no matter who held the territorial post of governor. Federal authorities, however, saw things differently. Young had no legal right to still be in office. So the U.S. Army was on its way to restore order and install the new governor, 54-year-old Alfred Cumming, whom they were bringing along with them.

Van Vliet also had traveled to Salt Lake City ahead of the troops to requisition needed supplies for the military expedition and negotiate a place in or near Salt Lake City, where the army could spend the winter. But much to Van Vliet's dismay, Young refused both requests. Moreover, Van Vliet was assured that "Governor Young and the people of Utah will prevent, if possible, the army for Utah from entering their Territory this season."[5] With this disturbing news, the Army's representative returned to Washington and informed the president that trouble lay ahead.

It did not take long for the Mormons to live up to Van Vliet's report. On September 15. 1857, Young issued a broadside proclamation to his people. "We are invaded by a hostile force," he warned his church. Young additionally confirmed implementation of the following:

> 1st:—Forbid all armed forces, of every description, from coming into this Territory under any pretense whatsoever.
>
> 2d:—[A]ll the forces in said Territory hold themselves in readiness to march, at a moment's notice, to repel any and all such invasion.
>
> 3d:—Martial law is hereby declared to exist in this Territory, from and after publication of this Proclamation; and no person shall be allowed to pass or repass into, or through, or from this Territory, without a permit from the proper officer.[6]

Young, for all intents and purposes, had severed Utah's ties with the U.S. government. The very next day he even held a strategy meeting with his top officer of the Nauvoo Legion, Lt. Gen. Daniel Wells. Together they agreed that Mormon soldiers would "waylay our enemies, attack them from ambush, stampede their animals, take the supply trains, cut off detachments, and parties sent to canyons for wood, or on other service."[7] Thus began the Utah War of 1857/58.

A WINTER OF CONFLICT

At the outset of their confrontation with America, the Mormons clearly had an advantage. The U.S. campaign had been badly mismanaged almost from its inception. First, the soldiers ordered to Utah had to be gathered from regiments scattered all over the country from Minnesota to Florida, which greatly delayed the army's departure. Second, the military force was held up even longer when no politician could be found to take Young's place in hostile Mormon country. Third, when the Tenth Infantry finally did leave Fort Leavenworth, it already was late July, far too close to winter to safely complete the 1,200 mile journey to Utah.

Then there was a change in the unit's command before the men could reach their destination. America's display of military might originally had been assigned to Brg. Gen. William Harney. But without warning, Harney and his Second Dragoons were detached and sent to Kansas to quell civil unrest, which left the advancing army with no capable commander and no cavalry support. Col. Johnston had been called upon, but he needed several weeks to catch up with the troops.[8] Until then, the army struggled under the highly inept Col. Edmund Alexander, who had neither the instincts, nor the experience, to effectively lead.

Before long, Alexander's entire brigade stretched disorganized across Wyoming, with their supply trains unguarded all along the way. The Mormons could not resist the temptation, and using small mounted companies of Nauvoo Legion soldiers, began making raids against the leaderless army. Under the command of Maj. Lot Smith, these tiny bands of Mormon marauders devastated Uncle Sam's supply trains. The first strike came on October 5, 1857, when Smith attacked after Col. Alexander's infantry march several miles beyond support distance:

> While the American soldiers helplessly watched the smoke, the Mormon
> major burned their bacon, more than forty-five tons of it. . . . He next
> captured another unprotected train on Big Sandy River, a few miles west

of present Farson, and destroyed it as well. . . . Smith and some two dozen men or so torched enough provisions to feed the federal expedition at least two months. Later that month, he teamed up with a company under noted plainsman Porter Rockwell to rustle more than a thousand head of cattle from government herds.[9]

PROCLAMATION
BY THE GOVERNOR.

CITIZENS OF UTAH—

We are invaded by a hostile force who are evidently assailing us to accomplish our overthrow and destruction.

For the last twenty five years we have trusted officials of the Government, from Constables and Justices to Judges, Governors, and Presidents, only to be scorned, held in derision, insulted and betrayed. Our houses have been plundered and then burned, our fields laid waste, our principal men butchered while under the pledged faith of the government for their safety, and our families driven from their homes to find that shelter in the barren wilderness and that protection among hostile savages which were denied them in the boasted abodes of Christianity and civilization.

The Constitution of our common country guarantees unto us all that we do now or have ever claimed.

If the Constitutional rights which pertain unto us as American citizens were extended to Utah, according to the spirit and meaning thereof, and fairly and impartially administered, it is all that we could ask, all that we have ever asked.

Our opponents have availed themselves of prejudice existing against us because of our religious faith, to send out a formidable host to accomplish our destruction. We have had no privilege, no opportunity of defending ourselves from the false, foul, and unjust aspersions against us before the nation. The Government has not condescended to cause an investigating committee or other person to be sent to inquire into and ascertain the truth, as is customary in such cases.

We know those aspersions to be false, but that avails us nothing. We are condemned unheard and forced to an issue with an armed, mercenary mob, which has been sent against us at the instigation of anonymous letter writers ashamed to father the base, slanderous falsehoods which they have given to the public; of corrupt officials who have brought false accusation against us to screen themselves in their own infamy; and of hireling priests and howling editors who prostitute the truth for filthy lucre's sake.

The issue which has been thus forced upon us compels us to resort to the great first law of self preservation and stand in our own defence, a right guaranteed unto us by the genius of the institutions of our country, and upon which the Government is based.

Our duty to ourselves, to our families, requires us not to tamely submit to be driven and slain, without an attempt to preserve ourselves. Our duty to our country, our holy religion, our God, to freedom and liberty, requires that we should not quietly stand still and see those fetters forging around, which are calculated to enslave and bring us in subjection to an unlawful military despotism such as can only emanate [in a country of Constitutional law] from usurpation, tyranny, and oppression.

Therefore I, Brigham Young, Governor and Superintendent of Indian Affairs for the Territory of Utah, in the name of the People of the United States in the Territory of Utah,

1st:—Forbid all armed forces, of every description, from coming into this Territory under any pretence whatever.

2d:—That all the forces in said Territory hold themselves in readiness to march, at a moment's notice, to repel any and all such invasion.

3d:—Martial law is hereby declared to exist in this Territory, from and after the publication of this Proclamation; and no person shall be allowed to pass, or repass into, or through, or from this Territory, without a permit from the proper officer.

{ L. S. }

Given under my hand and seal at Great Salt Lake City, Territory of Utah, this fifteenth day of September, A. D. Eighteen hundred and fifty seven and of the Independence of the United States of America the eighty second.

BRIGHAM YOUNG.

Brigham Young's 1857 proclamation forbidding the entrance of U.S. troops into Utah. The declaration effectively severed all ties with America and initiated the 1857/58 Utah War.

When Johnston finally arrived on the outskirts of Utah in November to take control of the forces now gathering there, he immediately knew his campaign would be difficult. Not only had his army's supplies been heavily plundered by Mormon raids, but there existed only two feasible ways for a large, heavily supplied unit to enter Young's territory—either through Echo Canyon, near present-day I-80; or Northward from Soda Springs, where the Bear River cut through the mountains. Both points of access were highly defensible.

Moreover, the winter blizzards had started and temperatures were already falling below zero. So before making any offensive moves, he pitched his army just outside Utah, establishing a base of operations called Camp Scott. The Colonel originally had planned to stay at nearby Fort Bridger. But this fortification was torched by its Mormon occupants before they abandoned it. These ruins would serve as the Saints' point of tolerance. Mormon officers were ordered to "make the first attack" if Johnston's men made an attempt to march west of the burned out post.[10] But as long the army stayed east of the old fort, they would remain unmolested.

Brigham's hope was that full-scale battles could be avoided by simply keeping the soldiers at bay long enough for the canyons to fill with snow, which in turn would block any invasion attempts. By spring, according to Young's plan, other pressing issues might distract Uncle Sam, prompting U.S. troops to withdraw. Johnston, understandably, was more than content to do nothing more than set up a safe and secure camp near Fort Bridger. In late 1857, his main concern was keeping his men alive, seeing to the safety of the new governor and his wife, and preparing for a long winter, after which time he would make a frontal assault on Salt Lake City. He knew it would be a bloody charge, but the expected arrival of perhaps 4,000 reinforcements would enable him to ultimately defeat Young's Nauvoo Legion, which numbered at least 7,000 soldiers.

A cold war of sorts ensued, with Young going so far as to taunt Johnston through letters sent by messenger. Johnston, although aching for a fight, had no choice but to bide his time at Camp Scott, an uncomfortable sprawl of tents and crude shacks. But nothing would deter him from finishing his mission. Johnston wrote Washington, saying:

> The Mormons have placed themselves in rebellion against the Union, and entertain the insane design of establishing a form of government thoroughly despotic, and utterly repugnant to our institutions . . . . I have ordered that wherever they are met in arms, that they be treated as enemies.[11]

Meanwhile, the anti-government rhetoric and bravado in Salt Lake City resounded from the church pulpit every Sunday. Orson Hyde remarked: "Whatever explanation may be given to the present movement of troops for Utah is immaterial. . . . The kingdom and government of God are the only legitimate jurisdiction that ever did exist."[12] Hyde promised that if the Saints remained faithful, the U.S. forces would be annihilated, or as Hyde put it, ground "to atoms."[13] Erastus Snow claimed the U.S. troop movement was nothing but another attempt expel the Mormons from their homes.[14]

Wilford Woodruff, however, gave assurances that the Saints had nothing to fear. "If the United States make war upon this people, the Lord will hold them responsible for it," he said. "[I]f they are ripe and the cup of their iniquity full, they will be shattered to pieces—their union broken up and destroyed. They will be visited with thunder and lightning and hail and the judgments of God."[15]

Brigham aimed his verbal attacks primarily at government officials, who were leading their troops and the Saints toward death. As far back as 1855, Young had called for blood atonement as the means by which Washington politicians and various other enemies would be punished:

> I will tell you how much I love those characters. If they had any respect to their own welfare, they would come forth and say, whether Joseph Smith was a Prophet or not, "We shed his blood, and now let us atone for it;" and they would be willing to have their heads chopped off, that their blood might run upon the ground, and the smoke of it rise before the Lord as an incense for their sins.[16]

Johnston's men, although none of them had their "heads chopped off," still bore a great deal of suffering. The winter of 1857 was terribly harsh and Camp Scott soon became known as Camp Death. Temperatures at the site repeatedly plunged to minus thirty degrees. "Horses, mules and cattle died in their tracks. Some wandered into campfires and refused to move though they were literally roasting."[17] The final march to Fort Bridger had itself been an ordeal, as Col. Cooke reported: "[T]he earth . . . contains scarcely a wolf to glut itself on the hundreds of dead and frozen animals which for thirty miles block the road."[18]

Making matters worse for Johnston's men was a frightening lack of security. Mormons actually had infiltrated the camp and were almost daily reporting back to Young about the army's condition and plans. On one occasion Young needled Johnston about his embarrassing plight by sending eight hundred pounds of salt to the Camp Scott as a gift. Mormon spies had informed their prophet that Johnston's army was out of the preservative. The gift came with a note assuring the commander that the salt was not laced with any "deleterious ingredients." Johnston rejected the offering because it had come from an enemy of his government.[19]

AN UNEASY TRUCE

The Saints were never going to surrender to the evil forces on their doorstep. According to Young and other LDS leaders, they would not have to because God was on their side. They were in the hands of the Almighty and he would be the one to fight their battles for them no matter how many troops were sent.[20] Since the first day the Saints learned that American soldiers were on the way, church members were assured that they would remain free of U.S. tyranny, or as Young promised, would "die in trying."[21] Heber C. Kimball asserted the following:

> Send 2,500 troops here, our brethren, to make a desolation of this people! God Almighty helping me, I will fight until there is not a drop of blood in my veins. Good God! I have wives enough to whip out the United States.[22]

Young's alternative plan, should the U.S. troops succeed in their offensive, was to flee to the mountains and burn Salt Lake City (as well as everything else in Utah) to the ground. Young went so far as to move "every willing inhabitant of Utah south" in preparations for the capital city's destruction.[23] On September 13, 1857, the Mormon prophet counseled his flock to be fully ready to see the destruction of their possessions, or else suffer the consequences:

> [W]hen the time comes to burn and lay waste our improvements, if any man undertakes to shield his, he will be sheared down. . . . [T]here shall not be one building, nor one foot of lumber, nor a stick, nor a tree, nor a particle of grass and hay, that will burn, left in reach of our enemies. I am sworn, if driven to extremity, to utterly lay waste, in the name of Israel's God.[24]

Fortunately, an opportunity to avoid such drastic measures came to Salt Lake City in February 1858, with the arrival of Thomas L. Kane, an unofficial emissary from President Buchanan.[25] Kane had earned Mormon friendship in 1846 as the mastermind behind President James Polk's offer to "enlist a battalion of five hundred Mormons to serve in the Mexican War," which largely financed the church's move to Utah a year later.[26] The young Democrat (35-years-old), far wiser and more diplomatic than many politicians, pled with Young for twelve days to accept Buchanan's generous offer: If the church would accept a new governor and allow the U.S. army to camp near Salt Lake City, a full pardon would be given to all Mormons for their various acts of rebellion and treason. This offer, however, was refused and Kane left on March 8.

But on that very day Young received a message that changed his mind. Word came from northern Utah that more than 200 Bannock and Shoshoni warriors had attacked Fort Limhi, a Mormon stronghold. They stole approximately two hundred head of cattle and as many as thirty horses. Two Mormons were killed and five others wounded.[27] The Indian uprising doomed Young's overall plan, which was to have the entire Mormon community flee from Johnston's invading army. But now the northern settlements were no longer safe. So on March 9, Young dispatched a letter to Kane, saying that he had changed his mind. Buchanan's offer would be

Engraving of Col. Sidney Johnston leading his 2,500 U.S. troops through Salt Lake City as a show of federal authority of Utah at the close of the 1857/58 Utah War (from T.B.H. Stenhouse, *The Rocky Mountain Saints*, 1873).

accepted. To show his goodwill, Young sent Johnston's starving troops two hundred head of cattle and twenty thousand pounds of flour.[28]

Four weeks later, Alfred Cumming entered Salt Lake City, under a Mormon escort. He made his first address (to a very hostile LDS crowd) in the tabernacle on Sunday, April 25, 1858. Young himself introduced Cumming as the new governor.[29] As for Johnston, after entering Utah he and his men went south to Cedar Valley to set up Camp Floyd, where they remained as a sort of peacekeeping force. Before departing the area, however, Johnston marched his entire 2,500-man force through the streets of Salt Lake City from about 10:00 a.m. to 5:30 p.m. as a show of federal authority.[30] The Utah War, a bloodless conflict, had ended. As Governor Cumming declared: "[P]eace is restored to our territory."[31]

Governor Cumming held his position for three years. Although not an ideal leader, he did seek to treat with fairness Mormon feelings as well as Gentile concerns. If anything he may have been a bit too yielding to the Mormons, who often manipulated him using their knowledge of his desire to maintain peace at almost any cost. Other federal appointees, however, refused to coddle the Mormons. There was 39-year-old John

The Bugle Corp of Johnston's Army at Camp Floyd (c. 1859, courtesy Utah State Historical Society).

Cradlebaugh, for instance, an attorney from Circleville, Ohio. He arrived in November 1858 to be a territorial supreme court judge.

Cradlebaugh seemed determined to immediately bring to trial all persons connected with the Mountain Meadows Massacre, the Aiken murders, and several other crimes. To accomplish his goal, he impaneled a grand jury and took sworn testimonies. It turned out to be a depressing affair as witnesses called by the court were "threatened and intimidated" by other Mormons. Some of them were so terrified that they "burst into tears in open court." Others fled town "compelled to fly from reasonably expected violence."[32]

The judge even called upon Johnston and his men (at least 200 of them) to help make arrests. But federal authorities were completely frustrated in their efforts to capture persons suspected of the many criminal acts that had been perpetrated since Utah gained territorial status. U. S. Marshal P. K. Dotson, in an letter to Cradlebaugh, explained:

> [I]t is not in my power to execute any of these processes. . . . So great is
> the number of persons engaged in the commission of these crimes, and

such the feeling of the Mormon Church, and the community in their favor, that I cannot rely on a civil posse to aid me in arresting them.[33]

Consider, too, the following statement from the remarks of Judge Cradlebaugh himself, who was forced to release his Grand Jury from further service in 1859:

> There seems to be a combined effort on the part of the community to screen the murderers from the punishment due for the murder they have committed. . . . [W]hen officers seek to arrest persons accused of crimes they are not able to do so; the parties are screened and secreted by the community. . . . Witnesses are screened; others are intimidated by persons in that community. . . . Such acts and conduct go to show that the community there do not desire to have criminals punished.[34]

Cradlebaugh's crusade ended when Cumming wrote to Washington, saying that the zealous judge's desire to bring justice to the land would only incite more rebellion and result in more bloodshed. Buchanan's decision to heed Cumming's words ended for many years the search for persons guilty of major crimes including: John D. Lee, Isaac Haight, Porter Rockwell, and dozens of others. All of them walked Utah streets knowing they had been granted virtual immunity.

To add insult to injury, Johnston was ordered to free the few Mormons he actually had managed to apprehend. Marshal Dotson in turn fired off an angry resignation to Buchanan, warning him that such actions would only strengthen Young's political and ecclesiastical powers.[35] But the U.S. government had far more important matters with which to deal; namely, those issues connected to the approaching Civil War.

BROTHER AGAINST BROTHER

Abraham Lincoln became the sixteenth U.S. president on March 4, 1861. But he did not inherit an undivided nation. Three months earlier South Carolina had seceded from the United States, followed eight weeks later by Mississippi, Florida, Alabama, Georgia, Louisiana and Texas.

These states eventually formed the Confederacy, under the leadership of their president, Jefferson Davis. Slavery and states' rights, once mere topics of heated debate, had evolved over the years into causes for which men would die. And so, barely a week after Lincoln was sworn into office, the Civil War began with a Confederate attack on Fort Sumter in Virginia. When four more states—Virginia, North Carolina, Arkansas, and Tennessee—seceded, the battle lines had clearly been drawn between the North and the South. America had been torn in two.

Meanwhile, Utah residents, especially Brigham Young, kept tabs on the conflict with bated breath. Prophecy, it seemed, was finally coming to pass. America was crumbling just as Joseph Smith had predicted in his "White Horse" prophecy (see Introduction), which had been cited by Brigham during the Saints' 1854 Independence Day celebration:

> Will the Constitution be destroyed? No: it will be held inviolate by this people; and, as Joseph Smith said, "The time will come when the destiny of the nation will hang upon a single thread. At that critical juncture, this people will step forth and save it from the threatened destruction." It will be so.[36]

According to Mormon opinion, then, America's destruction and Christ's appearing were both near at hand thanks to the 1861 Civil War. Consequently, no Saint was surprised, or sorrowful, over the tragedy that had engulfed the nation. Just one month after Lincoln took office, Young told his church that Joseph had been right all along:

> [God] is about to fulfil the prophecies of his ancient and modern Prophets. He will bring the nations into judgment, and deal with them and make a full end of them. . . . The whole Government is gone . . . I heard Joseph Smith say, nearly thirty years ago, "They shall have mobbing to their heart's content, if they do not redress the wrongs of the Latter-day Saints." . . . [E]ventually it will be State against State, city against city, neighbourhood against neighbourhood.[37]

Heber C. Kimball went so far as to promise that after all the secessions had ceased, in the end, the Mormons would come out as the sole rulers over every other government:

The South will secede from the North, and the North will secede from us, and God will make this people free as fast as we are able to bear it .... The day is not far distant when you will see us as free as the air we breathe, and we will be ruled by those men whom God Almighty appoints. . . . . We are going to be ruled by our Father in heaven, and the agents he sends and appoints for us, from this day henceforth and forever.[38]

Giving credence to this view was a prophecy Joseph Smith had uttered all the way back on December 25, 1832, while still living in Kirtland, Ohio. It actually seemed to predict the Civil War. This prophecy is still touted by twenty-first century Mormons "as a vindication of the prophetic powers of Joseph Smith."[39] The importance of the prophecy cannot be overstated since Smith himself declared that the information it contains came by way of an audible voice that spoke to him while he was deep in prayer.[40] Consequently, it deserves some degree of inspection.

SMITH'S CIVIL WAR PROPHECY

Although transcribed in 1832, this prophecy did not appear in any LDS publication until 1851 (in the *Pearl of Great Price*), and then again in 1854 (in *The Seer*). On both occasions, however, it was not considered holy scripture, as it is today. Only after the Civil War, when republished in the 1876 edition of *Doctrine and Covenants*, did the prediction receive scriptural status. When originally published in 1851 and 1854 it read as follows (bracketed numbers for reference purposes):

Verily thus saith the Lord, concerning the [1] wars that will shortly come to pass [2] beginning at the rebellion of South Carolina which will eventually terminate in the death and misery of many souls, and the days will come that [3] war will be poured out upon all Nations beginning at this place for behold the southern states shall be divided against the Northern States, and [4] the Southern States will call on other Nation[s] even the Nation of Great Britain as it is called and they shall also call upon other Nations in order to defend themselves against other Nations and thus war shall be poured out upon all Nations and it shall come to pass after many days [5] Slaves shall rise up against their Masters who shall be Marshaled and disciplined for war [6] and it shall come to pass also that the remnants who are left of the land will martial [marshal] themselves also and shall become exceeding angry and shall vex the Gentiles with a sore vexation and [7] thus with the sword and by bloodshed the inhabitants of the earth shall mourn and with famine and plague, and Earthquake and the thunder of heaven and the fierce and vivid lightning also shall the inhabitants of the earth be made to feel the wrath and indignation and chastening hand of an Almighty God until the consumption decreed hath made a full end of all Nations that the cry of the saints and of the blood of the saints shall cease to come up into the ears of the Lord of Sabaoth from the earth to be avenged of their enemies wherefore stand ye in holy places and be not moved until the day of the Lord come, for be hold it cometh quickly saith the Lord.[41]

A cursory reading of this prophecy would indeed seem to indicate that Joseph had an uncanny ability to foretell the future. But upon closer examination, the prediction falls significantly short of having any marks of divine foreknowledge, especially when considered in its historical context. In other words, in 1832 a civil war beginning with South Carolina would have surprised no one. It actually would have been more impressive to predict that a violent conflict between South Carolina and the federal government would *not* erupt within the near future.

First [1], just four weeks before Smith's so-called "prophecy" South Carolina had passed a tariff nullification ordinance (November 24, 1832), which invalidated "certain acts of the Congress of the United States."[42] Before that, in October, President Andrew Jackson actually had alerted U.S. forts in South Carolina for a possible confrontation. The president then made a December 10 proclamation that called the nullification movement absurd. He further pointed out that leaving the Union by force was nothing less than treason.[43] These comments were understandable since South Carolina already had organized regiments to fight against the federal government.[44]

Second [2], Smith's prediction merely echoed what every newspaper in America had been saying all through 1832. For example, the semiweekly *Morning Courier and New York Enquirer* ran five front page stories in three separate 1832 issues: September 8, December 8, and December 22. Each article expressed concern over a possible civil war, the Union's solidity, and treason.[45] Only ten miles from Smith's own home, the *Painesville Telegraph* ran a December 21, 1832, article titled "The Crisis," which detailed fears of a possible civil war and the Union's delicate state.[46] There is no question that the Saints monitored these periodicals. In fact, Smith's own newspaper, *The Evening and the Morning Star*, as far back as June 1832 repeatedly cited the *Morning Courier* and *New York Enquirer.*[47]

Third [3], Smith predicted South Carolina conflict would bring war to "all Nations." Obviously, a global catastrophe did not result from the Civil War. To excuse the falsity of this "all Nations" phrase, today's Mormons assert that Smith's words at this point refer to World Wars I and II, which allegedly somehow came about due to the North-South conflict.[48] But as Marvin W. Cowan observed in *Mormon Claims Answered* (1997): "[T]here is no more relationship between the Civil War and World Wars I and II than there is between the Spanish-American War and the Vietnam War!"[49]

Fourth [4], the southern states did indeed ask Great Britain for help against the Union, as Smith predicted. But contrary to the prophecy, Great Britain did not get directly involved in the Civil War, nor did Britain call on other countries "to defend themselves against other Nations."

Fifth [5], the Civil War did not result from slaves rising up *en masse* against their masters, as the prophecy foretells. The conflict emerged out of disagreements between whites. It cannot even be said that after the war began, all blacks rebelled. Some slaves actually fought for the Confederacy. Professor Ed Smith, director of American Studies at American University, calculated that Stonewall Jackson had 3,000 fully equipped black troops scattered throughout his corps at Antietam—the war's bloodiest battle. It has been further estimated that "between 60,000 and 93,000 blacks served the Confederacy in some capacity."[50]

Sixth [6], "the remnants," defined by Smith and Mormon doctrine as the Lamanites (i.e., Native Americans) did not "vex the Gentiles with a sore vexation" as a result of the Civil War. History, in fact, proves that the Indians were the ones, who for the most part, ended up being abused (or vexed) by the Gentiles.

Seventh [7], all nations did not come to a "full end" because of the Civil War, neither did the nations experience any marked increase in "famine and plague, and Earthquake and the thunder of heaven and the fierce and vivid lightning."

During the 1860s most of this information could not be discerned by the Latter-day Saints. Consequently, they remained confident that the end was near. But as Mormon expert Sandra Tanner has said, today we know that the statements in Smith's revelation about a war beginning at the rebellion of South Carolina "was probably inspired by the fact that South Carolina had *already* rebelled before the revelation was given."[51]

YEARS OF WAITING

Because the Saints saw the Civil War as a fulfillment of prophecy, its horrors actually brought them some degree of emotional satisfaction and comfort. They viewed the tragic conflict as judgment from God and the initial stages of their deliverance. In 1857, for instance, Orson Hyde preached: "Do I believe that the United States will be divided? Yes, I do; and the prayers of all the Saints throughout the world should be to that effect."[52] Brigham Young University history professor, Eugene E. Campbell, explains in *Establishing Zion* that the Saints steadfastly believed the battle between the North and South would open up a way for them to take back Missouri:

> Mormon leaders consistently expressed their feelings that the war had been brought on by the wickedness of the United States, which had rejected Mormonism and permitted the death of the prophet of God and his servants. . . . Although the waste of lives was lamentable, a war between the states would avenge the death of Joseph Smith. The Saints seemed especially gratified that Jackson County was a war zone and that Missouri would suffer the penalty of its cruelties to the Mormons. Besides avenging the blood of the innocent, the Lord would also prepare the way before his coming, which Mormons believed would occur in

Jackson County, Missouri. . . . William Clayton wrote that such a spirit seemed to operate on Brigham Young's mind: "All Latter-day Saints will not stay here [in Utah] forever. He [Young] talks much and frequently about Jackson County, Missouri."[53]

Utah's citizens also rejoiced over the fact that Johnston and his soldiers left Utah by July 1861, in order to join whichever side, North or South, was tugging at their allegiance. Kentucky-born Col. Johnston, ironically, ended up fighting against the very government he had spent time defending in Utah. He eventually became the Confederacy's second highest-ranking general under Robert E. Lee. In 1862, Johnston bled to death after being shot in the leg at the battle of Shiloh, where he almost defeated Ulysses S. Grant. His death on April 6, the anniversary of the Mormon church's organization, was interpreted by Mormons as a sign of divine judgment.

Although federal troops temporarily left Utah, politicians back east continued to aggravate Mormons with their appointees to government posts during this period. Some officials were less successful than others. John W. Dawson, for instance, who replaced Governor Cumming in late 1861, held his position only for nineteen days.[54] Dawson had no understanding of the territory or the people living in the territory. Consequently, he offended the Mormons immediately by:

1) seeking to levy against residents an annual "war tax" of $27,000;
2) calling for a survey of all land, to be put up for sale to settlers—land that "belonged" to God;
3) suggesting a form of public education for children more in line with the rest of the country;
4) vetoing a measure to form a "state" government in hopes of securing statehood.[55]

Shortly afterward, when Dawson tried to return to Indiana, he was confronted at the Mountain Dell stagecoach station by several Mormons and beaten so severely that he never fully recovered from his injuries.

Utah's third governor, Stephen S. Harding, did not appear on the

THE DESERET ALPHABET
In an effort to further identify Utah and the Mormons as a distinct nation and people from America and U.S. citizens, Brigham Young attempted to introduce a new alphabet to the Saints. Although a few text-books and the *Book of Mormon* were translated into this new script, the plan was a complete failure. The 1868 title page (*left*) reads "The Deseret First Book by the Regents of the Deseret University." Page three (*right*) shows the characters of the alphabet. Young also hoped that the new language would help foreign converts to more easily communicate with Utah Saints.

scene until July 1862, nearly six months after Dawson had fled. Like his predecessor, Harding was reviled by the Mormons and soon discovered one of the hallmarks of their religion—hatred for the U.S. government. After only six weeks, in a letter to Washington, he told of the curious position Mormons had taken with regard to the Civil War. It was almost beyond Harding's belief:

> Brigham Young and other preachers are constantly inculcating in the minds of the crowded audiences who sit beneath their teachings every Sabbath that the United States is of no consequence, that it lies in ruins, and that the prophecy of Joseph Smith is being fulfilled to the letter.

According to the prophecy, the United States as a nation is to be destroyed. That the Gentiles, as they call all persons outside of their church, will continue to fight with each other until they perish and then the Saints are to step in and quietly enjoy the possession of the land and also what is left of the ruined cities and desolated places. And that Zion is to be built up, not only in the valleys and the mountains but the great center of their power and glory is to be in Missouri where the Saints under the lead of their prophet were expelled many years ago.[56]

Harding also observed a shocking level of cold-heartedness among the Mormons toward the anguish and suffering taking place due to the war. For several Sundays in a row he attended church services and saw the Saints consistently "wink and chuckle" over each Civil War tragedy detailed for them from the pulpit.[57] Harding, appalled by their utter lack of sympathy, wrote:

In all the meetings that I have attended, not one word, not one prayer, has been uttered or offered up for the saving of our cause and for the restoration of peace, but on the contrary the God of the Saints has been implored to bring swift destruction on all nations, peoples, and institutions that stand in the way of the triumph of this people.[58]

The new governor also heard Heber C. Kimball state that the government of the United States was "dead, thank God, dead." Kimball then added that those who survived the Civil War would simply be destroyed by pestilence, famine, and earthquake; a sentiment to which the crowds "sent up a hearty Amen."[59] According to Eugene Campbell, Brigham had some choice words of his own to say about the war and America's future:

[Brigham] taught followers that the governments of the earth were false and should be overthrown, that God had only delegated to the priesthood the right to set up a government. God would appoint a ruler, and all persons who otherwise pretended to have authority to govern were usurpers. Young was said to have asserted that although the Constitution of the United States was a revelation, it had fulfilled its purpose—the formation of a government so that the Mormon church could be organized. According to Young, slavery had nothing to do with the present disturbances, which were in consequence of the persecution the Saints had suffered at the hands of the American people.[60]

Union Army officer Col. Patrick E. Conner concurred with Harding after coming to Salt Lake City, in September 1862. His assignment was to protect the Overland Mail Route through Utah to California. In a September 14 report to his commanding general in San Francisco, Conner expressed absolute disgust for Mormons, their society, and their attitude toward America:

> So as to make you realize the enormity of Mormonism suffice it that I found them a community of traitors, murderers, fanatics, and whores. The people publicly rejoice at the reverse to our arms and thank God that the American government is gone as they term it, while their prophet and bishops preach treason from the pulpit. Federal officers are entirely powerless and talk in whispers for fear of being overheard by Brigham's spies. Brigham Young rules with despotic sway and death by assassination is the penalty of disobedience to his command.[61]

Conner's observations, coupled with similar reports from others, led Washington, D.C., officials to agree that the Mormons had to be guarded. Only by keeping a watchful eye on them could the feds be sure that the church would not destabilize the Union any further in an effort to fulfill prophecy. Orders soon came for Conner to set up Camp Douglas, a base of operations overlooking Salt Lake City from which both the Overland mail and the Mormons could be monitored.[62] Utah was again under the watchful eye of the military.

The situation, however, according to LDS leaders, would not last for long. "The sayings of Joseph Smith are being literally fulfilled," Young promised. "Joseph Smith told the nations of the earth what would be their doom, unless they stopped rebelling against the kingdom of God" [i.e., Mormonism]."[63] Such assurances continued relentlessly throughout the war:

April, 1861: "[T]he North and the South will exert themselves against each other, and ere long the whole face of the United States will be in commotion, fighting one against another, and they will destroy their nationality. . . . I know that dissolution, sorrow, weeping, and distress are in store for the inhabitants of the United States, because of their conduct towards the people of God. . . . [Y]ou will strive to prepare for those things that are coming upon the earth in these last days."[64]

July, 1862: "[T]he things which the Lord has promised unto us thirty years ago are now being fulfilled to the very letter. . . . I copied a revelation more than twenty-five years ago, in which it is stated that war should be in the south and in the north, and that nation after nation would become embroiled in the tumult and excitement, until war should be poured out upon the whole earth, and that this war would commence at the rebellion of South Carolina. . . . These things are beginning to be made manifest, but the end is not yet; but it will come. . . . Who can stay this war that is devastating the whole nation both North and South? No human hand; it is out of the power of man, excepting by the repentance of the whole nation . . . . Will there ever be any more peace among them? No, not until the earth is drenched with the blood of the inhabitants thereof."[65]

June, 1863: "If a thousand Prophets had proclaimed to this nation what has come to pass since 1860 to the present time, who would have believed them? Not a man, unless they possessed the spirit of revelation. What the Prophet Joseph Smith foretold thirty years ago is now come to pass; and who can help it? . . . [T]he Lord has laid his hand on the nation. It is a consolation to the Saints when they contemplate upon what God has spoken through his servants which is now being fulfilled before their eyes. All that has been spoken by ancient and modern Prophets have had their fulfilment until now, and will have until the scene is wound up [i.e., the world ends]."[66]

Brigham Young during his final years (from *Brigham Young,* 1925).

But on April 9, 1865, as Mormon leaders patiently waited for their chance to come forth and save the Constitution, General Robert E. Lee surrendered his Confederate Army to Gen. Ulysses S. Grant at Appomattox, Virginia. The Civil War was over, and the nation reunited—but at a terrible cost. Approximately 620,000 Americans were killed, more losses than have been recorded in all other American wars combined from the Revolution War through Vietnam. About 50,000 survivors returned to their homes as amputees.[67]

As for the Mormons, they had not sent a single soldier into the conflict, but instead had prayed for Christ's return and the establishment of Zion. Lee's surrender indicated that neither expectation would transpire.

Nevertheless, in 1868, one day before the third anniversary of the Civil War's end, Brigham still had the temerity to promise his Salt Lake congregation that the end was near:

> [O]ur government, the best government in the world, is crumbling to pieces. Those who have it in their hands are the ones who are destroying it. How long will it be before the words of the prophet Joseph will be fulfilled? He said if the Constitution of the United States were saved at all it must be done by this people. It will not be many years before these words come to pass.[68]

Such rhetoric eventually was worked into a set of revised teachings on the Civil War that categorized the conflict as "just the beginning" of God's judgments near the end of the world, rather than the actual unfolding of the end of the world itself. Even so, toward the end of 1868 Orson Pratt continued making end of the world predictions:

> [New York City] will in a few years become a mass of ruins. . . . [T]here are some in this congregation who will live, to behold the fulfillment of these other things, and will visit the ruins of mighty towns and cities scattered over the face of this land destitute and desolate of inhabitants.[69]

By 1870, however, Mormon leaders had to admit that America was not on the verge of annihilation. The very opposite, in fact, was true. The Western frontier finally was being tamed from Wyoming to California. New states—e.g., Kansas (1861), Nevada (1864), and Nebraska (1867)—were being added to the Union, while at the same time Utah's size was being dramatically cut down by the federal government. And a new U.S. president, Ulysses S. Grant, was determined to bring all territories, especially Utah, into conformity with the rest of the nation. More significantly, an aging Brigham Young was nearing the end of his life.

THE END OF AN ERA

By the time Brigham reached his twilight years in the 1870s he had lived through some of the most tumultuous and progressive times in

American history. During his tenure as Mormonism's highest authority he saw the gold rush (c. 1848-1852); the migration of tens of thousands of Saints to Utah; the initiation and failure of the U.S. Pony Express mail system (1860/61); the completion of the first transcontinental railroad (1869); the founding of two major religious sects (Seventh-day Adventism and Christian Science); the admission of ten new states to the Union; two U.S. wars; and the terms of eight American presidents.[70] Through it all he never wavered in his faith.

But profound events were taking place in and around Utah that would eventually bring drastic changes to Mormonism as a religion and Mormon society as a whole:

- Blacks were emancipated (1860s), which in less than a hundred years would result in a backlash against Mormonism's racist spirituality;
- the Nauvoo Legion was outlawed and disbanded by federal orders (1870/71);
- more gentiles were migrating to Utah via the transcontinental railroad (Union-Pacific, 1869) and bringing with them new businesses, new ideas, and a new vision of Utah's future;
- federal law enforcement personnel were beginning to clamp down on Utah violence and earnestly seeking to bring Mormon criminals to justice;
- non-Mormon newspapers and magazines, which were beginning to be published in Utah, included exposés and criticisms of LDS leaders and Mormon beliefs.[71]

Brigham knew that these changes would bring many challenges. But he had every intention of meeting them head on. In fact, as late as his 76th birthday in June 1877, Young was keeping a highly active schedule. He seemed in excellent health. But then on August 23, he suddenly began experiencing severe nausea, vomiting, abdominal cramps, and an elevated temperature. Six days later, despite the prayers of his followers and the care of his best physicians, Brigham Young died. He had contracted what doctors back then called *cholera morbus*, a now non-existent diagnosis covering numerous gastrointestinal disorders.

On September 1, 1877, more than twenty-five thousand mourners paid one last visit to their beloved prophet in the Salt Lake City tabernacle. During the funeral, Daniel H. Wells described Young as "a friend to God . . . and a friend to humanity." Apostle George Q. Cannon said the church's Prophet, Seer, and Revelator was "the brain, the eye, the ear, the mouth, and hand for the entire people of the Church." Cannon added: "Nothing was too small for his mind; nothing was too large."[72] But the *Salt Lake Tribune*, a non-Mormon paper, voiced an entirely different opinion, noting that Young had for years unscrupulously used "the ignorance and credulity of his followers" to silence dissenters and prevent the execution of U.S. laws.[73] Adherents to both views agreed that Young's death marked the passing of fearless and dedicated leader.

Young left behind not only an incredible legacy of frontier accomplishments, but also a terribly controversial spiritual belief system that would, among other things, continue hindering Utah's bid for statehood. Besides blood atonement, the Mormon doctrine still offending American politicians and society was polygamy. This way of life, after all, had in 1856 been branded by Republicans as one of the "twin relics" of barbarism; the other relic being slavery. One had been crushed via the Civil War. The other would eventually be obliterated by political maneuvering. Brigham, of course, did not live to see polygamy's demise. That would not happen until more than a dozen years after his death, after the turbulent administrations of his two successors—John Taylor (third LDS president) and Wilford Woodruff (fourth LDS president).

THIRTEEN

Unholy Matrimony

We shall pull the wool over the eyes of the American people and
make them swallow Mormonism, polygamy and all.

Brigham Young (1875)[1]

NOT UNTIL THREE YEARS AFTER BRIGHAM'S DEATH, on October 10, 1880, did
sixty-nine-year-old John Taylor become Mormonism's new president. He
already had been leading the Saints as president of the Quorum of the
Twelve Apostles, but his official appointment to the church's presidency
was temporarily delayed by a disagreement among LDS apostles over
who should take Young's place.[2] Taylor was eminently qualified for the
job. He had joined the church in 1836, was ordained an apostle at age
thirty, and was with Joseph and Hyrum on the fateful day of their murder, he himself being wounded in the gunfire.

Taylor also was a staunch polygamist; one of the first apostles
allowed to enjoy the "privilege" of taking multiple wives. In fact, by the
time Taylor became church president in 1880, his household included
fifteen wives—considerably less, of course, than Brigham's collection
of fifty-five women. Taylor, like Young, vehemently condemned Washington, D.C., for attempting to curtail Mormon plural marriage, which
by the time of his administration had become a hallmark of Mormonism.[3]

But such was not always the case. Polygamy, when first introduced
by Smith, remained a closely guarded secret told only to Joseph's most
trusted allies (see Chapter Nine)—those "few that could bear it."[4] Smith
himself allegedly had a difficult time accepting plural marriage, acqui-

escing only after God commanded it of him. The prophet also said that the Lord went so far as to send to him an angel carrying a drawn sword with which Joseph would be slain if he did not take another wife.[5] He, therefore, reluctantly obeyed.

Ebenezer Robinson, recalled that the doctrine of multiple wives was talked about privately in Nauvoo as early as 1841, and that he was invited to join the select participants in 1843. Robinson recounted how Smith's brother initiated him into the elite group:

> [Hyrum] instructed me in Nov or Dec 1843 to make a selection of some young woman and he would seal her to me, and I should take her home, and if she should have an offspring [I was to] give out word that she had a husband, an Elder, who had gone on a foreign mission.[6]

Because secrecy had to be maintained, church leaders actually designated a place in Iowa (about a dozen or so miles from Nauvoo), where impregnated plural wives were sent to be shielded from inquisitive Gentiles.[7] Another subterfuge Joseph used to protect himself was to have his women feign marriage to other men. Historian George D. Smith related how Joseph resorted to this tactic during his marriage to seventeen-year-old Sarah Ann Whitney:

> She disguised her relationship to the prophet by pretending to marry Joseph Corodon Kingsbury . . . . Kingsbury wrote: "I according to Pres. Joseph Smith & Council & others agreed to stand by Sarah Ann Whitney as though I was supposed to be her husband and [participated in] a pretended marriage for the purpose of . . . [b]ringing about the purposes of God in these last days . . ." Three weeks later, while in hiding, Joseph Smith wrote a revealing letter which he addressed to her parents . . . inviting them to bring their daughter to visit him "just back of Brother Hyrums farm." He advised Brother Whitney to "come a little a head and nock [sic] at the south East corner of the house at the window." He assured them, especially Sarah Ann, that "it is the will of God that you should comfort me now." He stressed the need for care "to find out when Emma comes," but

"when she is not here, there is the most perfect safty [sic]." The prophet warned them to "burn this letter as soon as you read it."[8]

Not every woman, however, yielded to polygamy. Orson Pratt's first wife, Sarah, after leaving her husband and the church, declared plural marriage the "direst curse;" one that completely demoralized good men, and made bad men correspondingly worse. She added: "As for the women, well, God help them."[9] Sarah herself had been propositioned by Joseph, which partly led to her rejection of Mormonism. An 1886 interview with her enlightened many readers:

> [Joseph] used to state to his intended victims, as he did to me: "*God does not care if we have a good time, if only other people do not know it.*" He only introduced a marriage ceremony when he found out he could not get certain women without it. . . . If any woman, like me, opposed his wishes, he used to say: "Be silent, or I shall ruin your character. My character must be sustained in the interest of the Church."[10]

Despite such conduct, Mormonism's founder boldly denied all reports linking him to polygamy and/or adultery, especially if they came from dissidents, whom he denounced as shameless liars. Consider, for example, Joseph's May 26, 1844, public response to his accusers:

> [William Law] swears that I have committed adultery. I wish the grand jury would tell me who they are. . . I am quite tired of the fools asking me. A man asked me whether the commandment was given that a man may have seven wives. . . . I am innocent of all these charges. . . . What a thing it is for a man to be accused of committing adultery, and having seven wives, when I can only find one. I am the same man, and as innocent as I was fourteen years ago; and I can prove them all perjurers.[11]

When Smith made these statements, he indeed did not have seven wives. He had at least thirty-three wives, and using a more liberal estimate from *Dialogue: A Journal of Mormon Thought*, perhaps as many as forty wives.[12] Many of these women actually were teenaged girls acquired by Smith when he was well into his thirties. Nevertheless, Joseph's public renunciations of polygamy continued until his death. He also concealed from the outside world the fact that some thirty other men were enjoying the so-called privilege, which resulted in about eighty-four plural marriages in Nauvoo.[13]

During the next several years, especially after the exodus from Nauvoo, while the Saints were encamped at Winter Quarters (c. 1846/47), the privilege of plural marriage gradually was extended to a broader segment of the LDS community.[14] Then, once Young's followers arrived in far-away Utah, plural marriage became *the* standard of righteous living and faithfulness to God. Most Mormons began openly talking about polygamy, as evidenced by Brigham Young's 1851 comment from the pulpit about his "wives."[15]

Predictably, non-Mormons passing through Utah (e.g., California miners, military personnel, emigrants) could not help but notice the peculiar living arrangements of numerous Saints. U.S. Army officer John Gunnison, for instance, observed that many Mormons had "a large number of wives" and that polygamy was "perfectly manifest to anyone residing long among them."[16] Such rumors, along with newspaper reports about life in Utah, eventually mandated that the Latter-day Saints cease denying their polygamy.

Finally, five years after the Mormons arrived in Salt Lake City, Smith's 1843 plurality of wives revelation was published. And on August 29, 1852, Orson Pratt preached the first official sermon on the subject. He maintained that it was not a doctrine embraced "to gratify the carnal lusts and feelings of man."[17] It had a far nobler purpose. To understand that purpose, though, one must be familiar with several other LDS doctrines: i.e., pre-existence, the multiplicity of gods, eternal progression, and celestial marriage.

All of these beliefs not only served as the basis for polygamy, but when taken in conjunction with plural marriage, formed a cohesive worldview adopted by Mormons—one still held today by Latter-day Saints. This worldview answers all of life's mysteries for Mormons. As

Brigham Young declared so long ago: "[T]here is not a truth on earth or in heaven, that is not embraced in 'Mormonism.' "[18]

THE WORLD ACCORDING TO MORMONISM[19]

Mormons believe that untold years before this planet had been created, there existed a god named Elohim (a.k.a. Heavenly Father) and his wife, who is known to us only as Heavenly Mother.[20] Co-existing with these two deities was a limitless amount of cosmic spirit matter known as "intelligence," out of which Elohim and Heavenly Mother made countless spirit babies via celestial sex.[21] Their ethereal unions somehow siphoned off portions of that great ocean of cosmic "intelligence" and clothed each of these portions with a spirit body. The resulting offspring not only bore their image, but had resident within them the potential for godhood, an attribute of Heavenly Father and Mother.[22] All of these spiritual children were reared with the utmost care into "grown spirit men and women" somewhere in the cosmos.[23]

Millennia after millennia the celestial clan dwelt together in harmony near a planet named "KOLOB (as yet undiscovered)," where one day roughly translates into 1,000 earth years.[24] There they lived and interacted very much like a large family would on planet earth. Earth, by the way, in this Mormon scenario, was fashioned as part of a joint creative project supervised by the most faithful of Heavenly Father's spiritual progeny (e.g., Jesus, Joseph Smith, Noah, Adam, John the Baptist, etc.). Elohim's other spirit children included: Lucifer, who would become the Devil (a.k.a. Satan); Napoleon; George Washington; Joseph Smith; Louis Armstrong, Donny and Marie Osmond, Senator Orrin Hatch, U.S. President George W. Bush, and everyone else who has ever lived on this planet.[25] In other words, all people, before being born on Earth, "pre-existed" with Heavenly Father and Mother near KOLOB. We are their spirit children in human form.

Furthermore, everyone who will ever be born on this planet are their spirit children, since the two celestial deities are continuing to expand their family even now. Here it must be noted, however, that although most of us were born to "Heavenly Mother," some of us may have been spiritually birthed by one of Elohim's other wives, since he is a polygamous god.[26]

According to Mormonism, the first of Heavenly Father's spirit children to come here were Adam and Eve. They arrived in order to do what all of us are supposed to do—i.e., travel along the route of "eternal progression" toward godhood. As gods, we in turn will be able to have our own spirit babies, who will then populate other worlds as they progress toward godhood, all the while giving us the kind of worship bestowed on Elohim, the god of this planet.

Elohim himself, as it turns out, progressed toward godhood in a similar manner. He is a man just like us, albeit an exalted, glorified, and perfected man, but nevertheless a man with "a body of flesh and bones."[27] Mormonism teaches that Elohim is a god "whose perfection consists in eternal advancement—a Being who has attained His exalted state by a path which now His children are permitted to follow, whose glory it is their heritage to share."[28]

Basically, we humans are enduring the same kind of circumstances Elohim went through on his route to deification.[29] Joseph Smith put it this way:

> God himself was once as we are now, and is an exalted Man. . . . [I]f you were to see him to-day, you would see him like a man in form. . . . God came to be God. . . . [T]he Father of us all, dwelt on an earth. . . . and you have got to learn how to be Gods yourselves, and to be kings and priests to God, the same as all Gods have done before you—namely, by going from one small degree to another, . . . from exaltation to exaltation, until you attain to the resurrection of the dead, and are able to dwell in everlasting burnings. and to sit in glory, as do those who sit enthroned in everlasting power.[30]

Countless souls, say LDS leaders, have already attained godhood. Orson Pratt theorized: "If we should take a million of worlds like this and number their particles, we should find that there are more Gods than there are particles of matter in those worlds."[31] Brigham Young, much less willing to calculate the number of gods, admitted: "How many Gods there are, I do not know. But there never was a time when there were not Gods."[32] These teachings inspired the popular Mormons couplet: "As man is, God once was; as God is, man may become."[33]

Such exaltation, however, is available only in the LDS church because only in Mormonism can a person be sealed—i.e., married—*for time* (here on earth) and *for eternity* (in the afterlife). Sealing for eternity is the most crucial kind of marriage to Latter-day Saints because according to the Mormon gospel, a man cannot become a god without a wife (or wives) to bear him spirit children in the afterlife.[34] Each Mormon male, just like heavenly Father, needs spiritual offspring because only through receiving their worship and obedience can he be sustained as a god and acquire the power necessary to build up a celestial kingdom.[35] More spirit children means more power, which in turn pushes a Mormon male further up the hierarchical ladder of gods in our universe. Even the mighty Elohim is a god "simply because all of these intelligences honor and sustain Him as such."[36] LDS author W. Cleon Skousen explains:

> [S]ince God "acquired" the honor and sustaining influence of "all things" it follows as a correlary [sic] that if He should ever do anything to violate the confidence or "sense of justice" of these intelligences, they would promptly withdraw their support, and the "power" of God would disintegrate. . . . "He would cease to be God."[37]

Fortunately for Elohim, his firstborn son, Jesus, visited earth and died for humanity in order to point out and open up a way for everyone to follow Elohim's commandments; commandments by which their own godhood can be obtained. Jesus, because he was special, was born of the virgin Mary, an exceptionally righteous woman. This is not to say that Christ was conceived in any way that might be considered supernatural. He was not miraculously begotten, for instance, by the Holy Ghost, as Christianity teaches.[38]

According to LDS theology, Elohim visited earth and impregnated Mary by having sexual intercourse with her after making her his wife, even though she already was not only his daughter (i.e., one of his spirit children), but also the betrothed of Joseph.[39] Brigham said: "[Jesus] partook of flesh and blood—was begotten of his father, as we were of our fathers."[40] Heber C. Kimball agreed: "I was naturally begotten; so was my father, and also my Saviour Jesus Christ . . . [T]here was nothing unnatural about it."[41]

Later, as an adult, Jesus would become a polygamist, just like Elohim. According to Orson Pratt, Christ "followed the example of His Father, and became the great Bridegroom to whom kings' daughters and many honorable wives were to be married."[42] Among his many wives were Mary, Martha and Mary Magdalene.[43] Unlike most men, however, Jesus did not need these wives, nor temple rituals to become a god. He became a god before coming to earth through perfect obedience to Elohim's commands.[44]

For others the road to godhood is far more difficult and takes considerably longer. As previously mentioned, a Mormon male must be married in order to create an eternal family by which his heavenly kingdom can be established: "[E]xaltation consists in the continuation of the family unit in eternity. . . . Those who obtain it . . . have spirit children in the resurrection, in relation to which offspring they stand in the same position that God our Father stands to us."[45] The process by which all of this takes place is as follows:

> Each God, through his wife or wives, raises up a numerous family of sons and daughters. . . . [E]ach father and mother will be in a condition to multiply forever. As soon as each God has begotten many millions of male and female spirits . . . he, in connection with his sons, organizes a new world . . . where he sends both the male and female spirits to inhabit tabernacles of flesh and bones. . . . The inhabitants of each world are required to reverence, adore, and worship their own personal father who dwells in the Heaven which they formerly inhabited.[46]

This is what being a Mormon is all about—becoming a god to billions of worshipful souls through whom one's own godhood is sustained.[47] The ultimate reward is a powerful motivation for Mormons: "Godhood is to have the character, possess the attributes, and enjoy the perfections which the Father has. It is to do what he does, have the pow-

Late nineteenth century depiction of two women being sealed to a Mormon male as his plural wives (from Fanny Stenhouse, *Tell It All*, 1875).

ers resident in him, and live as he lives."[48] In other words, Mormons hope to become omnipotent.[49]

Herein lies the importance of LDS women, whose "primary place is in the home, where she is to rear children and abide by the righteous counsel of her husband."[50] According to the late BYU scholar Eugene England, Mormon women literally are to become "birth machines" so Mormon males can continue creating and populating various worlds without end.[51] In *Dialogue: A Journal of Mormon Thought*, LDS scholar Melodie Moench Charles publicly expressed her opposition to such teachings:

> Heavenly polygamy, more than anything else in our theology, reduces people to things. . . . The greater the number of wives and children a man has in heaven, the greater his power, kingdom, and eternal glory. In the worst materialistic sense rather than in the best metaphorical sense, wives and children were a man's riches. Benjamin F. Johnson remembered that "the Prophet taught us that Dominion & power in the great Future would be Commensurate with the no[.] of 'Wives, Children & Friends' that we inherit here."[52]

So if all goes well, each Mormon male will reach godhood and take his place among the other gods.[53] It is a "gradually unfolding course of advancement and experience," said LDS apostle Bruce McConkie. "[A] course that began in a past eternity [i.e., preexistence] and will continue in ages future."[54] In the nineteenth century one indispensable principle of this course of advancement was polygamy. First, it mirrored the ways of Elohim. Second, it followed the example supposedly set by Jesus. Third, it produced many children, which to Mormons, represented more spirits that could pursue godhood. Fourth, plural marriage provided additional wives through whom men could continue eternal progression.[55]

CONJUGAL COMPLEXITIES

One of the most enlightening volumes on polygamy ever published came from Ann Eliza Young, a plural wife of Brigham Young, who actually left the prophet and the church. Her 1875 book, *Wife No. 19*, revealed that in Utah plural marriage, rather than existing as an option, was a command. It was a duty and the "counseling" to get on with it was more like coercion.[56] According to Ann Young, men were constantly urged to "build up the kingdom" and in order to do that they were ordered to "take advantage of their privileges." If they did not do so, they quickly drew "Prophetic and Apostolic wrath onto their heads."[57]

LDS leaders went so far as to threaten men, saying that if they refused another wife, then in the afterlife the wife they did possess would go to another man—a polygamist—for all eternity.[58] It did not even matter whether there was a place to put a new spouse. Consequently, many men resided with their families in virtual squalor. One of Young's neighbors, for instance, had four wives, but only one room in which all of them could live during the winter. The tiny space was used for a sitting-room, kitchen, parlor, and bedroom. Ann Eliza wrote: "Modesty and decency forbid my throwing too strong a light on that habitation."[59]

Others enjoyed more luxurious arrangements. Brigham had a beautiful and spacious "Beehive House" built, complete with a separate rooms for each wife. It allowed for ample living space, as well as privacy when Young visited his women. Young also had his "Lion House," a supplemental home for his large family. Likewise, Kimball had his own "Big House," which not only included separate rooms for his forty-five wives, but also a nice "Girls' Parlor." William Clayton, too, had a "Big House" for his ten wives, as did many other powerful LDS men.[60]

Sketches showing the disparity between the living conditions of wealthy polygamists *(below)* and poor polygamists *(top)* in nineteenth century Utah. The lower drawing depicts Brigham's mansion (from *Tell It All*, 1875).

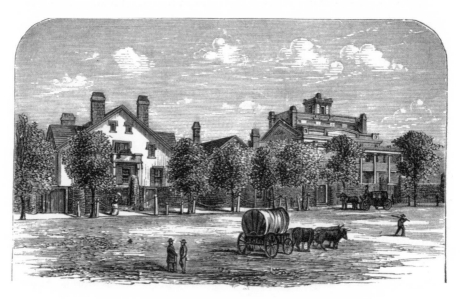

Once a Mormon male succumbed to the pressure, they resolutely followed the example of their leaders. Missionaries often returned from their trips with a new convert as a plural wife, very much to the surprise of the first wife in Utah, and very much to the shock of the second wife, who thought she was the missionary's only spouse.[61] Ann Eliza recalled:

> Men married in the most reckless fashion. . . . [M]en many times did not consider it at all necessary to inform the wives of their intentions, and the poor women would know nothing of the new marriage until the husband brought home his latest acquisition. . . . Those were the days when even the most trusting wives lost faith in their husbands; when solemn, oft-repeated promises were broken, evidently without the slightest qualm of conscience; when the tender, watchful affection of the husband and father was swallowed up in mad desire.[62]

Plural marriage also became a means of gaining status in the church. All bishops, stake presidents, and other ecclesiastical authorities were expected to abide by the "Law of Abraham" (i.e., polygamy). In response to one man who desired to marry two new arrivals from England, Brigham said: "Bring them on and I will seal them to you, for you are the kind of a man I like to see get ahead."[63] Such an attitude quickly fostered an atmosphere wherein men almost had to take more wives, or else suffer the consequences of perpetual low status.

Furthermore, contrary to Pratt's 1852 assertion of polygamy's nobleness, many LDS males seemed to relish their privilege as a means of satisfying their sexual appetites. They even composed songs about polygamy, singing: "Some men have a dozen wives, And some men have a score; The man that has but one wife, Is looking out for more."[64] This "looking out for more" often resulted in some highly irregular situations. In fact, the LDS marriage structure became extremely complex, and in many ways, somewhat confusing.

Unlike polygamy in other cultures, LDS plural marriage developed very rapidly, had few societal regulations, and presented no detailed methods for acquiring wives. There also existed no courtship patterns or limits on how many wives could be taken.[65] In the mad rush to acquire wives and solidify polygamous bonds, Mor-

Ann Eliza Young, plural wife of Brigham Young, who left the Mormon prophet and sought a divorce. When Ann Eliza asked for alimony and a portion of Young's estate, he countered by declaring that since polygamy was illegal, then their marriage was invalid, which meant that he should not have to pay her any support (from *The Mormon Monster*, 1901).

mon family units quickly became a tangled mass of inter-familial unions.

For example, Bishop Smith of Brigham City, married two of his own nieces. Bishop Johnson of Springville claimed six nieces, the eldest being only fifteen when they married. The other five remaining nieces ranged downward in age to two years old. Johnson asked that they be given to him as they grew up, which is exactly what happened, until he finally was sealed to that last one when she reached about thirteen.[66] Ann Eliza Young found it all rather unsettling:

> Uncles and nieces were married; one man would marry several sisters; and it was a very common thing for a mother and daughter to have the same husband. In one family, at least three generations were represented

among the wives—grandmother, mother, and daughter; and a case actually occurred in Salt Lake City where a man married his half sister, and that, too, with the full knowledge and approval of Brigham Young.[67]

LDS leadership had no problem with near relatives marrying. Joseph Smith's own diary, under October 26, 1843, records the sealing for eternity of John Bernhisel to his sister, Maria. Smith also sealed Bernhisel to four of his aunts and two cousins.[68] Brigham Young reasoned that since all people were brothers and sisters born to Heavenly Father, then earthly relationships were of little import when it came to sealing.[69]

Brigham Young University scholar, Jessie L. Embry, has acknowledged that as late as 1886 Lorenzo Snow—who became the fifth Mormon president—held that brothers and sisters could marry.[70] Fanny Stenhouse, who like Ann Eliza, defected from Mormonism after being a plural wife, witnessed the fruit of such teachings, which she described in her 1875 volume *Tell It All*:

Marriages have been contracted between the nearest of relatives; and old men tottering on the brink of the grave have been united to little girls scarcely in their teens; while unnatural alliances of every description, which in any other community would be regarded with disgust and abhorrence, are here entered into in the name of God.[71]

Stenhouse's book, which featured an impressive preface by the prestigious Harriet Beecher Stowe, highlighted yet another bi-product of Mormon polygamy—pedophilia.[72] In 1857, for instance, the *New York Times* reported on the sealing of old men to two girls aged ten and eleven. The article estimated that most girls married before they were fourteen.[73] Modern LDS scholar George D. Smith, in his study of 153 men who took plural wives in the early years of the LDS church, noted that two of the wives were only thirteen years old, more than a dozen girls were fourteen, twenty-one were fifteen; and fifty-three were only sixteen.[74]

Such behavior continued unabated throughout Mormonism's polygamous years as LDS leaders urged young girls to choose husbands of experience, who had the power to resurrect them after death, rather than a young man "whose position in the church was not fixed."[75] Thus polygamy thrived in the desert.

MORE IS NEVER ENOUGH

On February 1, 1857, Heber C. Kimball assured men: "In the spirit . . . world we will go to brother Joseph. . . . He will say to us, 'Come along, my boys, we will give you a good suit of clothes. Where are your wives.' [Answering Joseph] 'They are back yonder; they would not follow us.' 'Never mind,' says Joseph, 'here are thousands, have all you want.'"[76]

This cavalier attitude belied another rarely discussed aspect of polygamy—i.e., the Mormon male's perception of women as a commodity similar to livestock or property.[77] For instance, when Phineas Cook complained to Brigham about his circumstances, saying that his wife "was nearly tired out," Brigham said that "when his women got tired, he could take them home and change them for fresh ones."[78] Heber C. Kimball commonly referred to women as cows, explaining: "I think no more of taking another wife than I do of buying a cow, and if you want to build up the kingdom you must take more wives."[79]

Women were viewed as objects to be owned, as evidenced by a notation in John D. Lee's journal. He recounts his conversation with a new arrival to Utah named Nancy Gibbons. In explaining why he had not sought a relationship with her, Lee cites the fact that another individual had paid her way to the territory: "I told her . . . that inasmuch as he had brought her from Tennessee that he likely had claims on her."[80] This perception of women as little more than chattel was so pervasive throughout Utah that swapping of wives was looked upon as something acceptable if a high-ranking authority were to make such a request. Jedediah M. Grant admitted: "If President Young wants my wives I will give them to him without a grumble, and he can take them whenever he likes."[81] Grant also explained:

What would a man of God say, who felt aright, when Joseph [Smith] asked him for his money? He would say, "Yes, and I wish I had more to help to build up the kingdom of God." Or if he came and said, "I want your wife?" "O yes," he would say, "here she is; there are plenty more."[82]

The *Confessions of John D. Lee* reveals: "Some have mutually agreed to exchange wives."[83] One of Brigham's own brothers, Lorenzo Young, engaged in just such a trade with a Mr. Decker, whose wife Lorenzo wanted. Lorenzo simply swapped his wife for Mrs. Decker.[84]

Not surprisingly, many plural wives experienced depression, despair, anxiety, helplessness, abandonment, anger, psychosomatic illnesses, and low self-esteem. Todd Compton's *In Sacred Loneliness: The Plural Wives of Joseph Smith* notes: "Certainly polygamous marriage was accepted by nineteenth-century Mormons as thoroughly sacred—it almost defined what was most holy to them—but its practical result, for the woman, was solitude."[85]

Women saw their emotional torment and mental anguish as a cross they needed to bear for salvation. Polygamy was their duty and suffering was a test of faithfulness. They sincerely believed polygamy to be a divinely revealed necessity for spiritual advancement. The living of it, however, presented considerable suffering, as the following statements indicate (each is from a woman, who remained faithful to Mormonism):

- "[Polygamy] I could not have done if I had not believed it to be right in the Sight of god, and believed it to be one principal of his gospel once again restored to earth" (Sarah D. Rich)
- "God will be very cruel if he does not give us poor women adequate compensation for the trials we have endured in polygamy" (Mary Ann Angell Young).
- "O, if my husband could only love me even a little and not seem to be perfectly indifferent to any sensation of that kind. . . . O my poor aching heart when shall it rest its burden only on the Lord" (Emmeline B. Wells).[86]

Ann Eliza felt similarly, but she could not bear it. In 1882 she stated: "It is the very refinement of cruelty, this polygamy, and its hurts are deeper and more poisonous than any other wounds can be. They never heal, but grow constantly more painful, until it makes life unendurable."[87] Men, for the most part, seemed to flourish under such conditions. Their main problem was a lack of young girls in the territory, which called for drastic measures.

RESPECTING YOUR ELDERS

After several years in Utah, Mormon men began realizing that their supply of young women was dwindling. To remedy the situation, missionaries were instructed to bring back as many eligible females as possible in order to replenish the reservoir out of which LDS leaders could choose mates. But most of the men going on missions were young, strong, and handsome bachelors who posed a threat to the church's aging hierarchy. An obvious concern was that the missionaries would take the best women. Consequently, various safeguards were implemented. Missionaries, for instance, received warnings about not being greedy concerning women. Heber C. Kimball advised departing missionaries as follows:

> You are sent out as shepherds to gather the sheep together; and remember that they are not your sheep: they belong to Him that sends you. Then do not make a choice of any of those sheep; *do not make selections before they are brought home and put into the fold.*[88] The brother missionaries have been in the habit of picking out the prettiest women for themselves before they get here, and bringing on the ugly ones for us; hereafter you have to bring them all here before taking any of them, and let us all have a fair shake.[89]

For those men unwilling to heed Kimball's warning, LDS authorities resorted to a far more permanent means of having their wishes obeyed—castration. John D. Lee revealed in his confessions that such a practice dated back as far as Nauvoo. In Utah, according to Lee, it was a favorite revenge of "old, worn-out members of the Priesthood, who wanted young women sealed to them, and found that the girl preferred some handsome young man."[90]

Two cartoons depicting Mormon polygamy. The first (top) is titled "The Bishop's Family at Two A.M." The second is titled "Old Wife Washing the New Wife's Feet." Both are from William Jarman's 1884 anti-Mormon exposé *U.S.A.: Uncle Sam's Abscess, or Hell Upon Earth for U.S., Uncle Sam.* Jarman wrote: "All determined to lead a vicious life should leave their country for their country's good, and emigrate to Utah. . . . If you have a craving for Drink, Lust, Murder, go to Utah! your keenest appetite will there be fully satisfied, and your valuable services command a premium. A word to the wise is sufficient—to Christians I say, Beware! Beware! Beware!" (p. 9).

In the annals of Utah crime, one of the most well-known episodes involving such a heinous act centered around Warren Snow, Bishop of Manti. Although Snow already had several wives, he wanted another "buxom young woman" he knew. The girl thanked Snow for the offer, but told him she was then engaged to Thomas Lewis, a man much nearer her own age. Snow responded by telling her that it was God's will for her to marry him and that her beau could be gotten rid of; perhaps sent on a mission.

But the girl refused, which prompted church authorities to step in and counsel Lewis to give up his love. Lewis said no, and for his insolence, was attacked, held down by several men, and brutally castrated by Snow, who used a bowie knife to do the job.[91] The girl ended up marrying Snow, and Brigham Young moved that the entire episode be forgotten.[92] In fact, historian D. Michael Quinn found documented evidence showing that Young actually supported Snow's cruel deed.[93]

In addition to physical violence and verbal warnings against their own flock, LDS leaders resorted to deceptive evangelism techniques overseas in their efforts to procure more women for Utah. They knew that reaction to polygamy in Europe would be negative, so various public notices were used to assure potential converts that polygamy among the Saints was little more than an exaggerated rumor. For example, the 1866 European edition of the *Doctrine and Covenants* unabashedly denied polygamy, (as did the American edition until 1876, when its article advocating monogamous marriage was replaced by the polygamy-condoning Section 132).[94]

But during this very same year (1866), Brigham Young declared: "The only men who become Gods, even the Sons of God, are those who enter into polygamy."[95] Also in 1866 in Utah, John Taylor, who would become Brigham's successor, said: "Where did this commandment come from in relation to polygamy? It also came from God. . . . When I see any of our people, men or women, opposing a principle of this kind . . . I consider them apostates."[96]

John Taylor, interestingly, in 1850 sang a dramatically different tune during a debate held in France. During that event Taylor complained: "We are accused here of polygamy, and actions the most indelicate, obscene, and disgusting. . . . These things are too outrageous to admit of belief."[97] Taylor then read to his audience the old LDS marriage statement from the 1835 edition of *Doctrine and Covenants* disavowing polygamy.[98] Moreover, by 1850, the year of the debate, Taylor already had married twelve wives, who had borne him eight children.[99]

Mormon leaders were not the only ones to deliberately deceive European audiences. LDS missionaries routinely lied about plural marriage during their trips overseas.[100] Only by using half-truths and misinformation could these missionaries insure that potential converts would leave their homeland for Utah.[101] One tragic episode that resulted from such deception eventually led to a Supreme Court case (*Miles v. the United States*). It involved Caroline Owens, an English girl, who since her childhood had known a John D. Miles.[102]

Miles had immigrated to Utah as a Mormon, but during a visit to England he asked Owens to be his wife and return with him, promising to marry her in Salt Lake City. When asked about polygamy, Miles assured his intended bride that only a few old men were allowed more than one wife, but that young men like himself "had but one."[103] Upon Owens' arrival in Utah in 1878, the Mormons were cordial, loving, and supportive. She even was allowed to stay at the home of U.S. delegate George Q. Cannon. The entire charade gave way just hours after her wedding, as Owens recounted in 1893:

> I can never tell the horrors of the next few hours. . . . I went to my room and dressed for the reception, which took place at Cannon's other house, where he kept his three wives. When I went down, there was a crowd there, among the rest a plain looking girl in a calico dress, to whom I was introduced. It was Emily Spencer. . . . I told her to get up. Miles came forward and said, "Sit still, Emily Spencer, my wife." I felt as though I had been shot. I said, "Your wife! Then what am I?" He said, "You are both my wives." All at once my shame flashed over me. Here I was dishonored, the polygamous wife of a Mormon. I ran out of the house, bent only on escape, I did not think where. I could not do it, though, for Miles and young Cannon, a son of the Delegate, ran after me and dragged me back. . . . [B]ut I stole away and returned to the other house, where I had

been living the three weeks since my arrival from England. I noticed there was no key in the lock, but shot a little bolt and piled chairs against the door. I cried myself to sleep. The next thing I knew, I don't know what time it was, Miles stood in the room and was locking the door on the inside. I screamed . . . Miles said I need not take on, for Brother Cannon had anticipated that I would make trouble and had the house cleared of everyone else. I found out that it was so. He told me that I might as well submit; there was no law here to control the saints. There was no power on earth that would save me.[104]

Englishman William Jarman and his wife experienced a similar level of deception, and as a result emigrated to Utah in 1868. According to Jarman, the Elder who converted them never denied polygamy, but when asked about it, stated: "Polygamy is very rarely followed; the Prophet Brigham, and one or two others practise it. . . . But Mrs. Jarman it is not essential to salvation, as you seem to think, that men must become Polygamists." The missionary then added: "Even supposing the Lord revealed to the Prophet that Bro. Jarman should take another wife, before he can do so, you must be consulted and give your consent. If you refuse . . . your husband cannot become a Polygamist."[105]

Orson Pratt's 1852 lecture on plural marriage contradicts the missionary's claims: "[W]hat will become of those individuals who have this law taught unto them in plainness, if they reject it? [A voice in the stand, 'they will be damned.'] I will tell you: they will be damned, saith the Lord God Almighty."[106] Oddly, LDS apostle John Widtsoe affirmed in his volume *Evidences and Reconciliation* that Mormonism "ever operates in full light. There is no secrecy about its doctrine, aim, or work."[107]

WHY? WHY? WHY?

Mormons defended plural marriage primarily by saying that the Lord had commanded it. Monogamy was equated with a failure to obey God, which not only displeased the Almighty, but endangered one's eternal destiny. In reference to more temporal drawbacks of monogamy, Brigham said it was the "source of prostitution and whoredom" through-

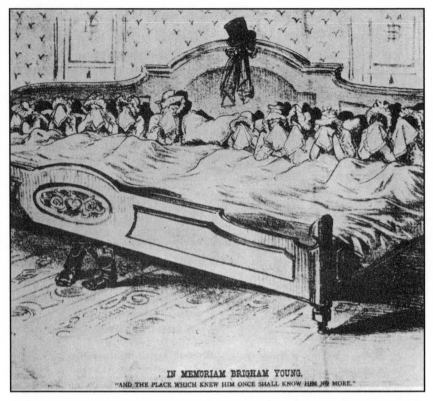

IN MEMORIAM BRIGHAM YOUNG.
"AND THE PLACE WHICH KNEW HIM ONCE SHALL KNOW HIM NO MORE."

A somewhat unsympathetic cartoon, published in *Puck* magazine, September 1877, soon after the death of Brigham Young.

out all Christendom.[108] Monogamy, therefore, allegedly was more detrimental to society. Closely linked to these motivations was a fear of punishment. Because the counsel of church leaders was to acquire plural wives, to do otherwise was tantamount to apostasy, a crime worthy of death, especially during Brigham's reformation.[109]

Such justifications were common to both men and women. Some reasons for plural marriage, however, seemed more gender-specific. Men were more influenced by direct appeals to their ego. The overriding issue for men might best have been summed up in the question: How is this going to affect me? Hence, single or monogamous men were often mocked and ridiculed as practically impotent, or at the very least, weak and unable to sustain a truly righteous family.

Additionally, Heber C. Kimball promised that polygamy would ensure longevity and youthfulness for men. "I would not be afraid to promise a man who is sixty years of age, if he will take the counsel of brother Brigham and his brethren, that he will renew his age," Kimball said. "[A] man who has but one wife, and is inclined to that doctrine, soon begins to wither and dry up, while a man who goes into plurality looks fresh, young, and sprightly. Why is this? Because God loves that man."[110]

A different method of coercion was used on women. Rather than appealing to self-interest, LDS authorities concentrated on the religious and maternal natures of the females in their flock. Women were told, for example, that they could only be saved through men, whose responsibility it would be to call them forth from the grave so that they could receive salvation and continue helping their husbands build up his kingdom.[111] Thus, their salvation depended on their cooperation in plural marriage and agreeableness to it.[112] One Utah pioneer song for women clearly articulated this belief:

> Now, sisters, list to what I say; with trials this world is rife.
> You can't expect to miss them all; help husband get a wife!
> Now this advice I freely give, if exalted you will be,
> Remember that your husband must, be blessed with more than thee.
> Chorus: Then, oh, let us say, God bless the wife that strives,
> And aids her husband all she can to obtain a dozen wives.[113]

Moreover, women were made to feel more than a fair amount of guilt for even thinking about wanting anything remotely corresponding to "happiness," which they were told should be rooted in getting married, serving their husbands, and making babies, whose spirits in heaven were longing for a body. Consider these comments from Brigham Young:

> I am now almost daily sealing young girls to men of age and experience. Love your duties, sisters. Are you sealed to a good man? Yes, to a man of God. It is for you to bear fruit and bring forth, to the praise of God, the spirits that are born in yonder heavens and are to take tabernacles [i.e., bodies] on the earth. You have the privilege of forming tabernacles for

those spirits, instead of their being brought into this wicked world that
God may have a royal Priesthood, a royal people, on the earth. That is
what plurality of wives is for, and not to gratify lustful desires. Sisters, do
you wish to make yourselves happy? Then what is your duty? It is for you
to bear children, . . . are you tormenting yourselves by thinking that your
husbands do not love you? I would not care whether they loved a parti-
cle or not; but I would cry out, like one of old, in the joy of my heart, "I
have got a man from the Lord!" "Hallelujah! I am a mother—I have
borne, an image of God!"[114]

Orson Pratt declared polygamy to be one of the greatest blessings
ever bestowed upon females because it gave many women an opportunity to be "united to a righteous man" instead of "being compelled to
remain single, or marry a wicked man."[115] But for the rebellious woman,
her lot was damnation and rejection. Kimball preached:

It is the duty of a woman to be obedient to her husband, and unless she
is, I would not give a damn for all her queenly right and authority, nor
for her either, if she will quarrel and lie about the work of God and the
principles of plurality.[116]

Kimball, Young, Pratt, Smith, and other LDS officials also used the
Bible to justify their beliefs. But Mormonism, as the following section
will show, legitimized their doctrines through the abuse—not the use—
of scripture.

THE BIBLE TELLS ME SO

Does the Bible advocate polygamy? That is a key question for anyone studying Mormonism's history and beliefs. Whether or not
polygamy is a positive or negative model of family living is not the issue;
at least not in a theological or historical study of Mormonism. The
importance of the question in a volume such as this one has more to do
with attempting to better understand how a faith (i.e., Mormonism) can
arrive at a certain belief (i.e., polygamy), even though that belief con-

tradicts the religious document appealed to for justification (in this case, the Bible).

History is filled with the misuse of holy writings by individuals committed to excusing their actions in the name of God. In the western world the Bible has been the book of choice for such activity. It has been used to rationalize all manner of behavior that in reality has little to do with the Bible's message. The Crusades, the Spanish Inquisition, the Salem witch trials were all justified using biblical verses; each of which were wrested from their historical, literary, cultural, and linguistic contexts. The Mormon use of the Bible in conjunction with polygamy falls into a similar category.

Polygamy, as previous chapters have indicated, began with Joseph Smith, who seemed to get the idea from reading the Old Testament. Apparently, the polygamous practices of various Hebrew patriarchs, kings, and leaders (e.g., Abraham, Jacob, David, and Solomon) led Smith and his successors to believe that having many wives was commanded by God. Here is where Joseph made his first mistake. Nowhere in the Bible does the Hebrew God sanction, let alone command, polygamy.

At best, the Old Testament God silently tolerates humanity's stubborn refusal to adhere to what appears to be the biblical ideal—i.e., monogamy. This pattern is set forth via the Genesis creation story, which states that after God decided the first man (Adam) should not be alone, Eve (one woman) was created for him. The singular pairing is reinforced by God declaring: "I will make a helper for him" (Gen. 2:18). In other words, God made one helper for Adam, the ideal relational coupling, rather than several helpers. The oft-quoted instructive passage that follows underscores for a third time the one to one union: "Therefore shall a man leave his father and mother, and shall cleave unto his wife [singular]: and they shall be one flesh [singular]" (Gen. 2:24).

Noteworthy is the first place polygamy appears in the Bible (Genesis 4:19). Here we find Lamech, the first polygamist. Far from being an admirable character, he is a member of the violent Cainite tribe, a descendant of the infamous Cain (Gen. 4:1-8), and a man in whom is seen "[t]he powerful development of the worldly mind and of ungodliness" six generations removed from Adam.[117] In his "sword song," for

instance, Lamech boasts of killing a man and a boy, then brags that anyone harming him would be avenged (Gen. 4:23-24).

After the time of Lamech (pre-2,100 B.C.), polygamy gradually developed among the Israelites, but was largely confined to the ruling and
upper classes. Although it was a social institution by the time of Moses,
the *Baker Encyclopedia of the Bible* observes that there were "no examples given of large polygamous marriages in the families of common-
ers."[118] The vast majority of the Israelites were monogamous. In fact,
monogamy remained not only the norm, but was viewed by the Israelites
as the most acceptable form of marriage, as is implied by various Hebrew
laws (Ex. 20:17; 21:5; Lev. 18:8, 16, 20; 20:10; Num. 5:12; Deut. 5:21).[119]

Herein lies another major departure that Mormons made from the
Old Testament in relation to plural marriage. The Hebrews never considered polygamy a standard practice for the general populace. It also is
highly significant that virtually every Old Testament story involving
polygamy included some tragedy, punishment, or suffering directly
related to plural marriage:

- Incessant fighting, bitterness, anger, and jealousy plagued Abraham's
  two wives—Sarah and Hagar—both of whom suffered great emotional
  anguish, especially Hagar (Gen. 21:8-16).
- Jacob's wives, Rachel and Leah, although sisters, were relationally
  torn by bitterness (Gen. 30:15).
- Friction between Elkanah's wives, Hannah and Peninnah, caused
  heartbreak and anger in Hannah (1 Sam. 1:1-10).
- David resorted to murder so he could have another wife (2 Sam. 11).
- Solomon's polygamy turned him into an idolater (1 Kings 11:1-8).

Such consistency suggests that these stories, far from being intended
as a promotion of polygamy, were presented to discourage the practice.
The Bible provides not a single instance of polygamy being extolled as
virtuous. On the contrary, Hebrew kings specifically were warned
against multiplying wives because it would turn their hearts away from
God (Deut. 17:17). Even in the renowned book of Proverbs, reportedly
written by Solomon, marriage related verses do not enjoin polygamy, but
rather, suggest monogamy.[120]

According to *The International Standard Bible Encyclopedia*, polygamy (no matter who practiced it) contradicted the established Old Testament pattern for marriage, which was intended to give men and women equal status as co-creations of God:

> [T]he Genesis dictum established monogamy as a working principle for mankind, and originally it was meant to signify the union of a male and a female who were counterparts to each other. The wife was in no way regarded as inferior to her husband, being considered in the first instance as specifically the "essence of his essence" (Gen. 2:23).[121]

Additionally, although Mormons call polygamy the "Law of Abraham," the story of Abraham actually portrays his acceptance of plural marriage as a mark of disobedience to, and a lack of faith in, God. Abraham accepted another wife from his first wife, Sarah, in order to father a child solely because he did not trust in God's promise to give him a son by Sarah. The Bible further states that Abraham embraced polygamy by listening to Sarah's counsel, rather than to God's counsel. Afterward Sarah recognized her mistake, saying: "My wrong be upon thee" (Gen. 16:5). Far from being Abraham's "Law," polygamy reflected Abraham's sin—i.e., his willingness to accept local pagan customs of ancient Mesopotamia instead of obeying the marriage pattern established at creation.[122]

Smith, Young, and other authorities of the LDS church further erred in believing that the New Testament teaches polygamy; more specifically, that Jesus and his apostles were polygamists. Jedediah M. Grant, Second Counselor to Brigham Young, asserted: "A belief in the doctrine of a plurality of wives caused the persecution of Jesus and his followers."[123] Orson Hyde taught: "Jesus Christ was married at Cana of Galilee, that Mary, Martha, and others were his wives, and that He begat children."[124] Orson Pratt plainly declared: "[T]he great messiah who was the founder of the Christian religion, was a polygamist."[125]

First, nothing in the New Testament remotely suggests that Jesus or any of his disciples were polygamists. Second, according to the gospel accounts of Christ's life, Jesus was persecuted and eventually crucified for committing what the Jews considered to be blasphemy, not for practicing polygamy (Matt. 26:63-66). Third, several New Testament verses teach that monogamy is the Judeo-Christian pattern of marriage:

- "A bishop then must be blameless, the husband of one wife" (I Tim.3:2).
- "[O]rdain elders in every city, as I had appointed thee: If any be blameless, the husband of one wife . . . For a bishop must be blameless" (Titus 1:6).
- "Every man should have his own wife" (1 Cor. 7:2).

The Bible also uses clear symbolism to depict the Christian Church as *the* bride of Christ; a bride, who is lovingly cared for by the Savior (Joel 2:16; John 3:29; 2 Cor. 11:2; Eph. 5:24-31; Rev. 19:7; 21:2-9). This illustration is transferred over as a picture of the marital relationship between one man and one woman. Such an illustration would be rendered meaningless by polygamy. The whole Christ/Church and Husband/Wife analogy would be invalidated. Ephesians 5:33 adds the following admonition:

> For this cause shall a man leave his father and mother, and shall be joined unto his wife, and they two shall be one flesh. . . . [L]et every one of you in particular so love his wife even as himself; and the wife see that she reverence her husband.

Other New Testament passages, in direct contrast to Mormonism, actually say that in certain instances it is better for a person to remain unmarried (1 Cor. 7:8-9; 11, 27). And one passage specifically declares that in the afterlife individuals "neither marry, nor are given in marriage" (Matt. 22:30; Mk. 12:25; Lk. 20:35).[126] Ironically, even the *Book of Mormon* condemns polygamy:

- "And now it came to pass that the people of Nephi . . . began to grow hard in their hearts, and indulge themselves somewhat in wicked practices, such as like unto David of old desiring many wives and concubines" (Jacob 1:15).

- "Behold, David and Solomon truly had many wives and concubines, which thing was abominable before me, saith the Lord. . . . [T]here shall not any man among you have save it be one wife; and concubines he shall have none" (Jacob 2:24-27).
- "Behold, the Lamanites . . . are more righteous than you; for they have not forgotten the commandment of the Lord, which was given unto our father—that they should have save it were one wife, and concubines they should have none, and there should not be whoredoms committed among them" (Jacob 3:5).

Even if just for the sake of discussion it is conceded that scripture tolerates polygamy, Mormons blatantly disobeyed Old Testament prohibitions on a man marrying either his wife's sister (Lev. 18:18) or his wife's mother (Lev. 20:14). Of this latter sin, the Bible says: "[I]f a man take a wife and her mother, it is wickedness; they shall be burnt with fire both he and they; that there be no wickedness among you." Despite all of these passages from the Bible and the *Book of Mormon*, contemporary Saints still assert that their spiritual forefathers were following God's command, adding: "For a person to say that he believes the Bible but does not believe the doctrine of plural marriage is something akin to saying that he accepts the Constitution but not the Bill of Rights."[127]

Of course, the U.S. government during the mid-nineteenth century cared little about whether polygamy was, or was not, biblical. Politicians simply decided that the concept was inconsistent with how America would be run. Moreover, the excesses and fanaticism associated with Mormon polygamy made it onerous in the sight of U.S. citizens. And politicians, always concerned with keeping voters happy, became determined to see polygamy's demise.

So a concerted effort began in 1862 to destroy the practice through the passage of various territorial statutes and federal laws. These political limitations would ultimately spell doom for the practice esteemed so sacred by Mormons. It also would place Mormon leadership in the uncomfortable position of having to explain why suddenly in 1890 polygamy, which was a requirement for godhood, was no longer to be practiced or taught as church doctrine.

FOURTEEN

The Politics of Compromise

[I]f a man has no divine right to marry two wives or more in this world, then marriage for eternity is not true, and your faith is all vain, and all the sealing ordinances and powers, pertaining to marriages for eternity are vain, worthless, good for nothing.

Orson Pratt (1880)[1]

LDS Apostle

WHEN JOHN TAYLOR ASSUMED the LDS presidency in 1880, he inherited a church facing extinction. Just one year earlier, Mormonism suffered a devastating legal blow by the U.S. Supreme Court in *Reynolds v. the United States*. Mormons thought they would be exonerated by the case, which directly challenged the constitutionality of the anti-bigamy Morrill Act (1862).[2] But America's highest court ruled against Reynolds, and in so doing, gave Mormonism notice that polygamy would have to be abandoned. It also placed George S. Reynolds, one of the church's most faithful Saints, behind bars.[3]

The government had tried for years to destroy polygamy by various statutes including the Wade Bill (1866), Cragin Bill (1867/1869), Ashley Bill (1869), Cullom Bill (1870), Voorhees Bill (1872), and Logan Bill (1872). Although none of these measures passed both the House and Senate to become law, they showed that the tide of opposition against polygamy was not receding. All of the bills sought to curtail polygamous activity in Utah by targeting how the territory handled persons guilty of breaking anti-bigamy laws. Some of them attempted to put the responsibility for prosecuting polygamists into the hands of U.S. authorities,

rather than leaving that task to local courts run by Mormons. Others
sought to increase penalties for polygamists.

Finally, in 1874, a new anti-polygamy measure—the Poland Bill—
made it beyond the political wrangling that had defeated every other
measure. Interestingly, this law made no mention whatsoever of
polygamy. Its purpose was to strip Utah's probate courts of local authority.[4] Furthermore, the offices of territorial marshal and attorney general
were abolished, and their duties assigned to the U.S. marshal and U.S.
attorney general. It was only the first of many steps the government
began taking to abolish the nation's last "relic" of barbarism.

More significant was the American government's desire to crush the
Mormon church's theocratic rule over Utah, which was closely linked to
its ongoing support and advancement of polygamy. This seemed to be
the primary concern of most U.S. officials, whose position was articulated well in 1880 by United States president Rutherford B. Hayes:

> [Utah] is virtually under the theocratic government of the Mormon
> Church. The Union of Church and State is complete. The result is the
> usual one[,] usurpation or absorption of all temporal authority and
> power by the Church. . . . Laws must be enacted which will take from
> the Mormon Church its temporal power. . . . [A]s a system of government
> it is our duty to deal with it as an enemy to our institutions, and its sup-
> porters and leaders as criminals.[5]

Hayes' observation came at a crucial point in the struggle between
Mormons and federal authorities. The two opposing forces had entered a
new phase of conflict, beginning around 1878 with the arrest of John
Miles, who had married Caroline Owens under false pretenses (see pp.
300–301). Although Miles was convicted by a Utah court, the U.S.
Supreme Court reversed the ruling because the lower court's decision
was based on the testimony of Owens. According to territorial law, a wife
could not testify against her husband. Consequently, Miles was released.[6]

One significant aspect of the case was the testimony of Daniel H.
Wells, the high-ranking LDS authority, who had wedded Miles to Owens.
Wells had no problem recalling that particular ceremony, but when

asked about Miles having another wife (or wives), the Mormon leader suddenly could "not remember." He refused to answer other questions because they involved "secret" Mormon ceremonies. Wells also denied the bloody oaths and threats of death contained in the temple rituals. He was fined $100 and jailed for two days on contempt of court charges.

The Miles case showed U.S. authorities that prosecuting polygamy would be virtually impossible given Mormon leadership's willingness to lie under oath. So a new approach was devised—arrest and convict Mormons for illegal cohabitation, rather than polygamy. The crime of cohabitation would be much easier to prove than polygamy. Thus began the "Decade of the Raids," a ten year period during which the United States unrelentingly hunted down Mormon polygamists and their wives.

THE MORMON UNDERGROUND

The campaign that ultimately ended polygamy started in late 1880, when George Q. Cannon won the Utah vote to become the territory's delegate to Congress. His opponent, Allen G. Campbell, represented Utah's fairly new Liberal Party, which had been organized by "opponents of the Mormon regime."[7] It was a landslide victory, with Cannon receiving 18,568 votes to Campbell's 1,357 votes. The decision, however, prompted a "flood of petitions from across the nation demanding his removal and action by Congress to stamp out, once and for all, the practice of polygamy."[8]

Cannon could do little except appeal to Congress, admitting: "I have taken plural wives, who now live with me, and have so lived with me for a number of years and borne me children." He further conceded: "[A]s a teacher of my religion in Utah territory, I have defended said tenet of said church as being in my belief a revelation of God."[9] Such admissions, rather than coming from any sincere desire on Cannon's part to be forthright, likely resulted from the excessive publicity engendered by the controversy. Back in 1873 he had retained his representative seat in Congress by boldly lying to the House Committee on Elections. Contradicting his lifestyle in Utah, he flatly denied that he was living with four wives, going so far as to maintain that he was not cohabitating with any wives,

Wanted poster for LDS president John Taylor and his Counselor George Q. Cannon.

"in defiant or willful violation of the laws of Congress." Cannon even
denied ever stressing the importance of polygamy as "paramount to all
human laws," and claimed that he had never said he would obey
polygamy "rather than the laws of any country."[10] All of it was untrue.

But after the Reynolds and Miles Supreme Court cases, politicians
were much more cautious with regard to polygamy. When the Elections
Committee finally issued its report to the House in 1882, it recommended
that Cannon be kept from representing Utah in Congress because he
practiced, taught, and advised people to engage in polygamy. The House
vote, taken April 19, 1882, unseated Cannon with a tally of 123 to 79, and
89 abstentions. This same year also saw passage of the potent anti-
polygamy Edmund's Law, which called for heavy fines and imprison-

ment for polygamists and those guilty of "unlawful cohabitation." It also stripped polygamists of their right to vote and barred them from public office and jury duty.[11]

Then, in 1884, a string of prosecutions began with Rudger Clawson, who in 1883 had married a second wife, twenty-one-year-old Lydia Spencer. He was the first of many to be convicted under the Edmunds Act. It began slow enough. That year saw convictions of only three men in Utah, one in Idaho, and five in Arizona. But by 1885 federal deputies were descending on Utah like packs of wild dogs sensing a wounded animal. They traveled in groups of two or three, armed with arrest warrants for Saints disdainfully labeled "polygs" and "cohabs."

Law enforcement pressure intensified so dramatically that in February 1885 LDS president John Taylor and his two counselors, George Q. Cannon and Joseph F. Smith, went into hiding. Taylor and Cannon stayed in Utah, while Smith fled to Hawaii. Moreover, rather than obey the laws of the land as commanded in *Doctrine and Covenants* 58:21, the church's First Presidency released an "epistle," promising: "They who fight against Zion shall be destroyed; and the pit which has been digged shall be filled by those who digged it."[12]

Hundreds of prominent Mormons subsequently followed the example of Taylor by disappearing into isolated parts of Utah or going on foreign missions. Their plural wives and children then hindered law enforcement officials as much as possible. They gave false testimony, denied marital relationships, and refused to answer questions posed by court authorities. Agnes W. Roskelley, for example, taught her children to tell strangers "that they didn't know what their name was; they didn't know where they lived; they didn't know who their dad or mother was."[13]

Despite these obstructions to justice, arrests and convictions continued.[14] By June 1886 dozens of Mormon leaders were in hiding throughout Utah, Europe, Canada, and Mexico. Some of them had even established polygamous communities in the latter two locations, hoping to return one day with their new wives and children. Polygamy was just as illegal in these other locales, but authorities there were less likely to interfere with the settlements.

As for Taylor, Mormons still looked to him for leadership and words of comfort. Only a few of them, however, would ever learn of the revelation from God he received on September 27. The Almighty promised him that polygamy would never be abandoned, saying: "[H]ave I not commanded men that if they were Abraham's seed & would enter into my glory, they must do the works of Abraham. I have not revoked this law nor will I for it is everlasting & those who will enter into my glory must obey the conditions thereof."[15] Three months later, in apparent demonstration of his confidence in God's promise, seventy-eight-year-old John Taylor took another plural wife, twenty-six-year-old Josephine Roueche.

But fulfillment of Taylor's revelation grew more doubtful when in March of 1887 politicians passed the powerful Edmunds-Tucker Act. It allowed wives to testify against their husbands in court during polygamy trials, made adultery a felony, and disincorporated the LDS church. Furthermore, the new legislation authorized federal seizure of church real estate valued in excess of a $50,000.

To make matters worse, on July 25, 1887, seventy-eight-year-old John Taylor passed away, while still in hiding. He had finished his course of leadership never having compromised the principle of plurality of wives. His successor, Wilford Woodruff, would not be as stubborn.

AN ETERNAL DOCTRINE

There existed no doubt in the minds of every nineteenth century Mormon that polygamy was an everlasting command.[16] In 1855 President Brigham Young warned: "[I]f any of you will deny the plurality of wives, and continue to do so, I promise that you will be damned."[17] He further explained in 1862 that to just believe in polygamy was inadequate. One had to practice it to be saved:

> Why do we believe in and practice polygamy? Because the Lord introduced it to his servants in a revelation given to Joseph Smith, and the Lord's servants have always practiced it. . . . [T]his is the religion of Abraham, and, unless we do the works of Abraham, we are not Abraham's seed and heirs according to promise.[18]

By 1870 the Saints no longer needed any convincing. In response to the passage that year of the Cullom Bill by the House of Representatives, Utah citizens sent a memorial to Congress describing plural marriage as "a principle revealed by God, underlying our every hope of eternal salvation and happiness in heaven."[19] Ten years later Wilford Woodruff received a supportive revelation that depicted polygamy as absolutely essential to godhood. This divine communication went so far as to damn anyone who would even hinder Mormons from obeying plural marriage.[20] Woodruff then told the Saints in 1881 that if they ever were to "give up polygamy," they also would have to give up revelation, prophets, apostles, temple ordinances, and the church itself.[21]

Woodruff was not alone. The year John Taylor took over as LDS president (1880), he insisted that polygamy was "a divine institution . . . handed down direct from God. The United States cannot abolish it. No nation on the earth can prevent it, nor all the nations of the earth combined. I defy the United States. I will obey God."[22] Then, at an October 1884 general conference, George Q. Cannon said that any appeal for a new revelation to "lay polygamy aside" was a "[v]ain thought" because such a revelation would be useless "unless indeed the people should apostatize."[23]

Clearly, Joseph Smith's revelation on plural marriage (*D&C* 132) was seen as irrevocable, having been instituted in this dispensation of time for the Saints as part of God's "restoration of all things" prior to Jesus' second advent.[24] Consequently, the Mormon position had always been that the practice of polygamy would never cease. For example, on August 19, 1866, Brigham Young strongly admonished his people to continue the practice of plural marriage, no matter what the cost:

> The only men who become Gods, even the Sons of God, are those who enter into polygamy. Others attain unto a glory and may even be permitted to come into the presence of the Father and the Son; but they cannot reign as kings in glory, because they had blessings offered unto them, and they refused to accept them. . . . 'Do you think that we shall ever be admitted as a State into the Union without denying the principle of polygamy?' If we are not admitted until then, we shall never be admitted.[25]

In April 1885, the *Deseret Evening News,* the LDS church's official publication, adamantly rejected any thoughts of giving up plural marriage. "Were the Church to do that as an entirety God would reject the Saints as a body," read the editorial. "[T]he authority of the Priesthood would be withdrawn . . . and the Lord would raise up another people of greater valor and stability."[26] In June the periodical lashed out again, criticizing anyone who would dare suggest that plural marriage could even be temporarily suspended.[27]

George Q. Cannon admitted that if the church ever accepted a cessation of polygamy, then it "would cease to be the Church of God, and the ligaments that now bind it together would be severed."[28] Woodruff posited: "[W]hat are we going to do under the circumstances? God says, 'we shall be damned if we do not obey the law [of Abraham].' Congress says, 'we shall be damned if we do' . . . Now who shall we obey? God or man? My voice is that we obey God."[29]

LDS leaders viewed America's opposition to polygamy as part of the "last days" persecution that would immediately precede Jesus' return. As late as the 1870s and 1880s Mormons still believing that the long-awaited millennial kingdom was near. Orson Pratt made the following prophecy in 1875:

> The time is coming, when we will not be fettered by unjust laws that are imposed upon us. Why? Because the Lord intends, by his judgment, by wars among the nations that will not serve him, by famines, and pestilence, and by various judgments that will be sent forth, to waste away the nations of the earth. . . . [W]e know their doom, and we know that it is very near at hand. It is not something to happen in a far distant period of the future, but it is right at the doors. . . . [H]e will speedily fulfill the prophecy in relation to the overthrow of this nation, and their destruction.[30]

That same year Woodruff warned that the world's end was so near the Saints needed to store up grain in preparation for the coming famine.[31] Doomsday was supposed to swiftly overtake America because of its opposition to polygamy. Then, in 1879 he predicted that America's actions would "sap the very foundation of our government" until it was "rent asunder." He added: "[T]here is no power beneath the heavens can save this nation from the consequences thereof."[32] Woodruff also prophesied:

> The American Nation will be broken in pieces. . . . [Y]ou live in the day and hour of the judgments of God Almighty. . . . [T]he hour of God's judgment is at the door. . . . I wish to warn all nations. . . . Thrones will be cast down, nations will be overturned, anarchy will reign, all legal barriers will be broken down, and the laws will be trampled in the dust. You are about to be visited with war, sword, famine, pestilence, plague, earthquakes, whirlwinds, tempests, and with the flame of devouring fire. . . . [T]he slain of the Lord will be many.[33]

Orson Pratt declared in 1879 that the approaching holocaust would be far worse than the Civil War, even though at one time he had said that the final conflict *would be* the Civil War. To describe the coming battle, Pratt even borrowed the same phrases and descriptions formerly used to describe the war between the states.[34] Such a prediction echoed the timetable Joseph Smith had set back in 1835, when he declared that most of the Saints then living would see Jesus' return by 1890/91. He promised them that "even fifty-six years should wind up the scene" (c. 1891).[35] Yet another revelation, allegedly from Jesus Christ to Joseph Smith, stated:

> My Son, if thou livest until thou art eighty-five years of age [i.e., December 1890], thou shalt see the face of the Son of Man. . . . [I]n the name of the Lord God, and let it be written—the Son of Man will not come in the clouds of heaven till I am eighty-five years old.[36]

In 1845 Parley P. Pratt understandably speculated that by 1945 workers building an LDS temple in New York City would erect it on the ruins of the former metropolis. He believed they probably would find "some coin of the old Government of the United States."[37] But a far more disappointing event would be the next landmark in Mormon history.

GOD CHANGES HIS MIND

After Taylor's death it seemed that LDS authorities were actually going to curtail Mormon polygamy in obedience to American laws. There really was no choice in the matter. The year 1887 had seen 327 Mormons convicted under the new anti-polygamy laws.[38] "Virtually every prominent Mormon was in prison, had served a sentence, or was a fugitive."[39] Finally, according to a plan proposed in 1888 by Frank Cannon (son of influential polygamist George Q. Cannon), it was decided that in return for light sentences, all fugitive Mormons would give themselves up and promise, along with every other Mormon, to cease practicing plural marriage.

After this solution was accepted by U.S. judge Elliot F. Sandford, the trek into court began for hundreds of polygamist, all of whom were slapped with minor fines and/or brief jail terms. George Q. Cannon, for instance, although he had jumped a $45,000 bail and had a price on his head, was fined only $450 and given seventy-five days in prison. In addition to the *en masse* surrender of fugitive Mormons, the new LDS leader—Wilford Woodruff—went a step further by demolishing the church's Endowment House, where plural marriages occurred.[40]

Soon, however, cynical onlookers noticed something very odd. It was true that church leaders had surrendered, the Endowment House had been destroyed, and official LDS posturing indicated the church's strict adherence to federal law. But new plural marriages were taking place all over Utah. How was it happening? Where was it happening? Who was officiating at the ceremonies? Answers to these questions might have remained a mystery were it not for Charles Mostyn Owen, a self-styled private investigator, who spent years tracking and exposing Mormon polygamists.

Owen catalogued hundreds of cases involving polygs and cohabs as he traveled incognito throughout Utah. He then swore out complaints against many of them. His activities quickly earned him a place alongside Missouri governor Lilburn Boggs and apostate Philastus Hurlbut as one of the most despised villains in Latter-day Saint history. Although Owen tended to be a bit mean-spirited about his work, he also uncovered

Mormon polygamists serving their sentences. High-ranking LDS apostle George Q. Cannon poses in the center of photo (courtesy of Utah State Historical Society).

the truth—i.e., high-ranking Mormons were not abiding by U.S. laws even after professing otherwise.

Owen remained baffled over the ongoing plural marriages, until one night in St. George, when an informant told Owen how non-Mormons had fallen for a semantic game played by LDS church authorities. Leadership had indeed stated that the church was no longer sanctioning polygamy, but they had never said anything about the priesthood authority within the church. This priesthood authority, considered as something entirely independent of the official church organization, was keeping polygamy alive. The church was merely the "agency created by the priesthood authority."[41]

This same authority had allowed polygamy to flourish for years in Kirtland, Nauvoo, and Utah, while at the same time the church as an organization denied and condemned it. In other words, the church could officially say just about anything as *the church*, and yet privately, by virtue of each individual's *priesthood authority*, members could engage in practices diametrically opposed to what had been officially stated. In Utah, after the Edmunds-Tucker Act, polygamy went underground as it had done in Nauvoo. In *Rocky Mountain Empire*, Samuel W. Taylor explains:

> In 1882 President John Taylor issued an Epistle, "On Marriage," author-izing church marriages outside the Endowment House and temples. Two years later he admitted in court testimony that he had authorized hundreds of men to perform secret marriages at any place convenient.[42]

Mormons excelled at drawing such distinctions by use of hair-split-ting tactics and clever word play. A perfect example would be the perjury court case of Mr. Brown, a Mormon who lied under oath during a jury selection process (*United States v. Brown*). Brown, when asked about his views on plural marriage, said he did not believe polygamy to be right. But the U.S. prosecutor knew Brown was a loyal Saint and challenged his testimony. At the perjury trial, Brown finally explained that his testimony was not false "because his adherence to polygamy was not a matter of 'belief'; rather, he 'knew it was right.'"[43]

And so the hunting of polygs and cohabs continued. The year 1889 saw 334 convictions, followed by another twelve-month span of even more convictions.[44] By 1890, approximately 1,300 Latter-day Saints had been jailed.[45] Woodruff, who had taken over the LDS presidency in 1889, knew something had to be done. But compromising on plural marriage would be terribly difficult for him. As a young convert he had prophecies spoken over him that indicated he would rule over nations, not bend to their whims. One such prophecy stated that he would become so power-ful that he would be able to literally fly through the air like a bird and travel to distant locations.[46] Another prophecy he received from LDS church leaders promised that even if he were imprisoned, he would be able to miraculously break his chains and perform other miracles. He was also told that he would perform various miracles, have kings seek him out for advice, and even visit KOLOB.[47]

Realistically, Woodruff had been put in charge of a church on the verge of ruin. And no kings were seeking his advice. Still, as late as

November 1889, he was betting on at least a favorable ruling from the U.S. Supreme Court on the LDS church's plea against the constitutionality of the Edmunds-Tucker Act (*Late Corporation of the Church of Jesus Christ of Latter-day Saints v. United States*). Ever the optimist, Woodruff had another revelation on November 24, 1889:

> Thus saith the Lord. . . . I the Lord hold the destiny of the courts in your midst, and the destiny of this nation, and all other nations of the earth, in mine own hands, and all that I have revealed and promised and decreed concerning the generation in which you live shall come to pass, and no power shall stay my hand. Let not my servants who are called to the Presidency of my Church deny my word or my law [i.e., plural marriage], which concerns the salvation of the children of men. . . . If the Saints will hearken unto my voice, and the counsel of my servants, the wicked shall not prevail. [48]

Despite Christ's assurances that the ruling would favor the Saints, May 19, 1890, saw a five to four decision by the Supreme Court to uphold the government's right to close the LDS church, seize its property, and redistribute it. There were only two choices: allow federal marshals to literally dismantle and sell off the unfinished Salt Lake Temple, or announce a discontinuation of polygamy. Woodruff chose the latter option, expressing it via an official Manifesto that was released on September 25, 1890.[49] The declaration admonished every Mormon to no longer enter into plural marriage.

"Inasmuch as laws have been enacted by Congress forbidding plural marriages," Woodruff said. "I hereby declare my intention to submit to those laws, and to use my influence with the members of the Church over which I preside to have them do likewise." He added: "[M]y advice to the Latter-day Saints is to refrain from contracting any marriage forbidden by the law of the land."[50]

Historical evidence suggests that the Manifesto was adopted only to save the church and that divine "revelation" had very little to do with the proclamation. Moreover, the LDS authorities who approved it knew that it would hardly affect them since they already had their plural wives.

Several prominent apostles, in fact, expressed only minor agitation over the Manifesto, adamantly agreeing that none of them would cease living with their plural wives. Joseph F. Smith, for instance, told his plural wife Sarah that she should not be troubled. "[Y]ou and the rest of us are all right," Smith wrote to her in a letter, adding that only "those who could and would not, and now can't" enter polygamy would be affected by the policy change.[51]

There also exists the possibility that Woodruff's Manifesto may have been adopted merely as a temporary stop-gap solution that Mormon leaders intended to repeal after statehood had been secured. Its wording and the way leaders publicly released it dramatically differed from every other "revelation" that had been given to the Saints:

- Before being issued, this so-called "revelation" was written, re-written, edited, and re-edited many times behind closed doors by various persons ranging from Mormon politicians, to LDS apostles, to non-Mormon legal advisors.[52]
- It was addressed "To whom it may concern," a decidedly secular phrase that failed to hold the authority of a "Thus saith the Lord" declaration.
- It was publicly issued as a press release from Washington by Utah delegate in Congress John T. Caine, rather than being presented to the congregation by church authorities at a church conference, which was how other revelations had been presented.
- It was not signed by the First presidency, but only signed by Wilford Woodruff.
- Woodruff carefully worded the Manifesto to read "I now publicly declare that *my advice* to the Latter-day Saints is to refrain from contracting any marriage forbidden by the law of the land [emphasis added]," which meant that the entire declaration was Woodruff's personal advice, rather than a command from God. Thus, a sort of theological loophole was given for disobedience.

The Manifesto also included blatantly false statements reminiscent of Joseph Smith's denials of polygamy. Consider the following falsehood, which remains in modern editions of the *Doctrine and Covenants* published by the Mormon church and considered scripture by today's Saints:

> [T]he Utah Commission . . . allege that plural marriages are still being solemnized and that forty or more such marriages have been contracted in Utah since last June or during the past year, also that in public discourses the leaders of the Church have taught, encouraged and urged the continuance of the practice of polygamy. I, therefore, as President of the Church of Jesus Christ of Latter-day Saints, do hereby, in the most solemn manner, declare that these charges are false. We are not teaching polygamy or plural marriage, nor permitting any person to enter into its practice, and I deny that either forty or any other number of plural marriages have during that period been solemnized in our Temples or in any other place in the Territory.

The Mormon church, of course, had for years been doing exactly what Woodruff was denying. Like Taylor, Young, and Smith before him, Woodruff apparently saw no problem in saying one thing publicly, while privately behaving otherwise. In fact, he himself continued practicing plural marriage after 1890, as did many other Saints. Supporting such an assertion are numerous historical records of more than two hundred plural marriages contracted *after* the declaration was issued.[53] Polygamy had been essential for Mormon salvation and not every Saint was eager to give it up—even for statehood.

NETWORK OF DECEPTION

"I live above the law, and so do this people," said Brigham Young in 1852.[54] A truer statement perhaps was never made by Young, as evidenced by the conduct of the Saints after the release of the 1890 Manifesto. Countless plural marriages continued to take place throughout Utah, Canada, and Mexico.[55] All of these illegal unions, of course, were veiled in secrecy. At the same time, LDS leaders penitently asked for the church's property to be returned, their status as a religion to be restored, and more importantly, their petition for statehood to be accepted.

Wilford Woodruff, Joseph F. Smith, and George Q. Cannon unflinch-
ingly swore in court to the Federal Master-in-Chancery, Charles Loof-
bourow, that the Manifesto: 1) prohibited plural marriages; and
2) required polygamous men to live with only one of their wives, thus ending illegal cohabitation in Utah. These LDS authorities gave assurances
that all Mormons were obeying the new policy. Woodruff remarked:
"As shepherds of a patient, suffering people we ask amnesty for them and
pledge our faith and honor for their future."[56] His testimony remains a
stunning example of perjury under oath by a high-profile witness.[57]

Lying, either to bring about a "greater good" or to protect the
church, has always been an acceptable practice within Mormonism, and
continues to be an unspoken tenet of the faith (see Chapter Eighteen).
Apostle Matthias F. Cowley, in his 1911 statements before the Council of
the Twelve, for instance, explained: "I have always been taught that
when the brethren were in a tight place that it would not be amiss to lie
to help them out. One of the Presidency of the Church made the statement some years ago . . . that he would lie like hell to help his
brethren."[58] In reference to Woodruff's false testimony, Abraham H. Cannon noted in his journal that the Mormon president told his apostles that
he "was placed in such a position on the witness stand that he could not
answer other than he did."[59]

And so, in 1896, the U.S. government in good faith granted Utah
statehood. The number of new plural marriages rose almost immediately, which prompted the ever vigilant anti-Mormon *Salt Lake Tribune*
to accuse LDS leaders of deception. The charges certainly were not
unfounded. The very year statehood was granted, Joseph F. Smith, who
would soon become Mormonism's president, boldly defied the Manifesto
during a dedication speech for the Payson, Utah, meeting house, saying:
"Take care of your polygamous wives; we don't care for Uncle Sam
now."[60]

By 1898 it had become apparent that the Saints were publicly saying
one thing, and privately doing something completely different. Many of
them believed that the end of the world was near, so it mattered almost
not at all to them whether they obeyed the law. As Lorenzo Snow put it:
"[T]here are many—hundreds and hundreds within the sound of my

voice—that will live to go back to Jackson County and build a holy temple to the Lord our God."[61]

This same year Wilford Woodruff suddenly passed away at the age of ninety-two and Lorenzo Snow took his place. He became the fifth president of the Mormon church; the one who would lead Mormonism into the twentieth century. Under his leadership polygamy continued to thrive. After all, he himself had served six months in jail for it back in 1885.[62] Like every other Mormon, Snow believed that plural marriage would never cease. But he also understood that times were changing and that trouble lay ahead. The very year he took over as LDS president, B.H. Roberts was denied his seat in the House of Representatives because he was a polygamist.

This event led to an actual attempt in 1901 by church authorities, via the state's legislature, to pass the Evans Bill—a measure designed to take the teeth out of federal anti-polygamy statutes by banning the prosecution of adultery except on the complaint of a close relative, and additionally stating that "no prosecution for unlawful cohabitation shall commence except on complaint of the wife or alleged plural wife of the accused."[63]

The bill was wisely vetoed by Governor Heber M. Wells, who feared severe reprisals from the U.S. government, the American people, and the press. But despite all his efforts to avert a public relations disaster, several national periodicals alerted the country to the LDS church's attempt to revive polygamy. The *Literary Digest* claimed that the bill's objective was to "gradually restore and continue" plural marriage. The *Outlook* pointed out that while Utah's state constitution made it impossible to legalize polygamy, the legislature had passed a law that would "practically prevent all prosecution for polygamy."[64]

A nationwide uproar developed, with a formal protest being sent to the U.S. president and Senate by the Ministers Association, which accused LDS leaders of "uniting in themselves authority of church and state" and using that authority to foster polygamy "regardless of pledges made for the purpose of attaining statehood."[65] This highly visible issue culminated in an exhaustive investigation of the LDS church by the U.S. Senate. On the line would be the future of Mormon Senator Reed Smoot, whose congressional seat was hung in the balance beginning in 1903.

Snow, however, would not live to endure the hearings. He died of old age in 1901. Taking his place was Joseph F. Smith, the son of Hyrum Smith. He was only one of many high-ranking Mormons who had not only taken more polygamous wives after the Manifesto, but encouraged others to do so. He tacitly approved at least sixty-three plural marriages between 1902–1904.[66] These were but a small portion of the documented 262 post-Manifesto marriages between October 1890 and December 1910 involving 220 different Mormon men.[67]

Despite his personal stand on polygamy, social forces and governmental pressure eventually compelled Joseph F. Smith to take drastic steps against Mormon polygamists. Smith, of course, like every other LDS president before him, would continue utilizing cunning prevarications to conceal his personal activities and anything else that might embarrass the church. Nevertheless, the Senate's Reed Smoot hearings would unearth not only his political deceptions, but also the hypocrisy and blatant lying of the entire LDS hierarchy. The church would recover, but only after implementing numerous public relations and organizational changes. These would gradually transform Mormonism's image from what it was, into what it is today—one of the wealthiest and most powerful religions the world has ever known.

PART FOUR

Going Mainstream
(1902–2002)

Headlines relating to modern Mormonism highlight the church's growth, public image, and ongoing controversial nature. LDS author Klaus Hansen, in the Spring 1969 issue of *Dialogue: A Journal of Mormon Thought*, noted: "[Mormonism is] yet another American success story in a society that measures success largely by material standards: Mormons have become eminently adept at imitating and assimilating American middle-class values; therefore, Mormons are okay."

FIFTEEN

Making the Transition

During its infancy and adolescence, the Mormon Church was a thing apart, subject to ridicule and persecution. The Mormons were collectivists under a dictator, almost on the communist model. Today the Mormons are just another religious group with large vested interests binding them to maintain the American system of economy.

M. R. Werner (May 1940)[1]
author, journalist

After the U.S. government granted amnesty to polygamous Mormons in 1891, the LDS church began to flourish. Then, once statehood had been secured in 1896, the door stood open for Utah to become a prosperous, political power-player, and an economic hub of the west. But the flow of opportunities temporarily slowed in 1901 with the passage of the Evans Bill by Utah's legislature (see p. 327). It was an obvious attempt by Mormons to circumvent federal laws against polygamy. The ensuing social uproar over the bill was an understandable reaction to decades of Mormon contempt for federal anti-polygamy laws, even after Woodruff's Manifesto:

In 1897, the first full year after Utah attained statehood, the number of plural marriages jumped nearly five-fold. Political pressures created by attempts for statehood subsided after Utah became a state, and church leaders realized they could allow more polygamous marriages than before because federal interference would be minimized. . . . There seems to have been little criticism of such marriages among those Latter-day Saints who knew about them.[2]

Caught in center of the commotion was Reed Smoot, the highly capable politician elected Utah's Senator in 1903. Smoot, an LDS monogamist supportive of Woodruff's Manifesto, found himself completely engulfed by the waves of anti-Mormon sentiment washing over the country. He lamented: "[T]he whole criticism is laid at the door of the church and myself."[3] The national hue and cry resulted in a formal demand from Salt Lake City businessmen, lawyers, and ministers for Smoot to be denied his senatorial seat. Petitions opposing Smoot contained as many as four million signatures.[4] Even President Teddy Roosevelt voiced opposition to Smoot.[5]

At first, accusations of polygamy, although unfounded, were hurled at Smoot. Then it was alleged that he would not be able to represent the needs of the people over the desires of LDS church authorities. After all, Smoot was not just any Mormon. He was a member of the Quorum of the Twelve Apostles—i.e., a General Authority. This fact greatly disturbed Smoot's opponents, who viewed his standing as dangerously close to a violation of the constitution's so-called "separation of church and state" provision, which forbids a national religion. Moreover, as a temple-going Mormon who had been initiated into all of LDS church's secret ceremonies, Smoot had taken an oath of vengeance against the U.S. for its complacency about the persecution of the Saints and the murder of Joseph Smith.

Mormon financial dealings were under suspicion as well, which again placed Smoot in a questionable position between loyalty to his church and loyalty to his country. Congress simply could not ignore the controversy, and a decision was made to hold hearings on whether or not Reed Smoot would be able to retain his political office. The investigation began in January 1904. Fortunately for Smoot, they did not prevent him from taking his seat in the Senate. Still, his political future was in jeopardy, and would remain so for three years.

THE REED SMOOT CASE

Were church and state truly separate in Utah? Did the church control the conduct of its members? Did it encourage polygamy and illegal cohabitation? Did any temple oaths supercede a Mormon's loyalty to the

American government? All of these questions were at the heart of the Reed Smoot hearings held by the Senate Committee on Privileges and Elections. The investigation would last three years, produce more than 3,000 pages of transcribed testimony, and bring out information on the history, theology, and culture of Mormonism.[6]

Mormonism's Oath of Vengeance

A chief concern of the committee was whether or not Smoot, as a high-ranking authority of the LDS church, could be loyal to America. It had been stated by various high-ranking Mormon leaders that Latter-day Saints were the sworn enemies of the United States. Was this true? Yes, according to William Smith, the brother of Joseph, Mormonism's murdered founder. In 1850 William sent a very revealing piece of information to Congress regarding the LDS church, which by then had come under the leadership of Brigham Young. Smith accused Young's followers of taking an oath to avenge Joseph' s death:

> [Y]ou do solemnly swear in the presence of Almighty God . . . that you will avenge the blood of Joseph Smith upon this nation, and so teach your children; that you will, from this day henceforth and forever, begin and carry out hostilities against this nation, and keep the same a profound secret now and forever. So help you God.[7]

John D. Lee, in his confessions volume, related how he had witnessed Brigham himself taking the oath and admonishing others to do the same:

> Brigham raised his hand and said, "I swear by the eternal Heavens that I have unsheathed my sword, and I will never return it until the blood of the Prophet Joseph and Hyrum, and those who were slain in Missouri, is avenged. This whole nation is guilty of shedding their blood, by assenting to the deed, and holding its peace." . . . Furthermore, every one who had passed through their endowments, in the Temple, were placed under the most sacred obligations to avenge the blood of the Prophet,

whenever an opportunity offered, and to teach their children to do the same, thus making the entire Mormon people sworn and avowed ene- mies of the American nation.[8]

This same oath, along with the doctrine of blood atonement, clearly served to motivate the Mormons involved in the terrible Mountain Mead- ows Massacre (see pp. 243–250). Not only had all of them taken the oath, but some of the same men also had received Patriarchal blessings proph- esying that they would be involved in "avenging the blood" of Joseph Smith and the prophets.[9] Revenge thus began to play a very prominent role in the Mormon belief system early in LDS history, even though the Bible condemns such actions (Lev. 19:18; Luke 6:27; Rom. 12:17,19; 1 Peter 3:9).

By the mid- to late 1800s, the Saints' actually were singing church hymns that glorified taking vengeance (see Table 15.1).[10] And it all seemed to begin on June 27, 1845, when the Quorum of the Twelve Apos- tles, while in their "prayer circle," introduced a prayer of vengeance against "those who shed the blood of the prophets."[11] Six months later it became part of the temple endowment ceremony for every Mormon.

"Lift Up Your Heads, Ye Scattered Saints"	"Awake, Ye Saints of God, Awake!"
The blood of those who have been slain; *For vengeance cries aloud;* *Nor shall its cries ascend in vain;* *For vengeance on the proud.*	*Though Zion's foes have counseled deep,* *Although they bind with fetters·strong,* *The God of Jacob will not sleep,* *His vengeance will not slumber long.*
"Wake, O Wake, the World From Sleeping"	"O! Ye Mountains High"
[T]he Lion's left his thicket; *Up, ye watchmen, be in haste,* *The destroyer of the Gentiles* *Goes to lay their cities waste,* *We're the true born sons of Zion*	*God will strengthen thy feet,* *On the necks of thy foes thou shalt tread . . .* *Thy deliverance is nigh,* *Thy oppressors shall die,* *And the Gentiles shall bow 'neath thy rod.*

Table 15.1

Obviously, such an oath posed a serious problem of allegiance and a conflict of interests for Smoot. To be obedient to the oath, he would have to consider himself an enemy of the U.S. government and do all he could against it in order to avenge the blood of the all the slain Saints. If Smoot either ignored or privately renounced his oath, then his integrity would be tarnished by proclaiming allegiance and faithfulness to the church, while at the same time disregarding a vow he had taken.

There is no doubt that Smoot took the oath, which existed in the temple ceremony as late as February 15, 1927, when Apostle George F. Richards sent a letter to all temple presidents directing them to "omit from the prayer circle all reference to avenging the blood of the prophets."[12] Even if this was merely a reiteration of an earlier directive, Stanley S. Ivins—the son of influential Mormon leader Anthony W. Ivins—stated many years ago that he had taken the oath in 1914.[13] And during the Smoot hearings it was revealed that the temple oath existed at that time.[14] So the oath probably existed until early 1927 and definitely still existed in 1914.

This means that numerous LDS leaders, after taking the oath during their temple endowment, went on to serve in the U.S. government. Ezra Taft Benson, for instance, U.S. Secretary of Agriculture from 1953–1961, took the oath. So, too, did Daken K. Broadhead, Benson's executive assistant (1953–1955). Every other Mormon who received their endowment prior to 1927 also would have taken this anti-government oath—every senator, representative, and judge. Noteworthy is the fact that every LDS president since Brigham Young has taken the oath as well, along with all current LDS church members over eighty years old. One can only wonder how these persons have reconciled their sacred oath with their pledge of allegiance to America.

Making this oath especially disturbing, even in the twenty-first century, is its ongoing nature. It required Mormons to promise that they would teach their children, grandchildren, and great-grandchild to take vengeance on "this nation." Exactly how many of today's Saints continue to harbor within their hearts this vow to take vengeance on the U.S. remains unclear, since it would be a secret not to be shared with outsiders. At the very least it may mean that when push comes to shove, every Mormon acquainted with the oath and taught to follow it will choose loyalty to the church (whatever form that may take) over loyalty to the United States. Even the Senate committee back in 1904–1906 could not ascertain the extent of LDS animosity toward America, although it did conclude:

> [T]he obligation hereinbefore set forth is an oath of disloyalty to the Government which the rules of the Mormon Church require, or at least encourage, every member of that organization to take. . . . the fact that the first presidency and twelve apostles retain an obligation of that nature in the ceremonies of the church shows that at heart they are hostile to this nation and disloyal to its Government.[15]

The controversy over Smoot's faith was further exacerbated by an equally controversial idea propagated by LDS church authorities involving their notion that non-Mormons are unfit to rule. By 1904, Mormons had for many years been declaring that: 1) a just political system can only originate with God; 2) the authority to lead humanity rests solely with the divinely-bestowed LDS priesthood; and 3) the keys of knowledge and power necessary to rule are resident only in the priesthood, which belongs exclusively to the LDS church. In other words, Mormons saw themselves as the only legitimate rulers of the United States and the world.

But loyalty to the U.S. was only one area where Mormons, it seemed, were being disingenuous. The old issue of polygamy also garnered a considerable amount of attention during the Smoot hearings.

Plural Marriage Problems[16]

Sixth LDS president Joseph F. Smith was the first witness called by the Senate committee. During his five days of testimony he confirmed that some church leaders had been violating federal laws by living with their plural wives and marrying additional women in direct disobedience to Woodruff's Manifesto. Smith defended his own illegal cohabitation with five wives, saying: "I have cohabited with my wives—not

Senator Reed Smoot (courtesy, Utah State Historical Society).

openly, that is, not in a manner that I thought would be offensive to my neighbors—but I have acknowledged them; I have visited them."[17]

What Smith did not reveal was how he had encouraged others to do likewise, again in direct disobedience to the Manifesto. Historical evidence suggests, for example, that while he was second counselor to Wilford Woodruff, Smith performed the 1896 plural marriage of Abraham H. Cannon to Lillian Hamlin.[18] Under LDS president Snow, Smith continued to know about, and approve of, many plural marriages.[19]

Then, during his own administration, he gave approval to polygamous unions solemnized in Mexico by Mormon authority Alexander F. MacDonald. In fact, when presented with MacDonald's marriage records by Orson Pratt Brown, a Mormon bishop in the Mexican colonies, Smith said the work had been "duly authorized" by him. He then told Brown to make sure the records stayed in Mexico "so that a search in Salt Lake City could not unearth the records if federal marshals were to get permission to look for just such materials."[20] As late as 1903 Smith had sent a letter to Anthony W. Ivins authorizing a plural marriage.[21]

But the Mormon president put on a different face for the public and certain LDS leaders. In 1902, for instance, he told Brigham Young, Jr. that no plural marriages were "taking place to his knowledge in the Church either in the U.S. or any other country" and that no one had for years been "authorized to perform any such marriages."[22] And at a 1903 meeting of the apostles he claimed that "he had not given his consent to anyone to solemnize plural marriages," nor did he "know of any such cases."[23]

During the Smoot hearings Smith gave equally false statements, saying: "[T]here has never been, to my knowledge, a plural marriage performed with the understanding, instruction, connivance, counsel, or permission of the presiding authorities of the church, or of the church, in any shape or form."[24] The Chairman later asked: "None whatever?" Smith answered: "None whatever." He then specified neither in Utah, Mexico, or anywhere else on earth. He added: "I wish to say again, Mr. Chairman, that there have been no plural marriages solemnized by and with the consent or by the knowledge of the Church of Jesus Christ of Latter-Day Saints by any man, I do not care who he is."[25]

Smith's testimony also included evasive answers, half-truths, and responses wherein he claimed to not remember some of his own statements, meetings he had had with church leaders, the words of fellow LDS authorities, and documents circulating throughout the church.[26] He even denied knowledge of the beliefs and practices of LDS church missionaries and elders.[27] Smith further claimed to have had no thoughts whatsoever when one of his apostles, Abraham H. Cannon, just showed up one day after the Manifesto with a new wife.[28]

The Mormon president additionally used narrowly-defined words to obscure facts. For example, he claimed to not know certain plural wives of an LDS apostle, only to later admit he did indeed know *of* them and had even seen them.[29] He then said the Manifesto was not *a law* of the church, only to later state that it was *a rule* of the church.[30] Smith also described a 1903 meeting (wherein he advocated polygamy) as merely a "select gathering of a few persons," until documentation was produced by the committee showing that in actuality it was a group of more than fifty high-ranking leaders of the church.[31]

Smith finally admitted that he had broken not only the laws of the land, but also the laws of God as given via the Manifesto and other revelations commanding obedience to the government.[32] Nevertheless, he was supposed to be Mormonism's spiritual leader; the beloved and trustworthy Prophet, Seer, and Revelator. Stanley S. Ivins recorded in his journal that the Mormons accepted Smith's actions by believing that he "had to say what he did in Washington to protect the Church."[33]

Other LDS leaders who testified did not present themselves in an any more reputable light. Apostle Marriner W. Merrill, for instance, who took a plural wife in 1901, swore that he had taken no additional wives since 1890.[34] Joseph F. Smith's son, Hyrum M. Smith, not as adept as his father at double-speak, seriously blundered. He first stated adamantly that he had no memory of the subject of new polygamous unions or illegal cohabitation being discussed at apostle meetings. But then he contradicted himself by assuring committee members that when the subject did come up in meetings, apostles were urged to do all they could to stop the practice.[35]

Polygamist George Reynolds testified that he did not know when his own daughter had been born, how old she was, or when she had become the plural wife of Benjamin Cluff (president of Brigham Young Academy). He also could not remember exactly when he found out about the marriage and claimed that even after he did find out about it, he never asked his daughter anything regarding the union. At the same time, he could not even remember why he had chosen not to ask her about the wedding.[36] Reynolds further stated that since 1890 he had spoken to absolutely no one either for or against polygamy and had never in *his life* ever preached either for or against it.[37]

Equally absurd testimony came from Mormon apostle John Henry Smith, who could remember very little about anything that had happened since 1890, including how many of his children had been born since that year.[38] He excused his inability to recall such details by explaining: "[I]t is a matter with which I have never charged myself in regard to dates. The date of my own birth has always been a little mixed in my own mind."[39]

And then there was Mrs. Margaret Geddes, who swore that she was an unmarried mother, while at the same time declining to identify the father of her youngest child.[40] The Senate believed her, not being able to see into the future to 1912, when David Eccles, the richest man in the LDS church, died. Geddes immediately filed suit as one of his plural wives for her share and her son's share of Eccles' estate, testifying that her marriage to him was performed by one of the apostles in 1898.[41] Exactly how many marriages like Geddes' took place may never be known because many polygamous unions were back-dated in church records to appear as if they had taken place before the Manifesto.[42]

Apostle Francis M. Lyman placed himself in perhaps the most comical light by first saying that although his continued cohabitation with plural wives was common knowledge in Utah, he still did not think Smoot was aware of it. Lyman soon found himself cornered by questions from Senator George Frisbie Hoar, who pointed out the absurdity of the general Utah population knowing about Lyman's polygamy, while at the same time Smoot—a fellow apostle—could remain ignorant of it. Lyman answered: "I think it is accepted as a fact by Mr. Smoot, but I do not think he knows it" which prompted laughter from the committee members.[43]

Lyman then admitted his contradiction and took back his prior statement, but compounded the problem by adding that he had been directed by the spirit of the Lord in giving his answers. Senator Hoar responded: "[D]id the spirit of the Lord direct you to make the answer which you just took back and said was a mistake?"[44] Lyman had no answer. The silence only accentuated his earlier clumsiness, which resulted when he admitted to disobeying the commands of the Lord on plural marriage (i.e., the 1890 Manifesto). When Senator Hoar asked, "Have you repented of that disobedience?," Lyman could only reply, "Not yet."[45]

It was painfully obvious to the Committee on Privileges and Elections that the Mormon hierarchy, which included Smoot, had for many years been practicing, encouraging, and solemnizing polygamy. The Manifesto, according to Walter M. Wolfe (a teacher for Brigham Young College and Brigham Young Academy), had been a ruse. During his testimony he stated that LDS apostle John Henry Smith told him: "'Brother Wolfe, don't you know that the manifesto is only a trick to beat the devil at his own game?'"[46] Wolfe also revealed that the Manifesto actually was being used by high-ranking church leaders as an excuse to bar undeserving Mormon males from entering into plural marriage, while at the same time giving an opportunity "for worthy men to take more wives."[47]

The Senate committee ended up voting seven to five against accepting Smoot as a senator. But by the time the committee's report and recommendation finally was debated before the senate in 1907, Smoot already had been in Congress for several years. He had formed political alliances, no doubt made *quid pro quo* agreements with various congressmen, and most importantly, during a private meeting had convinced U.S. president Teddy Roosevelt of his innocence. So when the full Senate voted, Smoot came out on top and he retained his congressional seat.

What the senators who voted for Smith may not have known at that time, however, was that Smoot himself had lied under oath. He claimed, for instance, that he had never heard a discussion of plural marriage in meetings of the apostles and had never himself "promulgated or advised the promulgation of the practice of polygamy."[48] But it is now known that Smoot, prior to 1904, had been present at sixteen meetings, where plural marriage was discussed by the apostles, including a January 1902 meeting, during which Smoot told fellow apostles that the plural order of marriage "if universally practiced would save the world much sorrow and distress." He also said he "looked forward to its restoration."[49] Then, in October 1903, Smoot was present when LDS leader Marriner W. Merrill advised three apostles to marry plural wives. Yet in 1904 Smoot testified before the U.S. Senate that he had never heard a discussion of plural marriage in the Temple. Also in 1904, Smoot advised the First Presidency to have post-Manifesto plural wives hide in order to avoid arrest.[50]

Despite these less than honorable acts, Smoot held his position in Washington for thirty years, eventually becoming one of the most powerful of all congressmen. Consider the following assessment of Smoot that was written in 1932 by syndicated columnist Raymond Clapper:

Utah has Senator Smoot and he has built up a dynasty of appointees which penetrates into a dozen or so of the most important branches of the government. . . . Ramifications of the Smoot dynasty are intricate enough to provide rich diggings for a political genealogist. Chairman of the mighty Senate Finance Committee, ranking member of the powerful committees on Appropriations, Public Lands, Public Buildings, and Rules, Smoot's influence extends in all directions. With it all, he is probably the hardest working man in Congress, tireless in dealing with a tariff or tax bill, a demon for efficiency, once described by President Harding as the most valuable public servant in Washington.[51]

Thus began the powerful political presence of Mormons in the nation's capital.[52] Meanwhile, back in Utah, the LDS church was facing yet another problem—a significant number of Mormons were continuing to practice plural marriage. Drastic steps would need to be taken; steps that would fracture Mormonism into two main groups: 1) the progressives, who agreed to follow the new anti-polygamy path of the church; and 2) the Fundamentalist, who refused to abandon the old ways and teachings of Joseph Smith, Brigham Young, and John Taylor.

RISE OF THE FUNDAMENTALISTS

The Smoot hearings and the embarrassing testimony it elicited from various church leaders resulted in pressure on Joseph F. Smith to decisively bring an end to Mormon polygamy. As soon as he returned to Utah from Washington, Smith faced a major power struggle taking place in the church between high-ranking polygamous officials and monogamy-inclined authorities. Those in the latter camp, like Smoot, wanted Smith to issue yet another anti-plural marriage pronouncement. Smoot warned that if Smith did not do so there would be "considerable trouble ahead for our people."[53]

Church attorney Franklin S. Richards similarly urged Smith to make some sort of declaration with regard to the Washington investigation. Leading apostle Anthony H. Lund also favored a statement making clear the anti-polygamy view of church leaders and the importance of all

Saints abiding by the official church position. Finally, in early April, after much debate, the Quorum of the Twelve Apostles decided that a statement should indeed be made in opposition to plural marriage. So on Sunday, April 7, 1904, Joseph F. Smith issued a Second Manifesto, which not only echoed Woodruff's Manifesto, but added a serious penalty for disobedience:

> If any officer or member of the church shall assume to solemnize or enter into any such marriage he will be deemed in transgression against the church, and will be liable to be dealt with according to the rules and regulations thereof and excommunicated therefrom.[54]

Unfortunately, Smith also included in his declaration a blatant untruth in an apparent attempt to propagate the ongoing myth that LDS authorities were in no way connected to post-Manifesto plural marriages, saying: "I, Joseph F. Smith, . . . do hereby affirm and declare that no such marriages have been solemnized with the sanction, consent, or knowledge of the Church of Jesus Christ of Latter-day Saints."[55] He further characterized as "nonsense" the charges that LDS authorities were "being dishonest and untrue to our word" respecting the 1891 amnesty. Smith then called for a church vote, which of course, passed the declaration just as it had passed Woodruff's Manifesto in 1890.[56]

This further departure from the foundational teachings delivered by Joseph Smith and Brigham Young, marked the true beginning of Mormonism's assimilation into society. But more had to be done. So in 1905 two scapegoats were chosen to be sacrificed as a show of good faith to the government: John W. Taylor and Matthias F. Cowley, both of whom were members of the Twelve Apostles. They also were polygamists, advocates of the practice, and had performed post-1890 plural marriages for numerous couples.

For obvious reasons both Taylor and Cowley had refused to testify in Washington. As a trade off for their continuing silence they tendered their resignations believing that they would be reinstated once the controversy had subsided.[57] These resignations, however, were not made public immediately, but were pocketed by the church's First Presidency until they were needed. Smoot, in a December 1904 letter, agreed with the decision, saying: "If you decide to use resignations do not make them public until I ask advice as to best time to do it."[58]

Even more important than saving Smoot's political hide, however, was preserving the church's legitimacy in the eyes of the government. As Quorum president of the Twelve Apostles, Francis M. Lyman wrote to Smoot: "You may feel at perfect liberty to use the resignations . . . where you need to use them. They were not given for your benefit, but for the relief of the church."[59] But before Smoot ever had the chance to use them, the church's First presidency decided to publicly accept them in April 1906, charging Taylor and Cowley with conduct "out of harmony" with their brethren.

Not everyone accepted the explanation, understanding all too well that the two popular apostles had become sacrificial lambs surrendered up by LDS authorities to protect the image of the church. Consequently, plural marriages continued so regularly that in 1910 the *Salt Lake Tribune* was able to publish a list of new polygamous marriages that had taken place among the Saints since the Manifesto of 1890. It included six members of the Quorum of Twelve and hundreds of others—mostly prominent men in both church and civic circles, including Cowley and Taylor.[60]

So many disillusioned Mormons dismissed both Manifestos on polygamy and continued practicing the sacred Law of Abraham, that for the next twenty-five years (throughout WWI and the Depression) efforts by LDS authorities to suppress polygamy were in vain. Dozens were excommunicated. But far too many Saints had grown up believing in the principle. Even Heber J. Grant—the successor of Joseph F. Smith (who died in 1918)—was a polygamist, although by the time he took office, only one of his three wives was still alive.

Grant, who remained LDS president until passing away in 1945, not only increased action against Utah polygamists, but continued the long-standing denials by church officials about post-1890 plural marriages.[61] In 1933, for instance, he released yet another official statement against plural marriage. This one denied that there ever was an 1886 revelation by John Taylor on polygamy (see p. 316) and claimed that there had never been any post-Manifesto plural marriages that occurred with the authorization of the First Presidency.[62]

Then, in March 1935, the Utah Legislature coincidentally passed a bill making unlawful cohabitation a felony. Even under the worst of Gentile persecutions cohabitation had only been a misdemeanor. Mormon leadership, however, knew that they had to take more extreme measures. So in 1936, to purge polygamists from Mormon congregations, LDS authorities adopted a loyalty oath for suspected polygamists in the church:

> "I . . . repudiate any intimation that any one of the Presidency or Apostles of the Church is living a double life; that I repudiate those who are falsely accusing them; that I denounce the practice and advocacy of plural marriage as being out of harmony with the declared principles of the Church at the present time; and that I myself am not living in such alleged marriage relationship.[63]

Although Mormon leaders continued excommunicating large numbers of polygamists, such action only created a full-blown movement of persons committed to following the old ways. They came to be known as Mormon Fundamentalists. In 1935 the major driving force of this movement, *Truth* magazine, began to be published by Joseph W. Musser. His publication provided irrefutable documentation showing that Joseph Smith, Brigham Young, John Taylor and other powerful leaders in early Mormonism had taught that polygamy was essential to celestial exaltation—i.e., Mormon salvation unto godhood. Their speeches, lectures, sermons, teachings, and writings clearly showed that the church's radical policy shift was nothing less than apostasy. In other words, the real apostates were the ones still in the church, including the entire First Presidency. Those still advocating polygamy, far from being in any way rebellious, actually were the ones remaining true to the teachings and revelations of Smith and Young.

Moreover, *Truth* revealed exactly what Gentile critics had been saying all along—that LDS church leaders publicly told their followers to not indulge in polygamy, while they themselves had been engaging in it, along with other select members of the church. The publication went so far as to accuse then LDS president Heber J. Grant of having practiced illegal plural marriage. Grant denied it, even though he had indeed been convicted of "unlawful cohabitation" in 1899 (nine years after the practice of polygamy was "officially" suspended). Moreover, in 1903, he had fled to England from the United States to avoid being arrested yet again.[64]

Such conduct incensed the Fundamentalists, who not only railed against the hypocrisy and deceit of church leaders, but also took great pains to try and convince others to join the faithful few still willing to be obedient to the Law of Abraham.[65] In the days of Brigham Young, of course, Musser and all of his supporters would no doubt have been murdered, or rather, blood atoned for their disobedience to, and criticisms of, the hierarchy. But by the 1940s the only thing LDS leaders could do was try and shut down Musser's press. They had him indicted on charges of publishing an obscene, lewd, and lascivious magazine. Ironically, the publication printed little more than quotations from the pioneer prophets and apostles. The judge, seeing the absurdity of the charges, threw the case out of court.

LDS leaders subsequently resorted to what has become a hallmark of Mormonism—revision of history. Even before Musser's arrest, the article "Leaves From An Old Scrapbook" had been published in the church's *Deseret News* (June 1, 1940). It stated that polygamy began among the Saints primarily because Mormons needed to rapidly increase their population in Utah to do the "work of subduing the deserts and building Zion." After that had been accomplished, said the article, plural marriage was no longer needed, and so it was discontinued.[66]

But this was not the reason given by Joseph and Brigham for polygamy's acceptance. Joseph said he was commanded to obey the Law of Abraham because it was part of God's restoration of all things before the world's end. Brigham essentially declared the same thing, adding that the practice was intricately linked to celestial glory and entrance into the highest of heavens as a god. Furthermore, the Manifesto that officially ended plural marriage was issued not because Utah's population had reached an adequate number, but for an altogether different reason: "Inasmuch as laws have been enacted by Congress forbidding plural marriage."[67]

The article also falsely claimed that only "Brigham and a limited number of the leading Mormons had more than one wife." In reality, *all* of the leading Mormons from the late-1840s through Woodruff's administration had plural wives. And perhaps has many as 20 to 25 percent of the entire LDS population was involved in polygamy. As the final report of the Smoot investigation concluded in 1906: "A majority of those who give the law to the Mormon Church are now, and have been for years, living in open, notorious, and shameless polygamous cohabitation."[68]

The ongoing battle between church authorities and Fundamentalists continued in like fashion until one of the most controversial anti-polygamy actions took place on July 26, 1953. On that date more than one hundred police officers raided a Mormon Fundamentalist colony at Short Creek, which straddled the Arizona-Utah border. Dozens of adults were arrested and hundreds of children were taken into custody and made wards of the state of Utah.

Of all the onlookers, Mormons should have been the most sympathetic. However, the very opposite proved to be true. Amid protests by social activists and concerned observers over the excessive measures taken at Short Creek, Mormon leaders hailed the action as practically a godsend. *The Deseret News* printed the following editorial:

> The existence of this community on our border has been an embarrassment to our people and a smudge on the reputations of our two great states. We hope Governor Pyle will make good his pledge to eradicate the illegal practices conducted there "before they become a cancer of a sort that is beyond hope of human repair."[69]

Eventually, after the Short Creek incident, an unspoken truce was accepted by both the Fundamentalists and the LDS church. Mormon leaders and law enforcement officials stopped harassing the Fundamentalists, while the polygamists in turn ceased active proselytizing and halted the publishing of *Truth*. A kind of don't-bother-us-and-we-won't-bother-you agreement had been reached, which still remains in effect to this day, for the most part.

POLYGAMY TODAY

Within contemporary Mormonism the *principle* of polygamy remains a sacred belief, despite the fact that the *practice* of it continues to be banned for Mormons in good standing with the church. In 1961, for instance, Mormon writer John J. Stewart affirmed that "plural marriage is the patriarchal order of marriage lived by God and others who reign in the Celestial Kingdom."[70] Consequently, although today's LDS leaders no longer allow the practice of polygamy here on the earth, they do maintain that it will be lived in heaven.

President Joseph Fielding Smith (d. 1972), the tenth LDS president, who remarried after the death of his first wife, remarked: "[M]y wives will be mine in eternity."[71] Harold B. Lee (d. 1973), the church's eleventh president, also remarried after his wife's death. In looking forward to his polygamous life in heaven, Lee wrote a poem:

> My lovely Joan was sent to me:
> So Joan joins Fern
> That three might be,
> more fitted for eternity.
> "O Heavenly Father, my thanks to thee."[72]

But polygamy in the afterlife was never good enough for Fundamentalists. So despite church efforts, plural marriage has continued in Utah, surrounding states, Mexico, and Canada. On June 7, 1998 the *Deseret News* ran an article pointing out the problem:

Utah usually ignores polygamy, hoping it will go away. But its scope and problems have grown and festered like cancer, according to an ex-wife . . . Polygamy is a relic of 19th-century Mormon fundamentalism, still thriving. Today, there are a dozen major clans consisting of hundreds of families. And there are small independent groups. Often the clans are eccentric and insular, while other polygamists blend unnoticed into contemporary American society. Estimates vary widely, but insiders claim that Mormon fundamentalism may involve 60,000 people scattered from

Canada to Mexico across seven Western states. Most of them are practicing some form of polygamy.[73]

In 2001 the issue of polygamy again pulled national media focus
when 53-year-old Tom Green was arrested, tried, and convicted on four
counts of felony bigamy for living with his five wives in a remote area of
Juab County, Utah. He also was found guilty of criminal non-support of
his more than two dozen children, failing to pay back $54,420 in state
assistance from the Aid to Families with Dependent Children fund.[74] In
August 2001 he was given five years in prison and began serving his sentence as the first polygamist convicted of bigamy in nearly five decades.[75]

Green, who prior to 1986 was a Mormon in good standing, embraced
polygamy after studying the teachings of early Mormon leaders. He was
heavily influenced particularly by John Taylor's 1886 revelation, wherein
God said polygamy would never be revoked. During an interview with
the LDS church's *Deseret News,* Green recalled how he had seen
"WANTED" fugitive posters of early church leaders, issued by the federal
authorities. He thought: "[H]ow could these men be prophets of God and
be criminals and lawbreakers?" Green now believes: "I'm no more a law-
breaker than they are, and if they were lawbreakers for keeping God's
commandments, they're my example."[76]

Interestingly, a sizable percentage of Utah's polygamists "reside in
urban Salt Lake County, where they typically keep a low profile."[77]
Green, however, was singled out because he flaunted his lifestyle on television shows and allowed various newspapers to photograph and write
stories about his wives (known to each other as sister-wives). According
to Juab County prosecuting attorney, David Leavitt, Green was prosecuted because of the extensive evidence against him.[78] Furthermore, he
was likely singled out among the many polygamists in Utah because
unlike most of them, who marry consenting adults, Green took a thir-
teen-year-old as a second bride.[79] As of September 2001, he was still facing an additional charge of statutory rape for having married this girl.

A similar child-abuse case took place in 1999, when polygamist
David Ortell Kingston was convicted not of bigamy, but of incest, for having sex with his 16-year-old niece who also was his fifteenth wife.

Kingston, a member of Utah's 1,000-member Latter Day Church of Christ, was fined $10,000 and ordered to serve two consecutive prison terms of up to five years. His brother, John Daniel Kingston, the young girl's father, was sentenced to seven months in jail on the charge of third-degree felony child abuse for beating his daughter with a horse-whip when she tried to escape the arranged marriage to her uncle.[80] Such unions were not uncommon. An investigation done by the *Salt Lake Tribune* "revealed several instances of Kingston leaders marrying half sisters, first cousins, nieces and aunts as part of their religious beliefs."[81]

Despite the many problems and abuses associated with plural marriage in America, as of January 2002 polygamists were enjoying near total freedom throughout Utah and other states.[82] As far back as 1955, a *Newsweek* article revealed, "[M]any a Utah Mormon takes quiet pride in his polygamous forbears and is inclined to be lenient toward the Fundamentalists."[83] Today, a similar attitude still holds sway in Utah. As long as polygamists do not make too much of a public spectacle of themselves, they are accepted by Mormon politicians and non-polygamous Latter-day Saints, who simply consider them somewhat wayward in their beliefs:

- In January 2000, Republican Representative Marlon Snow (Orem, UT) admitted that he has employed 60-70 polygamists in his construction firm.[84]
- Colorado City, Arizona, on the Utah-Arizona border, is home for approximately, 6,000 members of the polygamist-advocating Fundamentalist Church of Jesus Christ of Latter-day Saints sect.[85]
- In December 2000, Anne Wilde, graduate of Brigham Young University and second cousin to the late Ezra Taft Benson, published *Voices in Harmony: Contemporary Women Celebrate Plural Marriage*. This has begun a crusade by American polygamists to legalize the practice.[86]

Prosecuting polygamists remains a politically sensitive issue.[87] Attorney David Leavitt, who successfully prosecuted Tom Green, received numerous death threats against himself and his family.[88] Government offices also received threats during the trial. One menacing message e–mailed to the Utah Attorney General's office warned that anyone prosecuting polygamists would be "destroyed by God or one of God's servants." A second note delivered to the courthouse cautioned that "everyone in court would be utterly destroyed [because] God was displeased."[89]

Ironically, David Leavitt—brother of Utah Governor Mike Leavitt—is descended from Thomas Dudley Leavitt; a polygamist, who in the 1800s married his 15-year-old step-niece and 18-year-old stepsister.[90] This perfectly illustrates the unusual dilemma in which modern Mormon authorities find themselves. On the one hand, they must uphold polygamy as a righteous principle. On the other hand, they must discourage church members from practicing it, while at the same time avoiding any suggestion that Joseph Smith was wrong for advocating it. Then again, defending the doctrine too vigorously might encourage Saints to again start practicing it. And so LDS leaders try desperately to simply avoid the issue altogether.

Significant, however, is the fact that doctrinally speaking, Mormonism teaches that the current practice of monogamy is nothing but a brief interlude before polygamy resumes at the return of Christ in the last days. Potential converts, of course, will rarely, if ever, be taught this belief during the lessons they receive from LDS missionaries. But as apostle Bruce McConkie wrote in his *Mormon Doctrine*: "[T]he holy practice will commence again after the Second Coming of the Son of Man and the ushering in of the millennium."[91]

DECADES OF CHANGE

After Smith's second declaration against polygamy (1904) and the end of the Smoot hearings (1906), Mormon leaders began making a concerted effort at improving their church's public image. Part of their plan involved the implementation of various organizational changes, administrative alterations, and doctrinal revisions.[92] Use of the media also played an important role in their presentation of the church as a wholesome institution. The shift in the public's perception slowly began in 1905, even as the Smoot hearings were continuing.

By that year the Mormon Tabernacle Choir was drawing approximately 200,000 visitors annually to Salt Lake City. Then, from 1909 to 1915, popular LDS author, speaker, and general authority B. H. Roberts issued a series of articles on Mormon history in the magazine *Americana*. This highly biased history so influenced the public's perception of Mormonism that Americans increasingly began to defend the LDS church as a changed and acceptable religion. LDS president Heber J. Grant was especially interested in seeing Mormonism widely accepted:

> By the late 1920s Mormon president Grant conceded that virtually anything the church might request could be placed in the media. . . . *Time* magazine gave President Grant cover treatment, while Hollywood studios completed such favorable motion pictures as Union Pacific and Brigham Young.[93]

Other changes that took place during this era included the integration of Mormons into the larger American society, the interaction of church members with fellow U.S. citizens in urban settings, and the expansion of LDS agricultural settlements throughout the mountain West, Canada, and Mexico.[94] Then, throughout the 1920s and 1930s, non-Mormon businessmen (once shunned by the Saints) were wooed by lucrative partnerships with Mormons. Latter-day Saints increasingly started venturing into public affairs and government as well:

- Edgar B. Brossard became a member and then chairman of the United States Tariff Commission.
- J. Reuben Clark, Jr., was ambassador to Mexico.
- Marriner S. Eccles became chairman of the Federal Reserve System.
- James H. Moyle served as assistant secretary of the treasury from 1917 to 1921.
- William Spry was commissioner of public lands from 1921 to 1929.
- Heber M. Wells was the treasurer of the U.S. Shipping Board.
- Richard W. Young became a U.S. commissioner of the Philippines and returned from the First World War as Utah's first regular army general.[95]

Another contributing factor to Mormon church growth was the growing missionary force harvested from a new generation of Saints, who attracted young and unmarried individuals. Amazingly, LDS membership more than tripled during the first half of the twentieth century. Clearly, the church was well on its way to becoming America's most prosperous religion. But as the practice of polygamy faded away into the distant past for Mormons, a new controversy loomed on the horizon of the latter twentieth century—Mormonism's underlying white supremacist beliefs.

The church's racist doctrines would create a most troubling LDS controversy, especially during the Civil Rights movement of the 1960s. By 1978 the Mormon church would again be forced to make a significant change in its doctrinal practices in order to go forward in society. This time, however, the radical shift in religious policy would not revolve around Mormonism's views of marriage, but rather, of the Latter-day Saint perception of Blacks as humans cursed by God.

SIXTEEN

Mormon Racism:
Black Is *Not* Beautiful

*Had I anything to do with the negro, I would confine them by
strict law to their own species . . .*

Joseph Smith, Jr. (1843)[1]
Founder, Mormon Church

By 1960, the assimilation of Mormons into American society had long
been complete. No longer viewed by the general public as a "peculiar people," they were seen as patriotic citizens dedicated to the preservation of
conservative values and morality. Membership stood at approximately 1.7
million, Latter-day Saint temples were beginning to be built in other countries, and the Saints were gaining converts at an impressive rate per
decade of fifty-two to seventy-three percent.[2] And an inspirational evangelism slogan introduced in 1959 by then LDS president David O. McKay
had set a new standard for church work: "Every member a missionary."[3]

The LDS church also had access to, and was effectively using, powerful media tools capable of influencing millions; namely, television and
radio. Mormonism's world-renowned Tabernacle Choir, for instance,
had been broadcasting for many years over the radio. These broadcasts
in turn led to worldwide tours for the musical group. Then, in 1959, the
choir actually won a Grammy for its rendition of the "Battle Hymn of the
Republic." No organized faith appeared more American.

At the same time, the church was enjoying economic prosperity and
growth rivaling that of any large U.S. corporation. It owned prime real
estate throughout Salt Lake City, as well as major media outlets such as

Deseret News and KSL-TV. By 1966, the church held 300,000 shares of stock in the Times Mirror Corporation (worth $18,675,000), 80,000 acres of Canadian land near Cardston, Alberta, 220,000 acres of land in Florida (Deseret Farms Cattle Ranch, at a cost of $25 million on 1950), and was receiving financial contributions from its members totaling $100 million annually.[4]

Things had indeed changed since the Reed Smoot hearings half a century earlier. In fact, most of the social conflict Mormons had experienced between themselves and general society was over. Polygamy among LDS church authorities, for example, was no longer an issue. That controversy had died out in 1945 with the passing away of LDS president and one-time polygamist Heber J. Grant. But the 1960s did stir up another issue that would effect all of the Saints, especially LDS General Authorities—Mormon racism. Although allowed to flourish unchallenged throughout the nineteenth and early twentieth centuries, this aspect of Mormonism finally faced severe opposition with the beginning of the American Civil Rights movement.

PRIDE AND PREJUDICE

Mormonism and racism have for many years been synonymous terms to persons well acquainted with Latter-day Saint beliefs.[5] The prejudicial aspects of Mormonism, however, have been greatly obscured in recent decades thanks to a concerted effort by LDS leaders to portray their church as an equal-opportunity religion. This positive publicity push began in 1978, when in response to mounting social pressures, black males in the LDS church were granted access to Mormonism's priesthood. (They had previously been barred from that position.) But such a politically correct move could hardly eradicate the previous 148 years of Mormon racist/white supremacist teachings, all of which directly related to the LDS doctrine of pre-existence (see pp. 285–286).

According to Latter-day Saint beliefs, everyone's place in the world (e.g., country of birth, socio-economic status, etc.) is determined by their conduct in the pre-mortal world. This idea comes from Joseph Smith's *Book of Abraham*, which speaks of "the noble and great ones," who lived in the pre-existent realm as God's spirit children.[6] These admirable spirits served God well, followed his commands, and did the most with their talents before coming to earth. Consequently, they are rewarded by being born into favorable circumstances. To be specific, they are born as Mormons in America, or at the very least, somewhere in a predominantly Caucasian country. More righteous spirits are born with more advantages. Less commendable spirits, however, are born with fewer advantages, into lives of greater or lesser quality depending on how poorly they performed in the pre-earth world. Moreover, they are born as non-whites. This is their punishment for not having been all they could have been during the pre-existence.

Mormons also believe that performance in the pre-mortal realm not only determines one's race, but also the darkness of one's skin within that race. The darker the race and the skin, the less righteously a spirit behaved during their pre-mortal life. Apostle Mark E. Petersen explained this doctrine during a 1954 Brigham Young University lecture:

> [C]an we account in any other way for the birth of some of the children of God in darkest Africa, or in flood-ridden China, or among the starving hordes of India, while some of the rest of us are born here in the United States? We cannot escape the conclusion that because of performance in our pre-existence some of us are born as Chinese, some as Japanese, some as Latter-day Saints. These are rewards and punishments. . . . A Chinese, born in China with a dark skin, and with all the handicaps of that race seems to have little opportunity. But think of the mercy of God to Chinese people who are willing to accept the gospel. In spite of whatever they might have done in the pre-existence to justify being born over there as Chinamen, if they now, in this life, accept the gospel and live it the rest of their lives they can have the [Mormon] Priesthood.[7]

Of all the races and skin tones represented on earth, the lowest, most degrading form a spirit can receive, according to LDS teachings, is that of a Black. This body, because of its extremely dark skin, has always been viewed as not being an "honourable body."[8] Latter-day Saint John J. Stewart, who in the 1960s was billed as one of the most widely-read Mormon authors, further explained that the less-than-admirable behavior of some of these pre-existent spirits also caused them to be born into filth, poverty, and degradation—e.g., ghettos or third world countries.[9] Such souls, according to Stewart, actually penalized themselves "as to their circumstances in this world."[10] Tenth LDS president Joseph Fielding Smith presented a similar message in his book *Doctrines of Salvation*:

> *There is a reason why one man is born black* and with other disadvantages, while *another is born white* with great advantages. The reason is that we once had an estate before we came here, and were obedient, more or less, to the laws that were given us there. *Those who were faithful in all things there received greater blessings here, and those who were not faithful received less.*[11]

Blacks lucky enough to find themselves in more favorable conditions are enjoying God's mercy, says Stewart:

> There are Negroes born into families of wealth and refinement, others who are blessed with great talents, and there are those born into the lowest classes of society in Africa, in squalor and ignorance, living out their lives in a fashion akin to that of the animals. Does not this infinite variety of circumstance give further evidence of man's being assigned that station in life which he has merited by his performance in the pre-mortal existence?[12]

A person's skin color, more than anything else, is most commonly linked to one's actions during a great "rebellion," which supposedly took place in the pre-existent realm thousands (perhaps millions) of years ago. This celestial conflict, which culminated in a cosmic war between Lucifer and Christ, affected everyone in a very permanent way. Those who bravely fought on Christ's side were born as privileged Mormon whites, while those who were indecisive and/or less valiant in the celestial struggle were born black.[13] They were born through the lineage of Cain, the son of Adam and Eve who murdered his brother, Abel. "Cain was cursed with a dark skin," said LDS apostle Bruce McConkie. "[H]e became the father of the Negroes."[14] Brigham Young propagated this doctrine as early as 1859, saying:

> You see some classes of the human family that are black, uncouth, uncomely, disagreeable, and low in their habits, wild, and seemingly deprived of nearly all the blessings of the intelligence that is generally bestowed upon mankind. . . . Cain slew his brother. . . . [A]nd the Lord put a mark on him, which is the flat nose and black skin. . . . [T]hen, another curse is pronounced upon the same race—that they should be the "servant of servants;" and they will be, until that curse is removed.[15]

Prior to 1978, Latter-day Saints additionally believed that the greatest consequence of a sub-standard pre-mortal performance was the loss of one's right to both the Mormon priesthood and exaltation to godhood in the Celestial Kingdom. In reference to the priesthood, Mormon Elder George F. Richards made the following remarks:

> The Negro is an unfortunate man. He has been given a black skin. But that is as nothing compared with that greater handicap that he is not permitted to receive the Priesthood and the ordinances of the temple, necessary to prepare men and women to enter into and enjoy a fullness of glory in the celestial kingdom [i.e., godhood].[16]

Joseph Fielding Smith agreed that the Blacks could not hold the priesthood because they represented an inferior race "cursed with a black skin."[17] He also taught that Blacks, as added punishment, "have been made to feel *their inferiority* and have been separated from the rest of mankind from the beginning."[18] Most unfortunate for Blacks, however, was the loss of priesthood blessings, which meant that no Black could reproduce families in eternity like white Mormons.[19] Moreover, since priesthood membership is a prerequisite for holding any LDS church office, Blacks also were effectively barred from assuming any position in the Latter-day Saint hierarchy.

But if Blacks prior to 1978 could not attain godhood or hold any church office, then what could they look forward to as Mormons? Apostle Mark E.

Petersen answered this question in 1954: "If that Negro is faithful all his days, he can enter the celestial kingdom. He will go there as a servant."[20] Mormons, realizing the controversial nature of such a doctrine, for many years sought to keep its existence quiet. Although discussed among long-time members and LDS leaders, it certainly was not to be shared with potential converts, unbelievers, or Mormon critics. Apostle Petersen, for instance, tried to suppress from public release the lecture in which he made the previous statement.[21] And during a missionary conference in Oslo, Norway, LDS European Mission president Alvin R. Dyer warned his listeners to not reveal what he had to say about Blacks:

> I want to talk to you a little bit now about something that is not mission-ary work, and what I say is NOT to be given to your investigators [i.e., potential converts] by any matter of means. . . . Why is it that you are white and not colored? . . . [Remember that] God is not unjust to cause a righteous spirit to be born as a cursed member of the black race.[22]

In 1966, Bruce McConkie (ordained an apostle in 1972) agreed with this teaching in his popular *Mormon Doctrine*, saying: "The negroes are not equal with other races where the receipt of certain spiritual blessings are concerned . . . [B]ut this inequality is not of man's origin. It is the Lord's doing."[23] McConkie was merely echoing other Mormon leaders, such as Joseph Fielding Smith, who assured LDS critics: "It is not the authorities of the Church who have placed a restriction on him [i.e., the Black man] regarding the holding of the Priesthood. It was not the Prophet Joseph Smith. . . . It was the Lord!"[24] LDS sociologist Dr. Lowery Nelson, who understood the ramifications of such a doctrine, wrote a 1947 protest letter to the church's First Presidency:

> This doctrine pressed to its logical conclusion would say that Dr. George Washington Carver, the late eminent and saintly Negro scientist, is by virtue of the color of his skin, inferior even to the least admirable white person, not because of the virtues he may or may not possess, but because—through no fault of his—there is a dark pigment in his skin.[25]

Earlier this same year, the First Presidency had written to Nelson, telling him that his growing dissatisfaction with Mormonism was perhaps due to the erroneous idea that "all God's children stand in equal positions before Him in all things."[26] Predictably, such teachings have produced nothing less than a sense of racial superiority among Mormons. In her book, *Mormonism, Mama, and Me*, Thelma Geer—a fourth-generation Mormon who eventually left the LDS church—recounted exactly what it was like growing up as a Mormon:

> As a white Mormon, I proudly accepted the teaching that my fair skin and Mormon parentage signified that I had been one of God's most intelligent and obedient born-in-heaven spirit children. . . . As a reward for my superior attributes and attitudes, I had been singled out, trained, and qualified to be born a white Latter-day Saint, deserving of emulation, adulation, and eventual deification. All dark-skinned people, even darker-complexioned Caucasians . . . had been inferior spirits in heaven.[27]

Such a mindset inevitably led many Saints in the 1960s to conclude that segregation of the races, a point of heated controversy during the Civil Rights movement, was ordained of God. Mormon segregation, of course, included a prohibition on interracial marriage, which used to be considered one of the most heinous of deeds in the Mormon belief system. As the LDS *Juvenile Instructor* warned: "[W]e believe it to be a great sin in the eyes of our heavenly Father for a white person to marry a black one. And further, that it is a proof of the mercy of God that no such race appears able to continue for many generations."[28]

SEGREGATION ACCORDING TO GOD

Despite evidence to the contrary, Mormons have consistently argued that their church's doctrine has never been, nor currently is, racist. Apostle Mark E. Petersen, for instance, stated in 1954 that he had absolutely no problem with Blacks receiving an education, driving a Cadillac ("if they could afford it"), or obtaining other advantages. He then added: "But let them enjoy these things among themselves. I think the Lord segregated the Negro and who is man to change that segregation?"[29] In an ultimate example of blame-shifting, the 1963 volume titled *The Glory of Mormonism* argued that any suffering due to racism was more God's fault than anyone else's:

> When God allows a spirit to take on a Negroid body, do you suppose He is unaware of the fact that he will suffer a social stigma? Therefore, if you say this Church is unjust in not allowing the Negro to bear the Priesthood, you must, to be consistent, likewise say that God is even more unjust in giving him a black skin.[30]

To Mormons one of the most sensitive aspects of segregation related to the intermarriage of Blacks and Whites. Brigham Young certainly left no doubt as to his thoughts on the subject, preaching: "Shall I tell you the law of God in regard to the African race? If the white man who belongs to the chosen seed mixes his blood with the seed of Cain, the penalty, under the law of God, is death on the spot. This will always be so."[31] In a 1947 letter to a critic of Mormonism's racist views, the LDS First Presidency adamantly condemned any thoughts of interracial marriage:

> Your ideas, as we understand them, appear to contemplate the intermarriage of the Negro and white races, a concept which has heretofore been most repugnant to most normal-minded people from the ancient patriarchs until now. . . . [T]here is a growing tendency, particularly among some educators, as it manifests itself in this area, toward the breaking down of race barriers in the matter of intermarriage between whites and blacks, but it does not have the sanction of the Church and is contrary to Church doctrine.[32]

Prior to 1978, particularly strong language was frequently used by LDS leaders who believed that even one drop of "Negro blood" would disqualify a person from holding the priesthood. Apostle Petersen explained:

We must not intermarry with the Negro. Why? If I were to marry a Negro woman and have children by her, my children would all be cursed as to the priesthood. . . . If there is one drop of Negro blood in my children, as I have read to you, they receive the curse. . . . There are 50 million Negroes in the United States. If they were to achieve complete absorption with the white race, think what that would do. With 50 million Negroes inter-married with us, where would the priesthood be? . . .Think what that would do to the work of the church![33]

Petersen additionally exhorted members of his white audience to avoid marrying not only Blacks, but also dark-skinned individuals, such as persons of Hawaiian, Japanese, or Chinese descent.[34] To combat the danger posed by interracial marriage, the First Presidency recommended that Mormons not communicate with Blacks socially—even to share the LDS message of salvation:

No special effort has ever been made to proselyte among the Negro race, and social intercourse between the Whites and the Negroes should certainly not be encouraged because of leading to intermarriage, which the Lord has forbidden.[35]

Official LDS publications also presented highly racist mischaracterizations of Blacks. One article in the Mormon church's *Juvenile Instructor*, for instance, alleged that Blacks had the lowest intelligence of all humans, were the most barbarous of all people, advanced slower than anyone else, and was the least capable of improvement among the races.[36] This same article then described Blacks as looking like someone, or something, that had been overcooked:

[A Negro] looks as though he has been put in an oven and burnt to a cinder. . . .His hair baked crisp, his nose melted to his face, and the color of his eyes runs into the whites. Some men look as if they had only been burned brown; but he appears to have gone a stage further, and been cooked until he was quite black.[37]

Up through the early 1970s, Mormon leaders continued to promote not only anti-Black rhetoric, but also highly offensive stereotypes and segregationist policies. Eventually, however, church leaders slowly realized that their view of Blacks was harming Mormonism's expansion outside the United States. Moreover, the Civil Rights movement was placing Mormonism in a very bad light; so bad a light that protests against the church were beginning to occur. Organizations like the National Association for the Advancement of Colored People (NAACP) also were targeting the church as a hotbed of ongoing racism. The LDS ban on Blacks in the priesthood would soon have to be lifted. But such steps of progress were not well-received by all Mormon leaders.

BENSON'S BATTLE

In 1966, Wallace Turner's, *The Mormon Establishment*, stated: "The most serious problem facing the LDS church today is the Negro question."[38] Turner forcefully added that as long as the LDS church clung to its racist practices, it would be "a political and social cancer."[39] In Turner's estimation, the response of Mormons to the Civil Rights movement was lackadaisical at best. Their apathy was due in part to strong feelings of racial superiority infused into them by years of white supremacist teachings. Turner, a Pulitzer-Prize winning journalist, accused Mormons of "indifference, inattention, and irritation" toward the movement, as well as a "smug self-satisfaction" that very few Negroes lived in the Mormon centers of the country."[40]

But even as Turner wrote these words, events were taking place that would gradually lead to a drastic 1978 policy change for Mormons concerning Blacks and the priesthood. These events began unfolding as early as 1951, when David O. McKay took over as LDS president. He was quite unlike past General Authorities, according to Mormon sociologist Armand Mauss, who described McKay as being "remarkably free of traditional notions about marks, curses, and the like."[41]

In 1954 McKay went so far as to tell LDS philosopher Sterling M. McMurrin that the racial ban on the priesthood was not a *doctrine* of the church, but rather, only a *practice* of church; one that would someday be removed.[42] He had earlier admitted:

> I know of no scriptural basis for denying the Priesthood to Negroes other than one verse in the Book of Abraham (1:26) . . . Sometime in God's eternal plan, the Negro will be given the right to hold the Priesthood.[43]

But McKay's private conversation with McMurrin would remain secret for many years, leaving the average Saint to believe that the standing of Blacks in the church would not be changing anytime in the near future. The issue was pushed to the forefront of Mormon thought in 1959, however, when LDS officials learned that a small group of Nigerians had not only been receiving church materials since 1946, but also had built a Mormon church of several thousand members. This surprising information prompted McKay to send missionaries to Nigeria in 1963. The team, however, was refused entry into the country when the Nigerian government learned of Mormonism's anti-Black doctrines. McKay's counselors, apostles Hugh B. Brown and Henry D. Moyle, subsequently suggested that Blacks receive Mormonism's Aaronic priesthood.

Meanwhile, the Civil Rights movement was bringing to bear even more pressure on McKay, particularly through the efforts of Steve Holbrook, a young Mormon who in 1963 was working in Washington for Utah congressman Sherm Lloyd. Holbrook had given up his missionary work after being instructed by church leaders "not to work with the poor and to tell blacks that they should attend the church of their choice, but not the Mormon church."[44] He strongly disagreed with the directive, and headed back to Utah to work with the NAACP, an organization which by 1965 had not only staged several demonstrations in Utah against Mormonism's racist views, but had issued a condemnation of the church's "doctrine of non-white inferiority." It further stated that the church's policies fostered prejudice and perpetuated "the contention that Negroes deserve to be the subject of disadvantaged conditions during their lives on earth."[45]

Some observers of Mormonism believed that McKay would be the one to give Blacks access to the priesthood. But he was blocked from doing so by other high-ranking Mormon leaders; specifically, apostles Ezra Taft Benson, Harold B. Lee, and Joseph Fielding Smith. All three would eventually become Mormon presidents after McKay's death in 1970. Benson, a fanatical anti-communist and prominent supporter of the ultra-conservative John Birch Society, was by far the most outspoken bigot of the group. He condemned, for example, the 1965 Civil Rights demonstrations in Utah as proof positive that the communists were using the movement "to promote revolution and the eventual takeover of this country."[46]

Two years earlier Benson publicly declared that the drive in Southern states for equal rights also was "fomented almost entirely by the Communists."[47] This 1963 speech was little more than a parroting of Birch Society paranoia-inspired conspiracy theories. He said, for instance, that before 1973 the U.S. would be ruled by a Communist dictatorship, which would "include military occupation, concentration camps, tortures, terror and all that is required to enable about 3% of the population to rule the other 97% as slaves."[48]

Ezra's son, Reed Benson, not only shared his father's extremist views, but went several steps further. In 1965 he publicly endorsed the rantings of John Birch Society founder Robert Welch, who had publicly accused U.S. president Dwight D. Eisenhower of being a Communist agent.[49] Reed, a member of the Birch Society, then hatched a terribly destructive and deceptive plan to spread anti-Black hysteria throughout Utah using the Birch organization. The plan entailed spreading false stories about violent African-American demonstrations scheduled to be held at the LDS church's October 1965 conference.[50] He sent the following message to all Birch Society chapters in the state:

> [T]he Civil Rights Movement is Communist controlled, influenced and dominated. . . . It is urged that in the coming weeks the Utah Chapters begin a whispering campaign and foster rumors that the Civil Rights groups are going to organize demonstrations in Salt Lake City in connection with the forthcoming LDS conference. . . . A few well placed

comments will soon mushroom out of control and before the conference
begins there will be such a feeling of unrest and distrust that the populace will hardly know who to believe. The news media will play it to the
very hilt. No matter what the Civil Rights leaders may try to say to deny
it the seed will have been sown and again the Civil Rights movement will
suffer a telling blow.[51]

Unfortunately, the plan worked to a certain degree. Frightened Mormons in Utah believed rumors that armed Black Panthers were going to
invade the state. It was reported, too, that thousands of professional
demonstrators and Black Muslims stood ready to be imported under the
sponsorship of the NAACP.[52] Others had heard that assassination squads
were headed for prosperous Mormon neighborhoods and that black children were selling candy bars filled with broken glass.[53] Another widely
circulated story was that "all plane flights from Los Angeles to Salt Lake
[had been] chartered by 'Watts Negroes'" and that "3500 'transient
Negroes'" had already been shipped to Utah.[54] Some Saints even "spoke
of a prophecy attributed to [LDS president] John Taylor that blood would
run in the streets of Salt Lake City."[55] Of course, no catastrophes took
place at the conference. But the hysteria created by the rumors forever
prejudiced many Mormons against the NAACP.

Ezra Benson, meanwhile, continued to propagate his own
racist/anti-Communist views. Then, in early 1966, a national committee
guided behind-the scenes by none other than Robert Welch, began a
push to get Benson elected as U.S. president. For a running mate, the
committee chose South Carolina senator Strom Thurmond, who had
vehemently "opposed Congressional enactment of the Civil Rights Acts
of 1957, 1960, 1964, and the Voting Rights Act of 1965."[56] Benson's presidential bid, however, never materialized because he did not receive
enough Republican party support.

Interestingly, 1968 presidential candidate and third-party challenger
George Wallace of Alabama wanted Benson to be his vice-presidential
running mate. He actually wrote to McKay asking that the LDS apostle
be allowed to share the political ticket. McKay, however, denied Wallace's request, which served to illustrate the serious in-fighting and

strained relations between Benson and his supporters on one side, and more moderate high-ranking LDS authorities on McKay's side. The denial effectively ended Benson's political aspirations and directed him more toward church-only activities.

In subsequent years, Benson continued to advocate not only the John Birch Society, but anti-Communist conspiracy theories whenever speaking publicly. As a result, his popularity throughout the church remained constant amid the ongoing Civil Rights controversy that extended into the early 1970s. He would end up being an LDS church president following the administration of Spencer W. Kimball, under whose leadership Blacks finally were granted access to the LDS priesthood.

WELCOME TO THE TEMPLE

After the death of David O. McKay in 1970, ninety-three-year-old Joseph Fielding Smith inherited Mormonism's prophetic mantle. But he would only survive for two years (d. 1972), after which time Harold B. Lee took over the highest LDS office. Seventy-three-year-old Lee served an even shorter term, dying the following year on December 26, 1973. His successor was Spencer W. Kimball, a seventy-eight-year-old long-time church leader committed to seeing Mormonism spread throughout the world.

Kimball seemed to understand better than anyone that in order for Mormonism to continue its expansion, the church would need to change its policy on Blacks. By the time he took over, the church had been enduring non-stop pressure to conform with America's realization that racial inequality had to end. Consider the following measures taken against the LDS church to break its racist restrictions:

- The NAACP asked all Third World countries to deny visas to Mormon missionaries and representatives until their anti-Black doctrine was repealed.
- The Church of the Black Cross, under the leadership of Rev. Roy Flournoy, discouraged tourist travel to Utah and called for a boycott of Mormon goods including Mormon Tabernacle Choir record albums.

- A BYU basketball game was disrupted by a protest against the LDS church's policy on Blacks.
- A riot erupted at the University of Wyoming after black athletes were dismissed because they wore armbands protesting BYU's presence at the school.
- Stanford University and the University of Washington canceled all sporting events with BYU.
- Discrimination charges were brought against the LDS church for refusing to allow a Black Boy Scout to be a patrol leader, a position reserved for white LDS youths in church-sponsored troops.

By the mid 1970's, the Mormon church had made a number of concessions due to increasing public pressure. They allowed a few Blacks to join the Mormon Tabernacle Choir, Black Boy Scouts were allowed to be patrol leaders in LDS-sponsored troops, and a few Blacks were admitted to Brigham Young University. These token gestures within Mormonism might have remained just that had it not been for the fact that by the mid-1970s the church had expanded its missionary efforts to South America. There they were faced with an impossible task—distinguishing which converts, many of whom had very dark skin, had Blacks in their ancestral line.

The intensity of the problem dramatically increased when Kimball announced plans in 1974 to build a new temple in Brazil; a temple that could only be entered by priesthood holders. Potential priesthood holders in Brazil numbered well into the tens of thousands, but many of these same individuals were of a racially mixed background. The crisis point was reached in 1978 as the temple neared completion. Apostle LeGrand Richards acknowledged to Kimball: "All those people with negro blood in them have been raising money to build a temple." Although his point hardly needed to be spelled out, Richards continued: "[I]f we don't change, then they can't even use it after they've got it."[57]

Kimball responded by asking each of the Twelve Apostles for their arguments for and against giving Blacks the priesthood. One week later, on June 9, 1978, in a manner reminiscent of how Woodruff's 1890 Manifesto was issued, Kimball released a document to the media announc-

ing that Blacks henceforth would be granted the LDS priesthood. Like
the Manifesto, the 1978 policy change was billed as a "revelation" from
God:

> Aware of the promises made by the prophets and presidents of the
> Church who have preceded us that at some time, in God's eternal plan,
> all of our brethren who are worthy may receive the priesthood, and wit-
> nessing the faithfulness of those from whom the priesthood has been
> withheld, we have pleaded long and earnestly in behalf of these, our
> faithful brethren. . . . He has heard our prayers, and by revelation has
> confirmed that the long-promised day has come when every faithful,
> worthy man in the Church may receive the holy priesthood, with power
> to exercise its divine authority, and enjoy with his loved ones every
> blessing that flows therefrom, including the blessings of the temple.
> Accordingly, all worthy members of the Church may be ordained to the
> priesthood without regard for race or color.[58]

Mormons, by and large, were pleased that God had changed his
mind at such a convenient time in history. Even the more rigid, far right-
wing Saints, although not too pleased, took the declaration in stride.
After all, the doctrinal change would create a whole new world of opportunities not only in South America, but in the formerly cursed continent
of Africa. Lifting the ban also opened up missionary doors to the
Caribbean, Central America, Haiti, and other lands where Black ances-
try is prominent in the population. As a result, millions of dollars began
flowing into the church's coffers. Thus began Mormonism's move toward
becoming one of the world's wealthiest religions.

CURSED UNTIL WHEN?

Oddly, amid the rejoicing in the church, few Mormons seemed to
notice that Kimball's revelation directly contradicted the previous revelations of past LDS presidents. According to Brigham Young, Blacks were
not supposed to receive the priesthood until long after the resurrection
of the dead at the end of the world as we know it. He distinctly said:

When all the other children of Adam have had the privilege of receiving the Priesthood, and of coming into the kingdom of God, and of being redeemed from the four quarters of the earth, and have received their resurrection from the dead, then it will be time enough to remove the curse from Cain and his posterity.[59]

Joseph Fielding Smith, in addition to quoting Young on this issue, himself declared that the prohibition on Blacks in the priesthood would continue "while time endures."[60] Popular Mormon author John Lund, in his book *The Church and the Negro* likewise explained the church's position under the heading "When Will the Negroes Receive the Priesthood?" Lund labeled as absurd any thought of a revelation being issued that would remove the ban prior to the end of the world:

BRIGHAM YOUNG REVEALED THAT THE NEGROES WILL NOT receive the Priesthood until a great while after the second advent of Jesus Christ, whose coming will usher in a millennium of peace. . . . [I]t would be foolish indeed to give anyone the false idea that a new revelation is immediately forthcoming on the issue of the Negroes receiving the Priesthood. . . . [O]ur present prophets are in complete agreement with Brigham Young and other past leaders on the question of the Negro and the Priesthood. President McKay was asked by a news reporter at the dedication of the Oakland Temple, "When will the Negroes receive the Priesthood?" He responded to the question over a national television network saying, "Not in my lifetime, young man, nor yours."[61]

Lund further emphasized: "Social pressure and even government sanctions cannot be expected to bring forth a new revelation."[62] Ironically, this is exactly what had brought about not only the "revelation" on Blacks, but also the 1890 "revelation" on polygamy. The spiritual "out" for Mormons is the rather illogical belief that the words of a living prophet (i.e., church president) always supercede the teachings of a dead prophet. In other words, if a past prophet says by divine revelation or inspiration of God that doctrines "A," "B," and "C" are true, then a

Mormon must accept it. But once that prophet dies, if a new prophet of the church says doctrines "A," "B," and "C" are false, then Mormons must accept *that* teaching.[63] Of course, this places Mormons in yet another dilemma—trying to discern exactly what is, and what is not, truly true.

Noteworthy, too, is the fact that Kimball said the 1978 change was a fulfillment of "the promises made by the prophets and presidents of the Church who have preceded us."[64] This comment, however, is simply false. As the previous quotations so plainly show, the 1978 revelation actually was a *contradiction* of the promises made by the past LDS prophets and presidents. Nevertheless, Kimball's declaration was accepted and seemingly overnight Blacks went from being unworthy of the priesthood to being worthy of the priesthood.

But David Jackson, an African-American Saint, pointed out in 1998 that much is missing from Kimball's proclamation. "What [the 1978 revelation] doesn't say is we're no longer of the lineage of Cain, that we no longer did these things in preexistence. It does not say we are not cursed with black skin."[65] Consequently, several questions have never been adequately answered by Mormons:

1) If God has removed the curse that at one time kept Blacks from the priesthood, then why has he not removed the marks of that curse—i.e., a flat nose and black skin (per Brigham Young)?;

2) If some spirits continue to be cursed with black skin because of their unrighteous behavior in the pre-mortal world, then why does that same unrighteous behavior now no longer disqualify them from the priesthood?

3) If black skin is no longer a sign of a special curse, then does that mean white skin is no longer a sign of a special blessing?

4) If a racially mixed couple conceived a child before June 9, 1978, and in so doing sinned by mixing a cursed seed (Black) with an un-cursed seed (White), then after June 9, 1978, were they still guilty of the sin of race-mixing since Blacks were no longer cursed from the priesthood?

Jerald and Sandra Tanner, in their book *Mormonism: Shadow or Reality?*, suggest that by giving a "revelation" on the Blacks without explaining its implications, Mormon leaders are "leaving their people in a dense doctrinal fog."[66] According to the Tanners, if the church continues to hide behind a purported revelation on the Blacks and fails to come to grips with its racist doctrines, "thousands of people are going to continue believing these doctrines and the Church will be plagued with racism for many years to come."[67]

To date such issues remain unresolved. Mormon president Spencer W. Kimball (d. 1985), his successor, Ezra Taft Benson (d. 1994), and Benson's replacement, Howard W. Hunter (d. 1995) were far more concerned during their administrations with removing yet another thorn in Mormonism's side—the accusation that Mormonism is not Christian. The current LDS president-prophet, Gordon B. Hinckley, seems especially determined to do away with any doubts among the general public about whether or not Mormonism qualifies as a denomination of Christianity. Despite his efforts, though, Mormon critics continue to insist that Mormonism is at best a non-Christian faith, and at worst, little more than a religious "cult."

SEVENTEEN

Is Mormonism Christian?

[T]here are some of other faiths who do not regard us as Christians. That is not important. How we regard ourselves is what is important.

Gordon B. Hinckley (1998)[1]
President, Mormon Church

[Mormonism] now insists it be regarded as a Christian church, albeit one with doctrines about God, salvation and the priesthood that differ radically from traditional Christianity.

Newsweek[2]
September 10, 2001

Today's converts to Mormonism enter the LDS fold for a variety of reasons. First, the church is a highly social organization, where new members are warmly welcomed and can find friendship. Second, Mormonism offers a significant degree of self-satisfaction and high self-esteem to converts through the long-held Mormon notion that Latter-day Saints are innately better than non-Mormons. As tenth LDS president Joseph Fielding Smith noted in his *Doctrines of Salvation:* "SAINTS ARE THE BEST PEOPLE. . . . and in many ways superior to any other people."[3] Third, the LDS church advocates traditional values, family togetherness, and a healthy lifestyle (e.g., no alcohol consumption, no smoking, no illicit sex), which makes it one of society's most appealing bastions of conservatism.[4] Mormonism's current president, Gordon B. Hinckley, has noted several other reasons for his church's popularity:

> We give them [i.e., members] an assurance of who they are, sons and daughters of God. People find comfort. They find peace. They find strength in that. And in the organization they find sociability. They find friends. We're a very friendly church. We're a very happy church. We're a happy, go-ahead people. And others like it.[5]

The public's positive perception of the LDS faith as a wholesome alternative to secularism has clearly resulted in a marked membership increase, especially when such an image is coupled with the standard Mormon practice of not disclosing controversial doctrines to potential converts until they are well established within the church. But there exists another reason for Mormonism's incredible growth—the relentless effort that has been made by Latter-day Saints to appear "Christian."

Such a move radically departs from the staunchly anti-Christian stance taken by Mormonism's founders. In making the transition to appear Christian, twenty-first century LDS leaders have been able to capitalize on the world's acceptance of Christianity as an appealing belief system. Most new converts to Mormonism have no idea that the doctrines they are embracing have little to do with the historic Christianity founded centuries ago by Jesus of Nazareth.

AMERICA'S NON-CHRISTIAN CHRISTIANS

According to Mormonism expert Jan Shipps—emeritus history professor at Indiana-Purdue University—Latter-day Saints may at best be able to trace their roots to Christianity, but after that must be considered members of a new religion.[6] The well-known Lutheran Church Missouri Synod denomination asserts without reservation that Mormonism is definitely not Christian, explaining:

> The Lutheran Church—Missouri Synod, together with the vast majority of Christian denominations in the United States, does not regard the Mormon church as a Christian church. That is because the official writings of Mormonism deny fundamental teachings of orthodox Christianity.[7]

A rigid delineation between Christianity and Mormonism was originally drawn by none other than Joseph Smith. According to his First Vision (see pp. 11–14), God told Smith that the churches of Christendom "were all wrong;" that "all their creeds were an abomination;" and that Christian ministers "were all corrupt . . . having a form of godliness, but they deny the power thereof."[8] Smith maintained that Christianity existed only for a very short time after its emergence 2,000 years ago. The faith then allegedly disappeared from the earth through the wickedness of men, who proceeded to erect a false/corrupt Christianity—a product of what Mormons call the "Great Apostasy."

Smith claimed that he restored, under God's direction, the pure church, its doctrines, organizational structure, practices, rituals, priesthood, and ceremonies. As for all other churches, Smith said they were founded by the devil; representations of the "great and abominable church" of the satanic world system.[9] Smith made this all very clear through his *Book of Mormon,* which reads: "Behold there are save two churches only; the one is the church of the Lamb of God, and the other is the church if the devil, . . . the whore of all the earth."[10]

For more than 150 years (until the early 1990s) LDS leaders and publications consistently echoed these sentiments, going so far as to call Christians derogatory names and insult the views of Christians (see pp. 84–87). Brigham Young declared: "[T]he professing Christian world [is] like a ship upon a boisterous ocean without rudder, compass, or pilot."[11] LDS Apostle Heber C. Kimball stated: "Christians—those poor, miserable priests . . . some of them are the biggest whoremasters there are on the earth."[12] Mormon Apostle Orson Pratt ranted: "O, blush for modern Christianity!—a pious name for Atheism!"[13] As late as 1984, Mormonism's official *Ensign* magazine painted Christianity as satanic, saying:

God is not at its head, making that church [i.e., Christianity]—following the appearance in it of Satan—no longer the church of God. To say that Satan sits in the place of God in Christianity after the time of the apostles is not to say that all that is in it is Satanic.[14]

Mormons have repeatedly confirmed that their church is "the only true and living church upon the face of the whole earth" and that "the power of God unto salvation—(Rom. 1:16) is absent from all but the Church of Jesus Christ of Latter-day Saints."[15] LDS apostle Bruce McConkie additionally observed :

> [A]ll the millions of apostate Christendom have abased themselves before the mythical throne of a mythical Christ. . . . In large part the worship of apostate Christendom is performed in ignorance, as much so as was the worship of the Athenians who bowed before the Unknown God.[16]

The reason Mormons historically have made such statements is because Mormonism, as a religious belief system, varies significantly from Christianity, especially with regard to the person and work of Jesus Christ (Table 17.1). In a 1977 *Ensign* magazine article, published by the LDS church, high-ranking Mormon leader Bernard P. Brockbank revealed: "It is true that many of the Christian churches worship a different Jesus Christ than is worshipped by the Mormons."[17]

Mormon Beliefs About Jesus	Christian Beliefs About Jesus
A literal son (spirit child) of a god (Elohim) and his wife.	The uncreated, eternally existent, unique incarnation of God as "the Son."
The elder brother of all spirits born in the pre-existence to Heavenly Father.	The unique Son of God, with whom none can be compared.
A polygamous Jewish male.	An unmarried rabbi.
One of three gods overseeing this planet.	The Second Person of the Holy Trinity.
Atoned only for Adam's transgression by sweating blood in Gethsemene.[18]	Atoned for everyone's personal sins by being crucified on a cross.[20]
Is the literal spirit brother of Lucifer.	No relation to Satan, who is a mere angel.
Jesus' sacrificial death is not able to cleanse some people of all their sins.	Jesus' sacrifice on the cross is able to cleanse every person of all their sins.[21]
There is no salvation without accepting Joseph Smith as a prophet of God.[19]	Jesus alone is the way, truth, and life. No need to recognize or follow a prophet.

Table 17.1

Most recently (June 4, 1998), while speaking to 2,400 Latter-day Saints in Paris, LDS president Hinckley confessed that Mormons do not believe in the same "Jesus" in which Christians believe. The official Latter-day Saint publication *Church News* dramatically recounted the event:

> In bearing testimony of Jesus Christ, President Hinckley spoke of those outside the Church who say Latter-day Saints "do not believe in the traditional Christ. No I don't. The traditional Christ of whom they speak is not the Christ of whom I speak. For the Christ of whom I speak has been revealed in this Dispensation in the fullness of times [i.e., through Mormonism]."[22]

Mormons also have been instructed to not pray to Jesus, which is very unlike traditional Christianity that teaches prayer to Jesus is both desirable and appropriate due to the "personal relationship" Christians believe they have with Christ. LDS apostle Bruce McConkie, however, adamantly discouraged such beliefs during a controversial speech at BYU in 1982:

> [Some people] devote themselves to gaining a special, personal relationship with Christ that is both improper and perilous. I say perilous because this course, particularly in the lives of some who are spiritually immature, is a gospel hobby which creates an unwholesome holier-than-thou attitude. . . . Another peril is that those so involved often begin to pray directly to Christ because of some special friendship they feel has been developed. In this connection a current [1982] and unwise book, which advocates gaining a special relationship with Jesus, contains this sentence—quote: "Because the Savior is our mediator, our prayers go through Christ to the Father, and the Father answers our prayers through his Son." Unquote. This is plain sectarian nonsense. . . . [Y]ou have never heard one of the First Presidency or the Twelve . . . advocate this excessive zeal that calls for gaining a so-called special and personal relationship with Christ. . . . [S]ome who have prayed for endless hours feel they have a special and personal relationship with Christ that they never had before. I wonder if this is any or much different, however,

from the feelings of fanatical sectarians who with glassy eyes and fiery tongues assure us they have been saved by grace and are assured of a place with the Lord in a heavenly abode, when in fact they have never even received the fulness of the gospel. I wonder if it is not part of Lucifer's system to make people feel they are special friends of Jesus when in fact they are not following the normal and usual pattern of worship found in the true Church.[23]

At every doctrinal turn, Mormonism either contradicts or compromises a crucial tenet of Christianity (Table 17.2). For example, the LDS teaching that there exists more than one god is refuted by numerous biblical passages including Isaiah 43:10 and 44:8, wherein the Old Testament deity declares: "Before me there was no God formed, and there will be none after Me. . . . [Y]ou are My witnesses. Is there any God besides Me . . . ? I know of none" (KJV). Concerning the Mormon god's progression to godhood, the late LDS apostle James Talmage stated: "We believe in a God . . . who has attained His exalted state by a path which now His children are permitted to follow, whose glory it is their heritage to share."[24] Yet Isaiah 42:8 and 48:10-11 presents the classic Christian perspective that God will share His glory with no one.

Regarding our alleged existence in the spirit realm before being born, Brigham Young explained that people are "made first spiritual, and afterwards temporal [i.e., fleshly]."[25] Paul the apostle, however, stated differently: "[T]hat was not first which is spiritual, but that which is natural: and afterward that which is spiritual" (1 Cor. 15:46, KJV). Paul is simply saying here that the natural (or physical) comes first, then comes the spiritual. In the Old Testament, Zechariah 12:1 agrees with Paul, saying that God forms the spirit within the body of each man and each woman on earth, rather than in the womb of a celestial Heavenly Mother.

One biblical passage often cited by Mormons to support their doctrine of pre-existence is Jeremiah 1:5: "Before I formed thee in the belly I knew thee; and before thou camest forth out of the womb I sanctified thee, and I ordained thee a prophet" (KJV). This verse does say that God indeed knew us before we were born. Mormons assert, therefore, that for God to have had such knowledge, we must have existed with Him in heaven prior to being born. But in context, the passage is not referring to a pre-earth life with God. This verse is speaking of God's omniscience (cf. Ps. 139:11-12; 147:5; 1 John 3:19-20); specifically, God's *foreknowledge.* The Old Testament prophet is addressing the fact that even before our births, God knows everything about our lives—including our identity. He knows us as if we already existed. As Romans 4:17 puts it, "God . . . calleth those things which be not as though they were."

Concerning our identity as God's literal spirit children, Scripture nowhere says that we are procreated in the cosmic realm as literal sons and daughters of a Heavenly Father and his wife. Instead, we are described by the Bible as God's children by adoption (Rom. 8:15). Furthermore, Scripture explicitly states that God is not a man (Num. 23:19; 1 Sam. 15:29; Hos. 11:9). The Bible also says God did not evolve into deity as a man, who himself had to worship another god—i.e., *his* Heavenly Father. God, according to the Bible, has always been God (Is. 41:4; 57:15; Rom. 16:25-26). In the words of Psalms 90:2 and 93:2, God has been God "from everlasting to everlasting." He is unchanging (Mal. 3:6; Heb. 6:17-18; James 1:17). The LDS belief that God has a body of flesh and bones also is contradicted by Scripture. John 4:24 says, "God is spirit" and Jesus taught in Luke 24:39 that "a spirit does not have flesh and bones."

Even Mormonism's concept of the "gospel" (i.e., "good news") to be preached is far different than the one preached by Christians from the Bible. The Christian gospel is the death, burial, and resurrection of Jesus (1 Cor. 15:1-4). Compare this message with that of early LDS authority George Q. Cannon, who, after saying that the Saints believed in the "evolution of man until he shall become a god," revealed: "That is the Gospel of Jesus Christ, believed in by the Latter-day Saints."[26]

Whether or not one agrees with what the Bible says (e.g., about God, humanity, sin, salvation, Jesus, etc.) is not the point here. Relevant, however, is whether or not Mormonism is consistent with the Bible, and hence, Christianity Clearly, it is not, which means that Mormonism departs from historic Christian beliefs. Robert Millet—BYU's dean of religious education—admitted as much in a February 3, 1998 devotional address that the Bible alone is not Mormonism's primary source of doc-

Doctrines	Mormon Beliefs	Christian Beliefs
GOD	There are many gods—i.e., polytheism. The god of this planet is an exalted man with a body of flesh and bones. He has at least one wife, probably more.	There is one God—i.e., monotheism. God is not a man, nor does God have a body. God is not married. No Bible verses even hint at God being married.
PRE-EXISTENCE	We pre-existed in heaven as spirit children conceived via celestial sex between Heavenly Father and Heavenly Mother. Our actions in the pre-existence determined our race on earth.	Christians are children of God by adoption. One's spirit is formed on earth as they begin life within the womb. God is no respecter of persons and in Christianity there are no race distinctions.
JESUS	Jesus, the first spirit-child of Heavenly Father, is the spirit-brother of Lucifer. Jesus is only one of many created gods.	Jesus is not a created being, but rather, is the Creator—i.e., God in human flesh.
VIRGIN MARY	Jesus was conceived on earth via sexual intercourse between Heavenly Father and Mary (who was a virgin, until she had sexual relations with Heavenly Father).	Jesus was miraculously born of the virgin Mary in fulfillment of Old Testament prophecy (Is. 7:14). He was conceived without the aid of man, by the power of the Holy Ghost.
ETERNAL LIFE	There are three levels of eternal life, the highest level being godhood, which is available only to perfected Mormons.	There exist no other gods, nor can any person become a god, no matter how dedicated they are to the church.
SALVATION	Salvation is achieved only by those who do enough good deeds and obey all of God's laws (i.e. works of righteousness).	Salvation is not obtained through works of righteousness, but by simply asking God for forgiveness and giving one's life to God.
HOLY GHOST	A third god, like Heavenly Father and Jesus, but with a spiritual body only, rather than a physical body.	God, the Third Person of the Holy Trinity, co-equal and co-eternal with the Father and Jesus (i.e., not a separate entity, but rather, one being with the Father and Son). In other words, the Father, Son, and Holy Ghost are one eternal God (analogous to how a singular concept like "time" consists of three distinct units ([i.e., "past," "present," and "future.])"

Table 17.2

trine or authority. According to Millet, when it comes to certain beliefs, Latter-day Saints must look to those additional sources of revelation provided by Joseph Smith, which clarify, enhance, and supplement the "intended meaning of the Bible." As Millet stated:

> Joseph Smith loved the Bible. . . . From his earliest days, however, he did not believe the Bible was complete or that religious difficulties could necessarily be handled by turning to the Old or New Testaments for help (Joseph Smith-History 1:12). Nor did he believe in either the inerrancy or the infallibility of the Bible. . . . As the Lord declared through Nephi [*Book of Mormon*], "Wherefore, because that ye have a Bible ye need not suppose that it contains all my words; neither need ye suppose that I have not caused more to be written" (2 Nephi 29:10).[27]

Herein lies one of the very reasons why Mormonism is incompatible with Christianity—its acceptance of key doctrines from extra-biblical sources (i.e., Joseph Smith's revelations, the *Book of Mormon*, speeches of LDS presidents, etc.).[28] The Mormon view of scripture is so low, despite publicity statements to the contrary, that the Bible's teachings are invariably dismissed whenever they contradict official LDS beliefs. Bruce McConkie explained very well the superiority of Joseph Smith's writings over scripture, stating in his *Mormon Doctrine* that the Bible is accepted by Mormons, "coupled with a reservation that it is true only insofar as translated correctly. . . . The other three [*Book of Mormon*, *Doctrine and Covenants*, and *Pearl of Great Price*], having been revealed in modern times in English, are accepted without qualification."[29]

McConkie's volume further states that relegating scripture to a position below Smith's works is necessary because today's versions of the Bible "do not accurately record or perfectly preserve the words, thoughts, and intents of the original inspired authors."[30] LDS leaders, of course, were condemning the Bible long before McConkie expressed his opinions. In 1850, Mormon apostle Orson Pratt noted:

> [W]ho, in his right mind, could, for one moment, suppose the Bible in its present form to be a perfect guide? Who knows that even one verse of

the whole Bible has escaped pollution so as to convey the same sense now that it did in the original?[31]

Oddly, despite such declarations against the Bible, and contrary to the LDS notion that Christianity is an apostate/corrupt religion, since the early 1990s, Mormon leaders have stepped up their efforts to make Mormonism appear, of all things, more "Christian."

BLENDING IN

In a 2001 article titled "The Mormon Way," *Newsweek* journalist Ken Woodward highlighted how Mormons are indeed "looking more Christian" to the uninformed.[32] This has occurred, in part, through Mormon efforts to place a stronger emphasis on the name of Jesus, without actually changing any of their beliefs about the central figure of Christianity. In a letter to *Newsweek*, LDS church spokesman Michael Otterson "railed against the assertion that Mormons' emphasis on Jesus Christ is all about image."[33] He suggested that Mormons are not changing, but rather, that the world's perceptions of Mormons are changing. Otterson's statement is true. What he failed to mention, though, are the reasons *why* society's perception is changing. Washington and Lee University scholar O. Kendall White, Jr., has observed that the main reason for the perception change is less than admirable:

> [A] quest for respectability, the pursuit of converts, and expansion of Mormonism throughout the world tempt contemporary Mormons, especially officials, to present Mormonism as mainline Christianity.[34]

LDS leaders have Christianized their image primarily through clouding explanations of Mormon beliefs and adopting decidedly Christian terminology. Some LDS doctrines, it is true, have been modified over the years. But most of them have remained unchanged, even though they have been made to sound less incompatible with Christianity. Consider the following examples of the rewording/deletion of doctrinal views from the 1978 and 1997 editions of *Gospel Principles*, published by the LDS church:

Gospel Principles (1978)[35]	*Gospel Principles* (1997)[36]
"Our spirits resemble our heavenly parents although they have resurrected bodies."	THIS SENTENCE WAS DELETED IN THE 1997 EDITION.
"[O]bey the rules, laws, and commandments of the [LDS] Church."	"[K]eep your life in harmony with the laws and commandments of the gospel."
"We can become Gods like our Heavenly Father."	"We can become like our Heavenly Father."
"[O]ur Heavenly Father became a God."	"[O]ur Heavenly Father became God."

The Mormon church also has made various cosmetic changes that have no bearing whatsoever on the many LDS doctrines that separate Mormonism from Christianity. For instance, in 1982 the phrase "Another Testament of Jesus Christ" was added as a subtitle to the *Book of Mormon*; Mormon TV commercials now offer a free King James Version of the Bible, rather than a free *Book of Mormon*; and the church's official logo has been altered to more prominently feature the words "Jesus Christ."

This new presentation of Mormonism as a "Christian" organization has not only involved a dissemination of incomplete and deceptive information about LDS doctrines, but also a restriction of accurate information concerning Mormon beliefs. Consider the story of faithful Mormon Michael Barrett, an attorney for the Central Intelligence Agency. Barrett began in the early 1990s to send to various newspapers a series of letters in which he accurately explained Mormon doctrines and history. This action by Barrett prompted numerous warnings from LDS authorities, including a letter from T. LaMar Sleight (Director of LDS Church Public Communications, Washington, D.C.), reading: "The stake presidency is considering formal disciplinary action against you, including the possibility of disfellowshipment or excommunication, because you are considered to be guilty of apostasy."[37]

Sleight warned Barrett for three years to not write his letters. According to Barrett, Sleight revealed to him his belief that the general public had no business knowing about church doctrine or Mormon history. In his threatening letters, Sleight included information about two LDS General Authorities of the church who were not pleased: "F. Burton Howard and F. Enzio Busche came out on separate occasions and told me we have an obligation to conceal our doctrines; that we are trying to be a mainstream Christian Church."[38] For his efforts to be honest about the LDS church's beliefs, Barrett was excommunicated on April 24, 1994.[39]

As of 2002 the more controversial and non-Christian aspects of the Mormon faith were continuing to be downplayed, in contrast to Mormonism's more Christian-compatible beliefs: e.g., the importance of family, clean living, and conservative values. LDS president Gordon B. Hinckley, more than anyone else, has sought to diminish the differences between Mormonism and Christianity. Hinckley, along with Mormons in general, tend to pin the Christian label on themselves simply by virtue of the fact that they "believe in Christ."

What they do not wish to publicly recognize, however, is that the "Christ" in which they believe is not the "Christ" of Christianity. Numerous religions and widely differing sects also believe in a "Christ," but none of them would ever consider calling themselves Christian. Why? Because their view of Christ is at odds with Christianity (Table 17.3). Contemporary Mormons, however, refuse to acknowledge what past LDS prophets and presidents proudly admitted: i.e., the LDS concept of Jesus is vastly different than the concept of Jesus accepted by Christians.

Since taking the lead of Mormonism in 1995, ninety-one-year-old Gordon B. Hinckley has effectively distanced the Mormon church from anything that might make it appear non-Christian. Journalist Richard Ostling observes:

> Hinckley has held an unprecedented number of open press conferences from New York to Albuquerque to Seoul to Tokyo, and has granted interviews to newspapers, magazines, and TV's Mike Wallace and Larry King. In these appearances, ever the professional publicist, he conveys an upbeat philosophy and smoothes over the more controversial LDS teachings.[40]

Religions, Cults, and Sects	Different Ways of Believing In Christ
Christianity	Jesus was the unique God the Son, Second Person of the Holy Trinity, co-equal with the Father.
Mormonism	Jesus was a god, the firstborn spirit son of Heavenly Father, a polygamous deity.
Islam	Jesus was a highly esteemed messenger of God, but not as great as Muhammad.
Judaism	Jesus was man of remarkable wisdom, who gave insightful spiritual teachings.
New Age Movement	Jesus was a great teacher, who was filled with the cosmic "Christ" consciousness.
Heaven's Gate	Jesus was a good man, whose body was possessed by a space alien.
Hinduism	Jesus was a highly evolved avatar, or teacher, inhabited by the impersonal Brahman.
Baha'i Faith	Jesus was only one of nine manifestations of the divine being.
Hare Krishna	Jesus was the son of Krishna, a demi-god manifestation of a Hindu deity.
Buddhism	Jesus was a spiritual Master, who like Buddha, taught many truths.
Rastafarianism	Jesus was the third great avatar, a successor of Moses, then Elijah.
Raelians	Jesus was a messenger from extra-terrestrial beings.

Table 17.3

During some interviews, Hinckley has gone so far as to answer pointed doctrinal questions in a manner not altogether straightforward; one might even say, deceptively vague. For example, during a March 1997 interview with religion writer Don Lattin, Hinckley was asked about the LDS doctrine concerning God being a mortal man with a body (a belief highly offensive to Christians). To the question, "Don't Mormons believe that God was once a man?," the LDS president responded: "I wouldn't say that. . . . That gets into some pretty deep theology that we don't know very much about."[41] In actuality, this doctrine is one of Mormonism's key tenets about which a great deal is known, according to countless quotes from LDS leaders on the subject.

Later in 1997, during the PBS *NewsHour with Jim Lehrer*, Hinckley made an equally deceptive comment about the classic LDS doctrine affirming potential godhood for the Saints. Hinckley refused to say that Mormons hope to become a god, but instead, said: "[Latter-day Saints] can achieve to a godly status, yes, of course they can." He went on to side-step the godhood issue to say: "We believe in the eternity and the infinity of the human soul, and its great possibilities."[42]

Then, in August 1997, Hinckley again was evasive during an interview with *Time*. The magazine asked: "God the Father was once a man as we were. This is something that Christian writers are always addressing. Is this the teaching of the church today, that God the Father was once a man like we are?" Hinckley not only professed to have little knowledge of this cherished belief, but added that he did not even know if the LDS church taught such a thing! In response to the query about God once being a man, Hinckley answered:

> I don't know that we teach it. I don't know that we emphasize it. I haven't heard it discussed for a long time in public discourse. I don't know. I don't know all the circumstances under which that statement was made. I understand the philosophical background behind it. But I don't know a lot about it and I don't know that others know a lot about it.[43]

Making Hinckley's response all the more disingenuous is his self-professed role in the LDS church as a spiritual leader whose job it is to declare doctrine.[44] Interestingly, Hinckley sang a rather different tune shortly afterward when speaking to an all Mormon audience at the LDS church's General Conference. In an apparent reference to the prior interviews during which he feigned ignorance of key Mormon beliefs, Hinckley wryly commented: "None of you need worry because you read something that was incompletely reported. You need not worry that I do not understand some matters of doctrine. I think I understand them thoroughly."[45] At this comment his audience laughed with a sense of pride that they were indeed being led by a clever, as well as politically savvy, prophet.

OH WHAT A TANGLED WEB

The masking of Mormonism has continued unabated. On February 16, 2001, for instance, LDS officials urged journalists and media outlets to primarily refer to the LDS church as the "Church of Jesus Christ." Reporters also were asked to avoid as much as possible the labels Mormon, Latter-day Saint Church, and LDS church in news articles. High-ranking LDS apostle Dallin H. Oaks made perhaps one of the oddest and most logically inconsistent, remarks, saying: "I don't mind being called a Mormon, but I don't want it said that I belong to the Mormon Church."[46]

Jan Shipps feels that Oaks' comment fits in perfectly with the desire of many Latter-day Saints, especially leadership, "to be understood as a Christian tradition."[47] Mormon church member Kathleen Flake, an American history teacher at Vanderbilt University (Nashville, TN), observed in 2001 that the message now coming from Mormonism "is the language of traditional Christianity." She added: "You have to listen closely for that Joseph Smith twist on it."[48] It is this "twist" and its accompanying doctrines that are continually obscured by the more Christian-sounding terminology that Mormons are increasingly using to describe themselves and their faith.

Mormonism's smoke-screen of words has served to greatly confuse observers trying to determine where the church falls on the religious spectrum. Even Harvey Cox—renowned Harvard Divinity School professor—has succumbed to the Mormon publicity ploy, saying: "I do not at all exclude Mormons from their claims to be Christians."[49] Other individuals, such as Episcopal Bishop Carolyn Irish, are equally unconcerned about the vast differences between Christians and Mormons and take a decidedly simplistic approach, saying: "[I]f someone regards themselves as a Christian, I regard them as Christian."[50] Deacon Owen Cummings, theological consultant to the Roman Catholic Diocese of Salt Lake City, agrees, believing that "God is the final judge and arbiter of what it means to be a Christian."[51]

As politically correct as these sentiments may sound, the fact is that language and logic also can be used to determine what it means to be a Christian. Words we use to express our thoughts, feelings, beliefs, and attitudes about religion, or any issue for that matter, have meaning. It is the height of absurdity to say that a Christian believes doctrines "A" and "B," and then simultaneously assert that someone who denies doctrines "A" and "B" should still be considered a Christian just because they *say* they are a Christian.

To better understand the situation, one might consider Mormon claims in light of other religions. What classifies someone as a Muslim? A Hindu? A Buddhist? A Jew? Obviously, the religious beliefs sincerely held by them. Now, to the more relevant question: What would classify someone as a Christian? Again, that would be the religious beliefs held by that person. Logically, then, someone who does not hold "Christian" beliefs would not be a Christian; just as someone who does not hold Buddhist beliefs would not be a Buddhist.

Rather than asking "Are Mormons Christian?," a better question would be "Are Christians Mormon?" An affirmative answer to the first question certainly would mean an affirmative answer to the second one. But Latter-day Saints would be quick to voice countless objections to any Christian who claimed to be a Mormon and then demanded access to the temple. Why? Because Christians do not believe what Mormons believe. They are not Mormons, and therefore, are disqualified from temple entrance. Does it make sense for a Mormon to then turn around and claim to be Christian? It is simply unrealistic, and seemingly pointless, for anyone who does not accept the beliefs of a particular religion to continue claiming to be part of that world religion.

But this is exactly what Mormons are doing by claiming to be Christian, while at the same time denying or significantly diverging from key

Christian concepts. Noteworthy is the fact that when Mormons seek to justify their claim of Christianity they never mention doctrinal beliefs, but only external appearances and labels. In 1998, for example, apostles Boyd K. Packer and Robert Millet stressed that Mormons are Christian because: Latter-day Saint hymns contain the name of Jesus; prayers and sacraments invoke the name of Jesus, the name of Jesus appears in the *Book of Mormon*, and the church has "Jesus Christ" in its official name.[52] Exactly *what* Mormons believe about Jesus, however, was never mentioned. Why? Because that would have clearly placed Mormonism in a non-Christian light along with every other religious belief system that acknowledges "Jesus Christ" in a decidedly different way than Christians (e.g., Buddhists, Hindus, Muslims, etc.).

Latter-day Saints, in order to appear Christian, have gone so far as to infiltrate mainstream Christian churches in an effort "to convert Christian pastors to Mormonism, and thereby win not only one person, but the entire church to the LDS theology."[53] According to a March 1991 issue of the official LDS Church newspaper, *Church News*, Mormons by that time already had allied themselves with the Free Memorial Baptist Church in Atlanta, Georgia. Additionally, the speakers at a 1991 meeting of eight southeast Christian congregations included Mormon regional president Bryce Gibby and the Georgia-Atlanta Mission president John Fowler.[54] A year earlier in Hollister, California, Southern Baptist pastor Bill Habing actually had invited the local Mormon Stake Missionary to speak at his San Juan Road Baptist Church once a week.[55] Habing's critics felt that he had blatantly ignored Jesus' admonition: "Beware of the false prophets, who come to you in sheep's clothing, but inwardly are ravenous wolves" (Matt. 7:15).

THE CULT OF MORMONISM

Most people believe that "cults" are limited to two types of groups: 1) those that consist of members who shave their heads and dance around with tambourines in airports; and 2) those that gather together in isolated locations á la The People's Temple led by Jim Jones, or David Koresh's Branch Davidians. The majority of "cults," however, can be very attractive to sincere, clear-thinking, normal-looking seekers of spiritual fulfillment. But is it fair to put groups as dissimilar as the Branch Davidians and Mormonism into one large "cult" category? Some religion researchers believe so, as long as great care is taken when stating exactly why a certain religious body is a cult.

Scholars generally examine religious groups from three main perspectives: sociological, psychological, and theological. Each perspective focuses on a different aspect of a group's complex composition, including numerous "red flags" that may indicate whether an organization is cultic from that particular perspective. If one or more psychological, sociological, or theological red flag is present, then that group can properly be considered a cult.

Some groups might be cultic from only one perspective, while others might be cultic from all three perspectives. Unfortunately, this tri-faceted way of identifying cults can lead to confusion. For example, someone unfamiliar with the unique structure of religious organizations might conclude that a nonviolent group (e.g., Jehovah's Witnesses) is as murderous and socially deviant as the Jim Jones' People's Temple merely because both groups are referred to as cults. This would be a terrible mistake. To avoid such misunderstandings, various religion experts, such as Irving Hexham, believe that it is better to discard the term "cult" altogether in favor of a more neutral term like "new religious movement."[56]

Predictably, non-traditional religious bodies greatly prefer the less inflammatory language. Members of these groups strongly object to being called a cult, claiming that the term unfairly places them in an extremist category. They also claim that it damages their reputations, hinders their constitutional right to freedom of religion, and subjects them to religious persecution. Additionally, the "cult" label allegedly frightens away potential converts. Members maintain that the word's negative connotation slanders both their personal integrity and that of their organization. A few of these groups have even brought lawsuits against critics for using the term "cult" against them.[57]

Many sociologists have all but abandoned using the term in favor of nonjudgmental descriptions (e.g., alternative religion, unconventional faith). For these scholarly religion-watchers, making an extra effort to show impartiality by avoiding somewhat biased language might be acceptable. Often, however, their vague terminology fails to adequately help the average person, nor does it address an important issue—i.e., whether a group claiming to be Christian really is Christian. Moreover, sometimes these "alternative" faiths can be rather detrimental to a person's emotional, mental, spiritual, and physical well-being. Therefore, it behooves those interested in religious belief systems, in this case Mormonism, to understand the marks of a "cult." In other words, one should understand the various "red flags" present within three perspectives that can be used to identify cults.

A Sociological Cult

Identifying a religious organization as cultic from a sociological perspective involves determining whether that group's religious practices and day-to-day behavior are normative for the surrounding culture. From a sociological perspective, the primary indicator of a group's cultic nature is a complete withdrawal from society into a communal, isolated lifestyle (e.g., early Mormonism in Missouri, Illinois, and Utah). Secondary sociological marks of a cult, at least in America, would include polygamy, incest, pedophilia, use of illegal narcotics, physical abuse, murder, and the stockpiling of both legal and illegal weapons. Under Joseph Smith and Brigham Young, of course, early Mormonism engaged in several of these practices.

Obviously, sociological red flags tend to appear more frequently in groups that run afoul of the law, which is exactly what took place in early Mormon history. When dealing with sociological cults, however, the government must be careful to not infringe on constitutionally protected forms of religious expression simply because they diverge from societal norms. Debate regarding exactly how much freedom is too much freedom remains a heated and emotional topic that has sparked several court battles. In 1992, for instance, the U.S. Supreme Court heard a case centering on the ritualistic killing of animals in Florida by followers of Santeria, a fusion of Roman Catholicism and African tribal religions (*Church of the Lukumi Babalu v. City of Hialeah*). The Court ruled that

Santerians should be allowed to practice their sacrifices, even though such acts are technically illegal and contrary to societal norms.[58]

Another dilemma that presents itself when attempting to identify a cult from the sociological perspective emerges from a surprising source: sociologists and their literature. Sociologists rarely pass judgments on religious groups, but simply study them dispassionately—in the same way an entomologist might study a colony of ants. Unfortunately, these members of the academia usually end up sending an unclear message regarding the destructive nature of cults. They produce materials that do little more than explain the results of their studies, which tend to focus on simply the inner workings of a religious group and how that group relates to society as a whole. But their attempt at unbiased reporting helps few people understand if a group is a sociological cult, or more importantly, if a religious organization is harmful.[59]

A Psychological Cult

Psychologist Michael D. Langone, executive director of the American Family Foundation, notes that the term "cult" is often associated with thought reform (popularly known as "brainwashing"). According to Langone, this "mind control" model of cult involvement suggests "that cult environments, although certainly not 'robot factories,' are compellingly powerful."[60] They are so psychologically powerful, in fact, that cultists allegedly have their personalities radically altered. Furthermore, their ability to make free-will choices is said to be controlled to a large degree by the group's leadership. Psychologists who have adopted this position usually see cultists as victims of the group, rather than active participants responding with a totally free will. Langone offers his definition of a cult from this psychological perspective:

> A cult is a group or movement that, to a significant degree, (a) exhibits great or excessive devotion or dedication to some person, idea, or thing, (b) uses a thought-reform program to persuade, control, and socialize members (i.e., to integrate them into the group's unique pattern of relationships, beliefs, values, and practices), (c) systematically induces

states of psychological dependency in members, (d) exploits members to advance the leadership's goals, and (e) causes psychological harm to members, their families, and the community.[61]

Langone has been aggressively studying the psychological dynamics of cults since 1978, serving from 1984 to 1987 on the American Psychological Association Task Force on Deceptive and Indirect Techniques of Persuasion and Control. Through counseling hundreds of former cultists, Langone has discovered several psychological red flags common to cults. Each reveals the psychologically manipulative nature of cults:

- Information is withheld from new converts about the group's ultimate agenda.
- The presence of a dictatorial leadership that tells with "excruciating specificity" exactly how members are to think, feel and act.
- An absence of leader accountability to persons outside the group's power structure.[62]

Other religion experts and psychologists have discovered even more ways that a cult's leader(s) try to interrupt the normal thought processes of their followers:

1. Isolation of members—psychologically and/or physically—from individuals outside the group whose ideas and philosophies are contrary to those promoted by the group.
2. Intense "love-bombing" that so powerfully affects individuals with deep-seated emotional needs that those persons are psychologically thrown off balance. They are faced with an agonizing decision: stay with the group and receive love, or leave the group and lose love.
3. A systematic replacement of the pre-conversion identities of members with a new group-related identity. This sometimes includes the destruction of personal possessions and the destruction of family ties.
4. Rapid-fire teaching techniques that do not allow members to think critically about what is being said, coupled with an environment

wherein open discussion of relevant issues and the expression of contrary opinions is discouraged.

5. The use of fear and intimidation against members who desire to leave the group, or former members seeking to break ties with the group.

6. Use of deceptive recruitment techniques that include false information about the group's doctrinal beliefs and cover-ups of negative episodes in the group's history.

7. Total, unquestioning allegiance to a central leader or elite core of leaders.

8. The promotion of an "ends justifies the means" philosophy within the group.

9. An "us vs. them" mentality that stresses the group's unique hold on truth and demonizes anyone who opposes that alleged truth.

10. An inordinate emphasis on submission and obedience to group authority, which effectively "guilts" a person into submission.

11. Consistent stress on the importance of following the divinely revealed truths being taught by a group's leader or leaders.

12. A siege mentality that dismisses all criticisms of the group from outside sources as unwarranted "persecution."

13. Shunning and harsh criticism of "rebellious" members who question the teachings or practices of the group.

14 An elitist attitude that is drilled into members, which states that those outside the group are spiritually lukewarm, comprising, or entirely lost.

15. Excessive control over personal aspects of members' lives: e.g., where to live, where to work, who to date, who to marry, what literature to read, when vacations can be taken, etc.

16. Rigid restrictions relating to the sleeping habits, food intake, exercise, and leisure time of members.[63]

Not every technique must be used by a group in order for it to be cultic from a psychological perspective. Meeting only a few of these points might be enough to legitimately call a group cultic. According to psychologist Margaret Singer—another advocate of the mind control model—a cult is "basically a power structure wherein one person [or persons] has proclaimed himself [or herself, or themselves] to have some special knowledge. And if he [or she, or they] can convince others to let him [or her, or them] be in charge, he [or she, or they] will share that knowledge."[64]

But do these practices amount to "brainwashing"? Do cultists really have their wills rendered almost obsolete? Such thought-provoking questions highlight an extremely controversial area of cult studies. Countless debates between organizations trying to help persons involved in authoritarian groups have arisen over this issue. Many cult researchers disagree with the opinion of Langone and Singer, taking the position that cultists are not "brainwashed" at all, nor are they incapable of making free-will choices.

This alternative view proposes that the psychologically manipulative practices of cults and cult leaders merely disrupt a person's thinking pattern so that their ability to make rational, well-reasoned choices is somewhat hampered, not destroyed (e.g., if a cultist is deprived of sleep and food and encouraged to continue in a Bible study for ten hours straight, then that cultist's ability to make a good choice is certainly hindered, but he or she is still free at any time to simply say, "Look, I'm leaving. I need to get some sleep and food because I can't think clearly").

Cultists can, and often do, choose to leave a cult. Many cultists, despite being subjected to a vast array of psychologically manipulative techniques, continue processing information and making choices based on what they consciously want to do. During an interview I conducted in 1993, former Branch Davidian David Bunds explained to me that this was the case within David Koresh's group. Although Koresh used a number of psychologically manipulative techniques on his followers, each person was still able to reason. Some members left the group. Many others consciously chose to stay:

> [T]his idea that they [Davidians] were mindless, unthinking people is not true. They thought a lot. They did a lot of thinking, a lot of analyzing, and a lot of data processing, but their entire base, their entire worldview, their pre-suppositional base was completely crazy—It was false.

As for Mormonism, Bunds' observation and several of the previously listed "red flags" from the psychological perspective apply. Latter-day Saints, for instance, are discouraged from reading material critical of their faith, which would be consistent with psychological isolation (red flag #1). Deceptive recruitment tactics are used when Mormons fail to divulge LDS doctrines or cover up their church's history (red flag #6). As previously demonstrated, Latter-day Saint authorities (e.g., Joseph Smith, Brigham Young, Wilford Woodruff, Joseph F. Smith, Gordon B. Hinckley) typically have lived by an "ends justifies the means" philosophy whereby they lie, obscure the truth, and break laws to insure the church's well-being (red flag #8). And as Chapter Eighteen of this book will show, Mormon officials routinely have shunned and harshly treated (e.g., excommunicated) members simply for speaking the truth, questioning long-held beliefs, and exposing church secrets (red flag #13). Other psychological "red flags" applicable to Mormonism would include numbers seven, nine, twelve, and fourteen.

A Theological Cult

Religious groups such as the LDS church, which has had a cultic history from both a psychological and sociological perspective, always run the risk of evolving into a cult from a theological perspective. This leads us to the final, and to many, the most significant component of the definition of a cult: its theology (i.e., its teachings about God and related doctrines). Defining a cult from a theological perspective involves judging a group's doctrines against the beliefs of the major religion with which that cult claims association.[65]

This method of cult identification is used not only by Christians, but also by members of other major religions. For example, the Nation of Islam is a cult of Islam (see endnote #73). Aum Shinrikyo is a cult of Buddhism. The International Society for Krishna Consciousness (ISKCON), known as the Hare Krishnas, is a Hindu cult. Christianity, too, has its share of cults, which are appropriately termed pseudo-Christian. Several evangelicals have offered definitions for these groups. Although similar, each one provides a different shade to the overall picture of a cult from a Christian/theological viewpoint:

- "[A] group of people gathered about a specific person or person's interpretation of the Bible. . . . [C]ults contain not a few major deviations from historic Christianity. Yet, paradoxically, they continue to insist that they are entitled to be classified as Christians."[66]

- "[A]ny religious movement which claims the backing of Christ or the Bible, but distorts the central message of Christianity by 1) an additional revelation, and 2) by displacing a fundamental tenet of the faith with a secondary matter."[67]

- "[A group adhering to] . . . doctrines which are pointedly contradictory to orthodox Christianity yet which claim the distinction of either tracing their origin to orthodox sources or of being in essential harmony with those sources."[68]

- "[A] perversion, a distortion of biblical Christianity and/or a rejection of the historic teachings of the Christian church."[69]

- "A cult of Christianity is a group of people, which claiming to be Christian, embraces a particular doctrinal system taught by an individual, group of leaders, or organization, which (system) denies (either explicitly or implicitly) one or more of the central doctrines of the Christian faith as taught in the sixty-six books of the Bible."[70]

- "[A] group of persons polarized around a heretical interpretation of religious truth. Such groups typically cite the Bible and claim to be in harmony with Christianity, but deny such basic doctrines of the Christian faith as the Trinity, the unique deity of Jesus Christ, salvation by grace alone, and justification by faith."[71]

Mormonism, as previously shown, fits each of these definitions. And so, in answer to the question "Are Mormons Christian?," the only theologically accurate answer that can be given is no.[72] In reply to the question, "Is Mormonism a cult?," a very strong case can be made for saying yes—certainly from a theological perspective, and arguably, from a psychological perspective. Mormon leaders, of course, bristle at such accusations. In February 1998, for instance, LDS apostle Boyd K. Packer told a BYU audience of 15,000 students that those who refuse to classify Mormonism as Christian are "uninformed and unfair and not consistent with the spirit of Christian brotherhood."[73]

But Packer seems to have conveniently forgotten the words of his own church's prophets and apostles, who have claimed that Latter-day Saints are the only true followers of God and that the LDS church is the only true church. Mormon expert Eric Johnson of Southern California's Mormonism Research Ministry, insightfully responded:

> The fact that several LDS leaders have on numerous occasions used the expression "so-called Christianity" when speaking of Christendom, exposes the hypocrisy of Packer's complaints. His church can question the Christianity of others, but it is wrong to question his [church].[74]

Despite the many long-standing problems with Mormonism and its leaders, humanity may be witnessing the birth of the first new world religion since Islam. However, if this is going to occur, the LDS hierarchy will have to at some point, once and for all, completely sever its ties with Christianity. Only by taking such an approach will Mormonism be able to forever distance itself from the "cult" label and claim for itself some degree of legitimacy and integrity in the eyes of many religion researchers, especially those adhering to the historic Christian faith.

EIGHTEEN

Cover-Ups, Conspiracies, and Controversies

The story of the Mormon pioneers is in many ways the story of America. It is the story of everyone who has ever traveled to our shores seeking freedom to worship according to the dictates of their own conscience. And it is the story of a people who know that, with hard work and faith in God, they can accomplish anything.

U.S. President, Bill Clinton[1]

July 29, 1997

Mormonism stands on the threshold of achieving unparalleled prestige among government leaders, growth well beyond its current membership of eleven million, and wealth far exceeding its current global worth of approximately $25–$30 billion.[2] As the official *LDS Church News* correctly reported in 2001, most journalists no longer look upon Latter-day Saints as "a cult group with weird ideas running from the mobs in Missouri."[3]

Indeed, the church now appears about as conventional as any other mainstream religion, at least to casual observers with little knowledge of Mormonism's beliefs or inner workings. Enhancing this positive public image is the church's Visitors Center in Salt Lake City, which hosts five million guests each year. Another public relations boost comes from a force of nearly 61,000 full-time LDS missionaries scattered across the globe.[4] There also are various Mormon entertainers, such as The Osmonds (see photos, p. 402), who have used their popularity to spread the LDS message far and wide.

Possibly one of the oddest albums MGM Records ever produced. The inner sleeve of this 1973 release (*lower*) refers listeners to Abraham 3:3-16 (written just above the graphic of KOLOB held in Elohim's hand). *The Book of Abraham* (see Appendix C) is in the LDS church's *Pearl of Great Price* and details Mormonism's view of earth's creation. The inscription in the upper right corner (not visible in the image) is Lorenzo Snow's famous encapsulation of Mormon belief: "As man is, God once was; as God is, man may become." The record was released by MGM, but in association with Kolob Records, recorded at Kolob Studios. Kolob, according to Mormonism, is a planet near the celestial home of Heavenly Father and his wives. Interestingly, this album was re-released on October 16, 2001.

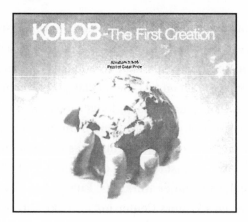

The ever-popular Mormon Tabernacle Choir, of course, has been one of the most effective tools of evangelism used by Latter-day Saints to proselytize unsuspecting music lovers and build a positive church image. The world-renowned group most recently performed at the inaugural celebration for President George W. Bush—"just as it did at the inauguration for his father and for four other U.S. presidential inaugurations."[5] Their invitation was secured by Mormon Sen. Orrin Hatch.[6]

LDS leaders have stopped at almost nothing to maintain Mormonism's sparkling image. One of their primary goals is to keep both Saints and non-believers focused on the positive, rather than the negative, aspects of the church. Such efforts have led to numerous cover-ups, conspiracies, and controversies.[7] Many of these black marks against the LDS church, however, have gone largely unnoticed by most people. Consequently, the general public, especially outside America, still possesses little knowledge of the unsavory nature of Mormonism. This lack of widespread information about LDS-related issues and what goes on in Utah have led detractors of Mormonism to describe America's Latter-day Saint stronghold of the west as being "Behind the Zion Curtain."[8]

Few Americans, for instance, know that in 1993 Mormons decided to baptize by proxy Adolf Hitler and seal him for eternity to his mistress, Eva Braun.[9] It was apparently done in order to give Hitler an opportunity to accept Mormonism in the afterlife and thereby become a god. This practice of baptizing dead individuals by proxy, which must take place inside LDS temples, is the prime reason for Mormonism's current push to build more temples worldwide. According to reporter Bob Mims of the *Salt Lake Tribune*, Mormons believe that proxy baptisms provide those in the after-life the choice to join, or reject, the LDS faith. The rite is intended as a way of offering salvation to non-Mormon ancestors, but sometimes "more zealous Mormons have sought baptism for prominent historical and religious figures."[10]

The zeal with which Mormons baptize the dead, which is a patently non-Christian practice, has led to baptisms by proxy of a wide range of notable non-Mormons including: all the signers of the Declaration of Independence, Abraham Lincoln, Paul Revere, William Shakespeare, Napoleon Bonaparte, Christopher Columbus, David Livingstone (a Christian Missionary), "Frederick the Great" (King of Prussia), Daniel Webster (American statesman), and John Wesley (Christian Evangelist).[11]

As odd as this practice may seem to outsiders, it has become nothing less than an *idée fixé* with Mormons, which accounts for their unwavering focus on genealogies and genealogical research.[12] The Saints have baptized hundreds of millions of deceased persons in this manner, many of whom had their names culled from obituaries, tombstones, state death records, and historical documents.[13] Any and all persons are fair game, so to speak, despite the faith they professed during their lives. Consequently, it is possible that many readers of this book have had their deceased relatives baptized by proxy into Mormonism, even though such persons might not have wanted anything to do with Mormonism during their lives.

Back in 1995, for example, it was learned that Mormons took it upon themselves to baptize by proxy a veritable Who's Who of the 20th century's most notable Jews, along with many deceased Jews who had perished in Nazi concentration camps. The list of Jewish persons baptized into the church by proxy (i.e., by having a Mormon standing in for them) included: Anne Frank, Sigmund Freud, David Ben-Gurion (Israel's first prime minister), and Ba'al Shem Tov, the 18th century Polish rabbi who founded the Hasidic Jewish movement.[14]

According to Aaron Breitbart, senior researcher for the Los Angeles-based Simon Wiesenthal Center, "[t]hese people were born Jews, they lived as Jews and many of them died because they were Jews. . . . They would not have chosen to be baptized Mormons in life, and there is no reason they would want to be baptized by proxy in death."[15] As of May 2001 the demand by Jewish organizations to remove the names of such individuals from LDS church baptism records still had not been met, although LDS spokespersons said the problem was being resolved. Equally troubling have been many other newsworthy events connected to Mormonism, especially those involving church-sanctioned censorship, suppression of information, and historical revisionism.

UNHISTORICAL HISTORY

According to former LDS church historian Leonard J. Arrington, "[f]rom its inception the Church of Jesus Christ of Latter-day Saints has sought to leave an accurate and complete record of its history."[16] But what is routinely presented by the church as official "history" has much more in common with well-crafted myths designed to tell uplifting stories about a specific LDS hero or set of heroes. It produces "faith" in church members, but bears little resemblance to historical fact. In 1999, long-time Mormon, Francis Nelson Henderson, a founding member of Comtel (a satellite communications company), publicly announced that he had left Mormonism because his trust in the church had been violated by LDS leaders' disreputable take on what constitutes good history:

> [C]hurch policy is that the only Mormon history told should be a so-called "faith promoting" history which conceals controversies and difficulties of the Mormon past and present. . . . [A] policy of changing, retelling, or withholding information, is willful manipulation of my ongoing right to an informed choice.[17]

Henderson's observation highlights an ongoing problem within Mormonism. LDS leaders, especially General Authorities and historians, are "not only anxious to forget the past, but actively suppress the activities of would-be researchers in Mormon archives."[18] Few issues trouble Latter-day officials as much as the constant threat of accurate Mormon history being revealed to the general public, potential converts, and/or church members. In his article "Truth and Mistruth in Mormon History," author B. Carmon Hardy additionally observed: "Apart from purposeful misrepresentation, there is also the practice, both past and present, of suppressing historical materials or, if not suppressing them, of discouraging their discovery."[19]

Journalist Richard Ostling agrees, having discovered that in official LDS publications sensitive issues "frequently are downplayed, avoided, or denied."[20] Such scholarly sins of omission are accentuated by blatant historical revisionism wherein LDS leaders re-write historical documents, deny that other documents exist, create fictitious historical data, add words to update old revelations so that they conform to current events/knowledge, and delete various sections of divine pronouncements said to have been transcribed perfectly when originally delivered. As a result, truth to Mormons "is not absolute or fixed; it is changeable, flexible, and additive."[21]

Numerous examples of looking at history in a "changeable" truth way is perhaps most pronounced in Mormonism's official *History of the Church*, supposedly written by Joseph Smith. In reality, the majority (approximately, 60 percent, or more than 2,000 pages) of this multi-volume set of books was composed by LDS officials and historians *after* Smith's death in an effort to build the faith of church members. Moreover, certain segments of the text that Smith actually did write were deleted in order to cover up embarrassing or contradictory statements.[22]

The behind-the-scenes authors also copied portions of various diaries, journals, and even newspaper articles, then changed them to read as if Joseph Smith himself had written the material (Table 18.1). Although such changes were drastic, no notations were added to the published text that would have alerted readers to the many liberties that had been taken with the original manuscripts. This was a flagrant breach of standard protocol for persons producing historical works.

As a result, Mormons perusing the official *History of the Church* are under the mistaken impression that what they are reading is accurate, original material. Yet this is not the case. For example, two Joseph Smith prophecies contained in the church's so-called history were not even uttered by Smith, but instead, were created after his death in an effort to glorify his accomplishments and confirm his prophetic abilities.

One of the forged predictions is about "a mighty people" (i.e., the Mormons) that would dwell "in the midst of the Rocky Mountains," while the other is a prediction about the political career of Senator Steven A. Douglas (1813–1861, D-Illinois).[23] Although both are impressive, neither one came from Smith. Yet most Mormons today enthusiastically point to them as proof of their prophet's divine powers and his appointment as God's representative on earth.

The Wasp	*History of the Church*
(original newspaper report)	(alleged Joseph Smith account)
Joseph Smith was arrested upon a requisition of Gov. Carlin, . . . in accordance with a process from Gov. Reynolds of Missouri, upon the affidavit of Ex-Governor Boggs, . . . [T]he Municipal court issued a writ of habeas corpus according to the constitution of the State, . . . *[T]hey left them* in care of the Marshal, without the original writ *by which they* were arrested, and by which *only they* could be retained, and returned back to Gov. Carlin for further instruction,—*and Messrs. Smith* and Rockwell went about their business. *As to Mr. Smith, we have yet to learn* by what rule of right *he was arrested* to be transported to Missouri for a trial of the kind stated [emphases added for clarity].[24]	*I was arrested* . . . on a warrant issued by Governor Carlin, founded on a requisition from Governor Reynolds of Missouri, upon the affidavit of ex-Governor Boggs, . . . [T]he municipal court issued a writ of habeas corpus according to the constitution of the state, . . . *[T]hey left us* in the care of the marshal, without the original writ *by which we* were arrested, and by which *only we* could be retained, and returned to Governor Carlin for further instructions, *and myself* and Rockwell went about *our business. I have yet to learn* by what rule of right *I was arrested* to be transported to Missouri for a trial of the kind stated [emphases added for clarity].[25]

Table 18.1

When carefully compared to the original handwritten documents from which the modern *History of the Church* was prepared, it seems that more than 62,000 words were either added or deleted, often leading to substantive changes in the meaning of the passages.[26] LDS author Samuel W. Taylor has found that vital facts have not only been omitted from the texts, but sometimes re-written to give a false impression of what took place.[27] Volume six of the *History*, for instance, contains the minutes from Smith's October 1843 church conference regarding Sidney Rigdon (vol. 6, pp. 47–48). But when compared to the minutes originally printed in the *Times and Seasons* (vol. 4, p. 330), the revised/modern version reveals an account exactly opposite of what actually happened.

Another tactic utilized by Mormon leaders has been to revise Smith's revelations so as to make the church's history more palatable. Some of the most drastic alterations to authoritative writings—e.g., paragraphs added/deleted, words added/deleted, wording changes to alter a meaning, phrases added/deleted—can be found by comparing sections of Smith's 1833 *Book of Commandments* with the text of the 1835 re-publication of these same revelations as the *Doctrine and Covenants* (Figure 18.1, 18.2, 18.3). Hundreds of changes were made to these revelations. In response to the discrepancies, famous Mormon scholar Hugh Nibley blithely stated: "Revelations have been revised whenever necessary. That is the nice thing about revelation—it is strictly open-ended."[28]

Not all Mormon officials have been so upfront. Apostle Hugh B. Brown, for instance, in a 1966 letter wrote: "None of the early revelations of the Church have been revised."[29] Consider a few of the other declarations made by high-ranking Mormon leaders over the years about Smith's revelations:

Apostle John A. Widtsoe (1951): "There has been no tampering with God's Word. . . . [T]he whole body of Church laws forms a harmonious unit, which does not anywhere contradict itself nor has it been found necessary to alter any part of it."[30]

LDS President Joseph Fielding Smith (1954): "Inspiration is discovered in the fact that each part, as it was revealed, dovetailed perfectly with what had come before. There was no need for eliminating, changing, or adjusting any part to make it fit."[31]

John J. Stewart (1966): "Joseph would dictate them to a clerk at as fast and steady a pace as the clerk was able to write, maintaining an even flow of delivery, and never altering the words spoken."[32]

This concerted attempt to cover-up significant alterations made to Smith's original revelations actually prompted some LDS officials in the early 1960s to suppress a copy of the *Book of Commandments* locked in their church archives. At one point Mormon leaders even contacted BYU, telling the school to not allow microfilmed pages of the rare book to be distributed to the public.[33] Eventually, however, a full copy of the revelations in the *Book of Commandments* was published.

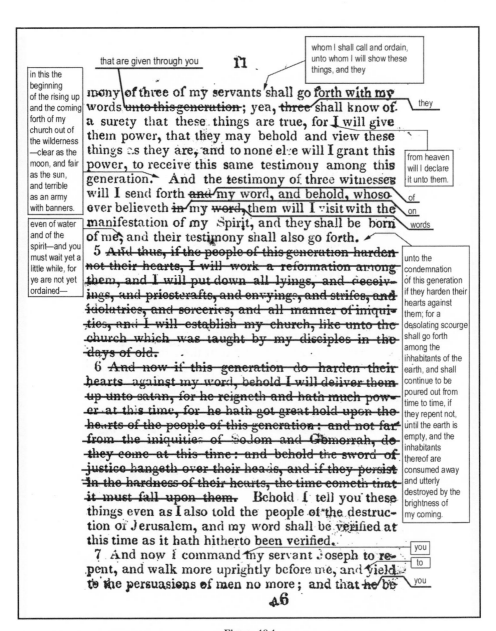

whom I shall call and ordain, unto whom I will show these things, and they

that are given through you

11

in this the beginning of the rising up and the coming forth of my church out of the wilderness —clear as the moon, and fair as the sun, and terrible as an army with banners.

even of water and of the spirit—and you must wait yet a little while, for ye are not yet ordained—

mony of three of my servants shall go forth with my words unto this generation; yea, three shall know of a surety that these things are true, for I will give them power, that they may behold and view these things as they are, and to none else will I grant this power, to receive this same testimony among this generation. And the testimony of three witnesses will I send forth and my word, and behold, whosoever believeth in my word, them will I visit with the manifestation of my Spirit, and they shall be born of me, and their testimony shall also go forth.

they

from heaven will I declare it unto them.

of
on
words

5 And thus, if the people of this generation harden not their hearts, I will work a reformation among them, and I will put down all lyings, and deceivings, and priestcrafts, and envyings, and strifes, and idolatries, and sorceries, and all manner of iniquities, and I will establish my church, like unto the church which was taught by my disciples in the days of old.

6 And now if this generation do harden their hearts against my word, behold I will deliver them up unto satan, for he reigneth and hath much power at this time, for he hath got great hold upon the hearts of the people of this generation: and not far from the iniquities of Sodom and Gomorrah, do they come at this time: and behold the sword of justice hangeth over their heads, and if they persist in the hardness of their hearts, the time cometh that it must fall upon them. Behold I tell you these things even as I also told the people of the destruction of Jerusalem, and my word shall be verified at this time as it hath hitherto been verified.

7 And now I command my servant Joseph to repent, and walk more uprightly before me, and yield to the persuasions of men no more; and that he be

unto the condemnation of this generation if they harden their hearts against them; for a desolating scourge shall go forth among the inhabitants of the earth, and shall continue to be poured out from time to time, if they repent not, until the earth is empty, and the inhabitants thereof are consumed away and utterly destroyed by the brightness of my coming.

you
to
you

46

Figure 18.1

Photocopy of page 11 from the 1833 *Book of Commandments* that shows where and how the original revelation (supposedly from God as first printed) has been changed for modern editions of *Doctrine and Covenants* (*D&C* 5:11–22). Boxed text marks words added, underlined words/phrases marks textual changes, and strike-thru text indicates words/phrases deleted.

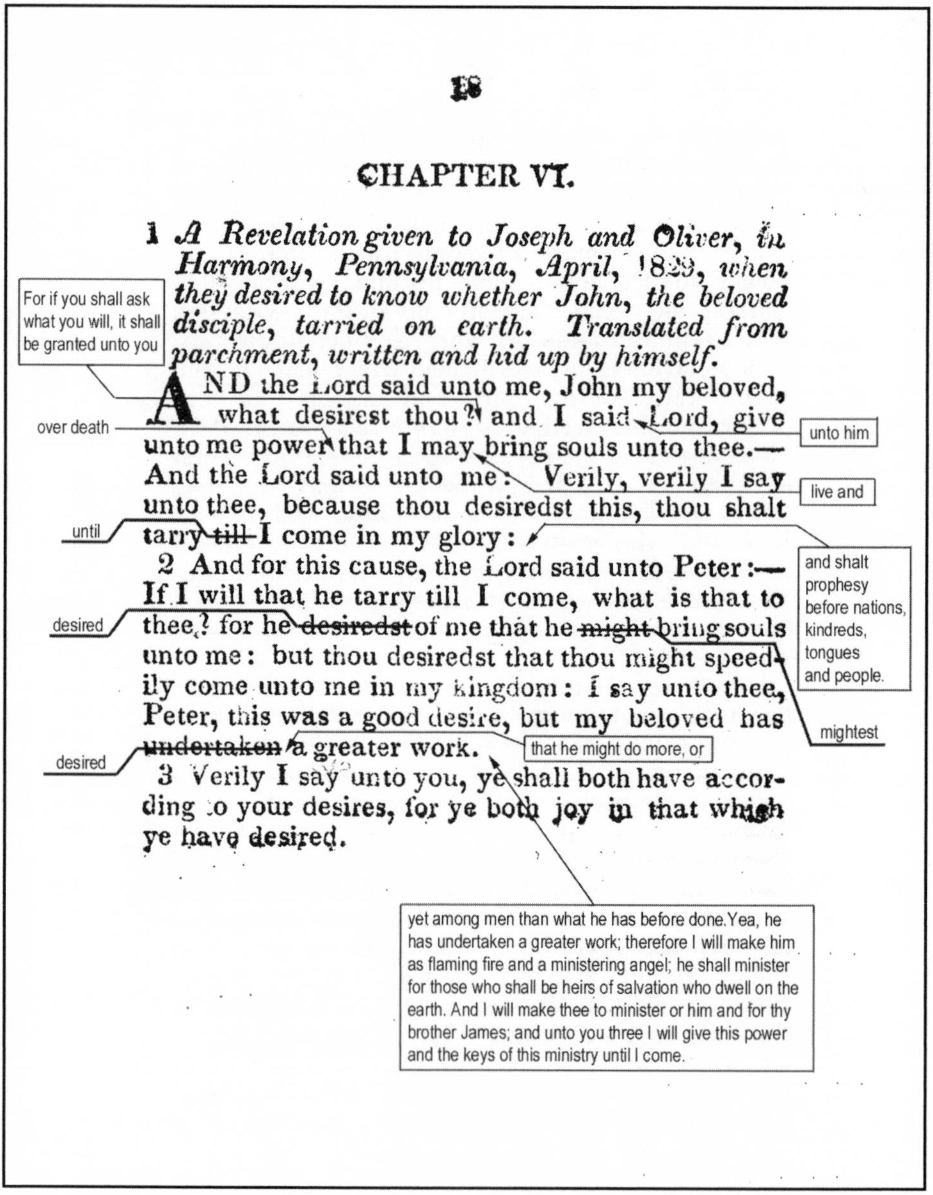

18

CHAPTER VI.

1 *A Revelation given to Joseph and Oliver, in Harmony, Pennsylvania, April, 1829, when they desired to know whether John, the beloved disciple, tarried on earth. Translated from parchment, written and hid up by himself.*

> For if you shall ask what you will, it shall be granted unto you

AND the Lord said unto me, John my beloved, what desirest thou? and I said Lord, give unto me power that I may bring souls unto thee.—
And the Lord said unto me: Verily, verily I say unto thee, because thou desiredst this, thou shalt tarry till I come in my glory:

over death

> unto him

> live and

until

2 And for this cause, the Lord said unto Peter:—If I will that he tarry till I come, what is that to thee? for he desiredst of me that he might bring souls unto me: but thou desiredst that thou might speedily come unto me in my kingdom: I say unto thee, Peter, this was a good desire, but my beloved has undertaken a greater work.

desired

desired

> and shalt prophesy before nations, kindreds, tongues and people.

> mightest

> that he might do more, or

3 Verily I say unto you, ye shall both have according to your desires, for ye both joy in that which ye have desired.

> yet among men than what he has before done. Yea, he has undertaken a greater work; therefore I will make him as flaming fire and a ministering angel; he shall minister for those who shall be heirs of salvation who dwell on the earth. And I will make thee to minister or him and for thy brother James; and unto you three I will give this power and the keys of this ministry until I come.

Figure 18.2

Photocopy of page 18 from the 1833 *Book of Commandments* that shows where and how the original revelation (supposedly from God as first printed) has been changed for modern editions of *Doctrine and Covenants* (*D&C* 7:1–8). Boxed text marks words added, underlined words/phrases marks textual changes, and strike-thru text indicates words/phrases deleted.

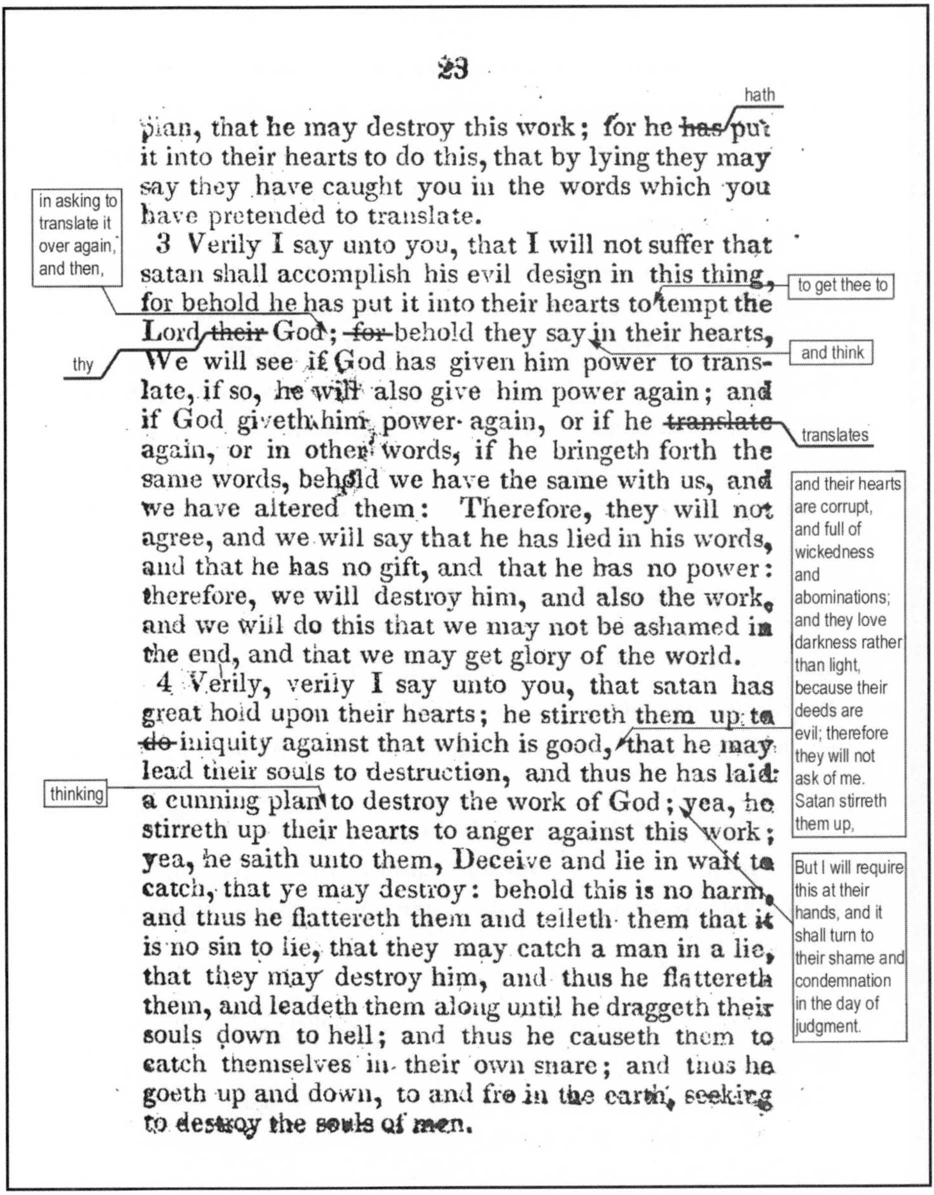

23

plan, that he may destroy this work; for he ~~has~~ /put [hath]
it into their hearts to do this, that by lying they may
say they have caught you in the words which you
have pretended to translate.

[in asking to translate it over again, and then,]

3 Verily I say unto you, that I will not suffer that
satan shall accomplish his evil design in this thing, [to get thee to]
for behold he has put it into their hearts to tempt the
Lord ~~their~~ God; ~~for~~ behold they say in their hearts, [and think]
[thy] We will see if God has given him power to trans-
late, if so, he will also give him power again; and
if God giveth him power again, or if he ~~translate~~ [translates]
again, or in other words, if he bringeth forth the
same words, behold we have the same with us, and
we have altered them: Therefore, they will not
agree, and we will say that he has lied in his words,
and that he has no gift, and that he has no power:
therefore, we will destroy him, and also the work,
and we will do this that we may not be ashamed in
the end, and that we may get glory of the world.

[and their hearts are corrupt, and full of wickedness and abominations; and they love darkness rather than light, because their deeds are evil; therefore they will not ask of me. Satan stirreth them up,]

4 Verily, verily I say unto you, that satan has
great hold upon their hearts; he stirreth them up to
~~do~~ iniquity against that which is good, /that he may
lead their souls to destruction, and thus he has laid
[thinking] a cunning plan to destroy the work of God; yea, he
stirreth up their hearts to anger against this work;
yea, he saith unto them, Deceive and lie in wait to
catch, that ye may destroy: behold this is no harm,
and thus he flattereth them and teileth them that it
is no sin to lie, that they may catch a man in a lie,
that they may destroy him, and thus he flattereth
them, and leadeth them along until he draggeth their
souls down to hell; and thus he causeth them to
catch themselves in their own snare; and thus he
goeth up and down, to and fro in the earth, seeking
to destroy the souls of men.

[But I will require this at their hands, and it shall turn to their shame and condemnation in the day of judgment.]

Figure 18.3

Photocopy of page 23 from the 1833 *Book of Commandments* that shows where and how the original revelation (supposedly from God as first printed) has been changed for modern editions of *Doctrine and Covenants* (*D&C* 10:12–27). Boxed text marks words added, underlined words/phrases marks textual changes, and strike-thru text indicates words/phrases deleted.

THINKING IS A SIN

Most of the academic dishonesty foisted upon church members by LDS scholars and leaders relates to the Mormon notion that all works of history must be "faith-promoting." In other words, books read by Mormons are intentionally designed to build up their faith, not challenge it in any way, especially on an intellectual basis. Since its earliest days, Mormonism has been an emotion-based religion opposed to intellectual, rational thought. Potential converts were told in the 1800s, just as they are instructed now, to "feel" the validity of Mormonism independent of reasoning.

This "feeling," often described as a "burning in the bosom," allegedly is the "witness of the Spirit" (i.e., God) that Mormonism is true. Although the "feeling" is completely subjective, its power over Mormons cannot be overstated. Even when faced with irrefutable facts that undermine the LDS church, a Saint will cling to their "witness" and often resort to simply repeating their personal testimony, as a kind of mantra that helps them sustain a state of unthinking, faith-bolstering denial. They will say something like: "I bear you my testimony that Joseph Smith was a prophet of God, that the Church of Jesus Christ of Latter-day Saints is the only true church, and that the *Book of Mormon* is true."

Such a response also shows obedience to LDS leaders, who have counseled their followers to not only shun anything that might shake their faith, but also to simply not think and obey church authorities. The church-published *Improvement Era* in 1945 warned:

> [Satan] wins a great victory when he can get members of the church to speak against their leaders and to do their own thinking. When our leaders speak, the thinking has been done. When they propose a plan— it is God's plan. When they point the way, there is no other which is safe. When they give direction, it should mark the end of controversy. God works in no other way.[34]

What about being led astray by an erring prophet? Circular reasoning helps alleviate any such concerns. Basically, the Mormon is taught: Since the church's prophet is directed by God, then he cannot lead the church astray. He cannot lead us astray because he is the church's prophet, who is directed by God. As Brigham Young said:

> The Lord Almighty leads this Church, and he will never suffer you to be led astray if you are found doing your duty. You may go home and sleep as sweetly as a babe in its mother's arms, as to any danger of your leaders leading you astray, for if they should try to do so the Lord would quickly sweep them from the earth.[35]

Little has changed since Young made these remarks. Apostle Bruce R. McConkie, for instance, at an October 7, 1984, church conference, announced:

> No true Latter-day Saint will ever take a stand that is in opposition to what the Lord has revealed to those who direct the affairs of his earthly kingdom. No Latter-day Saint who is true and faithful in all things will ever pursue a course, or espouse a cause, or publish an article or book that weakens or destroys faith.[36]

Amazingly, Mormons also have been taught that even if they are told to do something they know is wrong, they should *still* obey the instruction from their superiors. In 1960, Marion G. Romney of the LDS First Presidency quoted Mormon prophet-president Heber J. Grant, saying:

> Always keep your eye on the President of the church, and if he ever tells you to do anything, even if it is wrong, and you do it, the Lord will bless you for it but you don't need to worry. The Lord will never let his mouthpiece lead the people astray.[37]

Mormon apostle Boyd K. Packer echoed these teachings in 1992 saying: "Follow your leaders who have been duly ordained and have been publicly sustained, and you will not be led astray."[38] Some of the most disturbing instructions about blind obedience came from LDS president Ezra Taft Benson in his "Fourteen Fundamentals in Following the Prophet" speech. His fundamentals for living a righteous Mormon life left little room for independent thought (see this endnote for transcript).[39]

For those few who have ventured to take that forbidden step, the ultimate punishment awaiting them is excommunication. At one point in the mid- to late 1990s this drastic course of church discipline was used unsparingly against a cadre of Mormon scholars trying to break free of the intellectual confines into which they had been placed by LDS authorities.[40] Even more significant, many of them had dared to reveal various aspects of Mormon history that church leaders did not want released to the general public. It resulted in nothing less than a Latter-day Saint witch hunt.

THE MORMON PURGE

During his appearance on the popular *Larry King Live* show, LDS president Gordon B. Hinckley was asked: "Are people ever thrown out of your church?" After Hinckley answered, "yes," King responded: "For?" To this follow-up question, the Mormon president said:

> Doing what they shouldn't do, preaching false doctrine, speaking out publicly. They can carry all the opinion they wish within their heads, so to speak, but if they begin to try to persuade others, then they may be called in to a disciplinary council. We don't excommunicate many, but we do some.[41]

But Steve Benson, no less than the grandson of one-time Mormon president Ezra Taft Benson, expressed an altogether different opinion on CBS's *60 Minutes*. Benson, a Pulitzer Prize-winning cartoonist, stated that by enforcing group conformity, the LDS church stifles independent thought. He told newsman Mike Wallace: "The cultural mindset in the church is when the prophet has spoken, the debate is over. . . . When he has pronounced the church's position on any issue, it is incumbent upon the members of the church to pray, pay, and obey."[42]

Benson's perspective of the Mormon church has been demonstrated numerous times throughout LDS history, most recently, in the 1990s when LDS leaders moved against intellectuals and freethinkers within the Mormon community. During this "Mormon Purge," authors, journalists, historians, lecturers, feminists, and some Brigham Young University teachers were excommunicated on a variety of ecclesiastical charges: e.g., apostasy, questioning the validity of the *Book of Mormon*, revealing LDS doctrines without church permission, and not supporting church leaders. In other words, anyone who expressed a dissenting opinion of official church dogma was rooted out.

The crackdown on perceived dissidents began in late 1993, just before the October General Conference of the church. At that time six prominent Mormons (dubbed the "September Six" after the month of their persecution) were summoned to church courts to face disciplinary trials:

- Paul Toscano—an author and Salt Lake City attorney
- Avraham Gileadi—a theologian and writer
- Maxine Hanks—a journalist, ardent feminist, and author
- Lavina Fielding Anderson—author and former editor/writer for the LDS Church-published *Ensign* (1973–1981)
- Lynne Kanavel Whitesides—President of the Mormon Women's Forum
- D. Michael Quinn—BYU professor, author of several articles for *Ensign* and the Mormon journal *BYU Studies*

All of these individuals, except for Whitesides, were excommunicated in September 1993.[43] Whitesides was sentenced by church authorities to disfellowshipment (a lesser, but still very serious disciplinary action). Whitesides' spiritual crime stemmed from various feminist statements she had made on TV, which created "friction" in the church. She also dared to criticize a high-ranking LDS leader, apostle Boyd K. Packer, saying that she couldn't "find any evidence of Christ" in a speech he had delivered.[44] Her conduct was deemed "contrary to the laws of the church."[45]

As for the others, their offenses varied. Lavina Fielding Anderson was excommunicated for nothing more than an article titled "The LDS Intellectual Community and Church Leadership," which she had written for *Dialogue: A Journal of Mormon Thought*. It chronicled episodes of intimidation against LDS thinkers for the last 20 years.[46] Avraham Gileadi was disciplined for his writings about the apocalypse and the Bible's book of Isaiah.[47] Toscano was kicked out for criticisms he leveled at LDS leadership.[48] And Maxine Hanks received her discipline for espousing feminist views; specifically, that the priesthood should be opened to women.[49]

The most interesting case was that of D. Michael Quinn, one-time historian at BYU and highly adept defender of the LDS church. He started running into trouble after finding historical evidence that proved high-ranking Mormon leaders continued taking plural wives after the 1890 Manifesto. He then requested rare and highly guarded documents in the vaults of the LDS church's First Presidency. This request was denied in 1982. Then in 1984, church authorities (using Quinn's college dean as a liaison), asked Quinn to not publish the text of a lecture he had delivered on the activity of church General Authorities in business corporations. Quinn found himself experiencing what had only been hinted at in a conversation he had had with Apostle Boyd K. Packer in 1976:

> When Elder Packer interviewed me as a prospective member of Brigham Young University's faculty in 1976, he explained: "I have a hard time with historians because they idolize the truth. The truth is not uplifting; it destroys. I could tell most of the secretaries in the church office building that they are ugly and fat. That would be the truth, but it would hurt and destroy them. Historians should tell only that part of the truth that is inspiring and uplifting."[50]

Packer, head of the church's Quorum of the Twelve Apostles, would in late 1993 go so far as to name feminists, homosexuals and *intellectuals* as the three dangers facing the Mormon church.[51] His reputation as a harsh watchdog of LDS ranks left little doubt in many minds that he was personally behind the string of excommunications. *Private Eye Weekly* noted the following:

> All fingers seem to point to Elder Boyd Packer, acting president of the twelve apostles, as the prime force behind what has been called the "Mormon Inquisition." While Elder Packer, nicknamed "Darth Packer"

by the irreverent because of his cold and detached personal style, is a far cry from Torquemada . . . his speeches, instructions to lower ranking authorities, and direct contacts with local leaders have shown him to be the prime orchestrator of top-level-organized punishment.[52]

Quinn has not been the only BYU casualty.[53] John Beck, another ex-BYU business professor, left the church and his teaching position because of dishonesty at BYU. Beck told the *Arizona Republic* he departed because of BYU's penchant for not telling the truth. "My problems had to do with the ethics of the university," he said. "They are firing people not for the reasons they say."[54] Beck's wife, former BYU sociology professor Martha Nibley Beck, also left her position, saying: "The church is moving toward social isolation."[55] Paul Richards, former BYU spokesman, provided equally disturbing information based on his time at the church-affiliated university:

> The church wants to portray this image of being unified in all it does . . . . It wants Mormons to be unquestioning. . . . I worked in public affairs for the church for 13 years, and I had to lie all the time, and this has really battered my faith.[56]

The purge continued on April 9, 1994, with the excommunication of David P. Wright, a professor of Biblical Studies and Hebrew, who before he was kicked out of the church was dismissed from his BYU position. His mistake was questioning the origins of the *Book of Mormon* in an article for the volume *New Approaches to the Book of Mormon.* Wright suggested that Joseph Smith plagiarized from the Bible and noted that "there is evidence that Smith's other 'ancient' compositions are not actually ancient but arise out of his interactions with biblical texts and religious ideas of his period."[57]

Before April ended another visible Mormon had been excommunicated—CIA attorney Michael Barrett. As previously mentioned, his offense was nothing more than a letter writing campaign to accurately tell the public about Mormon doctrines and history (see pp. 385–386). Barrett's expulsion only mirrored what had been done to countless others who had tried to give the public a complete picture of Mormonism. This list of excommunicated members stretches back to 1945, when Fawn Brodie was kicked out of the church for her landmark biography of Joseph Smith titled *No Man Knows My History*.

In April 2000 LDS president Gordon B. Hinckley told a Mormon audience that all such enemies of the church deserve what they get as cursed servants of Satan, saying:

> I think the Lord had them in mind when he declared: 'Cursed are all those that shall lift up the heel against mine anointed, saith the Lord.' . . . [T]hey are the servants of sin, and are the children of disobedience themselves.[58]

The widespread crackdown on perceived enemies of the church brought to light another interesting piece of information—Mormon leaders operate a pseudo-clandestine group to spy on church members. This behind-the-scenes team, known as the Strengthening Church Members Committee, under the direction of two LDS apostles, monitors Mormons worldwide. The committee collects and files away for possible future reference "their letters to the editor, other writings, quotes in the media, and public activities."[59] Such monitoring of church members, a practice unheard of among America's other religious bodies, belies a long-held attitude by church leaders that has led to many Latter-day Saint excommunications as well as loss of employment at BYU:

- Journalist Deborah Laake, for her book *Secret Ceremonies: A Mormon Woman's Intimate Diary of Marriage and Beyond.*
- English teacher Cecilia Konchar-Farr, for her views on abortion laws.
- Anthropologist David Knowlton, for a Sunstone Symposium speech detailing the reasons behind terrorism against LDS missions in Latin America.
- English professor Gail Houston, for advocating prayer to "Heavenly Mother."
- Journalist Janice Allred, for her 1992 Sunstone Symposium paper "Toward a Mormon Theology of God the Mother."

These individuals suffered church-instigated discipline/persecution not necessarily for causing trouble, but simply for voicing an opinion contrary to the LDS party line.[60] The sin of sins, however, still seems to be revealing accurate LDS history, which runs contrary to today's ongoing attempt by the church's hierarchy to cover up as much of it as possible.

SKELETONS IN THE CLOSET

As late as 2001, leaders of the LDS church were still trying to conceal well-known aspects of LDS history. The facts behind Mormon polygamy, for example, are consistently downplayed through the dissemination of misinformation and disinformation about the practice. Official publications have gone so far as to omit all mention of polygamy, as if it never even existed. This tactic has become especially useful now that the church is reaching non-Americans all over the world, many of whom know virtually nothing about Mormonism or its past. Historian B. Carmon Hardy writes:

> Every scholar with whom I am acquainted agrees that there is yet official Church reticence when it comes to using certain records, diaries, and other materials in the church's archives and in the First Presidency's possession relating to polygamy.[61]

Hardy's observation was most recently confirmed in 1997 by the church's release of the new Relief Society manual in twenty-two languages. The material, which is based on the selected teachings of Mormonism's presidents, makes no mention at all of polygamy—as if it never was an early church doctrine. Moreover, when speaking of Brigham Young, who had more than fifty wives, the publication lists only his first wife, making it appear as if he had only one spouse. The manual mentions Young's first wife, Miriam Works, and her death. Then it says Young married Mary Ann Angell in 1834 (p. vii). On page 4, it states, "six children were born into their family." Nowhere does it go on to say that Young actually had fifty-five wives and fifty-six children during his life.

Interestingly, the official 2001–2002 LDS *Church Almanac* handles the issue in a similar, yet slightly different, manner. In this volume every LDS president (except the current one) is listed in the "Historical Listing of General Authorities" section, where they are each given a brief biography.[62] But out of all the presidents, only the monogamists have a wife listed (i.e., eighth LDS president George Albert Smith [d. 1951] and onward). Polygamist presidents Brigham Young, John Taylor, Wilford Woodruff, Lorenzo Snow, Joseph F. Smith, and Heber J. Grant have no wives or marriages mentioned in their write-ups at all. Joseph Smith does have the following included: "Married Emma Hale Jan. 18, 1827." But no more. None of his other 30-45 wives are mentioned.

Media-savvy Gordon B. Hinckley did his best to cover-up polygamy on *Larry King Live*, saying that only between two and five percent of Mormons in early Utah practiced it.[63] He added: "It was a very limited practice; carefully safeguarded. In 1890, that practice was discontinued."[64] The practice, however, as history reveals was not discontinued until many years after 1890, and it was hardly engaged in as a "very limited practice." Nevertheless, King dropped the issue and went on to discuss modern polygamy in the U.S., which Hinckley adamantly condemned as illegal.

Mormon racism, like polygamy, is another issue that church officials routinely try to hide. When Mike Wallace on *60 Minutes* asked Hinckley about Brigham Young's statement concerning African-Americans and their curse of black skin and a flat nose, Hinckley dismissed the quote. "It's behind us," he assured Wallace. "Look, that's behind us. Don't worry about those little flicks of history."[65] But contradicting Hinckley's response is the fact that Mormons still believe people with black skin are cursed by God, even though they can now hold the priesthood (see Chapter Sixteen).[66]

The *Book of Mormon*, in fact, originally stated that Lamanites (i.e., Native Americans) would miraculously turn Caucasian—i.e., "white and delightsome"—after embracing Mormon beliefs.[67] Then in 1981 the term "white" was changed to "pure" in an effort to conceal this bizarre belief. LDS leaders claimed that the alteration had nothing to do with the absurd notion that "Indians" physically would turn white-skinned. However, similar *Book of Mormon* passages indicate otherwise.[68]

Moreover, numerous pre-1981 statements from Mormon officials taught that the curse of dark skin, at least from Native Americans, would be removed one day. Brigham Young, in 1859, said that "by-and-by they will become a white and delightsome people."[69] At a 1960 LDS conference Spencer Kimball gleefully told listeners that they already were "fast becoming a white and delightsome people." He added that "[Native American] children in the home placement program in Utah are often lighter than their brothers and sisters in the hogans on the reservation."[70] Kimball also said he knew of one Indian girl, who because she was a Mormon, was "several shades lighter than her parents."[71]

In *Why I Believe*, Mormon writer George Edward Clark noted that he himself had been privileged to see the miraculous change in the skin pigmentation of Mormon American Indians. In reference to the Catawba tribe of South Carolina, Clark wrote:

> That tribe, or most of its people, are members of the Church of Jesus Christ of Latter-day Saints (Mormon). Those Indians, at least as many as I have observed, were white and delightsome; as white and fair as any group of citizens of our country. I know of no prophecy, ancient or modern, that has had a more literal fulfillment.[72]

Today, of course, such statements are rarely heard from Mormon leaders seeking to protect the LDS church, its history, leaders, and doctrines from criticism. But protecting the church at all costs has led to some rather sensational events in recent years; most notably, the Mark Hoffman murder and forgery case, the Paul Dunn controversy, and the Olympic bribery scandal.

HOFMANN'S DEADLY DOCUMENTS[73]

According to journalist Richard Ostling, one of the most infamous events in modern LDS history—the "Mormon Murders"—resulted from "the curious mixture of paranoia and obsessiveness with which Mormons approach church history."[74] The tragic series of events centered around a rare document dealer named Mark Hofmann, who approached Mormon leaders with a number of forged documents directly relating to

LDS history. Some of the bogus documents that he himself had created contained harmless bits of historical data. Into others, however, he placed what he knew was information that brought into question the validity of Mormonism and the historicity of Joseph Smith's claims. Hofmann, who understood that Mormon leaders would want to suppress such documents, began offering his well-crafted creations to the church for huge sums of money. Mormon researchers Jerald and Sandra Tanner explain:

> [Hofmann] noticed a weakness in them that he was able to exploit. This was that they were trying to hide the true history of the church from their people. He knew that church leaders were suppressing many early documents because they did not want members of the church to learn of their contents for fear that they would lose faith in Mormonism. Because of this Hofmann reasoned that there would be a market for controversial documents which the church leaders would buy up to suppress. In his confession, page 150, he noted that he felt "a controversial" document "always brings better money." Hofmann, therefore, perceived church leaders as easy marks for a blackmail type of operation. His plan was to create embarrassing documents and offer them to the church with the pretext that this would keep them from falling into the hands of the "enemy." The enemy, of course, would be those who would publish the contents of the documents to the world.[75]

The scheme worked. In 1983 Gordon B. Hinckley, who at that time was second counselor to LDS president Spencer W. Kimball, paid Hofmann $15,000 for a letter allegedly penned by Joseph Smith. The forged document, which appeared to be written to Josiah Stowell in 1825, included admissions from Smith about being an occultist/treasure-seeker, who used divination to find buried money. Another forged letter, this one supposedly written by Joseph Smith's mother, fetched $30,000.

The most sensitive document, known as the White Salamander Letter, supposedly was written in 1830 by Martin Harris to W.W. Phelps. It was acquired by the church through 31-year-old Steven Christensen, a Mormon bishop and acquaintance of Hofmann's. The letter, which cost

$40,000, repudiated the official church version of Smith's history by saying that Smith was led to the *Book of Mormon* by a seer stone, and there met a magic white salamander instead of the Angel Moroni.

Finally, an entire set of documents that Hofmann claimed to possess comprised the legendary McLellin Collection, named after early LDS apostate William E. McLellin (1806–1883). He was one of Smith's original twelve apostles. It had long been rumored that such a treasure trove of documents existed, but until Hofmann came up with them, no one knew their location. To obtain the collection, which allegedly contained information damaging to the church's reputation, high-ranking Mormon Hugh Pinnock secured a signature loan for $185,000, which was then given to Hofmann.

But what LDS officials did not know was that Hofmann had no collection. It was all a scam; one that continued to snowball, until Hofmann had sold the same non-existent collection to several parties. At the same time, Steven Christensen—who had been asked by Pinnock to be a middleman between Hofmann and the church—began applying pressure to close the deal. This forced Hofmann the document dealer to become Hoffman the murderer. If Christensen were killed, he thought, it might buy enough time to close other phony document deals, such as the sale of an unrelated document on the east coast for $1.5 million.

So on October 15, 1985, Hofmann planted a homemade "shrapnel bomb" encased in nails outside Christensen's Salt Lake City office. When Christensen picked up the booby-trapped package, it exploded, ripping a hole in his chest. He died at the scene. Later that morning another package exploded across town, killing 50-year-old Kathleen Sheets. Hofmann actually intended this bomb for her husband, J. Gary Sheets, another LDS bishop involved in the document deals. But Sheets' wife picked up the package before her husband could get to it. Then, on October 16, while on his way to commit a third murder, the bomb he was carrying accidentally went off in his car, seriously injuring him.

Eventually the pieces started coming together, until police realized that Hofmann had not been a third victim, but rather, was the lone perpetrator. As investigators began to uncover more information about the case, Mormon officials started to panic, afraid that the church would somehow be made to look bad. To prevent such an outcome, LDS officials actually began hindering the investigation by refusing to divulge information about the various transactions they had made with Hofmann. Mormon leaders also blocked efforts by police to see exactly what documents were in LDS church vaults, apparently knowing that some of their authentic documents not yet released to the public might further damage the church's reputation if the contents of them were to be revealed.

Salt Lake City detective Jim Bell, who spoke at a meeting that had been called to reveal what detectives knew, said that he suspected the church was concealing information about Hofmann and the murders. "They're hiding something; the church is doing everything it can to make this as difficult as possible. I've never seen anything like this in a homicide investigation."[76] Ironically, church leaders soon learned through private investigations that they already had the *real* McLellin Collection, having purchased it in 1908.

This important information, however, was kept from law enforcement authorities for six years after the murders. It came to light in *Victims: The LDS Church and the Mark Hofmann Case,* a 1992 book written by Richard Turley, managing director of the LDS Church Historical Department. According to Mormon experts Jerald and Sandra Tanner, "[a] close examination of Richard Turley's book shows that Mormon Church leaders were engaged in a conspiracy of silence with regard to the McLellin collection to save the church's image."[77] As for Mark Hofmann, he confessed, was convicted of murder, and sentenced to life in prison.

To Mormons one of the most disconcerting aspects of the whole tragedy was the way high LDS officials—i.e., Gordon B. Hinckley of the First Presidency, Apostle Dallin Oaks, Hugh Pinnock (member of the First Quorum of the Seventy), and bishop Steven Christensen—had all been utterly fooled by Hofmann. Their apparent lack of discernment with regard to Hofmann's legitimacy refuted in a most visible way the LDS belief that church leaders are divinely enabled by God to know deception when they see it. Apostle Bruce McConkie explained in *Mormon Doctrine*:

One of many forged documents sold to the Mormon church by Mark Hofmann. This one, allegedly from Joseph Smith to Josiah Stowell, includes statements that paint Smith as a money-digger, who in reference to a buried treasure, tells Stowell "the treasure must be guarded by some clever spirit."

Palmyra Octr 23d 1830

Dear Sir

Your letter of yesterday is received & I hasten to answer as fully as I can — Joseph Smith jr first come to my notice in the year 1824 in the summer of that year I contracted with his father to build a fence on my property in the cours of that work I approach Joseph & ask how it is in a half day you put up what requires your father & 2 brothers a full day working together he says I have not been with out assistence but can not say more onely you better find out the next day I take the older Smith by the arm & he says Joseph can see any thing he wishes by looking at a stone Joseph often sees Spirits here with great kettles of coin money it was Spirits who brought up rock because Joseph made no attempt on their money I latter learn I conversed with spirits which let me count their money when I awake I have in my hand a dollar coin which I take for a sign Joseph describes what I seen in every particular says he the spirits are grieved so I through back the dollar In the fall of the year 1827 I hear Joseph found a gold bible I take Joseph aside & he says it is true I found it 4 years ago with my stone but only just got it because of the enchantment the old spirit come to me 3 times in the same dream & says dig up the gold but when I take it up the next morning the spirit transfigured himself from a white salamander in the bottom of the hole & struck me 3 times & held the treasure & would not let me have it because I lay it down to cover over the hole when the spirit says do not lay it down Joseph says when can I have it the spirit says one year from to day if you obey me look to the stone after a few days he looks the spirit says bring your brother Alvin Joseph says he is dead shall I bring what remains but the spirit is gone Joseph goes to get the gold bible but the spirit says you did not bring your brother you can not have it look to the stone Joseph looks but can not see who to bring the spirit says I tricked you again look to the stone Joseph looks & sees his wife on the 22d day of Sept 1827 they get the gold bible I give Joseph $50 to move him

Page 1 from the "White Salamander" letter, yet another forged document of Hofmann's that was obtained by the LDS church (via the actual purchaser, Steve Christensen). This letter, allegedly from Martin Harris to W.W. Phelps, made it seem as if Smith met a magical white salamander when he found the *Book of Mormon* plates, rather than the Angel Moroni.

> [T]he gift of the discerning of spirits is poured out upon presiding offi-
> cials in God's kingdom; they have it given to them to discern all gifts and
> all spirits, lest any come among the saints and practice deception. . .
> Thereby even 'the thoughts and intents of the heart' are made known.[78]

But Mormons leaders, like everyone else, were unable to discover any deception in Hofmann. They, along with FBI forgery experts, hand-writing analysis specialists, and scholars of rare documents, were completely fooled. In fact, Mormon officials were not even able to tell that a lost "revelation" from God contained in a letter allegedly written by Joseph Smith to his brother ("The Far West Letter") was forged.[79] It seems their own desire to deceive the public through hiding controversial documents made them especially susceptible to Hofmann's schemes.[80]

DUNN IN GOD'S NAME

The Mormon habit of sometimes taking detours around truth to protect the church has not always led to murder. Sometimes it has resulted in embarrassment. Consider the case of Paul H. Dunn, a well-respected LDS general authority, popular teacher, author, and role model for young people. He was one of the church's most visible and motivational speakers. For decades, in fact, Dunn had illustrated the great "truths" of Mormonism using stories taken from his own life.

There was the tale about his best friend, who "died in his arms during a World War II battle, while imploring Dunn to teach America's youth about patriotism."[81] Then there was the riveting account of "how God protected him as enemy machine-gun bullets ripped away his clothing, gear and helmet without ever touching his skin."[82] Another inspirational yarn explained "how perseverance and Mormon values led him to play major-league baseball for the St. Louis Cardinals."[83] Unfortunately, none of these stories were true. Dunn's "dead" friend was still alive; only the heel of his boot was ever touched by a bullet; and he never played for the Cardinals.[84]

Nevertheless, Elder Dunn (Presidency of the Seventy) reveled in his stories, garnering fame and admiration from fellow Mormons until 1991 when he found himself being confronted by the media. Dunn eventually admitted that he had indeed exaggerated his accomplishments and experiences, but defended his actions, saying that the fabrications were necessary "to illustrate his theological and moral points."[85] For the sake of teaching his "moral points," Dunn had apparently found it necessary to ignore the Mormon church's 13th article of faith: "We believe in being honest."[86] A February 16, 1991 article that appeared in *The Arizona Republic* listed several of Dunn's tall tales:

- [He was] the sole survivor among 11 infantrymen in a 100-yard race against death, during which one burst of machine-gun fire ripped his right boot off, another tore off his ammunition and canteen belt and yet another split his helmet in half—all without wounding him.

- [He kept] a Japanese prisoner from being butchered by GIs bent on revenge for the torture slayings of American soldiers.

- [He wrestled] a dynamite pack off a child kamikaze infiltrator, saving himself and the child.

- [He] survived being run over by an enemy tank, while others were crushed.

- [He was] one of only six individuals in his 1,000-man combat group who survived a major battle, and was the only one of those six not wounded.[87]

Dunn's lies were discovered by Lynn Packer, a Brigham Young University teacher and free-lance writer who, after notifying the university's officials of the information, was told to "permit church leaders to deal privately with the Dunn matter."[88] Then, in a September 30, 1987, memo, Packer's BYU department chairman, Gordon Whiting, threatened him, saying:

> After providing the information, we accept the judgment of those responsible. We will not take accusations against a General Authority to the media. . . . [publication of such material] will damage the church, will damage the university, and will damage you.[89]

That same night Packer reportedly was offered a deal by church authorities: "[D]on't publish the story and you can teach at BYU as long as you want."[90] But Packer's integrity motivated him to ignore the warning and take his information to the *Arizona Republic* in 1991. The church still had not taken any action against Dunn, who was continuing to spread his stories. The move, however, cost Packer his teaching position. Whiting acknowledged that Packer's contract was "not renewed for the 1990-91 school year in part because Packer was violating church and university policies that prohibit public criticism of church leaders, even if the criticism is true."[91] The *Salt Lake Tribune* reported:

> [Packer] ultimately lost his teaching position at church-owned Brigham Young University and today, working on a one-year contract at the University of Dortmund in Germany, feels beaten 'to a pulp.' Why did the story that Republic reporter Richard Robertson calls the worst-kept secret in Salt Lake take so long to come out? The answer appears to lie in the church's effort to avoid a scandal and in Packer's own vulnerability as a BYU employee without tenure whose wife had been diagnosed with cancer early in 1987.[92]

What happened to Dunn? He was placed on early retirement and eventually issued a public apology in which he stated, "I confess that I have not always been accurate in my public talks and writings."[93] But even after his so-called retirement, Dunn continued to be "a popular public speaker and the most prolific author among current and former church leaders."[94] He also continued receiving royalties from approximately two dozen inspirational cassette tapes and nearly thirty books, many of which contained his war and baseball stories.

Amazingly, when Dunn passed away in 1998 his stories were still being circulated as true. Merrill Osmond, for example, of The Osmond Brothers, put up an Internet site in memory of Dunn, who was a close friend. Contrary to what is known about Dunn's many fabrications, Osmond wrote of him: "He was signed by the St. Louis Cardinals baseball club."[95] But the truth is that Dunn never played a single game for the St. Louis Cardinals or any other major-league team. The closest Dunn

ever came to the Cardinals was playing "six weeks 'off-roster' in several
practice and exhibition games in 1942 for the Pocatello (Idaho) Cardinals, a St. Louis Cardinal farm team. He was cut."[96]

MORMON GAMES

The most recent scandal to rock the Mormon church began when it
was discovered in 1998 that bribes had been paid to Olympic officials in
order to secure the 2002 Winter Games for Salt Lake City. The international event, which soon came to be known as the "Mormon Games," had
long been sought by Salt Lake City officials. LDS authorities, too, had
been praying for the honor of hosting the Olympics, knowing that it
would be a public relations dream come true.

Latter-day Saints received the good news from Olympic officials in
1995, just two years before the unparalleled publicity garnered by the
Mormons in 1997 through the church's sesquicentennial celebration of
the settling of Utah. "In my experience, it was an unprecedented public-
relations success," said Bret Walrath, senior vice president of Edelman
Public Relations Worldwide, the New York City-based firm the church
hired in the early 1990s to further its public-relations efforts.[97] A majority of publicity surrounding the celebration focused on the re-enactment
of the Mormon pioneers' 1847 trek from Nebraska to Utah. It drew hundreds of reporters and earned "glowing front-page coverage in *The
Washington Post, The New York Times* and *USA Today*."[98]

The choice of Salt Lake City as host of the 2002 Winter Games could
not have come at a better time. When the annual "Out of Obscurity: Public Affairs and the Worldwide Church" conference convened in 1997,
church leaders were ecstatic with joy. The more than 100 public-relations experts, who assembled to discuss Mormonism's future, knew that
hosting the Olympics would be the church's greatest opportunity for
widespread publicity.[99] Mark Tuttle, who oversees special projects for
Church Public Affairs, noted: "The limelight will be on Salt Lake City. It
is an incredible opportunity for us to let the light of the gospel shine out
of obscurity and darkness."[100]

To prepare for the onslaught of 10,000 journalists from around the world and hundreds of thousands of guests, LDS officials added two major exhibits to the main area of the Mormon Visitors Center—one about the building of Salt lake City, and the other about strengthening families.[101] Tours of the complex also were crafted to merge efficiently with regular showings of the church's historical film, "Legacy," a sterilized and distorted representation of Mormon history that glorifies the establishment of God's church in the latter days (since replaced by a new, updated film).[102]

But in 1998, widespread jubilation turned to anxiety as the media began reporting on bribes to Olympic officials that had been traced back to Salt Lake City.[103] It all began when KTVX revealed that the Salt Lake bid committee had paid tuition at American University for Sonia Essomba, daughter of the International Olympic Committe (IOC) member from Cameroon. Then, within a week, Salt Lake Olympic Committee (SLOC) president, Frank Joklik, admitted that there existed a program to send money to African national Olympic committees as "humanitarian aid."[104]

On December 8, the SLOC released a confirmation that six relatives of IOC members were among thirteen people, who received nearly $400,000 in financial aid from the bid committee. The SLOC, however, refused to identify them. The next day, in Switzerland, the controversy exploded into a scandal after International Olympic official Marc Hodler complained to the media about the sorry state of bidding to host the Olympics, adding that the SLOC payments were "not legitimate." Twenty-four hours later he leveled another charge: "Certainly it's a bribe."[105] Hodler's comments ignited a full-blown international investigation of the Salt Lake City bids.

As the months rolled by more evidence of apparent bribery was uncovered, including an admission from the Mormon church that businesses it owns gave $211,000 to the Olympic bid committee between 1985 and 1995. Other pieces of evidence continued to point to unethical, if not illegal transactions:

- Bid committee and SLOC tax returns were found not to have acknowledged scholarships.

- A list of bid-era improprieties included direct cash payments to IOC members.
- Utah Governor Michael Leavitt was accused of knowing that IOC members' children were receiving tuition assistance from the bid committee.[106]

Eventually it was learned that the amount given in gifts and payments to IOC members exceeded $1 million. In the wake of these revelations a number of individuals resigned from their positions: e.g., Frank Joklik (SLOC president); Dave Johnson (SLOC senior vice president); Alfredo La Mont (international-relations director for the United States Olympic Committee, who failed to disclose a business relationship with Olympic bid leader, Tom Welch); and Pirjo Haggman (IOC member in Finland, whose ex-husband had a questionable contract with the Salt Lake bid committee).

The scandal continued to rattle Utah, especially when on August 3, 1999, Salt Lake City businessman David Simmons pled guilty in federal court to filing a false tax return. It fraudulently accounted for at least $78,000 in Salt Lake bid committee funds that were used to pay for John Kim, (son of IOC vice president Un Yong Kim) to work for Simmons' former company—Keystone Communications. John Kim in turn was indicted by federal grand juries in Utah and New York on seventeen felony counts that included lying to federal agents and entering the U.S. on an illegally obtained visa. Then, to everyone's surprise, a Kim spokesman responded by identifying none other than Mormon Sen. Orrin Hatch as the one who helped Kim obtain the visa.[107]

In 2000, more controversy rippled through the LDS community when Alfredo La Mont, former director of international relations for the U.S. Olympic Committee, pled guilty to two federal counts of tax fraud. One count stemmed from his creation of a sham company to hide a consulting agreement with the Salt Lake bid committee in which he agreed to lobby IOC members. La Mont's guilty plea only accentuated the extensive corruption linked to the Salt Lake City bid, which developed into "the biggest scandal in the history of the modern Olympics, with ten IOC members expelled or quitting and sweeping changes made in how the multibillion-dollar Olympic community conducts its business."[108]

As of September 2001, Salt Lake City bid leaders Tom Welch and Dave Johnson—both Mormons—had eleven bribery-related felony charges still pending against them. These included conspiracy, mail fraud, and wire fraud.[109] They also stood accused of hiding or disguising cash payments, scholarships and gifts from trustees.[110] Fortunately for Salt Lake City, the defense was granted a trial postponement until after the Winter Games, thereby avoiding any negative publicity that might overshadow the long-awaited Mormon Olympics.

The year 2002 will no doubt be a time of great rejoicing for Latter-day Saint leaders, who will have the luxury of simply sitting back and letting the world come to them. As the LDS Minnesota public affairs director, Lynne Cropper, explained, Mormonism often has been "misunderstood," but the Olympics "will offer a good chance to clear up some of those misunderstandings."[111] LDS expert Gary Shepherd, an associate professor of sociology at Oakland University in Michigan, believes the Olympics, despite the bribery scandal, will do nothing but help Mormonism's image. "The obvious thing about the Olympics is that it will be a huge p.r. opportunity for them," said Shepherd. "Having an event like this taking place within the homeland of the Mormon church and that being such a prevalent backdrop for the Olympics will confer a certain amount of mainstream legitimacy."[112]

"Different athletes from different countries will come and go. But the church will remain on TV screens day after day, night after night as a larger and more enduring image," said Mark Crispin Miller, a New York University professor of media studies who specializes in advertising imagery. "I'd call that perfect product placement."[113] Jan Shipps, an expert in Mormonism and a professor emeritus of American history and religion at Indiana University-Purdue University, agrees. "They are seizing the day. That means they are taking advantage of the Olympics as a way of saying, 'We have the truth, and if you want to know the truth, we'll tell you,'" said Shipps.[114]

But prominent Mormon Mitt Romney, head of the Salt Lake Olympic

Organizing Committee, says "To be successful, we have to join all people, all races. . . . The Olympics won't be a reflection of any one faith."[115] Interestingly, though, as early as mid-2001 the church already was planning to offer free nightly shows in the world's largest religious auditorium, across from the Salt Lake City temple—"And missionaries will be on hand to answer spiritual questions."[116]

AMERICA'S MORMON DESTINY

Will The Church of Jesus Christ of Latter-day Saints ever succeed in taking over America, and eventually the world, as Joseph Smith prophesied? Brigham Young thought so, along with every other nineteenth century Mormon, especially the church's leadership. Throughout the twentieth century, and now into this twenty-first century, the belief has continued to be an integral part of Mormon teachings:

1912: "Joseph Smith . . . predicted that the time would come, 'when the Constitution of our country would hang as it were by a thread, and that the Latter-day Saints above all other people in the world would come to the rescue'" (LDS president, Joseph F. Smith).[117]

1928: "The Prophet Joseph told us that he saw the day when even the Constitution of the United States would be torn and hang as by a thread. . . . He saw the day when this people would be a balance of power to come to its defense" (LDS apostle, Melvin J. Ballard).[118]

1946: "[Joseph Smith] said if the Constitution of the United States were saved at all it must be done by this people. It will not be many years before these words come to pass. When the Constitution of the United States hangs, as it were, upon a single thread, they will have to call for the 'Mormon Elders to save it from utter destruction; and they will step forth and do it'" (Mark E. Petersen, LDS apostle).[119]

1950: "[The Prophet] said the time would come when this Constitution would hang as by a thread, and this is true. . . . 'Now I tell you it is time the people of the United States were waking up with the understanding that if they don't save the Constitution from the

dangers that threaten it, we will have a change of government'"
(Joseph Fielding Smith, president of the Quorum of the Twelve
Apostles and future Mormon president).[120]

1952: "Joseph Smith . . . [said] the time would come when the Constitution would hang as by a thread and at that time when it was thus
in jeopardy, the elders of this Church would step forth and save it
from destruction. Why the elders of this Church? . . . 'We alone
know by revelation as to how the Constitution came into being,
and we, alone, know by revelation the destiny of this nation'"
(Harold B. Lee, LDS apostle and future Mormon president).[121]

1961: "[I]f I were to guess as to how the Constitution may 'hang by a
thread' it would be because of the immense powers given to the
President and his opportunity for their abuse. Let us . . . resolve
that we will do all in our power to preserve these principles for
our posterity. This is our duty as citizens of the United States, and
pre-eminently our duty as Latter-day Saints" (Senator Wallace F.
Bennett, R–Utah).[122]

1966: "I gave the language and sources of the prophetic utterance made
by the Prophet Joseph that the Constitution of the United States
would hang by a single thread, but be saved by the elders of Israel.
I hope you will read those sources so you will be well-informed as
to this prophecy and be prepared to do your part in its fulfillment"
(Ernest L. Wilkinson, BYU president [1951–1971]).[123]

1975: "Thank God for the Constitution. And may God bless the elders of
Israel that when, as President John Taylor said, 'the people shall
have torn to shreds the Constitution of the United States, the
Elders of Israel will be found holding it up to the nations of earth
and proclaiming liberty'" (Ezra Taft Benson, president of the Quorum of the Twelve Apostles and future Mormon president).[124]

1988: "Joseph Smith predicted that the time would come when the Constitution would hang, as it were, by a thread, and at that time 'this
people will step forth and save it from the threatened destruction'" (Ezra Taft Benson, LDS president).[125]

1995: "LDS attachment to the Constitution has been further encouraged
by an important oral tradition deriving from a statement attrib-

uted to Joseph Smith, according to which the Constitution would
'hang by a thread' and be rescued, if at all, only with the help of
the Saints. Church President John Taylor seemed to go further
when he prophesied, 'When the people shall have torn to shreds
the Constitution of the United States the Elders of Israel will be
found holding it up to the nations of the earth.'"[126]

2000: "[LDS TV weatherman Thom Spencer] at a Republican rally . . .
broke with tradition that a journalist should remain objective and
spoke out at the rally because of a prophecy by Joseph Smith, who
founded the Church of Jesus Christ of Latter-Day Saints more than
150 years ago. Smith predicted that the time would come 'when the
Constitution and government would hang by a brittle thread and be
ready to fall into other hands, but this people, the latter-day saints,
will step forth and save it'" (*Seattle Times*, November 24, 2000).[127]

But what would such a scenario mean for America? Continued freedom? Greater liberty and prosperity? Widespread pluralism? That is
doubtful. The history of Mormonism is rife with nefarious deeds, corruption, vice, and intolerance. So far the fruits of Mormonism have
included lust, greed, theft, fraud, violence, murder, religious fanaticism,
bribery, and racism. Will Mormonism's future harvest be any different?
That question, of course, will have to be answered in years to come.

Until then, all of us might to do well to simply be watchful, and heed
the words of Jesus Christ, whom the Mormons claim to follow. "Beware
of false prophets, which come to you in sheep's clothing, but inwardly
they are ravening wolves," Jesus warned. "Ye shall know them by their
fruits. . . . [E]very good tree bringeth forth good fruit; but a corrupt tree
bringeth forth evil fruit. . . . Wherefore by their fruits ye shall know
them" (Matt. 7:1-20).

Glossary of Mormon Terms

Although Mormons use many terms that are very similar to those used by Christians, several words that are in the LDS vocabulary have no equivalent in Christendom. Moreover, sometimes a Christian term has an altogether different meaning to Mormons. For example, "Jehovah" to Mormons is simply another name for Jesus. Christians do not accept this definition. The following glossary provides definitions based on Mormon beliefs only, and may include brief comments on my part for clarity of terminology. Definitions have been adapted from the LDS *Encyclopedia of Mormonism* and other LDS sources.

Aaronic Priesthood—Mormonism's lesser priesthood, which consists of the offices of deacon, teacher, priest, and bishop. Holders of this priesthood are responsible for temporal needs of the church (e.g., ushering, passing out sacraments, teaching, baptizing, and ordaining others).

Adam—The first man, viewed by Saints as one of the "greatest and noblest of all men." Modern concept very different from that of Brigham Young, who taught that Adam was God.

Adamic Language—The perfect language given by God to Adam.

Adam-ondi-Ahman—Daviess County, Missouri, where Adam and Eve fled after being expelled from the Garden of Eden.

Agency (a.k.a. free agency)—The God-given right to choose good or evil, and our responsibility for the choices we make.

Apostates—Mormons who "seriously oppose or ignore cardinal teachings of the Church, publicly or privately."

Apostle—A high office in the Melchizedek Priesthood; a member of the Quorum of the Twelve Apostles.

Articles of Faith—Thirteen statements of LDS belief written by Joseph Smith. Originally, there were fourteen articles, but these were significantly revised and edited unto the present format.

Babylon—A term signifying the collective ungodly world.

Baptism for the Dead—Vicarious baptism on behalf of the deceased, performed by proxy so that dead individuals in the spirit world can accept Mormonism and join the church.

Bear Testimony—When Mormons express their personal convictions of the truthfulness of the LDS church, its teachings, the *Book of Mormon*, and Joseph Smith's claims. One's testimony of "knowing" that Mormonism is true is usually based on subjective feelings rather than an acknowledgment of objective facts.

Bishop—An Aaronic priesthood office whose bearer has been ordained and set apart to preside over a ward (i.e., an organizational partition of several hundred church members in a specific geographical area).

Blood Atonement—The doctrinal teaching that to receive forgiveness for some sins (e.g., murder), one must have their own blood shed.

Book of Abraham—The writings of Abraham, revealed to Joseph Smith, who claimed to have produced the book by translating ancient Egyptian scrolls (see Appendix C). The *Book of Abraham* is contained in the *Pearl of Great Price*.

Book of Commandments—The earliest published collection of revelations to Joseph Smith (1833); re-published in 1835 and thereafter as the *Doctrine and Covenants*.

Book of Mormon—An account of ancient inhabitants in the Western Hemisphere, recorded on gold plates and translated by Joseph Smith.

Book of Moses—A record about the creation of the world and mankind up to the time of the great flood of Noah's time. It was revealed to Joseph Smith, while he was translating the Bible, and is contained in the *Pearl of Great Price*.

Burning in the Bosom—A supernatural manifestation of a burning sensation in the chest that is sometimes experienced by Mormons. It is said to be a confirmation by God that Mormonism is true.

Celestial Kingdom—The highest of three degrees of glory in the kingdom of heaven, where faithful Mormons become gods.

Church of Jesus Christ of Latter-day Saints, The—The official name of the Mormon church.

Conference Reports—The published proceedings of the general conferences of the church.

Counselor—Someone called to be an adviser, assistant, and occasional substitute for a church officer or leader.

Danites—A covert militia-like unit of Mormons active during early years of the church. They "protected" the church by harassing, threatening, and sometimes murdering "enemies," including church critics and dissidents.

Deacon—The lowest office of the Aaronic Priesthood, usually given to boys aged twelve to thirteen.

Degrees of Glory—The celestial, terrestrial, and telestial kingdoms in heaven.

Deseret—A *Book of Mormon* word that supposedly means "honey bee." It is often used in titles of LDS institutions, businesses, and organizations in areas with a dense LDS population.

Disfellowshipment—A disciplinary action against a Church member that severely restricts their participation in church activities.

Doctrine and Covenants—A volume of LDS scripture containing revelations and declarations given to Joseph Smith and his successors.

Elder—The lowest office in the Melchizedek Priesthood, as well as a title designating: 1) a holder of this priesthood; 2) a General Authority; 3) a male missionary. Most LDS young men are ordained to this office at the age of eighteen.

Elohim—God the Father.

Endowment—A significant ritual performed in the temple for worthy members of the church.

Eternal Marriage—Marriage by two Mormons that takes place in the temple, and will continue after death. It is an indispensable part of the LDS teaching that marriages and procreation are eternal in order to reach godhood (also known as celestial marriage or sealing).

Eternal Progression—The path of evolution on which Mormons believe themselves to be, which will one day lead them to godhood.

Eve—The first woman.

Exaltation—Attainment to the highest degree of glory in the celestial kingdom—i.e., godhood.

Excommunication—A disciplinary action against an LDS church member in which church membership is involuntarily withdrawn, after which time the individual is considered disgraced. Re-instatement is possible after repentance and a period of waiting time determined by church authorities on a case by case basis.

First Presidency—A hierarchical group consisting of the Mormon president and his two counselors; they are the highest-ranking LDS leaders. On rare occasions (e.g., during the terms of LDS presidents David O. McKay and Spencer W. Kimball) the president has taken on additional counselors.

First Vision—The term officially used to designate the appearance of God the Father and Jesus Christ to Joseph Smith in the spring of 1820 near Palmyra, New York.

Fulness of the Gospel—The doctrines, ordinances, authority, and organizational structure present only in the Mormon church.

Garden of Eden—The dwelling place of Adam and Eve, located in Jackson County, Missouri.

Garments—Sacred ceremonial undergarments worn by Temple Mormons. Mormons believe that this clothing protects them from harm.

General Authorities—The highest church leaders: the First Presidency, Quorum of the Twelve Apostles, Quorums of the Seventy, and Presiding Bishopric.

General Conference—A general assembly of church members in Salt Lake City, regularly convened the first weekend of every April and October.

Gentile(s)—(1) one not of the lineage of Israel; (2) a non-Mormon; (3) one who is not Jewish; (4) one who is not a Lamanite.

God the Father—Elohim, the god of this planet, but only one of innumerable gods that exist throughout the universe. He has at least one wife (perhaps more), is our *literal* father, and possesses a body of flesh and bones as tangible as our own. He is an exalted man.

Godhead—The three glorified, exalted, and resurrected personages known as the Father, Son, and Holy Ghost—i.e., the three gods associated with this planet. They are the "supreme presidency of the universe." The Father and Son have bodies of flesh and bone, while the Holy Ghost is a personage of spirit.

Gold Plates—Alleged source of the *Book of Mormon*.

Great and Abominable Church—All religious assemblies, congregations, churches, or associations of people that are not Mormon.

Heavenly Mother—One of the wives of Elohim, God the Father.

High Priest—The highest office in the Melchizedek Priesthood.

Holy Ghost—The third god of this planet, a personage of Spirit.

Inspired Version of the Bible—Another name for the Joseph Smith "translation" of the Bible, which Smith produced to support some of his doctrinal views. Technically, it is not a translation at all, but rather, a revision of the King James Bible.

Israel—(1) Mormons; (2) the Old Testament patriarch Jacob and his descendants.

Jehovah—Another name for Jesus Christ, particularly in the Old Testament.

Joseph Smith Translation of the Bible (JST)—The flawed "translation" of the Bible by Joseph Smith, which he began in 1830 (see Inspired Version).

Journal of Discourses—A collection of sermons by early LDS leaders that cover the early to late 1800s (26 volumes).

Lamanites—(1) The Israelite people of the *Book of Mormon*, descended from Joseph of Egypt through Lehi and Ishmael; (2) disobedient Israelites in the *Book of Mormon*; and 3) today's Native Americans, descendants from the *Book of Mormon* Israelites who turned away from God and forgot their origins.

Latter-day Saint—A Mormon.

Manifesto of 1890—The official announcement by Wilford Woodruff that was supposed to end polygamy, although most LDS leaders continued practicing polygamy for many years thereafter.

Marvelous Work and A Wonder—A reference to a prophecy in Isaiah (29:1-14) that applies to the emergence of Mormonism in 1830 and the coming forth of the *Book of Mormon*. It is also the title of an extremely popular book by the late LDS apostle, LeGrand Richards.

Melchizedek Priesthood—The higher priesthood, including the offices of Elder, Seventy, High Priest, and Apostle. This priesthood, unlike the Aaronic priesthood, focuses on the spiritual needs of the church.

Michael—The archangel, the pre-earthly name for Adam.

Moroni—(1) A Nephite military leader in the *Book of Mormon*; (2) a *Book of Mormon* prophet, who in 1827, as a resurrected being, appeared to Joseph Smith and gave him gold plates from which was translated the *Book of Mormon*. A golden statue of Moroni is placed atop most LDS temples.

Mountain Meadows Massacre—The 1857 massacre of more than one hundred and twenty Arkansans and Missourians by Mormons enroute to California. They were brutally murdered by Mormons, aided by a small band of Indians.

Pearl of Great Price—One of the four standard works of the LDS church. It contains the *Book of Moses*, the *Book of Abraham*, Joseph Smith—Matthew (Smith's supposed "translation" of Matthew 24), Joseph Smith—History (portions from the church's official *History of the Church*), and the Articles of Faith.

Pioneer Day—The annual July 24 celebration of the anniversary of the arrival of Latter-day Saints in Salt Lake Valley in 1847.

Plural Marriage—The more technical and less offensive term Mormons use in reference to polygamy.

Pre-existence/Pre-mortal Life—The belief that everyone existed in a cosmic spirit realm before coming to earth.

Priest—The highest office in the Aaronic Priesthood, usually given to boys aged sixteen to seventeen.

Priesthood—(1) The power of God; (2) the authority to act in God's name; (3) the right and responsibility to preside within the church organization; (4) a term referring to the men of the church in general.

Prophet—(1) When capitalized, Joseph Smith; (2) when not capitalized, it usually refers to the Mormon president, or any authorized spokesman for God.

Prophet, Seer, and Revelator—The special powers and functions held by members of the First Presidency and the Quorum of the Twelve Apostles. Often used to refer exclusively to the Mormon president.

Quorum of the Twelve Apostles—The body of twelve men who, under the direction of the First Presidency, constitute the second-highest presiding quorum of the LDS church.

Quorums of the Seventy—General Authorities organized in bodies of up to seventy members. Under supervision of the quorum's presidential board, the First Presidency, and the Quorum of the Twelve, the Seventy direct missionary and other administrative activities of the Mormon church.

Reformed Egyptian—The language Joseph Smith said he saw on the golden plates from which he translated the *Book of Mormon*. No evidence for any such language exists.

Reorganized Church of Jesus Christ of Latter Day Saints (RLDS)—A church that emerged after Joseph Smith's death, founded in 1860 by those who did not follow Brigham Young to Utah. It was headed by Joseph's son, Joseph Smith III. The RLDS denied polygamy. It is now known as the Community of Christ, and is based in Independence, Missouri.

Restoration—(1) The re-establishment of the "pure" Christian gospel through Joseph Smith; (2) the culmination of God's work on the earth.

Saints—Mormons.

Seventy—The second office in the Melchizedek Priesthood, with a special calling to missionary service or to administrative duties.

Sons of Perdition—Individuals who knowingly and willingly have rejected Mormonism after fully understanding its teachings and beliefs.

Stake—A unit of the church consisting of several wards in a specific geographical location.

Stake President—The presiding authority of a stake.

Standard Works—The four works that Mormons look to for doctrinal truth: *Book of Mormon*, *Doctrine and Covenants*, *Pearl of Great Price*, and the Bible. All of these works, except the King James Bible, are believed without reservation. The Bible, however, is accepted only "as far as it is correctly translated." It must be read in light of the other works (see pp. 381, 383).

Stick of Joseph—A biblical term, which according to Mormons, refers to the *Book of Mormon*, the LDS alleged record of a remnant of the posterity of Joseph who was sold into Egypt (Ezek. 37:15-19).

Stick of Judah—A biblical term, which according to Mormons, refers to the Bible, the record of the Jews, as preserved by the prophets of Judah (Ezek. 37:15-19).

Tabernacle—(1) The physical body in which a person's spirit dwells while on earth; (2) a special building used for assemblies, such as the Tabernacle on Temple Square.

Teacher—The Second office in the Aaronic Priesthood, usually given to boys aged fourteen to fifteen.

Telestial Kingdom—The lowest of three degrees of glory; the place where the wicked go after they die and have been judged.

Temple—A sacred Mormon building, also known as the "House of the Lord," in which Mormons are married, hold secret ceremonies, and perform baptisms for the dead.

Temple Marriage—A term for a marriage solemnized in a Mormon temple; also known as marrying for eternity (see Eternal Marriage).

Temple Ordinances—Secret ceremonies performed in Mormon temples.

Temple Recommend—A certificate of worthiness needed by a Mormon before they can enter and participate in temple ordinances.

Terrestrial Kingdom—The middle of the three degrees of glory; the afterlife destination of "honorable" people, who did not become Mormons during their life on earth or afterward.

Testimony—An expression of one's positive convictions or beliefs about Mormonism.

Time and Eternity—A term suggesting that gospel ordinances and blessings are valid forever, both on earth and in the heavens.

Urim and Thummim—Two stones set in "silver bows," used by Joseph Smith to translate portions of the *Book of Mormon*. It also is a euphemism used for Joseph's seer stone, the means by which he translated the original edition of *Book of Mormon*.

War in Heaven—According to LDS teachings, the conflict between Lucifer and Jesus Christ that took place during the pre-existence.

Ward—An organizational partition of several hundred church members in a specific geographical area.

Word of Wisdom—A health code for Mormons that forbids consumption of alcohol, tobacco, coffee, and tea.

Zion—Originally, the place where God would begin establishing his earthly kingdom (i.e., Independence, Missouri). Then, it meant the whole of North America. It eventually came to mean anywhere the LDS church was established.

Notable Mormons

Bennett, John C. (1804–1867), powerful LDS leader, Assistant President to Joseph Smith, major general of the Nauvoo Legion, mayor of Nauvoo, but ultimately became one of the church's most troublesome opponents. APOSTATIZED/EXCOMMUNICATED.

Benson, Ezra Taft (1899–1994), thirteenth Mormon president, noted for his extensive church service and his distinguished career in government (U.S. Secretary of Agriculture, 1953–1961).

Brodie, Fawn (1915–1981), biographer, social critic, and author of the landmark book on Joseph Smith's life, *No Man Knows My History*. EXCOMMUNICATED.

Cannon, George Q. (1827–1901), First Counselor in the First Presidency, went to prison for polygamy.

Clayton, William (1814–1879), secretary to Joseph Smith, treasurer of Nauvoo, polygamist, and member of original pioneer company to Utah in 1847.

Cowdery, Oliver (1806–1850), one of Joseph Smith's scribes, assistant president under Joseph Smith and at one time (c. 1830) next in authority to Smith (*D&C* 21:10-12), witnessed many critical events in early Mormon history.

Dunn, Paul H. (1924–1997), a general authority, became a controversial figure after it was discovered he had lied about his life's accomplishments.

Emma Smith (1804–1879), first wife of Joseph Smith, did not follow Brigham Young to Utah, helped establish the Reorganized Church of Jesus Christ if Latter Day Saints (now known as Community of Christ). APOSTATIZED.

Faust, James E. (1920–), an apostle, Second Counselor to current LDS president, Gordon B. Hinckley.

Ferguson, Thomas Stuart (1915–1983), LDS scholar, founded the Archaeology Department at Brigham Young University, tried in vain to find archeological evidence for the *Book of Mormon*, lost his faith in the church, but remained a member out of deference to his family and friends.

Grant, Heber J. (1856–1945), seventh Mormon president, a polygamist, and instrumental in beginning to utilize the media in order to improve Mormonism's public image.

Grant, Jedediah M. (1816–1856), powerful apostle, polygamist, first mayor of Salt Lake City, instigator of the bloody Mormon Reformation (1856–1857), Second Counselor to Brigham Young.

Harris, Martin (1783–1875), a New York farmer, one of the Three Witnesses to *Book of Mormon*, financed the first publication of the *Book of Mormon* in 1830 at a cost of $3,000. APOSTATIZED.

Hatch, Orrin (1934–), Republican Senator from Utah.

Hickman, Bill (1815–1883), bodyguard of Joseph Smith, murdered numerous individuals at the behest of Brigham Young, Indian fighter, left the church and published the tell-all book of his exploits, *Brigham's Destroying Angel: Being the Life, Confession, and Startling Disclosures of the Notorious Bill Hickman.* APOSTATIZED.

Hinckley, Gordon B. (1910–), fifteenth Mormon president, currently leading the church as of 2002, media-savvy and committed to making the LDS church appear like just another Christian denomination.

Hunter, Howard W. (1907–1995), fourteenth Mormon president, took over the church at the age of eighty-six and served the shortest term of any LDS president—nine months.

Hurlbut, Philastus (1809–1883), one of the most despised apostates, after leaving the church he attacked Mormonism relentlessly, acquired numerous anti-Joseph Smith statements from personal acquaintances of Smith's during Mormonism's formative years, and had them published by E.D. Howe in *Mormonism Unvailed* (1834).

Hyde, Orson (1805–1878), a member of the first twelve apostles who took the LDS message to continental Europe and the Near East.

Kimball, Heber C. (1801–1868), an apostle, polygamist, First Counselor to Brigham Young, extremely influential, popular preacher, and avid supporter of Young.

Kimball, Spencer W. (1895–1985), twelfth Mormon president, under whose administration Blacks were given the priesthood.

Lee, Harold B. (1899–1973), eleventh Mormon president.

Lee, John D. (1812–1877), Danite, Nauvoo policeman, major in the Nauvoo Legion, member of the Council of Fifty, leader of the Mountain Meadows Massacre, used as a scapegoat by the LDS church, the only Mormon convicted of anything having to do with the massacre. EXECUTED.

Maxwell, Neal A. (1926–), important LDS apostle, often in the middle of controversial issues as a church spokesperson.

McConkie, Bruce R. (1915–1985), well-known LDS apostle, whose widely circulated *Mormon Doctrine* proved in some cases to be an embarrassment to the church because of its candor.

McKay, David O. (1873–1970), ninth Mormon president, who spearheaded the move by the church to become more international.

McLellin, William E. (1806–1883), one of the original members of the Quorum of the Twelve Apostles, apostatized from the church, wrote numerous documents feared to contain damaging information on the church, which many years later led twentieth century Mormons to seek out the mythical "McLellin Collection," which played an integral part of the Mark Hofmann murders.

Monson, Thomas S. (1927–), an apostle, First Counselor to current LDS president Gordon B. Hinckley.

Oaks, Dallin H. (1932–), influential LDS apostle, often a spokesperson for the church and a key leader.

Packer, Boyd K. (1924–), powerful LDS apostle, acting president of the Quorum of the Twelve Apostles, nicknamed "Darth Packer" for his authoritarian ways and strict adherence to LDS beliefs, thought to be behind the string of excommunications of intellectuals in the early 1990s.

Parker, LeRoy (1866–1937), a.k.a. Butch Cassidy, famous outlaw, "King of the Wild Bunch," born in Beaver, Utah, baptized a Mormon at the age of eight, never followed LDS teachings, instead left Utah to live a life of crime, died of rectal cancer.

Petersen, Mark E. (1900–1984), high-ranking LDS apostle, very visible during the racist controversies of the 1960s, made some highly prejudicial comments.

Phelps, W.W. (1792–1872), publisher of Mormon newspapers, briefly excommunicated, eulogized Joseph Smith, died a faithful member of the church in Utah.

Pratt, Orson (1811–1881), famous LDS apostle, prolific author, responsible for establishing the publication of Mormon pamphlets focused on explaining LDS theology.

Pratt, Parley P. (1807–1857), renowned LDS apostle, and one of the most significant LDS missionaries, writers, poets, and thinkers to emerge during the early years of the church. His publications set a standard for future pamphleteers. MURDERED.

Richards, LeGrand (1886–1983), influential LDS apostle, threatened Jerald and Sandra Tanner in the early 1960s after they began disseminating accurate history and information damaging to the LDS church.

Rigdon, Sidney (1793–1876), First Counselor to Joseph Smith, one of Smith's closest friends and advisers, persuasive orator during early Mormon period, attempted to take over the church after Smith's death. APOSTATIZED/EXCOMMUNICATED.

Roberts, B. H. (1857–1933), widely-known General Authority, a historian, and prolific writer, who eventually lost his faith in the *Book of Mormon* by investigating its historicity. Never left the church.

Rockwell, Orrin Porter (1813–1878), Joseph Smith's bodyguard, known as the "Destroying Angel," thought to have made an attempt on the life of Missouri governor Boggs, committed countless murders and other crimes at the behest of various LDS leaders.

Smith, George Albert (1870–1951), eighth Mormon president.

Smith, Hyrum (1800–1844), brother of Joseph Smith, served as Assistant President, polygamist, and highly regarded as a martyr by Latter-day Saints. MURDERED.

Smith, Joseph F. (1838–1918), sixth Mormon president, polygamist, son of Hyrum Smith, led the Church into the first two decades of the twentieth century and helped establish Mormonism as a mainstream religion.

Smith, Joseph Fielding (1876–1972), tenth Mormon president, the first-born son of Joseph F. Smith.

Smith, Joseph, Jr. (1805–1844), first Mormon president and founder of the LDS church, proven to be a money-digger, occultist, and polygamist. MURDERED.

Smoot, Reed (1862–1941), LDS apostle, changed the political course of the church by becoming the first major political figure within Mormonism, served in U.S. Senate from 1903–1932, endured a three-year-long investigation by the Senate Oversight Committee to determine whether he would be allowed to keep his congressional seat.

Snow, Lorenzo (1814–1901), fifth Mormon president, penned the popular Mormon couplet: "As man is, God once was; as God is, man may become."

Stout, Hosea (1810–1889), Chief of Police in Nauvoo, murderer, close associate of Joseph Smith and Brigham Young.

Talmage, James E. (1862–1933), high-ranking LDS apostle, prolific writer, and LDS theologian.

Taylor, John (1808–1887), third Mormon president, steadfastly defied the U.S. government's demands to cease polygamy, fled into hiding to avoid arrest, and died while still eluding law enforcement authorities.

Whitmer, David (1805–1888), one of the three witnesses to the *Book of Mormon*, very important in early Mormonism, occasionally served as the church's clerk. APOSTATIZED.

Whitmer, John (1802–1878), brother of David Whitmer, fourth of the Eight Witnesses to the *Book of Mormon*. APOSTATIZED

Widtsoe, John A. (1872–1952), influential LDS apostle, and prolific author defending the Mormon faith.

Woodruff, Wilford (1807–1898), fourth Mormon president, convinced the end of the world would occur around 1890, was forced to issue the famous Manifesto banning polygamy.

Young, Brigham (1801–1877), second Mormon president, ruthless and calculating, governed Utah and the LDS church for thirty years, a period during which the horrific doctrine of blood atonement was practiced.

Abraham's Book?

The June 30, 1835, arrival in Kirtland, Ohio of a traveling exhibitor named Michael H. Chandler would lead to the emergence of some of Mormonism's most crucial doctrines. More precisely, the cargo Chandler had brought with him—i.e., four Egyptian mummies and several ancient papyrus scrolls—would be the source of many Mormon beliefs. The four mummies certainly were awesome to behold, but more significant to the Latter-day Saints were the scraps of papyri in Chandler's possession. At that time, no scholars were able to translate Egyptian writings, but the *Book of Mormon*, they recalled, said a *seer* was gifted by God with the ability to "translate all records that are of ancient date" (Mosiah 8:13). Mormons, of course, had their own seer—Joseph Smith. Who better to translate the ancient documents?

So, after careful consideration, members of Smith's church pooled their resources and purchased Chandler's entire exhibit for $2,400. The ancient treasures were then delivered to Joseph. Surely Smith would be able to translate the writings, thereby proving his God-given abilities. Joseph's followers were not disappointed. According to Smith, the scrolls were not only ancient, but were penned by none other than Abraham, the Hebrew patriarch, and Joseph, the renowned son of Jacob, yet another famous biblical figure. Moreover, the inscriptions were so similar to those on the *Book of Mormon* golden plates that Smith was positive he could translate them. Surely, this was a miracle intended to bring more divine truth to God's faithful followers.

Smith immediately began translating the documents. The information the scrolls revealed was revolutionary, relating to the origin of Blacks, the doctrine of pre-existence, the nature of Deity, the way Earth was created, and insights on the priesthood. So important were the documents and their teachings that Smith made three sketches of the papyri's main images. These drawings, the interpretation of them, and Smith's "translation" of the scrolls were first published in the LDS *Times and Seasons* in March 1842.

Then, after being re-published and re-distributed in 1851 and 1878, the *Book of Abraham* was finally canonized by the Mormon church in 1880 and included in the *Pearl of Great Price*. To modern Mormons the divine authenticity of this *Book of Abraham* is crucial because it not only "proves" Joseph Smith's powers of translation, but also provides information for several LDS doctrines that can be found nowhere else.

As it turns out, however, the ancient documents Smith acquired were only copies of common Egyptian funeral texts; namely, the *Book of Breathings* (which Smith turned into the *Book of Abraham*) and *Book of the Dead* (which Smith said had been written by the Bible's Joseph). The first challenges to his *Book of Abraham* were lodged as far back as 1912. At that time Egyptologists and other scholars already were able to recognize Smith's interpretations of the illustrations as highly flawed (see Figures C-1, C-2, C-3 and C-4):[1]

Dr. A. H. Sayce (Oxford, England): "It is difficult to deal seriously with Joseph Smith's impudent fraud. . . . Smith has turned the Goddess [Isis] into a king and [the god] Osiris into Abraham."

Dr. W. M. Flinders Petrie (London University): "To any one with knowledge of the large class of [Egyptian] funeral documents to which these belong, the attempts to guess a meaning are too absurd to be noticed. It may be safely said that there is not one single word that is true in these [i.e., Smith's] explanations."

James H. Breasted, Ph.D. (Haskell Oriental Museum, University of Chicago): "To sum up, then, these three fac-similes of Egyptian documents in the 'Pearl of Great Price' depict the most common objects in the mortuary religion of Egypt. Joseph Smith's interpretations of them as part of a unique revelation through Abraham, therefore, very clearly demonstrates that he was totally unacquainted with the significance of these documents and absolutely ignorant of the simplest facts of Egyptian Writing and civilization."

Dr. Arthur C. Mace (Assistant Curator, Metropolitan Museum of Art, New York, Department of Egyptian Art): "I return herewith, under separate cover, the 'Pearl of Great Price! The 'Book of Abraham,' it is hardly necessary to say, is a pure fabrication. . . . Joseph Smith's interpretation of these cuts is a farrago [i.e., a confused mixture] of nonsense from beginning to end."

Professor S. A. B. Mercer, Ph.D. (Western Theological Seminary, Custodian Hibbard Collection, Egyptian Reproductions): "[Smith] knew neither the Egyptian language nor the meaning of the most commonplace Egyptian figures. . . . the explanatory notes to his fac-similes cannot be taken seriously by any scholar, as they seem to be undoubtedly the work of pure imagination."

Despite such scathing appraisals of Smith's work, Mormons continued to steadfastly support their prophet's rendering of the hieroglyphics, claiming that none of the scholars had examined the *original* documents from which Smith made his drawings. Moreover, his drawings represented only a few of the many papyri fragments used to produce the entire *Book of Abraham*. The bulk of the translation, in fact, was taken from papyri that contained actual writing rather than just pictures. Consequently, Mormons felt no negative judgment could legitimately be passed on their prophet's volume of scripture.

For many years it seemed that these arguments would indefinitely protect LDS claims about the *Book of Abraham* because the original papyri fragments Smith "translated" had been destroyed in the great Chicago fire of 1871. The *Book of Abraham* would forever be beyond a thorough scholarly investigation. Then in 1967, to everyone's great surprise, Smith's original papyri fragments were recovered from an old, dusty storage bin located in New York's Metropolitan Museum of Art. Egyptologists, religion scholars, and other interested parties hailed the discovery.

Figure C-1

Figure C-2

Facsimile No. 1 from the LDS *Book of Abraham*, which includes numbered explanations of the images shown. Smith's original papyri found at New York's Metropolitan Museum of Art (*top image*) reveals that this section was missing its top segment. So he crudely drew in the missing parts (*barely visible*), which were reproduced in the official version of the *Book of Abraham* (*bottom image*). But when compared to how the papyri should appear, based on the modern Egyptology and other copies of the *Book of Breathings* (*see next page*), it is clear that Smith seriously erred in depicting the missing papyri segment. He gave the standing figure a human head, instead of a jackal head (#3). He gave the flying bird (#1) a bird's head instead of a human head. He missed drawing in the falcon altogether. And he incorrectly drew the hand positioning of the figure lying down (#2). Smith also mislabeled every part of the Egyptian scene, having no clue as to what the images actually meant (see comparison chart after Figure C-3).

Figure C-3

This is an accurate reconstruction of the *Book of Breathings* papyri segment used by Smith, except unlike Smith's papyri, this reconstruction includes those portions that were missing from Smith's scroll (from Charles M. Larson, *By His Own Hand Upon Papyrus: A New Look At the Joseph Smith Papyri*, 1985, 1992 edition).

Smith's Identifications of Images (Supposedly About Abraham)	Accurate Egyptian Scene Depictions (The Embalming/Resurrection of Osiris)
1. Angel of the Lord.	1. The soul of Osiris, *ba*, hovering over the body, waiting to enter it.
2. Abraham fastened on altar.	2. The god, Osiris, one hand pointing upward (palm down as a sign of grief), and one hand holding his phallus, in preparation for the impregnation of his wife, Isis (in the form of a falcon).
3. Evil priest Elkenah attempting to sacrifice Abraham.	3. The jackal-headed god, Anubis, who is embalming Osiris
4. The altar of sacrifice.	4. Traditional lion-headed embalming couch.
5. The idolatrous god Elkenah	5. A grandson of Osiris and Isis.
6. The idolatrous god Libnah	6. A grandson of Osiris and Isis.
7. The idolatrous god Mahmackrah	7. A grandson of Osiris and Isis.
8. The idolatrous god Korash	8. A grandson of Osiris and Isis.
9. The idolatrous god Pharaoh	9. The crocodile god, Sobek.
10. Abraham in Egypt	10. A libation platform bearing wines, oils, and a stylized papyrus plant.
11. Pillars of heaven, as understood by Egyptians	11. Stones bordering the front of a pool of water.
12. Represents the height of the heavens	12. A pool in which Sobek is swimming.

Figure C-4

Facsimile No. 3 from the *Book of Abraham*, like Facsimile No. 1, has a numbered explanation of the images represented. It, too, has been completely misrepresented by Joseph Smith (see comparison chart below). The original of this papyri used by Smith has not been found. However, it is one of the most common funeral scenes represented in Egyptian burial texts.

Smith's identifications of Images (Abraham in the King's Court)	Accurate Egyptian Scene Depictions (About the Court of Osiris in Underworld)
1. Abraham sitting on throne.	1. Osiris, wearing a double-plumed crown, holding royal flail and crook across chest.
2. King Pharaoh.	2. Isis, wearing customary solar disc and cow horn.
3. Signifies Abraham in Egypt.	3. Standard libation platform common in all Egyptian sketches featuring major deities.
4. Prince of Pharaoh, King of Egypt.	4. Maat, goddess of justice.
5. Shulem, one of the king's principle waiters.	5. Deceased individual wearing traditional perfumed cone and lotus flower on head, being led by Maat to Osiris.
6. Olimlah, a slave belonging to the prince.	6. Anubis, guide of the dead.

Unfortunately for Mormons, careful examination of the scrolls vindicated LDS church critics, not Joseph Smith. The texts were indeed Egyptian funeral scrolls belonging to the *Book of Breathings* and the *Book of the Dead*. The *Book of Breathings*, which Smith claimed had been written by Abraham, was actually penned around the second century B.C.—approximately 2,000 years after Abraham had died.

With regard to the writing on the papyri, an accurate translation of the characters using modern-day knowledge of the Egyptian language does not match Joseph's *Book of Abraham* "translation." In fact, Smith's entire narrative consists of nothing but lengthy paragraphs falsely attributed to simple hieroglyphics, each of which represents little more than one or two short words or ideas (see Table C-1 and Figure C-5, pp. 458–459).

To date, numerous books have been written cataloguing and explaining the inaccurate information, mistranslated texts, and erroneously interpreted drawings associated with Smith's *Book of Abraham*.[2] In *Mormonism: Shadow or Reality?* Jerald and Sandra Tanner have aptly commented: "That the Utah Mormon leaders would continue to endorse the *Book of Abraham* in the face of the evidence which has been presented is almost beyond belief."[3]

Correct Translations	Joseph Smith's "translation" *Book of Abraham* 1:11-15
"the, this" ⯗	11. Now, this priest had offered upon this altar three virgins at one time, who were the daughters of Onitah, one of the royal descent directly from the loins of Ham. These virgins were offered up be-cause of their virtue; they would not bow down to worship gods of wood or of stone, therefore they were killed upon this altar.
"pool" ⯗	and it was done after the manner of the Egyptians. 12. And it came to pass that the priests laid violence upon me, that they might slay me also, as they did those virgins upon this altar; and that you may have a knowledge of this altar, I will refer you to the representation at the commencement of this record.
"water" ⯗	13. It was made after the form of a bedstead, such as was had among the Chaldeans, and it stood before the gods of Elkenah, Libnah, Mahmackrah, Korash, and also a god like unto that of Pharaoh, king of Egypt. 14. That you may have an understanding of these gods, I have given you the fashion of them in the figures at the beginning, which manner of the figures is called by the Chaldeans Rahleenos, which signifies hieroglyphics.
"great" ⯗	15. And as they lifted up their hands upon me, that they might offer me up and take away my life, behold, I lifted up my voice unto my God, and the Lord hearkened and heard, and he filled me with the vision of the Almighty, and the angel of his presence stood by me, and unloosed my bands.

Table C-1

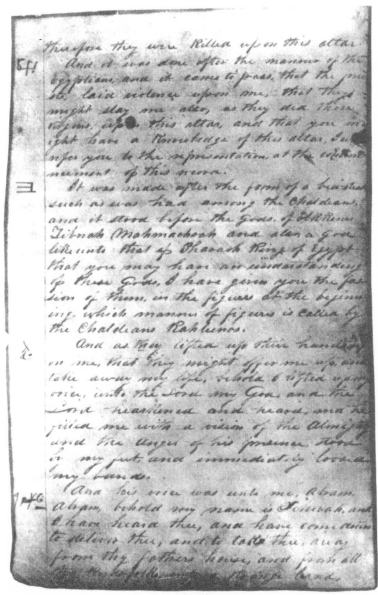

Figure C-5

Page three of Joseph Smith's Manuscript No. 1 (c. 1835), in the handwriting of Smith's scribe. It shows how much *Book of Abraham* material was "translated" from the corresponding Egyptian characters in the column on left of page. Egyptologists and scholars say the so-called translations are not merely incorrect, but ludicrous.

Failed Joseph Smith Prophecies

Mormons believe they are led by prophets of God, who have received divine revelations as appointed leaders of the LDS church. This is especially true of Joseph Smith, the church's founder. A legitimate question is: "Did the predictions/prophecies made by Smith come true?" According to Bible, a true prophet must be correct in his/her predictions 100 percent of the time (Deut. 18:21-22). Even the *Doctrine and Covenants* promises that every prophecy it contains "shall all be fulfilled" (*D&C* 1:37). Hyrum Smith, Joseph's brother, was a bit more forgiving, saying that any prophet, if they "hit once in 10 times that is alright."[1] In light of these criteria, the following partial list of failed prophecies/predictions by Joseph Smith is significant.

Date of Prophecy	Prophecy/Prediction	Outcome
1823, Sept. 21	The angel Moroni tells Smith that Isaiah 11 is "about to be fulfilled." Isaiah 11:6-11 says that the wolf and the lamb, the calf and the lion, will dwell in peace together, that nothing will "hurt or destroy," and that the earth shall be "full of the knowledge of the Lord."[2]	This prophecy has not yet come to pass, and the phrase "about to be fulfilled" no longer applies.
1829/1830, Winter	Joseph received a revelation that Hiram Page and Oliver Cowdery were to raise money by going to Canada, where they would find a buyer for the copyright of the *Book of Mormon*.[3]	Cowdery and Page went to Canada, but never found a buyer for the copyright.

1830, Sept.	In a revelation, God decrees that the elect shall be gathered into one place "against the day when tribulation and desolation are sent forth upon the wicked."[4]	The one place to which Mormons were to gather changed as the Saints were driven from one location to another. Mormons remain a scattered people.
1830, Sept.	Smith declares by revelation that "the hour is nigh and the day soon at hand" when the wicked will burn, all prophecies will be fulfilled, and Jesus will return to begin a 1,000-year reign.[5]	The terms "nigh" and "soon" can no longer be applied to this prophecy.
1831, Mar. 7	By God's command and revelation the Saints were to gather riches and purchase an inheritance (i.e., the New Jerusalem, a.k.a. Zion), a place of refuge and safety, where the wicked would not come, and against which the wicked would refuse to battle because of fearing the Mormons.[6]	Most of the Missouri property that the Saints had acquired was either sold or abandoned.
1831, July 20	Missouri is named as the land consecrated for the gathering of the Saints, the place for the City of Zion and the building of a temple. It will be purchased by the saints "for an everlasting inheritance."[7]	The "City of Zion," including its temple, was never built up.
1830, Sept.	Zion, along with its temple, will be built at Independence, Missouri, "in this generation." This generation "shall not all pass away" until the temple will be built upon the spot chosen.[8]	The generation to which Smith refers died out many years ago, without seeing the building of a temple in Independence.

1832, Sept.	New York, Albany and Boston will be destroyed if they reject the gospel. The "hour of their judgment is nigh."[9]	Newell K. Whitney and Joseph Smith went to New York, Albany, and Boston and preached the LDS message. The cities did not accept it. They have not yet been destroyed.
1832, Dec. 25	Civil War Prophecy	see Chapter Twelve
1833, Jan. 4	Joseph Smith says "by the authority of Jesus Christ" that "not many years shall pass away" before the wicked "of this generation" will be swept from off the face of the land and the Lost Ten Tribes will be gathered to Missouri, and that "there are those now living upon the earth whose eyes shall not be closed in death until they see all these things, which I have spoken, fulfilled."[10]	Smith's generation has died out, and yet Jesus has not returned.
1833, August 2	Promise that if the saints are obedient the City of Zion (in Missouri) will prosper and become glorious, great and terrible, honored by the nations of the earth. Zion cannot fall or "be moved" out of its place.[11]	The City of Zion never prospered in Missouri. The Saints fled the state.
1833, Dec. 10	Joseph Smith tells the saints that they should retain their lands in Missouri and seek legal redress against their enemies. If they should not obtain it, God will avenge them with "ten thousand of his Saints" and all their adversaries would be destroyed.[12]	The Mormons sought redress of their losses, but were unsuccessful. Wrongs against them were not avenged, nor were their enemies destroyed.

1834, Spring	Smith prophesies to Zion's Camp that "within three years they should march to Jackson County and there should not be a dog to open his mouth against them."[13]	Jackson County was never redeemed and Zion's Camp never marched again.
1834, Apr. 23	Revelation received stating Smith's United Order would be "everlasting," "immutable and unchangeable," to benefit the church "until I [i.e., Jesus] come." Through Smith, Jesus said: "This is the way that I, the Lord, have decreed to provide for my saints."[14]	The United Order failed in Ohio and Missouri.
1834, June 22	The Lord says regarding Missouri: "I will fight your battles. . . the destroyer I have sent forth to destroy and lay waste mine enemies; and *not many years hence* they shall not be left to pollute mine heritage, and to blaspheme my name upon the lands which I have consecrated for the gathering together of my saints."[15]	Enemies in Missouri were not destroyed, nor were they ever driven from the land. The Mormons, on the other hand, were driven from Missouri within five years.
1834, Aug. 16	Smith said the Spirit of the Lord told him that the Saints should be ready to move into Jackson County, Missouri, on September 11, 1836, "the appointed time for the redemption of Zion."[16]	The Latter-day Saints fled Missouri in 1839.
1835, Feb. 14	"[T]he coming of the Lord, which is nigh—even fifty-six years should wind up the scene."[17]	1835 + 56 years = 1890/91. Jesus did not return.

1835, Feb. 14	Smith prophesied that Orson Hyde would go to Jerusalem, and "by thy hands shall the Most High do a great work, which shall prepare the way and greatly facilitate the gathering of that people [i.e., the Jews]."[18]	Orson Hyde went to Jerusalem, but did nothing to facilitate the gathering of the Jews, which did not occur until over 100 years later (i.e., 1948).
1836, Aug. 6	Smith received a revelation to go to Salem, Massachusetts, where he was supposed to receive "its wealth pertaining to gold and silver."[19]	Smith returned in September to Kirtland, without having seen the prophecy fulfilled.
1837, July 23	Smith issued a revelation saying that Thomas B. Marsh, then the president of the quorum of the Twelve Apostles, would be "exalted," would preach to Jews and Gentiles "unto the ends of the earth," among "the mountains, and among many nations." Smith said that by marsh's word "many high ones shall be brought low, and . . . many low ones shall be exalted." Through Smith, God tells Marsh: "I know thy heart."[20]	Less than two years later, on March 17, 1839, Marsh was excommunicated. The prophecy was not fulfilled.
1838, Apr.17	Smith, via a revelation, says Apostle David W. Patten should settle his business so that he can go on a mission "next spring . . . to testify of my name and bear glad tidings unto all the world."[21]	Less than eight months later, Patten was killed at the Battle of Crooked River (October 25, 1838). The revelation never came to pass, even though Patten died "strong in the faith" (HC 3:171).
1839, Mar. 20	While in prison, Smith prophesied that his enemies would be taken "in their own craftiness" and that "not many years hence, . . . [his enemies] and their posterity shall be swept from under heaven, saith God, that not one of them is left to stand by the wall."[22]	None of these prophecies came to pass.

1842, Apr. 28	At a Relief Society meeting, Smith says; "I now prophecy that before ten years shall roll around, the queens of the earth shall come and pay their respects to this Society."[23]	No queens have ever fulfilled this prophecy.
1843, Jan. 20	Joseph Smith prophesies that he and Orson Hyde will drink wine together in Palestine.[24]	Smith never went to Palestine. And drinking wine would have been against Smith's Word of Wisdom command.
1843, Apr. 6	"I prophesy in the name of the Lord God, and let it be written—the Son of Man will not come in the clouds of heaven till I am eighty-five years old."[25] "[T]he 14th chapter of Revelation . . . '[T]he hour of His judgment is come.' And Hosea, 6th chapter. After . . . 2,520 years; which brings it to 1890."[26]	1805 + 85 years = 1890/91. Jesus did not return in 1890 based on the either of these calculations.
1843, Apr. 6	"There are those of the rising generation who shall not taste death till Christ comes."[27]	All persons of Joseph's generation, as well as those of the rising generation alive when he was speaking, are deceased. None of them saw Christ's return.
1843, May 18	"I prophecy in the name of the Lord God of Israel, unless the United States redress the wrongs committed upon the Saints in the state of Missouri and punish the crimes committed by her officers that in a few years the government will be utterly overthrown and wasted, and there will not be so much as a potsherd left for their wickedness."[28]	The U.S. government did not redress any of the wrongs committed against the Mormons in Missouri. Nevertheless, it has not been "overthrown and wasted."

1843, Dec. 16	"While discussing the petition to Congress, I prophesied, by virtue of the holy Priesthood vested in me, and in the name of the Lord Jesus Christ, that, if Congress will not hear our petition and grant us protection, they shall be broken up as a government, and god shall damn them. And there shall nothing be left of them—not even a grease spot."[29]	The United States rejected the Mormons' petitions; their wrongs were not redressed. America has not been "broken up." When this was reprinted in the *HC* (vol. 6, 116), 18 words were omitted in order to read: "While discussing the petition to Congress, I prophesied, by virtue of the holy Priesthood vested in me, and in the name of the Lord Jesus Christ, that, if Congress will not hear our petition and grant us protection, they shall be broken up as a government.* * * *" Notice how the comma after the word "government" was changed to a period in order to make it appear as if the sentence was complete.
1844, Feb. 6	Smith prophesied "that 5 years would not roll round before the company would all be able to live without cooking."[30]	Mormons are still cooking their food.
1844, Apr.–May	Joseph Smith prophesies that his unborn child will be called David, and will be "church president and king over Israel."[31]	Smith's son, David, was never "church president and king over Israel." He died in 1904, at the age of 60, having spent the last 27 years of his life in an insane asylum.

Recommended Resources

Studying Mormonism is a difficult task given the fact that much of the historical documents dealing with LDS history are extremely difficult to obtain, even for a trained researcher. Thanks to the Internet, however, many of these documents are available as never before. The following Internet resources and sites should be helpful for anyone wanting access to detailed information on Mormonism. It should be remembered, however, that websites by devout Mormons tend to be overtly biased and permeated with LDS propaganda. Consequently, they are listed separately since it is this author's opinion that such sources of information are highly skewed and can be unreliable. (These pro-Mormon sites, including the official LDS church website, are listed for research purposes only and their contents are not necessarily endorsed as being a full or accurate representation of Mormon history, LDS doctrines, world history, the sciences, or Christianity).

> **Utah Lighthouse Ministry**, Jerald and Sandra Tanner, extensive research materials provided including rare documents made available for purchase and online. Specializes in the historical aspects of Mormonism. http://www.utlm.org/.
>
> *Salt Lake Tribune,* news from inside Utah, accurate journalism, no favoritism, handles controversial LDS-related issues regularly, current events, online archives. http://www.sltrib.com/.
>
> **Concordance.com**, a highly useful site that provides searchable databases of numerous rare and important works on Mormonism, including Mormon works, the full twenty-six volumes of the *Journal of Discourses, Book of Mormon* (1830 and modern editions), *Doctrine*

and Covenants, and the *Book of Commandments*. Dozens of similar texts. http://www.concordance.com/mormon.htm.

Mormon Classics Library, features countless rare books and newspapers from early Mormons as well as early Mormon critics, maintained by RLDS member Dale Broadhurst, books include E.D. Howe's *Mormonism Unvailed* (1834), *Mountain Meadow's Massacre* (Gibbs, 1910), *Illustrations of Freemasonry* (Morgan, 1826), *Remarkable Visions* (Orson Pratt, 1848), *Rocky Mountain Saints* (Stenhouse, 1873), and *Wife No. 19* (Young, 1875). http://SidneyRigdon.com/Classics1.htm.

Making of America Books, approximately 8,500 books and 50,000 journal articles written between 1800 and 1925, many of which deal with Mormonism. An invaluable resource with well-crafted and accurate search engines. For Mormon-related materials, go to http://moa.umdl.umich.edu/, then click on either "Go to MoA Books" or "Go to MoA Journals." At these two sites either browse the collection titles, or run key word searches on Mormon related words and phrases (e.g., Mormon, Brigham, Joseph Smith, etc.).

Anti-Mormon Preservation Society, although its name leaves much to be desired, this site offers excellent resources, rare books, interesting facts. http://antimormon.8m.com/.

Mormonism Research Ministries, an evangelical site with a vast amount of research and information that looks at Mormonism from a religious perspective, also has a great deal on history, research, a newsletter, feedback, weekly quotes, search engine, newspaper articles about Mormonism updated regularly. http://www.mrm.org/.

Ex-Mormons, excellent site to get information from and about former Mormons, specializes in analyzing Mormon doctrines, personal stories, bulletin boards, newsgroups, and tips for people interested in leaving Mormonism, counseling available. http://www.exmormon.org/.

Mormonism Web Ministries, offers in-depth articles examining Mormon doctrines in light of Christianity, excellent research covering nearly every Mormon doctrine, quotations of the day from LDS leaders, free e-mail newsletter. http://mormonism-web.com/index.htm.

Alpha & Omega, site of Christian scholar James White, an expert on Mormonism, highly involved in debates with other Mormon scholars, academic approach, philosophical assessment of LDS faith, answers to Mormon apologists. http://aomin.org/Mormonism.html.

Mormon Central, very important site started by well-known Mormon scholar, H. Michael Marquardt, extremely knowledgeable, current and relevant, bibliography, frequently asked questions, scholarly papers. http://www.xmission.com/~research/central/index.htm.

Real Mormon History, a bit sensationalistic in tone, but accurate, well-organized. Specializes in controversial Mormon history, countless quotes from historical sources, fascinating LDS trivia, maintained by a former Mormon who grew up in the church, disillusioned after looking into LDS history. http://www.realmormonhistory.com/.

LDS-Mormonism, a valuable site established by a former Mormon, up-to-date information, controversial issues, history, reviews of Mormon-related books, links, bulletin boards. http://www.lds-mormon.com/.

Mormons in Transition, sponsored by the Institute for Religious Research, good scholarly information, a wide range of issues, book reviews, updated reports on Mormon studies, site not as user-friendly, best to use search engine on site. http://www.irr.org/mit/.

Christian Research Institute, does not specialize in Mormonism, but is the largest "counter-cult" organization in the world, a storehouse of cult-related materials ranging from A-Z, scholarly journal, tapes, books, pamphlets, tracts, CDs, videos, solidly evangelical Christian in its approach. http://equip.org/.

Watchman Fellowship, does not necessarily specialize in Mormonism, but contributes a great deal of information on cults worldwide, extensive database index of cults, brief descriptions for easy perusal, in-depth articles, books, videos, tapes, CDs, publications, speaking engagements, excellent resource, solidly evangelical Christian in its approach. http://watchman.org/watchman.htm.

Utah Missions, Inc., a solidly evangelical Christian organization, long-time distributor of LDS information, specializes in materials dealing with the religious/doctrinal aspects of Mormonism. http://www.umi.org/.

Mormons / Fundamentalists / RLDS

The Church of Jesus Christ of Latter-day Saints, official site of the Mormon church. http://www.lds.org/.

Deseret News, official news publication of the Mormon church, biased, and unabashedly pro-LDS. http://deseretnews.com/dn.

LDS Church News, official publication of the Mormon church, specializes in news specifically related to the church, highly biased. http://www.desnews.com/cn/.

Kingdom of Zion, interesting site set up by a Mormon Fundamentalist named Ogden Kraut, who is a polygamist. Excellent documents showing the original teachings of Mormonism. http://www.kingdomofzion.org.

Restoration Website, extremely well-designed, countless links to Mormon related sites, especially sites related to acquiring and collecting rare Mormon books and memorabilia, maintained by John Hajicek, a Strangite (follower of James Strang, who claimed to be the legitimate successor to Joseph Smith). Hajicek is a dealer in rare Mormon books and manuscripts, a great site to visit and explore. http://restoration.org/.

An Unofficial Introduction to the Church of Jesus Christ of Latter-day Saints, a good example of an average Mormon's attempt to defend the LDS faith, numerous self-published articles, not scholarly, extremely biased, articles often based on misinformation. This site will provide great insights into the LDS mindset, especially through the answers to critics articles. http://www.jefflindsay.com/LDS_Intro.shtml.

Foundation for Ancient Research and Mormon Studies (F.A.R.M.S.), under BYU auspices, highly scholarly site, seeks to validate Mormonism on an academic/intellectual level, highly biased, very unreliable, can be confusing to average reader due to use of technical terminology, often misleading due to its use of historical, archeological, and linguistic arguments unverifiable by persons not possessing higher education. Very controversial. http://farms.byu.edu/splash4.html.

Community of Christ, formerly known as the Reorganized Church of Jesus Christ of Latter Day Saints, established church by Mormons refusing to follow Brigham Young, and have always disavowed polygamy. http://CofChrist.org/.

Notes

ABBREVIATIONS

AOF   The *Articles of Faith* are thirteen statements that outline the more socially acceptable Mormon beliefs, usually discussed openly by Latter-day Saints when explaining Mormonism to potential converts. None of the articles deal with any doctrines that might be viewed as offensive or controversial to non-Mormons. The *Articles of Faith* are contained in modern LDS editions of the *Pearl of Great Price*, one of the Standard Works of the Mormon church. The *AOF* are online at http://www.exmormon.org/fourteen.htm. A searchable text version of the *Articles of Faith* is online at http://www.concordance.com/mormon.htm, under the *Pearl of Great Price*.

BMO   The *Book of Moses* was supposedly received by direct revelation from God. It is Joseph Smith's re-write of the first several chapters of the Bible's book of Genesis, which according to Smith, is textually corrupted. Contained in modern LDS editions of the *Pearl of Great Price*, one of the Standard Works of the Mormon church. A searchable text version of the *Book of Moses* is online at http://www.concordance.com/mormon.htm, under the *Pearl of Great Price*.

BOA   The *Book of Abraham* was allegedly written on ancient scrolls by the Hebrew Patriarch Abraham; scrolls which Joseph Smith acquired in 1835 and supposedly translated. In actuality, the scrolls were common funeral texts from the Egyptian *Book of Breathings* (see Appendix C). A searchable text version of the *Book of Abraham* is online at http://www.concordance.com/mormon.htm, under the *Pearl of Great Price*.

BOC   The *Book of Commandments* was originally published in 1833, containing many of Smith's earliest revelations. A searchable text version of the *Book of Commandments* is online at http://www.concordance.com/mormon.htm.

BOM   The *Book of Mormon*, originally published in 1830, allegedly was translated from golden plates Joseph Smith said he found in the Hill Cumorah in New York. The plates supposedly contained the history of America's ancient inhabitants and the fullness of God's everlasting gospel (*Doctrine and Covenants*, 27:5). Searchable text versions of both the 1830 edition of the *BOM* and the current edition are online at http://www.concordance.com/mormon.htm.

BYU   Brigham Young University, named after the Mormon church's second president.

CHC   *A Comprehensive History of the Church* was produced by celebrated Mormon historian, B.H. Roberts. It is similar to the *HC*, but contains additional information and commentary (six volumes). It is more reliable than the official *HC*, but is still biased.

D&C   *Doctrine and Covenants* is a re-printing of the original *Book of Commandments*. It has been significantly revised, updated and amended over the course of its many editions, beginning in 1835. The *D&C* also includes Wilford Woodruff's 1890 Manifesto banning polygamy and the 1978 "revelation" that opened up the LDS priesthood to persons of African descent. A searchable text version of the *D&C* is online at http://www.concordance.com/mormon.htm.

E&MS   *The Evening and the Morning Star*, the first Mormon periodical, originally was published in Independence, MO, from June 1832 to July 1833. After being destroyed by a Missouri mob, its publication site was relocated to Kirtland, OH, where it continued from December 1833 to September 1834. A searchable text version of *E&MS* is online at http://www.concordance.com/mormon.htm.

EJ   The *Elders' Journal of the Church of Latter Day Saints*, an early Mormon periodical, originally was published in Kirtland, OH, from October 1837 to November 1837, then in Far West, MO, from July 1838 to August 1838. A searchable text version of the *EJ* is online at http://www.concordance.com/mormon.htm.

HC   The *History of the Church*, also known as the *Documentary History of the Church*, is the official history of the LDS church, published by the church. It supposedly was written by Joseph Smith himself, but in actuality, was written by Smith, various scribes, and later historians, who revised and "updated" the original text in an effort to conceal unflattering events in Mormon history. The *HC* is highly biased and unreliable (seven volumes). A searchable text version of the *HC* is online at http://www.concordance.com/mormon.htm.

HR   *The Historical Record* was an LDS periodical devoted to the historical, biographical, chronological, and statistical matters of the church (nine volumes, 1882–1890). They were edited by assistant Mormon church historian, Andrew Jenson.

JOD   The *Journal of Discourses*, published by the LDS church, are the lectures/sermons given by Mormon church leaders from 1843 to 1886 (twenty-six volumes). A searchable text version of the *JOD* is online at http://www.concordance.com/mormon.htm.

LDSCA   The Church of Jesus Christ of Latter-day Saints, Church Archives, Salt Lake City, UT.

MS   The *Millennial Star* was an early LDS periodical published in England. The *MS*, volumes one through seven (1840–1846), are available for purchase online at http://www.utlm.org/booklist/titles/ up035_millenialstarvol1.htm.

MS&AD   *The Latter-day Saints' Messenger & Advocate* was an early Mormon periodical published in Kirtland from October 1834 to August 1837. A searchable text version of the *MS&AD* is online at http://www.concordance.com/mormon.htm.

PGP   The *Pearl of Great Price* is one of the Mormon church's Standard Works, a compilation of various documents including the *Book of Moses, Book of Abraham*, a section from the *HC* about Smith's first visions, a portion of Smith's re-translation of the biblical passages Matthew 23:39–Matthew 24, and Smith's *Articles of Faith*. A searchable text version of the *Pearl of Great* is online at http://www.concordance.com/mormon.htm.

RLDSCA   The Reorganized Church of Jesus Christ of Latter Day Saints, Church Archives, Independence, MO. On April 6, 2001, the Reorganized Church of Jesus Christ of Latter-day Saints (RLDS) officially changed its name to the Community of Christ. However, for the sake of consistency when citing documents from previously published resources, I have chosen to retain the RLDS designation.

Proceedings The *Proceedings Before the Committee On Privileges and Elections of the United States Senate in the Matter of the Protests Against the Right of Hon. Reed Smoot, A Senator from the State of Utah, to Hold His Seat* is the testimony to determine whether polygamist Reed Smoot could retain his senatorial seat (1904).

T&S   The *Times and Seasons* was an early Mormon periodical issued from Commerce/Nauvoo, IL, from November 1839 to February 1846. A searchable text version of the *T&S* is online at http://www.concordance.com/mormon.htm.

ULM   The Utah Lighthouse Ministry of Salt Lake City, Utah, is a veritable storehouse of information on Mormonism from former Mormons Jerald and Sandra Tanner. Jerald is a descendant of John Tanner, who in the 1830s was an associate of Joseph Smith, Jr. and a large financial contributor to his activities. Sandra is the great-great grandchild of Brigham Young.

AUTHOR'S PREFACE: ABOUT MORMON HISTORY

1. D. Michael Quinn, lecture before the Mormon Historical Association, BYU, November 4, 1981, published as "On Being a Mormon Historian (and Its Aftermath)," 8, reprinted in George D. Smith, ed., *Faithful History: Essays On Writing Mormon History* (Salt Lake City: Signature Books, 1992), 69–111. Quinn's lecture and related stories are online at http://www.xmission.com/~country/reason/mormhist.htm (transcript) and from the ULM, online at http://www.utlm.org/newsletters/no85.htm (Jerald Tanner and Sandra Tanner, "Mormon Inquisition?: LDS Leaders Move to Repress Rebellion," *Salt Lake City Messenger* [#85], November 1993, 3–5). Quinn's article is available for purchase online at http://www.utlm.org/booklist/titles/ub057_onbeingamormonhistorian.htm.

2. Mormon church officials have routinely insisted that any materials written on LDS history by Mormons must be "faith promoting," which means they must support Mormon beliefs and official teachings, even at the risk of being historically inaccurate. In 1981, for instance, LDS apostle Boyd K. Packer warned Mormon historians against publishing objective history, even in professional journals because such works destroy and weaken the faith of Mormons (Boyd K. Packer, "The Mantle Is Far, Far Greater Than the Intellect," *BYU Studies* [Summer 1981], vol. 21, 264–265). Eventually, in June 1986, the staff of the LDS church's historical department were made to "sign a form which Elder Packer declared gave the right of pre-publication censorship for any archival research completed before signing the form" (Smith, 109, footnote #52; quoted in Tanner and Tanner, 3, http://www.utlm.org/newsletters/no85.htm).

3. See Smith, 69–111.

4. See Quinn, http://www.xmission.com/~country/reason/mormhist.htm.

5. Allen Roberts, *Private Eye Weekly*, October 20,1993, 12. Quoted in Jerald Tanner and Sandra Tanner, "Legacy: A Distorted View of Mormon History," *Salt Lake City Messenger* (#88), May 1995, 4, online at http://www.utlm.org/newsletters/no88.htm.

6. John E. Hallwas and Roger D. Launius, *Cultures in Conflict: A Documentary History of the Mormon War in Illinois* (Logan, UT: Utah State University Press, 1995), 2–3. For in-depth information on the debate among Mormon and non-Mormon scholars over LDS history that has been falsified by LDS scholars and how such practices relate to the writing of what has been called "faithful history," see Jerald Tanner and Sandra Tanner, *Falsification of Joseph Smith's History* (Salt Lake City: ULM, 1971), available for purchase online at http://www.utlm.org/booklist/titles/ub071_falsificationofjosephsmiths history.htm; Robert B. Flanders, "Writing the Mormon Past," *Dialogue. A Journal of Mormon Thought* (Autumn 1966), vol. 1, 47–61; Moses Rischin, "The New Mormon History," *The American West* (March 1969), vol. 5, 49; Richard D. Poll, "God and Man in History," *Dialogue. A Journal of Mormon Thought* (Spring 1972), vol. 7, 101–109; Thomas G. Alexander, "Toward the New Mormon History. An Examination of the Literature on the Latter-day Saints in the Far West," in Michael P. Malone, ed., *Historians and the American West* (Lincoln: University of Nebraska Press, 1983), 344–368; Thomas G. Alexander, "Historiography and the New Mormon History: A Historian's Perspective," *Dialogue: A Journal of Mormon Thought* (Fall 1986), vol. 19, 25–50; Jerald Tanner and Sandra Tanner, Falsifying History" subheading in "Magic in Mormonism," *Salt Lake City Messenger* (#65), November 1987, online at http://www.utlm.org/newsletters/no65.htm#FALSIFYING %20HISTORY; Marvin S. Hill, "The 'New Mormon History' Reassessed in Light of Recent Books on Joseph Smith and Mormon Origins," *Dialogue. A Journal of Mormon Thought* (Fall 1988), vol. 21, 115–127; Paul M. Edwards, "The New Mormon History," *Saints' Herald* (November 1986), vol. 133, 13; Davis Bitton and Leonard J. Arrington, *Mormons and Their Historians* (Salt Lake City: University of Utah Press, 1988); George D. Smith, ed., *Faithful History*; and D. Michael Quinn, ed., *The New Mormon History* (Salt Lake City: Signature Books, 1992).

7. Roberts, 12. A number of individuals have been excommunicated like Quinn for similar expressions of doubt over certain aspects of Mormon history. In December, 1994, for example, Brent Metcalfe, editor of *New Approaches to the Book of Mormon* (Salt Lake City: Signature Books, 1993) was excommunicated for questioning the authenticity of the *Book of Mormon*.

8. See Linda King Newell and Valeen Tippetts Avery, *Mormon Enigma: Emma Hale Smith* (New York: Doubleday & Co., 1984). When Newell met with Apostle Dallin H. Oaks to discuss the contents of her controversial book on Smith's polygamous adventures and the subsequent ban on her and Avery, Oaks—a former Utah Supreme Court justice and past president of BYU—said: "My duty as a member of the Council of the Twelve is to protect what is most unique about the LDS church, namely the authority of priesthood, testimony regarding the restoration of the gospel, and the divine mission of the Savior. Everything else may be sacrificed in order to maintain the integrity of those essential facts. Thus, if *Mormon Enigma* reveals information that is detrimental to the reputation of Joseph Smith, then it is necessary to try to limit its influence and that of its authors" (Linda King Newell, "The Biography of Emma Hale Smith," 1992 Pacific Northwest Sunstone Symposium, audiotape #J976).

INTRODUCTION: A THREAD OF PROPHECY

1. Joseph Smith. Quoted in John J. Roberts, *Journal of John J. Roberts* (Paradise, UT), online at http://www.helpingmormons.org/white_horse.htm. References to this prophecy by various LDS leaders are online at http://www.2eternity.com/mormon/whitehorse.html. There is considerable controversy surrounding this prophecy. Some LDS officials consider it to be fraudulent. However, historical evidence indicates that Smith did indeed make the prophecy, or at least prophesied something extremely close to it. For example, Orson Hyde, one of Smith's contemporaries and an early leader of the Mormon church, made the following statement: "It is said that brother Joseph in his lifetime declared that the Elders of this Church should step forth at a particular time when the Constitution should be in danger, and rescue it, and save it. This may be so; but I do not recollect that he said exactly so. I believe he said something like this—that the time would come when the Constitution and the country would be in danger of an overthrow; and said he, [i]f the Constitution be saved at all, it will be by the Elders of this Church. I believe this is about the language, as nearly as I can recollect it" (Orson Hyde, January 3, 1858, *JOD* [Liverpool: Asa Calkin, 1859; lithographed reprint of original edition, 1966], vol. 6, 152). Another contemporary of Smith's, James Burgess, recorded the following: "In the month of May 1843. Several miles east of Nauvoo. The Nauvoo Legion was on parade and review. At the close of which Joseph Smith made some remarks upon our condition as a people and upon our future prospects contrasting our present condition with our past trials and persecutions by the hands of our enemies. Also upon the constitution and government of the United States stating that the time would come when the Constitution and Government would hang by a brittle thread and would be ready to fall into other hands but this people the Latter day Saints will step forth and save it. General Scott and part of his staff on the American Army was present on the occasion. I James Burgess was present and testify to the above" (James Burgess, *James Burgess Notebook*, LDSCA, vol. 1, as cited in Andrew F. Ehat and Lyndon W. Cook, *The Words of Joseph Smith: The Contemporary Accounts of the Nauvoo Discourses of the Prophet Joseph* [Orem, Utah: Grandin, 1991], 279, see note under May 6, 1843). Whatever Smith's exact wording may have been, a significant number of Mormons—including LDS church presidents, high-ranking church officials, and persons closely associated with Smith (e.g., Brigham Young, Joseph F. Smith, Charles Penrose, J. Reuben Clark, Joseph Fielding Smith, Harold B. Lee)—endorsed the prophecy as genuine. Several of these same individuals have gone so far as to quote it verbatim in their lectures and writings (see end-

notes #7, #8, #9). LDS leaders have reiterated the prophecy by referring to either the "constitution" or the "nation," either "hanging by a thread" or being "torn to shreds," after which time either "the Saints" or "the Elders" would save America. For a listing of these references see Sandra Tanner, "Joseph Smith's 'White Horse' Prophecy," Internet article online at http://www.utlm.org/onlineresources/whitehorseprophecy.htm.

2. Senator Orrin Hatch, "The Doug Wright Show" (KSL), November 9, 1999. Quoted in John Heilprin, "Did Hatch Allude To LDS Prophecy?," *Salt Lake Tribune*, November 11, 1999, online at http://www.sltrib.com (archives).

3. The Doug Wright Show and the Mormon church-owned KSL radio are both based in Salt Lake City, Utah.

4. Marvin S. Hill, "Quest for Refuge: An Hypothesis as to the Social Origins and Nature of the Mormon Political Kingdom," *Journal of Mormon History* (1975), vol. 2, 3–4; also see James R. Clark, "The Kingdom of God, the Council of Fifty, and the State of Deseret," *Utah Historical Quarterly* (April 1958), vol. 26, 131–150 and Klaus Hansen, "The Political Kingdom of God as a Cause for Mormon-Gentile Conflict," *BYU Studies* (Spring–Summer 1960), vol. 2, 241–260.

5. Fred Esplin, "The Saints Go Marching On," *Utah Holiday*, June 1981, 34.

6. D. Michael Quinn, *The Mormon Hierarchy: Origins of Power* (Salt Lake City: Signature Books, 1994), ix.

7. Brigham Young, February 18, 1855, *JOD* (London: F.D. Richards, 1855; lithographed reprint of original edition, 1966), vol. 2, 182.

8. George Q. Cannon, April 3, 1881, *JOD* (Liverpool: John Henry Smith, 1883; lithographed reprint of original edition, 1966), vol. 23, 123; cf. George Q. Cannon, November 20, 1881, *JOD*, vol. 23, 104.

9. Preston Nibley, *Deseret News*, December 15, 1948. Quoted by Ogden Kraut, a fundamentalist Mormon (and a polygamist), in his self-published book titled *The White Horse Prophecy* (Salt Lake City: Pioneer Press, 1993), 65, online at http://www.kingdom ofzion.org/doctrines/gospellibrary/kraut/kraut.html, click on the link marked "White Horse Prophecy, The."

10. Esplin, 33.

11. Some individuals interpret the prophecy to mean that all Mormons collectively will rescue America.

12. Doug Wright. Quoted in Heilprin.

13. Jan Shipps. Quoted in Heilprin.

14. Jan Shipps. Quoted in Glen Warchol and John Heilprin, "Mormon Myth Stalks Hatch in Presidential Race" *Salt Lake Tribune*, July 15, 1999, online at http://www.sltrib.com (archives).

15. Bruce McConkie, *Mormon Doctrine* (Salt Lake City: Bookcraft, 1958; second edition, 1966), 855. During a December 23, 1866 sermon, Brigham Young declared that at Christ's second coming, he would return to "the land of America" (Brigham Young, December 23, 1866, *JOD* [Liverpool: B. Young, Jr., 1867; lithographed reprint of original, 1966], vol. 11, 249).

16. Orson Hyde, n.d., *JOD* (Liverpool: Amasa Lyman, 1860; lithographed reprint of original edition, 1966), vol. 7, 53.

17. Joseph Smith, statement of December 30, 1842, *HC* (Salt Lake City: Deseret Book Company, 1976/1980), vol. 5, 212.

18. Ezra Taft Benson, *Teachings of Ezra Taft Benson* (Salt Lake City: Bookcraft, 1988), 619. Quoted in Tanner (see this chapter, endnote #1). Benson often quoted the prophecy. Consider the following quotations (additional examples are online at http://www.utlm.org/onlineresources/whitehorseprophecy.htm):

   • "[Joseph Smith] foresaw the time when the destiny of the nation would be in danger and would hang as by a thread. Thank God he did not see the thread break. He also indicated the important part that this people should yet play in standing for the principles embodied in these sacred documents—the Declaration of Independence and the Constitution" (Ezra Taft Benson, *Conference Report*, April 1948, 85).

- "[T]he Lord told the Prophet Joseph Smith there would be an attempt to overthrow the country by destroying the Constitution. Joseph Smith predicted that the time would come when the Constitution would hang, as it were, by a thread, and at that time "this people will step forth and save it from the threatened destruction. . . . It is my conviction that the elders of Israel, widely spread over the nation will at that crucial time successfully rally the righteous of our country and provide the necessary balance of strength to save the institutions of constitutional government" (Ezra Taft Benson, *Conference Report*, October 1961, 70).

- "The Prophet Joseph Smith said the time would come when the Constitution would hang as it were by a thread. Modern-day prophets for the last thirty years have been warning us that we have been rapidly moving in that direction. Fortunately, the Prophet Joseph Smith saw the part the elders of Israel would play in this crisis" (Ezra Taft Benson, *Conference Report*, April 1963, 113).

19. George Romney, interview in "A Man's Religion and American Politics: An Interview with Governor Romney," *Dialogue: A Journal of Mormon Thought* (Autumn 1967), vol. 2, 25.

20. David B. Magleby, "Contemporary American Politics," in Daniel H. Ludlow, ed., *Encyclopedia of Mormonism* (New York: Macmillan Publishing Company, 1992), vol. 3, 1108.

21. It is common knowledge that the CIA and FBI routinely draw recruits from the Mormon church. Both of these law enforcement agencies have instituted Mormon-recruitment plans (see David Van Biema, "Kingdom Come," *Time*, August 4, 1997, 52, online at http://www.time.com (archives).

22. Robert Gottlieb and Peter Wiley, *America's Saints: The Rise of Mormon Power* (New York: G.P. Putnam's Sons, 1984), 65.

23. Gottlieb and Wiley, 65.

24. Gottlieb and Wiley, 89.

25. National Archives and Records Administration, "Appendix A—Digest of Other White House Announcements," online at http://bushlibrary.tamu.edu/papers/1992/app_a.html.

26. As of 2000, sixteen LDS Senators and Representatives were serving on Capitol Hill. The religious affiliation listing of members of the 107th Congress (2000) is online at http://www.adherents.com/adh_congress.html.

27. John Heinerman and Anson Shupe, *The Mormon Corporate Empire* (Boston: Beacon Press, 1985), 139.

28. Heinerman and Shupe, 139.

29. Heinerman and Shupe, 141.

30. Heinerman and Shupe, 129.

31. Jeffery L. Sheler "The Mormon Moment," *U.S. News*, November 13, 2000, online edition, online at http://www.usnews.com (archives).

32. Richard N. Ostling and Joan K. Ostling, *Mormon America: The Power and the Promise* (San Francisco: Harper San Francisco, 1999), 115; cf. Kenneth L. Woodward, "The Mormon Way." *Newsweek*, September 10, 2001, 46.

33. Ostling and Ostling, 124.

34. Ostling and Ostling, 118.

35. Catherine Pepinster, "Mormons Spend Millions On UK Farmland," *The Independent—London*, July 15, 2001, PSA-2890, News Section. This article is online at http://www.northernlight.com (Special Collections). The article also states: "Although mainly based in the United States, it now has 180,000 members in Britain, based in 40

regional centers, or stakes. It first began buying land in Britain in 1995. . . . The Mormons say they are buying land to produce income for the sect as a long-term investment. Chris Jolliffe, general manager of the sect's farming company, Agreserves, said the crops it grows, such as wheat, provide food for the Third World. Other crops such as sugar beet are sold, with profits funding other humanitarian projects. In the past three years, pounds 2.5m [$3.5 million] has been made from the farms and used to support Mormon work in Ethiopia and Kenya."

36. Pepinster, http://www.northernlight.com.

37. Jeffrey Kaye, "An Invisible Empire: Mormon Money in California," *New West*, May 8, 1978, 36.

38. Ostling and Ostling, 115.

39. Brigham Young, March 8, 1857, *JOD* (Liverpool: S. W. Richards, 1857; lithographed reprint of original edition, 1966), vol. 4, 269.

40. Joseph Fielding Smith, *Doctrines of Salvation* (Salt Lake City: Bookcraft, 1954), vol. 1, 236. Mormons also believe that their church is "the only true and living church upon the face of the whole earth" and that "the power of God unto salvation—(Rom. 1:16) is absent from all but the Church of Jesus Christ of Latter-day Saints" (McConkie, 136 and Kent P. Jackson, "Early Signs of the Apostasy," *Ensign*, December 1984, 9).

41. Dan Erickson, *As A Thief in the Night* (Salt Lake City: Signature Books, 1998), 102.

42. McConkie, 321.

43. Joseph Smith, April 6, 1844, *JOD*, vol. 6, 4.

44. Spencer W. Kimball, "The Privilege of Holding the Priesthood," *Ensign*, November 1975, 80.

45. B.H. Roberts, *The Rise and Fall of Nauvoo* (Salt Lake City: Deseret News, 1900), 180.

46. Duane S. Crowther, *Prophetic Warnings to Modern America* (Bountiful, UT: Horizon Publishers, 1977; second edition, 1979), 315–316.

47. Joseph Smith, July 19, 1840, as recorded by Martha Jane Knowlton; ms. in LDSCA. Quoted in Ezra Taft Benson, "Our Divine Constitution," October 3, 1987 (General Conference), reprinted in *Ensign*, November 1987, online at http://www.etext.org/Politics/Essays/Conspiracy/LWB/LDS/god.planned.founding.fathers. Knowlton's entire report is as follows: "A few Item[s] from a discourse delivered by Joseph Smith July 19 - 1840. . . . 'We shall build the Zion of the Lord in peace until the servants of that Lord shall begin to lay the foundation of a great and high watch Tower and then shall they begin to say within themselves, what need hath my Lord of this tower seeing this is a time of peace &c. Then the Enemy shall come as a thief in the night and scatter the servants abroad. When the seed of these 12 Olive trees are scattered abroad they will wake up the Nations of the whole Earth. Even this Nation will be on the very verge of crumbling to pieces and tumbling to the ground and when the constitution is upon the brink of ruin this people will be the Staff up[on] which the Nation shall lean and they shall bear the constitution away from the very verge of destruction'" (see "The Historians Corner," *BYU Studies* [Spring 1979], vol. 19, 391–392); cf. D. Michael Stewart, "I Have A Question," *Ensign*, June 1976, 64–65. Stewart provides several additional quotations that support this prophecy and the White Horse prophecy as genuine, saying: "The documents show that Joseph Smith did prophecy a number of times that the United States and the Constitution would be imperiled and that the elders would have a hand in saving them" (Stewart, 64). The complete acceptance of the validity of Smith's prophecy is evident in countless statements by LDS leaders (see previous endnotes)—e.g., Joseph Fielding Smith, who in 1936, stated: "[Joseph Smith] predicted that the time would come when the Constitution of our country would hang as it were by a thread, and that the Latter-day Saints above all other people in the world would come to the rescue of that great and palladium of our liberty" (Joseph Fielding Smith, *The Progress of Man* [Salt Lake City: Deseret News Press, 1936], 342).

CHAPTER ONE: VAGABOND VISIONARIES

1. Pomeroy Tucker, "The Mormon Imposture—The Mormon Aborigines," *Wayne Democratic Press* (Lyons, New York), June 2, 1858, 2, reprinted in Dan Vogel, ed., *Early Mormon Documents*, (Salt Lake City: Signature Books, 2000), vol. 3, 67–68. Tucker was a Palmyra resident who, beginning in 1823, co-owned and operated the *Wayne Sentinel* newspaper for thirty years. He published his own book on Mormonism titled *Origin, Rise and Progress of Mormonism* (New York: D. Appleton and Co., 1867), online at http://moa.umdl.umich.edu/cgi/sgml/moa-idx?notisid=AGU9642. Tucker provides invaluable information about the Smiths because he knew them as early as 1816, the year they first moved to Palmyra. In the preface to his book, Tucker says he "was equally acquainted with Martin Harris and Oliver Cowdery, and with most of the earlier followers of Smith, either as money-diggers or Mormons," and that during the printing of the *BOM* he "had frequent and familiar interviews with the pioneer Mormons, Smith, Cowdery, and Harris" (Tucker, 4).

2. Joseph Fielding Smith, *Doctrines of Salvation* (Salt Lake City: Bookcraft, 1954), vol. 1, 188.

3. *HC* (Salt Lake City: Deseret Book Company, 1976/1980), vol. 6, 317. Mormon leaders claim that this official *HC* was written by Joseph Smith himself and that it is not only "an unusually accurate historical document," but it is "the most accurate history in all the world" (John Widtsoe, *Joseph Smith-Seeker After Truth* [Salt Lake City: Bookcraft, 1951], 255–257 and Joseph Fielding Smith, *Doctrines of Salvation* [Salt Lake City: Bookcraft, 1955], vol. 2, 199). It also is claimed by LDS leaders that "no historical or doctrinal statement has been changed" in the seven-volume history (*HC*, vol. 1, vi). Religion researchers, however, have discovered that this particular history of the LDS church has been significantly altered over the years in an effort to: 1) conceal negative aspects of Smith's personal life; 2) delete crude language and profanity he used; and 3) cover-up doctrinal changes and false prophecies that Smith presented to his followers. Moreover, most of the history was not even written by Smith. An excellent treatment of this issue can be found in Jerald Tanner and Sandra Tanner, *The Changing World of Mormonism* (Chicago: Moody, 1981), 398–416. The Internet version of this entire volume is online at http://www.utlm.org/onlinebooks/changecontents.htm. The specific chapter dealing with the *HC* is online at http://www.utlm.org/onlinebooks/changech13.htm.

4. The doctrine of "divine election," which is an essential tenet of Calvinism—so named after Protestant Reformation leader John Calvin (1409–1564)—teaches that it is God's sovereign will alone that "elects" people to salvation (i.e., the state wherein one has been forgiven for their sins, and via their subsequent relationship with God, may enter heaven after death). In other words, according to Calvinism, no one can contribute anything of their own to the salvation process.

5. Daniel G. Reid, coordinating editor, *Dictionary of Christianity in America* (Downers Grove, IL: InterVarsity Press, 1990), 781.

6. Benjamin Latrobe, *Journal of Benjamin Latrobe* (August 23, 1806–August 8, 1809). Quoted in the summary of the "Religion and the Founding of the American Republic" exhibition by the Library of Congress that toured America from 1999–2001 (an exhibition of more than 200 items), online at http://www.loc.gov/exhibits/religion/rel07.html.

7. James Finley. Quoted in "The 'Second Great Awakening,'" Internet article produced by the Center for History and New Media (an organization jointly developed by George Mason University [GMU] and the American Social History Project [ASHP] at the Center for Media and Learning at the City University of New York [CUNY]), online at http://chnm.gmu.edu/courses/jackson/revival/revival.html.

8. "The 'Second Great Awakening.'"

9. Reid, 639.

10. John Noyes, "Free Love," *Handbook of the Oneida Community—1875* (Oneida, NY: Wallingford Printing, 1875), 40–43, online at http://www.binghamton.edu/~womhist/oneida/doc18.htm.

11. Fawn M. Brodie, *No Man Knows My History* (New York: Vintage Books, 1995; original edition by Alfred A. Knopf, 1945), 12.

12. Nathaniel Lewis, statement of March 21, 1834, in E.D. Howe, *Mormonism Unvailed* (Painesville, OH: author, 1834), 267, online at http://www.solomonspalding.com/docs/1834howf.htm#pg267. This entire volume is online at http://www.solomon spalding.com/docs/1834howb.htm. A searchable text version is online at http://www.concordance.com/mormon.htm.

13. Asa B. Searles, a biographical sketch of Asa Searles in *History of Lee County* (Chicago, 1881), 387. According to Searles, Smith was "lazy, but kind-hearted, had a large brain and a good deal of ability" (p. 387). Quoted in David Persuitte, *Joseph Smith and the Origins of the Book of Mormon* (Jefferson, NC: McFarland & Co., 2000), 15.

14. Orasmus Turner, *History of the Pioneer Settlement of Phelps and Gorham's Purchase* (Rochester: William Alling, 1852), 213–214, online at http://home1.gte.net/dbroadhu/RESTOR/Lib/Tur1851a.htm.

15. Brodie, 26–27.

16. C.G. Webb. Quoted in W. Wyl, *Mormon Portraits* (Salt Lake City: Tribune Printing & Publishing Company, 1886), 25. A photo-mechanical reprint of this volume is available for purchase online at http://www.utlm.org/booklist/titles/up016_mormonportraits.htm.

17. Howe, 12, http://www.solomonspalding.com/docs/1834howc.htm#pg012a.

18. Persuitte, 1.

19. Kenneth H. Winn, *Exiles In A Land of Liberty* (Chapel Hill: University of North Carolina Press, 1989), 6.

20. Richard L. Bushman, *Joseph Smith and the Beginnings of Mormonism* (Urbana: University of Illinois press, 1984), 29.

21. Winn, 6; cf. Bushman for a detailed explanation of the financial disasters that hit the Smiths (pp. 30ff) .

22. Lucy had actually given birth to ten children by this time. But her first child died in 1797 soon after birth, and her seventh child (Ephraim) died only days after being born in 1810.

23. Brodie, 10.

24. Brodie, 10–11.

25. Joseph Capron, statement of November 8, 1833, reprinted in Howe, 260, online at http://www.solomonspalding.com/docs/1834howf.htm#pg260.

26. Roswell Nichols, statement of December 1, 1833, reprinted in Howe, 257, online at http://www.solomonspalding.com/docs/1834howf.htm#pg257. The severe debt of the Smiths has been substantiated by many sources and in various ways. For example, at one point in 1830 (c. October/November), Joseph Smith, Sr. was arrested and jailed for failure to pay a four dollar debt (see Vogel, vol. 3, 3–4).

27. Nichols, reprinted in Howe, 257, http://www.solomonspalding.com/docs/1834howf.htm#pg257.

28. Parley Chase, statement of December 2, 1833, reprinted in Howe, 248, online at http://www.solomonspalding.com/docs/1834howf.htm#pg248.

29. Citizens of Palmyra/Manchester, joint statement, December 4, 1833, reprinted in Howe, 261–262, online at http://www.solomonspalding.com/docs/1834howf.htm#pg261.

30. Richard L. Anderson, "Joseph Smith's New York Reputation Reappraised," *BYU Studies* (Spring 1970), vol. 10, 283–314. Howe's volume, including the affidavits that Philastus Hurlbut secured from acquaintances of Smith family, has been sharply criticized by numerous Mormon historians who say the work is biased and unreliable. They have attempted to discredit the book by charging that Philastus Hurlbut, because he was an

apostate, actually fabricated some of the statements for the signers. However, the probability of such accusations being correct is very low. In *Joseph Smith and the Origins of the Book of Mormon*, David Persuitte provides just a few of the many reasons why the statements in question are probably reliable and accurate: "In the first place, most of the statements were sworn to before judges or justices of the peace. Furthermore, one could perhaps understand why the signers might harshly magnify any earlier idiosyncrasies that Joseph Smith and his family had displayed, but one wonders what they would gain by signing completely false and therefore easily disprovable statements. It is possible that Hurlbut might have helped to draft some of the statements, but the content of those statements must have met with the approval of the signers. In the second place, Hurlbut did not collect the statements from Joseph's in-laws and acquaintances in the Harmony, Pennsylvania, area. These statements were first published in the May 1, 1834, *Susquehanna Register*, and subsequently republished by Howe in *Mormonism Unvailed*. The statement that Joseph's father-in-law, Isaac Hale, made is particularly important because it deals with several significant events leading up to the production of the *Book of Mormon*. If all of this testimony were part of a conspiracy to discredit Joseph, it is remarkable that so many people were in on it. The conspiracy would have had to encompass not only those living in the Palmyra-Manchester area, but also the Harmony, Pennsylvania, area" (p. 34).

Jan Shipps—professor emeritus of history and religious studies at Indiana University–Purdue University at Indianapolis—also affirms the probable accuracy of Howe's documents, pointing out that "newspaper articles and first-hand accounts written by Obadiah Dogberry [a.k.a. newspaper man Abner Cole], the Reverend Diedrich Willers, and James Gordon Bennett published in 1831—a full two years before the preparation of *Mormonism Unvailed*—contain precisely the same information" (Jan Shipps, "The Prophet Puzzle: Suggestions Leading Toward A More Comprehensive Interpretation of Joseph Smith," *Journal of Mormon History* [1974], vol. 1, 3–21, reprinted in D. Michael Quinn, ed., *The New Mormon History* [Salt Lake City: Signature Books, 1992], 63).

31. Milton V. Blackman, Jr., *Joseph Smith's First Vision* (Salt Lake City: Bookcraft, 1971; second edition, 1980), 116.

32. Rodger I. Anderson, *Joseph Smith's New York Reputation Reexamined* (Salt Lake City: Signature Books, 1990), 6.

33. Eduard Meyer, *Ursprung und Geschichte der Mormonen* (Halle: Max Niemeyer, 1912). Heinz F. Rahde and Eugene Seaich, trans., *The Origin and History of the Mormons* (Salt Lake City: University of Utah, n.d.), 4. The statements appearing in Howe's book are by no means the only harsh recollections of the Smith family. Negative descriptions of the Smiths, particularly of Joseph, have been published in a wide variety of documents stretching back to the early 1830s. One particularly scathing memory of the Smith's comes from Pomeroy Tucker in the June 2, 1858 edition of the *Democratic Press* (see this chapter, endnote #1). It reads: "JOE SMITH junior, who became the world-renowned translator of the recovered Israelitish records or scriptures—the publisher of the new revelation, in the Book of Mormon or Golden Bible, and founder of the politico-religious institution of Mormonism—was, at the period referred to, a dull-eyed, flaxen-haired, ragged boy. He was of taciturn habits—seldom speaking unless first spoken to while out among folks—but apparently a thinking, calculating, mischief-brewing genius, whose whole secretive mind seemed devoted to some mysterious scheme or marvelous invention. In his mental composition, the organ of 'conscientiousness' might have been marked by phrenologists as not there. His word, by reason of his propensity for exaggeration, was never received with confidence by any body who knew him, (excepting of course his bigoted dupes.) He was proverbially considered by his neighbor co[n]temporaries 'the meanest boy' of the family" (reprinted in Vogel, vol. 3, 69).

34. *HC*, vol. 1, 4.

35. *HC*, vol. 1, 4.

36. *HC*, vol. 1, 5–6; also in *PGP*, Joseph Smith—History, 1:16–20.

37. *HC*, vol. 1, 7.

38. Joseph Smith, "History of Joseph Smith," *T&S*, March 15, 1842, vol. 3, no. 10, 726–728 and *T&S*, April 1, 1842, vol. 3, no. 11, 748–749.

39. David O. McKay, *Gospel Ideals* (Salt Lake City, UT: Deseret News Press, 1953), 85.

40. Gordon B. Hinckley, *Ensign*, November 1998, 70–71. More than thirty years earlier, a much younger Hinckley had stated: "I would like to say that this cause is either true or false. Either this is the kingdom of God, or it is a sham and a delusion. Either Joseph Smith talked with the Father and the Son or he did not. If he did, not, we are engaged in a blasphemy" (Gordon B. Hinckley, *Improvement Era*, December 1961, 907).

41. John A. Widtsoe, *Joseph Smith—Seeker After Truth* (Salt Lake City: Deseret Book Company, 1951), 19.

42. This directly contradicts the Mormon claim that "Joseph Smith lived a little more than twenty-four years after the first vision. During this time he told but one story" (Preston Nibley, *Joseph Smith the Prophet* [Salt Lake City: Deseret News, 1944], 30).

43. James B. Allen, "The Significance of Joseph Smith's 'First Vision' in Mormon Thought," *Dialogue, A Journal of Mormon Thought* (Autumn 1966), vol. 1, 30–34. All of the issues of *Dialogue, A Journal of Mormon Thought* can be found on the *New Mormon Studies CD ROM: Comprehensive Resource Library* (Salt Lake City: Signature Books, 2000).

44. H. Michael Marquardt and Wesley P. Walters, *Inventing Mormonism: Tradition and Historical Record* (San Francisco: Smith Research Associates, 1994), 15–41. This in-depth study of early Mormonism contains an irrefutable compilation of facts from numerous historical documents that conclusively prove no 1820 revival took place in the Palmyra-Manchester area. According to Oliver Cowdery's 1834/1835 *Latter Day Saints' Messenger and Advocate* version of Smith's initial vision (see Chapter Two, endnotes #19 and #20), the Palmyra-Manchester revival began when Reverend Lane, a presiding Elder of the Methodist church, "visited Palmyra, and vicinity" (Oliver Cowdery, "Letter III," Oliver Cowdery to W.W. Phelps, *MS&AD*, December 1834, vol. 1, no. 3, 42, reprinted in Dan Vogel, ed., *Early Mormon Documents* [Salt Lake City: Signature Books, 1998], vol. 2, 424). But Methodist church records show that Reverend Lane did not receive an appointment to "serve as Presiding Elder of the Ontario District in which Palmyra is located" until July 1824. Moreover, Lane's own account of the Palmyra-Manchester revival, which appeared in *The Methodist Magazine* (April 1825, vol. 8, 159ff) states that it began in 1824, rather than 1820. Furthermore, in 1819/20 the Reverend Lane was still serving the Susquehanna District in Central Pennsylvania, more 150 miles from Palmyra. Mormon apologists have asserted that a revival involving Reverend Lane did indeed occur from 1819 to 1820, but that it took place in Vienna, some thirteen miles from Joseph's home (see Bushman, 53). Although historical records do show that Lane was in Vienna in July 1819 in order to attend the annual meeting of the Methodist Genesee Conference, there is no indication that he preached there or that camp meetings were held in connection with the conference, nor is there any evidence that there was a revival at that time. Wesley Walters and Michael Marquardt have shown that the idea of a revival at Vienna during these years can only result from a misreading and conjoining of two unrelated sources (Marquardt and Walters, 28–31). Regarding the many converts that supposedly came into the Methodist, Presbyterian, and Baptist churches during 1820, no such numbers exist in church records. Wesley P. Walters found membership records from each of these churches that actually list the number of converts for 1820. Palmyra's Presbyterian church lists no revival. The Palmyra Baptist church, which also did not report a revival, baptized only six people. Baptist churches in nearby Farmington, Lyons, and Canandaigua actually lost members. The Methodist churches in the entire area circuit recorded a net loss of six people for 1820 (cf. Persuitte, 300, endnotes). For a point-counterpoint article on this issue, see "Wesley P. Walters and Richard L. Bushman, "The Question of the Palmyra Revival," *Dialogue: A Journal of Mormon Thought* (Spring 1969), vol. 4, 59–100.

45. Marvin S. Hill, "The First Vision Controversy: A Critique and Reconciliation," *Dialogue: A Journal of Mormon Thought* (Summer 1982), vol. 15, 31–46. Hill, a Mormon, concluded in this article that the great revival to which Smith alludes in his First Vision story must be the 1824 revival. However, in an effort to reconcile the obvious discrepancy of timing between the official year of the First Vision (1820) and the year of the revival (1824), Hill also concludes that Smith *must* have been influenced by *some* kind of religious excitement around 1819/1820.

46. A listing of several more First Vision versions that are contradictory and rather confusing can be found in Sandra Tanner, "Evolution of the First Vision and Teaching On God In Early Mormonism," Internet article online at http://www.utlm.org/online resources/firstvision.htm. This article also discusses the evolution of Joseph Smith's concept of God and how it affected Mormon beliefs. Latter-day Saint historians and theologians have attempted to justify the many different versions of Smith's First Vision (even those he himself related) by theorizing that each version was simply emphasizing a different aspect of the vision. In reference to the 1832 version, for instance, Richard Bushman claims that it makes no mention of God the Father because in 1832 Joseph did not see this particular element of the story as very significant (Bushman, 56). He goes on to theorize that suddenly by 1838, Joseph realized "how significant it was that God the Father had appeared to introduce the Son" (p. 57). Consequently, Smith began talking about how he had seen God the Father, too. Such theories have been dismissed by non-Mormon historians and religion scholars.

47. Joseph Smith, *1832 History*, original manuscript, contained in Joseph Smith Letterbook 1, 1–6, Joseph Smith Papers, LDSCA, reprinted in Dean C. Jessee, ed., *The Papers of Joseph Smith* (Salt Lake City: Deseret Book Company, 1989), vol. 1, 5–7, and Dan Vogel, ed., *Early Mormon Documents* (Salt Lake City: Signature Books, 1996), vol. 1, 27–29. The 1832 version of the First Vision, as reprinted by Dan Vogel, reads in part as follows (original text has been retained where possible, but some misspellings, extraneous editorial marks, and confusing punctuation has been deleted in order to preserve the reading flow of the original document. Text that appears within < > indicates additional words above the line that do appear in the original manuscript. Words with a strike-through have been retained):

> "At about the age of twelve years my mind become Seriously imprest with regard to the all importent concerns for the wellfare of my immortal Soul which led me to Searching the Scriptures believeing as I was taught, that they contained the word of God thus applying myself to them and my intimate acquaintance with those of differant denominations led me to marvel excedingly for I discovered that <they did not ~~adorn~~ ~~instead~~> of adorn~~ing~~ their profession by a holy walk and Godly conversation agreeable to what I found contained in that sacred depository this was a grief to my Soul thus from the age of twelve years to fifteen I pondered many things in my heart concerning the sittuation of the world of mankind the contentions and divi[si]ons the wicke[d]ness and abominations and the darkness which pervaded the ~~of the~~ minds of mankind my mind become excedingly distressed for I become convicted of my Sins and by Searching the Scriptures I found that ~~mand~~ <mankind> did not come unto the Lord but that they had apostatised from the true and liveing faith and there was no society or denomination that built upon the Gospel of Jesus Christ as recorded in the new testament and I felt to mourn for my own Sins and for the Sins of the world for I learned in the Scriptures that God was the Same yesterday to day and forever that he was no respecter to persons [Heb. 13:8; Acts 10:34–35]. . . . [T]herefore I cried unto the Lord for mercy for there was none else to whom I could go and ~~to~~ obtain mercy and the Lord heard my cry in the wilderness and while in <the> attitude of calling upon the Lord <in the 16th year of my age> a piller of ~~fire~~ light above the brightness of

the sun at noon day come down from above and rested upon me and I was filled with the spirit of God and the <Lord> opened the heavens upon me and I saw the Lord and he spake unto me saying Joseph <my Son> thy Sins are forgiven thee. go thy <way> walk in my statutes and keep my commandments behold I am the Lord of glory I was crucifyed for the world that all those who believe on my name may have Eternal life <behold> the world lieth in sin ~~and~~ at this time and none doeth good no not one they have turned asside from the Gospel and keep not <my> commandments they draw near to me with their lips while their hearts are far from me and mine anger is kindling against the inhabitants of the earth to visit them acording to th[e]ir ungodliness and to bring to pass that which <hath> been spoken by the mouth of the prophets and Ap[o]stles behold and lo I come quickly as it [is] written of me in the cloud <clothed> in the glory of my Father and my soul was filled with love and for many days I could rejoice with great Joy and the Lord was with me but [I] could find none that would believe the hevnly vision nevertheless I pondered these things in my heart."

48. Joseph Smith, *Joseph Smith Diary* (Ohio Journal, 1835–1836), November 9, 1835, Joseph Smith Papers, LDSCA, reprinted in Dean C. Jessee, *The Papers of Joseph Smith* (Salt Lake City: Deseret Book Company, 1992), vol. 2, 68–69. The November 9, 1835, version of the First Vision, as reprinted by Dean Jessee, reads in part as follows (the editorial note *wr.ov.* means that the preceding word has been written over by the subsequent word):

     "[B]eing wrought up in my mind, respecting the subject of religion, and look-ing at ["at" *wr.ov.* by "upon"] the different systems taught the children of men, I knew not who was right or who was wrong and I considered ["I considered" *wr.ov.* by "considering"] it of the first importance that I should be right, in mat-ters that involve eternal consequ[e]nces; being thus perplexed in mind I retired to the silent grove and bow[e]d down before the Lord, under a realising sense that he had said (if the bible be true) ask and you shall receive knock and it shall be opened seek and you shall find [Matt. 7:7] and again, if any man lack wisdom let him ask of God who giveth to all men libarally and upbradeth not [Jas. 1:5]; information was what I most desired at this time, and with a fixed determination to obtain it, I called upon the Lord for the first time, in the place above stated. . . . I called on the Lord in mighty prayer, a pillar of fire appeared above my head, it presently rested down upon me ["me" *wr.ov.* by "my"] ~~head~~, and filled me with Joy unspeakable, a personage appeared in the midst of this pillar of flame which was spread all around, and yet nothing consumed, another personage soon appeared like unto the first, he said unto me thy sins are forgiven thee, he testifyed unto me that Jesus Christ is the Son of God; <and I saw many angels in this vision> I was about 14 years old when I received this first communication."

49. Smith, *Joseph Smith Diary* (Ohio Journal, 1835–1836), November 14, 1835, Joseph Smith Papers, LDSCA, reprinted in Jessee, vol. 2, 79. The event described under November 14, 1835 is a meeting that took place between Smith and Erastus Holmes. It appears to be an extremely abbreviated summary of the First Vision that was detailed on November 9. Jessee's reprint of the original diary manuscript, originally transcribed by Warren Par-rish, reads: "I commenced and gave him a brief relation of my experience while in my juvenile years, say from 6 years old up to the time I received the first visitation of Angels which was when I was about 14 years old." Interestingly, when this text was later re-written by Warren Cowdery (i.e., copied into the History, 1834–1836), it was transcribed in the Third Person, as follows: "He (Smith) commenced and gave him a brief relation of his experience while in his youthful days, say from the age of six years up to the time he received his first visitation of Angels which was when he was about 14 years old" (Jessee, vol. 1, 137). Then, still later, this entry was further altered (for today's official

HC published by the LDS church). The passage not only was changed to again read in the First Person, but the "first visitation of Angels" phrase was re-written as "my first vision" (see *HC*, vol. 2, 312). LDS leaders apparently felt that the discrepancy between today's official version of the First Vision and the original November 14 version needed reconciling. Moreover, the November 9, 1835 account (see previous endnote) was deleted altogether from the modern *HC*.

50. Orson Pratt, *Interesting Account of Several Remarkable Visions, and of the Late Discovery of Ancient American Record* (Edinburgh: Ballantyne and Hughes, 1840), 3–5; reprinted in Vogel, vol. 1, 149–160 (for specific sections quoted, see Vogel, 150–151). A searchable text version of *Interesting Account of Several Remarkable Visions* is online at http://www.concordance.com/mormon.htm.

51. Orson Hyde, *Ein Ruf aus der Wüste, eine Stimme aus dem Schoose der Erde (A Cry from the Wilderness, A Voice from the Dust of the Earth*, Frankfurt: 1842), reprinted in Jessee, vol. 1, 402–425 (for specific sections quoted, see Jessee, 405–409), translation in *The Papers of Joseph Smith* completed by Marvin H. Folsom, professor of German, BYU. Although published in 1842, this work actually was completed by Hyde in 1841, as evidenced by a letter he wrote to Smith informing him of the pamphlet's completion (see Orson Hyde, letter to Joseph Smith, June 15, 1841, published in *T&S*, October 1, 1841, vol. 2, no. 23, 551–555; cf. *HC*, vol. 4, 372–374).

52. Orson Pratt, sermon by Orson Pratt (c. 1837–1839), as recorded by William I. Appleby, "Biography and Journal of William I. Appleby, Elder in the Church of Latter Day Saints," 1848, 30–33, LDSCA, Salt Lake City, Utah, reprinted in Vogel, vol. 1, 146–147.

53. Andrew Jenson, "Joseph Smith, The Prophet," *HR*, January 1888, vol. 3, nos. 1–3, 355. When this document was reprinted two years later by the church, Mormon leaders attempted to cover-up the discrepancy by changing "The angel" to "The Holy Being" and "(the angel)" to "(the Christ)." The rest of the text and its formatting remained exactly as it appeared in the original version, and no notation was made to alert readers to the fact that the text had been altered.

54. Joseph Smith, letter to John Wentworth, *T&S*, March 1, 1842, vol. 3 no. 9, 706–707, reprinted in Jessee, vol. 1, 430.

55. Joseph Smith, *T&S*, March 15, 1842, vol. 3, no. 11, 727–728 and *T&S*, April 1, 1842, vol. 3, no. 11, 748–749. This version of Smith's First Vision has usually been accepted as part of the "final" *HC* that was completed around 1839.

56. Joseph Smith, "Latter Day Saints," in I. Daniel Rupp, *An Original History of the Religious Denominations at Present Existing in the United States* (Philadelphia, 1844), 404–410, reprinted in Jessee, vol. 1, 448–458. This statement by Joseph Smith, although sent to Rupp in July 1843, was not published until 1844. On June 5, 1844—three weeks before he was murdered—Smith acknowledged receiving a copy of Rupp's book. Smith expressed that he was "very thankful for so valuable a treasure" (Joseph Smith, letter to I. Daniel Rupp, June 5, 1844, published by Smith, *HC*, vol. 6, 428).

57. Joseph Smith, interview with David Nye White, August 29, 1843, reprinted in Jessee, vol. 1, 443–444. This interview with Smith, although it took place August 1843, was not published until September 15, 1843. White's interview, although published before Rupp's book, actually took place after Rupp received his letter from Smith.

58. Joseph Smith, as related by Alexander Neibaur, *Alexander Neibaur Journal*, May 24, 1844, ms., LDSCA, reprinted in Jessee, vol. 1, 459–461.

59. John Taylor, letter to the Editor of the *Interpreter Anglais et Français*, June 25, 1850, *MS*, August 1, 1850, vol. 12, 235–237, reprinted in Vogel, vol. 1, 191. Taylor somehow blended the first and second visions into a single event. Although he failed to identify the personages as the Father and Son, he did say that the two heavenly beings told Joseph about the golden plates, which actually took place during Joseph's so-called "second" vision. This type of blending occurred on numerous occasions (see two prior endnotes). Another example of this error can be seen in the writings of William McLellin, who in

an 1832 letter mentioned two Mormon missionaries preaching that "in September 1827 and Angel appeared to Joseph Smith . . . and showed to him the confusion on the earth respecting true religion" (William McLellin, letter to Samuel McLellin, August 4, 1832, reprinted in Vogel, vol. 3, 300).

60. John Taylor, December 7, 1879, *JOD* (Liverpool: Albert Carrington, 1881; lithographed reprint of original edition, 1966), vol. 21, 161.

61. Wesley Walters, "New Light On Mormon Origins From the Palmyra N.Y. Revival," originally published in the *Evangelical Theological Society* (Fall 1967), vol. 10, no. 4, 227–244; cf. the revised version of this article published in *Dialogue: A Journal of Mormon Thought,* (Spring 1969), vol. 4, no 1, 60–81.

62. Joseph Smith, Sr. Quoted by Fayette Lapham, "Interview with the Father of Joseph Smith, the Mormon Prophet, Forty Years Ago. His Account of the Finding of the Sacred Plates," *Historical Magazine* (May 1870), 2nd Series, vol. 7, 305–306, reprinted in Vogel, vol. 1, 458. A searchable text version of this interview is online at http://www.concordance.com/ mormon.htm (under "Interview with Father of Jos. Smith—Fayette Lapham"). The 1824 date is derived from the explanation of Joseph's father, who stated to Lapham that his son turned to the Baptists about two years after digging a well for Willard Chase (the well-digging occurred in 1822). Joseph's involvement with the Baptist church is supported by an article about the history of the Manchester Baptist Church, which in part reads: "Joe occasionally attended the stone church; especially the revivals, sitting with the crowds—the "sinners"—up in the gallery" (Mitchell Bronk, "The Baptist Church at Manchester," *The Chronicle: A Baptist Historical Quarterly* (January 1948), vol. 11, 23–24. This article's contents included reminiscences of conversations with old Manchester townspeople (reprinted in Vogel, vol. 3, 259).

63. This information comes from Orasmus Turner (see this chapter, endnote #14), who knew Smith in Palmyra and had accompanied Smith to Methodist camp meetings on Vienna Road. According to an article by Turner that was published in the *Lockport Daily Courier,* May 5, 1854, Turner left the Palmyra area in 1822, which would put his experiences with Smith as an "exhorter" before that date. The "Deeds of Ontario Co. Bk G, 345" show that the Methodists did not acquire their property in the woods on the Vienna Road until July of 1821, which would mean that the camp meetings were held sometime between 1821 and 1822 (see Wesley P. Walters, "A Reply to Dr. Bushman," *Dialogue: A Journal of Mormon Thought,* [Spring 1969], vol. 4, 99).

64. Sophia Lewis, *Susquehanna Register,* May 1, 1834 (reprinted in Howe, 269), online at http://www.solomonspalding.com/docs/1834howf.htm#pg269. According to Hiel and Joseph Lewis, cousins of Emma Hale (Smith's wife), Joseph Smith requested that his name be put on a roster for a membership class. But it was removed three days later when church members asked Smith to either renounce his previous money-digging/occult activities or strike his name from the class book. He chose to do the latter (see Persuitte, 76).

65. Persuitte, 21. As late as 1840, few people had heard about Smith meeting God and Jesus Christ in the woods. For example, in a letter to the editor appearing in the *Ohio Observer* (Hudson, Ohio, August 11, 1836) and reprinted in the *Cincinnati Journal and Western Luminary* (August 25, 1836), Kirtland, Ohio resident Truman Coe detailed his knowledge of Smith's visionary experiences. Coe makes no mention whatsoever to any 1820 vision of the Father and the Son (see this chapter, endnote #80; cf. Vogel, vol. 1, 46-47).

66. Brodie, 25.

67. Brodie, 25.

68. Solomon Chamberlain, *A Sketch of the experience of Solomon Chamberlin, to Which Is Added a Remarkable Revelation or Trance, of His Father-in-Law, Philip Haskins: How His Soul actually Left His Body and Was Guided by a Holy Angel to Eternal Day* (Lyons, New York: Solomon Chamberlain, 1829). BYU obtained an extremely rare copy of this pamphlet in 1989. Its contents were republished in Larry C. Porter, "Solomon Chamberlain's

Missing Pamphlet: Dreams, Visions, and Angelic Ministrants," *BYU Studies* (1997–1998), vol. 37, 131–140.

69. Solomon Chamberlain, "A Short Sketch in the Life of Solomon Chamberlin," 4–12, LDSCA, reprinted in Vogel, vol. 3, 43.

70. Chamberlain, "A Short Sketch," reprinted in Vogel, vol. 3, 43–44.

71. Chamberlain, "A Short Sketch," reprinted in Vogel, vol. 3, 44.

72. Chamberlain, "A Short Sketch," reprinted in Vogel, vol. 3, 44.

73. Elias Smith, *The Life, Conversion, Preaching, Travels, and Sufferings of Elias Smith* (Portsmouth, New Hampshire: Beck & Foster, 1816), 58–59, online at http://www.mun.ca/rels/restmov/texts/esmith/es2.html#Ch5. This entire volume is online at http://www.mun.ca/rels/restmov/texts/esmith/es1.html.

74. Asa Wild, *Wayne Sentinel*, October 22, 1823. Quoted in Jerald Tanner and Sandra Tanner, "Dunn in the Name of God!," *Salt Lake City Messenger* (#78), June 1991, 9, online at http://www.utlm.org/newsletters/no78.htm.

75. Alexander Campbell, March 1, 1824 (*The Christian Baptist*, 1955 reprint, vol. 1, p. 148); Quoted in Tanner and Tanner, "Dunn in the Name," 9.

76. *Christian Guide* (Utica, New York, 1826), 71. Quoted in Brodie, 22.

77. Stephen Bradley. *A sketch of the life of Stephen H. Bradley, from the age of five to twenty-four years, including his remarkable experience of the power of the Holy Spirit on the second evening of November, 1829* (Madison, CT: Stephen Bradley, 1830). Cited in William James, *The Varieties of Religious Experience* (New York: MacMillan Publishing Company, 1997 reprint [original edition, 1902]), 157–58, online at http://www.psywww.com/psyrelig/james/james8.htm#189.

78. This author could find no reports on Mormonism dated prior to 1840 that mentioned Joseph having a vision of God the Father and Jesus Christ in the woods due to a revival in the Palmyra-Manchester area. Many of the accounts produced during Smith's earliest years as a Mormon leader included interviews with some of his closest/newest converts, yet none of these individuals mentioned anything about their leader having an encounter with two personages in a secluded grove. A prime example of such an account comes from Joseph's mother, Lucy Mack Smith. In a January 6, 1831 letter to her older brother—Solomon Mack, Jr.—Lucy explains that Joseph's first vision connected to the *Book of Mormon* andthe formation of the Mormon church was that of a "holy Angel." No mention is made of God the Father and Jesus Christ appearing to Joseph (see Vogel, vol. 1, 216). Several other examples can be found in Dan Vogel's *Early Mormon Documents*, volumes 1, 2, and 3. Dozens of similar stories can be found in old newspaper articles (c. 1829–1836) on Mormonism, money-digging, and Smith's early visions that are online at http://www.lavazone2.com/dbroadhu/artindex.htm.

CHAPTER TWO: MORONI, MAGIC, AND MASONRY

1. George Hamilton Combs, *Some Latter Day Religions* (New York, Fleming H. Revell, c. 1900). Quoted in Edgar E. Folk, *The Mormon Monster* (New York: Fleming H. Revell, 1901), 17.

2. In Mormonism's official seven-volume *HC* (Salt Lake City: Deseret Book Company, 1976/1980), allegedly written by Joseph Smith, an obvious three-year gap of information occurs in volume one between the conclusion of the 1820 "first" vision story (p. 8) and the beginning of the 1823 "second" vision (p. 11). The pages in between these two accounts provides only a brief reference to the intervening years during which time it is alleged that Smith continued to pursue his "common vocation in life." The *HC* also mentions in passing that Smith "fell into many foolish errors, and displayed the weaknesses of youth" (p. 9). The narrative, however, is careful to assure the reader that Smith was never "guilty of any great or malignant sins," but that he was simply guilty of "levity, and sometimes associated with jovial company, etc., not consistent with that character which

ought to be maintained by one who was called of God" as he had been (p.9). Even this minor criticism of Smith is softened by an additional note indicating that such behavior and associations simply resulted from Smith's "native cheery temperament" (p. 10). These latter comments were added to the text in December 1842.

3. *HC*, vol. 1, 11.

4. *HC*, vol. 1, 11.

5. Mormons define angels in a number of ways: 1) pre-existent spirits; 2) individuals, who by virtue of their holiness, are "translated"—i.e., they are changed from their mortal state to an immortal state without having died; 3) righteous individuals who have died, and are waiting in the afterlife to receive their resurrected bodies when Jesus Christ returns at the end of the world; 4) individuals who have died, but due to their right-eousness, have already received their resurrected bodies of glorified flesh and bones, and are used by God to contact persons on earth through visions and dreams; 5) right-eous persons now living on earth who are properly called "angels" in the way that some-one might call a special friend or a loved one "an angel" (Bruce McConkie, *Mormon Doctrine* [Salt Lake City: Bookcraft, 1958; second edition, 1966], 35–36).

6. *HC*, vol. 1, 12.

7. *HC*, vol. 1, 12.

8. *HC*, vol. 1, 6.

9. *HC*, vol. 1, 12. In the Old Testament, the Urim and Thummim was a means of revelation used by the priests of Israel (Ex. 28:30; Lev. 8:8; Deut. 33:8; Ezra 2:63) to discern God's will regarding various inquiries (Num. 27:21). They were kept in the breastplate of the high priest's ephod and used in conjunction with the ephod (1 Sam. 2:18ff.; 23:9–12; 30:7ff.). Use of them seems to have ended after the time of King David. Joseph and his Mormon followers usually described the Urim and Thummim as two stones set in silver bows, very similar to a pair of spectacles. Joseph described them as "'two transparent stones set in a rim of a bow fastened to a breastplate'" (Joseph Smith. Quoted in B.H. Roberts, *CHC* [Salt Lake City: Deseret News Press, 1930], vol. 1, 128). Joseph's mother described them as "two smooth three-cornered diamonds set in glass, and the glasses were set in silver bows, which were connected with each other in much the same way as old fashioned spectacles" (Lucy Mack Smith, *Biographical Sketches of Joseph Smith the Prophet, and His Progenitors for many Generations* [Liverpool: S.W. Richards, 1853], 101, reprinted in Dan Vogel, ed., *Early Mormon Documents* [Salt Lake City: Signature Books, 1996], vol. 1, 328–329). The Old Testament, however, provides no such descrip-tion of them, nor does the Bible depict exactly how they were used (Geoffrey W. Bromi-ley, gen. ed., *The International Standard Bible Encyclopedia* [Grand Rapids: William B. Eerdmans Publishing Company, 1988], vol. 4, 957–958).

10. *HC*, vol. 1, 13.

11. *HC*, vol. 1, 14.

12. *HC*, vol. 1, 14.

13. *HC*, vol. 1, 16.

14. *HC*, vol. 1, 16.

15. Oliver Cowdery (under the supervision of Joseph Smith), "History of Joseph Smith," *T&S*, April 15, 1842, vol. 3, no. 12, 753. The variant portion of text in the 1842 version reads: "[I]mmediately a personage appeared at my bedside, standing in the air. . . . He called me by name, and said unto me that he was a messenger sent from the presence of God to me, and that his name was Nephi; that God had a work for me to do." The 1851 edition of *The Pearl of Great Price* (Liverpool: F.D. Richards, 1851) similarly stated: "He called me by name and said unto me, that he was a messenger sent from the presence of God to me, and that his name was Nephi" (p. 41).

16. Joseph Smith, *1832 History*, original manuscript, contained in Joseph Smith Letterbook 1, 1–6, Joseph Smith Papers, LDSCA, reprinted in Dean C. Jessee, ed., *The Papers of Joseph Smith* (Salt Lake City: Deseret Book Company, 1989), vol. 1, 8; cf. Vogel, vol. 1, 29–30.

17. An 1840 version of the "second" vision by Mormon leader Orson Pratt also stated that Joseph's heavenly visitor was merely "an Angel of God," rather than Moroni (Orson Pratt, *Interesting Account of Several Remarkable Visions, and of the Late Discovery of Ancient American Record* [Edinburgh: Ballantyne and Hughes, 1840], 3–5), reprinted in Jessee, vol. 1, 389–401 (for Pratt's specific citation about the angel, see Jessee, vol. 1, 393).

18. *MS&AD* is available on the *New Mormon Studies CD ROM: Comprehensive Resource Library* (Salt Lake City: Signature Books, 2000); cf. Dan Vogel, ed., *Early Mormon Documents* (Salt Lake City: Signature Books, 1998), vol. 2, 422–450.

19. Oliver Cowdery, "Letter III," *MS&AD*, December 1834, vol. 1, no. 3, 41–43, reprinted in Vogel, vol. 2, 423 and "Letter IV," *MS&AD*, February 1835, vol. 1, no. 5, 77–80, reprinted in Vogel, vol. 2, 427. The text of Cowdery's second letter reads: "I mentioned the time of a religious excitement, in Palmyra and vicinity to have been in the 15th year of our brother J. Smith Jr's, age—that was an error in the type—it should have been in the 17th.—You will please remember this correction, as it will be necessary for the full understanding of what will follow in time. This would bring the date down to the year 1823" (p. 78; Vogel, vol. 2, 427). Cowdery supplied another interesting bit of information about Smith's experience: "[H]e continued to call upon the Lord in secret for . . . the all important information, if a Supreme being did exist, to have an assurance that he was accepted of him" (p. 78; Vogel, vol. 2, 427). An obvious question arises: How could Smith question the existence of a Supreme Being in 1823 (per this particular account), if in 1820 he had already seen that Supreme Being face to face?

20. Cowdery, "Letter IV," 78–79 (Vogel, vol. 2, 428). This portion of Cowdery's letter reads: "On the evening of the 21st of September, 1823, previous to retiring to rest, our brother's mind was unusually wrought up on the subject which had so long agitated his mind— his heart was drawn out in fervent prayer, . . . While continuing in prayer for a manifestation in some way that his sins were forgiven . . . a sudden a light like that of day, only of a purer and far more glorious appearance and brightness, burst into the room . . . . [A]nd in a moment a personage stood before him. . . . [H]e heard him declare himself to be a messenger sent by commandment of the Lord, to deliver a special message, and to witness to him that his sins were forgiven. . . . [He] gave a general account of the promises made to the fathers, and also gave a history of the aborigines of this country, . . . He said this history was written and deposited not far from that place, and that it was our brother's privilege, if obedient to the commandments of the Lord, to obtain, and translate the same by the means of the Urim and Thummim, which were deposited for that purpose with the record."

21. William Smith, *William Smith on Mormonism* (Lamoni, IA: Herald Steam Books and Job Office, 1883), 6, reprinted in Vogel, vol. 1, 494. William Smith's account reads as follows: "In 1822 and 1823, the people in our neighborhood were very much stirred up with regard to religious matters by the preaching of a Mr. Lane, an Elder of the Methodist Church, and celebrated throughout the country as a 'great revival preacher.' . . . My mother, who was a very pious woman and much interested in the welfare of her children, both here and hereafter, made use of every means which her parental love could suggest, to get us engaged in seeking for our souls' salvation, or (as the term then was) 'in getting religion.' She prevailed on us to attend the meetings, and almost the whole family became interested in the matter, and seekers after truth. I attended the meetings with the rest, but being quite young and inconsiderate, did not take so much interest in the matter as the older ones did. This extraordinary excitement prevailed not only in our neighborhood but throughout the whole country. Great numbers were converted. it extended from the Methodists to the Baptists, from them to the Presbyterians; and so on until finally, almost all the sects became engaged in it; and it became quite the fashion to 'get religion.' My mother continued her

importunities and exertions to interest us in the importance of seeking for the salvation of our immortal souls, until almost all of the family became either converted or seriously inclined. After the excitement had subsided, in a measure, each sect began to beat up for volunteers; each one saying, "'We are right,' 'Come and join us,' 'Walk with us and we will do you good,' etc. . . . Joseph, then about seventeen years of age, had become seriously inclined, though not 'brought out,' as the phrase was, began to reflect and inquire, which of all these sects was right. Each one said that it was right; which he knew could not be the case; and the question then was which one of the whole taught the true gospel of Jesus Christ, and made known the plan of salvation." This same account, using slightly different wording, also appeared in William Smith, "The Old Soldier's Testimony. Sermon preached by Bro. William B. Smith in the Saints' Chapel, Detroit, Iowa, June 8th, 1884. Reported by C.E. Butterworth," *Saints Herald*, October 4, 1884, vol.31, 643–644. It reads: "[J]ust before the angel appeared to Joseph, there was an unusual revival in the neighborhood. It moved from town to town, from city to city, and from state to state. . . . Joseph and myself did not join; I had not sown all my wild oats . . . . [I]t was at the suggestion of the Rev. M–, that my brother asked of God. . . . Accordingly, he went and bowed down in prayer to God" (see Vogel, vol. 1, p. 503–505).

22. William Smith, *William Smith on Mormonism*, 8–10 (see Vogel, vol. 1, 495–496); cf. William Smith, "The Old Soldier's Testimony" (see Vogel, vol. 1, 504), which reads: "While he was engaged in prayer, he saw a pillar of fire descending. Saw it reach the top of the trees. He was overcome, became unconscious, did not know how long he remained in this condition, but when he came to himself, the great light was about him, and he was told by the personage whom he saw descend with the light, not to join any of the churches. . . . [T]here was a record hidden in the hill Cumorah which contained the fulness of the Gospel."

23. George A. Smith, November 15, 1863, *JOD* (Liverpool: Albert Carrington, 1869; lithographed reprint of original edition, 1966], vol. 12, 334, and June 20, 1869, *JOD* (Liverpool: Horace S. Eldredge, 1871; lithographed reprint of original edition, 1966], vol. 13, 78.

24. Lucy Mack Smith, "Preliminary Manuscript" of *Biographical Sketches of Joseph Smith the Prophet, and His Progenitors for many Generations*, the unedited 1845 version, as reprinted in Vogel, vol. 1, 289–291. The text has recently been published in Lavina Fielding Anderson, ed., *Lucy's Book: A Critical Edition of Lucy Mack Smith's Family Memoir* (Salt Lake City: Signature Books, 2001). Lucy's account reads as follows (original text has been retained where possible, but some misspellings, extraneous editorial marks, and confusing punctuation has been deleted in order to preserve the reading flow of the original document. Text that appears within < > indicates additional words that do appear in the original manuscript. Words with a strike-through have been retained):

"One evening we were sitting till quite late conversing upon the subject of the diversity of churches that had risen up in the world and the many thousand opinions in existence as to the truths contained in scripture[.] Joseph who never said many words upon any subject but always seemed to reflect more deeply than common persons of his age upon everything of a religious nature This After we ceased conversation he went to bed and was pondering in his mind which of the churches were the true one and but he had not laid there long till he saw a bright light entered the room where he lay he looked up and saw an angel of the Lord stood standing by him The angel spoke[:] I perceive that you are enquiring in your mind second which is the true church[.] there is not a true church on Earth[,] No not one. . . . The churches that are now upon the Earth are all man made churches. Joseph there is a record for you and you must get it one day get it There is a record for you and Joseph when you have

learned to keep the commandments of God but you cannot get it untill you
learn to keep the commandments of God. . . . Now Joseph beware or when you
go to get the plates your mind will be filled with darkness and all maner of evil
will rush into your mind To keep <prevent> you from keeping the commandments of God . . . and you must tell your father of this for he will believe every
word you say[.] the record is on a side hill on the Hill of cumorah 3 miles from
this place remove the Grass and moss and you will find a large flat stone[,] pry
that up and you will find the record under it laying on 4 pillars of cement then
the angel left him."

In an even earlier account (a January 6, 1831 letter to her brother), Lucy wrote that
Joseph's first vision was that of "an holy Angel whose countenance was as lightening
and whose garments were white above all whiteness and gave unto him commandments which inspired him from on high. and gave unto him by means of which was
before prepared that he should translate this book, and by <reading> this our eyes are
opened that we can see the situation in which the world now stands that the eyes of the
whole world are blinded, that the churches have all become corrupted, yea every church
upon the face of the earth; that the Gospel of Christ is nowhere preached. this is the situation which the world is now in, and you can judge" (see Vogel, vol. 1, 216).

25. Smith, *HC*, vol. 1, 16–17.

26. For Joseph Smith's and other early Mormons' direct involvement, see D. Michael Quinn,
Early Mormonism and the Magic World View (Salt Lake City: Signature Books, 1998),
30–65; Dan Vogel, "The Locations of Joseph Smith's Early Treasure Quests," *Dialogue: A
Journal of Mormon Thought*, (Fall 1994), vol. 27, 197–231; H. Michael Marquardt and
Wesley P. Walters, *Inventing Mormonism: Tradition and the Historical Record* (San Fran-
cisco: Smith Research Associates, 1994), 83–87; and John L. Brooke, *The Refiner's Fire:
The Making of Mormon Cosmology, 1644–1844* (New York: Cambridge University Press,
1994; paperback edition, 1996). For an excellent survey of money digging in America
prior to Joseph Smith's era, see Herbert Leventhal's *In the Shadow of the Enlightenment:
Occultism and Renaissance Science in Eighteenth–Century America* (New York: New York
University Press, 1976), 110–18. Contemporary references to money digging include:
Palmyra Herald, July 24, 1822; *Ontario Repository*, February 9, 1825; *Wayne Sentinel*
(Palmyra), February 16 and December 27, 1825; *Rutland Herald* (Vermont*)*, 22 Aug.
1826; *Rochester Gem*, 15 May 1830; *Palmyra Reflector*, 1 Feb. 1831; Thurlow Weed, *Life
of Thurlow Weed: Autobiography of Thurlow Weed* (Boston: Houghton, Mifflin and Company, 1883), vol. 1, 84); Barnes Frisbie, *The History of Middleton, Vermont in Three Discourses . . .* (Rutland, VT: Tuttle & Co., Printers, 1867), 43–64; and Nathan O. Hatch, *The
Democratization of American Christianity* (New Haven, CT: Yale University Press, 1989),
114.

27. David Persuitte, *Joseph Smith and the Origins of the Book of Mormon* (Jefferson, NC:
McFarland & Co., 2000), 35.

28. Brooke, 30–31

29. Brooke, 77.

30. Joseph Smith, Sr. Quoted in Fayette Lapham, "Interview with the Father of Joseph
Smith, the Mormon Prophet, Forty Years Ago. His Account of the Finding of the Sacred
Plates," *Historical Magazine* (May 1870), 2nd Series, vol. 7, 305–306, reprinted in Vogel, vol.
1, 458. A searchable text version of this interview is online at http://www.concordance.com/
mormon.htm (under "Interview with Father of Jos. Smith—Fayette Lapham").

31. Lapham (see Vogel, vol. 1, 457), online at http://www.concordance.com/mormon.htm
(under "Interview with Father of Jos. Smith—Fayette Lapham").

32. Brooke, 78.

33. It has been suggested that the Smith's move to Palmyra was determined in part by a
prior connection (i.e., in Vermont) to a network of money-digging families "stretching
from Tunbridge to Poultney to Andover" (Brooke, 362, endnote #2).

34. Martin Harris, "Mormonism—No. II" (an interview), *Tiffany's Monthly*, August 1859, vol. 5, 164, online at http://www.utlm.org/onlineresources/sermons_talks_interviews/harrisinterviewtiffanysmonthly.htm.

35. During his *Tiffany's Monthly* interview (see previous endnote), Harris related the following:

> "It was reported by these money-diggers, that they had found boxes, but before they could secure them, they would sink into the earth. A candid old Presbyterian told me, that on the Susquehannah flats he dug down to an iron chest, that he scraped the dirt off with his shovel, but had nothing with him to open the chest; that he went away to get help, and when they came to it, it moved away two or three rods into the earth, and they could not get it. There were a great many strange sights. One time the old log school-house south of Palmyra, was suddenly lighted up, and frightened them away. Samuel Lawrence told me that while they were digging, a large man who appeared to be eight or nine feet high, came and sat on the ridge of the barn, and motioned to them that they must leave. They motioned back that they would not; but that they afterwards became frightened and did leave. At another time while they were digging, a company of horsemen came and frightened them away. These things were real to them, I believe because they were told to me in confidence, and told by different ones, and their stories agreed, and they seemed to be in earnest—I knew they were in earnest" (p. 165).

36. Joshua Stafford, statement of November 15, 1833, in E.D. Howe, *Mormonism Unvailed* (Painesville, OH: author, 1834), 258, online at http://www.solomonspalding.com/docs/1834howf.htm#pg258b. This entire volume is online at http://www.solomonspalding.com/docs/1834howb.htm. A searchable text version is online at http://www.concordance.com/mormon.htm.

37. "Gold Bible, No. 3," *Palmyra Reflector*, February 1, 1831, reprinted Vogel, vol. 2, 242.

38. William Stafford, statement of December 8, 1833, reprinted in Howe, 238, online at http://www.solomonspalding.com/docs/1834howf.htm#pg238.

39. Jesse Townsend, letter to Phineas Stiles, December 4 1833, reprinted in Pomeroy Tucker, *Origin, Rise and Progress of Mormonism* (New York: D. Appleton and Co., 1867), 288–291. This volume is online at http://moa.umdl.umich.edu/cgi/sgml/moa-idx?notisid=AGU9642 (also see Dan Vogel, ed., *Early Mormon Documents* [Salt Lake City: Signature Books, 2000], vol. 3, 21. Testimony describing Smith as a fortune-teller appears in several statements from various individuals besides Townsend. For example, C.M. Stafford recalled: "Jo claimed to have revelations and tell fortunes. He told mine by looking in the palm of my hand and said among other things that I would not live to be very old" (C. M. Stafford, statement of March 23, 1885, reprinted in A.B. Deming, ed., *Naked Truths About Mormonism* (April 1888), vol. 1, no. 2, 1, online at http://www.lavazone2.com/dbroadhu/CA/natruths.htm; cf. Henry Harris, statement to Justice of the Peace Jonathan Lapham, n.d., reprinted in Howe, 251, online at http://www.solomonspalding.com/docs/1834howf.htm#pg251.

40. Joseph Capron, statement of November 8, 1833, reprinted in Howe 259, online at http://www.solomonspalding.com/docs/1834howf.htm#pg259.

41. John Sherer, letter to American Home Missionary Society, November 18, 1830. Quoted in Persuitte, 36. Original letter in Amistad Research Center, Dillard University, New Orleans, LA.

42. Stafford, in Howe, 238, online at http://www.solomonspalding.com/docs/1834howf.htm#pg238.

43. Emily M. Austin, *Mormonism; or, Life Among the Mormons* (Madison, WI: M. J. Cantwell, 1882), 32ff, online at http://www.olivercowdery.com/smithhome/1882Astn.htm#pg031b. Quoted in Wesley P. Walters, "Joseph Smith's Bainbridge, N.Y., Court Trials," *Westminster Theological Journal* (Winter 1974), vol. 36, 125.

44. Hiel Lewis, comments published in *Amboy Journal*, June 4, 1879. Quoted in Jerald Tanner and Sandra Tanner, *Mormonism, Magic and Masonry* (Salt Lake City: ULM, 1988), 33. Another sacrifice by Smith occurred while he was hunting for treasure on William Stafford's property. The account, related by William Stafford, reads as follows:

> "[T]hey devised a scheme, by which they might satiate their hunger, with the mutton of one of my sheep. They had seen in my flock a sheep, a large, fat, black weather. Old Joseph and one of the boys came to me one day, and said that Joseph Jr. had discovered some very remarkable and valuable treasures, which could be procured only in one way. That way, was as follows:—That a black sheep should be taken to the ground where the treasures were concealed—that after cutting its throat, it should be led around in a circle while bleeding. This being done, the wrath of the evil spirit would be appeased. the treasures could then be obtained, and my share of them was to be four fold. To gratify my curiosity, I let them have a large fat sheep. They afterwards informed me, that the sheep was killed pursuant to commandment; but as there was some mistake in the process, it did not have the desired effect. This, I believe, is the only time they ever made money-digging a profitable business" (see Howe, 238–239, online at http://www.solomonspalding.com/docs/1834howf.htm#pg237b).

This story is corroborated by C.R. Stafford, who testified concerning the same incident: "Jo Smith, the prophet, told my uncle, William Stafford, he wanted a fat, black sheep. He said he wanted to cut its throat and make it walk in a circle three times around and it would prevent a pot of money from leaving" (C. R. Stafford, statement of March 1885, reprinted in A.B. Deming, ed., *Naked Truths About Mormonism* (January 1888), vol. 1, no. 1, 3, online at http://www.lavazone2.com/dbroadhu/CA/natruths.htm. Significant is Joseph's choice of a black sheep for the sacrifice. *The Greater Key of Solomon*, page 122, reads: "Sometimes white animals are sacrificed to the good Spirits and black to the evil." Making a sacrifice to an evil spirit would be consistent with a money-digger's attempt to appease that spirit in order to have the entity release the treasure in their care. Additional confirmation of this particular episode comes from Mormon history professor Richard L. Anderson. In his 1970 article "Joseph Smith's New York Reputation Reappraised," (*BYU Studies*, Spring 1970, vol. 10, 294), Anderson quotes a Wallace Miner as saying: "I once asked [William] Stafford if Smith did steal a sheep from him. He said no, not exactly. He said, he did miss a black sheep, but soon Joseph came and admitted he took it for sacrifice but he was willing to work for it" It should be noted Anderson's article, although it provides some interesting and useful historical data, contains highly biased conclusions that downplay Smith's more undesirable characteristics and activities."

45. William Stafford, in Howe, 239, http://www.solomonspalding.com/docs/1834howf.htm#pg239.

46. Capron, in Howe, 259-260, http://www.solomonspalding.com/docs/1834howf.htm#pg259.

47. Brooke, 31.

48. Joshua Stafford, in Howe, 258, http://www.solomonspalding.com/docs/1834howf.htm#pg258.

49. Martin Harris, speaking to a group of Latter-day Saints in Clarkston, Utah (c. 1870s). Quoted in testimony of Mrs. Comfort Godfrey Flinders, *Utah Pioneer Biographies*, (Genealogical Society of Utah), vol. 10, 65, as cited in the unpublished version of a manuscript by LaMar Petersen (see Tanner and Tanner, 38). The text was published by Petersen in *The Creation of the Book of Mormon: A Historical Inquiry* (Salt Lake City: Freethinkers Press, 1998), 90; cf. Ole A. Jensen, statement of July 1875 (Clarkston, Utah: Archives, Historical Department, Church of Jesus Christ of Latter-day Saints), which reads as follows (original text has been retained where possible, but some misspellings, extraneous editorial marks, and confusing punctuation has been deleted in order to preserve the reading

flow of the original document. Text that appears within < > indicates additional words that do appear in the original manuscript. Words with a strike-through have been retained):

> "Brother Harris then turned himself as though he had no more to say and we made ready to go. He then spoke again and said. 'I Will tell you a wonderful thing that happened after Joseph had found the plates: three of us took a notion to take some of tools and go to the hill and hunt for some more boxes or gold or something, and Indeed we found a stone box; we got quiet excited about it; and dug quiet [quite] carefully around it; we were ready to take it up: but behold <by> some unseen power it slipped and back into the hill; we stood there and looked at it; One of us took a crowbar and tried to ~~hold~~ <drive> it through the lid to hold it; but it glanced and only broke one corner off of the box'" (reprinted in Vogel, vol. 2, 376).

Rockwell's version was re-told by Brigham Young (Brigham Young, June 17, 1877, *JOD* [Liverpool: William Budge, 1878; lithographed reprint of original edition, 1966], vol. 19, 36-39).

50. Lucy Mack Smith, reprinted in Vogel, vol. 1, 285. This paragraph, which appears in the 1845 preliminary manuscript version of *Biographical Sketches of Joseph Smith the Prophet, and His Progenitors for many Generations*, did not make it into the 1853 published edition. Dan Vogel writes: "One possible reason is that Lucy alludes to folk magic, which was a sensitive subject for those not wishing to give credence to claims made in affidavits collected in 1833 by Philastus Hurlbut. D. Michael Quinn has noted, 'Joseph Smith's mother did not deny her family's participation in occult activities but simply affirmed that these did not prevent family members from accomplishing other, equally important work. More significantly, she also affirmed that these folk magic activities were part of her family's religious quest.'" (see Vogel's quote from Quinn's 1987 edition of *Early Mormonism and the Magic World View*, vol. 1, 285, footnote #85; cf. Quinn, 1998 ed., 68).

51. Julien Tondriau, L'OCCULTISME (Verviers, FRANCE: Gerard & Co., 1964), transl. edition by Bay Bocks Pty. Ltd., *The Occult: Secrets of the Hidden World* (New York: Pyramid Communications, 1972), 195–196.

52. Lewis de Claremont, *The Ancients Book of Magic*, 10. Quoted in Tanner and Tanner, 31.

53. Tondriau, 127.

54. Tanner and Tanner, 55.

55. Albert G. Mackey, *Mackey's Encyclopedia of Freemasonry*, (Richmond: Macoy, 1921), 202 (1929 edition, 269).

56. Joseph Fort Newton, *The Religion of Masonry: An Interpretation* (Richmond: Macoy, 1969), 116.

57. Henry Wilson Coil, *A Comprehensive View of Freemasonry* (Richmond: Macoy, 1973), 234.

58. John E. Thompson, "The Facultie of Abrac: Masonic Claims and Mormon Beginnings," *The Philalethes*, December 1982, 9. Quoted in Tanner and Tanner, 21.

59. W.W. Phelps, August 25, 1830, *Ontario Phoenix*. Quoted in Thompson, 9, 15 (see Tanner and Tanner, 21).

60. Among the many Freemasons drawn into Mormonism were William Cowdery, Warren Cowdery, Heber C. Kimball, Elijah Fordham, Newel K. Whitney, James Adams, and John C. Bennett.

61. Thompson, 9, 15 (see Tanner and Tanner, 21).

62. Thomas S. Webb, *The Freemason's Monitor* (New York: Southwick and Crooker, 1802), 245–254. The links existing between Mormonism and Freemasonry are far too numerous to include under the cover of *One Nation Under Gods*. Therefore, the reader is encouraged to refer to the many extensive and well-documented works already published on Freemasonry and its connection to Mormonism: e.g., Tanner and Tanner, Quinn, and Brooke.

63. Reed C. Durham, "Is There no Help for the Widow's Son," Presidential Address, Mormon History Association Conference, April 20, 1974, re-printed in "Reed C. Durham, Jr.'s Astounding Research on the Masonic Influence on Mormonism," *Mormon Miscellaneous*,

October 1975, 16, online at http://www.xmission.com/~country/reason/widowson.htm. Durham additionally stated: "How does a Mormon historian interpret Joseph Smith and the Masonic Enoch legend? The parallels demand an answer. Was Joseph Smith the fruition of Enoch's prophecy? Was this an extreme "grabbing on" by the Prophet? Or did mysterious and divine, even magical, forces attach themselves to him? Can anyone deny that Masonic influence on Joseph Smith and the Church, either before or after his personal Masonic membership? The evidence demands comments" (p. 16).

64. The temple endowment ceremony is a ritualized drama of the Genesis creation story, fall of humanity, and redemption of Adam. During the ceremony participants make specific promises regarding obedience to Mormonism's commandments and pledge their loyalty to the Mormon church. This ritual also includes various passwords and their signs, which Mormons believe will one day enable them to enter into the celestial (or highest) kingdom of heaven. In other words, these rites of spiritual passage will enable them eventually to become gods. An extensive list of similarities between the Masonic ceremony and the Mormon temple ritual can be found Jerald Tanner and Sandra Tanner, "Captain Morgan and the Masonic Influence in Mormonism," this article is based on excerpts from Jerald Tanner and Sandra Tanner, *The Mormon Kingdom* (Salt Lake City: ULM, 1969), vol. 1, 161–169, online at http://utlm.org/onlineresources/mormonkingdomvol1ch13masonicinfluence.htms.

65. W.M. Paden, *Temple Mormonism—Its Evolution, Ritual and Meaning* (New York: A.J. Montgomery, 1931), 18. At some point in the early twentieth century, this bloody vow was changed to read: "[I] do covenant and promise that I will never reveal the First Token of the Aaronic Priesthood, together with its accompanying name, sign and penalty. Rather than do so I would suffer my life to be taken." However, the accompanying penalty sign remained until it, too, was removed in 1990. Similarly gruesome vows and imagery were removed at that time as well, even though Smith and other Mormon leaders defined such aspects of the ceremony as "most sacred." Jerald and Sandra Tanner ask a thought-provoking question with regard to the 1990 Temple ceremony changes that removed its more offensive/Masonic aspects:

> "Now that the Mormon leaders have completely removed both the gruesome wording and the penalties from the temple ritual, it places these apologists on the horns of a dilemma. If God really instructed Joseph Smith to lift the bloody oaths and penalties from the Masonic ritual and insert them into the endowment ceremony, how can the present leaders of the church, who are supposed to be guided by revelation, tear them out of the temple ritual without offending God? It would appear that either the present leaders of the church feel that they know more than the God who was supposed to have spoken to Joseph Smith, or else they realize that Smith made a serious mistake when he borrowed this embarrassing material from the Masons. The action of church authorities in dropping out some of the elements which were once believed to be 'most sacred' will undoubtedly raise some serious questions in the minds of many faithful LDS people. If Joseph Smith was in error when he included these things, then it is obvious that we have no assurance that the other material he took from the Masons is really inspired. If a portion of the Masonic material he plagiarized is found to be defective, it throws suspicion on all the rest of the Masonic ritual which was incorporated into the endowment, and since there is so much Masonry in the ceremony, it would lead one to the suspicion that the entire ceremony is man-made" (Jerald Tanner and Sandra Tanner, "Temple Ritual Altered: Mormon Leaders Delete Some of the 'Most Sacred' Parts Of Ceremony," *Salt Lake City Messenger* [#75], July 1990, 10, online at http://www.utlm.org/newsletters/no75.htm).

66. William Morgan, *Illustrations of Freemasonry* (Batavia, NY, 1827), 21–22, online at

http://www.utlm.org/onlinebooks/captmorgansfreemasonry2.htm. This entire volume is online at http://www.utlm.org/booklist/titles/up025_expositionoffreemasonry.htm.

67. Morgan, 23, online at http://www.utlm.org/onlinebooks/captmorgansfreemasonry2. htm.

68. Morgan, 52–53, online at http://www.utlm.org/onlinebooks/captmorgansfreemasonry3. htm.

69. Paden, 20.

70. Morgan, 75–77, online at http://www.utlm.org/onlinebooks/captmorgansfreemasonry4. htm.

71. LDS Endowment Ceremony (1931), online at http://home.teleport.com/~packham/ endow31.htm and http://www.geocities.com/Athens/Forum/2081/temple0.htm. Although these words were replaced with less offensive vows (see endnote #65) many years ago, Mormons continued until 1990 to execute the *sign* of the penalty, as follows: "The sign of the first token of the Melchizedek Priesthood or sign of the nail is made by bringing the left hand in front of you with the hand in cupping shape, the left arm forming a square, the right hand is also brought forward, the fingers close together, and the thumb is placed over the left hip. This is the sign. The execution of the penalty is represented by drawing the thumb quickly across the body and dropping the hands to the side" (Quoted in Tanner and Tanner, "Temple Ritual Altered," 9, http://www.utlm.org/newsletters/no75. htm).

72. E. Cecil McGavin, *Mormonism and Masonry* (Salt Lake City: Bookcraft, 1947), 6.

73. Durham listed most of these similarities during his 1974 speech before attendees of the Mormon History Association in Nauvoo, Illinois: "conferences, councils, priesthood, temples, anointing with oil, the issuance of licenses, certificates for identifying legitimate fellow workers, elders, high priests, and even the Book of the Law. . . . The Kirtland Temple also reflected an influence of Masonry. . . . It is also obvious that the Nauvoo Temple architecture was in part, at least Masonically influenced. Indeed, it appears that there was an intentional attempt to utilize Masonic symbols and motifs. The sun stones, and the moon and star stones, were examples. An additional example was the angel used on the weather vane on the top of the Temple" (see endnote #62). Another similarity involves Freemasonry's "Five Points of Fellowship" and Mormonism's "Five Points of Fellowship" (the five points were removed from the LDS ceremony as of 1990). The following comparison of original texts are from Tanner and Tanner, *The Mormon Kingdom*, vol. 1. 159:

Freemasonry (Morgan, 84-85)	Mormonism (Paden, 22)
"He (the candidate) is raised on what is called the five points of fellowship, . . . This is done by putting the inside of your right foot to the inside of the right foot of the person to whom you are going to give the word, the inside of your knee to his, laying your right breast against his, your left hands on the back of each other, and your mouths to each other's right ear (in which position alone you are permitted to give the word), and whisper the word Mahhahbone . . . He is also told that Mahhahbone signifies marrow in the bone."	The five points of fellowship are given by putting the inside of the right foot to the inside of the Lord's, the inside of your knee to his, laying your breast close to his, your left hands on each other's backs, and each one putting his mouth to the other's ear, in which position the Lord whispers: "Lord—'This is the sign of the token: "'Health to the navel, marrow in the bones. . .'"

74. Durham, 16, online at http://www.xmission.com/~country/reason/widowson.htm.

75. Durham, 14, online at http://www.xmission.com/~country/reason/widowson.htm; cf. Heber C. Kimball, November 9, 1858, quoted in Brooke, 91.

76. Kimball. Quoted in Brooke, 91. Mormons claim that Freemasonry dates all the way back to King Solomon of Israel, who originally instituted the temple ceremony. According to Smith, this ceremony was gradually perverted and changed over time, until he was initiated into Freemasonry, and through revelation, was able to again obtain the undefiled ceremony, which he subsequently inserted into the Mormon temple ritual. Historically, however, Masonic rituals can be documented only as far back as the 1700s. They emerged as a blending of Egyptian rites, alchemic symbolism, astrology, occultism, Rosicrucianism, the Bible, and Jewish Cabala mysticism (see John J. Robinson, *Born In Blood: The Lost Secrets of Freemasonry* [New York: M. Evans & Company, 1989] and John Ankerberg and John Weldon, *The Secret Teachings of the Masonic Lodge* [Chicago: Moody Press, 1990]).

77. For an in-depth look at the *Book of Mormon* and its reflection of anti-Masonic thought of the early nineteenth century, see Persuitte, 192–197.

CHAPTER THREE: FROM PROFIT TO PROPHET

1. John L. Brooke, *The Refiner's Fire: The Making of Mormon Cosmology, 1644–1844* (New York: Cambridge University press, 1994; paperback edition, 1996), 4.

2. Smith eventually obtained two additional seer stones, and perhaps more, before his death in 1844. There is no solid information, however, as to how he may have used these other stones (see D. Michael Quinn, *Early Mormonism and the Magic World View* [Salt Lake City: Signature Books, 1998], 245). Quinn's book provides an incredibly thorough and in-depth look at Joseph Smith's occult practices including his use of seer stones, magical ritual, amulets, and astrology. Quinn also discusses the importance of occultism throughout Mormonism's first 100 years.

3. "E. W. Vanderhoof remembered that his Dutch grandfather once paid Smith seventy-five cents to look into his "whitish, glossy, and opaque" stone to locate a stolen mare" (E. W. Vanderhoof, *Historical Sketches of Western New York*, Buffalo: Matthews–Northrup Works, 1907, 13–39. Quoted in Quinn, 43).

4. Quinn, 43.

5. Lucy Mack Smith, *Biographical Sketches of Joseph Smith the Prophet, and His Progenitors for many Generations* (Liverpool: S.W. Richards, 1853), 91–92, reprinted in Dan Vogel, ed., *Early Mormon Documents* (Salt Lake City: Signature Books, 1996), vol. 1, 309–310.

6. Isaac Hale, statement of March 20, 1834, in E.D. Howe, *Mormonism Unvailed* (Painesville, OH: author, 1834), 262–263, online at http://www.solomonspalding.com/docs/1834howf.htm#pg262. This entire volume is online at http://www.solomonspalding.com/docs/1834howb.htm. A searchable text version is online at http://www.concordance.com/mormon.htm.

7. Hale, 263. Hale's statement is supported by Martin Harris: "When Joseph found this stone, there was a company digging in Harmony, Pa., and they took Joseph to look in the stone for them, and he did so for a while, and then he told them the enchantment was so strong that he could not see, and they gave it up" (Martin Harris, "Mormonism—No. II" [an interview], *Tiffany's Monthly*, August 1859, vol. 5, 164), online at http://www.utlm.org/onlineresources/sermons_talks_interviews/harrisinterviewtiffanysmonthly.htm.

8. Alva Hale. Quoted in Joseph Lewis, "Review of Mormonism," *Amboy Journal*, June 11, 1879, cited in David Persuitte, *Joseph Smith and the Origins of the Book of Mormon* (Jefferson, NC: McFarland & Co., 2000), 38.

9. According to an 1877 letter published in the *Chenango Union*, May 3, 1877 (Chenango

was the county in which Bainbridge was located), a trial eye-witness named Dr. William Purple stated that the sons of Stowell had been instrumental in getting Smith arrested (see William Mulder and A. Russell Mortensen, *Among the Mormons* [New York: Alfred A. Knopf, 1958], 35–38 and James H. Smith, *History of Chenango and Madison Counties*, New York [Syracuse, NY: D. Mason & Co., 1880], 153); cf. Persuitte, 46–47.

10. Charles Marshall, "The Original Prophet, By A Visitor to Salt Lake City," *Fraser's Magazine* (February 1873), vol. 2, 229–230. For an in-depth look at exactly how the transcript came to be published, see Persuitte, 45–47.

11. The court transcript was printed again by a Bishop Daniel Tuttle (Episcopal Church, Salt Lake City) in the *New Schaff-Herzog Encyclopedia* (New York: 1883, vol. 2, 1576) with the announcement that it had never before been published. Tuttle apparently did not know about the transcript's appearance in *Fraser's Magazine*. The Schaff-Herzog transcript included a segment deleted from Marshall's printing. The deleted portion reads as follows: "Horace Stowel sworn. Says he see prisoner look at hat through stone, pretending to tell where a chest of dollars were buried in Windsor, a number of miles distant; marked out size of chest in the leaves on ground." The transcript reads as follows (bracketed words are Marshall's additions, emphases added for reading clarity):

STATE OF NEW YORK v. JOSEPH SMITH

Warrant issued upon written complaint upon oath of Peter G. Bridgeman, who informed that one Joseph Smith of Bainbridge was a disorderly person and an imposter. Prisoner brought before Court March 20,1826.

Prisoner examined: says that he came from the town of Palmyra, and had been at e house of Josiah Stowel in Bainbridge most of time since; had small part of time been employed in looking for mines, but the major part had been employed by said Stowel on his farm, and going to school. That he had a certain stone which he had occasionally looked at to determine where hidden treasures in the bowels of the earth were; that he professed to tell in this manner where gold mines were a distance under ground, and had looked for Mr. Stowel several times, and had informed him where he could find these treasures, and Mr. Stowel had been engaged in digging for them. That at Palmyra he pretended to tell by looking at this stone where coined money was buried in Pennsylvania and while at Palmyra had frequently ascertained in that way where lost property was of various kinds; that he had occasionally been in the habit of looking through this stone to find lost property for three years, but of late had pretty much given it up on account of its injuring his health, especially his eyes, making them sore; that he did not solicit business of this kind, and had always declined having anything to do with this business.

Josiah Stowel sworn: says that prisoner had been at his house something like five months; had been employed by him to work on farm part of time; that he pretended to have skill of telling where hidden treasures in the earth were by means of looking through a certain stone; that prisoner had looked for him sometimes; once to tell him about money buried in Bend Mountain in Pennsylvania, once for gold on Monument Hill, and once for a salt spring; and that he positively knew that the prisoner could tell, and did possess the art of seeing those valuable treasures through the medium of said stone; that he found the [word illegible] at Bend and Monument Hill as prisoner represented it; that prisoner had looked through said stone for Deacon Attleton for a mine, did not exactly find it but got a p-[word unfinished] of ore which resembled gold, he thinks; that prisoner had told by means of this stone where a Mr. Bacon had buried money; that he and prisoner had been in search of it; that prisoner had said it was in a certain root of a stump five feet from the surface of the earth, and with it would be found a tail feather; that said Stowel and prisoner thereupon commenced digging, found a tail feather, but money was gone; that he supposed the money moved down. That prisoner did offer his services; that he never deceived him; that prisoner looked through stone and described Josiah Stowel's house and outhouses, while at Palmyra at Simpson

Stowel's, correctly; that he had told about a painted tree, with a man's head painted upon it, by means of said stone. That he had been in company with prisoner digging for gold, and had the most implicit faith in prisoner's skill.

Arad Stowel sworn: says that he went to see whether prisoner could convince him that he possessed the skill he professed to have, upon which prisoner laid a book upon a white cloth, and proposed looking through another stone which was white and transparent, hold the stone to the candle, turn his head to look, and read. The deception appeared so palpable that witness went off disgusted.

McMaster sworn: says he went with Arad Stowel, and likewise came away disgusted. Prisoner pretended to him that he could discover objects at a distance by holding this white stone to the sun or candle; that prisoner rather declined looking into a hat at his dark colored stone, as he said that it hurt his eyes.

Jonathon Thompson: says that prisoner was requested to look for chest of money; did look, and pretended to know where it was; and prisoner, Thompson and Yeomans went in search of it; that Smith arrived at spot first; was at night; that Smith looked in hat while there, and when very dark, and told how the chest was situated. After digging several feet, struck something sounding like a board or plank. Prisoner would not look again, pretending that he was alarmed on account of the circumstances relating to the trunk being buried [which] came all fresh to his mind. That the last time he looked he discovered distinctly the two Indians who buried the trunk, that a quarrel ensued between them, and that one of said Indians was killed by the other, and thrown into the hole beside the trunk, to guard it, as he supposed. Thompson says that he believes in the prisoner's professed skill; that the board he struck his spade upon was probably the chest, but on account of an enchantment the trunk kept settling away from under them when digging; that notwithstanding they continued constantly removing the dirt, yet the trunk kept about the same distance from them. Says prisoner said that it appeared to him that salt might be found at Bainbridge, and that he is certain that prisoner can divine things by means of said stone. That as evidence of the fact prisoner looked into his hat to tell him about some money witness lost sixteen years ago, and that he described the man that witness supposed had taken it, and the disposition of the money: And therefore the Court find the Defendant guilty.

Costs: Warrant, 19c. Complaint upon oath, 25-c. Seven witnesses, 87-c. Recognisances, 25c. Mittimus, 19c. Recognisances of witnesses, 75c. Subpoena, 18c.-$2.68

12. See court transcript, previous endnote.

13. A.W. Benton, letter to Editor, *Evangelical Magazine and Gospel Advocate* (Utica, New York), April 9, 1831, New Series 2, 120, Benton reported: "For several years preceding the appearance of his book, he [i.e., Joseph Smith] was about the country in the character of a glass-looker: pretending, by means of a certain stone, or glass, which he put in a hat, to be able to discover lost goods, hidden treasures, mines of gold and silver, &c. Although he constantly failed in his pretensions, still he had his dupes who put implicit confidence in all his words. In this town, a wealthy farmer, named Josiah Stowell, together with others, spent large sums of money in digging for hidden money, which this Smith pretended he could see, and told them where to dig; but they never found their treasure. At length the public, becoming wearied with the base imposition which he was palming upon the credulity of the ignorant, for the purpose of sponging his living from their earnings, had him arrested as a disorderly person, tried and condemned before a court of Justice."

14. Joel K. Noble, letter to Jonathan B. Turner, March 8, 1842. The original of this letter is in the Turner Collection of the Illinois State Historical Library in Springfield, Ill. Wesley P. Walters discussed this document and provided a copy of it in "From Occult to Cult with Joseph Smith, Jr.," *Journal of Pastoral Practice* (Summer 1977), vol. 1, 121–137.

15. Francis Kirkham, *A New Witness for Christ in the America* (Salt Lake City: Utah Printing Co., 1942; 1960 edition), 386.

16. *Deseret News*, Church Section, May 11, 1946, as cited in Kirkham, enlarged edition, 430–431. Quoted in Jerald Tanner and Sandra Tanner, "State of New York vs. Joseph Smith," Salt *Lake City Messenger* (#68), July 1988, 1, online at http://www.utlm.org/newsletters/no68.htm.

17. John Widtsoe, *Joseph Smith-Seeker After Truth* (Salt Lake City: Bookcraft, 1951), 78.

18. Hugh Nibley, *The Myth Makers* (Salt Lake City: Bookcraft, 1967),142.

19. Leonard J. Arington and David Bitton, *The Mormon Experience* (Champaign, IL: University of Illinois Press, 1992), 10–11.

20. Kirkham, 387.

21. Hale, in Howe, 263, online at http://www.solomonspalding.com/docs/1834howf.htm#pg263.

22. *HC* (Salt Lake City: Deseret Book Company, 1976/1980), vol. 3, 29.

23. Parley Chase, letter to James T. Cobb, April 3, 1879, as quoted in Wilhelm Ritter von Wymetal, *Joseph Smith, the Prophet, His Family, and His Friends* (Salt Lake City: Tribune Printing and Publishing Co., 1886), 276.

24. Abner Cole, "Gold Bible, No. 4," *Palmyra Reflector*, February 14, 1831, reprinted in Dan Vogel, ed., *Early Mormon Documents* (Salt Lake City: Signature Books, 1998), vol. 2, 245.

25. For more information on the desperate economic situation of Joseph and Emma Smith, see Marvin S. Hill, *Quest for Refuge: The Mormon Flight From American Pluralism* (Salt Lake City: Signature Books, 1989), 19–20. In *No Man Knows My History* (New York: Vintage Books, 1995 [original edition by Alfred A. Knopf, 1945]), Fawn Brodie comments: "What had been originally conceived as a mere money-making history of the Indians had been transformed at some point early in the writing, or possibly even before the book was begun, into a religious saga" (Brodie, 83). Interestingly, Hiram Page (one of the "Eight Witnesses" to the *Book of Mormon*) and David Whitmer (one of the "Three Witnesses" to the *Book of Mormon*) noted in later years that at one point Joseph actually tried to sell the copyright to the *Book of Mormon*, which would have been an odd decision if Smith did indeed believe the book was divine. Smith supposedly sent several men, including Oliver Cowdery, to Kingston, Canada because he had received a revelation through his seer stone that indicated the copyright would be sold there for $8,000. The men returned unsuccessful (see Hiram Page, letter to William McLellin, February 2, 1848, Fishing River, Missouri, photocopy, RLDSCA; cf. David Whitmer, an interview published in the *DesMoines Daily News*, October 16, 1886 and David Whitmer, *An Address to All Believers in Christ* (Richmond, MO: author, 1887), 30–31; also see William McLellin, letter to Joseph Smith III, July 1872, RLDSCA, and William McLellin, letter to John L. Traughber, May 7, 1877, copied by Traughber, Traughber Collection, Accession 1446, Box 2, Marriot Library). For more information on this revelation to sell the *Book of Mormon* copyright, see H. Michael Marquardt, *The Joseph Smith Revelations: Text and Commentary* (Salt Lake City: Signature Books, 1999), 372–374.

26. Joseph Capron, statement of November 8, 1833, reprinted in Howe, 260, online at http://www.solomonspalding.com/docs/1834howf.htm#pg260.

27. Parley Chase, statement of December 2, 1833, reprinted in Howe, 248, online at http://www.solomonspalding.com/docs/1834howf.htm#pg248.

28. W. R. Hine, n.d., reprinted in Arthur B. Deming, ed., *Naked Truths About Mormonism*, January 1888, vol. 1, no. 1, 2, online at http://www.lavazone2.com/dbroadhu/CA/natruths.htm. Hine's full statement reads: "Jo Smith claimed to be a seer. He had a very clear stone about the size and shape of a duck's egg, and claimed that he could see lost or hidden things through it. He said he saw Captain Kidd sailing on the Susquehanna River during a freshet, and that he buried two pots of gold and silver. He claimed he saw writing cut on the rocks in an unknown language telling where Kidd buried it, and he translated it through his peep-stone. . . . Jo dug next for Kidd's money, on the west bank of the Susquehanna, half a mile from the river, and three miles from his salt wells." This same edition of *Naked Truths About Mormonism* also includes a statement by K. A. E.

Bell (May 1885), who said: "I attended the first Mormon meeting Pratt and Cowdery held in Painesville. My brother Milo, from Broome County, N.Y., was present. They told about Prophet Jo Smith finding the gold plates, and said they saw them. My brother ridiculed them after the meeting. He told me he knew Jo Smith when he was digging near the Susquehanna River for Captain Kidd's money" (vol. 1, no. 2, 3); also see Quinn, 42.

29. Hiel Lewis, letter to James T. Cobb, *Amboy Journal*, April 30, 1879, 1. Quoted in Wesley P. Walters, "The Mormon Prophet Attempts to Join the Methodists," online from ULM at http://www.utlm.org/onlineresources/josephsmithmethodist.htm, reprinted in W. Wyl, *Mormon Portraits* (Salt Lake City: Tribune Printing & Publishing Company, 1886), 79–80. A reprint of Wyl's volume is available for purchase online at http://www.utlm.org/booklist/titles/up016_mormonportraits.htm.

30. Fayette Lapham, "Interview with the Father of Joseph Smith, the Mormon Prophet, Forty Years Ago. His Account of the Finding of the Sacred Plates," *Historical Magazine* (May 1870), 2nd Series, vol. 7, 305–307, reprinted in Vogel, vol. 1, 459.

31. Lapham, reprinted in Vogel, vol. 1, 459.

32. Lapham, reprinted in Vogel, vol. 1, 459.

33. Willard Chase, statement of December 11 1833, reprinted in Howe, 242, online at http://www.solomonspalding.com/docs/1834howf.htm#pg242.

34. Chase, see this chapter, endnote #33.

35. Chase, see this chapter, endnote #33.

36. Chase, see this chapter, endnote #33.

37. "Golden Bible," *Rochester Gem*, September 5, 1829, vol. 1, 70, reprinted in Vogel, vol. 2, 272. An earlier, but very similar version of this article, was printed in the *Palmyra Freeman* (c.1829). The original cannot be located, but it was reprinted in the *Advertiser and Telegraph* (Rochester, August 31, 1829) and again in the *Painesville Telegraph* (Ohio, September 22, 1829): "The text contained herein is a copy of the text as it was reprinted in the fall of 1827, a person by the name of Joseph Smith, of Manchester, Ontario county, reported that he had been visited in a dream by the spirit of the Almighty, and informed that in a certain hill in that town, was deposited the golden Bible, containing an ancient record of a divine nature and origin. After having been thrice visited, as he states, he proceeded to the spot, and after penetrating "mother earth" a short distance the Bible, was found, together with a huge pair of spectacles!" (reprinted in Vogel, vol. 2, 221).

38. O. Turner, *History of the Pioneer Settlement of Phelps and Gorham's Purchase, and Morris Reserve* (Rochester: William Alling, 1852), 216, http://home1.gte.net/dbroadhu/RESTOR/Lib/Tur1851a.htm.

39. Hosea Stout, *On the Mormon Frontier: The Diary of Hosea Stout*, Juanita Brooks, ed. (Salt Lake City: University of Utah Press, 1964), vol. 2, 593.

40. Harris' interview with Joel Tiffany, 163 and 169 (see this chapter, endnote #7), online at http://www.utlm.org/onlineresources/sermons_talks_interviews/harrisinterview tiffanysmonthly.htm; cf. statements by non-Mormons that confirm Harris' recollection are numerous, including those by Willard Chase, Henry Harris, and Orasmus Turner.

41. Turner, 214, online at http://home1.gte.net/dbroadhu/RESTOR/Lib/Tur1851a.htm.

42. Hiel Lewis, online at http://www.utlm.org/onlineresources/josephsmithmethodist.htm.

43. Oliver B. Huntington, a faithful follower of Smith's, noted: "As far back as 1837, I know he [Smith] said the moon was inhabited by men and women the same as this earth, and that they lived to a greater age than we do—that they live generally to near the age of 1000 years. He described the men as averaging near six feet in height, and dressing quite uniformly in something near the Quaker style" (Oliver B. Huntington, "The Inhabitants of the Moon," *The Young Woman's Journal*, published by the Young Ladies' Mutual Improvement Association of Zion, 1892, vol. 3, 263–264). Joseph's father—Joseph Smith, Sr.—went so far as to prophecy that Huntington would one day preach the Mormon gospel to "the inhabitants of the moon" (Huntington, 264). In February 1881, Huntington recorded the following in his journal: "Inhabitants of the Moon are more of a uni-

form size than the inhabitants of the Earth, being about 6 feet in height. They dress very much like the Quaker Style & are quite general in Style, or the one fashion of dress. They live to be very old; comeing [sic] generally, near a thousand years. This is the description of them as given by Joseph the Seer, and he could 'See' whatever he asked the Father in the name of Jesus to see (Oliver B. Huntington, *Journal of Oliver B. Huntington*, book 14, original at Huntington Library, San Marino, Calif.; also vol.3, p.166 of typed copy at Utah State Historical Society).

44. William Smith, Joseph's brother, recounted: "'I did not see them uncovered, but I handled them and hefted them while wrapped in a tow frock and judged them to have weighed about sixty pounds. . . . Father and my brother Samuel saw them as I did while in the frock. So did Hyrum and others of the family.' When the interviewer asked if he didn't want to remove the cloth and see the bare plates, William replied, 'No, for father had just asked if he might not be permitted to do so, and Joseph, putting his hand on them said; 'No, I am instructed not to show them to any one. If I do, I will transgress and lose them again.' Besides, we did not care to have him break the commandment and suffer as he did before'" (*Zion's Ensign*, January 13, 1894, 6, cited in Church of Christ broadside, online at http://www.exmormon.org/file9.htm).

45. Harris' interview with Joel Tiffany (see this chapter, endnotes #7 and #40), 167, online at http://www.utlm.org/onlineresources/sermons_talks_interviews/harrisinterview tiffanysmonthly.htm. David Whitmer, one of the three "witnesses" to the *Book of Mormon*, may have first heard about the golden plates from some of Smith's money-digging companions. During an 1881 interview with the *Kansas City Journal*, Whitmer related that he had "had conversations with several young men who said that Joseph Smith had certainly golden plates, and that before he attained them he had promised to share with them, but had not done so, and they were very much incensed with him(David Whitmer, interview in *Kansas City Journal*, June 5, 1881, reprinted in *MS*, July 4, 1881, vol. 43, no. 27, 421–423 and *MS*, July 11, 1881, vol. 43, no. 28, 437–438; modern reprint in Fred C. Collier, *Unpublished Revelations* [Salt Lake City: Collier's Publishing, Co., 1993], vol. 2, 114).

46. Harris remembered a "black hollow oak tree top" (Harris's interview with Joel Tiffany, 165 and 167), online at http://www.utlm.org/onlineresources/sermons_talks_interviews/ harrisinterviewtiffanysmonthly.htm.

47. Joseph Smith claimed that the golden plates were seen by eleven specially chosen individuals whose names were written at the end of his 1830 edition of *Book of Mormon*. Attached to the names were short paragraphs attesting to the authenticity of the plates. The names appeared in two groups as "The Testimony of Three Witnesses" (Oliver Cowdery, David Whitmer, and Martin Harris) and "The Testimony of Eight Witnesses" (Christian Whitmer, Jacob Whitmer, Peter Whitmer, Jr., John Whitmer, Hiram Page, Joseph Smith, Sr., Hyrum Smith, and Samuel H. Smith). The Three Witnesses claimed: "[W]e have seen the engravings which are upon the plates; and they have been shown unto us by the power of God, and not of man" (Statement, *BOM*, opening page). The Eight Witnesses claimed: " Joseph Smith, Jun., the translator of this work, has shown unto us the plates of which hath been spoken, which have the appearance of gold; and as many of the leaves as the said Smith has translated we did handle with our hands; and we also saw the engravings thereon" (Statement, *BOM*, opening page). Mormons have assumed that these statements mean that the individuals named actually saw the golden plates with their own eyes. However, numerous historical documents demonstrate that these men only saw through visionary experiences. None of them actually ever saw the plates with their natural sight in the same way anyone would be able to see or pick up a book on a table. The Three Witnesses, as it turns out, had the plates shown to them by an angel who appeared to them while they were praying in the woods. The Eight Witnesses only "saw" the plates as long as they were covered with a cloth of some kind. Martin Harris, one of the so-called "Three Witnesses," went so far as to admit that

none of the eight witnesses ever saw the plates. In a document suppressed for many decades by the Mormon church, a former Latter-day Saint wrote the following account of a lecture by Harris: "[W]hen I came to hear *Martin Harris* state in public that *he never saw the plates with his natural eyes only in vision or imagination*, neither Oliver nor David & also that the eight witnesses never saw them & [that he] hesitated to sign that instrument for that reason, but were persuaded to do it, the last pedestal gave way, in my view our foundation was sapped & the entire superstructure fell in heap of ruins, I . . . renounced the Book of Mormon . . . [A]fter we were done speaking M Harris arose & said he was sorry for any man who rejected the Book of Mormon for he knew it was true, he said he had hefted the plates repeatedly in a box with only a tablecloth or a hand-kerchief over them, but he never saw them only as he saw a city throught [sic] a moun-tain" (Stephen Burnett, letter to Br Johnson, April 15, 1838, Joseph Smith Papers, Let-terbook, April 20, 1837–February 9, 1843, 64–66, typed copy). Quoted in Jerald Tanner and Sandra Tanner, *The Changing World of Mormonism* (Chicago: Moody, 1981), 108, online at http://www.utlm.org/onlinebooks/changech5a.htm. This entire volume is available from ULM, online at http://www.utlm.org/onlinebooks/changecontents.htm. Smith himself explained that the Three Witnesses saw the plates in a vision (Joseph Smith, "History of Joseph Smith—Continued," *T&S*, September 1, 1842, vol. 3, no. 21, 897–898). David Whitmer agreed that neither he, nor the other Three Witnesses, ever physically saw or handled the plates. They "saw" the plates in a vision (David Whitmer, interview recorded by P. Wilhelm Poulson, c. early 1878, reprinted in *Deseret Evening News*, August 16, 1878; cf., modern reprint in Collier, vol. 2, 104–107). For information and documentation demonstrating this little known aspect of the supposed "witnesses" to the golden plates, see the following resources: Brodie, 77–80; Jerald Tanner and San-dra Tanner, *Mormonism: Shadow or Reality?* (Salt Lake City: ULM, 1987), 50–55; and "The Book of Mormon," Internet article online at http://www.exmormon.org/file9.htm.

48. According to Brigham Young: "When Joseph got the plates, the angel instructed him to carry them back to the hill Cumorah, which he did. Oliver [Cowdery] says that when Joseph and Oliver went there, the hill opened, and they walked into a cave, in which there was a large and spacious room. He says he did not think, at the time, whether they had the light of the sun or artificial light; but that it was just as light as day. They laid the plates on a table; it was a large table that stood in the room. Under this table there was a pile of plates as much as two feet high, and there were altogether in this room more plates than probably many wagon loads; they were piled up in the corners and along the walls" (Brigham Young, Special Conference Speech, June 17, 1877, *JOD* [Liverpool: William Budge, 1878; lithographed reprint of original edition, 1966], vol. 19, 38). David Whitmer stated more specifically that the cave was located "near" the hill Cumorah (Whitmer, in Collier, vol. 2, 107).

49. Pomeroy Tucker, "The Mormon Imposture—The Mormon Aborigines," *Wayne Democ-ratic Press* (Lyons, New York), June 2, 1858, 2, reprinted in Dan Vogel, ed., *Early Mor-mon Documents*, (Salt Lake City: Signature Books, 2000), vol. 3, 71.

50. Albert Chandler, letter to William Linn, December 22, 1898, reprinted in Vogel, vol. 3, 223.

51. Stephen S. Chandler, letter to Thomas Grigg, reprinted in Thomas Grigg, *The Prophet of Palmyra* (New York: John B. Alden, 1890), 46, reprinted in Vogel, vol. 3, 160. In 1831, newspapers would report that Harris had again started seeing the devil around the Kirt-land area. He described Satan as "very much like a jack-ass, with very short, smooth hair, similar to that of a mouse" (Howe, 14, reprinted in Vogel, vol. 2, 285). Moreover, Harris had "seen Jesus Christ and that he is the handsomest man he ever did see. He has also seen the Devil, whom he described as a very sleek fellow with four feet, and a head like that of a Jack-ass" (*Guernsey Times*, April 16, 1831 and *American Friend and Marietta Gazette*, April 30, 1831, reprinted in Vogel, vol. 2, 271, footnote#32).

52. John A. Clark, letter to Dear Brethren, August 24, 1840, *The Episcopal Recorder* (Philadelphia: W.J. & J.K. Soimon, 1842), 217, 222–31, reprinted in Vogel, vol. 2, 271.

53. Harris, 163, see this chapter, endnote #45 for online resource.

54. Harris, 169, see this chapter, endnote #45 for online resource.

55. Chase, in Howe, 236, online at http://www.solomonspalding.com/docs/1834howf. htm#pg236; cf. similar statement in Jesse Townsend, letter to Phineas Stiles, December 4 1833, reprinted in Pomeroy Tucker, *Origin, Rise and Progress of Mormonism* (New York: D. Appleton and Co., 1867), 288–291. This volume is online at http://moa. umdl.umich.edu/cgi/sgml/moa-idx?notisid=AGU9642 (also see reprint in Vogel, vol. 3, 21).

56. Charles Anthon, letter to E.D. Howe, February 17, 1834, reprinted in Howe, 271, online at http://www.solomonspalding.com/docs/1834howf.htm#pg270. This entire volume is online at http://www.solomonspalding.com/docs/1834howb.htm. A searchable text version is online at http://www.concordance.com/mormon.htm.

57. Brodie, 52.

58. There is evidence that Smith actually may have orchestrated the outcome of Harris' trip to New York so he could manipulate Harris into thinking that a prophecy had been fulfilled. No one could have translated Smith's characters, even if they had indeed been real Egyptian, since Egyptology in the early 1800s had not yet evolved far enough to translate anything other than simple names. So why did Smith send Harris on his trip? The following explanation appears in Persuitte's excellent work, *Joseph Smith and the Origins of the Book of Mormon*: "The answer to that question can perhaps be suggested as follows: First, Anthon could not (as we know) have translated the characters. Second, because he had made them up, Joseph knew that Anthon could not translate the characters. Third, Joseph told Harris what to expect when "the learned" tried to translate them. Fourth, what Joseph told Harris to expect, in fact, came to pass: the learned could not read the characters and Joseph could (or so he claimed). But Joseph was just an "ignorant" young man. Harris therefore concluded that "God had chosen the foolish things of the world to confound the wise [1 Cor. 1:27]" (Persuitte, 74).

59. Anthon, reprinted in Howe, 270. A much lengthier extract from Anthon's letter, including the already quoted text, reads as follows:

"Upon examining the paper in question, I soon came to the conclusion that it was all a trick, perhaps a *hoax*. When I asked the person, who brought it, how he obtained the writing, he gave me, as far as I can now recollect, the following account: A "gold book," consisting of a number of plates of gold, fastened together in the shape of a book by wires of the same metal, had been dug up in the northern part of the state of New York, and along with the book an enormous pair of "gold spectacles"! . . . The farmer [Harris] added, that he had been requested to contribute a sum of money towards the publica-tion of the "golden book," the contents of which would, as he had been assured, produce an entire change in the world and save it from ruin. . . . I changed my opinion about the paper, and, instead of viewing it any longer as a hoax upon the learned, I began to regard it as part of a scheme to cheat the farmer of his money, and I communicated my suspicions to him, warning him to beware of rogues. . . . This paper was in fact a singular scrawl. It consisted of all kinds of crooked characters disposed in columns, and had evidently been prepared by some person who had before him at the time a book containing various alphabets. Greek and Hebrew letters, crosses and flourishes, Roman letters inverted or placed sideways, were arranged in perpendicular columns, and the whole ended in a rude delineation of a circle divided into various compartments, decked with various strange marks, and evidently copied after the Mexican Calender. . . . [T]he paper contained any thing else but "Egyptian Hieroglyphics." Some time after, the same farmer paid me a second visit. He brought with him the golden book in print, and offered it to me for sale. I declined purchasing. He then asked permission to leave the book with me for examination. I declined receiving it, although his manner was strangely urgent. I adverted once more to the roguery which had been in my opinion practised upon him, and asked him what had become of the gold plates. He informed me that they were in a trunk with the large pair of spectacles. I advised him to go to a magistrate and have the trunk examined. He said the "curse of God" would come upon him should he do this. On my pressing him, however, to pursue the course which I had recommended, he told me that he would open the trunk, if I would take the "curse of God" upon myself. I replied that I would do so with the greatest willingness, and would incur every risk of that nature, provided I could only extricate him from the grasp of rogues. He then left me" (Howe, 270–272, online at http://www.solomonspalding.com/docs/1834howf.htm#pg270).

Anthon wrote another letter to John A. Clark, in which he reiterated the statements he made in his communication to Howe (Charles Anthon, letter to John A. Clark, April 3, 1841. Quoted in John A. Clark, *Gleanings by the Way* [New York: 1842], 233–38). Mormons often try to discredit Anthon by pointing out an alleged discrepancy between his letters, but there exists no such discrepancy (see Persuitte, 303–304, endnote#19).

60. John A. Wilson, letter to Marvin Cowan, March 16, 1966. Quoted in Tanner and Tanner, *The Changing World*, 144. The Internet versions of this entire volume is online at http://www.utlm.org/onlinebooks/changecontents.htm. The specific chapter dealing with Wilson's letter and *Book of Mormon* archeology is online at http://www.utlm.org/onlinebooks/changech5c.htm. Additionally, in 1966, Richard A. Parker of Brown University's Egyptology department, wrote a letter to at Marvin Cowan, March 16, 1966. Quoted in Tanner and Tanner, *The Changing World*, 144, online at http://www.utlm.org/onlinebooks/changech5c.htm). University of Chicago Egyptologist Klaus Baer has gone so far as to refer to Smith's *Book of Mormon* characters as senseless "doodlings."(*Sunstone*, May–June 1980, 30. Quoted in Tanner and Tanner, *The Changing World*, 144, online at http://www.utlm.org/onlinebooks/changech5c.htm).

61. B.H. Roberts, *CHC* (Salt Lake City: Deseret News Press, 1930), vol. 1, 129.

62. Hiel Lewis, "Review of Mormonism: Rejoinder to Elder Cadwell." *Amboy Journal*, June 4, 1879. Quoted in Quinn, 172.

63. Emma Smith Bidamon, Interview with Joseph Smith, III, February 1879, Miscellany, RLDS Church Library-Archives, Independence, Missouri, reprinted in Vogel, vol. 1, 539. In a letter dated March 27, 1870, Emma indicated that the entire published version of the *Book of Mormon* was translated through her husband's seer stone. Emma's letter states: "Now the first that my husband translated, was translated by use of the Urim and Thummim, and that was the part that Martin Harris lost, after that he used a small stone, not exactly black, but was a rather dark color" (Emma Smith Bidamon, letter to Emma Pilgrim, March 27, 1870, reprinted in Vogel, vol. 1, 532).

64. Martin Harris, Interview with Anthony Metcalf, c. 1873–1874. Quoted in A. Metcalf, *Ten Years Before the Mast. Shipwrecks and Adventures at Sea! Religious Customs of the People of India and Burmah's Empire. How I became a Mormon and Why I Became an Infidel!* (Malad City, ID: n.p., 1888), 70–71, reprinted in Vogel, vol. 2, 346–347; cf. Emma Smith Interview with Joseph Smith III, Feb. 1879 (see Vogel, vol. 1, 539). Isaac Hale, Emma's father, remembers a slightly an additional piece of information: "The manner in which he pretended to read and interpret, was the same as when he looked for the money-diggers, with the stone in his hat, and his hat over his face, while the Book of Plates were at the same time hid in the woods!" (Hale, in Howe, 264, online at http://www.solomonspalding.com/docs/1834howf.htm#pg264).

65. David Whitmer, *An Address to all believers in Christ* (Richmond, MO: author, 1887), 12.

66. Edward Stevenson, letter to the editor, November 30, 1881, *Deseret Evening News*,

December 13, 1881, reprinted in Vogel, vol. 2, 318–321; cf. "On Sunday, Sept. 4, 1870, Martin Harris addressed a congregation of Saints in Salt Lake City. He related an incident which occurred during the time that he wrote that portion of the translation of the Book of Mormon which he was favored to write direct from the mouth of the Prophet Joseph Smith, and said that the Prophet possessed a seer stone, by which he was enabled to translate as well as from the Urim and Thummim, and for convenience he then used the seer stone" (Andrew Jenson, "The Three Witnesses," May 1887, *HR*, vol. 6, no. 3-5, 216).

67. Roberts, *CHC*, vol. 1, 128–129. Mormon Apostle George Q. Cannon agreed with Roberts, stating: "One of Joseph's aids in searching out the truths of the record was a peculiar pebble or rock which he called a seer stone, and which was sometimes used by him in lieu of the Urim and Thummim" (George Q. Cannon, *Life of Joseph Smith*, 1888 edition, 56). In more current editions of Cannon's volume, which are published by the LDS church-owned Deseret Books, this passage has been deleted without a footnote to indicate the change (see George Q. Cannon, *Life of Joseph Smith* [Salt Lake City: Deseret Book Company, 1958]). Another statement confirming Joseph's use of a seer stone in his translating of the *Book of Mormon* can be found in *Joseph Smith-Seeker After Truth* (Widtsoe, 267).

68. Mormon Apostle Orson Pratt stated in 1878 that Joseph often used his seer stone to receive revelations: "Elder Pratt gave a plain, simple narration of his early experience in the Church, relating many interesting incidents connected with its rise; explained the circumstances under which several revelations were received by Joseph, the Prophet, and the manner in which he received them, he being present on several occasions of the kind. Declared [that] at such times Joseph used the Seerstone when inquiring of the Lord, and receiving revelation, but that he was so thoroughly endowed with the inspiration of the Almighty and the spirit of revelation that he often received them without any instrument, or other means than the operation of the spirit upon his mind" (see *HC*, introduction, vol. 5, xxxi); cf. "Joseph received several revelations to which I was a witness by means of the Seerstone, but he could receive also without any instrument" (Orson Pratt, *MS*, vol. 40, no. 49. Quoted in Tanner and Tanner, *Shadow or Reality?*, 42; also see Quinn, 243–245. In 1842, Smith commented that he and Oliver Cowdery used the seer stone (i.e., the "Urim and Thummim," a common euphemism for the peepstone) to receive a revelation that settled a difference of opinion between the two men over whether or not John the Apostle ever died (Joseph Smith, "History of Joseph Smith—Continued," *T&S*, July 15, 1842, vol. 3, no. 18, 853). Another early "revelation" received through the stone related to a promise that Martin Harris, Oliver Cowdery , and David Whitmer would at some point see the golden plates (Joseph Smith, "History of Joseph Smith—Continued," *T&S*, September 1, 1842, vol. 3, no. 21, 897–898).

69. Joseph Fielding Smith, *Doctrines of Salvation* (Salt Lake City: Bookcraft, 1956), vol. 3, 225. In reference to the brown seer stone, this volume reads: "This seer stone is now in the possession of the Church." David C. Martin also has presented evidence to show that the LDS church president keeps Smith's seer stone locked in a safe: "Dean Hooper, Rockford. Illinois, in a conversation with Joseph Anderson, Assistant to the Council of the Twelve of the 'Utah' Church, at a Chicago Stake Conference, January, 1971, quotes Anderson as saying that the 'Seer' Stone that Joseph Smith used in the early days of the church is in the possession of the church and is kept in a safe in Joseph Fielding Smith's office. Anderson has seen it a number of times there. Slightly smaller than a chicken egg, oval, chocolate in color. (*Restoration Reporter*, vol. 1, no. 2, June, 1971, 8. Quoted in Tanner and Tanner, *Shadow or Reality?*, 44). As recently as 1991, members of the LDS church with access to the president's vault saw *three* seer stones in the secured location: one unidentified stone (origin unknown); one brown stone matching the description of the one Smith used to translate the *BOM*; and one whitish stone comparable to the one Smith used to receive revelations and prophecies (see Quinn, 245–246).

CHAPTER FOUR: SMITH'S GOLDEN BOOK

1. Dan Erickson, *As A Thief in the Night* (Salt Lake City: Signature Books, 1998), 53–54.

2. *Gospel Principles* (Salt Lake City: The Church of Jesus Christ of Latter-day Saints, 1979), 351, online at http://www.lds.org/library/display/0,4945,11-1-13-1,00.html (see "Book of Mormon" under GLOSSARY); cf. John Widtsoe and Franklin S. Harris, Jr., *Seven Claims of the Book of Mormon: A Collection of Evidences* (Independence: Zion's Printing and Publishing Co., 1937), 13–14.

3. *What is the Book of Mormon* (Salt Lake City: The Church of Jesus Christ of Latter-day Saints, 1982), 1.

4. Bruce McConkie, *Mormon Doctrine* (Salt Lake City: Bookcraft, 1958; second edition, 1966), 528.

5. Joseph Smith, *Book of Mormon* (Palmyra, NY: E.B. Grandin, 1830), 71–72; 2 Nephi 5:1-18, modern edition.

6. McConkie, 528.

7. *BOM*, 1830 ed., 73 (2 Nephi 5:21, modern edition).

8. *BOM*, 1830 ed., 73 (2 Nephi 5:22, modern edition); cf. 1 Nephi 12:23, modern edition.

9. *BOM*, 1830 ed., 73 (2 Nephi 5:24, modern edition).

10. *BOM*, 1830 ed., 73 (2 Nephi 5:23, modern edition).

11. *BOM*, 1830 ed., 456 (3 Nephi 2:14-16, modern edition). In the original *BOM* text, Smith consistently neglected to add an "ly" to words where such an addition was grammatically necessary. Hence, this passage in the 1830 edition reads " . . . and their young men and their daughters became exceeding fair." This particular kind of grammatical error in connection the word "exceeding" occurs 222 times in the 1830 *BOM* edition. They have since been corrected by LDS church leaders.

12. *BOM*, 1830 ed., 473–474 (3 Nephi 9:14-21, modern edition).

13. *BOM*, 1830 ed., 476–477 (3 Nephi 11:1-17, modern edition).

14. *BOM*, 1830 ed., 515 (4 Nephi 1:16-17, modern edition). Joseph's use of the term "Ites" as a proper noun in this passage reveals his incorrect notion that the suffix "ites" could be used as a descriptive noun for a group of people. LDS leaders corrected this error in subsequently editions by re-writing the term as a hyphenated word: i.e., "-ites." This is only one example of the atrocious grammar that LDS leaders had to correct in subsequent editions of the *BOM*, the text of which was allegedly written by God.

15. Smith's scribe, Oliver Cowdery, in a letter to W.W. Phelps, wrote the following statement about the fate of the Lamanites: "[T]he land was left to the possession of the red men, who were without intelligence, only in the affairs of their wars; and having no records, only preserving their history by tradition from father to son, lost the account of their true origin, and wandered from river to river, from hill to hill, from mountain to mountain, and from sea to sea, till the land was again peopled, in a measure, by a rude, wild, revengeful, warlike and barbarous race.—Such are our Indians" (Oliver Cowdery, "Letter VII," *MS&AD*, July 1835, vol. 1, no. 10, 158, reprinted in Dan Vogel, ed., *Early Mormon Documents* [Salt Lake City: Signature Books, 1998], vol. 2, 450.

16. *BOM*, modern ed., introduction.

17. *BOM*, 1830 ed., 512–513 (3 Nephi 29, modern edition).

18. David Persuitte, *Joseph Smith and the Origins of the Book of Mormon* (Jefferson, NC: McFarland & Co., 2000), 102.

19. Fawn M. Brodie, *No Man Knows My History* (New York: Vintage Books, 1995; original edition by Alfred A. Knopf, 1945), 34. Brodie also writes: "[T]he Mound builders had been not a lost race, but the direct ancestors of certain of the upper Mississippi Indian tribes. But at that time only a few antiquarians knew that the Indians had made a practice of exhuming, collecting together, and reburying in mounds all the bones of the recently dead" (p. 36).

20. *Palmyra Register*, May 26, 1819. Quoted in Jerald Tanner and Sandra Tanner, *The Chang-*

ing World of Mormonism (Chicago: Moody, 1981), 125, online at http://www.utlm.org/onlinebooks/changech5b.htm. This entire volume is online at http://www.utlm.org/onlinebooks/changecontents.htm.

21. *Palmyra Herald*, February 19, 1823. Quoted in Tanner and Tanner, 125, online at http://www.utlm.org/onlinebooks/changech5b.htm. The article reads: "[F]ortifications and the remains of antiquity in Ohio and elsewhere prove them to be the work of some other people than the Indians . . . . The first settlers of North America were probably the Asiatics, the descendants of Shem [a son of Noah]. . . . [A]t an early period, [they] might easily have crossed the Pacific Ocean, and made settlements in North America. . . . The descendants of Japheth [another son of Noah] might afterwards cross the Atlantic."

22. Brodie, 34.

23. Brodie, 35.

24. Lucy Mack Smith, *Biographical Sketches of Joseph Smith the Prophet, and His Progenitors for many Generations* [Liverpool: S.W. Richards, 1853], 85, reprinted in Dan Vogel, ed., *Early Mormon Documents* [Salt Lake City: Signature Books, 1996], vol. 1, 296.

25. Persuitte, 103.

26. For a more in-depth look at the myths surrounding the Ten Tribes of Israel, see Richard Abanes, *American Militias: Rebellion, Racism, and Religion* (Downers Grove: InterVarsity Press, 1996), 155–159.

27. For a more in-depth look at British-Israelism and its racist/white supremacist/neo-Nazi effect in America, see Abanes, 159–168.

28. John Wilson, *Our Israelitish Origin* (London: James Nisbet & Co., 1840; 1843 edition), 114.

29. Wilson, 80.

30. Edward Hine, *Forty-Seven Identifications of the British Nation* (London: S.W. Partridge & Co., 1871), v. Hine wrote: "The main point of my differing with the late Mr. John Wilson, author of "Our Israelitish Origin," is, that he sought to identify all the Modern Teutonic Nations as parts of Israel. . . . I maintain that God requires the whole Ten Tribes to be consolidated in an Island Nation."

31. Alexander Campbell, "The Mormonites," *Millennial Harbinger*, February 1830, 93.

32. Joseph Smith, letter to John Wentworth, *T&S*, March 1, 1842, vol. 3 no. 9, 708, online at http://www.concordance.com/mormon.htm.

33. Theories about Israel's lost Ten Tribes were so common by 1833 that Josiah Priest observed: "The opinion that the American Indians are descendants of the Lost Ten Tribes is now a popular one and generally believed" (Josiah Priest, *American Antiquities*, quoted in Brodie, 45). Brodie commented: "Fantastic parallels were drawn between Hebraic and Indian customs, such as feasts of first fruits, sacrifices of the first-born in the flock, cities of refuge, ceremonies of purification, and division into tribes. The Indian 'language' (which actually consisted of countless distinct languages derived from numerous linguistic stocks) was said to be chiefly Hebrew. The Indian belief in the Great Spirit (which originally had been implanted by French and Spanish missionaries) was said to be derived in a direct line from Jewish monotheism. One writer even held that syphilis, the Indian's gift to Europe, was an altered form of Biblical leprosy" (p. 45).

34. Dan Vogel, ed., *Early Mormon Documents*, (Salt Lake City: Signature Books, 2000), vol. 3, 279, footnote #3.

35. Mordecai M. Noah, *Wayne Sentinel*, October 4, 1825. Quoted in Vogel, vol. 3, 279 (see footnote #3).

36. *Wayne Sentinel*, October 11, 1825, reprinted in Larry Jonas, *Mormon Claims Examined*, 45. Quoted in Tanner and Tanner, 126, online at http://www.utlm.org/onlinebooks/changech5b.htm.

37. Brodie, 46.

38. John L. Brooke, *The Refiner's Fire: The Making of Mormon Cosmology, 1644–1844* (New York: Cambridge University press, 1994; first paperback edition, 1996), 35. According to Brooke, many writers obtained their chief arguments from Thorowgood.

39. Elias Boudinot, *A Star in the West; or, a Humble Attempt to Discover the Long Lost Tribes of Israel, Preparatory to Their Return to Their Beloved City, Jerusalem* (1816), 279–280. Quoted in Jerald Tanner and Sandra Tanner, *Mormonism: Shadow or Reality?* (Salt Lake City: ULM, 1987), 82.

40. Brodie, 49.

41. Josiah Priest and his works were known to Smith since he quoted from Priest's 1835 *American Antiquities* in "From Priest's American Antiquities," *T&S*, June 1, 1842, vol. 3, no. 15, 813–14, online at http://www.concordance.com/mormon.htm. Moreover, *The Wonders of Nature and Providence Displayed* (1825) was available in Smith's neighborhood prior to the time the *BOM* was translated. Jerald and Sandra Tanner received from Wesley P. Walters a photograph of an original copy of *The Wonders of Nature* that contained a sticker showing it belonged to the library in Manchester, New York (where Smith lived). The library's records confirm that it was checked out by many people in Smith's hometown during the year 1827, which means it must have been very well-known in the area of Palmyra and Manchester (see Tanner and Tanner, *Shadow or Reality?*, 84).

42. Josiah Priest, *The Wonders of Nature and Providence Displayed* (1825 ed.). Quoted in Tanner and Tanner, *Shadow or Reality?*, 84–85. The first passage cited from Priest's volume is taken from page 598; the second from page 469; and the third from page 524.

43. *BOM* (1830 ed.). The first passage cited is taken from page 560 (Ether 10:20, modern edition); the second from page 61 (2 Nephi 1:14, modern edition); and the third from page 471–472 (3 Nephi 8:20-23, modern edition).

44. Ethan Smith, *View of the Hebrews; or the Tribes of Israel in America* (Poultney, VT: 1st ed., 1823; 2nd ed., 1825), 172. Quoted in Persuitte, 107. A searchable text version of *View of the Hebrews* is online at http://www.concordance.com/mormon.htm.

45. Persuitte, 122.

46. An extremely concise look at the many similarities between the *BOM* and *View of the Hebrews* can be found in Sandra Tanner, "Where Did Joseph Smith Get His Ideas for the Book of Mormon?," Internet article online at http://www.utlm.org/onlineresources/bomindianorigins.htm. For a highly detailed and in-depth comparison of the *Book of Mormon* and *View of the Hebrews*, see Persuitte.

47. Ethan Smith. Quoted in Persuitte, 171, 155, 163, 162 (in order of quotations). The first passage cited from Ethan Smith's volume is taken from page 103; the second from pages 232–233; the third from pages 235, 241–242; and the fourth from page 56.

48. *BOM* (1830 ed.). The first passage cited is taken from page 275 (Alma 18:28-29, modern ed.); the second from page 85 (2 Nephi 10:20, modern ed.); the third from page 115 (2 Nephi 29:2, modern ed.); and the fourth from page 104 (2 Nephi 25:17, modern ed.). Regarding Smith's use of the term "Great Spirit," Persuitte makes the following observation: "The problem with this is that the term "Great Spirit" was invented by the European settlers in America to describe their own god to the Indians. Some of the Indians subsequently took up the term for their own use! Therefore, its use in the *Book of Mormon* (which is supposedly a pre-Columbian record) is incongruous and anachronous" (Persuitte, p. 171).

49. According to Mormon historian Andrew Jenson, Oliver Cowdery did not leave Poultney, Vermont for New York until about 1825 (Andrew Jenson, "The Three Witnesses," *HR*, May 1887, vol. 6 nos. 3-5, 196).

50. Ethan Smith was installed as minister of the church on Nov. 21, 1821. Records of the Poultney Congregational Church indicate that on August 2, 1818, a "Mr. Cowdery" (i.e., William) had three of his four daughters (Rebecca, Maria, Lucy, and Phoebe) baptized "on the faith of their mother," which would have been a Mrs. Keziah Pearce Austin, to whom William was wed in 1810 after his first wife died in 1809. Under the date of May 26, 1810, the church's records also reveal that a vote was taken "to give Mrs. Keziah Cowdery a letter of recommendation" (Persuitte, 7, 298, endnote#3).

51. According to Mormon historian Reed Durham, Oliver Cowdery bought a Bible containing the Apocrypha on October 8, 1829: "It was a large family Bible. . . . It was an edition of the Authorized Version 'together with the Apocrypha,' which was located between the two testaments, and was an 1828 edition, printed in Cooperstown, New York, by H. and E. Phinney Company" (Reed C. Durham, Jr., Ph.D. dissertation, "A History of Joseph Smith's Revision of the Bible," BYU, 1965, 25). For more information on the Smith's plagiarism of the Apocrypha, see Jerald Tanner and Sandra Tanner, "Joseph Smith's Use of the Apocrypha," *Salt Lake City Messenger* (#89), December 1995, online at http://www.utlm.org/newsletters/no89.htm.

52. Brodie, 62–63. For an excellent in-depth look at Joseph Smith's plagiarism of the Bible, see Jerald Tanner and Sandra Tanner, *Joseph Smith's Plagiarism of the Bible* (Salt Lake City: ULM, 1998), available for purchase online at http://www.utlm.org/booklist/titles/ub007_ josephsmithsplagiarismofthebible.htm.

53. An extensive listing of *BOM* names/words that are apparently nothing more than variations on Bible names/words is online at http://www.lds-mormon.com/names.shtml. An extensive listing of *BOM* names/words that are apparently nothing more than variations on Apocrypha names/words is online at http://www.utlm.org/newsletters/no89.htm. The following lists only several of the most obvious examples from each site (names from Apocrypha are taken from the King James Version of the Bible, online at http://www.ebible.org/bible/kjv/):

Bible	*Book of Mormon*		*Apocrapha*
Omer (Exodus 16:16)	Omner (Mosiah 27:34)	Nephi (1 Nephi 1:1)	Nephi (2 Maccabees 1:36)
Nahum (Nahum 1:1)	Nahom (1 Nephi 16:34)	Laban (1 Nephi 3:3)	Laban (Judith 8:26)
Gershon (Genesis 46:11)	Jershon (Alma 27:22)	Zedekiah (1 Nephi 1:4)	Zedechias (1 Esdras 1:46)
Helam (2 Samuel 10:16)	Helaman (Mosiah 1:2)	Ezias (Helaman 8:20)	Ezerias / Ezias (1 Esdras 8:1-2)
Ham (Genesis 5:32)	Hem (Mosiah 7:6)		

54. Wesley P. Walters, *The Use of the Old Testament in the Book of Mormon* (Salt Lake City: ULM, 1990), 30. Smith also used terms such as "Methought" (1 Nephi 8:4), which could hardly be considered an accurate rendering of any "Reformed Egyptian" character. This book by Walters is available for purchase online at http://www.utlm.org/booklist/titles/ ub012_useoftheoldtestamentinthebookofmormon.htm.

55. The first passage cited from the Apocrypha is 2 Maccabees 2:23, 26, 28, 31; the second is 1 Maccabees 14:48–49 (cf. 1 Maccabees 8:22; 14:18–19, 27); the third is 2 Maccabees 1:34, 36; the fourth is 2 Esdras 13:1 (see Apocrypha, online at http://www.ebible.org/bible/ kjv/).

56. The first passage cited from the *Book of Mormon* (modern edition) is a compilation from 1 Nephi 1:17, Words of Mormon 3, Mormon 5:9, and Moroni 1:1; the second is 1 Nephi 4:20, 24; the third is 2 Nephi 5:8; and the fourth is 1 Nephi 8:2.

57. The first passage cited from the Bible is Malachi 4:1; the second is Malachi 4:2; the third is Matthew 3:10; the fourth is Acts 8:23; the fifth is Romans 7:24; the sixth is 1 Corinthians 15:58; and the seventh is Galatians 5:1.

58. The first passage cited from the *Book of Mormon* (modern edition) is 1 Nephi 22:15; the second is 2 Nephi 25:13; the third is Alma 5:52; the fourth is Mosiah 27:29; the fifth is 2 Nephi 4:17; the sixth is Mosiah 5:15; and the seventh is Mosiah 23:13.

59. *BOM*, 1830 edition, 444, (Helaman 13:35, modern edition).

60. *BOM*, 1830 edition, 8, (1 Nephi 2:11-12, modern edition).

61. Vogel, vol. 1, 321, footnote #128.

62. *BOM*, 1830 edition, 529–530 (cf. spelling in Mormon 6:2-11, modern edition).

63. See http://www.primenet.com/~heuvelc/bom1830/changes.htm#CAMORA for more information on Moroni and Cumorah.

64. For information on the Italian painter, Moroni, see http://www.lds-mormon.com/names.shtml.

65. For more examples of *BOM* events that correspond to aspects of Joseph Smith's life, see Tanner and Tanner, *Shadow or Reality?*, 85–88.

66. For more examples of these types of errors, see Tanner and Tanner, *Shadow or Reality?*, 92–93.

67. For example, the name modern name "Sam," in the *BOM*, 1830 ed., 69, 71 (2 Nephi 4:11; 5:6, modern edition) and the French word, *adieu*, *BOM*, 1830 ed., 143 (Jacob 7:27, modern edition).

68. For a detailed look at the *Book of Mormon*, see Jerald Tanner and Sandra Tanner, *3,913 Changes in the Book of Mormon* (Salt Lake City: ULM, 1996) available for purchase online at http://www.utlm.org/booklist/titles/ub003_3913changesinthebookofmormon.htm.

69. *HC* (Salt Lake City: Deseret Book Company, 1976/1980), vol. 4, 461. No changes should have been made to the first edition of the *Book of Mormon*. Smith claimed that while he and his "witnesses" to the *BOM* (see Chapter Three, endnote#47) were praying about the volume, a voice spoke from heaven, which told them that the translation of the *BOM* was correct: "[W]e heard a voice from out of the bright light above us, saying, 'These plates have been revealed by the power of God, and they have been translated by the power of God. The translation of them which you have seen is correct, and I command you to bear record of what you now see and hear.'" (*HC*, vol. 1, 54–55). Nevertheless, substantive changes began to made to the volume as early as the 1837 second edition.

70. *BOM*, 1830 ed., 268 (Alma 16:13, modern edition).

71. J.D. Douglas, rev. ed. and Merrill C. Tenney, gen. ed., *The New International Dictionary of the Bible* (Grand Rapids: Zondervan Publishing House, 1987), 972.

72. Thomas D.S. Key, Sc.D., Ed.D. (Biology), Th.D. (1985), "A Biologist Looks at the Book of Mormon," *Journal of the American Scientific Affiliation*, June 1985, XXX-VIII, 3. Dr. Thomas Key, Box 43, East Central Community College, Decatur MS 39227-0129. This article has since been expanded and renamed *The Book Of Mormon In The Light Of Science*. It is sold by Utah Missions, Inc. (UMI), P.O. Box 348, Marlow, OK 73055, 1-800-654-3992, www.umi.org/.

73. Key, 3. In an attempt to reconcile this problem, Mormon apologist John Sorenson has suggested that Smith mistranslated numerous words from the *Book of Mormon* golden plates. For example, *cattle* and *oxen* should have been rendered deer and bison. Moreover, *horses* should also have been translated deer, while *swine* more accurately refers to the wild pig. Other supposed mistranslations also are listed by Sorenson (John L. Sorenson, *An Ancient American Setting for the Book of Mormon* [Salt Lake City: Deseret Book, 1985], 191–276, 299). As appealing as this resolution may be to some Mormons, it is countered by Joseph Smith himself, who claimed that a voice spoke to him from heaven, saying that the translation of the *BOM* was correct (see this chapter, endnote #69).

74. Michael Coe, "Mormons & Archeology: An Outside View," *Dialogue: A Journal of Mormon Thought* (Summer 1973), vol. 8, 46.

75. Michael Coe, letter to William McKeever, Aug. 17,1993, printed in William McKeever, "Yale Anthropologist's Views Remain Unchanged," *Mormonism Researched* (Winter, 1993), 6.

76. Bradley Lepper. Quoted in Ben Fulton, "Burden of Proof," *Weekly Wire*, October 6, 1997, online at http://weeklywire.com/ww/10-06-97/slc_story.html.

77. This original statement from the Smithsonian Institute was released in 1965: "The Smithsonian Institution has never used the *Book of Mormon* in any way as a scientific guide. Smithsonian archeologists see no direct connection between the archeology of the New World and the subject matter of the book," online at http://www.utlm.org/onlineresources/smithsonianletter2.htm. An updated statement (March 1998) was released by the Smithsonian Institution after complaints were received from Mormon apologists associated with FARMS (Foundation for Ancient Research and Mormon Studies), a BYU affiliate dedicated to finding objective evidence that supports the historicity of the *Book of Mormon*. The new statement reads: "Your recent inquiry concerning the Smithsonian Institution's alleged use of the Book of Mormon as a scientific guide has been received in the Smithsonian's Department of Anthropology. The Book of Mormon is a religious document and not a scientific guide. The Smithsonian Institution has never used it in archeological research and any information that you have received to the contrary is incorrect" (Quoted in Richard N. Ostling and Joan K. Ostling, *Mormon America: The Power and the Promise* [San Francisco: Harper San Francisco, 1999], 260–261).

78. Dee F. Green, "Book of Mormon Archeology: the Myths and the Alternatives," *Dialogue: A Journal of Mormon Thought* (Summer 1969), vol. 4, 72–80. Green stated: "The first myth we need to eliminate is that Book of Mormon archaeology exists. . . . no Book of Mormon location is known with reference to modern topography. Biblical archaeology can be studied because we do know where Jerusalem and Jericho were and are, but we do not know where Zarahemla and Bountiful (nor any other location for that matter) [from the *Book of Mormon*] were or are. It would seem then that a concentration on geography should be the first order of business, but . . . years of such an approach has left us empty-handed" (p. 78).

79. For more information on Roberts and his views on the *Book of Mormon*, see Jerald Tanner and Sandra Tanner, "B. H. Robert's Doubts," *Salt Lake City Messenger* (#84), April 1993, online at http://www.utlm.org/newsletters/no84.htm#B.%20H.%20Robert's%20Doubts. For an in-depth look at Ferguson's changing attitudes toward the histpricity of the *Book of Mormon*, see Jerald Tanner and Sandra Tanner, "Ferguson's Two Faces," *Salt Lake City Messenger* (#69), September 1988, online at http://www.utlm.org/newsletters/no69.htm (also Jerald Tanner and Sandra Tanner, "Ferguson's Rejection of the *Book of Mormon* Verified," *Salt Lake City Messenger* (#76), November 1990, online at http://www.utlm.org/newsletters/no76.htm#Ferguson's%20Rejection, and Jerald Tanner and Sandra Tanner, "Quest for the Gold Plates," *Salt Lake City Messenger* (#91), November 1996, online at http://www.utlm.org/newsletters/no91.htm).

80. For a detailed look at Roberts' views and his manuscript, see *An Examination of B.H. Roberts' Secret Manuscript* (Salt Lake City: ULM, 1979), available for purchase online at http://www.utlm.org/booklist/titles/ub070_examinationbhrobertssecretmanuscript.htm.

81. B.H. Roberts, *Studies of the Book of Mormon*, Brigham D. Madsen and Sterling M. McMurrin, eds., (Urbana, IL: University of Illinois Press, 1985), 243. Roberts stated: "[W]as Joseph Smith possessed of a sufficiently vivid and creative imagination as to produce such a work as the Book of Mormon from such materials as have been indicated in the preceding chapters? . . . That such power of imagination would have to be of a high order is conceded; that Joseph Smith possessed such a gift of mind there can be no question" (Roberts, 243). Roberts also wrote: "In the light of this evidence, there can be no doubt as to the possession of a vividly strong, creative imagination by Joseph Smith, the Prophet, an imagination, it could with reason be urged, which, given the suggestions that are found in the 'common knowledge' of accepted American antiquities of the times, supplemented by such a work as Ethan Smith's *View of the Hebrews*, would make it possible for him to create a book such as the Book of Mormon is. . . . If from all that has gone before in Part 1, the view be taken that the Book of Mormon is merely of

human origin . . . if it be assumed that he is the author of it, then it could be said there is much internal evidence in the book itself to sustain such a view. In the first place there is a certain lack of perspective in the things the book relates as history that points quite clearly to an undeveloped mind as their origin. The narrative proceeds in characteristic disregard of conditions necessary to its reasonableness, as if it were a tale told by a child, with utter disregard for consistency" (Roberts, 250, 251).

82. Roberts, 271.

83. Wesley P. Lloyd, *Private Journal of Wesley P. Lloyd*, August 7, 1933, quote is online at http://www.lds-mormon.com/bhrlettr.shtml.

84. Lloyd's quote is online at http://www.lds-mormon.com/bhrlettr.shtml. Mormon church leaders and LDS apologists have desperately tried to dispute the idea that Roberts changed his position on the *Book of Mormon*. For example, representatives of the Mormon-owned and operated FARMS (Foundation for Ancient Research and Mormon Studies), which is the most prestigious of all organizations seeking to defend Latter-day Saint claims, said the editors of *Studies of the Book of Mormon*—Brigham D. Madsen and Sterling M. McMurrin—had misrepresented Roberts' final views. Madsen and McMurrin responded by offering to hold a public panel discussion of the issues. Their offer, however, was refused by members of FARMS, who simply continued to maintain that Roberts was indeed misrepresented and that he was only playing the "devils-advocate" role by making the statements he had made. No documentation was ever provided by FARMS to prove this assertion. Other LDS writers have sought to denounce the Roberts-lost-his-faith opinion by citing several instances of Roberts affirming the *Book of Mormon* after he began his in-depth study of it. But these attempts fail to adequately address some of Roberts' later statements, choosing instead, to concentrate on declarations he made *before* he had reached his final conclusion (see Truman G. Madsen, "B.H. Roberts and the Book of Mormon," *BYU Studies* [Summer 1979,] vol. 19, 427–445.

85. Thomas Stuart Ferguson, *One Fold And One Shepherd* (1962, p. 263). Quoted in Tanner and Tanner, "Ferguson's Two Faces," 3, http://www.utlm.org/newsletters/no69.htm.

86. Quoted in "Ferguson's Two Faces," 3, http://www.utlm.org/newsletters/no69.htm.

87. Thomas Stuart Ferguson, letter to Harold Hougey, June 5, 1972. Quoted in Stan Larson, "The Odyssey of Thomas Stuart Ferguson," *Dialogue: A Journal of Mormon Thought* (Spring 1990), vol. 23, 76.

88. Ferguson, "Written Symposium on Book-of-Mormon Geography: Response of Thomas S. Ferguson to the Norman & Sorenson Papers," 4, 7, 29, reprinted in Jerald Tanner and Sandra Tanner, *Ferguson's Manuscript Revealed* (Salt Lake City: ULM, 1988). In a Feb. 20, 1976 letter to Mr. & Mrs. H. W. Lawrence, Ferguson said the *BOM* to be fictional: "Herewith is a copy of my recent (1975) paper on Book of Mormon matters. . . . It was one of several presented in a written symposium on Book of Mormon georgraphy [sic]. (My thesis is that Book of Mormon geography involves a lot more than playing with topography and terrain.) The real implication of the paper is that you can't set Book of Mormon geography down anywhere—because it is fictional and will never meet the requirements of the dirt-archeology, I should say—what is in the ground will never conform to what is in the book."

89. Thomas Stuart Ferguson, letter dated February 9, 1976.

90. Ferguson, letter dated February 9, 1976.

91. Pierre Agrinier Bach. Quoted in Stan Larson, *Quest for the Gold Plates: Thomas Stuart Ferguson's Archaeological Search for the Book of Mormon* (Salt Lake City: Freethinker Press, 1996), 158 . Larson is CEO of Freethinker Press, and curator for the Utah History, Philosophy, and Religion Archives at the Marriott Library, University of Utah; cf. Tanner and Tanner, "Quest for the Gold Plates," online at http://www.utlm.org/newsletters/no91.htm.

92. Larson, 158; cf. Tanner and Tanner, "Quest for the Gold Plates," online at http://www.utlm.org/newsletters/no91.htm.

93. For a highly detailed, complex, and scholarly study on the *Book of Mormon*, see Brent Lee Metcalfe, ed., *New Approaches to the Book of Mormon* (Salt Lake City: Signature Books, 1993).

94. Erickson, 31–32.

CHAPTER FIVE: PEOPLE OF ZION

1. "The Pilgrim's Hymn," *E&MS*, July 1832, vol. 1, no. 2, 16, photomechanical reprint (1969), republished by Eugene Wagner (Basil, Switzerland), online at http://www.centerplace.org/history/ems/v1n01.htm. All volumes are online at http://www.centerplace.org/history/ems/vol1.htm.

2. There is some confusion over exactly where the church was organized. Some accounts place the event in Manchester, New York. Others place it in Fayette, New York. The existing evidence favors the Manchester location (see H. Michael Marquardt, "An Appraisal of Manchester as Location for the Organization of the Church," *Sunstone* (February 1992), vol. 16, 56. It also should be noted that the Mormon church's official name evolved from The Church of Christ (April 1830) to The Church of the Latter Day Saints (May 1834) to The Church of Jesus Christ of Latter-day Saints (April 1838). The church's first members were Joseph Smith, Jr., Hyrum Smith, Samuel Harrison Smith, Oliver Cowdery, Peter Whitmer Jr., and David Whitmer. Within days Joseph Smith, Sr., Lucy Mack Smith, Martin Harris, Orrin Porter Rockwell, and Solomon Chamberlain joined the flock.

3. Dean May, "A Demographic Portrait of the Mormons, 1830–1980," *After 150 Years: The Latter-day Saints in Sesquicentennial Perspective*, Thomas G. Alexander and Jessie L. Embry, eds. (Provo: Charles Redd Center for Western Studies, 1983), reprinted in D. Michael Quinn, ed., *The New Mormon History* (Salt Lake City: Signature Books, 1992), 121. Interestingly, Joseph's own wife, Emma, failed to join the church until six weeks after it had been organized. According to Fawn Brodie's research in *No Man Knows My History* (New York: Vintage Books, 1995; original edition by Alfred A. Knopf, 1945), Emma was not at all interested in Joseph starting a new church, nor was she comfortable with the prospect of living off "the dubious and intermittent charity of Joseph's followers" (Brodie, 89). Emma finally joined the church only after Smith spoke a revelation from "God" that was specifically addressed to her. It basically gave Emma two choices: 1) stay with Joseph, toe the line by joining the church, and be financially provided for "from the Church"; or 2) continue in rebellion, and as a result, be damned ("A Revelation to Emma, given in Harmony; Pennsylvania, July, 1830," XXVI:8, *Book of Commandments* [Zion: W.W. Phelps, 1833], 58). In order to remove any suggestion that Smith originally had planned to make his livelihood "from the church" (i.e., live off the money of his followers), this revelation was changed when reprinted in the 1835 edition of the *Doctrine and Covenants*—the phrase "from the church" was changed to "in the church" (*D&C* 48:2).

4. Smith's revelations were first released in book form as the *Book of Commandments* (1833). They were later re-published as the *Doctrine and Covenants* (1835). Because Smith's revelations allegedly came verbatim from the Lord, Joseph was viewed as a mouthpiece for God, whose words were recorded as nothing less than holy scripture. Nevertheless, Smith's revelations underwent hundreds of revisions after initially being transcribed. Some of these changes were made decades after he had died. All of the alterations appeared in subsequent editions of the *Doctrine and Covenants* with no footnoting to indicate the textual revisions, many of which greatly altered the meaning of the revelation. Sometimes the revisions served to cover-up original doctrines, false prophecies, and other material embarrassing to church leaders. This is important for the reader to bear in mind when reviewing endnotes throughout the remainder of this book. Modern editions of the *D&C* will be cited when possible. However, in cases where

modern editions of the *D&C* have been significantly altered from the original revelations as printed in the *BOC*, the *BOC* will be cited. For an in-depth look at these
changes, see H. Michael Marquardt, *The Joseph Smith Revelations: Text & Commentary*
(Salt Lake City: Signature Books, 1999) and Jerald Tanner and Sandra Tanner, *Mormonism: Shadow or Reality?* (Salt Lake City: UTL, 1987), 14–31D.

5. *D&C* 6:1-2, 6. This is one of the Mormon church's official "Standard Works" (i.e., books
    of holy scripture). The four standard works are the *Book of Mormon* (BOM), *Doctrine
    and Covenants (D&C)*, *Pearl of Great Price*, and the King James Version of the Bible.

6. University of San Diego, "The Burned-Over District" (Civil War Index), online at
    http://history.acusd.edu/gen/civilwar/01/burned.html.

7. John L. Brooke, *The Refiner's Fire: The Making of Mormon Cosmology, 1644–1844* (New
    York: Cambridge University press, 1994; paperback edition, 1996), 65.

8. Smith's young age might have been yet another factor in his success. When he organ-
    ized the church in April 1830, he was only 24-years-old. Like the young preachers who
    attracted thousands of college-aged persons during the "Jesus Movement" of the late
    1960s to early 1970s, Smith attracted the youth of his day. More than eighty percent of
    Mormon converts before 1846 were under the age of thirty, with the median age falling
    between twenty and twenty-five (see Kenneth H. Winn, *Exiles in a Land of Liberty*
    [Chapel Hill, NC: University of North Carolina Press, 1989], 47.

9. Marvin S. Hill, "Quest for Refuge: An Hypothesis as to the Social Origins and Nature of
    the Mormon Political Kingdom," *Journal of Mormon History* (1975), vol. 2, 4–5.

10. Hill, 13. Hill also notes: "Such leaders as Wilford Woodruff, Brigham Young, Lyman
    Wight, Parley and Orson Pratt, John Taylor, and Lorenzo Snow, to say nothing of the
    members of the Smith family, were poor farmers, or artisans and down on their luck at
    the time of conversion (see Hill, 13, footnote #57). According to D. Michael Quinn, "40
    per cent of those appointed to high office by Joseph Smith had little education, and that
    one third of the early leaders had been Methodists and nearly that many members of no
    church" ("Organizational Development and Social Origins of the Mormon Hierarch,
    1832–1932: A Prosopographical Study," [M.A. thesis, University of Utah, 1973], 102, 11,
    cited in Hill, 13).

11. Joseph himself admitted as much in his 1832 handwritten account of the First Vision,
    wherein he explains that before having any visions of God, he found that mankind "did
    not come unto the Lord but that they had apostatised [sic] from the true and liveing [sic]
    faith and there was no society or denomination that built upon the gospel of Jesus Christ
    as recorded in the new testament" (see Joseph Smith, *1832 History*, original manuscript,
    contained in Joseph Smith Letterbook 1, 1–6, Joseph Smith Papers, LDSCA, reprinted in
    Dean C. Jessee, ed., *The Papers of Joseph Smith* [Salt Lake City: Deseret Book Company,
    1989], vol. 1, 5; cf. Dan Vogel, ed., *Early Mormon Documents* [Salt Lake City: Signature
    Books, 1996], vol. 1, 28).

12. Martin Harris, September 4, 1870, as dictated by Martin Harris to Edward Stevenson,
    reprinted in Dan Vogel, ed., *Early Mormon Documents* (Salt Lake City: Signature Books,
    1998), vol. 2, 331–332.

13. W.W. Phelps, letter to Oliver Cowdery, December 25, 1834, "Letter No. 4," *MS&AD*, Feb-
    ruary 1835, vol. 1, no. 5, 65–67, reprinted in Dan Vogel, ed., *Early Mormon Documents*
    (Salt Lake City: Signature Books, 2000), vol. 3, 29.

14. Thomas B. Marsh, "History of Thomas Baldwin Marsh (written by himself in Great Salt
    Lake City, November 1857)," *Manuscript History of Brigham Young*, vol. G, 107–112,
    LDSCA. Published in Thomas B. Marsh, "History of Thos. Baldwin Marsh," *Deseret News*,
    March 24, 1858, vol. 8, 18, reprinted in *MS*, June 11, 1864, vol. 26, 375 and in Vogel, vol.
    3, 347. Smith's longtime friend, Joseph Knight, previous to the publication of the *BOM*,
    already called himself a "Restorationar"—i.e., one who "wished to restore the doctrines
    and practices of the new Testament church and eliminate all else" (Richard L. Bushman,

Joseph Smith and the beginnings of Mormonism [Urbana: University of Illinois Press, 1984], 154).

15. Lucy Mack Smith, *Biographical Sketches of Joseph Smith the Prophet, and His Progenitors for many Generations* [Liverpool: S.W. Richards, 1853], 37, reprinted in Vogel, vol. 1, 234. Lucy confirmed her views in an 1831 letter to her brother, Solomon Mack. She wrote: "[W]e can see the situation in which the world now stands that the eyes of the whole world are blinded, that the churches have all become corrupted, yea every church upon the face of the earth; that the Gospel of Christ is nowhere preached" (Lucy Mack Smith, letter to Solomon Mack, January 6, 1831, reprinted in Vogel, vol. 1, 216). Lucy later reversed herself on this point and joined the Presbyterians. But this may have been in reaction to the death of her son, Alvin, rather than in response to sincere belief in Presbyterianism.

16. Brodie, 5.

17. *BOM*, Mormon 8:22-41, modern edition.

18. *D&C* 10:56, modern edition; cf. textual differences, *BOC* (IX:14), 26.

19. *BOC* (IV:5), 11; cf. textual differences in *D&C* 5:18-19.

20. *D&C* 5:9-10; cf. textual differences in *BOC* (IV:4), 10-11.

21. *D&C*, 24:1, modern edition; cf. *BOM*, modern ed., Mormon 8:14-15.

22. Brigham Young, July 26, 1857 and September 13, 1857, *JOD* (Liverpool: Asa Calking, 1858; lithographed reprint of original edition, 1966), vol. 5, 73, 229; Brigham Young, September 16, 1860 and October 7, 1860, *JOD* (Liverpool: George Q. Cannon, 1861; lithographed reprint of original edition, 1966), vol. 8, 171, 199.

23. John Taylor, November 1, 1857 and January 17, 1858, *JOD* (Liverpool: Asa Calkin, 1859; lithographed reprint of original edition, 1966), vol. 6, 25, 167; John Taylor, May 6, 1870, *JOD* (Liverpool: Horace S. Eldredge, 1871; lithographed reprint of original edition, 1966)), vol. 13, 225.

24. Bruce McConkie, *Mormon Doctrine* (Salt Lake City: Bookcraft, 1958; second edition, 1966), 132.

25. Kent P. Jackson, "Early Signs of the Apostasy," *Ensign*, December 1984, 9.

26. Using *Webster's Third New International Dictionary*, Quinn defines the "occult" and "magic" as follows: "[occult] 'deliberately kept hidden, not revealed to others, secret, undisclosed; not to be apprehended or understood, demanding more than ordinary perception or knowledge, abstruse, mysterious, recondite; hidden from view, not able to be seen, concealed; of, relating to, or dealing in matters regarded as involving the action or influence of supernatural agencies or some secret knowledge of them, not manifest or detectable by clinical methods alone.' For magic, Webster's states: 'the use of means (as ceremonies, charms, spells) that are believed to have supernatural power to cause a supernatural being to produce or prevent a particular result (as rain, death, healing) considered not obtainable by natural means and that also include the arts of divination, incantation, sympathetic magic ['magic based on the assumption that a person or thing can be supernaturally affected through its name or an object (as a nail paring, image, or dancer) representing it'], and thaumaturgy ['the performance of miracles'], control of natural forces by the typically direct action of rites, objects, materials, or words considered supernaturally potent; an extraordinary power or influence seemingly from a supernatural source; something that seems to cast a spell or to give an effect of otherworldliness, enchantment; the art of producing unusual illusions by legerdemain" (D. Michael Quinn, *Early Mormonism and the Magic World View* [Salt Lake City: Signature Books, 1998], xxiii).

27. Quinn, *Early Mormonism*, 239.

28. Quinn, *Early Mormonism*, xxii.

29. Brooke, 71-72

30. Brooke, 4.

31. Quinn, *Early Mormonism*, 247–258; cf. Ogden Kraut, *Seers and Seer Stones*, 55, online at http://www.kingdomofzion.org/doctrines/kraut/books/Seers%20&%20Seer%20Stones. txt. Joseph's mother, Lucy Mack Smith, apparently used seer stones as well, according to New York neighbor Samantha Payne: "[Lucy] once came to my mother to get a stone the children had found, of curious shape. She wanted to use it as a peepstone" (Samantha Payne, Affidavit, June 29, 1881, Ontario County Clerk's Office, Canandaigua, New York, published in *Ontario County Times*, July 27, 1881, 3, photocopy in fd 31, box 149, Marquardt papers, Marriott Library)

32. Samuel F. Whitney, statement of March 6, 1885, reprinted in A. B. Deming, ed., *Naked Truths About Mormonism* (January 1888), vol. 1, no. 1, 3, online at http://www. lavazone2.com/dbroadhu/CA/natruths.htm.

33. Quinn, *Early Mormonism*, 248–251.

34. Elaine Mullins, "Statement by Elaine Mullins," reprinted in Kraut, 55, online at http://www.kingdomofzion.org/doctrines/kraut/books/Seers%20&%20Seer%20Stones. txt. It is interesting to note that Pulsipher's daughter eventually passed this peep stone on to her daughter to use, which she did, until someone asked her to try seeing Satan in it. She did so, "but that was the last time that stone ever worked for anyone" (Quinn, *Early Mormonism*, 249.)

35. Kraut, 62, see endnote #31 for Internet reference; cf. Quinn, *Early Mormonism*, 250.

36. Quinn, *Early Mormonism*, 294–295.

37. Quinn, *Early Mormonism*, 39.

38. Quinn, *Early Mormonism*, 33.

39. There is evidence that Joseph Smith, Sr. was connected to this group. If so, it would further explain his obsession with money-digging. For information on Smith's possible link to the New Israelites, see and Barnes Frisbie, *The History of Middleton, Vermont in Three Discourses* . . . (Rutland, VT: Tuttle & Co., Printers, 1867), 43–64; also see Quinn, *Early Mormonism*, 123.

40. Quinn, *Early Mormonism*, 35.

41. Quinn, *Early Mormonism*, 35.

42. Frisbie, 56–59. Quoted in Brooke, 103.

43. Frisbie, 56–59. Quoted in Brooke, 103.

44. Frisbie, 56–59. Quoted in Brooke, 103

45. Brooke, 103

46. Quinn, *Early Mormonism*, 121.

47. *BOC* (VII:3), 19. When this revelation was re-published in the *D&C*, it was substantially changed to conceal the original statement about Oliver working with the divining rod, an obvious reference to an occult practice. Modern editions of the *D&C* read: "[Y]ou have another gift, which is the gift of Aaron; behold, it has told you many things; Behold, there is no other power, save the power of God, that can cause this gift of Aaron to be with you" (*D&C* 8:6-7, modern edition).

48. Marvin S. Hill, "Brodie Revisted: A Reappraisal," *Dialogue: A Journal of Mormon Thought* (Winter 1972), vol. 7, 78.

49. Stanley B. Kimball, *Heber C. Kimball: Mormon Patriarch and Pioneer* (Urbana: University of Illinois Press, 1981), 248–249.

50. Kimball, 256 (see footnote); cf. Brooke, 143.

51. Anthon H. Lund, *Anthon H. Lund Journal*, under July 5, 1901. Lund's journal reads: "[I]n the revelation to Oliver Cowdery in May 1829, Bro. [B. H.] Roberts said that the gift which the Lord says he has in his hand meant a stick which was like Aaron's Rod. It is said Bro. Phineas Young [brother-in-law of Oliver Cowdery and brother of Brigham Young] got it from him [Cowdery] and gave it to President Young who had it with him when he arrived in this [Salt Lake] valley and that it was with that stick that he pointed out where the Temple should be built" (Quoted in D. Michael Quinn, *BYU Studies*, Fall 1978, vol. 18, 82, cited in Jerald Tanner and Sandra Tanner, *The Changing World of Mormonism*

[Chicago: Moody, 1981], 87, online at http://www.utlm.org/onlinebooks/changech4. htm).

52. Description of Artifact 1076, Donation Book I, Daughters of Utah Pioneers Museum, Salt Lake City, UT. Cited in Quinn, *Early Mormonism*, 271.

53. Quinn, *Early Mormonism*, 107, 113,115.

54. Quinn, *Early Mormonism*, 111.

55. Quinn, *Early Mormonism*, 110

56. Quinn, *Early Mormonism*, 104–105, 115.

57. Quinn, *Early Mormonism*, 104, 108, 112.

58. Quinn, *Early Mormonism*, 176. The popularity of astrology among Mormons continued well into the 1970–80s, until church authorities began criticizing it as incompatible with the LDS faith. Nevertheless, in 1998, Apostle David B. Haight "reinvoked the astrological principle that people should 'do nothing without the assistance of the moon'" (Quinn, *Early Mormonism*, 291).

59. Since the first century Christians have looked forward to this event because it will mark not only their savior's reappearance (Titus 2:13), but the resurrection of the dead, the final judgment of every soul, and the establishment of a "new heaven and a new earth" (Rev. 21). Christians further hold that every follower of Jesus will receive a "glorified" (i.e., perfected) body designed for immortality (1 Cor. 15:50–53). Christ's second advent also will cause the world, along with its accompanying evil and suffering, to end. In reference to this day of destruction, the apostle Paul said that the heavens would pass away "with a roar" and that the elements would be "destroyed with intense heat" (2 Peter 3:10–13).

60. Dan Erickson, *As A Thief in the Night* (Salt Lake City: Signature Books, 1998), 18.

61. *BOM*, 1830 edition, 535. As far back as August 28, 1830, Joseph had been announcing that doomsday was very near. In a letter to followers at Colesville, New York, he wrote: "[T]he day of your deliverance is not far distant for the judgements [sic] of the Lord are already abroad in the earth and the cold hand of death will soon pass through your neighborhood, and sweep away some of your most bitter enemies. . . . [T]he day is fast hastening on when the restoration of all things shall be fulfilled (Joseph Smith, letter to the Colesville Saints, August 28, 1830. As copied by Newel Knight, *Newel Knight Journal*, 132–136, reprinted in Vogel, vol. 1, 14).

62. Parley P. Pratt, *Autobiography of Parley P. Pratt*, Parley P. Pratt, Jr., ed. (New York: Russell Brothers, 1874; modern reprint in Salt Lake City: Deseret Book Company, 1979), 39.

63. Phineas Howe Young, "History of Brigham Young," *MS*, June 13, 1863, vol. 25, 375, reprinted in Vogel, vol. 3, 353.

64. Russell Chandler, *Doomsday* (Ann Arbor, MI: Servant Publications, 1993), 71.

65. Richard Abanes, *End Time Visions: The Road to Armageddon?* (New York: Four Walls Eight Windows, 1998; paperback edition, 1999, published as *End-Time Visions: The Doomsday Obsession* [Nashville: Broadman & Holman, 1999]), 209.

66. Nathan O. Hatch, *The Democratization of American Christianity* (New Haven CT: Yale University Press, 1989), 184; Ernest R. Sandeen, *The Roots of Fundamentalism British and American Millenarianism 1800–1930* (Chicago: University of Chicago Press, 1970), 42.

67. Joseph Smith, letter to George A. Smith. Quoted in Donna Hill, *Joseph Smith: The First Mormon* (Salt Lake City: Signature Books, 1999), 83-84.

68. *Wayne Sentinel*, October 23, 1823. Quoted in Marvin S. Hill, *Quest for Refuge: The Mormon Flight from American Pluralism* (Salt Lake City: Signature Books, 1989), 8.

69. Cosma Shalizi, "Millennarianism," online at http://www.santafe.edu/~shalizi/ notebooks/millenarian.html.

70. Abanes, 304–325; cf. Joseph M. Hallman, "God and the End of Civilization," *American Journal of Theology and Philosophy* (Sept. 1983), vol. 4, 114, Michael Barkun, *Crucible of the Millennium: The Burned-Over District of New York in the 1840s* (Syracuse: Syracuse University Press, 1986), 9–10.

71. According to the 1883 volume *American Progress, or The Great Events of the Greatest Century* by R. M. Devens, Miller published a series of sixteen articles in the *Vermont Telegraph* (p. 308). However, according to the 1990 *Dictionary of Christianity in America*, Miller only published eight articles in the *Vermont Telegraph* (p. 740). The discrepancy may be the result of how the editors of these two reference volumes counted the various segments of the Miller's articles. For an in-depth look at the story of Miller and his followers, see Abanes, 209–228.

72. W.W. Phelps, letter to E.D. Howe, January 15, 1831, in E.D. Howe, *Mormonism Unvailed* (Painesville, OH: author, 1834), 274, online at http://www.solomonspalding.com/docs/1834howf.htm#pg274. This entire volume is online at http://www.solomonspalding.com/docs/1834howb.htm. A searchable text version is online at http://www.concordance.com/mormon.htm.

73. Albert Chandler, letter to William Linn, December 22, 1898, reprinted in Vogel, vol. 3, 222.

74. Chandler, reprinted in Vogel, vol. 3, 222–223.

75. Nathaniel W. Howell and Others, letter to Ancil Beach, Walter Hubbell Collection, 1831–1833 Correspondence, Princeton University Library, Princeton, New Jersey, reprinted in Vogel, vol. 3, 15.

76. Calvin Stoddard. Cited in Stephen S. Harding, letter to Thomas Gregg, February 1882, originally reproduced in Thomas Gregg, *The Prophet of Palmyra* (New York: John B. Aldeen, 1890), 34–56, reprinted in Vogel, vol. 3, 162.

77. Oliver Cowdery. Cited in Ashbel Kitchell, *Ashbel Kitchell Journal*. This individual, a Shaker, noted in his journal that among the missionaries who visited his village (situated a short distance east of Cleveland, Ohio) was "Oliver Lowdree [Cowdery]." Copy in Elisha D. Blakeman, *Elisha D. Blakeman Journal*, Shaker Museum, Old Chatham, New York.

78. Joseph Smith alluded to these events in his December 1830 letter to the Colesville, New York Saints. Joseph Smith, letter to the Colesville Saints, December 2, 1830, as copied by Newel Knight, *Newel Knight Journal*, 197–207, reprinted in Vogel, 1, 20.

79. Joseph Smith, letter to Colesville, reprinted in Vogel, vol. 1, 21.

80. Joseph Smith, letter to Colesville, reprinted in Vogel, vol. 1, 21.

81. *BOC* (Preface, I:3), 4.

82. *BOC* (XXIX:10, 18–24), 62–63. Joseph's mother stressed her son's teaching in much plainer terms, simply explaining that all who rejected the *BOM* would be cursed and receive God's wrathful punishment on the fast-approaching day of judgment (see Lucy Mack Smith, letter to Soloman Mack, Jr., January 6, 1831, LDSCA, reprinted in Vogel, 1, 215.).

83. *BOC* (XXXIX:1–4), 79–80. James Gordon Bennett, in his 1831 Diary, confirmed that Smith and his followers left the Palmyra/Manchester area because the people there "would not pay any attention to them" (James Gordon Bennett, *James Gordon Bennett Diary*, under August 7, 1831. Quoted in Leonard J. Arrington, "James Gordon Bennett's 1831 Report on 'The Mormonites,'" *BYU Studies* [Spring 1970], vol. 10, 355).

84. Rigdon subsequently converted most of his own church to Mormonism. In a letter to E.D. Howe, W.W. Phelps stated that Rigdon told him he believed Mormonism was true by the power of the Holy Ghost, which again had been given to man "in preparation for the millennium" (W.W. Phelps, letter to Howe, reprinted in Vogel, vol. 3, 7).

85. Joseph Smith, letter to Colesville, reprinted in Vogel, vol. 1, 21.

86. *BOC* (XL:10), 81; *D&C* 38:12.

87. *BOC* (XLI:8, 14, 19–20, 23), 85–87.

88. *The Telegraph* [Painesville, Ohio], March 15, 1831, vol. 2, no. 39, see this article and other rare newspaper stories from the period online at http://www.lavazone2.com/dbroadhu/OH/paintel2.htm#031531.

89. George A. Smith, May 11, 1862, *JOD* (Liverpool: George Q. Cannon, 1862; lithographed reprint of original edition, 1966), vol. 9, 346.

90. John Whitmer, *The Book of John Whitmer Kept by Commandment: Being an History of the Church of Jesus Christ from 1831–1838*, typescript by Pauline Hancock, BYU-A. Holograph located in RLDSCA, online at http://www.centerplace.org/history/misc/jwhitmer.htm. This text is now published in Bruce N. Westergren, ed., *From Historian to Dissident: The Book of John Whitmer* (Salt Lake City: Signature Books, 1995).

91. Erickson, 64.

92. *BOC* (XXX:9), 68; *D&C* 28:9.

93. Jesse Townsend, letter to Phineas Stiles, December 24, 1833, reprinted in Vogel, vol. 3, 23.

94. *BOC* (LXV:27), 159.

95. *BOC* (XLIII:9), 88.

96. *BOC* (XVI:13–21, 27, 33–39), 40–42.

97. This text is now included in the LDS church's *Pearl of Great Price* as the *Book of Moses*.

98. The Aaronic Priesthood holds "the keys of the ministering of angels," and members who hold it are to watch over the church, teach the gospel, and perform baptism.

99. Brooke, 193.

100. Joseph Smith, *Far West Record*, October 25, 1831. Quoted in Lauritz G. Peterson, "The Kirtland Temple," *BYU Studies* (Summer 1972), vol. 12, 401; cf. Brooke, 193–194.

101. *BOC* (XLV: 24, 31, 36), 98–99.

102. *BOC* (XLVIII:59), 110 ; cf. *D&C* 45:66.

103. *BOC* (LIV:43), 127; cf. *D&C* 52: 42.

104. *BOC* (LIX:64), 138; cf. *D&C* 58:52.

105. *BOC* (LIX:45), 136; cf. *D&C* 58:35. Martin Harris complied to Joseph's command, and as a result, ended up dying a pauper many years later.

106. *D&C* 64:23.

107. *BOC* (XLIV:26–30), 92–93; cf. *D&C* 42:29–36. Although this system allowed each person to "technically" retain control of their property, each individual was ultimately responsible to the church for how that property was used (Thomas G. Alexander, "An Ambiguous Heritage," *Dialogue: A Journal of Mormon Thought* [Autumn 1967], vol. 2, 127).

108. *BOC* (LVIII:19–20), 132: cf. *D&C* 56:16.

109. *BOC* (LIX:38), 136; cf. *D&C* 58:29.

110. William McLellin, letter to relatives, August 4, 1832, typescript, RLDSCA, Independence, Missouri, see "History and Selected Writing, online at http://www.math.byu.edu/~smithw/Lds/LDS/Early-Saints/Mcllelin.html.

111. *D&C* 57:1–3. By 1826, Jackson County was founded and Independence became the county seat in 1827.

112. *D&C* 52:42.

113. Ezra Booth, "Letter II," *Ohio Star*, in Howe, 180, http://www.solomonspalding.com/docs/1834howe.htm#pg180.

114. Erickson, 102.

CHAPTER SIX: NO REST FOR THE RIGHTEOUS

1. Martin Harris, handwritten statements. Quoted in E.D. Howe, *Mormonism Unvailed* (Painesville, Ohio: E.D. Howe, 1834), 14, online at http://www.solomonspalding.com/docs/1834howc.htm#pg014. This entire volume is online at http://www.solomon spalding.com/docs/1834 howb.htm. A searchable text version is online at http://www.concordance.com/mormon.htm.

2. In February 1832, for example, Smith and Sidney Rigdon supposedly had a joint vision of the afterlife, which appeared to them as three separate kingdoms—telestial, terrestrial, and celestial—each having its own degree of glory (*D&C* 76:70–98). The first degree of glory, which provides a very limited amount of glory/reward, is reserved for non–Mormons whose lives are marked primarily by immorality. The second degree,

which offers a slightly greater glory/reward, is granted to non-Mormons and Mormons alike who live good lives marked primarily by kindness, goodness, and trying to live the best life possible. Finally, the third degree, which is basically the highest heaven attainable, is reserved for faithful Mormons who lived an exemplary life as "priests of the Most High, after the order of Melchizadeck."

3. In July 1831, Smith gave the following revelation: "[T]he land of Missouri, which is the land which I have appointed and consecrated for the gathering of the saints. Wherefore, this is the land of promise, and the place for the city of Zion. And thus saith the Lord your God, if you will receive wisdom here is wisdom. Behold, the place which is now called Independence is the center place" (*D&C* 57: 1–3).

4. W.W. Phelps, "To Man," *E&MS*, June 1832, vol. 1, no. 1, 6, photomechanical reprint (1969), republished by Eugene Wagner (Basil, Switzerland), online at http://www. centerplace.org/history/ems/v1n01.htm. All volumes are online at http://www. centerplace.org/history/ems/vol1.htm.

5. *Western Monitor* (Fayette, Missouri), August 2, 1833. Quoted in Fawn M. Brodie, *No Man Knows My History* (New York: Vintage Books, 1995; original edition by Alfred A. Knopf, 1945), 131.

6. There are many examples of early converts to Mormonism explaining that they came to "know" Smith's claims were valid by revelation and/or and inner feeling that the new faith was true. Oliver Cowdery, for instance, had such an experience when he decided to pray about the validity of Smith's claims. He subsequently told Smith that "the Lord manifested to him that they were true . . . [A]fter this revelation having been given he knew that the work was true" (Joseph Smith, "History of Joseph Smith—Continued," *T&S*, July 15, 1842, vol. 3, no. 18, 853). According to Joseph, his claims also were accepted by his brother, Samuel H. Smith, who like Cowdery, "obtained revelations for himself sufficient to convince him of the truth of our assertions" (Joseph Smith, "History of Joseph Smith—Continued," *T&S*, August 1, 1842, vol. 3, no. 19, 866).

7. Letter to Editor, *Ohio Atlas*, March 18, 1836, reprinted in "Mormonism," *Painesville Telegraph*, May 20, 1836, online at http://www.lavazone2.com/dbroadhu/OH/paintel5.htm.

8. Citizens of Jackson County, Anti-Mormon Manifesto (c. July 18, 1833). Quoted in "To His Excellency, Daniel Dunklin, Governor of the State of Missouri," *E&MS* (Kirtland Edition), December 1833, vol. 2, no. 15, 114. This periodical, after having been destroyed in Jackson County, relocated to Kirtland, where it resumed publication.

9. Kenneth H. Winn, *Exiles in a Land of Liberty* (Chapel Hill, NC: University of North Carolina Press, 1989), 90.

10. *BOC* (XLIV:32), 93.

11. Winn, 90.

12. "The Last Days," *E&MS*, February 1833, vol. 1, no. 10, 65.

13. *D&C* 84:51-53. In 1840, Grant Underwood—associate professor of religion at BYU (Provo)—agrees, stating: "[T]he Saints used the word 'wicked' as a sort of generic term for all unbelievers, regardless of their personal ethics" (Grant Underwood, *The Millenarian World of Early Mormonism* [Urbana: University of Illinois Press, 1993], 44). Parley Pratt defined the "wicked" as all people who "were not of the Kingdom of God" (Parley P. Pratt, *An Answer to Mr. William Hewitt's Tract Against the Latter-day Saints* [Manchester, U.K.: W.R. Thomas, 1840], 8).

14. Dan Erickson, *As A Thief in the Night* (Salt Lake City: Signature Books, 1998), 55.

15. James West Davidson, *The Logic of Millennial Thought: Eighteenth-Century New England* (New Haven, CT: Yale University Press, 1977), 163–65, 281–87. Cited in Erickson, 55; cf. Grant Underwood, "Millennarianism and the Early Mormon Mind," *Journal of Mormon History* (1982), vol. 9, 43. Several other sources that discuss this issue are listed in Erickson's book (see Erickson, 55, footnote #95).

16. Erickson, 55.

17. Mormons also drew a parallel between themselves and righteous Noah, who had been

mocked by his neighbors for building an ark. An 1841 article in the LDS publication *Times and Seasons* explained that *"precisely* as it was" in the days of Noah, so it would be in the days of earth's final days before Christ's second coming: "Revelations shall preceed [sic] his coming, the whole world shall ridicule them and cast them off, for so it was in the days of Noah, and the consequences were, inevitable destruction; and so it will be with this generation, the righteous only, will be saved" ("Truth Prevailing," *T&S*, March 15, 1841, vol. 2, no. 10, 351).

18. D. Michael Quinn. Quoted by Vern Anderson, *Klamath Falls Herald and News*, January 20, 1995, cited in Jerald Tanner and Sandra Tanner, "Quinn's New Book," *Salt Lake City Messenger* (#88), May 1995, 4, online at http://www.utlm.org/newsletters/no88.htm.

19. "Israel Will Be Gathered," *E&MS*, June 1833, vol. 2, no. 13, 101, which mentions the gathering of Indians by the government as a sign of the last days; cf. *HC* (Salt Lake City: Deseret Book Company, 1976/1980), vol. 2, 358–362 and Brodie, 121.

20. Brodie, 121.

21. Erickson, 96; cf. *Book of Mormon*, 3 Nephi 20:10–22 and 21:14, 22–25, modern edition.

22. Howe, 145–46, 197. In his 1842 report to Iowa's governor, Indian agent Henry King clearly expressed the prevailing fears among non-Mormons scattered throughout the western frontier: "[F]rom all that I can learn from the leading men among the *Mormons* and from various other sources that a grand conspiracy is about to be entered into between the Mormons and Indians to destroy all white settlements on the frontier" (John King, letter to John Chambers, July 14, 1843, as cited in Ronald W. Walker, "Seeking the 'Remnant': The Native American During the Joseph Smith Period," *Journal of Mormon History* (Spring 1993), vol. 19, 1–33; see Underwood, 81.

23. Donna Hill, *Joseph Smith: The First Mormon* (Midvale, UT: Signature Books, 1999), 135.

24. Winn, 93.

25. See the Bible (Is. 5:26, 27:1–12, 51:11; Jer. 31:10, 50:19; Ezek. 28:25, 37:12, 21, 27), the *BOM* (1 Nephi 10:14, 19:16, 21:18), and *D&C* (29:7, 39:11; 77:14). The Mormon *Articles of Faith* explain: "We believe in the literal gathering of Israel" (*AOF*, #10, see *PGP*; cf. *HC*, vol. 4, 535–541).

26. Underwood, 30.

27. Brigham Young, April 8, 1855, *JOD* (Liverpool: F.D. Richard, 1855; lithographed reprint of original edition, 1966), vol. 2, 269.

28. Young, in *JOD*, vol. 2, 268–269. Young declared: "It is Ephraim that I have been searching for all the days of my preaching, and that is the blood which ran in my veins when I embraced the Gospel."

29. *D&C* 64:36. Another important revelation linked to the issue of literal descent from Israel is *D&C* 86:8–10, which states that the Mormon priesthood has continued through history via the lineage of Israel. According to this revelation, it will go on being passed down from father to son until the "restoration of all things."

30. *HC*, vol. 3, 380.

31. Young, in *JOD*, vol. 2, 269.

32. Dean L. May, "A Demographic Portrait of the Mormons, 1830–1980," in Thomas G. Alexander and Jessie L. Embry, ed., *After 150 Years: The Latter-day Saints in Sesquicentennial Perspective* (Provo, UT: Charles Redd Center for Western Studies, 1983), 39–69. By 1845/46, there were 30,000–50,000 British members worldwide. By 1870, nearly twenty-five years after the Mormons had fled to Utah, one-third of the population of Salt Lake City had been born in Britain and the church had baptized nearly 100,000 people in England (see Underwood, 197, footnote#1 and Erickson, 82).

33. See Jerald Tanner and Sandra Tanner, "Excommunication: Mormon Leader Expelled After Charging Church with Racism," *Salt Lake City Messenger* (#73), October 1989, online at http://www.utlm.org/newsletters/no73.htm.

34. "A Prophecy Given to the Church of Christ, March 7, 1831," *E&MS*, June 1832, vol. 1, no. 1, 2.

35. "The Far West," *E&MS*, October 1832, vol. 1, no. 5, 37.

36. "The Indian," *E&MS*, December 1832, vol. 1, no. 7, 54; cf. "Indian Treaties," *E&MS*, January 1833, no. 8, 62 and "Israel Will Be Gathered," *E&MS*, June 1833, vol. 2, no. 13, 101.

37. "Sacred Poetry," *E&MS*, November 1832, vol. 1, no. 6, 45.

38. Simeon Carter, letter to Brother Sidney, *E&MS*, November 1832, vol. 1, no. 6, 46.

39. Joseph Smith, letter to N.E. Seaton (a.k.a Sexton, as spelled in Ms. History, LDSCA), January 4, 1833, *HC*, vol. 1, 315. "When Smith observed that his letter had appeared in the newspaper in an abbreviated form, he wrote to Saxton [sic] a second time urging publication of his letter in its entirety" (Erickson, 77).

40. Smith, *HC*, vol. 1, 315–316. In 1840, while "[u]nder the spirit of prophecy," Wilford Woodruff told potential converts in England that they would remain on earth "until the coming of Christ" (Wilford Woodruff, *Wilford Woodruff's Journal*, under January 26, 1840. Quoted in Erickson, 83). Heber C. Kimball told his English audiences that he "would not suffer death before Christ's second coming," and prophesied that "within ten or fifteen years the sea between Liverpool and America would dry up" (Heber C. Kimball. Quoted in Walter Armytage, *Heaven's Below: Utopian Experiments in England, 1560–1960* [Toronto: Toronto University Press, 1961], 260).

41. *D&C* 45:21.

42. "Signs of the Times," *E&MS*, October 1832, vol. 1, no. 5, 38; "Signs of the Times," *E&MS*, January 1833, vol. 1, no. 8, 62; "Memorandum Of Signs," *E&MS*, May 1833, vol. 1, no. 12, 95; Seymour Brunson, letter to the Editor, *E&MS*, June 1833, vol. 2, no. 13, 100.

43. "Signs of the Times," *E&MS*, January 1833, vol. 1, no. 8, 62.

44. Winn, 94

45. W.W. Phelps, "Free People of Color," *E&MS*, June 1833, vol. 2, no. 14, 109; cf. HC 1:377–378.

46. Phelps, 109.

47. "The Elders Stationed in Zion, to the Churches Abroad," *E&MS*, June 1833, vol. 2, no. 14, 111.

48. Citizens of Jackson County. Quoted in "To His Excellency," 113; cf. *HC* 1:374–376.

49. Citizens of Jackson County. Quoted in "To His Excellency," 113; cf. *HC* 1:374–376.

50. *HC*, vol. 1, 376.

51. Brodie, 133.

52. *HC*, vol. 1, 378–379.

53. *HC*, vol. 1, 379.

54. Quoted in Brodie, 133.

55. Peter Crawley, "A Bibliography of The Church of Jesus Christ of Latter–day Saints in New York, Ohio, and Missouri," *BYU Studies* (Summer 72), vol. 12, 483.

56. Mary E. Rollins Lightner, letter to the Editor, *Deseret Evening News*, February 12, 1904, 24. Quoted in Crawley, 483. According to Mormon leader David Whitmer, publishing Smith's commandments greatly contributed to animosity against Mormons in Missouri. He wrote the following in 1887: "The main reason why the printing press was destroyed, was because they published the *Book of Commandments*. It fell into the hands of the world, and the people of Jackson county, Missouri, saw from the revelations that they were considered by the church as intruders upon the land of Zion, as enemies to the church, and that they should be cut off out of the land of Zion and sent away. The people seeing these things in the Book of Commandments became the more enraged, tore down the printing press, and drove the church out of Jackson county" (David Whitmer, *An Address to All Believers in Christ* [Richmond, MO: David Whitmer, 1887], 54).

57. Brodie, 134.

58. "To His Excellency," 114.

59. *D&C* 97:11.

60. *D&C* 97:26

61. *D&C* 97:19

62. Brodie, 129.

63. *D&C* 98:16.

64. D. Michael Quinn, *The Mormon Hierarchy: Origins of Power* (Salt Lake City: Signature Books, 1994), 81.

65. Brodie, 136.

66. Winn, 97 and Brodie, 136.

67. Brodie, 137.

68. Benjamin F. Johnson, *Autobiography (1818–1846), From Benjamin F. Johnson, My Life's Review* (Independence, Missouri: Zion's Printing and Publishing Co., 1947), 7–107, online at http://www.math.byu.edu/~smithw/Lds/LDS/Early–Saints/BFJohnson.html. Johnson incorrectly dates this event as November 14. It actually occurred on November 13 (R.M. Devens, *America Progress: or The Great Events of the Greatest Century* [Chicago: Hugh Hurons, 1883], 228). Devens describes the celestial phenomenon as a universal and wonderful event during which time *"the whole firmament, over the United States, being then, for hours, in fiery commotion!"* It was estimated that no less than 240,000 meteors were visible at the same time above the horizon of Boston (Devens, 229).

69. Winn, 97.

70. *D&C* 101:57–58. This revelation further reads: "And now, I will show unto you a parable, that you may know my will concerning the redemption of Zion. A certain nobleman had a spot of land, very choice; . . . and the enemy came by night, and broke down the hedge; and the servants were affrighted, and fled; and the enemy destroyed their works. . . . And the lord of the vineyard said unto one of his servants: Go and gather together the residue of my servants, and take all the strength of mine house, which are my warriors. . . . And go ye straightway unto the land of my vineyard, and redeem my vineyard; for it is mine; I have bought it with money. Therefore, get ye straightway unto my land; break down the walls of mine enemies; throw down their tower, and scatter their watchmen. And inasmuch as they gather together against you, avenge me of mine enemies, that by and by I may come with the residue of mine house and possess the land" (*D&C* 101:43–44. 51, 55–58).

71. *D&C* 101:89.

72. *D&C* 103:22, 24, 26.

73. Joseph Smith, "Joseph Smith Recital to Kirtland (OH) High Council," *Kirtland Council Minute Book* (1832–37), April 21,1834, 44, reprinted in Dan Vogel, ed., *Early Mormon Documents* (Salt Lake City: Signature Books, 1996), vol. 1, 33–34.

74. For an in-depth description of Zion's Camp, its organization, and experiences during the march to Zion, see Brodie, 148–157.

75. W.W. Phelps, letter to the brethren, May 1, 1834, *E&MS*, May 1834, vol. 2, no. 20, 160.

76. Phelps, letter to the brethren, 160.

77. Erickson, 108.

78. Robert T. Divett, "His Chastening Rod: Cholera Epidemics and the Mormons," *Dialogue: A Journal of Mormon Thought* (Fall 1979), vol. 12, 12; cf. Warren A. Jennings, "The Army of Israel Marches Into Missouri," *Missouri Historical Review* (January 1968), vol. 62, 133.

79. Winn, 101.

80. Quinn, 85.

81. Reed Peck, *Reed Peck Manuscript* (written by a Mormon eye-witness to the events), 3, online at http://www.connect-a.net/users/drshades/reedpeck.htm.

82. *D&C* 105: 2-17; cf. Wilford Woodruff, 1836–1837 Diary, under December 11, 1836, reprinted in Dean Jessee, "The Kirtland Diary of Wilford Woodruff," *BYU Studies* (Summer 1972), vol. 12, 374.

83. *HC*, vol. 2, 144.

84. *D&C* 105:28

85. *D&C* 105:19

86. Brodie, 157.

87. Joseph Smith, letter to the High Council of Zion, August 16, 1834, in *HC*, vol. 2, 145.

88. *D&C* 88:119.

89. LaMar Peterson, *Hearts Mad Glad* (Salt Lake City: LaMar Peterson, 1975), 121.

90. Brodie, 160.

91. Brodie, 176.

92. Brodie, 178.

93. *MS&AD*, March 1836, vol. 2, no. 6, 278, online at http://www.centerplace.org/history/ma/v2n06.htm.

94. George A. Smith, March 18, 1855, *JOD* (Liverpool: F.D. Richards, 1855; lithographed reprint of original edition, 1966), vol. 2, 216.

95. *MS*, vol. 15, 727. Quoted in Jerald Tanner and Sandra Tanner, *The Mormon Kingdom* (Salt Lake City: ULM, 1969), vol. 1, 5. When this statement by Smith was re-printed in the LDS church's *HC* (vol. 2, 431), the word "cursings" was removed with no notation indicating that the text had been altered. Mormon apostle George A. Smith remembered that even before the temple's opening, Saints had been petitioning the Lord "to kill the mob." This referred primarily to the mobs in Kirtland (George A. Smith, August 2, 1857, *JOD* [Liverpool: Asa Calkin, 1858; lithographed reprint of original edition, 1966], vol. 5, 107).

96. Brodie, 180.

97. *D&C* 110:2.

98. *D&C* 110:3-7.

99. *D&C* 110: 16.

100. *D&C* 110:11; cf. *D&C* 133:26–34. Smith's ideas about the location of Israel's Lost Ten Tribes being at the North Pole must be pieced together from a variety of sources that include testimony from persons who knew Smith and heard him teach on the subject. For example, in a letter to Oliver Cowdery, W.W. Phelps postulated, based on the *BOM*, that there existed a continent at the North Pole of approximately 1,300 square miles "containing thousands of millions of Israelites" (W.W. Phelps, "Letter No. 11," *MS&AD*, October 1835, vol. 2, no. 1, 194). Faithful Mormon, Benjamin Johnson, wrote the following account of an occasion on which Smith made his beliefs known: "I was then really 'the bosom friend and companion of the Prophet Joseph.' . . . Sometimes when at my house I asked him questions relating to past, present and future; . . . one of which I will relate: I asked where the nine and a half tribes of Israel were. 'Well,' said he, 'you remember the old caldron or potash kettle you used to boil maple sap in for sugar, don't you?' I said yes. 'Well,' said he, 'they are in the north pole in a concave just the shape of that kettle. And John the Revelator is with them, preparing them for their return'" (Benjamin Johnson, *My Life's Review* [1947], 93). Oliver B. Huntington, a close associate of Smith, in 1892 remembered being told by Joseph that just beyond the North Pole there existed "a warm fruitful country," inhabited by the ten tribes of Israel. Huntington further recalled: "At the same time he described the shape of the earth at the poles as being a rounded elongation and drew a diagram of it" (Oliver B. Huntington, "The Inhabitants of the Moon," *The Young Woman's Journal*, published by the Young Ladies' Mutual Improvement Association of Zion, 1892, vol. 3, 264). Huntington, in his journal, stated: "I have heard Joseph say that 'John was among the Ten Tribes beyond the North Pole'" (*Oliver B. Huntington Journal*, under January 13, 1881); cf. Heber C. Kimball, letter to Addison Everett, in *Oliver B. Huntington Journal*, under January 13, 1881 (quoted online at http://www.eagle-net.org/enoch144/tribes.txt), and Levi Ward Hancock, *Life of Levi Ward Hancock*, under June 4, 1831 (online at http://www.math.byu.edu/~smithw/Lds/LDS/Early-Saints/LHancock.html).

101. There are several sources that present this view as having come from Smith. Consider the following quotations, all of which are online at http://www.code-co.com/rcf/mhistdoc/enoch.htm; also see Wandle Mace, *Journal*, 1809–1890, 38–39, original in library of BYU; Eliza R. Snow, "Address to Earth", *MS*, vol. 13, Sep 1, 1851; Charles L.

Walker, *Journal*, original in BYU library, edited version printed in A. Karl Larson and Katharine Miles Larson, eds., *Diary of Charles Lowell Walker* (Logan, UT: Utah State University Press, 1980) vol. 2, 532 [Feb. 1881], 539 [Mar. 1881], 540 [Mar. 1881], 868 [Apr. 1898]. More examples are online at http://www.eagle-net.org/enoch144/tribes.txt.

- "President Young said he herd [sic] Joseph Smith say that the Ten Tribes of Israel were on a Portion of Land separated from this Earth" (Wilford Woodruff, *Wilford Woodruff Journal*, September 8, 1867, reprinted in Susan Staker, ed., *Waiting for World's End, The Diaries of Wilford Woodruff* [Salt Lake City: Signature Books, 1993], 291).
- "The evening was spent in conversing upon the subject of the Ten tribes in the North Country . . . . [A] portion of the North Country Containing the ten tribes may be separated from the Earth. O[rson] Hyde & others believed they would soon return" (Woodruff, Sep 25, 1859, reprinted in Staker, 238)
- "I heard Joseph Smith preach baptism for the dead. . . . I heard him say, '[T]he Ten Tribes were not on this globe, but a portion of this earth had cleaved off with them and went flying into space, and when the time comes when the 'earth reels to and fro like a drunken man and the stars from heaven fall,' it would join on again'" (Bathsheba W. Smith, "Recollections of the Prophet Joseph Smith." *The Juvenile Instructor*, June 1, 1892, vol. 27. 34).
- The Prophet Joseph [Smith] once in my hearing advanced his opinion that the Ten Tribes were separated from the Earth; or a portion of the Earth was by a miracle broken off, and that the Ten Tribes were taken away with it, and that in the latter days it would be restored to the Earth or be let down in the Polar regions. Whether the Prophet founded his opinion upon revelation or whether it was a matter of mere speculation with him, I am not able to say" (Orson Pratt, Letter Box of Orson Pratt, LDS Church Historian's Office, letter to John C. Hall, December 13, 1875. Quoted in R. Clayton Brough, "The Lost Tribes," Horizon Publishers, 1979, 50).

102. In a Patriarchal blessing given by Oliver Cowdery to Joseph Smith, God said (through Cowdery) that Joseph would one day "go forth toward the north, and by the power of his word shall the deep begin to give way: and the ice melt before the Sun. By the keys of the kingdom shall he lead Israel into the land of Zion, while the house of Jacob shouts in the dance and in the song" (Oliver Cowdery, "A Patriarchal blessing given by Oliver Cowdery to the Prophet Joseph Smith at Kirtland," September 22, 1835, reprinted in Fred C. Collier, ed., *Unpublished Revelations* (Salt Lake City: Collier's Publishing Co., 1979; 2nd edition, 1981), vol. 1, 76.

103. Brodie, 180.

104. John Corrill, *A Brief History of the Church of Christ of Latter Day Saints (Commonly Called Mormons, Including an Account of their Doctrine and Discipline, with the Reasons of the Author for Leaving the Church)* (St. Louis, n.p., 1839). online at http://www.math.byu.edu/~smithw/Lds/LDS/Early-Saints/Corrill-history.html.

CHAPTER SEVEN: WOE IN OHIO

1. Joseph Smith. Quoted in David Whitmer, *An Address to All Believers in Christ* (Richmond, MO: author, 1887), 31; cf. David Whitmer, interview in *Omaha Herald*, October 17, 1886, reprinted in Lyndon W. Cook, ed., *David Whitmer Interviews: A Restoration Witness* (Orem, UT: Grandin Book Co., 1991), 203. A similar statement appears in one of Smith's revelations (*D&C* 46:7). A searchable text version of Whitmer's pamphlet is online at http://www.concordance.com/mormon.htm.

2. *MS&AD*, May 1836, vol. 2, no. 8, 278, online at http://www.centerplace.org/history/ma/v2n08.htm.

3. See previous endnote. In his journal, Wilford Woodruff—the LDS church's fourth president—noted that he interpreted a red sky at sunset as being a clear sign of the world's end: "At early Candlelight the heavens began to show forth the signs in fulfillment of the Prophecy of JOEL recorded in the 2nd chap 30th vers [sic] of the Book of Joel. [T]he clouds of fire & blood began to arise in the N.E & reached unto the N.W which principly [sic] covered the horizon the reflection of the clouds upon the earth which was covered with snow presented a vary red appearance"(Wilford Woodruff, *1836-1837 Diary*, under January 25, 1836, reprinted in Dean Jessee, "The Kirtland Diary of Wilford Woodruff," *BYU Studies* [Summer 1972], vol. 12, 384.)

4. Orson Hyde, "A Prophetic Warning," *MS&AD*, July 1836, vol. 2, no. 10, 345, online at http://www.centerplace.org/history/ma/v2n10.htm; also see Edward Partridge, letter to Friends and Neighbors," *MS&AD*, Jan 1835, vol. 1, no. 4, 58 ("[T]he day of the Lord: the coming of the Son of God, is near at hand: probably he will make his appearance in the clouds of heaven within the present generation"), Orson Hyde and William E. McLellin, letter to 'Brother,' *MS&AD*, October 1835, vol. 2, no. 1, 205 ("[W]e left the brethren much encouraged and pursued our course easterly, calling upon the inhabitants publicly, and from house to house, to repent and prepare for the day of wrath, which will overtake this generation as a thief in the night; and for the coming of the Lord Jesus Christ, which is nigh at hand").

5. Joseph Smith, *HC* (Salt Lake City: Deseret Book Company, 1976/1980), vol. 2, 182. In 1843, Smith again prophesied that Christ would return in 1890 (*HC*, vol. 5, 336).

6. In reference to the Mormons, one non-Mormon resident of Kirtland, wrote: "Their object is to acquire political Power as fast as they can, without regard to the means they made use of. They are ready to harness in with any party that is willing to degrade themselves by asking their assistance. They now carry nearly a majority of this township, and every man votes as directed by the prophet and elders" (unsigned, letter to the Editor dated, April 14, 1835, *Painesville Telegraph*, April 17, 1835), online at http://www.lavazone2.com/dbroadhu/OH/paintel4.htm#041735. Mormon apostle Orson Hyde, in an 1864 sermon, said that one of the main reasons for the Saints' expulsion from Ohio, Missouri, and Illinois, was the political power non-Mormons saw in the united bock of voters represented by the Mormons: "The world dreaded the germs of greatness which they saw in the Saints. They dreaded the power that seemed to attend them. They were almost at war with us because we were united. They disliked the idea of our being politically one, they wanted us to be of different parties. But when they saw we were united, they said, 'There is a power that is destined to make them great, to exalt them'" (Orson Hyde, December 18, 1864, *JOD* [Liverpool: Daniel H. Wells, 1865; lithographed reprint of original edition, 1966], vol. 10, 376.

7. This event took place in the spring of 1835, before the temple's opening. Anti-Mormon sentiment continued to build in following years as the Mormon population of Kirtland increased and Mormons began seeking political offices (c. 1834–1837).

8. George A. Smith, "Memoirs of George A. Smith," 59–60. Quoted in Jessee, 393 (see this chapter, endnote #3).

9. Fawn M. Brodie, *No Man Knows My History* (New York: Vintage Books, 1995; original edition by Alfred A. Knopf, 1945), 141.

10. H. Michael Marquardt, *The Joseph Smith Revelations: Text & Commentary* (Salt Lake City: Signature Books, 1999), xv.

11. Marquardt, xv.

12. These same revelations would undergo additional revisions before being reprinted again in subsequent editions of the *D&C*, a text still used by Latter-day Saints as Holy Writ. Most of the changes, however, were made to the 1835 edition of the *D&C*. For an extremely detailed look at the hundreds of changes that were made to Smith's revelations, see Jerald Tanner and Sandra Tanner, *Mormonism: Shadow or Reality?* (Salt Lake City: ULM, 1987), 14–31D; also see Marquardt. Another excellent Internet

resource demonstrating these changes—i.e., chapter three from *The Changing World of Mormonism* (Chicago: Moody, 1981) by Jerald Tanner and Sandra Tanner—is online at http://www.utlm.org/onlinebooks/changech3.htm. This entire volume is online at http://www.utlm.org/onlinebooks/changecontents.htm.

13. Quinn, *The Mormon Hierarchy: Origins of Power* (Salt Lake City: Signature Books, 1994), 88.
14. Quinn, 88. This marriage occurred on November 23, 1835.
15. Joseph Smith. Quoted in Quinn. 88.
16. Brodie, 183. Disruptions of the family unit and marriage break-ups are often seen among religious groups commonly termed "cults." Mormon leadership today continues to encourage divorce when the spouse of a faithful Mormon begins to doubt the validity of the Mormon faith. This unfortunate pattern has been partly responsible for charges of "cultism" against the Mormon church.
17. Joseph Smith, *HC*, vol. 2, 377–378.
18. *D&C* 58:21
19. Smith's acceptance of polygamy may have resulted from his 1831 studies of the Old Testament, which presents several examples of Jewish patriarchs and kings having multiple wives and concubines (see Todd Compton, *In Sacred Loneliness* [Salt Lake City: Signature Books, 1997], 27); cf. biblical texts (Gen. 29-30; 1 Sam. 1:2; 1 Kings 11:3; 1 Chron. 14:3; 2 Chron. 11:21; 2 Chron. 13:21).
20. Smith's revelation advocating polygamy reads as follows:

"Verily, thus saith the Lord unto you my servant Joseph, that inasmuch as you have inquired of my hand to know and understand wherein I, the Lord, justified my servants Abraham, Isaac, and Jacob, as also Moses, David and Solomon, my servants, as touching the principle and doctrine of their having many wives and concubines—Behold, and lo, I am the Lord thy God, and will answer thee as touching this matter. Therefore, prepare thy heart to receive and obey the instructions which I am about to give unto you; for all those who have this law revealed unto them must obey the same. For behold, I reveal unto you a new and an everlasting covenant; and if ye abide not that covenant. . . then are ye damned; for no one can reject this covenant and be permitted to enter into my glory. . . . And again, verily I say unto you, if a man marry a wife by my word, which is my law, and by the new and everlasting covenant, they shall pass by the angels, and the gods, which are set there, to their exaltation. . . . Then shall they be gods, because they have no end....God commanded Abraham, and Sarah gave Hagar to Abraham to wife. . . . Was Abraham, therefore, under condemnation? Verily I say unto you, Nay; for I, the Lord, commanded it. . . . Abraham received concubines, and they bore him children; and it was accounted unto him for righteousness . . . . David also received many wives and concubines, and also Solomon and Moses my servants, . . . and in nothing did they sin save in those things which they received not of me. David's wives and concubines were given unto him of me. . . . And let mine handmaid, Emma Smith, receive all those that have been given unto my servant Joseph, and who are virtuous and pure before me; and those who are not pure, and have said they were pure, shall be destroyed, saith the Lord God. . . . Let no one, therefore, set on my servant Joseph; for I will justify him. . . . And again, as pertaining to the law of the Priesthood—if any man espouse a virgin, and desire to espouse another, and the first give her consent, and if he espouse the second, and they are virgins, and have vowed to no other man, then is he justified; he cannot commit adultery for they are given unto him; for he can not commit adultery with that that belongeth unto him and to no one else. And if he have ten virgins given unto him by this law, he cannot commit adultery, for they belong to him, and they are given unto him; therefore is he justified" (*D&C* 132:1-4, 19, 20, 34, 35, 37, 38, 39, 52, 60–62).

21. Mormon historian B. H. Roberts stated that the "date in the heading of the Revelation on the Eternity of the Marriage Covenant, including the Plurality of Wives, notes the time at which the revelation was committed to writing, not the time at which the principles set forth in the revelation were first made known to the Prophet." (*CHC*, vol. 5, 1843).

22. Levi Lewis, *Susquehanna Register*, May 1, 1834, reprinted in E.D. Howe, *Mormonism Unvailed* (Painesville, OH: author, 1834), 268, online at http://www.solomonspalding.com/docs/1834howf.htm#pg268. This entire volume is online at http://www.solomonspalding.com/docs/1834howb.htm. A searchable text version is online at http://www.concordance.com/mormon.htm.

23. Joseph Smith, "Revelation Received West of Jackson County, Missouri, On 17 July 1831." Transcribed by W.W. Phelps, manuscript in LDSCA, reprinted in Marquardt, 375; cf. W.W. Phelps, letter to Brigham Young, August 12, 1861, Joseph Smith Collection, LDSCA, reprinted in Fred C. Collier, comp., *Unpublished Revelations* (Salt Lake City: Collier's Publishing CO., 1979; 2nd ed., 1981), vol. 1, 58; also see Tanner and Tanner, *The Changing World*, 210, online at http://www.utlm.org/onlinebooks/changech9a.htm#Chapter%209. Smith's Indian "Polygamy" revelation recorded by W.W. Phelps can be found through Utah Lighthouse ministry, http://www.utlm.org/onlineresources/indianpolygamyrevelation.htm. No one knows when Phelps recorded this revelation or when he wrote the follow-up paragraph. It is certain that both were written sometime before 1861, the year Phelps quoted it to Brigham Young in a letter.

24. W.W. Phelps, manuscript in LDSCA, reprinted in Marquardt, 375. As an added note, there is reason to believe that Smith may not have clearly advocated the practice of polygamy at the time he gave the revelation, but merely suggested its possible necessity in conjunction with marrying Indian women, which would open up access to Indian territories for Mormon males despite opposition that might be voiced by government agents. This latter reason for marrying Indian women would certainly be more important to Smith than simply satiating carnal desires.

25. Martin Harris. Quoted in S.F. Whitney, *Naked Truths About Mormonism* (January 1888), 3, online at http://www.lavazone2.com/dbroadhu/CA/natruths.htm#010088-3b2.

26. Andrew Jenson, "Plural Marriage," *HR*, May 1887, vol. 6, nos. 3-5, 219.

27. Ezra Booth, "Letter No. IX," *Ohio Star*, December 8, 1831, reprinted in Howe, 220, online at http://www.solomonspalding.com/docs/1834howe.htm#pg220.

28. Orson Pratt, October 7, 1869, *JOD* (Liverpool: Horace S. Eldredge, 1871; lithographed reprint of original edition, 1966), vol. 13, 193. Orson Pratt made a very similar comment during an 1878 lecture. Pratt said Lyman Johnson told him that Smith, as early as 1831, had explained that "plural marriage was a correct principle. Joseph declared to Lyman that God had revealed it to him, but that the time had not come to teach or practice it in the Church, but that the time would come" (Orson Pratt, "Report of Elder Orson Pratt and Joseph F. Smith," *MS*, December 16, 1878, vol. 30, 788).

29. Andrew Jenson (an assistant LDS church historian), when making his list of women who were married to Joseph Smith, said Fanny Alger was "one of the first plural wives sealed to the Prophet" (Jenson, 233). John A. Widtsoe stated: "It seems that Fannie Alger was one of Joseph's first plural wives" (John A. Widtsoe, *Joseph Smith-Seeker After Truth* [Salt Lake City: Deseret News, 1951], 237).

30. Benjamin F. Johnson, "Autobiography of Benjamin F. Johnson (1818–1846)," in *My Life's Review* (Independence, MO: Zion's Printing and Publishing Co., 1947), 7-107, online at http://www.math.byu.edu/~smithw/Lds/LDS/Early-Saints/BFJohnson.html. Johnson stated: "Without a doubt in my mind, Fanny Alger was, at Kirtland, the Prophet's first plural wife, in which, by right of his calling, he was justified of the Lord" (also see *D&C* 132:59-60).

31. Richard Van Wagoner, *Mormon Polygamy: A History* (Salt Lake City: Signature Books, 1989; paperback edition), 6.

32. Van Wagoner, 7.

33. Compton, 34.

34. Levi Hancock, as told by his son, Mosiah Hancock, *Autobiography of Mosiah Hancock*, ms. 570, LDSCA. Quoted in Compton, 31.

35. Mosiah Hancock. Quoted in Compton 32.

36. Compton, 33.

37. William McLellin, letter to Joseph Smith III, July 1872, RLDSCA. Quoted in Compton, 35. McLellin recounted this same story to J.H. Beadle, who interviewed McLellin for an article that appeared in the *Salt Lake City Tribune*, October 6, 1875, online at http://www.xmission.com/~country/reason/beadle1.htm. The article reads: "He [McLellin] also informed me of the spot where the first well authenticated case of polygamy took place in which Joseph Smith was 'sealed' to the hired girl. The 'sealing' took place in a barn on the hay mow, and was witnessed by Mrs. Smith through a crack in the door! The Doctor was so distressed about this case, (it created some scandal at the time among the Saints,) that long afterwards when he visited Mrs. Emma Smith at Nauvoo, he charged her as she hoped for salvation to tell him the truth about it. And she then and there declared on her honor that it was a fact—'saw it with her own eyes.'"

38. Ann Eliza Web Young, *Wife No. 19* (Hartford, CT: Dustin, Gilman & Co., 1875), 66–67.

39. Young, 66–67.

40. William McLellin, letter to Joseph Smith III, July 1872. Quoted Jerald Tanner and Sandra Tanner, *The Mormon Church and the McLellin Collection* (Salt Lake City: ULM, 1993), 53.

41. Daniel S. Miles, "To Our Readers," *MS&AD*, May 1837, vol. 3, no. 8, 511 ("[W]e will have no fellowship whatever with any Elder belonging to the quorums of the Seventies who is guilty of polygamy or any offence [offense] of the kind, and who does not in all things conform to the laws of the church contained in the Bible and in the Book of Doctrine and Covenants"), online at http://www.centerplace.org/history/ma/v3n08.htm, and *Kirtland Council Minute Book*, September 7, 1836, LDSCA.

42. *D&C* CL:4, 1835 edition, 251. Photo of this page from the *D&C* is located online at http://www.utlm.org/images/changingworld/chwp206dcsection101.gif.

43. Linda King Newell and Valeen Tippetts Avery, *Mormon Enigma: Emma Hale* (New York: Doubleday & Co., 1984), 62. Newell and Tippetts note: "[T]he Mormon population increased twenty-fold while the landholdings only quadrupled."

44. Ebenezer Robinson, "The Return" (1888–1890), July, 1889, vol. 1, no. 7, online at http://www.math.byu.edu/~smithw/Lds/LDS/Early-Saints/ERobinson.html.

45. Heber C. Kimball could hardly believe how land speculation had affected the city: "On our arrival in Kirtland we were much grieved to see the spirit of speculation prevailing in the church; trade and traffic seemed to engross the time and attention of the Saints: when we left Kirtland a City lot was worth about 150 dollars, but on our return to our astonishment the same lot was said to be worth from 500 to 1000 dollars according to location; and some men who when I left could hardly get food to eat, I found on my return to be men of supposed great wealth; in fact every thing in the place seemed to be moving in great prosperity, and all seemed determined to become rich; in my feelings they were artificial or imaginary riches"(Heber C. Kimball, "History of Heber Chase Kimball by his own Dictation," 47–48. Quoted in Jessee, 397–398, see this chapter, endnote #3 for reference).

46. "The Growth of the Mormon Church in Kirtland, Ohio," Unpublished Ph.D. dissertation by Robert Kent Fielding, Indiana University, 1957, typed copy, 202–204. 206–208, 211–212. Quoted in Jerald Tanner and Sandra Tanner, *The Mormon Kingdom* (Salt Lake City: ULM, 1969), vol. 1, 9.

47. Fielding. Quoted in Tanner and Tanner, *The Mormon Kingdom*, vol. 1, 9.

48. Fielding. Quoted in Tanner and Tanner, *The Mormon Kingdom*, vol. 1, 9. Not every Mormon was willing to enter into such transactions with Joseph. Isaac McWithy refused to sell his land to Joseph for $3,000, with a suggested down payment of $300–$400 so

McWithy could settle in Zion, where he would wait for the remainder of the selling price to come at a later date. For his refusal, McWithy was brought to trial before the church's High Council for insolence (*HC*, vol. 2, 446).

49. Mormon historian B.H. Roberts admitted in his history of the church that the Saints purchased "an extensive stock of goods" on credit and that many Mormons "lived extravagantly on borrowed money" (B.H. Roberts, *CHC* [Salt Lake City: Deseret Book Co., 1930], vol. 1, 398). For more documentation on the Mormon practice of purchasing goods on credit, see Tanner and Tanner, *The Mormon Kingdom*, vol. 1, 20–21.

50. Brodie, 192.

51. Warren Parrish, letter dated March 6, 1838, *Zion's Watchman*, March 24, 1838 (see Brodie, 195). For numerous quotations relating to this claim, see Tanner and Tanner, *The Mormon Kingdom*, vol. 1, 14.

52. "In the past it has been suggested by most Mormon authors that the reason for the lack of a charter was religious persecution. Joseph Smith himself declared 'Because we were 'Mormons,' the legislature raised some frivolous excuses on which they refused to grant us those banking privileges they so freely granted to others.' There is little evidence that the Church in this instance was subject to religious persecution. . . . In 1835, all requests for additional charters were refused, while in 1836 only one of seventeen requests was granted" (Marvin S. Hill, C. Keith Rooker, and Larry T. Wimmer, "The Kirtland Ecomony: A Market Critique of Sectarian Ecomomics," *BYU Studies* [Summer 1977, vol. 17], 437–38, 458).

53. Jessee, 381 (see this chapter, endnote #3 for reference).

54. Brodie, 196–197. Quotations taken from W. Wyl, *Mormon Portraits* (Salt lake City: Tribune Printing and Publishing Company, 1886), 36; cf. Oliver Olney, *Absurdities of Mormonism Portrayed* (Hancock, IL: author, 1843), 4, and Cyrus Smalling in E.G. Lee, *The Mormons, or Knavery Exposed* (Philadelphia: author, 1841),14; see reprint texts in Tanner and Tanner, *The Mormon Kingdom*, 17–18.

55. Warren Parrish, letter dated March 6, 1838, *Zion's Watchman*, March 24, 1838, and Cyrus Smalling in E.G. Lee, 14 (see Brodie, 195).

56. Brodie, 196.

57. Jessee, 381 (see this chapter, endnote #3 for reference).

58. "Anti-Banking Company," *Painesville Republican*, January 19, 1837, online at an excellent source for rare newspaper articles on Mormonism, http://www.lavazone2.com/dbroadhu/OH/painerep.htm#011937.

59. Dale W. Adams, "Chartering the Kirtland Bank," *BYU Studies* (Fall 1983), vol. 23, 472; cf. Hill, Rooker, and Wimmer, 445–449.

60. Adams, 472.

61. Hill, Rooker, and Wimmer, 445–449.

62. Jessee, 393 (see this chapter, endnote #3 for reference).

63. Jessee, 393 (see this chapter, endnote #3 for reference).

64. N.K. Whitney, R. Cahoon, and V. Knight, letter of September 18, 1837, "To the Saints scattered abroad, the Bishop and his Counselors of Kirtland send greeting," *MS&AD*, September 1837, vol. 3, no. 1, 563–564.

65. Grant Underwood, *The Millenarian World View of Early Mormonism* (Urbana: University of Illinois Press, 1993), 28.

66. Parley P. Pratt, *A Voice of Warning and Instruction to All People* (New York: W. Sanford, 1837), iii, x, online at http://www.solomonspalding.com/docs/prt1837b.htm.

67. Roberts, vol. 1, 401–402.

68. "Thirteen suits were brought against him between June 1837 and April 1839, to collect sums totaling nearly $25,000. The damages asked amounted to almost $35,000. He was arrested seven times in four months, and his followers managed heroically to raise the $38,428 required for bail. Of the thirteen suits only six were settled out of court—about

$12,000 out of the $25,000. In the other seven the creditors either were awarded damages or won them by default. Joseph had many additional debts that never resulted in court action. Some years later he compiled a list of still outstanding Kirtland loans, which amounted to more than $33,000. If one adds to these the two great loans of $30,000 and $60,000 borrowed in New York and Buffalo in 1836, it would seem that the Mormon leaders owed to non-Mormon individuals and firms well over $150,000" (Brodie, 201–202).

69. Anderson Wilson. Quoted in Kenneth H. Winn, *Exiles in a Land of Liberty* (Chapel Hill: University of North Carolina, 1989), 102–103.
70. Wilson. Quoted in Winn, 103.
71. Joseph Thorp, *Early Days in the West: Along the Missouri One Hundred Years Ago* (Liberty, MO: Liberty Tribune, 1924), 79. Quoted in Stephen C. LeSueur, *The 1838 Mormon War in Missouri* (Columbia, MO: University of Missouri Press, 1987), 18.
72. Clay County citizens. Quoted in Brodie, 191.
73. Clay County citizens. Quoted in Brodie, 191
74. Quoted in Brodie, 191.
75. Winn, 105.
76. *EJ*, November 2, 1837, vol. 1, no. 2, 28, reprinted in Collier, vol. 1, 86.
77. Brodie, 205.
78. Those arrested were eventually released on the grounds that there was no cause for action (see Brodie, 206).
79. Brodie, 207.
80. As told by L. E. Miller (see Brodie, 207).
81. Joseph Smith, Joseph Smith Collection, LDSCA, Salt Lake City, reprinted in Collier, vol. 1, 88.
82. *HC*, vol. 3, 1.
83. *HC*, vol. 3, 1.
84. Brodie, 207.
85. Warren Parrish, letter to the Editor dated February 5, 1838, *Painesville Republican*, February 22, 1838, online at http://www.lavazone2.com/dbroadhu/OH/painerep.htm.

CHAPTER EIGHT: BIG TROUBLE IN LITTLE MISSOURI

1. Thomas B. Marsh, sworn affidavit, October 24, 1838, Ray County, Missouri, reprinted in *Document Containing the Correspondence, Orders, &c., in Relation to the Disturbances with the Mormons and the Evidence Given Before the Hon. Austin A. King, Judge of the Fifth Judicial Circuit of the State of Missouri, at the Court-House in Richmond, in a Criminal Court of Inquiry, Begun November 12, 1838 on the Trial of Joseph Smith Jr., and Others for High Treason and Other Crimes Against the State* (Fayette, MO: Published by order of the General Assembly at the office of *Boon's Lick Democrat*, 1841), 57–59. This document eventually was sent to the Senate Judiciary Committee in Washington, D.C., where it was labeled *Senate Document 189*.
2. Stephen LeSueur, *The 1838 Mormon War in Missouri* (Columbia, MO: University of Missouri Press, 1987), 26.
3. LeSueur, 29.
4. John Corrill, *A Brief History of the Church of Jesus Christ of Latter Day Saints* (St. Louis: author, 1839), 26, online at http://www.math.byu.edu/~smithw/Lds/LDS/Early-Saints/Corrill-history.html and http://www.olivercowdery.com/smithhome/1839Corl.htm.
5. Fawn M. Brodie, *No Man Knows My History* (New York: Vintage Books, 1995; original edition by Alfred A. Knopf, 1945), 210.
6. According to Joseph Smith, the phrase "Adam-ondi-Ahman" is from the pure language

spoken by Adam and Eve. It supposedly means "The place of God where Adam dwelt" (Bruce McConkie, *Mormon Doctrine* [Salt Lake City: Bookcraft, 1958; second edition, 1966], 19–20).

7. This event occurred c. June 1838 at Spring Hill, MO.

8. *D&C* 117:8. Heber C. Kimball, a close associate of Smith's, declared: "[T]he spot chosen for the garden of Eden was Jackson County, in the State of Missouri; where Independence now stands" (Heber C. Kimball, June 27, 1863, *JOD* [Liverpool: Daniel H. Wells, 1865], vol. 10, 235). Joseph Smith also claimed that Far West was the exact spot where Cain killed Abel (Gen. 4:4-10). For an extensive listing of quotes by Mormon leaders about the Garden of Eden in Missouri, see Sandra Tanner, "Was The Garden of Eden in Missouri?," Internet article online at http://www.utlm.org/onlineresources/garden ofeden.htm.

9. *D&C* 116. Apostle John A. Widtsoe stated: "[T]he Prophet designated 'Spring Hill,' a hill of eminence about fifty or sixty miles north and somewhat to the east of Independence, as Adam-ondi-Ahman, '. . . the place where Adam shall come to visit his people, or the Ancient of Days shall sit, as spoken of by Daniel the prophet'" (John A. Widtsoe, arranged by G. Homer Duncan, *Evidences and Reconciliation* [Salt Lake City: Bookcraft, 1960], volumes 1–3 combined, 395).

10. *D&C* 107:41-53. Brigham Young testified: "In the beginning, after this earth was prepared for man, the Lord commenced his work upon what is now called the American continent, where the Garden of Eden was made. In the days of Noah, in the days of the floating of the ark, he took the people to another part of the earth" (Brigham Young, October 7, 1860, *JOD* [Liverpool: George Q. Cannon, 1861], vol. 8, 195). Mormon Apostle John A. Widtsoe, wrote: "That is the position of the Latter-day Saints today, with respect to the much-discussed location of the Garden of Eden. Adam, after his expulsion from the Garden of Eden, lived in the vicinity of the great Missouri and Mississippi rivers. As his descendants multiplied, they would naturally settle along the fertile and climatically acceptable river valleys. When the flood came in the days of Noah, the Mississippi drainage must have increased to a tremendous volume, quite in harmony with the Biblical account. Noah's ark would be floated on the mighty, rushing waters, towards the Gulf of Mexico. With favorable winds, it would cross the Atlantic to the Eastern continents. There the human race, in its second start on earth, began to multiply and fill the earth. The location of the Garden of Eden in America, and at Independence, Missouri, clears up many a problem, which the Bible account of Eden and its garden has left in the minds of students" (Widtsoe, 396–397).

11. LeSueur, 30.

12. LeSueur, 35.

13. Joseph Smith and Sidney Rigdon, letter to Stephen Post, September 17, 1838. Quoted in LeSueur, 36.

14. Alanson Ripley, letter to the Elders abroad, dated May 1838, *EJ* (July 1838), vol. 1 no. 3, 39, online at http://www.concordance.com/cgi–bin/1wrdr.pl. A searchable text version of the *Elders' Journal* is online at http://www.concordance.com/mormon.htm.

15. Benjamin Johnson. Quoted in Dean R. Zimmerman, ed., *I Knew the Prophets: An Analysis of the Letter of Benjamin F. Johnson to George F. Gibbs, Reporting Doctrinal Views of Joseph Smith and Brigham Young* (Bountiful: UT: Horizon Publishers, 1976). Johnson's original 1903 letter is in LDSCA, MS 1289, online at http://www.math.byu.edu/~smithw/Lds/LDS/Early-Saints/BFJohnson.html. The relevant text is as follows: "And there was some trouble with Oliver Cowdery, and whisper said it was relating to a girl then living in his (the Prophet's) family; and I was afterwards told by Warren Parish, that he himself and Oliver Cowdery did know that Joseph had Fannie Alger as wife, for they were spied upon and found together. And I can now see that at Nauvoo, so at Kirtland, that the suspicion or knowledge of the Prophet's plural relation was one of the causes of apostasy and disruption at Kirtland, although at the time there was little said publicly on the subject" (in

this online version, misspellings have been corrected); cf. William McLellin, letter to Joseph Smith III, September 8, 1872, 2, RLDSCA and William McLellin, interview of September 28, 1875, *Salt Lake Tribune*, October 6, 1875, online at http://www.xmission.com/~country/reason/beadle1.htm. The *Salt Lake Tribune* text reads: "Joseph Smith was "sealed" to the hired girl. The "sealing" took place in a barn on the hay mow, and was witnessed by Mrs. Smith through a crack in the door! The Doctor was so distressed about this case, (it created some scandal at the time among the Saints,) that long afterwards when he visited Mrs. Emma Smith at Nauvoo, he charged her as she hoped for salvation to tell him the truth about it. And she then and there declared on her honor that it was a fact—"saw it with her own eyes."

16. *HC* (Salt Lake City: Deseret Book Company, 1980), vol. 5, 412.
17. Oliver Cowdery, "Oliver Cowdery Letterbook," under January 30, 1838, located at Huntington Library, San Marino, California. In a follow-up letter to Mormon leaders, Cowdery wrote: "I will not be influenced, governed, or controlled, in my temporal interests by any ecclesiastical authority or pretended revelation whatever, contrary to my own judgment" (Oliver Cowdery, letter to church leaders, April 12, 1838, online at http://www.math.byu.edu/~smithw/Lds/LDS/Early-Saints/OCowd-his.html.
18. Oliver Cowdery, letter to Warren Cowdery, January 21, 1838. Original located in the Huntington Library in San Marino, California. Xerox copy at RLDSCA and microfilm copy in the Historical Department of the LDS church; see photocopy in Jerald Tanner and Sandra Tanner *The Mormon Kingdom* (Salt Lake City: ULM, 1969), vol. 1, 27.
19. Oliver Cowdery, letter dated February 24, 1838, located in Huntington Library, San Marino, California.
20. Minutes of the Proceedings of the Committee of the Whole Church in Zion, in General Assembly, February 5, 1838, reprinted in Smith, *HC*, vol. 3, 3–4.
21. Kenneth H. Winn, *Exiles in a Land of Liberty* (Chapel Hill, NC: University of North Carolina Press, 1989), 123; cf. detailed information on these excommunications may be found in Marvin S. Hill, *Quest for Refuge: The Mormon Flight from American Pluralism* (Salt Lake City: Signature Books, 1989), 70-71 and Donald Q. Cannon and Lyndon W. Cook, eds., *Far West Record: Minutes of The Church of Jesus Christ of Latter-day Saints, 1830–1844* (Salt Lake City: Deseret Book, Co., 1983), 162–163.
22. Ripley, 39.
23. *HC*, vol. 3, 232.
24. *HC*, vol. 3, 228.
25. Sidney Rigdon, "Argument to argument where I find it; Ridicule to ridicule, and scorn to scorn," *EJ* (August 1838), vol. 1, no. 4, 55–59. This scathing missive is online at http://www.concordance.com/cgi-bin/1wrdr.pl. The following is only a partial excerpt:
"[A]t the appearance of every new liar, not only the prince himself [i.e., Satan] but all the flunkies that fly at his knell whether in the flesh or out of the flesh, take new courage and put forth new efforts, and it would seem that they really believe that by the assistance of a few more liars, they will be able to dethrone Jehovah and upset His kingdom, and with Satan at their head, establish an empire that shall forever defy the Son of God and so completely destroy the Zion of the last days that He never will come down and reign in Mount Zion . . . Poor simpletons! . . . Within the last six months, they have been making one of their greatest efforts. The Church in accordance with her laws, excluded from her fellowship a set of creatures whose behavior would have disgraced a heathen temple, and as might have been expected, they had recourse to the foulest lying and basest slander in order to hide their iniquity. . . . All these pious soul's papers were put into requisition and this gang of liars, thieves and drunkards were called upon immediately to write their lies on paper and let them print them, so that all the world might have as great a feast of lies as they had . . . . From the bowels of Mr. Warren Parrish and the priest's papers have flown

abroad to tell the world of it. . . . [A]ll the devils whelps in Geauga and Cuyahoga
counties in Ohio were running together to hear what was about to come forth
from the womb of Granny Parrish. . . . In all this grunting business, he was aided
by Leonard Rich who, however, was generally so drunk, that he had to support
himself by something to keep him from falling down, but then it was all for conscience sake. Also a pair of young blacklegs, one of them a Massachusetts
shoemaker by the name of John F. Boynton, a man notorious for nothing but
ignorance, ill breeding and impudence. And the other by the name of Luke
Johnson, whose notoriety consisted, if information be correct, in stealing a bar-
rel of flour from his father and other acts of a similar kind. Thus aided, Mamma
Parrish made a monstrous effort to bring forth. And when the full time of gesta-
tion was come, the wonder came forth, and the priests who were in waiting
seized the animal at its birth, rolled it up in their papers and sent it abroad to
the world. But Rich, Boynton, and Johnson in the character of midwives, waited
around the bed of Mamma Parrish to get away the afterbirth; but awful to relate!
They no sooner got it away than mamma expired and the poor bantling was left
on the hands of the priests to protect and nurse it without any other friend. A
short time after the delivery of Granny Parrish, a little ignorant blockhead by the
name of Stephen Burnet, whose heart was so set on money, that he would at any
time sell his soul for fifty dollars and then think he had made an excellent bargain; and who had got wearied of the restraints of religion and could not bear to
have his purse taxed, hearing of the delivery of Granny Parrish, ran to Kirtland,
got into the temple and tried withal his powers to bring forth something, nobody
knows what, nor did he know himself. But he thought as Granny Parrish had
been fruitful, so must he, but after some terrible gruntings and finding nothing
coming but an abortion, rose up in his anger, proclaimed all revelation lies, and
ran home to his daddy with all his might, not leaving even an egg behind, and
there sat down and rejoiced in the great victory he had obtained over the great
God and all the holy angels, how he had discovered them liars and impostors
. . . . There was also a kind of secondary attendant that waited upon this granny
of modern libels, whose name is Sylvester Smith. In his character there is something notorious and that is that at a certain time in Kirtland, he signed a libel in
order to avoid the punishment due to his crimes. That libel can be forthcoming
at any time when called for. And in so doing, has disqualified himself for taking
an oath before any court of justice in the United States. Thus armed and
attended, this modern libeler has gone forth to the assistance of the priests, to
help them fight against the great God and against His work. . . . A poor perse-
cuting booby by the name of Grandison Newel and who in fact was scarcely a
grade above the beast that perish, went and swore out a state's warrant against
the editor of this paper, saying that he was afraid of his life. In so doing, he swore
a palpable lie and everybody knew it, and so did the court and decided accordingly. . . . There is another character who has figured somewhat in the affairs of
Granny Parrish, Doctor W. A. Cowdery. This poor pitiful beggar came to Kirtland
a few years since with a large family, nearly naked and destitute. It was really
painful to see this pious doctor's (for such he professed to be) rags flying when
he walked the streets. He was taken in by us in this pitiful condition and we put
him into the printing office and gave him enormous wages, not because he
could earn it, or because we needed his service, but merely out of pity. We knew
the man's incompetency all the time and his ignorance and inability to fill any
place in the literary world with credit to himself or to his employers. But
notwithstanding all this, out of pure compassion, we gave him a place and afterwards hired him to edit the paper in that place and gave him double as much as

he could have gotten anywhere else. . . . Granny Parrish had a few others who acted as lackeys, such as Martin Harris, Joseph Coe, Cyrus P. Smalling, etc. but they are so far beneath contempt that a notice of them would be too great a sacrifice for a gentleman to make."

26. Corrill, 59.

27. John Whitmer. Quoted in *Correspondence & Orders*, 138–139.

28. John Whitmer (one of the Eight Witnesses to the *BOM*), *Book of John Whitmer*, RLDSCA, online at http://www.math.byu.edu/~smithw/Lds/LDS/Early-Saints/JWhitmer history.html.

29. Hill, 75.

30. William Edwin Berrett, *The Restored Church* (Salt Lake City: Deseret Book Company, 1949), 198. Interestingly, although Berrett admits to the existence of the Danites, he falsely claims that the organization was formed entirely by Avard, who was "cut off from the church when his guilt was discovered" (Berrett, 197). Such historical revisionism is typical of Mormon historians, who must at all costs, preserve the integrity of early Mormon leaders (see Author's Preface and Chapter Eighteen).

31. Sampson Avard, *Correspondence, Orders*, 97-98; cf. Richard Van Wagoner, *Sidney Rigdon: Portrait of Religious Excess* (Salt Lake City: Signature Books, 1994), 250–252.

32. Winn, 123.

33. David Whitmer, *An Address to All Believers in Christ* (Richmond, MO: David Whitmer, 1887), 27–28. Numerous statements by non-Mormon and Mormon sources unquestionably verify the existence of the Danites. These documents include, but are by no means limited to, Oliver B. Huntington, *Diary of Oliver B. Huntington*, vol. 1, 36, typed copy at Utah State Historical Society, online at http://www.math.byu.edu/~smithw/Lds/LDS/Early-Saints/OBHuntington.html, and Albert P. Rockwood, "Albert P. Rockwood Papers," letter dated October 29, 1838, Coe Collection, Yale University Library. Rockwood explains in his letter that Smith's clandestine group was called "Danites" because "[the] Prophet Daniel has said the Saints shall take the Kingdom & possess it for ever." Testimony by several individuals before the Richmond, Missouri court also has established beyond doubt the existence of the Danites and Smith's role in forming the group and issuing orders to it (see *Senate Document 189*, reprinted in Jerald Tanner and Sandra Tanner, *Senate Document 189* [Salt Lake City: ULM, n.d.], 97–151. This document is available for purchase online at http://www.utlm.org/booklist/titles/ub060_senate document189.htm.).

34. *D&C* 103:10.

35. Winn, 124. There is some disagreement over whether the Danites were organized in June or July of 1838. It may be that a few founding members met several times in June, but did not official organize themselves until July. David Whitmer claims the group was formed in June (Whitmer, *An Address*, 27–28). Sampson Avard testified that the group was formed four months before his November 1838 testimony against Smith, which would have placed its organization in July (see B.H. Roberts, *A Comprehensive History of The Church of Jesus Christ of Latter-day Saints* [Salt Lake City: Deseret News Press, 1930], vol. 1, 500–501).

36. Reed Peck, *Reed Peck Manuscript* (written by a Mormon eye-witness tothe events), 3, online at http://www.connect-a.net/users/drshades/reedpeck.htm.

37. Peck (see previous endnote). William Harris mentioned this same speech, adding that Rigdon expounded on Smith's assertion saying that the apostles threw Judas down from where he had been hung and then trampled upon him until his bowels gushed out. Apparently, Rigdon went on to claim that Ananias and his wife, Sapphira (see the Bible, Acts 5), also were slain by Peter and John (William Harris, *Mormonism Portrayed; Its Errors and Absurdities* [Warsaw, IL: author, 1841], 32–33, quoted by Jerald Tanner and Sandra Tanner, *Mormonism: Shadow or Reality?* [Salt Lake City: ULM, 1987], 428.

38. D. Michael Quinn, *The Mormon Hierarchy: Origins of Power* (Salt Lake City: Signature Books, 1994), 99.

39. Joseph Smith, *Missouri Journal, 1838, March to September,* under July 27, 1838, LDSCA, reprinted in Dean Jessee, ed., *The Papers of Joseph Smith* (Salt Lake City: Deseret Book Co., 1992), vol. 2, 262. (The words quoted in this manuscript were literally crossed out at a later date to indicate that they were not to appear in the LDS church's official history.) Danite Ebenezer Robinson verified that "[b]oth Joseph Smith, Jr. and Sidney Rigdon sanctioned and favored" the Danites (Ebenezer Robinson, *The Return* [February 1890], vol. 2, 217; cf. Corrill, 31). It has been suggested that Smith himself was a Danite because he apparently knew the Danite secret signs and passwords. Danite Luman A. Shurtliff revealed this information about Smith in his autobiography, see Luman A. Shurtliff, *Manuscript Autobiography (1807–51),* 120, 122, 125, under August 1838, LDSCA; cf. Quinn, 337, endnote #77.

40. Winn, 123.

41. Peck (see this chapter, endnote #36). Several loyal Mormon sources detail this Danite oath as well as the willingness of many Danites to break the law in order to protect the church (see Morris Phelps, "Reminiscences," 4–5, typescript, LDSCA; David Lewis, "Excerpt From the Journal of David Lewis," 5, typescript, LDSCA; and Abner Blackburn, "Diary," 2; cf. Corrill, 30–32; William Swartzell, *Mormonism Exposed, Being A Journal Of A Residence In Missouri from the 28th of May to the 20th of August 1838* [Pekin, OH: author, 1840, 22; and Thomas B. Marsh, affidavit of October 24, 1838, in *Correspondence, Orders,* 58).

42. LDS Elders, letter to dissenters, reprinted in Tanner and Tanner, *Senate Document 189,* 6–9. Mormon historian B.H. Roberts confirms in his own *A Comprehensive History of The Church of Jesus Christ of Latter-day Saints* that this letter was drafted by Rigdon and sent to the dissenters (Roberts, vol. 1, 438–439).

43. LDS Elders, quoted in Tanner and Tanner, *Senate Document 189,* 6.

44. LDS Elders, quoted in Tanner and Tanner, *Senate Document 189,* 7–9.

45. John Whitmer, *Book of John Whitmer* (see this chapter, endnote #28).

46. Peck (see this chapter, endnote #36).

47. Corrill, 32.

48. Peck (see this chapter, endnote #36).

49. Quinn, 479–485. Quinn has identified about 230 of these Danites by name.

50. Anson Call, "Statement, December 30, 1885," 2. Quoted in LeSueur, 46; cf. Albert P. Rockwood, "Journal," 7–8 (see LeSueur, 46).

51. Peck (see this chapter, endnote #36).

52. Swartzell, 22.

53. For more information on the activities of the Danites, the regularity with which they met, and their interaction with Mormon church leadership, see LeSueur, 43–45.

54. Sidney Rigdon, speech of July 4, 1838, reprinted in Peter Crawley, "Two Rare Missouri Documents," *Brigham Young University Studies* (Summer 1974), vol. 14, 527.

55. Rigdon, in Crawley, 527. Rigdon made various additional statements that indicated the Mormons might not have actually resorted to aggression. These points, however, were overlooked by non-Mormons whose fears were fueled by Rigdon's various incendiary declarations. Rigdon's milder sentiments were expressed as follows: "We will never be the agressors [sic] we will infringe on the rights of no people; but shall stand for our own until death. We claim our own rights, and are willing that all others shall enjoy theirs. . . . We therefore, take all men to record this day, that we proclaim our liberty on this day, as did our fathers. And we pledge this day to one another, our fortunes, our lives, and our sacred honors, to be delivered from the persecutions which we have had to endure, for the last nine years, or nearly that. . . . We this day then proclaim ourselves free, with a purpose and a determination, that never can be broken, no never! no never!! NO NEVER!!!"

56. Peter Crawley, "A Bibliography of The Church of Jesus Christ of Latter-day Saints in New York, Ohio, and Missouri," *BYU Studies* (Summer 1972), vol. 12, 523. Mormon leaders

agree almost unanimously that the terrible problems Smith and his followers faced in Missouri in 1838/39 were a direct result of Rigdon's inflammatory speech. LDS Apostle Jedediah M. Grant acknowledged that the lecture "was the main auxiliary that fanned into flame the burning wrath of the mobocratic portions of the Missourians" (Jedediah M. Grant, *A Collection of Facts, Relative to the Course Taken by Elder Sidney Rigdon . . .* [Philadelphia, 1844], 11). However, it must be recognized that Smith approved of Rigdon's speech, and therefore, shares responsibility for the ensuing troubles. According to Mormon historian B.H. Roberts, "[t]he unwisdom of the utterance has been quite generally recognized by our writers, and by them responsibility for it has been placed upon the rather fervid imagination of Sidney Rigdon, who delivered the speech, and who quite generally is supposed to have been mainly or wholly responsible for it. This is not true. The speech was carefully prepared . . . and read by other presiding elders of the church before its delivery. It immediately appeared in *The Far West*, a weekly newspaper . . . and was also published . . . on the press of the *Elders' Journal*. Joseph Smith in his journal speaks of it approvingly; and in the *Elders' Journal*, of which he was the editor, and in the editorial columns under his name, the speech is approvingly recommended to the saints. In view of these facts, if the 'declaration' was of doubtful propriety, and unwise and impolitic, responsibility for it rests not alone on Sidney Rigdon, but upon the authorities of the church who approved it, and the people who accepted it by their acclamation" (Roberts, vol. 1, 443).

57. *Missouri Argus*, September 27, 1838. Quoted in Van Wagoner, 221.

58. LeSueur, 56.

59. LeSueur, 59.

60. LeSueur, 60.

61. LeSueur, 61.

62. LeSueur, 61–62.

63. John L. Butler, as recorded in *Journal History of the Church of Jesus Christ of Latter-day Saints*, under August 6, 1838, 3, 246 reels, microforms, Marriot Library; cf. Quinn, 96.

64. *Story of the Grand River Country*, n.p. Quoted in LeSueur, 63.

65. LeSueur, 101-111.

66. Many 21st century Mormons deny that their spiritual forefathers committed such crimes, but historical documents written by 19th century Saints supports the allegations. Oliver B. Huntington, for example, recorded in his journal that Smith's followers plundered huge amounts of merchandise and property from non-Mormons (Huntington, vol. 1, 31-32, 34, see this chapter, endnote #33 for bibliographic information).

67. LeSueur, 118. Apostle Thomas B. Marsh, horrified by these actions, drew up a formal affidavit against the Saints who had taken part in the crimes. For his actions, the church excommunicated him as an apostate. In a letter to his brother and sister, Marsh noted: "[T]he disposition manifested in J. Smith and S. Rigdon to pillage, rob, plunder, assassinate and murder, was never equalled [sic] in my estimation, unless by some desperate Bandit" (Thomas B. Marsh, letter to Brother and Sister Abbot," October 25, 1838, in Joseph Smith Letterbook, vol. 2, 18, Smith Papers, microfilm at RLDSCA, Lee Library, and Marriot Library).

68. LeSueur, 129.

69. Joseph Smith. Quoted in LeSueur, 138, footnote #24.

70. LeSueur, 138.

71. David Patten. Quoted by Nathan Tanner, in George S. Tanner, *John Tanner and His Family* (Salt Lake City: John Tanner Family Association/Publishers Press, 1974), 386.

72. Quinn, 100.

73. James H. Hunt, *Mormonism . . . Their Troubles In Missouri and Final Expulsion From the State* (St. Louis: Ustick & Davies, 1844), 190-191.

74. Andrew Jenson, "Caldwell County, Missouri," *HR*, January 1888, vol. 8, no. 1, 702.

75. E.M. Ryland, letter to Messengers Amos Rees and Wiley C. Williams, October 25, 1838.

76. Lilburn Boggs, letter to General John B. Clark, October 27, 1838.

77. Joseph Young. Quoted in Parley P. Pratt, *Autobiography of Parley P. Pratt*, (Salt Lake City: Deseret Book Co., 1938; 1979 edition), 202–203.

78. LeSueur, 164–165.

79. LeSueur, 165.

80. Amanda Smith, account in Edward W. Tullidge, *The Women of Mormondom* (New York: Tullidge and Crandall, 1877), 121–132, reprinted in Fred C. Collier, ed., *Unpublished Revelations* (Salt Lake City: Collier's Publishing Co., 1993), vol. 2, 287.

81. LeSueur, 166.

82. LeSueur, 166.

83. LeSueur, 166.

84. Quinn, 100.

85. The non–Mormon, named Walker, may have been passing through Haun's Mill on his way to Far West or somewhere else (LeSueur, 167).

86. Amanda Smith, in Collier, 287–288; cf. Quinn, 100.

87. Amanda Smith, in Collier, 290.

88. LeSueur, 155

89. John Taylor, March 5, 1882, *JOD* (Liverpool, John Henry Smith, 1883; lithographed reprint of original edition, 1966), vol. 23, 37.

90. Taylor, in *JOD*, vol. 23, 37.

91. Corrill, 24 and Peck (see this chapter, endnote #36).

92. George Hinkle, letter to W.W. Phelps, August 14, 1844, in S.J. Hinkle, "A Biographical Sketch of G.M. Hinkle," *Journal of History* (October 1920), vol. 13, 449.

93. LeSueur, 178.

94. Peck (see this chapter, endnote #36).

95. According to historian Fawn Brodie, six thousand men visited Far West in less than a week and shot livestock for sport, killed some leading Elders, and raped several girls who had been "bound to the benches in the schoolhouse and violated by a score of men (Brodie, 242). However, recent research has shown that "all reports of rape are based on hearsay and rumors" (LeSueur, 181, footnote #7). LeSueur writes: "Charles Morehead, the representative to the state legislature from Ray County, said during a debate that 'he was in Far West when one of these reports [of rape] was started, and he assisted in attempting to ascertain the truth, and the Mormons themselves admitted that it was false'" (Charles Morehead, *Missouri Republican*, December 29, 1838. Quoted in LeSueur, 181, footnote#7). Whether or not such atrocities of war actually took place in Far West will remain in debate until solid evidence for such actions can be examined.

96. General John B. Clark, reprinted in *History of Caldwell and Livingston Counties* (St. Louis, 1886), 140.

97. Grant Underwood, *The Millenarian World of Early Mormonism* (Urbana: University of Illinois Press, 1993), 34.

98. Brodie, 244.

99. LeSueur, 205.

100. Brodie, 244.

101. Brodie, 246.

102. Brodie, 255.

103. *HC*, vol. 3, 321.

104. Brodie, 255.

CHAPTER NINE: MARCH TO MARTYRDOM

1. Joseph Smith, *HC* (Salt Lake City: Deseret Book Company, 1976/1980) vol. 6, 78, 319–320, 408–409.

2. Roger D. Launius and John E. Hallwas, eds., *Kingdom on the Mississippi Revisited* (Urbana: University of Illinois Press, 1996), 2.

3. The Nauvoo temple cost Smith's followers more than $1 million.

4. Robert Flanders, *Nauvoo: Kingdom on the Mississippi* (Urbana: University of Illinois Press, 1965), 104; James L. Kimball, Jr., "The Nauvoo Charter: A Reinterpretation," *Journal of the Illinois State Historical Society* (Spring 1971), vol. 64, 66-78; James L. Kimball, Jr., "A Wall to Defend Zion: The Nauvoo Charter," *BYU Studies* (Summer 1975), vol. 15, 499–526.

5. Laws of Illinois, 12 G.A., 52–57, includes printed transcript of Nauvoo Charter, Illinois State Archives. Quoted in James L. Kimball, Jr., "The Nauvoo Charter: A Reinterpretation," in Launius and Hallwas, 41.

6. Marvin S. Hill, "Religion in Nauvoo: Some Reflections," in Launius and Hallwas, 123.

7. *D&C* 124:49.

8. Jospeh Smith, Sidney Rigdon, Hyrum Smith, "A Proclamation to the Saints Scattered Abroad," *T&S*, July 15, 1841, vol. 2, no. 6, 276.

9. Dean Jessee, "Joseph Smith's 19 July 1840 Discourse," *BYU Studies* (Spring 1979), vol. 19, 392 and Andrew F. Ehat and Lyndon Cook, *The Words of Joseph Smith: The Contemporary Accounts of the Nauvoo Discourses of the Prophet Joseph Smith* (Provo: Utah: BYU Religious Studies Center) 363; cf. *HC*, vol. 6, 318–319, 321.

10. Ronald K. Esplin, "The Significance of Nauvoo for Latter-day Saints," *Journal of Mormon History* (1990), vol. 16, 72.

11. Robert Flanders, "Dream and Nightmare: Nauvoo Revisited," in F. Mark McKiernan, Alma R. Blair, and Paul M. Edwards, eds., *The Restoration Movement: Essays in Mormon History*, (Lawrence, Kansas: Coronado Press, 1973), 156. Quoted in Ronald K. Esplin, "The Significance of Nauvoo for Latter-day Saints," in Launius and Hallwas, 27.

12. Launius and Hallwas, 4.

13. John Emerich Edward Dalberg Acton, personal letter, quoted in *Encyclopedia Britannica*, online at http://www.britannica.com/seo/j/john-emerich-edward-dalberg-acton-1st-baron-acton-of-aldenham-8th-baronet/.

14. Wilford Woodruff, *1836-1837 Diary*, under December 11, 1836, reprinted in Dean Jessee, "The Kirtland Diary of Wilford Woodruff," *BYU Studies* (Summer 1972), vol. 12, 382.

15. Heber C. Kimball, cited in Helen Mar Whitney, "Scenes and Incidents from H.C. Kimball's Journal," *Woman's Exponent*, August 1, 1883, vol. 12, 34.

16. Woodruff, under April 9, 1836, reprinted in Jessee, 384.

17. Brigham Young, August 13, 1871, *JOD* (Liverpool: Albert Carrington, 1872; lithographed reprint of original edition, 1966), vol. 14, 203.

18. Brigham Young, July 11, 1852, *JOD* (Liverpool: F.D. Richards, 1855; lithographed reprint of original edition, 1966), vol. 1, 41.

19. Heber C. Kimball, July 26, 1857, *JOD* (Liverpool: Asa Calking, 1858; lithographed reprint of original edition, 1966), vol. 5, 88.

20. Brigham Young, October 9, 1859, *JOD* (Liverpool: Amasa Lyman, 1860; lithographed reprint of original edition, 1966), vol. 7, 289.

21. Levi Edgar Young, letter dated April 14, 1961. Quoted in Jerald Tanner and Sandra Tanner, *Mormonism: Shadow or Reality?* (Salt Lake City: ULM, 1987), 252.

22. John J. Stewart, *Joseph Smith: The Mormon Prophet* (Salt Lake City: Mercury Publishing, 1966), 1.

23. Brigham Young, September 9, 1860, *JOD* (Liverpool: Amasa Lyman, 1861; lithographed reprint of original edition, 1966), vol. 8, 176; Young said essentially the same thing in 1844: "Every spirit that confesses that Joseph Smith is a prophet, that he lived and died a prophet and that the Book of Mormon is true, is of God, and every spirit that does not is of anti-christ" (Brigham Young, "October Conference Minutes [October 6, 1844]," *T&S*, October 15, 1844, vol. 5, no. 19, 683).

24. Robert D. Anderson, *Inside the Mind of Joseph Smith: Psychobiography and the Book of Mormon* (Salt Lake City: Signature Books, 1999), xxxix, 222–242.

25. "Diagnostic Criteria for 301.81 Narcissistic Disorder," Diagnostic and Statistical Manual of Mental Disorders, 4th edition (Washington, D.C.: American Psychiatric Association, 1994), 661.

26. Hezekiah McKune, n.d., in E.D. Howe, *Mormonism Unvailed* (Painesville, OH: author, 1834), 268, online at http://www.solomonspalding.com/docs/1834howf.htm#pg268. This entire volume is online at http://www.solomonspalding.com/docs/1834howb.htm. A searchable text version is online at http://www.concordance.com/mormon.htm.

27. Sophia Lewis (a cousin of Emma Smith), n.d., in Howe, 269, online at http://www.solomonspalding.com/docs/1834howf.htm#pg269. This entire volume is online at http://www.solomonspalding.com/docs/1834howb.htm. A searchable text version is online at http://www.concordance.com/mormon.htm.

28. Levi Lewis (a cousin of Emma Smith), statement in Howe, 268–269, online at http://www.solomonspalding.com/docs/1834howf.htm#pg268. This entire volume is online at http://www.solomonspalding.com/docs/1834howb.htm. A searchable text version is online at http://www.concordance.com/mormon.htm.

29. *HC*, vol. 6, 408–409.

30. Charlotte Haven, "A Girl's Letters from Nauvoo," *Overland Monthly*, December 1890, 621.

31. Haven, 623.

32. *The New York Spectator*, September 23, 1843. Tanner and Tanner, 255.

33. D. Michael Quinn, *The Mormon Hierarchy: Origins of Power* (Salt Lake City: Signature Books, 1994), 261–262.

34. *HC*, vol. 5, 302.

35. *HC*, vol. 5, 316.

36. *HC*, vol. 5, 466.

37. *HC*, vol. 5, 524, 531.

38. Benjamin F. Johnson, letter to George S. Gibbs, 1903, LDSCA, cited in E. Dale LeBaron, "Benjamin Franklin Johnson: Colonizer, Public Servant, and Church Leader," M.A. thesis, Brigham Young University, 1967, 325–46, online at http://www.math.byu.edu/~smithw/Lds/LDS/Early-Saints/BFJohnson.html.

39. Jedediah M. Grant, September 24, 1854, *JOD* (Liverpool: Orson Pratt, 1856; lithographed reprint of original edition, 1966), vol. 3, 67.

40. According to Johnson, Smith attacked the Baptist preacher simply because the clergyman had "called Joseph a hypocrite, a liar, an imposter and a false prophet, and called upon him to repent" (Luke S. Johnson, "History of Luke Johnson [by himself]," under February the 14, 1835, online at http://www.math.byu.edu/~smithw/Lds/LDS/Early-Saints/LUJohnson.html.

41. Quinn, 91–92.

42. John D. Lee, *Mormonism Unveiled* (St. Louis: Bryan, brand and Co., 1877), 287, online at http://antimormon.8m.com/leechp19b.html.

43. *HC*, vol. 3, 291.

44. Josiah Quincy, *Figures of the Past* (Boston: Little, Brown, 1883), 377–400, reprinted in John E. Hallwas and Roger D. Launius, *Cultures in Conflict: A Documentary History of the Mormon War in Illinois* (Logan, UT: Utah State University Press, 1995), 46. Quincy was the nephew of U.S. President John Quincy Adams. Josiah met with Smith in his travels through Nauvoo, and wrote: "The past had shown him that a military organization was necessary."

45. Hamilton Gardner, "The Nauvoo Legion, 1840–45: A Unique Military Organization," in Launius and Hallwas, *Kingdom . . .*, 55, 57.

46. Hosea Stout, *On the Mormon Frontier: The Diary of Hosea Stout*, Juanita Brooks, ed. (Salt Lake City: University of Utah Press, 1964), vol. 1, 140–141, 197, 259.

47. Flanders, *Nauvoo*, 100.

48. There exist various estimates as to the size of the Nauvoo Legion, including 3,000 (Quinn, 106); 4,000 (Dan Erickson, *As A Thief in the Night* [Salt Lake City: Signature Books, 1998], 128 and Kenneth H. Winn, *Exiles in a Land of Liberty* [Chapel Hill, NC: University of North Carolina Press, 1989], 162); and 5,000 (Gardner, in Launius and Hallwas, *Kingdom . . .*, 57).

49. "Mormon Visitors," *Warsaw Signal*, July 21, 1841, http://www.lavazone2.com/dbroadhu/ IL/sign1841.htm#0721.

50. Flanders, *Nauvoo*, 112–113.

51. *HC*, vol. 4, 382. Mormons often have pointed to Smith's rank of Lieutenant-General with great pride, noting that no other officer in the U.S. held such a high rank. However, Joseph's rank actually meant very little, as Joseph M. O'Donnell (Chief, Archives & History Division, United States Military Academy at West Point) points out: "[A]lthough the Nauvoo Legion was chartered by the State of Illinois, it was not considered to be part of the state militia. . . . Joseph Smith, Jr., was not a Lieutenant General in the state militia, but of a small Mormon Army established to police Nauvoo, Illinois and to defend the state of Illinois" (Joseph M. O'Donnell, letter to Ralph L. Foster, August 29, 1963, photo reproduction in Ralph Leonard Foster, *The Book of Mormon On Trial*, facing page 20. Quoted in Tanner and Tanner, 254).

52. Gardner, in Launius and Hallwas, *Kingdom . . .*, 53. George Washington was given the rank lieutenant general on July 3, 1798 (see Francis B. Heitman, *History Register and Dictionary of the United States Army from Its Organization September 29, 1789, to March 2, 1903* [Washington, D.C.: Government Printing Office, 1903], vol. 1, 1004–1007). Ulysses S. Grant was given the rank of lieutenant general only through a special act of Congress on February 28, 1864 (Ulysses S. Grant, *Personal Memoirs of U.S. Grant* [New York: Charles L. Webster and Co., 1885–1886], vol. 2, 114–115). Interestingly, for some reason, Smith's official request for the exquisitely high rank of lieutenant general was recommended by Illinois Adjutant General Moses K. Anderson, the commission issued by Secretary of State Lyman Trumball, and signed/approved by Governor Thomas Carlin. As Gardner notes: "Just why all this was done still remains unexplained."

53. Fawn M. Brodie, *No Man Knows My History* (New York: Vintage Books, 1995; original edition by Alfred A. Knopf, 1945), 271.

54. Ebenezer Robinson, "The Return," (1888–1890), vol. 2, 298–302, typed copy only. Quoted in Tanner and Tanner, 254.

55. *HC*, vol. 4, 40.

56. *HC*, vol. 4, 80.

57. *HC*, vol. 4, 89.

58. Parley P. Pratt, *Mormonism Unveiled: Zion's Watchman Unmasked, And Its Editor, M R. L. R. Sunderland: Exposed: Truth Vindicated: The Devil Mad, And Priestcraft In Danger!* (New York: O. Pratt & E. Fordham, 1838), 15, online at http://www.solomonspalding.com/ docs/prt1838b.htm#pg15b. This entire volume is online at http://www.solomon spalding.com/docs/prt1838b.htm.

59. Pratt, 15.

60. Wilford Woodruff, in Scott G. Kenney, ed., *Wilford Woodruff's Journal*, 1833–1898 (Midvale, UT: Signature Books, 1983–85), under February 12, 1841, vol. 2, 43–44.

61. Joseph Smith, July 19, 1840, as recorded by Martha Jane Knowlton; ms. in LDSCA. Quoted in Ezra Taft Benson (thirteenth LDS president), "Our Divine Constitution," October 3, 1987, reprinted in *Ensign*, 1987, online at http://www.etext.org/Politics/ Essays/Conspiracy/LWB/LDS/god.planned.founding.fathers.

62. Joseph Smith. Quoted by Orson Pratt, letter to George A. Smith, January 21, 1841, Orson Pratt file, LDSCA.

63. Smith's belief that he would be asked to save America was in the context of a prophecy now being presented by the LDS church as a prophecy of the Civil War. Obviously,

Smith's role as America's deliverer from utter ruin via the Civil War never came about because he had been dead for nearly twenty years by the time the war between the states broke out. Consequently, the text about Smith coming to America's aid has been deleted from the official *History of the Church* produced by the Mormon church (see *HC*, vol. 5, 324). The inclusion of the excised text would have rendered Smith's "Civil War" prophecy a failed prediction (see "Suppressed Material Concerning The Civil War Prophecy," Tanner and Tanner, 195-H, online at http://www.concordance.com/cgi-bin/1wrdr.pl). Note: It seems Orson Hyde originally gave the dream's interpretation, which Smith eventually accepted.

64. Klaus J. Hansen, "The Political Kingdom of God as a Cause of Mormon–Gentile Conflict," in Launius and Hallwas, 63.

65. *HC*, vol. 6, 116.

66. Joseph Smith, letter to John C. Calhoun, *T&S*, January 1844, vol. 5, no. 1, 395.

67. *HC*, vol. 6, page 322.

68. *HC*, vol. 6, 282. Smith's request to raise this number of soldiers included an interesting provision that would deal with anyone seeking to hinder his plans: "Sec. 2. And be it further ordained that if any person or persons shall hinder or attempt to hinder or molest the said Joseph Smith from executing his designs in raising said volunteers . . . [he] shall be punished by a fine not exceeding one thousand dollars . . .or by hard labor on some public work not exceeding two years, or both" (*HC*, vol. 6, page 277).

69. John D. Lee, *A Mormon Chronicle: The Diaries of John D. Lee, 1848–1876*, Robert Glass Cleland and Juanita Brooks, eds. (San Marino, CA: Arthur H. Clark, 1955), vol. 1, 80.

70. Woodruff, in Kenney, under March 11, 1844, vol. 2, 366.

71. Sidney Rigdon, April 6, 1844, Conference Address, reprinted in "Conference Minutes," *T&S*, May 1, 1844, vol. 5, no. 9, 524.

72. Quinn, 123; cf. Sidney Rigdon, 524.

73. Quinn, 129.

74. Quinn, 128. For a more detailed look at the activities of the Council of Fifty and Smith's political aspirations during this era, see Quinn, 120–136.

75. George T.M. Davis, *An Authentic Account of the Massacre of Joseph Smith, the Mormon Prophet, and Hyrum Smith, His Brother, Together with a Brief History of the Rise and Progress of Mormonism, And All the Circumstances Which Led to Their Deaths* (St. Louis: Chambers and Knapp, 1844), 7; cf. Quinn, 128.

76. Sampson Avard, testimony transcribed in *Document Containing the Correspondence, Orders, &c., in Relation to the Disturbances with the Mormons and the Evidence Given Before the Hon. Austin A. King, Judge of the Fifth Judicial Circuit of the State of Missouri, at the Court-House in Richmond, in a Criminal Court of Inquiry, Begun November 12, 1838 on the Trial of Joseph Smith Jr., and Others for High Treason and Other Crimes Against the State* (Fayette, MO: Published by order of the General Assembly at the office of *Boon's Lick Democrat*, 1841), 97.

77. William Marks, letter to Beloved Brethren, June 15, 1853, in *Zion's Harbinger and Baneemy's Organ*, July 1853, vol. 3, 53.

78. John Taylor, "A Revelation on the Kingdom of God in the Last Days given through President John Taylor at Salt Lake City," June 27, 1882, reprinted in Fred C. Collier, ed., *Unpublished Revelations* (Salt Lake City: Collier's Publishing Co., 1979; 2nd edition, 1981), vol. 1, 133.

79. Lyman Wight and Heber C. Kimball, letter to Joseph Smith, June 19, 1844, LDSCA. This passage was deleted from the published text appearing in Mormonism's official *History of the Church* (see vol. 7, 139). Interestingly, Smith had always advocated monarchy as the best form of government. The *Book of Mormon*, published in 1830, stated that "if it were possible that ye could have just men to be your kings, which could establish the laws of God, and Judge this people according to his commandments . . . then it would be

expedient that ye should always have kings to rule over you" (*BOM*, 218, 1830 edition; Mosiah 29:13, modern edition).

80. Kenneth W. Godfrey, "The Road to Carthage Led West," *BYU Studies* (Winter 1968), vol. 8, 212–213. Godfrey also refers to the "Diary of George A. Smith, May 9,1844," stored in the "Library of the [LDS] Church Historian." In his dissertation written at BYU, Godfrey observed: "Joseph Smith had himself anointed King and Priest . . . [I]n a revelation dated 1886 given to President John Taylor, mention is made of Joseph Smith being crowned a king in Nauvoo. Not only was he ordained a king but the leading members of the Church were assigned governmental responsibilities. Brigham Young was to be president, John Taylor vice president, members of the Church were assigned to represent different states in the house and senate of the United States, and a full cabinet was appointed" ("Causes of Mormon Non-Mormon Conflict in Hancock County, Illinois, 1839–1846," Ph.D. dissertation, BYU, 1967, 63–65).

81. Smith and the high-ranking leaders of his church urged all of the Mormons to vote as one. For example, just before the congressional race of 1843, John Taylor stressed to the Saints the "necessity of unanimity." He warned: "It can answer no good purpose if half the citizens should disenfranchise the other half, thus rendering Nauvoo powerless as far as politics are concerned. In this city we have one interest alone and should not be divided" (John Taylor, *Nauvoo Neighbor*, August 2, 1843. Quoted in Winn, 178).

82. Quinn, 120.

83. Joseph Smith, "The Government of God," *T&S*, July 15, 1842, vol. 3, no. 18, 856–857.

84. Hallwas and Launius, *Cultures in Conflict*, 85. This volume gives extensive treatment to the political activities and ensuing fallout of Mormon politics in Illinois.

85. Quinn, 119.

86. Quinn, 119.

87. Anson G. Henry, letter to John J. Hardin, January 24, 1844, Hardin Collection, Chicago Historical Society.

88. *Sangamo Journal*, July 15, 1842. Quoted in Tanner and Tanner, *Shadow or Reality?*, 255.

89. *Quincy Whig*, in *Nauvoo Expositor*, June 7, 1844, 4, http://www.utlm.org/online resources/nauvooexpositor.htm.

90. Quinn, 130.

91. Quinn, 130.

92. *HC*, vol. 6, 105, emphases added. After passing this ordinance, the city council passed another ordinance "imprisoning and/or defining any legal officer attempting to arrest a Nauvoo resident without first having his writ countersigned by the mayor" (*Nauvoo Neighbor*, December 27, 1843). Governor Thomas Ford would later write: "[W]hen these ordinances were published they created general astonishment. Many people began to believe in good earnest that the Mormons were about to set up a separate government for themselves in defiance of the laws of the state" (Thomas Ford, *A History of Illinois: From Its Commencement as a State in 1818 to 1847*, Milo Quaife, ed. (Chicago: The Lakeside Press, 1945), vol. 2, 155–156.

93. Alanson Ripley, letter to Joseph Smith, April 10, 1839, Joseph Smith Letterbook 2:17, Smith papers, microfilm at Lee Library, at Research Library and Archives, RLDSCA, and at Marriot Library. Quoted in Marvin S. Hill, *Quest for Refuge: The Mormon Flight From American Pluralism* (Salt Lake City: Signature Books, 1989), 100.

94. *The Wasp* [Nauvoo, IL], May 28, 1842.

95. William Law, statement of July 31, 1887, in Lyndon W. Cook, ed., *William Law: Biographical Essay, Nauvoo Diary, Correspondence, Interview* (Orem, UT: Grandin Book Co., 1994), 116–117. Law repeated this charge in several documents including a sworn affidavit of July 17, 1885, published in Charles A Shook, *The True Origins of Mormon Polygamy* (Cincinnati: author, 1914), 125–129; also see Law's interview with William Wyl, published in the *Salt Lake Tribune* and reprinted in Thomas Gregg, *The Prophet of*

Palmyra (New York: John B. Alden, Publisher, 1890), 505, online at http://www.solomon spalding.com/docs1/1890GrgE.htm#pg505. This entire volume is online at http://www.solomonspalding.com/docs1/1890GrgA.htm.

96. Joseph Smith. Quoted in John C. Bennett, letter to Editor dated July 2, 1842, *Sangamo Journal* (Springfield, Illinois), July 5, 1842, reprinted in Hallwas and Launius, *Cultures in Conflict*, 117.

97. Joseph Smith. Quoted in John C. Bennett, letter to Editor dated July 2, 1842, *Sangamo Journal* (Springfield, Illinois), July 5, 1842, reprinted in Hallwas and Launius, *Cultures in Conflict*, 118.

98. Orrin Porter Rockwell. Quoted in Harold Schindler, *Orrin Porter Rockwell, Man of God, Son of Thunder* (Salt Lake City: University of Utah Press, 1966), 80, also see 74–109; cf. Richard S. Van Wagoner and Steven C. Walker, *A Book of Mormons* (Salt Lake City: Signature Books, 1982), 250.

99. Hallwas and Launius, *Cultures in Conflict*, 88–89.

100. Smith's public sermon on baptism for the dead, for instance, appeared in print in *T&S*, April 15, 1841, vol. 2, no. 12, 387.

101. Todd Compton, *In Sacred Loneliness: The Plural Wives of Joseph Smith* (Salt Lake City: Signature Books, 1997), 4.

102. According to several contemporary accounts, Smith claimed that he had to proceed with polygamy because an angel had declared to him that he must do so or risk having his call from God given to another (see Daniel W. Bachman, "A Study of the Mormon Practice of Plural Marriage before the Death of Joseph Smith," M.A. thesis, Purdue University, 1975, 74–75. Quoted in Launius and Hallwas, *Kingdom . . .*, 49.

103. According to Mormon researcher Todd Compton, most of these women, eleven to be precise, were teenagers (aged fourteen to twenty). Nine of the women were in the twenty-one to thirty-year-old age range. Eight of the wives were in Smith's own peer group, aged thirty-one to forty. Only two women fell into the forty-one to fifty-year-old age range, and three of his wives were in the aged fifty-one to sixty group.

104. Compton, 15.

105. Compton, 4, 15–16.

106. Quotes of Joseph Smith, John Taylor, and Wilford Woodruff taken from Richard Van Wagoner, *Mormon Polygamy: A History* (Salt Lake City: Signature Books, 1989; paperback edition), 62; cf. Jedediah Grant, February 19, 1854, *JOD* (Liverpool: F.F. Richards, 1855), vol. 2, 14. Grant, Second Counselor to Brigham Young, stated that Smith's "grand object in view" of asking for other men's wives, then relenting when they agreed to it, was "to try the people of God, to see what was in them."

107. Orson Whitney, *Life of Heber C. Kimball* (Salt Lake City: Kimball Family, 1888; Stevens & Wallis edition, 1945), 93–94; cf. Compton, 495.

108. Whitney, 333–335; cf. Compton, 495. After Heber received his wife back, he was so grateful that he himself, at Joseph's command, agreed to take his own plural wife—a thirty-year-old English convert named Sarah Peake Noon. Moreover, Smith forbade Heber to tell Vilate about the second marriage for fear that she would not accept the teaching and cause trouble. Heber struggled with the idea, but eventually capitulated. Vilate ultimately found out about Heber's new wife, accepted it, and allowed him to have even more wives.

109. See Compton, 499.

110. See Compton, 499.

111. Van Wagoner, *Mormon Polygamy*, 51–54, 59–60.

112. *D&C* 132:52.

113. By 1845, only about twenty-five families among 20,000 people living in Nauvoo knew about polygamy. The others thought that the charges of polygamy being leveled at church leaders by dissenters was nothing but vicious and unfounded anti-Mormon slander (George D. Smith, "Mormon Plural marriage," *Free Inquiry* [Summer 1992], vol. 12, no. 3), 34–35.

114. William Clayton, "William Clayton's Testimony," dated February 16, 1874, in Andrew Jenson, "Plural Marriage," May 1887, *HR*, 226, reprinted in Andrew Jenson, *HR* (Salt Lake City: Andrew Jenson, 1887; bound volumes), vol. 6, 226; cf. Joseph F. Smith, July 7, 1878, *JOD* (Liverpool: William Budge, 1880), vol. 20, 29.

115. Clayton, in Andrew Jenson, vol. 6, 226. In his diary, William Clayton related how Smith initiated him into the inner circle of leaders allowed to practice polygamy: "[T]he Prophet invited me to walk with him. During our walk, he said he had learned that there was a sister back in England, to whom I was very much attached. I replied there was, but nothing further than an attachment such as a brother and sister in the Church might rightfully entertain for each other. He then said, 'Why don't you send for her?' I replied, 'In the first place, I have no authority to send for her, and if I had, I have not the means to pay expenses.' To this he answered, 'I give you authority to send for her, and I will furnish you with means,' which he did. This was the first time the Prophet Joseph talked with me on the subject of plural marriage. He informed me that the doctrine and principle was right in the sight of our Heavenly Father, and that it was a doctrine which pertained to celestial order and glory. After giving me lengthy instructions and information concerning the doctrine of celestial or plural marriage, he concluded his remarks by the words, 'It is your privilege to have all the wives you want'" (William Clayton, see Robert C. Fillerup, compiler, *William Clayton's Nauvoo Diaries and Personal Writings*, under March 9, 1843, "Diary for November 27, 1842–April 28, 1843 and September 25, 1844–March 31, 1845," original in LDSCA, online at http://www.math.byu.edu/~smithw/Lds/LDS/Early-Saints/clayton-diaries, also online at http://www.code-co.com/rcf/mhistdoc/clayton.htm).

116. Jan Shipps. Cited in B. Carmon Hardy, *Solemn Covenant: The Mormon Polygamous Passage* (Urbana: University of Illinois Press, 1992), 9.

117. *T&S*, March 15, 1843, vol. 4, no. 9,143.

118. Thomas C. Sharp, "Matters and Things at Nauvoo," *Warsaw Signal*, May 8, 1844, 2 and untitled articles in the *Warsaw Signal*, May 15, 1844, 2, reprinted in Hallwas and Launius, *Cultures in Conflict*, 131–132; cf. John C. Bennett and others, various exposés, reprinted in Hallwas and Launius, *Cultures in Conflict*, 115–132.

119. *HC*, vol. 6, 363.

120. See the "Prospectus Of The Nauvoo Expositor," (see *HC*, vol. 6, 443–444); cf. online at http://www.utlm.org/onlineresources/nauvooexpositor.htm.

121. *Nauvoo Expositor*, June 7, 1844 (the only issue of this publication that was ever released), 2, online at http://www.utlm.org/onlineresources/nauvooexpositor.htm

122. Clayton, see Robert C. Fillerup, under June 22, 1844, in "Nauvoo Temple History Journal, William Clayton, 1845," original in LDSCA, online at http://www.math.byu.edu/~smithw/Lds/LDS/Early-Saints/clayton-diaries and also online at http://www.code-co.com/rcf/mhistdoc/clayton.htm; cf. quotation in Andrew F. Ehat, "'It Seems Like Heaven Began On Earth': Joseph Smith and the Constitution of the Kingdom of God," *BYU Studies* (Spring 1980), vol. 20, 268.

123. *Nauvoo Expositor*, 1–2.

124. *Nauvoo Expositor*, 2.

125. *Nauvoo Expositor*, 2.

126. *Nauvoo Expositor*, 2.

127. *Nauvoo Expositor*, 3.

128. *HC*, vol. 6, 441–445.

129. Charles A. Foster, "Tremendous Excitement—Unparalleled Outrage. On Board Steamer 'Osprey,'" St. Louis Evening Gazette, June 12, 1844, 2, reprinted in as "Dissenter Reports the Destruction of the 'Expositor,'" in Hallwas and Launius, *Cultures in Conflict*, 157.

130. William Edwin Berrett, *The Restored Church* (Salt Lake City: Deseret Book Company, 1949), 255.

131. Joseph Smith, letter to Emma, June 27, 1844. Quoted in Brodie, 391.

132. Brodie, 392.

133. Brodie, 392.

134. The entire Masonic call for distress is "Oh Lord, my God. Is there no help for a widows son?"

135. Brodie, 394. Smith reportedly also had a bayonet run through him by one of the vigilantes (Samuel Williams, second lieutenant in the Carthage Militia, letter to John Prickett, July 10, 1844, reprinted in Hallwas and Launius, *Cultures in Conflict*, 225).

136. Eliza R. Snow, "The Assassinations of Generals Joseph Smith and Hyrum Smith," *T&S*, July 1, 1844, 575, reprinted in Hallwas and Launius, *Cultures in Conflict*, 238–240.

CHAPTER TEN: A NEW BEGINNING

1. Orson Pratt, "Second Epistle of Orson Pratt," dated October 1, 1853, in *The Seer*, November 1853, vol. 1, no. 11, reprinted in *The Seer: 1853–1854* (Salt Lake City: Eborn Books, 1990), 168.

2. William Law, letter dated July 20, 1844. Quoted in Richard S. Van Wagoner, *Mormon Polygamy: A History* (Salt Lake City: Signature Books, 1989; paperback edition), 72.

3. Nauvoo would be renamed "The City of Joseph" on April 7, 1845 in response to the city's charter being terminated in January 1845.

4. George Morris, "Autobiography of George Morris," 22, typescript, Special Collections, Harold B. Lee Library, Brigham Young University, online at http://www.math. byu.edu/~smithw/Lds/LDS/Early-Saints/GMorris.html.

5. Henry W. Bigler, "Diary of a Mormon in California," 14, Bancroft Library, University of California, Berkeley.

6. "The City of Nauvoo," *T&S*, December 15, 1844, vol. 5, no. 23, 744.

7. D. Michael Quinn, "The Mormon Succession Crisis of 1844," *BYU Studies* (Winter 1976), vol. 16, 187.

8. Davis Bitton, "The Martyrdom of Joseph Smith in Early Mormon Writings," in Roger D. Launius and John E. Hallwas, eds., *Kingdom on the Mississippi Revisited* (Urbana: University of Illinois Press, 1996), 186–189.

9. W.W. Phelps, Willard Richards, and John Taylor, letter "To the Church of Jesus Christ of Latter Day Saints," *T&S*, July 1, 1844, vol. 5, no. 12, 568.

10. William Clayton, see Robert C. Fillerup, compiler, *William Clayton's Nauvoo Diaries and Personal Writings*, under July 6, 1844, "Diary for April 27, 1843–September 24, 1844," original in LDSCA, online at http://www.math.byu.edu/~smithw/Lds/LDS/Early-Saints/clayton-diaries, also online at http://www.code-co.com/rcf/mhistdoc/clayton.htm.

11. D. Michael Quinn, *The Mormon Hierarchy: Origins of Power* (Salt Lake City: Signature Books, 1994), 149.

12. Quinn, *The Mormon Hierarchy: Origins of Power*, 153. Although Quinn explains in great depth the various reasons why it is probable that Stout killed Samuel, he adds a word of caution: "This troubling allegation should not be ignored but cannot be verified."

13. Van Wagoner, 78.

14. Quinn, "The Mormon Succession," 189–190.

15. Wilford Woodruff, in Scott G. Kenney, ed., *Wilford Woodruff's Journal*, 1833–1898 (Midvale, UT: Signature Books, 1983–85), under August 7, 1844, vol. 2, 434. Woodruff's journals, edited by Kenney, can be found on the *New Mormon Studies CD ROM: Comprehensive Resource Library*.

16. William Clayton, "William Clayton Diary," in George D. Smith, ed., *An Intimate Chronicle: The Journals of William Clayton* (Salt Lake City: Signature Books/Smith Research Associates, 1995), under July 12, 1844, 138. Clayton's diary, edited by Smith, can be found on the *New Mormon Studies CD ROM: Comprehensive Resource Library*.

17. Quinn, *The Mormon Hierarchy: Origins of Power*, 152.

18. Quinn, *The Mormon Hierarchy: Origins of Power*, 164.

19. Clayton, under August 8, 1844, *An Intimate Chronicle*, 142; cf. Heber C. Kimball, "Heber C. Kimball Diary," under August 8, 1844, in Stanley B. Kimball, ed., *On the Potter's Wheel: The Diaries of Heber C. Kimball* (Salt Lake City: Signature Books/Smith Research Associates, 1987), 79. *On the Potter's Wheel* can be found on the *New Mormon Studies CD ROM: Comprehensive Resource Library*.

20. Brigham Young, "An Epistle of the Twelve," *T&S*, August 15, 1844, vol. 5, no. 15, 618.

21. Marvin S. Hill, *Quest for Refuge* (Salt Lake City: Signature Books, 1989), 158–159.

22. Quinn, "The Mormon Succession," 193.

23. The Mormon succession crisis of 1844–1846 produced numerous other splinter groups, much less notable, that came under the leadership of various Mormons including Alpheus Cutler, William Smith (Joseph's brother), Charles Blanchard Thompson, James Brewster, Austin Cowles, Granville Hedrick, and others (see Kate B. Carter, *Denominations that Base Their Beliefs On the Teachings of Joseph Smith* [Salt Lake City: Daughters of Utah Pioneers, 1969 and Steven L. Shields, *Divergent Paths of the Restoration* [Los Angeles: Restoration Research, 1990]).

24. For an in-depth look at these and other individuals who formed Mormon factions, see Quinn, *The Mormon Hierarchy*, 187–243; also see Steven L. Shields, *Divergent Paths of the Restoration* (Bountiful, UT: Restoration Research, 1990), available for purchase from Utah Lighthouse Ministry, online at http://www.utlm.org/booklist/titles/xb063_divergent pathsoftherestoration.htm.

25. Brigham Young, "October Conference Minutes [October 6, 1844]," *T&S*, October 15, 1844, vol. 5, no. 19, 683,; cf. *HC* (Salt Lake City: Deseret Book Company, 1976/1980), vol. 7, 288. Brigham Young originally stated that no one would ever take Smith's place as prophet-leader of the church (Young, "An Epistle of the Twelve," 618). But by December 1847, Young had become so powerful that he was able to re-organize the church's leadership structure in such a way as to place himself at the absolute head of the church. He accomplished this by reorganizing the First Presidency with himself installed as church president, backed by two counselors. This structure continues to be used in today's Mormon church.

26. Hill, 172–173.

27. Marshall Hamilton, "From Assassination to Expulsion: Two Years of Distrust, Hostility, and Violence," in Launius and Hallwas, 216.

28. Quinn, *The Mormon Hierarchy: Origins of Power*, 637.

29. Orson Hyde. Quoted in John Bennion, "John Bennion Journal," under October 13, 1860, Special Collections and Manuscripts Department, Lee Library; cf. Brigham Young Office Journal, April 3, 1860, copies in fd 2, box 26, Donald R. Moorman papers, archives, Stewart Library, Weber State University, Ogden, UT, and in fd 1, box 93, H. Michael Marquardt papers, Manuscripts Division, Marriot Library.

30. Hyde. Quoted in John Bennion Journal.

31. Allen J. Stout, "Allen J. Stout Journal," under June 28, 1844, Utah State Historical Society, 14, online at http://www.math.byu.edu/~smithw/Lds/LDS/Early–Saints/AStout.html; cf. Quinn, *The Mormon Hierarchy: Origins of Power*, 151.

32. Hosea Stout, under February 22, 1845, in Juanita Brooks, ed., *On the Mormon Frontier: The Diary of Hosea Stout* (Salt Lake City: University of Utah Press, 1964), vol. 1, 22.

33. Hosea Stout, under March 13, 1847, vol. 1, 241.

34. Quinn, *The Mormon Hierarchy: Origins of Power*, 643.

35. *HC*, vol. 7, 446–447.

36. Quinn, *The Mormon Hierarchy: Origins of Power*, 653.

37. George Rockwell, letter to Thomas Rockwell, September 23, 1845, Special Collections and Manuscripts Department, Lee Library. Quoted in Quinn, *The Mormon Hierarchy: Origins of Power* , 181.

38. Quinn, *The Mormon Hierarchy: Origins of Power*, 181.

39. Orrin Rhodes, affidavit of October 1, 1845, reprinted in John E. Hallwas and Roger D. Launius, eds., *Cultures in Conflict* (Logan: Utah: Utah State University Press, 1995), 279–280.

40. Thomas Ford, *A History of Illinois, from its Commencement as a state in 1818 to 1847* (Chicago: S.C. Griggs and Co., 1854), 409, http://www.solomonspalding.com/docs/frd1854a.htm; cf. Hallwas and Launius, *Cultures in Conflict*, 279.

41. William Hall, *The Abominations of Mormonism Exposed* (Cincinnati, 1852), 31–34; cf. Quinn, *The Mormon Hierarchy: Origins of Power*, 651.

42. Quinn, *The Mormon Hierarchy: Origins of Power*, 217.

43. Brigham Young. Quoted on an undated page of statements by Jehiel Savage, Charles B. Thompson, George J. Adams, and Joseph Younger, RLDSCA, a portion of the minutes of the high council at Voree, Wisconsin, April 6, 1846, of the followers of James J. Strang, Document 6, Strang Manuscripts, Beinecke Library (see Quinn, *The Mormon Hierarchy: Origins of Power*, 217).

44. Oliver B. Huntington, statement in "Seymour B. Young Diary," under May 23, 1903, LDSCA; see Quinn, *The Mormon Hierarchy: Origins of Power*, 179.

45. Clayton, under July 5, 1845, see Quinn, *The Mormon Hierarchy: Origins of Power*, 179, 652.

46. Hosea Stout, under September 14, 1845, in Brooks, vol. 1, 63.

47. Hosea Stout, under January 9, 1846, in Brooks, vol. 1, 103.

48. Hosea Stout, under April 3, 1845, in Brooks, vol. 1, 32.

49. William B. Pace, *William B. Pace Autobiography*. Quoted in Dean Moody, "Nauvoo's Whistling and Whittling Brigade," *BYU Studies* (Summer 1975), vol. 15, 487.

50. Jehiel Savage statement in minutes of the high council of James Strang's followers at Voree, Wisconsin, April 6, 1846.

51. Hosea Stout, under April 27, 1845, in Brooks, vol. 1, 36.

52. William Clayton, "William Clayton Diary," under the date February 28, 1845, in James B. Allen, *Trials of Discipleship: The Story of William Clayton, a Mormon* (Urbana: University of Illinois Press, 1987), 176. Allen's book can be found on the *New Mormon Studies CD ROM: Comprehensive Resource Library*; cf. Allen Stout, under February 27, 1845, 15, online at http://www.math.byu.edu/~smithw/Lds/LDS/Early-Saints/AStout.html.

53. Clayton, in Allen, 176.

54. John Taylor, "Deacon Reports," *Nauvoo Neighbor*, May 7, 1845, 2, available at Kansas City Public Library, Special Collections Department, Newspapers on Microfilm, accessible online at http://www.kcpl.lib.mo.us/sc/history/newspapers.htm.

55. *Quincy Signal*, September 17, 1845. Quoted in Hill, 174

56. Hill, 175–176.

57. Hamilton, in Launius and Hallwas, 214.

58. "Nauvoo: By Order of the Council, Brigham Young Pres. Willard Richards Clerk," September 24, 1845, online at http://library.byu.edu/~imaging/into/lvnauvoo/10denfs.html.

59. Quinn, *The Mormon Hierarchy: Origins of Power*, 176.

60. Brigham Young. Quoted Heber C. Kimball, "Journal of Heber C. Kimball," under January 2, 1846, in possession of LDSCA.

61. Hill, 180.

62. Jerald Tanner and Sandra Tanner, *The Mormon Kingdom* (Salt Lake City: ULM, 1971), vol. 2, 51–64.

63. Quinn, *The Mormon Hierarchy: Origins of Power*, 127.

64. Tanner and Tanner, vol. 2, 54–56, 61 and Quinn, *The Mormon Hierarchy: Origins of Power*, 650–651. The Tanners' book quotes numerous historical documents from the period that discuss the arrest and detention of various Mormons for passing counterfeit money that apparently was created in Nauvoo (e.g., *Warsaw Signal*, June 5, 1844 and *St. Louis American*, December 2, 1845).

65. Tanner and Tanner, vol. 2, 54–56, 61.

66. Norma Baldwin Ricketts, *The Mormon Battalion: U.S. Army of the West, 1846–1848* (Logan, UT: Utah State University Press, 1996), 1.

67. Thomas Ford, December 7, 1846, address to state legislature, reprinted in Illinois State Register, December 11, 1846.

68. Nels Anderson, *Desert Saints: The Mormon Frontier in Utah* (Chicago: University of Chicago Press, 1942; paperback edition, 1966), 56.

69. Orson Pratt, "Extracts from O. Pratt's Private Journal," *MS*, June 15, 1850, 177–180. Quoted in David L. Bigler, *Forgotten Kingdom: The Mormon Theocracy in the American West, 1847–1896* (Logan, Utah: Utah State University Press, 1998), 21.

70. Edwin Brown Firmage and Richard Collin Mangrum, *Zion in the Courts* (Urbana: University of Illinois Press, 1988), 125–126.

71. Firmage and Mangrum, 213.

72. Firmage and Mangrum, 126.

73. Dale L. Morgan, *The State of Deseret* (Logan, UT: Utah State University Press/Utah State Historical Society, 1987), 125. According to Mormons, the word Deseret (from the *Book of Mormon*) means "honeybee." It supposedly is an ancient term dating back to the building of the tower of Babel. However, there exists no cultural or linguistic evidence anywhere in the world supporting this contention.

74. Bigler, 46. To bolster his assertion about Deseret's constitution, Bigler notes that although the initial elections for the state's legislative body and other officers was to be held on May 7, 1849, the election had already been mapped out and officers chosen before the constitutional convention even met. Then, when the open election was held, Brigham Young easily won the governorship without opposition and other officers were unanimously elected as well.

75. Bigler, 47.

76. Brigham Young. Quoted in *Deseret News*, September 17, 1856, 220.

77. Brigham Young, August 13, 1871, *JOD* (Liverpool: Albert Carrington, 1872; lithographed reprint of original edition, 1966), vol. 14, 205.

78. Brigham Young, April 6, 1862, *JOD* (Liverpool: George Q. Cannon, 1862; lithographed reprint of original edition, 1966), vol. 9, 267.

79. Heber C. Kimball, July 16, 1854, *JOD* (Liverpool: Amasa Lyman, 1860; lithographed reprint of original edition, 1966), vol. 7, 19.

80. Clayton, under July 25, 1847, *An Intimate Chronicle*, 365.

81. Brigham Young, February 3, 1867, *JOD* (Liverpool: B. Young, Jr., 1867; lithographed reprint of original edition, 1966), vol. 11, 298.

82. Brigham Young, November 29, 1868, JOD (Liverpool: Albert Carrington, 1869; lithographed reprint of original edition, 1966), vol. 12, 315; cf. Young, October 8, 1868, vol. 12, 301.

83. Noteworthy is the fact that control of Utah's creeks and canyons, the most valuable and useful land in the desert climate, was given to Young and other high-ranking church leaders.

84. Brigham Young, June 3, 1855, *JOD* (Liverpool: F.D. Richards, 1855; lithographed reprint of original edition, 1966), vol. 2, 298–308.

85. S[olomon] N. Carvalho, *Incidents of Travel and Adventure in the Far West; with Col. Fremont's Last Expedition* (New York: Derby & Jackson, 1857), 142–143, online at http://moa.umdl.umich.edu:80/cgi/pageviewer?frames=1&coll=moa&view=75&root= mm000007%2F0182inci%2Fv0000%2Fi000&tif=01420142.tif&cite=http%3A%2F%2F moa.umdl.umich.edu%2Fcgi%2Fsgml%2Fmoa-idx%3Fnotisid%3DAAW4596.

86. Joseph Smith, *HC* (Salt Lake City: Deseret Book Company, 1976/1980), vol. 1, 150; cf. *D&C* 42:37.

87. John Taylor, who would become the LDS church's 3rd president, in 1852 wrote: "[T]his earth is properly the dwelling-place, and rightful inheritance of the Saints. Inasmuch as it belongs to Jesus Christ, it also belongs to his servants and followers. . . . It is

therefore their rightful inheritance, and the usurpation before referred to, while it is unjust to God, is also as unjust to his Saints" (John Taylor, *The Government of God* [London: Latter-day Saints' Book Depot, 1852], 72). LDS officials not only prevented private ownership of Utah land by Mormons, but passed various ordinances that made ownership of land illegal for non-Mormons. For example, in order to exploit a federal law exempting land within municipalities from claims, LDS leaders expanded city limits to include all available farm land, thus rendering such lands unobtainable. They also passed a law forbidding transfer of land to anyone until a certificate of survey had been approved and countersigned by one or more of the "Selectmen of the county." Such measures, along with the verbal threats and violent intimidation tactics used by Mormons, effectively prevented outsiders from owning land (see Bigler, 248). *The Government of God* can be found on the *New Mormon Studies CD ROM: Comprehensive Resource Library.*

88. Young, July 8, 1855, in *JOD*, vol. 2, 310.

89. Young, July 8, 1855, in *JOD*, vol. 2, 317.

90. Andrew Cahoon. Cited in Klaus J. Hansen, *Quest for Empire: The Political Kingdom of God and the Council of Fifty in Mormon History* (East Lansing, MI: Michigan State University Press, 1967), 200, footnote #74.

91. William Willes and other composers, *The Mountain Warbler* (Salt Lake City: Deseret News Book and Job Establishment, 1872), 91. According to its title page, this hymnbook was "sanctioned" by the authorities of the church, and distributed primarily for use by LDS choirs, Sabbath schools, and families.

92. William Jarman, *USA—Uncle Sam's Abscess or Hell Upon Earth for U.S.* (Exeter, England: H. Leduc's Steam Printing Works, 1884), 34. The extended subtitle of this work is extremely interesting and revealing: *By William Jarman . . . Knight of the Grand Legion of North America, who suffered twelve years in the Mormon hell on earth, as one of the "Virgins Without Guile," and a priest after the order of Melchizedek: where Polygamy, Incest, and Murder are taught and practised as religion under the "All Seeing Eye," and the sign "Holiness unto the Lord."*

93. Heber C. Kimball, November 9, 1856, *JOD*, vol. 4, 81 and October 5, 1856, *JOD*, vol. 4, 119. In his riveting 1873 book *The Rocky Mountain Saints*, T.B.H. Stenhouse reprinted the following eye-witness account from a Mormon in Utah: "[Heber C. Kimball] declared to the people that Brigham Young was his God, and their God, and the only God they would ever see if they did not obey him: 'Joseph Smith was God to the inhabitants of the earth when he was amongst us, and Brigham is God now.' This strain was caught up and reiterated by many of the elders, from Orson Hyde, the president of the twelve apostles, down to the most ignorant teacher, and to question it openly was to be put under the ban" (T.B.H. Stenhouse, *The Rocky Mountain Saints* [New York: D. Appleton & Co., 1873; 1904 edition, published in Salt Lake City, Shepard Book Company], 294). This volume is online, along with several other historical books, at http://antimormon.8m.com/index.html.

94. Quoted in Nelson Winch Green, *Mormonism: its rise, progress, and present condition. Embracing the narrative of Mrs. Mary Ettie V. Smith* (Hartford, CT: Belknap & Bliss, 1858; 1870 edition), 201, online at http://moa.umdl.umich.edu/cgi/pageviewer?frames=1&cite=http%3A%2F%2Fmoa.umdl.umich.edu%2Fcgi%2Fsgml%2Fmoa-idx%3Fnotisid%3DAJK2869&coll=moa&view=75&root=mm000044%2F1206morm%2Fv0000%2Fi000%2F&tif=00190017.tif&pagenum=201.

95. Hubert Howe Bancroft, *History of Utah, 1540–1886* (San Francisco: The History Company Publishers, 1890), 505.

96. John Taylor, September 20, 1857, in *JOD* (Liverpool: Asa Calkin, 1858; lithographed reprint of original edition, 1966), vol. 5, 266.

97. Heber C. Kimball, August 13, 1853, in *JOD*, vol. 2, 107.

98. One of Brigham Young's own wives stated: "There is no despotic monarchy in the world

where the word of the sovereign is so absolute as in Utah. And never, in the whole history of Mormonism, has the despotic rule been so arbitrary as it was during the period of, and for a short time after, the Reformation" (Ann Eliza Young, *Wife No. 19, or the Story of A Life In Bondage, Being A Complete Exposé of Mormonism, and Revealing the Sorrows, Sacrifices and Sufferings of Women in Polygamy* [Hartford, Ct: Dustin, Gilman & Co., 1875], Chapter Eighteen, online at http://www.antimormon.8m.com/youngchp18.html. This entire volume is online at http://www.antimormon.8m.com/youngindex.html).

CHAPTER ELEVEN: BLOODY BRIGHAM

1. Aaron DeWitt, letter to Elizabeth Durrant, January 31, 1875, available online at http://www.saintsalive.com/mormonism/murder.html. The story behind this letter is a fascinating tale. On March 8, 1987, with much fanfare and media hype, a time-capsule originally sealed in 1889 was opened at Old Main on the Utah State University campus. Inside were found several interesting trinkets associated with mid- to late nineteenth century Utah. The most curious item was a copy of DeWitt's letter to his sister. DeWitt— a prominent Cache Valley resident, businessman and poet—apparently slipped his communiqué into the capsule without anyone noticing it. The letter describes how he saw life in Utah, under Brigham Young. Its complete text reads as follows:

> Logan, Utah, Jan. 31,1875
> To Mrs. Elizabeth Durrant
>
> My Dear Sister:
>
> I low to commence this letter I have promised you so long. I hardly know, but will say in the first place I have been deceived, led into error, imposed upon, deluded, beguiled into a false religion in my youth and spent the best part of my life in a wilderness, a desert, a land of sage and salt, away from all enlightenment and civilization, among the most degraded tribes of Indians on the Western hemisphere. And what is still more worse, I have had to mingle with
>
> **A BEASTLY, BLACKHEARTED, BLOODLY PRIESTHOOD;**
>
> A set of treacherous villains, as full of meanness as old Satan, and as thirsty for blood as a stinted leech.
>
> > *While these are facts, they are not half told;*
> > *For hundreds have been killed for gold;*
> > *Both men and women have been slain*
> > *And robbed to add to Brigham's gain.*
>
> I will here mention a few of the most inhuman and cruel acts ever committed by any man-eating savage in the darkest ages, and which none but a corrupt priesthood could ever perpetrate. All of these have been done in Utah since I came here by men claiming to hold
>
> **THE HOLY PRIESTHOOD OF THE SON OF GOD,**
>
> And sent by their great Prophet and leader to do these deeds of blood and plunder in the name of Cod Almighty. On the 12th day of September, 1857, two days after I arrived in this accursed land,119 men, women and children were murdered while traveling to California, by a band of Mormons painted as Indi-

ans, and led by a Mormon high priest, a pious president of a stake of Zion, and a wise ward bishop. After the emigrants had defended themselves against those wretches for three days beneath a burning sun in a sandy desert,

WITHOUT A DROP OF WATER,

They dressed two beautiful little girls in white and sent them to a spring near by. But as they tripped along towards the sparkling stream they met the bullets of those merciless Mormons and fell dead into the water they were trying to secure to save their own lives and quench the parched throats of their beloved parents. Finally John D. Lee, a Mormon bishop, who had just been anointed

A KING AND PRIEST TO GOD,

And who had eighteen wives given to him for being so great and good, sent a flag of truce to the poor parched up, bleeding emigrants and promised them protection if they would give up their arms and go back to the nearest town. This they gladly agreed to; but mark the next act of this sanctified saint. They had not gone a half mile from their camp, when this great deliverer gave the command to his men to fire, and every man was shot down and every woman screamed and ran. The terrible, sorrowful scene that ensued no tongue can tell. Every woman was caught ravished, murdered, robbed of her jewelry, stripped naked and left unburied on the burning sand. In a few days nothing was left of all those beautiful forms but the bleaching bones the prairie wolf could not devour. Then every child those bloodhounds thought could tell the tale of their infernal villainy was beheaded or cut to pieces, and scattered quivering with its bleeding friends, Then those pure-souled priests plunged their hands into the gory clotted blood of their victims, and with outstretched arms toward heaven,

EXPRESSED THEIR GRATITUDE TO GOD

For so great a favor; to Him who doeth all things well; but who will undoubtedly, when they meet Him, hear His laugh re-echo through the caverns of the damned, saying, "I told you I would laugh at your calamity and mock when your fear cometh." All the property of those murdered men and women was gathered together the value of one hundred and fifteen thousand dollars, besides thirty-five thousand dollars in gold, and sent to their old master-murderer Brigham And this is how he sits in his office, wags his big toe, and makes his means, and then boasts that he is

THE GREATEST FINANCIER ON EARTH,

And owns nothing but what the Lord has given him. Another and similar case is that of the murdered Morrisites, a religious body of simple minded souls, who had met together for devotional exercise in a small valley on the banks of the Weber River in the summer of 1862, when a corps of the Nauvoo Legion, led by cowardly Captain Burton, who is now on a mission preaching the Gospel of Mercy to you dark benighted Britons and inviting you to the home of the free and the land of the brave, but he is not gallant enough to come home himself. He is the dastardly dog who crawled on his belly, like his ancient progenitor which tempted Mother Eve, until he was near enough to fire a cannon and blow down the house where those poor souls had met. Then, after they had surrendered, and given up their few fire arms, the paltroon shot and killed Joseph Morris, Mr. Banks, and two women, one with a beautiful baby nursing at her breast, took the rest of the camp prisoners, put them in the penitentiary, and finally fined them one hundred dollars each, just because they did not believe in the rascality of Brigham Young, and do as they were told.

> *What bloody deeds, what sin and strife,*
> *What sacrifice of human life,*
> *What deeds of plunder have been done,*
> *To raise a gory throne for Young.*

I will next mention the most perfidious act coupled with the foulest murder ever committed since the world began.

IT WAS IN THE DEAD OF NIGHT,

when three of the Salt Lake City police were sent by the great Seer and Revelator of all the world, to see Dr. Robinson and ask him to set a broken limb for a poor man who, they said was writhing in agony. The Doctor had just retired to bed, but at his murderers' entreaties, he dressed himself, and in a few moments was on his errand of mercy. He had not gone far when one of the villains, who walked behind, struck him on the head with a meat chopper he had stolen for the purpose, and cleft open his skull. The others fired their pistols immediately, and blowing out their victim's brains, fled.

But my soul sickens at these dreadful deeds, or I would tell you of the brutal murder of Yates, the killing of McNiel, the assassination of Borman, the shooting of Brassfield, the slaughter of the Akins party, the emasculation of Jones, and finally the butchering of him and his poor old mother. I would also mention the dead man in the meat market, the three men in the barn, the murder near the Warm Springs, the shooting. of Pike in the streets of Salt Lake City in broad daylight, the murder of the Potters and Parishes, of Rhodes and Roberts, and hundreds of others who

HAVE BEEN MURDERED IN COLD BLOOD,

And robbed to satisfy the avaricious cravings of as foul a man and as false a Prophet as ever disgraced this sin stained earth. These horrible deeds have all been committed in our holy Zion, and not one of the perpetrators ever brought to justice. In fact, there has been no justice in the land. A few years ago a man's life was not worth a cent who durst utter such words as there is evil in the land, or sin among the Priesthood. "You do as you are told!" has been the Gospel preached in this priest-ridden place for the last quarter of a century.

In the fall of 1857, I heard our Prophet in a congregation of three thousands souls, tell his bishops they were to "counsel" the brethren to do as they were told; and, said he "if they don't do it, lay righteousness to the line and judgment to the pummel. If you don't know what that is, come to me and I will tell you." He then threw back his head and with a revolting grin,

DREW HIS FINGER ACROSS HIS THROAT,

A sign the anointed ones well understood. And yet, the old bilk, with his smooth slang will make his innocent dupes believe he is free from guilt, and that he is

THE LIGHT, THE TRUTH, AND THE WAY,

And that he has a place prepared for them, where the waters are flowing placidly-a land of milk and honey.

> *But the waters are stained with blood, and the milk is turned to whey,*
> *And the honey has lost its sweetness, the people seem to say;*
> *And dupes are getting scarcer, and obedience is dead,*
> *And all the old man's judgments and plummets, too, have fled.*

THE HAND-CART EXPEDITION

Then there was the hand-cart company that crossed the plains in 1856. The details of their distress caps the climax of all horrors. Could I portray that terrible journey and the sufferings of those poor souls, your very heart would bleed. Three ounces of flour per day was all they had to eat. Upon this scanty fare they dragged their carts with 100 pounds of luggage over the worst kind of road, and more than five hundred miles through snow, fording rivers whose currents are of the swiftest kind, and their waters always cold. Then at night, when those poor, wet, shivering souls came into camp they had no wood to make a fire. At times a few small willows could be obtained, just enough to bake their scanty cake. It did not take them long to eat their supper, for a mouthful each was all they had. So hungry were they, that some gnawed the flesh off their own arms, eat roasted hide, or fed upon their shoes. One-fourth of all who started,

DIED OF STARVATION ON THE WAY

From five to fifteen died every night for over 300 miles of the road. So weak and weary were these living skeletons that they could scarcely bury their dead. Every night a pit would be dug just large enough to place the dead in, and a shallow covering of dirt thrown over them. Those that dug the grave one night expected to be placed in theirs the next. Many a one prayed that his spirit might leave his frame of bones for a berth among the blessed.

Why did they start in this way? do you inquire. Because this false prophet had told them that it was the Lord's plan of emigration, and the only way to secure salvation. They believing him to be a true prophet, had faith in all he said, and started on their journey, 1,400 miles, as late in the season as August. As they traveled on Westward toward the Zion of their hopes, songs could be heard from every cart and prayers from every camp. But before they got five hundred miles on their weary pilgrimage,

THE SNOWS BEGAN TO FALL,

The wintry winds to blow, and the keen frost and piercing cold set in. Then their suffering commenced in earnest. Still they trudged along day after day, full of faith in God and holy priesthood, and day after day endured greater pain. Finally their limbs began to freeze, and pieces fell from their worn-out bodies. They became dispirited and pined away and died, as I have already told you.

So sad and sickening is this gospel plan
As taught by Brigham, to poor fallen man,
That every time I mention his ill name.
It sends a shudder quivering through my frame.
I also tremble for the deeds he's done;
For life destroyed, for blood he caused to run;
For victims frozen on the plains, through him,
While starving, suffering, falling limb from limb.

Dear Sister, in this sad letter I have told you the truth.

AS IT IS IN JESUS CHRIST,

And as I expect to meet at the final bar of retribution. All these deeds and a thousand others equal to them in baseness and brutality, have all been committed under the cloak of religion. But I must tell you more of them at another time.

I will now tell you the reason why we could not leave this blood-stained land, I mean ten or twelve years ago. In the first place, we were a thousand miles from the nearest town East, eight hundred miles to the nearest settlement West, and God only knows how far to any place north and south. On all this vast tract of land.

NO WHITE MAN DWELT,

No civilization was known, none but the red men roamed the dreary solitudes. To travel such a space required considerable food, a good wagon and team, in fact, everything necessary for a three month's pilgrimage. Nor was it safe for a few men to go together, unless they were well-armed. Again, every Bishop knew your business

AND WAS ALWAYS ON THE LOOKOUT.

If you started they would send men to drive off your stock, and thus you would be compelled to return. Then, if you did not behave and act the hypocrite, the bishop would send the Danites to use you up, send you across lots to that bright brimstone home we read about. Thus you see it was almost impossible to get away. But now we have a railroad across the plains and settlements every little way and civilization is coming to Zion. If the Lord won't come the law will, and if Jesus is not approaching, justice is. Then all who want can leave. But now the priests want us to go, and we wish to stay.

Burst off every fetter, remove this Priestly yoke.
And never rest contented, till every link is broke.
For every man in Utah and woman shall be free,
And shouts shall echo through the
land for God and liberty!

Hoping to meet you soon on earth life and finally beyond the confines of time measured out to mortal man. I am affectionately, Your Brother, AARON DEWITT.

* * *

The late A. J. Simmonds—curator of Special Collections at Utah State University (Logan, Utah), author, and an authority on Cache Valley history—delivered a very insightful lecture about DeWitt's letter to Saints Alive Capstone Conferences in 1987. His paper is available online in its entirety at http://www.saintsalive.com/mormonism/murder.html.

2. David L. Bigler, *Forgotten Kingdom: The Mormon Theocracy in the American West, 1847–1896* (Logan, Utah: Utah State University Press, 1998), 49. One of Brigham Young's many wives noted as much in her book about life in Utah, stating: "For many years the Mormons rejected the aid of physicians altogether. They applied oil, and 'laid hands' on all sick persons, without regard to their ailments. If a person was ill, the elders were called, and they anointed him with consecrated oil; then. they rubbed or manipulated him, much after the manner of the modern 'magnetic treatment,' the elders praying audibly all the time" (Ann Eliza Young, *Wife No. 19, or the Story of A Life In Bondage, Being A Complete Exposé of Mormonism, and Revealing the Sorrows, Sacrifices and Sufferings of Women in Polygamy* [Hartford, Ct: Dustin, Gilman & Co., 1875], chapter 7, online at http://www.antimormon.8m.com/youngchp7.html. This entire volume is online at http://www.antimormon.8m.com/youngindex.html).

3. Bigler, 49.

4. *Acts, Resolutions and Memorials, Passed at the Several Annual Sessions of the Legislative Assembly of The Territory of Utah, from 1851 to 1870 Inclusive*, 32. Quoted in Bigler, 50.

5. Orson Pratt, January 24, 1858, *JOD* (Liverpool: Asa Calkin, 1859; lithographed reprint of original edition, 1966), vol. 6, 204. Brigham Young stated the following about America's fate: "Joseph Smith escaped many conspiracies against his life. . . . But the Lord said— 'Now let my servant seal up his testimony with his blood;' and that sealed up the damnation of the United States, not of individuals, but of the nation. . . . I am prophet enough to prophesy the downfall of the government that has driven us out. . . . Wo to the United States! I see them going to death and destruction" (Brigham Young, "Manuscript History of Brigham Young," under July 8, 1849 and August 26, 1849, reprinted in William S. Harwell, ed., *Manuscript History of Brigham Young, 1847–1850* (Salt Lake City: Collier's Publishing Co., 1997), 221, 238.

6. Daniel H. Wells, April 6, 1861, *JOD* (Liverpool: George Q. Cannon, 1861; lithographed reprint of original edition, 1966), vol. 8, 374.

7. Orson Hyde, January 3, 1858, *JOD*, (Liverpool: Asa Calkin, 1859; lithographed reprint of original edition, 1966), vol. 6, 153.

8. Joseph Young, October 11, 1857, in *JOD*, vol. 6, 207.

9. Lorenzo D. Young, October 25, 1857, in *JOD*, vol. 6, 225.

10. Brigham Young, June 6, 1858, *JOD* (Liverpool: Amasa Lyman, 1860; lithographed reprint of original edition, 1966), vol. 7, 64.

11. Brigham Young, September 13, 1857, *JOD* (Liverpool: Asa Calkin, 1858; lithographed reprint of original edition, 1966), vol. 5, 232; August 9, 1857, in *JOD*, vol. 5, 126; and April 6, 1861, *JOD* (Liverpool: George Q. Cannon, 1862; lithographed reprint of original edition, 1966), vol. 9, 4.

12. Brigham Young. Quoted in Stanley P. Hirshon, *The Lion of the Lord: A Biography of the Mormon Leader, Brigham Young* (New York: Alfred A. Knopf, Publisher, 1969), 278–279.

13. Bigler, 57–58; cf. Harold Schindler, "Saints Invited To Flock To Zion," *Salt Lake Tribune*, http://www.sltrib.com (archives).

14. Bigler, 58.

15. Brigham Young. Quoted by Perry Brocchus, "Utah Officials' Report to President Fillmore," *Congressional Globe*, new series, vol. 25, 87, as cited in B.H. Roberts, *CHC* (Salt Lake City: Deseret News Press, 1930], vol. 3, 520 (footnote #3).

16. David H. Burr, letter to Thomas A. Hendricks, General Land Office, August 30, 1856, located in the annual land reports of the General Land Office for 1856 and 1857; cf. Nels

Anderson, *Desert Saints: The Mormon Frontier in Utah* (Chicago: University of Chicago Press, 1942; paperback edition, 1966), 149.

17. Hirshon, 127.

18. Burr, letter to Hendricks.

19. William A. Linn, *Story of the Mormons* (New York: The MacMillan Company, 1902), 474, online at http://www.thedigitalvoice.com/enigma/1902LinG.htm. The Internet version of this entire volume is online at http://thedigitalvoice.com/enigma/1902LinA.htm.

20. David H. Burr, letter to Thomas A. Hendricks, General Land Office, February 4, 1857, located in the annual land reports of the General Land Office for 1856 and 1857 (see Bigler, 135).

21. David H. Burr, letter to Thomas A. Hendricks, General Land Office, March 28, 1857, located in the annual land reports of the General Land Office for 1856 and 1857 (see Bigler, 135).

22. Anderson, 160. Stiles had angered LDS leaders by a judicial opinion that favored U.S. Marshals (usually non-Mormons) over territorial Marshals (usually LDS).

23. Bigler, 56.

24. Jacob H. Holeman, letter to Commissioner of Indian Affairs, December 28, 1851. Quoted in Anderson, 107.

25. Holeman. Quoted in Anderson, 111.

26. W.W. Drummond, charges given to U.S. Attorney General, March 30, 1856, in House Executive Document No. 71 (35th Cong., 1st session), X, 212–214. Eugene E. Campbell, *Establishing Zion: The Mormon Church in the American West, 1847–1869* (Salt Lake City: Signature Books, 1988; second printing 1989), 130–131.

27. Bigler, 142.

28. News of the U.S. Army's approach had been brought to Young on July 24, 1857 in the midst of the Saints' tenth anniversary celebration of their arrival in Utah (see Campbell, 236–237).

29. Republican Platform, The Republican Convention at Philadelphia, June 13, 1856, online at http://www.furman.edu/~benson/rep1856.htm

30. Brigham Young, September 21, 1856, *JOD* (Liverpool: S.W. Richards, 1857; lithographed reprint of original edition, 1966), vol. 4, 52.

31. Bigler, 121–122.

32. Despite Hickman's title, he was never a Missouri Danite. See Jerald Tanner and Sandra Tanner, "Brigham Young And Wild Bill Hickman," *Salt Lake City Messenger* (#77), February 1991, online at http://www.utlm.org/newsletters/no77.htm#HICKMAN'S%20WORK%20FOUND. For an in-depth study of Hickman, see Hope A. Hilton, *"Wild Bill" Hickman and the Mormon Frontier* (Salt Lake City: Signature Books, 1988). According to Hilton, in 1857 "hands were laid on Hickman's head and he was given a blessing by church patriarch, John Young: 'You shall have power over all your enemies, even to set your feet upon their necks, and no weapon that is formed against you shall prosper. . . . If you are faithful you shall assist in avenging the blood of the prophets of God, and assist in accomplishing the great work of the last days'" (p. 65). On April 25, 1865, Hickman wrote a letter to Brigham Young in which he confided: "If you want me to do anything, just let me know it. . . . If you want this or that, or whatever you may think, I will try. Or if you want my life you can have it without a murmer [sic] or a groan, just let me know late or early. I will be there, and there will be no tale left behind . . . I am on hand" (p. 113).

33. Brigham Young, January 17, 1858, *JOD*, vol. 6, 176.

34. Brigham Young. Quoted by Wilford Woodruff, in Scott G. Kenney, ed., *Wilford Woodruff's Journal*, 1833–1898 (Midvale, UT: Signature Books, 1983–85), under August 7, 1844, vol. 4, 448. Woodruff's journals, edited by Kenney, can be found on the *New Mormon Studies CD ROM: Comprehensive Resource Library*.

35. *Deseret News*, September 24, 1856, 228. Quoted in Forgotten, 123.

36. Young, September 21, 1856, in *JOD*, vol. 4, 53; cf. Brigham Young, March 16, 1856, *JOD* (Liverpool: Orson Pratt, 1856; lithographed reprint of original edition, 1966), vol. 3, 247.

37. Young, September 21, 1856, in *JOD*, vol. 4,4, 53.

38. Young, September 21, 1856, in *JOD*, vol. 4,4, 53.

39. Young, September 21, 1856, in *JOD*, vol. 4,4, 53–54.

40. Jedediah M. Grant, September 21, 1856, in *JOD*, 4, 49.

41. Woodruff, in Kenney, under October 7, 1856, vol. 4, 468–469.

42. Juanita Brooks, ed., *On the Mormon Frontier: The Diary of Hosea Stout* (Salt Lake City: University of Utah Press, 1964), vol. 2:613 and Garland Hurt, letter to Cumming, letter dated December 17, 1857, Territorial Papers, Utah Series (quoted in Forgotten, 130–131); cf. Chapter X in Ann Eliza Young's 1875 volume titled *Wife No. 19, or the Story of A Life In Bondage, Being A Complete Exposé of Mormonism, and Revealing the Sorrows, Sacrifices and Sufferings of Women in Polygamy*, online at http://www.antimormon.8m.com/youngindex.html. A photo-mechanical reproduction of this rare book is available for purchase online at http://www.utlm.org/booklist/titles/ub081_wifeno19.htm (see this chapter, endnote #71).

43. List of questions found in the diary of John Moon Clements, under November 4, 1856, as quoted in Gene A. Sessions, *Mormon Thunder: A Documentary History of Jedediah Morgan Grant* (Urbana: University of Illinois Press, 1982), 220–221. The list of questions included the following:
    • Have you ever committed adultery?
    • Have you ever spoken evil of Authorities or anointed of the Lord?
    • Have you ever betrayed your brethren?
    • Have you ever stolen or taken anything that was not your own?
    • Have you ever took [sic] the name of God in vain?
    • Have you ever been drunk?
    • Do you pay all your Tithing?
    • Do you attend your Ward meetings?
    • Do you pray in your families night and morning?
    • Do you wash your bodies once a week?

44. Jedediah M. Grant, November 2, 1857, in JOD, vol. 4, 72. Hannah Tapfield King remembered the interrogation as "a fearful ordeal" ("Journals of Hannah Tapfield King," MS 628, LDSCA. Quoted in Bigler, 127).

45. Brigham Young, February 8, 1857, in *JOD* 4, 219–220.

46. Heber C. Kimball, November 2, 1856, in *JOD*, vol. 6, 34–35.

47. Heber C. Kimball , December 13, 1857, in *JOD*, vol. 6, 125–126. In this same lecture, Heber also invoked Sidney Rigdon's old "salt sermon" analogy, saying: "Do you understand me? Judas was like salt that had lost its saving principles—good for nothing but to be cast out and trodden under foot of men. It is just so with you men and women, if you do not honour your callings and cultivate the principles you have received. It is so with you, ye Elders of Israel, when you forfeit your covenants" (p. 126).

48. Joseph Smith wrote: "In debate, George A. Smith said imprisonment was better than hanging. I replied, I was opposed to hanging, even if a man kill another, I will shoot him, or cut off his head, spill his blood on the ground, and let the smoke thereof ascend up to God; and if ever I have the privilege of making a law on that subject, I will have it so" (*HC*, vol. 5, 296).

49. John D. Lee, *Mormonism Unveiled; Including The Remarkable Life And Confessions Of The Late Mormon Bishop. John D. Lee* (St. Louis: N.D. Thompson and Company, 1877), 284, online at http://www.helpingmormons.org/Rare_Books.htm.

50. The following represents an extremely small sampling of the many statements made by leaders, who called for death as punishment for sins:
    Adultery - "The principle, the only one that beats and throbs through the heart

of the entire inhabitants of this Territory, is simply this: The man who seduces his neighbors wife must die, and her nearest relative must kill him!" (George A. Smith, plea of 1851, *JOD* [Liverpool: F.D. Richards, 1855; lithographed reprint of original edition, 1966], vol. 1, 97; cf. Heber C. Kimball, in *JOD*, vol. 7, 20, where Kimball recommends that adulterers be beheaded; also see Brigham Young, March 16, 1856, in *JOD*, vol. 3, 247). Consider the following:

Stealing - "If you want to know what to do with a thief that you may find stealing, I say kill him on the spot, and never suffer him to commit another iniquity . . . [I]f I caught a man stealing on my premises I should be very apt to send him straight home, and that is what I wish every man to do. . . . this appears hard, and throws a cold chill over our revered traditions . . . but I have trained myself to measure things by the line of justice. . . . If you will cause all those whom you know to be thieves, to be placed in a line before the mouth of one of our largest cannon, well loaded with chain shot, I will prove by my works whether I can mete out justice to such persons, or not. I would consider it just as much my duty to do that, as to baptize a man for the remission of his sins (Brigham Young, May 8, 1853, in *JOD*, vol. 1, 108–9);

Covenant Breaking - "What disposition ought the people of God to make of covenant breakers. . . . What does the Apostle say? He says they are worthy of death. . . . Putting to death transgressors would exhibit the law of God, no difference by whom it was done; that is my opinion. . . . [H]as not the people of God a right to carry out that part of his law as well as any other portion of it? It is their right to baptize a sinner to save him, and it is also their right to kill a sinner to save him, when he commits those crimes that can only be atoned for by shedding his blood. . . . We would not kill a man, of course, unless we killed him to save him. . . . Do you think it would be any sin to kill me if I were to break my covenants? . . . Do you believe you would kill me if I broke the covenants of God, and you had the Spirit of God? Yes; and the more Spirit of God I had, the more I should strive to save your soul by spilling your blood, when you had committed sin that could not be remitted by baptism (Jedediah M. Grant, *Deseret News*, July 27, 1854. Quoted in Tanner and Tanner, 498, online at http://www.utlm.org/onlinebooks/changech20.htm);

Intermarriage - "And if any man mingle his seed with the seed of Cane [i.e., Blacks, a.k.a. seed of Cain] the only way he could get rid of it or have salvation would be to come forward and have his head cut off & spill his Blood upon the ground it would also take the life of his children" (Brigham Young, recorded by Wilford Woodruff, in "Wilford Woodruff's Journal," under January 16,1852, typed copy, original in LDSCA. Quoted in Jerald Tanner and Sandra Tanner, *The Changing World of Mormonism* (Chicago: Moody, 1981), 497, online at http://www.utlm.org/onlinebooks/changech20.htm. The Internet versions of this entire volume is online at http://www.utlm.org/onlinebooks/change contents.htm;

Rejecting Mormonism - "The time is coming when justice will be laid to the line and righteousness to the plummet; when we shall take the old broad sword and ask, 'Are you for God?' and if you are not heartily on the Lord's side, you will be hewn down" (Brigham Young, March 2, 1856, in *JOD*, vol. 3, 226).

51. Brigham Young, March 16, 1856, in *JOD*, Vol. 3, 247.
52. Heber C. Kimball, August 16, 1857, in *JOD*, vol. 4, 375.
53. Brigham Young, July 8, 1855, in *JOD*, vol. 2., 311.
54. Brigham Young, October 6, 1855, in *JOD*, Vol. 3, 50.
55. Quoted in Nelson Winch Green, *Mormonism: its rise, progress, and present condition. Embracing the narrative of Mrs. Mary Ettie V. Smith* (Hartford, CT: Belknap & Bliss, 1858; 1870 edition), 273, online at http://moa.umdl.umich.edu/cgi/pageviewer?

frames=1&cite=http%3A%2F%2Fmoa.umdl.umich.edu%2Fcgi%2Fsgml%2Fmoa–idx%3Fnotisid%3DAJK2869&coll=moa&view=75&root=mm000044%2F1206morm%2Fv0000%2Fi000%2F&tif=00190017.tif&pagenum=273.

56. Green, 275, see endnote #55 for Internet reference, change last characters "pagenum=273" to "pagenum=275."

57. Quoted in Green, 309, see endnote #55 for Internet reference, substitute last characters "pagenum=273)" for "pagenum=309."

58. In reference to apostates, Brigham Young stated: "I say, rather than that apostates should flourish here, I will unsheath my bowie knife, and conquer or die. [Great commotion in the congregation, and a simultaneous burst of feeling, assenting to the declaration.] Now, you nasty apostates, clear out, or judgment will be put to the line, and righteousness to the plummet. [Voices, generally, 'go it, go it.'] If you say it is right, raise your hands. [All hands up.] Let us call upon the Lord to assist us in this, and every good work" (Brigham Young, March 27, 1853, in *JOD*, vol. 1, 83).

59. William Hickman, *Brigham's Destroying Angel: Being the Life, Confession, and Startling Disclosures of the Notorious Bill Hickman* (Salt Lake City: Shepard Publishing Company, 1872; 1904 edition; lithographed reprint of original edition, 1964), 97–98. When Hosea Stout was informed of the murder, he told Hickman he had done a good job. Hyde, likewise, said the deed had been "well done." Hartly's widow made the following comments:

"I married Jesse Hartly, knowing he was a 'Gentile' in fact, but he passed for a Mormon, but that made no difference with me, although I was a Mormon, because he was a noble man, and sought only the right. By being my husband, he was brought into closer contact with the members of the Church, and was thus soon enabled to learn many things about us, and about the Heads of the Church, that he did not approve, and of which I was ignorant, although I had been brought up among the Saints; and which, if known among the Gentiles, would have greatly damaged us. I do not understand all he discovered, or all he did; but they found he had written against the Church, and he was cut off, and the Prophet required as an atonement for his sins, that he should lay down his life. That he should be sacrificed in the endowment rooms; where human sacrifices are sometimes made in this way. This I never knew until my husband told me, but it is true. They kill those there who have committed sins too great to be atoned for in any other way. The Prophet says, if they submit to this he can save them; otherwise they are lost. Oh! that is horrible. But my husband refused to be sacrificed, and so set out alone for the United States: thinking there might be at least a hope of success. I told him when he left me, and left his child, that he would be killed, and so he was. William Hickman and another Danite, shot him in the canyons; and I have often since been obliged to cook for this man, when he passed this way, knowing all the while, he had killed my husband. My child soon followed after its father, and I hope to die also; for why should I live? They have brought me here, where I wish to remain, rather than to return to Salt Lake where the murderers of my husband curse the earth, and roll in affluence unpunished" (Miss Bullock of Provo, Utah. Quoted by Mary Ettie V. Smith [while at Green River], in Green, 310–311, see endnote #55 for Internet reference, change last characters "pagenum=273" to "pagenum=310."

Hickman detailed this murder, as well as many other murders, after leaving the Mormon church. He eventually confessed to a plethora of crimes committed with the knowledge of, and often at the request of, some of the highest ranking leaders of the LDS church. Hickman made his confessions during at least two separate interviews with R.N. Baskin, former Mayor of Salt Lake City and a member of the Utah State Supreme Court (see R.N. Baskin, *Reminiscences of Early Utah* [Salt Lake City: author, 1914]).

60. Forgotten, 131–132.

61. DeWitt, letter online at http://www.saintsalive.com/mormonism/murder.html.

62. DeWitt, letter online at http://www.saintsalive.com/mormonism/murder.html.

63. Hickman, 124–125.

64. That some Mormons did confiscate Yates' property is shown in the diary of Newton Tuttle "'Sat 24 . . . Lewis Robinson got back from Green river he took 48 Horse & colts 36
pair of blankets &c that belonged to Yates'" (Brooks, vol. 2, 643, footnote #13). That
Hosea Stout was on the scene at the time of the murder is verified by his own diary:
"Sunday 18 Oct 1857. . . . Some 700 head of the captured cattle passed to day being driven
by teamsters who left the enemy. At dark W. A. Hickman came in with Mr. Yates a prisoner" (Stout, in Brooks, vol. 2, 643).

65. Stout, in Brooks, vol. 2, 653.

66. Nathaniel Case, affidavit of April 9, 1859, sworn before John Cradlebaugh, Judge 2nd
Judicial District, Utah, reprinted in *The Valley Tan*, April 19, 1859. Quoted in Jerald Tanner and Sandra Tanner, "Blood Atonement: Fact or Fantasy?," *Salt Lake City Messenger*
(#92), April 1997, 13, online at http://www.xmission.com/~country/reason/blood.htm.

67. Hickman made his confessions primarily to R.N. Baskin, a non-Mormon chief justice of
Utah's supreme court. (see Baskin, *Reminiscences of Early Utah*, 150).

68. Mormon writer Harold Schindler has done an excellent job of compiling the evidence
concerning the Aiken massacre. His research points to the unmistakable conclusion that
Rockwell was involved in the bloody deed (see Harold Schindler, *Orrin Porter Rockwell:
Man of God, Son of Thunder* [Salt Lake City: University of Utah Press, 1966; second edition, 1983], 268–279).

69. Bigler, 309.

70. Hickman, 210.

71. Baskin, 154–155. For a very explicit and in-depth look at the numerous murders committed at the orders of Young and other high-ranking LDS leaders, it is recommended
that the reader consult Chapter X–XVI of Ann Eliza Young's 1875 volume titled *Wife No.
19, or the Story of A Life In Bondage, Being A Complete Exposé of Mormonism, and
Revealing the Sorrows, Sacrifices and Sufferings of Women in Polygamy*, online at
http://www.antimormon.8m.com/youngindex.html. A photo-mechanical reproduction
of this rare book is available for purchase online at http://www.utlm.org/booklist/titles/
ub081_wifeno19.htm.

72. Brigham Young, "Citizens of Utah" proclamation, September 15, 1857. A copy is located
in the Special Collections, Marriot Library, University of Utah.

73. Roberts, *CHC*, vol. 4, 274.

74. The exact number of emigrants, and the final number of victims massacred remains
unclear because the wagon-train picked up additional members as it traveled to California. There is evidence that some Mormons actually may have joined the caravan in
hopes of escaping Utah.

75. Bigler, 160.

76. Bigler, 162.

77. John H. Baker, deposition regarding John T. Baker, "Territorial Papers of the United
States Senate 1789–1873, Roll 15, Utah December 31, 1849–June 11, 1870," National
Archives. Quoted in Roger V. Logan, Jr., "Long Overlooked Documents In National
Archives Reveal Details About Mountain Meadows Massacre Victims From North
Arkansas," *Utah Historical Quarterly*, online at http://www.mtn-meadows-
assoc.com/Depo%20and%20Journals/Depos/DEPOS-3.html (cf. Roger V. Logan, Jr.,
"New Light On The Mountain Meadows Caravan," *Utah Historical Quarterly* [Summer
1992], vol. 60, 224ff.

78. Logan, see previous endnote for Internet reference.

79. Pratt was killed by Hector McLean, a particularly violent man, who afterward boasted in
a letter to a San Francisco relative about his crime. The letter, which ended up being
printed in the *Daily Alta California*, stated: 'My duty to myself, demanded it; my duty to
my children demanded it; my duty to my relations, demanded it; and my duty to society,

demanded it. And the people of West Arkansas agree with me in this view of the commission of the deed" (July 9, 1857). It has been theorized that Mormon knowledge of this letter may have significantly contributed to a desire for vengeance upon the Arkansans.

80. Bigler, 167.

81. Hickman, 284.

82. On August 2, 1857, just one month before the massacre, Brigham Young wrote to a letter to church leaders telling them to make sure that no one sold as much as "one kernal" of food to the Saints "enemies" (Brigham Young, letter to Bronson and Haight, August 2, 1857, MS 1234, LDSCA).

83. Lee, 218–219, 233, online at http://www.helpingmormons.org/Rare_Books.htm; cf. Ralph R. Rea, *The Mountain Meadows Massacre and Its Completion as a Historic Episode* (Boone County Historical & Railroad Society), online at http://members.tripod.com/tfancher/rea.htm. This charge seems to have originally come from Isaac Haight, who told it to John D. Lee. It may very well have been a trumped up charge, since Haight also told Lee that the emigrants were planning to kill Brigham Young and all of the apostles.

84. Cedar City Ward Records, September 6, 1857. Quoted by Juanita Brooks, *The Mountain Meadows Massacre* (Norman, OK: University of Oklahoma Press, 1991), 52.

85. Lee, 218, online at http://www.xmission.com/~country/reason/lee_mm.htm.

86. Bigler, 167. Kanosh, Mormon convert chief of the Pahvants; Tutsegabit, head chief of the Piedes; and Youngwuds, another Piede chief; and various other heads of desert bands along the Santa Clara and Virgin Rivers.

87. Dimick B. Huntington, "Dimick B. Huntington Journal," under September 1, 1857, copied from microfilm, original in LDSCA, Ms d. 1419, online at http://www.mtn-meadows-assoc.com/Depo%20and%20Journals/Dimick/Dimick-2.htm.

88. Christopher Smith, "Mountain Meadows Massacre: Part III, The Dilemma of Blame," *Salt Lake Tribune*, March 14, 2000, online at http://www.sltrib.com (archives).

89. Bigler, 169.

90. Lee, 228, online at http://www.xmission.com/~country/reason/lee_mm.htm.

91. J. H. Carleton, "Special Report on the Mountain Meadow Massacre," May 25, 1859, eyewitness testimony, online at http://www.mtn-meadows-assoc.com/Carelton/maj.htm.

92. Lee, 228.

93. Lee, 237.

94. Carleton, online at http://www.mtn-meadows-assoc.com/Carelton/maj.htm.

95. Carleton, online at http://www.mtn-meadows-assoc.com/Carelton/maj.htm.

96. Lee, 241–242.

97. In the summer of 1999, after nearly two dozen skeletons were accidentally unearthed at Mountain Meadows, forensic experts did tests on the bones and discovered that most of the males they found had been shot, while most of the females and children had been bludgeoned to death (Shannon Novak, "Mountain Meadows Forensics," January 21, 2001, *Salt Lake Tribune*, online at http://www.sltrib.com [archives]).

98. Jacob Hamblin, in Carleton, online at http://www.mtn-meadows-assoc.com/Carelton/maj.htm.

99. Robert Briggs, cited in Bob Mims, "Mountain Meadows Debated Anew," May 19, 2001, *Salt Lake Tribune*, online at http://www.sltrib.com (archives). Briggs made his statement at a 2001 Mormon History Conference held at Southern Utah University.

100. Christopher Smith, "Massacre: Forensic Analysis Supports Tribe's Claim of Passive Role," January 21, 2001, *Salt Lake Tribune*, online at http://www.sltrib.com (archives).

101. Smith, "Massacre: Forensic Analysis," online at http://www.sltrib.com (archives).

102. Carleton, online at http://www.mtn-meadows-assoc.com/Carelton/maj.htm.

103. Woodruff, in Kenney, under May 25, 1860, vol. 5, 577.; cf. Brooks, *Mountain Meadows*, 183.

104. Carleton, online at http://www.mtn-meadows-assoc.com/Carelton/maj.htm.

105. Bigler, 173 and Carleton, online at http://www.mtn-meadows-assoc.com/Carelton/maj.htm.

106. In 1863, for instance, Young preached a sermon wherein he blamed the massacre entirely on Indians (Brigham Young, March 8, 1863, in *JOD* vol. 10, 109–110). This tactic continues to be used by present-day Mormons to shift blame away from the church (see this chapter, endnote #112).

107. A very interesting film documentary on the Mountain Meadows massacre was presented in 2000 at the Eclipse Film Festival in St. George, Utah. The documentary, produced by Dixie State College film professor Eric Young, portrayed Lee as a scapegoat. The following article about the film appeared in the *Salt Lake Tribune*:

> "A documentary about the Mountain Meadows Massacre is headlining the Eclipse Film Festival in St. George. The hour-long film details how a group of southern Utah Mormons and Paiute Indians killed 120 members of an Arkansas wagon train heading to California in September of 1857. It also suggests that John D. Lee, who participated in the massacre and was the only person ever tried for the crime, was a scapegoat—stemming from a conflict between the federal government and The Church of Jesus Christ of Latter-day Saints. Produced by Dixie State College film professor Eric Young, and some of his students, the documentary relies heavily on The Mountain Meadows Massacre, by the late Mormon author Juanita Brooks, and presents a sympathetic picture of Lee. It took two trials, 20 years after the massacre, before Lee was convicted and sentenced to death. Many believe he was made a scapegoat by the LDS Church to appease the federal government as Utah sought statehood. The documentary includes interviews with several historians and St. George lawyer Fay Reber, who has studied the transcripts of Lee's two trials. Young, whose great-great-grandfather was Brigham Young's brother, said he has wanted to make the documentary ever since a date he had planned with a girl in St. George 20 years ago was canceled. 'I went to pick her up for our first date,' Young says, 'and her mother told me that because of what [Brigham Young] did to her ancestor, John D. Lee, she wouldn't let me date her daughter.' Young's intention was to clear his relative's name of wrongdoing in the trials, but after researching the documentary he was unable to do so to his satisfaction" (Lin Alder, "Documentary on Massacre Headlines Eclipse Festival," *Salt Lake Tribune*, November 11, 2000, online at http://www.sltrib.com [archives]).

108. John D. Lee, final statement to execution observers, March 23, 1877, in Lee, 387–389.

109. Thelma Geer, *Mormonism, Mama & Me* (Chicago: Moody, 1986), 171.

110. Harold Schindler, "Porter Rockwell," in Allen Kent Powell, ed., *Utah History Encyclopedia* (Salt Lake City: University of Utah Press, 1994), online at http://www.onlineutah.com/historyrockwell.shtml.

111. Quoted in Tony Yapias, "Statue Honors Pioneer Figure Rockwell," *Salt Lake Tribune*, September 11, 2000, online at http://www.sltrib.com (archives).

112. Gordon B. Hinckley. Quoted in Smith, "Mountain Meadows Massacre: Part III" (see this chapter, endnote #88) online at http://www.sltrib.com (archives). The ongoing Mormon mindset regarding the Mountain Meadows massacre was articulated well by Russell R. Rich in his highly biased "history" of the LDS church titled *Ensign to the Nations: A History of the LDS Church from 1846 to 1972* (Salt Lake City: Brigham Young University Publications, 1972). This volume actually places most of the blame for the atrocity on the Baker-Fancher company, and names the Indians as the primary murderers (p. 239), falsely stating that "a number of the [Mormon] militia objected to killing and were allowed to shoot in the air" (p. 240). The book also repeats the untrue accusation that the emigrants poisoned water along their route (p. 238). Russell Rich goes so far as to say that the primary reason the Saints were involved at all in the massacre was because they "feared for their lives" (p. 237) from the emigrant train of men, women, and children.

Rich's take on the event is concluded with a fairly obvious attempt to exonerate Brigham Young, the LDS church, and even to some degree, the very perpetrators of the crime. He writes: "[T]hose who committed the Mountain Meadows atrocity were not heartless, cold-blooded killers. They were ordinarily good men who committed a tragic crime in the name of safeguarding their homes. . . . Perhaps the most important point to remember is that no matter whom we might think guilty of the crime in this tragic affair, their descendants had nothing to do with it. . . . [N]ot a single descendant of any man who participated in the massacre bears a shred of guilt, nor does any other living Latter-day Saint. And neither Brigham Young nor any other general authority of the Church was guilty of perpetrating the deed (pp. 241–242). In a similar fashion, Rich blames apostate Joseph Morris for his own murder, and the murder of several of his followers, by Mormon soldiers. Morris (see photo, *One Nations Under God,* p. 236) was killed after declaring himself to be a prophet, in opposition to Brigham Young. According to *Ensign to the Nations,* Morris "became the cause of a tragic and misunderstood affair in Utah" (p. 299). For an excellent look at the Mountain Meadows massacre, see Josiah F. Gibbs, *Mountain Meadows Massacre* (Salt Lake City: Salt Lake Tribune Publishing Company, 1910), online at http://www.utlm.org/onlinebooks/meadowscontents.htm.

113. Rex E. Lee, September 15, 1990, online at ttp://www.sonic.net/~caddpro/mmassacr.htm.

CHAPTER TWELVE: WARS AND RUMORS OF WARS

1. Hosea Stout. Quoted in David L. Bigler, *Forgotten Kingdom: The Mormon Theocracy in the American West, 1847–1896* (Logan, Utah: Utah State University Press, 1998), 141. Young made such comments on numerous occasions: e.g., "I shall take it as a witness that God designs to cut the thread between us and the world, when an army undertakes to make their appearance in this Territory to chastise me or to destroy my life from the earth. . . . I shall take a hostile movement by our enemies as an evidence that it is time for the thread to be cut (Brigham Young, August 2, 1857, *JOD* [Liverpool: Asa Calkin, 1858; lithographed reprint of original edition, 1966], vol. 5, 99); "As to the world's being in fellowship with us, it never was and it never can be. We cut off the Gentiles just before we left Nauvoo; and they have cut us off from their fellowship. The thread is cut that has hitherto connected us; and now we have to act for ourselves and build up the kingdom of God on the earth" (Brigham Young, September 20, 1857, *JOD*, vol. 5, 256–257).

2. John Taylor, April 13, 1862, *JOD* (Liverpool: George Q. Cannon, 1862; lithographed reprint of original edition, 1966), vol. 9, 342.

3. Brigham Young, September 13, 1857, *JOD*, vol. 5, 227. Van Vliet arrived in Salt Lake City on September 8 (see Stewart Van Vliet, in H. Exec. Doc., 35th Cong., 1st Session, ii., pt. 2, 25.), and held his first official meeting with Young the following day at the social hall (*Deseret News*, September 16, 1857, description of Van Vliet's visit, cited in Hubert Howe Bancroft, *History of Utah, 1540–1886* [San Francisco: The History Company Publishers, 1890], 505–506, see footnote #47).

4. Bigler, 148.

5. Stewart Van Vliet, letter to Pleasanton, September 16, 1857, House Exec. Doc. 2 (35-I), Serial 943, 24–27, reprinted in LeRoy R. Hafen and Ann W. Hafen, eds., *The Utah Expedition, 1857–1858: A Documentary Account of the United States Military Movement under Colonel Albert Sidney Johnston, and The Resistance by Brigham Young and the Mormon Nauvoo Legion* (Glendale, CA: Arthur H. Clark, Co., 1958), 50–55.

6. Brigham Young, "Citizens of Utah" proclamation, September 15, 1857. A copy is located in the Special Collections, Marriot Library, University of Utah.

7. Brigham Young and Daniel Wells, letter to David Evans, September 16, 1857, David Evans Papers, Utah State Historical Society. Quoted in Bigler, 148.

8. Eugene E. Campbell, *Establishing Zion: The Mormon Church in the American West, 1847–1869* (Salt Lake City: Signature Books, 1988; second printing 1989), 235.

9. Bigler, 152–153

10. Daniel Wells, letter to Brigham Young, November 15, 1857, Brigham Young Collection, MS 1234, LDSCA.

11. Sidney Johnston, letter dated November 5, 1857, House Exec. Doc. 71, 46, 47.

12. Orson Hyde, November 1, 1857, in *JOD* (Liverpool: Asa Calkin, 1859; lithographed reprint of original edition, 1966), vol. 6, 49.

13. Hyde, c. 1857, in *JOD*, vol. 6, 14. The text of Hyde's speech reads: "If we continue in all humility before the Lord, full of faith and diligent in prayer, with hearts full of integrity, and honor the words of our Prophets and leaders, and the United States continue their hostile movements against the Saints, it shall be with them as it was with the man upon the scaffold lifting at the granite rock, when the scaffolding gave way and fell, and with it the man; and the stone, falling on the top of him, ground him to atoms."

14. Erastus Snow, November 29, 1857, in *JOD*, vol. 6, 90.

15. Wilford Woodruff, September 27, 1857, in *JOD*, vol. 5, 269.

16. Brigham Young, February 18, 1855, *JOD* (Liverpool: F.D. Richards, 1855; lithographed reprint of original edition, 1966), vol. 2, 179. Brigham went so far as to claim that the term "United States" was synonymous with "united hell," promising that the Saints never would submit to letting go of their rights and religious freedom (Brigham Young, October 7, 1857, in *JOD*, vol. 5, 331).

17. Harold Schindler, "Utah War Broke Mormon Hold On Territory," *Salt Lake Tribune*, *Salt Lake Tribune* Centennial Collection Series, online at http://www.sltrib.com (archives).

18. Col. Cooke. Quoted in Schindler.

19. Brigham Young, letter to Col. Sidney Johnston and Col. Edmund Alexander, November 26, 1857, House Exec. Doc. 71, 110–111.

20. The Saints believed that since they represented the kingdom of God on earth, anyone choosing to fight against them would have to "fight God, and Jesus Christ, and the Holy Ghost, and they fight all the Prophets that have been from the creation down to the present time" (Heber C. Kimball, August 2, 1857, in *JOD*, vol. 5, 130).

21. Brigham Young, October 18, 1857, in *JOD*, vol. 5, 342.

22. Heber C. Kimball, July 26, 1857, in *JOD*, vol. 5, 95.

23. John Hajicek, "The Sale and Burning of the Nauvoo Temple," a paper delivered to 25th annual meeting of the John Whitmer Historical Association (Kirtland, Ohio), online at http://www.NauvooTemple.org/Loss.htm.

24. Brigham Young, September 13, 1857, in *JOD*, vol. 5, 232. On this same day, the following exchange occurred during the sermon of John Taylor (bracketed text appears in original *JOD* transcription): "Would you, if necessary, brethren, put the torch to your buildings, and lay them in ashes, and wander houseless into the mountains? I know what you would say and what you would do. [President Brigham Young: Try the vote.] All you that are willing to set fire to your property and lay it in ashes, rather than submit to their military rule and oppression, manifest it by raising your hands. [The congregation unanimously raised their hands.] I know what your feelings are" (John Taylor, September 13, 1857, in *JOD*, vol. 5, 247). A Mormon War song from this period included the following lyrics:

> *If Uncle Sam's determined*
> *On his very foolish plan,*
> *The Lord will fight our battles*
> *And we'll help Him if we can.*

> *If what they now propose to do*
> *Should ever come to pass,*
> *We'll burn up every inch of wood*
> *And every blade of grass.*

We'll throw down all our houses,
Every soul shall emigrate.
And we'll organize ourselves
Into a roving mountain state.

25. For an in-depth look at Kane's mission, see Richard D. Poll, *Quixotic Mediator: Thomas L. Kane and the Utah War* (Ogden, UT: Weber State College Press, 1985).

26. Bigler, 185.

27. Bigler, 186.

28. Brigham Young, letter to Thomas Kane, March 9, 1858, House Exec. Doc. 2, vol. 2, pt. II (35-2), 1858, serial 998, 87, 88; also see Hafen and Hafen, 269–270 and Bigler, 187.

29. Bigler, 187

30. Interestingly, as evil, corrupt, and insanely barbaric as LDS officials portrayed the coming enemy, Young publicly admitted that Johnston's army marched through Salt Lake City with the utmost decency. He stated: "Probably many of you have already learned that General Johnston passed through Great Salt Lake City with his command under the strictest discipline. Not a house, fence, or side-walk has been infringed upon by any of his command. Of course, the camp-followers are not under his control; but so far as his command is concerned while passing through the city, he has carried out his promises to the letter" (Brigham Young, June 27, 1858, *JOD* [Liverpool: George Q. Cannon, 1862; lithographed reprint of original edition, 1966], vol. 7, 56–57.

31. Campbell, 246, 247.

32. Cradlebaugh and Sinclair to James Buchanan, April 7, 1859, Se. Exec. Doc. 32 (36-1), serial 1031, 5–9.

33. P.K. Dotson, letter to John Cradlebaugh, June 3, 1859, U.S. Attorney General, "Records Relating to the Appointment of Federal judges, Attorneys, and Marshals for the Territory and State of Utah." One example would be that of Bishop Aaron Johnson, whom Johnston and Cradlebaugh tried to arrest with a company of U.S. dragoons on the night of March 25, 1859. When they arrived the bishop had already fled, leaving only his wives to give the troops a verbal rebuke. Several other Mormon church leaders similarly retreated into the mountains and hid from authorities, until the hunt for them was called off by President Buchanan. Those who went into hiding included John D. Lee, Philip Klingensmith, Isaac Haight, and William Stewart.

34. John Cradlebaugh, in *The Valley Tan*, March 29, 1859, 3. Quoted in Jerald Tanner and Sandra Tanner, "Brigham Young and Wild Bill Hickman," *Salt Lake City Messenger* (#77), February 1991, 9, online at http://www.utlm.org/newsletters/no77.htm.

35. P.K. Dotson. Cited by John Cradlebaugh, "Utah and the Mormons," Speech of Hon. John Cradlebaugh, of Nevada, on the Admission of Utah As A State, Delivered in the House of Representatives, February 7, 1863, 25, 26.

36. Brigham Young, July 4, 1854, in *JOD*, vol. 7, 15.

37. Brigham Young, April 6, 1861, in *JOD*, vol. 9, 2, 5,

38. Heber C. Kimball, April 6, 1861, in *JOD*, vol. 9, 7.

39. Paul H. Peterson, "Civil War Prophecy," in Daniel H. Ludlow, ed., *Encyclopedia of Mormonism* (New York: Macmillan Publishing Company, 1992), vol. 1, 288.

40. *D&C* 130:12–13.

41. This prophecy, as originally transcribed, included numerous spelling errors that have been corrected for easier reading (see *D&C* 87).

42. "South Carolina Ordinance of Nullification," November 24, 1832, in Paul Leicester Ford, *The Federalist: A Commentary on the Constitution of the United States by Alexander Hamilton, James Madison and John Jay* (New York: Henry Holt and Company, 1898), online at http://www.yale.edu/lawweb/avalon/states/sc/ordnull.htm.

43. "President Jackson's Proclamation Regarding Nullification," December 10, 1832, in Ford, online at http://www.yale.edu/lawweb/avalon/presiden/proclamations/jack01.htm.

44. Carol Bleser, ed., *Secret and Sacred: The Diaries of James Hummond, A Southern Slave-holder* (New York: Oxford University Press, 1988). Cited in James David, "Response to K.," online at http://www.lds-mormon.com/civilwar.shtml.

45. John Farkas, "False Prophecies Of Joseph Smith," Internet article online at http://www.frontiernet.net/~bcmmin/falsprop.htm.

46. Farkas, online at http://www.frontiernet.net/~bcmmin/falsprop.htm.

47. Between June 1832 and April 1834, the *E&MS* cited or quoted from the *Morning Courier and New York Enquirer* no less than a dozen times in several issues (1832—June, July, August, December; 1833—January, February, March, May, June; 1834—April). List of issues, and citations online at http://www.concordance.com/cgi-bin/methr.pl. In *Mormonism: Shadow or Reality?*, Jerald and Sandra Tanner point out a particularly interesting bit of historical trivia relating to Smith and his possible use of newspaper accounts to formulate the 1832 prophecy: "On December 10, 1832, the *Boston Daily Advertiser & Patriot* printed 'Extracts from the Message of the Governor of South Carolina at the opening of the Legislature, November 27, 1832.' . . . [The Governor's] message warned that South Carolina was prepared to resist the U.S. Government by force if necessary. The same day that this was printed (Dec. 10, 1832), Orson Hyde "left Boston." On December 22, 1832, he 'arrived at Kirtland, Ohio' (*Journal of Orson Hyde*, typed copy, pp. 56–57). We cannot, of course, prove that Orson Hyde brought a copy of the *Boston Daily Advertiser & Patriot* with him, but it is interesting to note that just three days after his arrival (Dec. 25, 1832), Joseph Smith gave his revelation on 'the rebellion of South Carolina' (Jerald Tanner and Sandra Tanner, *Mormonism: Shadow or Reality?* [Salt Lake City: ULM, 1987], 190).

48. The rationale for making such an assertion has been articulated well by Mormon apologist Jeff Lindsay, who writes: "The Civil War was the bloodiest this country has ever seen. . . . The South did enlist the aid of Great Britain and also sought help from France (Great Britain, as I recall, also encouraged France to assist the South). Later, after war had been poured out on the nations of the earth, Great Britain found herself threatened by Nazi Germany and called upon other nations of the earth for her defense. After the Civil War, international intrigues and wars grew to increasing severity, with ghastly international scenes of horror during World War I and World War II, with dozens of other wars having been fought and going on at the moment. War has always been on the earth, but the scale of destruction since the Civil War has grown sharply, and war in the past century has become increasingly multinational rather than bilateral. Truly, war has been poured out on all nations," online at http://www.jefflindsay.com/LDSFAQ/FQ_prophecies.shtml#war.

49. Marvin W. Cowen, *Mormon Claims Answered* (Salt Lake City: Utah Christian Publications, 1997), http://www.utlm.org/onlinebooks/mclaims5.htm. Cowen's entire volume is available from ULM online at http://www.utlm.org/onlinebooks/mclaimscontents.htm.

50. Walter Williams, "Blacks Who Fought For The South," *Washington Times*, online at http://www.civilwarhome.com/blacks.htm. Also see "Annals of the War" article by Edward Spencer, online at http://www.civilwarhome.com/negroenlistments.htm. It must be noted that there is some degree of controversy surrounding the assertion that Blacks fought for the Confederacy. Much of the disagreement may be semantic in nature—e.g., What exactly do the terms "slave," "Black," or "fight" mean? An article highlighting the opposing view was written by Kristen Peterson and published in the August 19, 2000 edition of the *Las Vegas Sun* ("Black Confederates: Slaves or Soldiers?"). It is online at http://www.innercitynews.com/black%20confederates.htm. To access a number of articles dealing with this heated issue, an Internet search engine should be used on the search phrase: "Blacks Who Fought For The South."

51. Tanner and Tanner, *Shadow or Reality?*, 190.

52. Orson Hyde, c. 1857, in *JOD*, vol. 6, 13.

53. Campbell, 290–291. One example of Mormon leaders preaching such an idea can be found in an 1861 sermon of Brigham Young: "How is the Lord going, to empty the earth?

Will it be done in a week or a year? No. He has begun to do it. President Lincoln called out soldiers for three months, and was going to wipe the blot of secession from the escutcheon of the American Republic. . . . Now they are beginning to enlist men for three years. . . . [T]hey have begun to empty the earth, to cleanse the land, and prepare the way for the return of the Latter-day Saints to the center Stake of Zion. . . . When I left the State of Missouri, I had a deed for five pieces of as good land as any in the State, and I expect to go back to it. . . . There are also a few others in the Territory who received theirs. A few will remain and receive their inheritance. Will we return and receive an inheritance there? Many of the Saints will return to Missouri, and there receive an inheritance" (Brigham Young, July 28, 1861, in *JOD*, vol. 9, 142).

54. Cumming left after years of an impotent administration. Speaking of himself in the Third Person, he wrote in an 1860 letter: "There is nothing to do. Alfred Cumming is Governor of the Territory, but Brigham Young is Governor of the people" (Alfred Cumming, letter dated March 1, 1860, Alfred Cumming Papers).

55. Dawson's education idea brought an especially interesting objection from Mormons. Apparently, the Saints felt that too much education could be damaging to their children. Young had stated: "We should never crowd and force the minds of our children beyond what they are able to bear. If we do we ruin them for life" (Brigham Young. Quoted in Scott G. Kenney, ed., *Wilford Woodruff's Journal*, 1833–1898 (Midvale, UT: Signature Books, 1983–85), under January 1, 1861, vol. 5, 536.

56. Harding. Quoted in Campbell, 292.

57. Campbell, 292.

58. Harding. Quoted in Campbell, 292.

59. Harding. Quoted in Campbell, 292.

60. Campbell, 292.

61. Patrick E. Conner, letter dated September 14, 1862. Quoted in Campbell, 293–294.

62. Lincoln removed Harding from office in 1863, and replaced him with James Duane Doty, a brilliant statesman, who was admitted to the Michigan Bar at 19-years-old and in 1841 served as the youngest governor of Wisconsin Territory. He died in office in 1864 from an illness. After Doty came a series of governors, which have extended to present-day. For a list and short biography of all territorial governors, see information online at http://www.sltrib.com (archives).

63. Brigham Young, June 4, 1864, *JOD* (Liverpool: Daniel H. Wells, 1865; lithographed reprint of original edition, 1966), vol. 10, 304.

64. Heber C. Kimball, April 14, 1861, in *JOD*, vol. 9, 55.

65. Wilford Woodruff, July 27, 1862, in *JOD*, vol. 10, 13, 15.

66. Wilford Woodruff, June 12, 1863, in *JOD*, vol. 10, 217.

67. For an excellent Internet site that provides a user-friendly overview of the Civil War, including its major personalities, battles, costs, and other historical data, see "Home of the American Civil War" online at http://www.civilwarhome.com/index.htm.

68. Brigham Young, April 8, 1868, *JOD*, (Liverpool: Albert Carrington, 1869; lithographed reprint of original edition, 1966), vol. 12, 204.

69. The full relevant excerpt from Pratt's sermon is as follows:

"This great war is only a small degree of chastisement, just the beginning; nothing compared to that which God has spoken concerning this nation, if they will not repent. For the Lord has said in this book, (the Book of Mormon) which has been published for thirty eight years, that if they will not repent He will throw down all their strongholds and cut off the cities of the land, and will execute vengeance and fury on the nation, even as upon the heathen, such as they have not heard. That He will send a desolating scourge on the land; that He will leave their cities desolate, without inhabitants. For instance the great, powerful and populous city of New York, that may be considered one of the greatest cities of the world, will in a few years become a mass of ruins. The people will wonder while gazing on the ruins that cost hundreds of millions to build, what has become of its inhabitants, Their houses will be there, but they will be left desolate. So saith the Lord God. That will be only a sample of numerous other towns and cities on the face of this continent. Now I am aware that it is almost impossible for even some of the Latter-day Saints to get that confidence and that strong faith in the events which God intends to accomplish on this land in the future to believe in such a thing, to say nothing about outsiders, that do not believe a word of it. Outsiders do not believe it any more than they believed me when I was a boy and took that revelation which was given in 1832, and carried it forth among many towns and cities and told them there was to be a great and terrible war between the North and the South, and read to them the revelation. Did they believe it? Would they consider that there was any truth in it? Not in the least, "that is a Mormon humbug" they would say. "What! this great and powerful nation of ours to be divided one part against the other and many hundreds of thousands of souls to be destroyed by civil wars!" Not a word of it would they believe. They do not believe what is still in the future. But there are some in this congregation who will live, to behold the fulfillment of these other things, and will visit the ruins of mighty towns and cities scattered over the face of this land destitute and desolate of inhabitants. . . . Thus will He pour out His wrath and indignation upon them and make manifest to the people that that which he has spoken must be fulfilled" (Orson Pratt, December 27, 1868, *JOD*, vol. 12, 344–345.)

70. Iowa (29th state, December 28, 1846); Wisconsin (30th state, May 29, 1848); California (31st state, September 9, 1850); Minnesota (32nd state, May 11, 1858); Oregon (33rd state, February 14, 1859; Kansas (34th state, January 29, 1861); West Virginia (35th, June 20, 1863); Nevada (36th state, October 31, 1864); Nebraska (37th state, March 1, 1867); Colorado (38th state, August 1, 1876). Presidents: James K. Polk (1845–1849); Zachary Taylor (1849–1850); Millard Fillmore (1850–1853); Franklin Pierce (1853–1857); James Buchanan (1857–1861); Abraham Lincoln (1861–1865); Andrew Johnson (1865–1869); Ulysses S. Grant (1869–1877).

71. For an in-depth look at many of these issues, the reader should consult Campbell and Bigler, as well as Ernest H. Taves, *This is the Place: Brigham Young and the New Zion* (Buffalo: Prometheus Books, 1991), 237–249.

72. Quoted in B.H. Roberts, *CHC* (Salt Lake City: Deseret News Press, 1930), vol. 5, 516–517.

73. *Salt Lake Tribune*, August 30, 1877. Quoted in Bigler, 307.

CHAPTER THIRTEEN: UNHOLY MATRIMONY

1. Brigham Young, July 12, 1875, originally quoted in E.A. Folk, "Story of Mormonism," cited in *Proceedings Before The Committee On Privileges And Elections Of The United States Senate In The Matter Of The Protests Against The Right Of Hon. Reed Smoot, A Senator From Utah, To Hold His Seat* (Washington, D.C.: Government Printing Office, 1904), vol. 1, 15.

2. D. Michael Quinn, *The Mormon Hierarchy: Origins of Power* (Salt Lake City: Signature Books, 1994), 253–255 and D. Michael Quinn, *The Mormon Hierarchy: Extensions of Power* (Salt Lake City: Signature Books, 1997), 40–43.

3. In 1880 Taylor announced: "The people of the rest of the country are our enemies. . . . [W]hen the Government conflicts with heaven, we will be ranged under the banner of heaven and against the Government. . . . I defy the United States. I will obey God" (John Taylor, *Salt Lake Tribune*, January 6, 1880. Quoted in Samuel W. Taylor, *Rocky Mountain Empire* [Macmillan Publishing Co., Inc., 1978], 29.

4. "A Sketch of the Life of Nancy Naomi Tracy," n.d., 20. Quoted in George D. Smith, "Nau-

voo Roots of Mormon Polygamy, 1841–46: A Preliminary Demographic Report," *Dialogue: A Journal of Mormon Thought* (Spring 1994), vol. 27, no. 1, 26.

5. Mary Elizabeth Lightner, speech delivered April 14, 1905, Brigham Young University, typed copy.

6. Ebenezer Robinson, letter to Jason W. Briggs, Jan. 28, 1880, LDSCA. On December 29, 1873, Ebenezer and Angeline Robinson signed an affidavit saying that Hyrum Smith had come to their house in the fall of 1843 to teach them the doctrine of polygamy and that he had been wrong to oppose it.

7. Robinson, see previous endnote.

8. Smith, 27. Joseph married Sarah Ann Whitney on July 27, 1842. Sources used include: Joseph Smith, letter to Whitney family, Aug. 18, 1842, photocopy, George Albert Smith papers, Special Collections, Marriott Library; "History of Joseph Kingsbury, Written by His Own Hand, 1846, 1849, 1850," Stanley Snow Ivins Collection, vol. 15, 74–76, Utah State Historical Society.

9. Richard S. Van Wagoner, *Mormon Polygamy: A History* (Salt Lake City: Signature Books, 1989; paperback edition), 29–36 98–100.

10. W. Wyl, *Mormon Portraits* (Salt Lake City: Tribune Printing & Publishing Company, 1886), 62. A photo-mechanical reprint of this volume is available for purchase online at http://www.utlm.org/booklist/titles/up016_mormonportraits.htm.

11. *HC* (Salt Lake City: Deseret Book Company, 1976/1980), vol. 6, 410–411.

12. Smith, 9.

13. Smith, 13.

14. Van Wagoner, 83 and Quinn, *The Mormon Hierarchy: Origins of Power*, 176.

15. Wilford Woodruff, in Scott G. Kenney, ed., *Wilford Woodruff's Journal, 1833–1898* (Midvale, UT: Signature Books, 1983–85), under February 4, 1851, vol. 4, 12.

16. John W. Gunnison, *The Mormons or the Latter-day Saints, in the Valley of the Great Salt Lake* (London: Sampson, Low, Son, & Co., 1852), 66–67, online at a UK site with numerous 17th and 18th century tests, http://www.ee.surrey.ac.uk/Contrib/manx/fulltext/gu1852/ch06.htm. This entire volume is online at http://www.ee.surrey.ac.uk/Contrib/manx/fulltext/gu1852/index.htm.

17. Similarly, Brigham Young often preached on how sexual desire had little to do with taking wives: "The time is coming when the Lord is going to raise up a holy nation. . . .[H]e has introduced a plurality of wives for that express purpose, and not to gratify lustful passion in the least. . . . I never entered into the order of plurality of wives to gratify passion. And were I now asked whether I desired and wanted another wife, my reply would be, It should be one by whom the Spirit will bring forth noble children. I am almost sixty years old; and if I now live for passion, I pray the Lord Almighty to take my life from the earth" (Brigham Young, April 7, 1861, *JOD* [Liverpool: George Q. Cannon, 1862; lithographed reprint of original edition, 1966], vol. 9, 36).

18. Brigham Young, July 24, 1853, *JOD* (Liverpool: F.D. Richards, 1855; lithographed reprint of original edition, 1966), vol. 1, 244.

19. For detailed information on the theological beliefs of Mormonism, see "General Information FAQ," online at http://utlm.org/faqs/faqgeneral.htm, the ULM's "Terminology Differences," online at http://utlm.org/onlineresources/terminologymain.htm, and "Mormons Hope to Become Gods of Their Own Worlds," online at http://utlm.org/onlineresources/mormonshopetobecomegods.htm. For an excellent evaluation of, and in-depth look at, Mormon doctrine and practice from an evangelical Christian perspective, see: Bill MacKeever and Eric Johnson, *Mormonism 101: Examining the Religion of the Latter-day Saints* (Grand Rapids: Baker Book House, 2000; Bill MacKeever and Eric Johnson, *Questions to Ask Your Mormon Friend* (Minneapolis: Bethany House, 1994); and Bill MacKeever, *Answering Mormons Questions* (Minneapolis: Bethany House, 1991). Also very useful is Chapter Six on Mormonism in Walter Martin, Hank Hanegraaff, gen. ed.,

The Kingdom of the Cults (Minneapolis: Bethany House, 1997 updated and revised edition), 179ff.

20. LDS Apostle Bruce McConkie wrote: "This doctrine that there is a Mother in Heaven was affirmed in plainness by the First Presidency of the Church (Joseph F. Smith, John R. Winder, and Anthon H. Lund) when, in speaking of pre-existence and the origin of man, they said that 'man, as a spirit was begotten and born of heavenly parents, and reared to maturity in the eternal mansions of the Father'" (Bruce McConkie, *Mormon Doctrine* [Salt Lake City: Bookcraft, 1958; second edition, 1966], 516). An official LDS church manual reads: "For as we have a Father in heaven, so also we have a Mother there, a glorified, exalted, ennobled Mother" (Achieving a Celestial Marriage, *LDS Church Manual*, 1976, 129). James E. Talmage, declared, "We, the human family, literally the sons and daughters of Divine Parents, the literal progeny of God our Eternal Father, and of our God Mother, are away from home for a season" (James E. Talmage, *The Philosophical Basis of "Mormonism"* [Independence, MO: Missions of the Church Of Jesus Christ of Latter-Day Saints, 1928], 9). Milton R. Hunter said: "The stupendous truth of the existence of a Heavenly Mother, as well as a Heavenly Father, became established facts in Mormon Theology" (Milton R. Hunter, *Gospel Through the Ages* [Salt Lake City: Deseret Book Company, 1958], 98. Hunter then quotes the Mormon hymn, "O My Father." The third verse declares, "[T]he tho't makes reason stare! Truth is reason, Truth eternal, Tells me I've a Mother there" (Hunter, 99–100). The LDS teaching of a Heavenly Mother clearly indicates she has a body just like the Heavenly Father, so that they can procreate offspring. But if they have resurrected bodies of flesh and bones, why are their children born as baby spirits without bodies?

21. McConkie, 387, which reads: "[I]ntelligence or spirit element became intelligences after the spirits were born as individual [spirit] entities." He also states: "Our spirit bodies had their beginning in pre-existence when we were born as the spirit children of God our Father. Through that birth process spirit element was organized into intelligent entities." (McConkie, 750). Brigham Young stated: "[God] created man, as we create our children; for there is no other process of creation in heaven, on the earth, in the earth, or under the earth, or in all the eternities, that is, that were, or that ever will be" (Brigham Young, June 18, 1865, *JOD* [Liverpool: B. Young, Jr., 1867; lithographed reprint of original, 1966], vol. 11, 122. In 1853, Orson Pratt estimated that perhaps as many as 70 billion spirit babies were born to Heavenly Father and Mother (Orson Pratt, "The Pre-Existence of Man," *The Seer*, March 1853, vol. 1, no. 3, 38).

22. Hunter, 127–129; cf. McConkie, 516.

23. Hunter, 127–129 and Joseph F. Smith, John R. Winder, and Anthon H. Lund, *Improvement Era*, vol. 13, 80 (quoted in Hunter, 99).

24. McConkie taught: "Kolob means 'the first creation.' It is the name of the planet 'nearest to the celestial, or the residence of God.' It is 'first in government, the last pertaining to the measurement of time. . . . One day in Kolob is equal to a thousand years according to the measurement of this earth" (McConkie, 428). A fascinating bit of trivia associated with this particular Mormon belief is the fact that the old 1970s TV series Battlestar Gallactica was probably based on Latter–day Saint beliefs. Consider the following:

BATTLESTAR:	Kobol, the mother world of all humans. The planet where all life started. The inhabitants that lived on it before it 'died' are often referred to as the 'Lords of Kobol' or the 'Gods of Kobol.'
MORMONISM:	"These are the governing ones; and the name of the great one is Kolob, because it is near unto me" (*PGP*, Abraham 3:3) and "Kolob is the greatest . . . because it is nearest unto me" (*PGP*, Abraham 3:16). Notice the similarity between the names 'Kobol' and 'Kolob.'

BATTLESTAR:	The people are led by Commander Adama and the Council (also known as Quorum) of Twelve. The head of which is called the president.
MORMONISM:	Led by the "prophet" who has a Council (also known as Quorum) of Twelve under him. The prophet also is referred to as the president.
BATTLESTAR:	Instead of being married, characters are sealed, "not for now, but for all ages."
MORMONISM:	Men and women are sealed together in the marriage for time and eternity (McConkie, 684).
BATTLESTAR:	A ship of lights appeared and took several people inside of it. When they were confronted by the "angel-like" crew they asked them who they were. They responded with, "You are as we once were, we are as you may become" (from the episode "War of the Gods," part 2).
MORMONISM:	"As man is, God once was: as God is, man may become" (Hunter, 105, 106).
BATTLESTAR:	Egyptian hieroglyphics were the written language of the people of Kobol.
MORMONISM:	In the *PGP*, the book of Abraham supposedly was translated from a papyrus scroll that was written in Egyptian hieroglyphics. The *Book of Mormon* allegedly was translated from golden plates containing Reformed Egyptian.
BATTLESTAR:	There are thirteen tribes. Twelve of the tribes are known, but one of these tribes left for a shining star known as earth, and is now lost.
MORMONISM:	"But now I go unto the Father, and also to show myself unto the lost tribes of Israel" (*BOM*, 3 Nephi 17:4) and "The leading of the ten tribes from the north" (*D&C* 110:11).

25. See McConkie, 169. Jesus is "the First Spirit Child born to God the Father in Pre-existence" (McConkie, 281). In *PGP*, Moses 5:13, Satan declares: "I am also a son of God." Hunter wrote, "The appointment of Jesus to be the Savior of the world was contested by one of the other sons of God. He was called Lucifer, son of the morning. Haughty, ambitious, and covetous of power and glory, this spirit-brother of Jesus desperately tried to become the Savior of mankind" (Hunter, 15).

26. "God the Father had a plurality of wives, one or more being in eternity, by whom He begat our spirits as well as the spirit of Jesus His Firstborn (Orson Pratt, "Celestial Marriage," *The Seer*, November 1853, vol. 1, no. 11, 172). In 1961, Mormon writer John J. Stewart affirmed that "plural marriage is the patriarchal order of Marriage lived by God and others who reign in the Celestial Kingdom" (John J. Stewart, *Brigham Young and His Wives and The True Story of Plural Marriage* [Salt Lake City: Mercury Publishing Company, Inc., 1961], 41).

27. McConkie, 751 and *D&C* 130:22. McConkie stated: "[God] is a personal Being, a holy and exalted man, a glorified, resurrected Personage having a tangible body of flesh and bones, an anthropomorphic Entity" (McConkie, p. 250).

28. James E. Talmage, *Articles of Faith* (Salt Lake City: The Church of Jesus Christ of Latter-day Saints, 1890; modern reprint, 1948], 430). Hunter writes: "Mormon prophets have continuously taught the sublime truth that God the Eternal Father was once a mortal man who passed through a school of earth life similar to that through which we are now passing. He became God—an exalted being—through obedience to the same eternal Gospel truths that we are given opportunity today to obey" (Hunter, 104). And again: "[W]e must accept the fact that there was a time when Deity was much less powerful than He is today. Then how did He become glorified and exalted and attain His present

status of Godhood? In the first place, aeons ago God undoubtedly took advantage of every opportunity to learn the laws of truth. . . . From day to day He exerted His will vigorously, . . . he gained more knowledge. . . . Thus he grew in experience and continued to grow until He attained the status of Godhood. In other words, He became God by absolute obedience to all the eternal laws of the Gospel. . . . No prophet of record gave more complete and forceful explanations of the doctrine that men may become Gods than did the American Prophet" (Hunter, 114–15).

29. McConkie, 64.

30. Joseph Smith, April 6, 1844, *JOD* (Liverpool: Asa Calkin, 1859; lithographed reprint of original edition, 1966), vol. 6, 3–4.

31. Orson Pratt, February 18, 1855, *JOD* (Liverpool, F.D. Richards, 1855; lithographed reprint of original edition, 1966), vol. 2, 345. In *The Seer*, Pratt wrote: "We were begotten by our Father in Heaven; the person of our Father in Heaven was begotten on a previous heavenly world by His Father; and again He was begotten by a still more ancient Father, and so on, from generation to generation, from one heavenly world to another still more ancient, until our minds are wearied and lost in the multiplicity of generations and successive worlds, and as a last resort, we wonder in our minds, how far back the genealogy extends, and how the first world was formed, and the first Father was begotten" (Orson Pratt, "The Pre-Existence of Man," *The Seer*, September 1853, vol. 1, no. 9, 132; cf. Orson Pratt, "The Pre-Existence of Man," *The Seer*, February, 1853, vol. I, no. 2, 23–24).

32. Brigham Young, October 8, 1859, *JOD* (Liverpool: Amasa Lyman, 1860; lithographed reprint of original edition, 1966), vol. 7, 333.

33. Lorenzo Snow, *MS*, vol. 54, 404. Quoted in Hunter, 105–106.

34. "[F]ull salvation is obtained in and through the continuation of the family unit in eternity, and those who obtain it are gods"(McConkie, 670).

35. "Baptism is the gate to the Celestial Kingdom. Celestial Marriage is the gate to an exaltation in the highest heaven within the Celestial World" (McConkie, 118).

36. W. Cleon Skousen, *The First 2000 Years* (Salt Lake City: Bookcraft, 1953; 1977 edition), 355.

37. Skousen, 355.

38. These explanations of Jesus' conception are clearly unbiblical. Scripture indicates that Christ was miraculously conceived in the womb of the virgin Mary by the power of the Holy Spirit. One may not agree with the assertion, but one cannot legitimately argue that the assertion is not there. The Bible explicitly states: "When as his mother Mary was espoused to Joseph, before they came together, she was found with child of the Holy Ghost. . . . the angel of the Lord appeared unto him Joseph in a dream, saying, 'Joseph, thou son of David, fear not to take unto thee Mary thy wife: for that which is conceived in her is of the Holy Ghost'" (Matthew 1:18–20, KJV). Contrast this passage with what was preached by Brigham Young in 1852: "Now, remember from this time forth, and for ever [sic], that Jesus Christ was not begotten by the Holy Ghost" (Brigham Young, April 9, 1852, in *JOD*, vol. 1, 51).

39. Brigham Young had this to say concerning the birth of Christ: "The man Joseph, the husband of Mary, did not, that we know of, have more than one wife, but Mary the wife of Joseph had another husband" (*Deseret News*, October 10, 1866); cf. Brigham Young, August 19, 1866, *JOD* [Liverpool: B. Young, Jr., 1867; lithographed reprint of original edition, 1966], vol. 11, 268). Orson Pratt explained the event as follows:

"The fleshly body of Jesus required a Mother as well as a Father. Therefore, the Father and Mother of Jesus, according to the flesh, must have been associated together in the capacity of Husband and Wife; hence the Virgin Mary must have been, for the time being, the lawful wife of God the Father: we use the term lawful Wife, because it would be blasphemous in the highest degree to say that He overshadowed her or begat the Saviour unlawfully. It would have been unlawful for any man to have interfered with Mary, who was already espoused to Joseph; for such a heinous crime would have subjected both the guilty parties to death, according to the law of Moses. But God having created all men and women, had the most perfect right to do with His own creation, according to His holy will and pleasure: He had a lawful right to overshadow the Virgin Mary in the capacity of a husband, and beget a Son, although she was espoused to another; for the law which He gave to govern men and women was not intended to govern Himself, or to prescribe rules for his own conduct. It was also lawful in Him, after having thus dealt with Mary, to give her to Joseph her espoused husband. Whether God the Father gave Mary to Joseph for time only, or for time and eternity, we are not informed. Inasmuch as God was the first husband to her, it may be that He only gave her to be the wife of Joseph while in this mortal state, and that He intended after the resurrection to again take her as one of his own wives to raise up immortal spirits in eternity (Orson Pratt, "Celestial Marriage," *The Seer*, October 1853, vol. 1, no. 10, 158).

40. Brigham Young, July 8, 1860, *JOD* (Liverpool: George Q. Cannon, 1861; lithographed reprint of original edition, 1966), vol. 8, 115.

41. Heber C. Kimball, September 2, 1860, in *JOD*, vol. 8, 211. McConkie explained: "Christ was begotten by an Immortal Father in the same way that mortal men are begotten by mortal fathers" (McConkie, 547).

42. Pratt, "Celestial Marriage, *The Seer*, 172 (see this chapter, endnote #26 for additional reference information).

43. Pratt, *The Seer*, 158, (see this chapter, endnote #39 for additional reference information).

44. McConkie, 129.

45. McConkie, 257.

46. Pratt, *The Seer*, 37, (see this chapter, endnote #21 for additional reference information). According to *D&C* 132:18–22: "[I]f a man marry a wife, and make a covenant with her for time and for all eternity, . . . they shall [have]. . . a continuation of the seeds [children] forever and ever. Then shall they be gods, because they have no end; therefore shall they be from everlasting to everlasting, . . . Then shall they be gods, because they have all power, . . . and continuation of the lives, . . . [endless procreation of spirit children]." Moreover, the LDS church's publication, *Doctrines of the Gospel, Student Manual*, declares: "[A] man and his wife when glorified will have spirit children who eventually will go on an earth like this one we are on and pass through the same kind of experiences, being subject to mortal conditions, and if faithful, then they also will receive the fullness of exaltation and partake of the same blessings. There is no end to this development; it will go on forever. We will become gods and have jurisdiction over worlds, and these worlds will be peopled by our own offspring" (LDS Church, Salt Lake City, *Doctrines of the Gospel, Student Manual* [Salt Lake City: The Church of Jesus Christ Of Latter–day Saints, 1986]); also see Joseph Fielding Smith, *Doctrines of Salvation* (Salt Lake City: Bookcraft, 1955, vol. 2, 48).

47. Brigham Young made further statements about men becoming gods: "The Lord created you and me for the purpose of becoming Gods like himself. . . . We are created . . . to become Gods like unto our Father in heaven" (Brigham Young, August 8, 1852, *JOD* [Liverpool: Orson Pratt, 1856; lithographed reprint of original edition; 1966], vol. 3, 93). "[M]an is the king of kings and lord of lords in embryo." (Brigham Young, 1863, *JOD* [Liverpool: Daniel H. Wells, 1865, vol.10, 223).

48. McConkie, 321.

49. McConkie, 544.

50. McConkie, 844.

51. Jessie L. Embry, "Burden or Pleasure?: A Profile of LDS Polygamous Husbands," *Dialogue: A Journal of Mormon Thought* (Winter 1987), vol. 20, no. 4, 148.

52. Melodie Moench Charles, "The Need for a New Mormon Heaven," *Dialogue: A Journal of Mormon Thought* (Autumn 1988), vol. 21, no. 3, 76, 78–82, 84–86.

53. Brigham taught: "Intelligent beings are organized to become Gods, even the sons of God, to dwell in the presence of the Gods, and become associated with the highest intelligencies [sic] that dwell in eternity"(Brigham Young, September 2, 1860, *JOD* [Liverpool: George Q. Cannon, 1861; lithographed reprint of original edition, 1966], vol. 8, 160).

54. McConkie, 238.

55. Orson Pratt concluded that a Mormon polygamist "could increase his kingdoms with his own children, in a hundred fold ratio above that of another who had only secured to himself one wife." Pratt reasoned thusly:

> "As yet, we have only spoken of the hundred fold ratio as applied to his own children; but now let us endeavor to form some faint idea of the multiplied increase of worlds peopled by his grandchildren, over which he, of course, would hold authority and dominion as the Grand Patriarch of the endless generations of his posterity. If... only one million of sons were redeemed to the fulness. . . . they, in their turn, would now be prepared to multiply and people worlds the same as their Father. . . . While their Father, therefore, was peopling the second world, these millions of redeemed sons would people one million of worlds . . . the number in the third generation amounts to one billion three million and three worlds. The fourth generation would people over a trillion, and the fifth over a quadrillion of worlds; while the one-hundredth generation would people more worlds than could be expressed by raising one million to the ninety-ninth power. Any mathematician who is able to enumerate a series of 595 figures, will be able to give a very close approximation to the number of worlds peopled by the descendants of one Father in one hundred thousand million of years, according to the average ratio given above. Now this is the period in which only one world could be peopled with one wife. While the Patriarch with his hundred wives, would multiply worlds on worlds, systems on systems, more numerous than the dust of all the visible bodies of the universe, and people them with his descendants to the hundredth generation of worlds; the other, who had only secured to himself one wife, would in the same period, just barely have peopled one world." (Pratt, *The Seer*, 39 [see this chapter, endnote #21 for additional reference information]).

56. Ernest H. Taves, *This is the Place: Brigham Young and the New Zion* (Buffalo: Prometheus Books, 1991), 153.

57. Ann Eliza Young, *Wife No. 19, or the Story of A Life In Bondage, Being A Complete Exposé of Mormonism, and Revealing the Sorrows, Sacrifices and Sufferings of Women in Polygamy* [Hartford, Ct: Dustin, Gilman & Co., 1875], Chapter Seven, online at http://www.antimormon.8m.com/youngchp7.html.

58. N.B. Lundwall, comp., *Inspired Prophetic Warnings* (Salt Lake City: author, 1940), 117. In 1873 Brigham Young gave this stem warning: "Now, where a man in this church says, 'I don't want but one wife, I will live my religion with one,' he will perhaps be saved in the Celestial kingdom; but when he gets there he will not find himself in possession of any wife at all. He has had a talent that he has hid up. He will come forward and say, 'Here is that which thou gavest me, I have not wasted it, and here is the one talent,' and he will not enjoy it but it will be taken and given to those who have improved the talents they received, and he will find himself without any wife, and he will remain single forever and ever" (*Deseret News*, Sept. 17, 1873). Also in 1873, during a meeting at Paris, Idaho, Brigham Young said: "[A] man who did not have but one wife in the Resurrection that woman will not be his but [be] taken from him & given to another" (Quoted by Woodruff, in Kenney, under August 31, 1873, vol. 7, 152). Francis M. Lyman, eventual

president of the Quorum of the Twelve, remarked in 1883 that "Celestial marriage is for the fulness of the glory of god. It is the crowning glory. A man has no right to one wife unless he is worthy of two. . . . [T]here is no provision made for those who have had the chance & opperternity [sic] and have disregarded that law. Men who disregard that law are in the same situation as if they broke any other law. they are transgressors" (Van Wagoner, 97).

59. Ann Young, Chapter Seven, online at http://www.antimormon.8m.com/youngchp7.html.
60. George D. Smith, 20.
61. Nels Anderson, *Desert Saints: The Mormon Frontier in Utah* (Chicago: University of Chicago Press, 1942; paperback edition, 1966), 118.
62. Ann Young, Chapter Seventeen, online at http://www.antimormon.8m.com/youngchp17. html.
63. Quoted in Anderson, 402.
64. Ann Young, Chapter Seven, online at http://www.antimormon.8m.com/youngchp7.html.
65. Most Mormon males took only 1–3 wives. Less than ten percent took four wives. Approximately the same percentage took five or more wives (Eugene E. Campbell, *Establishing Zion: The Mormon Church in the American West, 1847–1869* [Salt Lake City: Signature Books, 1988; second printing 1989], 166). Theological factors caused additional complexities:

  • Mormons married—i.e., were "sealed" to each other—not only for time (i.e., their lives on earth until death), but also for eternity (i.e. the afterlife).
  • Sometimes people were "sealed" to different spouses. Female A, for example, might be sealed both for time and eternity to Male A, but after Male A died, she married Male B, to whom she was sealed only for time. Thus, after death, she would need to go back to Male A because she had been sealed to him for eternity.
  • A living Mormon could actually be sealed for eternity to a deceased Mormon by "proxy." This was accomplished via a special ceremony whereby the living individual was married to the departed individual, with a living partner (i.e., the proxy) standing in for the deceased spouse-to-be. This sealing by proxy for eternity continues to be practiced today by Mormons.
  • If necessary, an individual could be "unsealed" from one person, then sealed to another one.
  • No stipulations were placed on who could be sealed to whom, the proper age for sealing, or relational prohibitions on persons sealed for time or eternity.

66. Ann Young, Chapter Eighteen, online at http://www.antimormon.8m.com/youngchp18. html. Many families, perhaps as many as 10% of the polygamous population, included two or more sisters as plural wives to one man (Stanley S. Ivins, "Notes On Mormon Polygamy," in D. Michael Quinn, *The New Mormon History* [Salt Lake City: Signature Books, 1992], 175.) Two sets of Brigham's spouses were sisters (Clara/Lucy Decker and Mary/Lucy Bigelow), while eight of his daughters shared husbands: Luna and Fanny wed to George Thatcher; Mary and Caroline were given to Mark Croxall; Alice and Emily married Hiram Clawson; and Polly and Lovina were sealed to John D. Lee. Heber C. Kimball married fives sets of sisters (Clarissa/Emily Cutler; Amanda/Anna Gheen; Harriet/Ellen Sanders; Hannah/Dorothy Moon; and Laura/Abigail Pitkin).
67. Ann Young, Chapter Eighteen, online at http://www.antimormon.8m.com/youngchp18. html. Eliza's recollections are supported by numerous historical documents. Samuel Bowles, for instance, in *Across the Continent: A Summer's Journey to the Rocky Mountains, the Mormons, and the Pacific States* (1865), observed: Polygamy introduces many curious cross-relationships, and intertwines that branches of the genealogical tree in a manner greatly to puzzle a mathematician, as well as to disgust the decent-minded. The marrying of two or more sisters is very common; one young Mormon merchant in Salt Lake City has three sisters. . . . There are several cases of men marrying both mother (widow) and her

daughter or daughters; taking the "old woman" for the sake of getting the young ones. (Samuel Bowles, *Across the Continent: A Summer's Journey to the Rocky Mountains, the Mormons, and the Pacific States* [Springfield, MA: Samuel Bowles & Company, 1865], 123.

68. Scott H. Faulring, ed., *An American Prophet's Record: The Diaries and Journals of Joseph Smith* (Salt Lake City: Signature Books,1987), 424.

69. On October 8, 1854, Brigham commented: "I believe in sisters marrying brothers, and brothers having their sisters for wives. . . . This is something pertaining to our marriage relation. The whole world will think what an awful thing it is. What an awful thing it would be if the Mormons should just say we believe in marrying brothers and sisters (Fred C. Collier, ed., *The Teachings of President Brigham Young* [Salt Lake City: Collier's Publishing Co., 1987], vol. 3, 362, 368). This book is available for purchase online at http://www.utlm.org/booklist/titles/xb024_teachingsofpresidentbrighamyoung.htm.

70. Embry discovered information in the journal of Apostle Abraham H. Cannon, which records a relevant experience Cannon had in 1886: "[I talked to] Pres. Snow about various doctrines. Bro Snow said I would live to see the time when brothers and sisters would marry each other in this church. All our horror at such an union was due entirely to prejudice and the offspring of such union would be healthy and pure as any other. These were the decided views of Pres. Young when alive, for Bro. S. talked to him freely on this matter" (*Journal of Mormon History*, 1992, 106).

71. Fanny Stenhouse, *Tell It All* (Hartford, CT: A.D. Worthington & Co., 1875), 468–469. Stenhouse added: "I know also another man who married a widow with several children; and when one of the girls had grown into her teens he insisted on marrying her also . . . . and to this very day the daughter bears children to her step-father, living as wife in the same house with her mother" (p. 469).

72. The definition of pedophilia presented by the American Psychiatric Association, as found in the *Diagnostic and Statistical Manual of Mental Disorders* (fourth edition), is as follows: "Over a period of at least 6 months, recurrent, intense sexually arousing fantasies, sexual urges, or behaviors involving sexual activity with a prepubescent child or children (generally age 13 years or younger)," online at http://mentalhelp.net/disorders/sx63.htm.

73. Stanley P. Hirshon, *The Lion of the Lord* (New York: Knopf, 1969), 126–27.

74. George D. Smith. Cited in Jerald Tanner and Sandra Tanner, "Joseph Smith and Women," *Salt Lake City Messenger* (#91), November 1996, 7, online at http://www.utlm.org/newsletters/no91.htm#JOSEPH%20SMITH%20AND%20WOMEN.

75. Ann Young, Chapter Nineteen, online at http://www.antimormon.8m.com/youngchp19.html.

76. Heber Kimball, February 1, 1857, in *JOD*, vol. 4, 209.

77. During a conversation with Henry Jacobs—the husband of Zina Huntington, who had been married to Joseph Smith at the same time she was married to Jacobs—Brigham Young told Jacobs: "The woman you claim for a wife does not belong to you. She is a spiritual wife of brother Joseph, sealed to him. I am his proxy, and she, in his behalf, with her children, are my property. You can go where you please and get another" (William Hall, *The Abominations of Mormonism Exposed* [Cincinnati, 1852], 43–44. Hall Claims to have heard this statement from Young. It was confirmed by T.B.H. Stenhouse in *The Rocky Mountain Saints* [New York: D. Appleton & Co., 1873; 1904 edition, published in Salt Lake City, Shepard Book Company], 185–186).

78. Rhea Allred Kunz, *Voices of Women Approaching Celestial or Plural Marriage* (Draper, UT: Review and Preview Publishers, n.d.), 87. Quoted in Van Wagoner 83.

79. Heber C. Kimball. Quoted in Jennie Anderson Froiseth, ed., *The Women of Mormonism: or the Story of Polygamy As Told by the Victims Themselves* (Detroit: C.G.G. Paine, 1886), Chapter Two, online at http://www.biblebelievers.net/Cults/Mormonism/Womenof Mormonism/kjcwom2.htm or also online at http://www.polygamyinfo.com/wom_book_ contents.htm. The latter site, an especially fascinating one, is maintained by a modern-day former plural wife of a Mormon fundamentalist / polygamist.

80. John D. Lee, Journal, under February 23, 1847, published at Salt Lake City in 1938 by
    Charles Kelly. Quoted in Anderson, 404.
81. Jedediah Grant. Quoted in T.B.H. Stenhouse, 294.
82. Jedediah Grant, February 19, 1854, in *JOD*, vol. 2, 14.
83. John D. Lee, *Mormonism Unveiled; Including The Remarkable Life And Confessions Of
    The Late Mormon Bishop. John D. Lee* (St. Louis: N.D. Thompson and Company, 1877),
    165, online at http://www.helpingmormons.org/Rare_Books.htm.
84. Lee, 165, and Ann Young, Chapter Seven, ttp://www.antimormon.8m.com/youngchp7.
    html. Obviously, love rarely played a role in polygamy, except during the early years of
    a relationship between a man with his first wife. Afterward, however, once a new plural
    wife arrived, a more sterile view of marriage was adopted. Vilate Kimball, Heber's wife,
    advised younger wives to "lay aside wholly all interest or thought in what her husband
    was doing while he was away from her . . . . [To be] pleased to see him when he came
    in as she was pleased to see any friend" (Vilate Kimball. Quoted in Mrs. S.A. Cooks, *The-
    atrical and Social Affairs in Utah* [Salt Lake City: n.p., 1884], 5–6). Another of Kimball's
    wives confessed, "I never asked him whether he had more wives than me or not, There
    was not any love in the union between myself and Kimball" (Temple Lot Case, 375.
    Quote in Jerald Tanner and Sandra Tanner, *Mormonism: Shadow or Reality?* [Salt Lake
    City: ULM, 1987], 209). Annie Clark Tanner, plural wife to Joseph Tanner, said that when
    her husband came home, "he was more like a guest" (Annie Clark Tanner. Quoted in
    Todd Compton, *In Sacred Loneliness* [Salt Lake City: Signature Books, 1997], xiv). Zina
    Huntington Young, one of Brigham's wives, admitted: "[A] successful polygamous wife
    must regard her husband with indifference, and with no other feeling than that of rev-
    erence, or love we regard as a false sentiment; a feeling which should have no existence
    in polygamy" (Zina Huntington Young. Quoted in *New York World*, November 19, 1869,
    cited in Van Wagoner, 101).
85. Compton, xiv–xv. The fact that plural marriage brought great sorrow to many of the
    women involved can hardly be denied. Heber C. Kimball once stated: "There is a great
    deal of quarrelling in the houses, and contending for power and authority; and the sec-
    ond wife is against the first wife, perhaps, in some instances" (Heber C. Kimball, Janu-
    ary 11, 1857, *JOD*, vol. 4,178). Brigham Young made the following statements: "Our sis-
    ters need not be worried about any doctrine. Brother Penrose said it would be better for
    them if they believed in the doctrine of polygamy. But they do believe it; they know it is
    true, and that is their torment. It perplexes and annoys many of them, because they are
    not sanctified by the spirit of it; if they were there would be no trouble" (Brigham Young,
    November 29, 1868, *JOD* [Liverpool: Albert Carrington, 1869; lithographed reprint of
    original edition, 1966], vol. 12, 312).
86. Sarah D. Rich. Quoted in Leonard J. Arrington, *Charles C. Rich: Mormon General and
    Western Frontiersman* (Provo: Brigham Young University Press, 1974), 288; Mary Ann
    Angell Young. Quoted in *Anti-Polygamy Standard*, August 1882, 36; Emmeline B. Wells,
    diary date of September 30, 1874, quoted in Van Wagoner, 94. The heartache of
    polygamy for Mormon women is perhaps most striking in the writings of Wells, who
    remained a faithful Latter-day Saint all her life. On their twenty second wedding
    anniversary she wrote in her diary, "Anniversary of my marriage with Pres. Wells. 0 how
    happy I was then how much pleasure I anticipated and how changed alas are things
    since that time, how few thoughts I had then have ever been realized, and how much
    sorrow I have known in place of the joy I looked forward to" (October 10, 1874). The
    autumn years of Emmeline's life brought a bittersweet unexpected reunion with her
    erstwhile husband. Wells, then seventy-six, became attentive to the sixty-two-year-old
    wife he had essentially ignored for nearly four decades. After his death in 1891, she
    wrote, "Only memories, only the coming and going and parting at the door. The joy
    when he came the sorrow when he went as though all the light died out of my life. Such
    intense love he has manifested towards me of late years. Such a remarkable change

from the long ago—when I needed him so much more" (March 24, 1891). Quoted from Van Wagoner, 94.

87. Ann Young, letter to Mormon Women, "Letter Number Two," in Froiseth, Chapter Fourteen, 169–170, online at http://www.polygamyinfo.com/wom_book_ch14.htm.

88. Heber C. Kimball, August 28, 1852, *JOD*, vol. 6, 256.

89. Heber C. Kimball. Quoted in Hirshon, 129–130.

90. Lee stated: "In Utah it has been the custom with the Priesthood to make eunuchs of such men as were obnoxious to the leaders. This was done for a double purpose: first, it gave a perfect revenge, and next, it left the poor victim a living example to others of the dangers of disobeying counsel and not living as ordered by the Priesthood. In Nauvoo it was the orders from Joseph Smith and his apostles to beat, wound and castrate all Gentiles that the police could take in the act of entering or leaving a Mormon household under circumstances that led to the belief that they had been there for immoral purposes. . . . In Utah it was the favorite revenge of old, worn-out members of the Priesthood, who wanted young women sealed to them, and found that the girl preferred some handsome young man. The old priests generally got the girls, and many a young man was unsexed for refusing to give up his sweetheart at the request of an old and failing, but still sensual apostle or member of the Priesthood" (pp. 284–285, online at http://antimormon.8m.com/leechp19b.html.

91. John D. Lee described what happened next: "[H]e refused to consent to give up the girl. The lights were then put out. An attack was made on the young man. He was severely beaten, and then tied with his back down on a bench, when Bishop Snow took a bowie-knife, and performed the operation in a most brutal manner, and then took the portion severed from his victim and hung it up in the school-house on a nail, so that it could be seen by all who visited the house afterwards. The party then left the young man weltering in his blood, and in a lifeless condition. During the night he succeeded in releasing himself from his confinement, and dragged himself to some hay-stacks, where he lay until the next day, when he was discovered by his friends. The young man regained his health, but has been an idiot or quite lunatic ever since, and is well known by hundreds of both Mormons and Gentiles in Utah" (p. 286).

92. Lee; cf. Gustive O. Larson, professor of church history at Brigham Young University, *Utah Historical Quarterly*, January 1958, 284–286.

93. "In May 1857 Bishop Warren S. Snow's counselor wrote that twenty-four-year-old Thomas Lewis 'has now gone crazy' after being castrated by Bishop Snow for an undisclosed sex crime. When informed of Snow's action, Young said: 'I feel to sustain him.' . . . In July Brigham Young wrote a reassuring letter to the bishop about this castration: 'Just let the matter drop, and say no more about it,' the LDS president advised, 'and it will soon die away among the people'" (Quinn, *The Mormon Hierarchy: Extensions of Power*, 250–251).

94. *D&C* Section CIX:4 (European edition) "Inasmuch as this Church of Christ has been reproached with the crime of fornication and polygamy; we declare that one man should have one wife; and one woman but one husband, except in case of death, when either is at liberty to marry again."

95. Brigham Young, August 19, 1866, in *JOD*, vol. 11, 269.

96. John Taylor, April 7, 1866, in *JOD*, vol. 11, 221.

97. John Taylor, *Three nights' public discussion between the Revds. C. W. Cleeve, James Robertson, and Philip Cater, and Elder John Taylor, of the Church of Jesus Christ of Latter-day Saints, at Boulogne-sur-mer, France* (Liverpool: Taylor, 1850).

98. *D&C*, 1835 edition, 330 (see quote in *One Nation Under Gods*, Chapter Seven, p. 134).

99. Taylor's marriages were recorded at Nauvoo Temple and the Salt Lake City Endowment House; cf. Nellie T. Taylor, "John Taylor, His Ancestors and Descendants," *Utah Genealogical and Historical Magazine* (July 1930), vol. 21, 105–107. The year 1850 even saw the *MS*, Mormonism's English periodical, print the following denial of polygamy in

response to Mormon detractors: "12th Lie—Joseph Smith taught a system of polygamy. 12th Refutation—The Revelations given through Joseph Smith, state the following . . . 'We believe that one man should have one wife.'"

100. Individuals knowledgeable about Mormonism often asked missionaries why they denied polygamy. In response, they excused their subterfuge by saying that potential converts could not bear such strong doctrine. Consequently, the teaching was reserved for time when the Lord would open their heart to greater truth, usually after they had left their country and were half-way across the United States. Pressed further, missionaries would say that although polygamy was indeed a church institution, it was not mandatory, but simply an option for those so led.

101. In 1875 Eliza Young revealed the following: "[M]en who go on missions are very guarded in preaching the doctrine, and advocate it only where they are very certain that it will be received. They admit its existence, but they by no means are willing to confess to what an extent it is practiced; and to this day many of them win wives under false pretences. . . . [A] gentleman living in the British Provinces . . . spoke of a visit he had received quite recently from a lady friend from England . . . who had become converted to Mormonism, and married one of the elders of the church, and was on her way to Utah with him. . . . [She] deplored the existence of polygamy as its only drawback to a perfect faith. Yet she said her husband had told her that it was only a doctrine of the church that was rarely practiced, except by the older Saints, who had received the Revelation directly from Joseph, and had considered the adoption of the system a duty; that in time it would, be entirely done away with, except in theory, and that at all events she need have no fear. . . . [S]he, who so fondly believed herself the only wife of her husband, [actually] made Number 5 or 6 of his plural wives" (Ann Eliza Young, Chapter Nine, online at http://www.antimormon.8m.com/youngchp9.html).

102. *Miles v. United States*, decision, online lat http://laws.lp.findlaw.com/getcase/us/103/304.html.

103. Matilda Joslyn Gage, *Women, Church and State* (Carmichael, CA: Sky Carrier Press, 1998), 238–240.

104. Gage, see previous endnote. For several weeks Owens was abused and repeatedly exhorted to bear her condition patiently as a "sister" to be exalted. She finally escaped with the help of "Gentiles" and filed suit against Miles. She reconciled for a very brief period of time, but again had left him by the time his case went to court.

105. William Jarman, *USA—Uncle Sam's Abscess or Hell Upon Earth for U.S.* (Exeter, England: H. Leduc's Steam Printing Works, 1884), 45.

106. Pratt, August 29, 1852, in *JOD*, vol. 1, 64.

107. John A. Widtsoe, *Evidences and Reconciliation* (Salt Lake City: Bookcraft, 1960; Single-Volume Edition), 282.

108. Brigham Young, June 18, 1865, in *JOD*, vol. 11, 128.

109. Not surprisingly, the reformation period (1856–1857) was marked by a noticeable increase in polygamous marriages. Stanley Ivins documented that there were "sixty-five more [polygamous] marriages during 1856 and 1857 than in any other two years" (Marie Cornwall, Camela Courtright, and Laga Van BeekHow, "Common the Principle?: Women As Plural Wives in 1860," *Dialogue: A Journal of Mormon Thought* (Summer 1993), vol. 26, 142.

110. Heber C. Kimball, April 6, 1857, *JOD* (Liverpool: Asa Calkin, 1858; lithographed reprint of original edition, 1966), vol. 5, 22.

111. For extensive documentation and in-depth explanations of this beliefs, see Sandra Tanner, "How the LDS Husband Hopes to Resurrect His Wife According to the LDS Temple Ceremony," article online at http://www.utlm.org/onlineresources/resurrectwife.htm.

112. Mary Ettie V. Smith described her temple experience as follows: "We were next led into what is called the Terrestrial Glory; where Brigham Young received us, . . . he gave each a pass-word and grip necessary, he said, to admit us into the "Celestial Glory;" . . . there are

many gods, and they do not acknowledge the one Triune God of the Bible, but that every man will sometime be a "god;" and that women are to be the ornaments of his kingdom, and dependent upon him for resurrection and salvation; and that our salvation is dependent upon the recollection of these passwords" (Mary Ettie V. Smith, in Nelson Winch Green, ed., *Mormonism: its rise, progress, and present condition. Embracing the narrative of Mrs. Mary Ettie V. Smith* [Hartford, CT: Belknap & Bliss, 1858; 1870 edition], 42–48, online at http://moa.umdl.umich.edu/cgi/pageviewer?frames=1&cite=http%3A%2F%2Fmoa.um dl.umich.edu%2Fcgi%2Fsgml%2Fmoa–idx%3Fnotisid%3DAJK2869&coll=moa&view=7 5&root=mm000044%2F1206morm%2Fv0000%2Fi000%2F&tif=00190017.tif&pagenum= 42. In her Ph.D. dissertation, Vicky Burgess–Olson, noted several additional reasons for women entering into polygamy: 1) dedication to the principle; 2) pressure from a third party; 3) economic forces; and 4) increased status in the community (see "Family Structure and Dynamics in Early Utah Mormon Families—1847–1885," Ph.D. dissertation, Northwestern University, 1975, cited in Cornwall, Courtright and BeekHow, 140–141).

113. *Songs of Zion*, published by the LDS Church, quoted in Green, 217, online at http://moa.umdl.umich.edu/cgi/pageviewer?frames=1&cite=http%3A%2F%2Fmoa. umdl.umich.edu%2Fcgi%2Fsgml%2Fmoa–idx%3Fnotisid%3DAJK2869&coll=moa &view=75&root=mm000044%2F1206morm%2Fv0000%2Fi000%2F&tif=02070201.tif &pagenum=217.

114. Brigham Young, April 7, 1861, *JOD*, vol. 9, 37. Helen Mar Whitney, a faithful plural wife, revealed: "I told her of our future hopes, which I knew we should enjoy, and they would be reward enough for the sacrifice we were making for the great good it would accomplish, not only for ourselves but for generations unborn" (Helen Mar Whitney, *Why We Practice Plural Marriage* [Salt Lake City, Juvenile Instructor Office, 1884), online at http://website.lineone.net/~mahonri/hwplural.txt). Eliza Young recalled that Mormon leaders additionally taught the following: "[We] were also told that floating through space were thousands of infant spirits, who were waiting for bodies; that into every child that was born one of these spirits entered, and was thereby saved; but if they had no bodies given them, their wails of despair would ring through all eternity; and that it was, in order to insure their future happiness, necessary that as many of them as possible should be given bodies by Mormon parents. If a woman refused to marry into polygamy, or, being married, to allow her husband to take other wives, these spirits would rise up in judgment against her, because she had, by her act, kept them in darkness" (Ann Eliza Young, Chapter Eighteen, online at http://www.antimormon.8m.com/youngchp18.html).

115. Pratt, *The Seer*, 155, (see this chapter, endnote #39 for additional reference information).

116. Heber C. Kimball, November 9, 1856, in *JOD*, vol. 4, 82; cf. *Deseret News*, vol. 6, 291. Quoted in Jarman, 112.

117. C.F. Keil and F. Delitzsch, *Commentary on the Old Testament* (Peabody, MA: Hendrickson Publishers, 1996 edition), vol. 1, 73.

118. Walter A. Elwell, ed., *Baker Encyclopedia of the Bible* (Grand Rapids: Baker Book House, 1988; 1995 edition), vol. 2, 1406.

119. Despite numerous examples of polygamy cited in the OT, there is no doubt that the vast majority of the Israelites were monogamous.

120. "A virtuous woman [not virtuous women] is a crown to her husband" (Prov. 12:4) and "Who can find a virtuous woman? [not women] for her price is far above rubies. The heart of her husband doth safely trust in her [not in them]. . . . Her husband [not their husband] is known in the gates, when he sitteth among the elders (Prov. 31:10–11, 23).

121. Geoffrey W. Bromiley, gen. ed., *The International Standard Bible Encyclopedia* (Grand Rapids: William Eerdmans Publishing, 1986; 1990 edition), vol. 3, 901.

122. Bromiley, 901.

123. Jedediah M. Grant, August 7, 1853, in *JOD*, vol. 1, 346. Ann Eliza remembered being taught that Jesus Christ "was a practical polygamist; Mary and Martha, the sisters of Lazarus, were his plural wives, and Mary Magdalen was another. Also, the bridal feast

at Cana of Galilee, where Jesus turned the water into wine, was on the occasion of one of his own marriages (Ann Eliza Young, Chapter Eighteen, online at http://www.antimormon.8m.com/youngchp18.html).

124. Orson Hyde, March 18, 1855, in *JOD*, vol. 2, 210.

125. Pratt, *The Seer*, 172, (see this chapter, endnote #26 for additional reference information).

126. Contrary to this Bible verse, Heber C. Kimball taught that marriages would take place in the spirit world: "Supposing that I have a wife or a dozen of them. . . . Suppose that I lose the whole of them before I go into the spirit world, but that I have been a good, faithful man all the days of my life, and lived my religion, and had favour with God, and was kind to them, do you think I will be destitute there [in the spirit world]? No, the Lord says there are more [women] there [in the spirit world] than there are here. . . . In the spirit world there is an increase of males and females, there are millions of them, and if I am faithful all the time, and continue right along with brother Brigham, we will go to brother Joseph [Smith] and say, 'Here we are brother Joseph'. . . . He will say to us, ... 'Where are your wives?' 'They are back yonder; they would not follow us.' 'Never mind,' says Joseph, 'here are thousands, have all you want.' Perhaps some do not believe that, but I am just simple enough to believe it. . . . I am looking for the day, and it is close at hand, when we will have a most heavenly time, one that will be romantic, one with all kinds of ups and downs, which is what I call romantic, for it will occupy in full all the time" (Kimball, *JOD*, vol. 4, 209).

127. Stewart (writing in 1961), 26. Latter-day Saints completely reject the argument that that the *Book of Mormon* prohibits polygamy. They commonly respond by claiming that although God did indeed forbid polygamy to the people he was addressing in the *BOM*, he was not making a blanket condemnation of it. Also, they claim that the appropriateness of polygamy is somewhat of a fluid issue, meaning that when God says it is acceptable, then it is acceptable and must be obeyed (c. 1841–1890). But when God says it is not acceptable, then it must not be practiced, otherwise one is in disobedience to God (c. 1890–present). Although this answer seems to make their God appear somewhat fickle, it is how Mormons view the discrepancy between the practice at one time being necessary for righteous living, and then suddenly, having to accept the very opposite as true.

CHAPTER FOURTEEN: THE POLITICS OF COMPROMISE

1. Orson Pratt, July 18, 1880, *JOD* (Liverpool: Albert Carrington, 1881; lithographed reprint of original edition, 1966), vol. 21, 296. In 1883 LDS apostle Charles Penrose, likewise stated: "[I]f the doctrine of plural marriage was repudiated so must be the glorious principle of marriage for eternity, the two being indissolubly interwoven with each other" (Charles Penrose. Quoted in "Plural Marriage," *MS*, vol. XLV, no. 29, July 16, 1883, 454).

2. This measure outlawed not only polygamy, but also any marital unions falling in the category of "ecclesiastical solemnities, sacraments, ceremonies, consecrations, or other contrivances."

3. The Reynolds case began on June 18, 1875 with the arrest of Reynolds for bigamy. However, his case was thrown out on a technicality. A second trial, which began in October 1875, resulted in the conviction. Reynolds was fined $500 and sentenced to two years at hard labor. The Supreme Court appeal began in November 1878. The final ruling against Reynolds came from the high court on January 6, 1879.

4. The Poland Bill was signed by President Ulysses S. Grant on June 24, 1874.

5. Rutherford B. Hayes. Quoted in T. Harry Williams, ed., *The Diary of a President, 1875–1881* (New York: David McKay Co., Inc. 1964), under January 9, 1880, 258–259.

6. This decision came just months after the George S. Reynolds case had been decided.

7. David L. Bigler, *Forgotten Kingdom: The Mormon Theocracy in the American West, 1847–1896* (Logan, Utah: Utah State University Press, 1998), 279.

8. Bigler, 316.

9. B.H. Roberts, *CHC* (Salt Lake City: Deseret News Press, 1930), vol. 6, 19.

10. House Misc. Doc. 49 (43-1), 1873, Serial 1617, 5.

11. Few Mormons were prosecuted for bigamy because the government had difficulty obtaining testimony about plural wedding ceremonies. Rather, they were charged with bigamous cohabitation, a misdemeanor created by the Edmunds Act (1882). The Edmunds Law took the 1862 Morrill Act and simply replaced the word bigamy with polygamy. Those guilty were to be fined no more than $500 and given not more than five years in jail, or both the fine and jail. The law also defined polygamous living as "unlawful cohabitation," a misdemeanor punishable by a fine not exceeding $300, and imprisonment for not more than six months, or both the fine and jail.

12. First Presidency (John Taylor, George Q. Cannon, and Joseph F. Smith). Quoted in James R. Clark, *Messages of the First Presidency* (Salt Lake City: Bookcraft, 1965–1975), 5 volumes, cited in Samuel W. Taylor, *Rocky Mountain Empire* (Macmillan Publishing Co., Inc., 1978) , 13.

13. Jesse Embry, *Mormon Polygamous Families: Life in the Principle* (Salt Lake City: University of Utah Press, 1987), 22.

14. On March 23, 1885, the Edmunds measure was given full constitutional standing by the United States Supreme Court, after which prosecutions of the Saints became more vigorous. Lorenzo Snow was jailed for more than six months on illegal cohabitation charges in December 1885.

15. John Taylor, revelation given to Taylor on the night of September 27, 1886, online at http://www.kingdomofzion.org/doctrines/library/tlc/GospelDiscussionsFolder/Plural Marriage/PM4HiddenRev.htm; also see Fred C. Collier, ed., *Unpublished Revelations* (Salt Lake City: Collier's Publishing Co., 1979; 2nd edition, 1981), vol. 1, 145–146, 180–183. This highly volatile and controversial revelation continues to be disputed by LDS leaders. Several sources, however, including witnesses present when the revelation was given and John W. Taylor (John Taylor's son), have produced evidence that indicates the LDS president did indeed receive this revelation and accept it as having come from God:

    "My Son John. You have asked me concerning the new and everlasting covenant [i.e., polygamy] & how far it is binding upon my people. [T]hus saith the Lord all commandments that I give must be obeyed by those calling themselves by my name unless they are revoked by me or by my authority, and how can I revoke an everlasting covenant; for I the Lord am everlasting and my everlasting covenants cannot be abrogated nor done away with; but they stand for ever. Have I not given my word in great plainness on this subject? . . . I the Lord do not change & my word & my covenants & my law do not, & as I have heretofore said by my servant Joseph all those who would enter into my glory must & shall obey my law & have I not commanded men that if they were Abraham's seed & would enter into my glory, they must do the works of Abraham. I have not revoked this law nor will I for it is everlasting & those who will enter into my glory must obey the conditions thereof."

16. For an extensive listing of quotes from high-ranking LDS authorities on the essential nature of polygamy for exaltation, see the Internet article "Was Plural Marriage A Requirement for Exaltation in the Celestial Kingdom" by Perry L. Porter, online at http://www.ldshistory.net/pc/required.htm.

17. Brigham Young, July 14, 1855, *JOD* (Liverpool: Orson Pratt, 1856; lithographed reprint of original edition, 1966), vol. 3, 266. Some Mormons argue that Young was not speaking here about the practice of polygamy, but merely referring to the belief or acceptance of it in one's heart. However, after stating that a person would be damned for denying polygamy, he goes on to state that those who deny it even in their feelings will also be damned. Consequently, Young must be referring to the practice of polygamy in the first

part of his statement. His entire remarks are as follows: "[I]f any of you will deny the plurality of wives, and continue to do so, I promise that you will be damned; and I will go
still further and say, take this revelation, or any other revelation that the Lord has given,
and deny it in your feelings, and I promise that you will be damned."

18. Brigham Young, July 6, 1862, *JOD* (Liverpool: George Q. Cannon, 1862; lithographed
    reprint of original edition, 1966), vol. 9, 322

19. U.S. Congress, Memorial Adopted by Citizens of Salt Lake City, Utah Territory, 41st
    Cong., 2nd Sess., Senate Misc. Document No. 12, Serial 1408, 1.

20. Wilford Woodruff, in Scott G. Kenney, ed., *Wilford Woodruff's Journal*, 1833–1898 (Mid-
    vale, UT: Signature Books, 1983–85), under January 26, 1880, vol. 7, pages 546, 615–617,
    621. This revelation was accepted as the "word of the Lord" by John Taylor and the Quo-
    rum of the Twelve. It stated: "[W]o unto that Nation or house or people who seek to hin-
    der my People from obeying the Patriarchal Law of Abraham which leadeth to a Celes-
    tial Glory . . . for whosoever doeth those things shall be damned Saith the Lord."
    Ironically, this condemnation would eventually pertain to Woodruff himself.

21. Wilford Woodruff, April 3, 1881, *JOD* (Liverpool: Albert Carrington, 1882; lithographed
    reprint of original edition, 1966), vol. 22, 147–148.

22. John Taylor, *Salt Lake Tribune*, January 6, 1880. Quoted in Richard S. Van Wagoner, *Mor-
    mon Polygamy: A History* (Salt Lake City: Signature Books, 1989; paperback edition),
    112–113.

23. George Q. Cannon, October 5, 1884, *JOD* (Liverpool: John Henry Smith, 1884; litho-
    graphed reprint of original edition, 1966), vol. 25, 321–322. Cannon stated: "Men say,
    'Oh, if you will only get a revelation concerning polygamy, if you will only lay polygamy
    aside, you will no longer have any opposition to contend with; if you will only conform
    to modern ideas concerning your domestic institutions, we shall have nothing to say
    against you. The opposition that finds now such strong support will be deprived of its
    war-cry and of the sympathy of thousands which sustain it at the present time—they will
    be deprived of this and you will go along like the rest of the churches, without having to
    suffer from the opposition and the hatred that are now manifested against you.' Vain
    thought!—a thought that is only expressed by those who know nothing of the character
    of this work, who are not familiar with the history of this dispensation, and who judge
    of the effects of such movements by their human knowledge and the experience that
    they have with other systems. This system which God has established, this great work
    of our God, cannot be measured by human thoughts. . . . Therefore, those who under-
    stand this work, know very well that anything of this kind—unless indeed the people
    should apostatize—would have no such effect as our friends in many instances think it
    would have."

24. It must be noted that there exists a few sporadic comments from various leaders that
    polygamy as a practice was optional, as long as a person believed in their heart that it
    was a true principle from God. For example, Brigham Young apparently announced at
    one point that "a man may embrace the law of celestial marriage in his heart and not
    take the second wife and be justified before the Lord" (Brigham Young, quoted by
    Woodruff, in Kenney, under September 24, 1871, vol. 7, 31). However, such comments
    were rendered virtually meaningless because they were so greatly overshadowed by
    remarks encouraging polygamy to be practiced as a condition of salvation/exaltation.
    Consider the following remark from Brigham Young: "We are told that if we would give
    up polygamy which—we know to be a doctrine revealed from heaven, and it is of God
    and the world for it—but suppose this Church should give up this holy order of mar-
    riage, then would the devil, and all who are in league with him against the cause of God,
    rejoice that they had prevailed upon the Saints to refuse to obey one of the revelations
    and commandments of God to them . . . Will the Latter-day Saints do this? No; they will
    not to please anybody" (Brigham Young, June 3, 1866, *JOD* [Liverpool: B. Young, Jr.,
    1867; lithographed reprint of original edition, 1966], vol. 11, 239).

25. Brigham Young, August 19, 1866, in *JOD*, vol. 11, 269.

26. Editorial, *Deseret News*, April 23, 1885.

27. "No Relinquishment," *Deseret News*, June 5, 1885. For an extensive listing of similar remarks from LDS leaders, see "Celestial Plural Marriage: References," online at http://website.lineone.net/~mahonri/cpmr.htm. The quotations wherein LDS leaders stated that polygamy would continue until Christ returns are far too long and numerous to include in this volume. Only a few references to the most important statements can be given: Brigham Young (*JOD*, vol. 2, 267; *JOD*, vol. 4, 371–372; *JOD*, vol. 9, 322; *JOD*, vol. 11, 269 and Young's Sermon at Dedication of St. George Temple), William Clayton (*HR*, vol. 6, 225–227), Joseph F. Smith (*JOD*, vol. 20, 29; *JOD*, vol. 21, 10), Heber C. Kimball (*JOD*, vol. 4, p. 224; *MS*, vol. 28, 190), John Taylor (*JOD*, vol. 11, p. 221), Wilford Woodruff (*MS*, vol. 41, p. 242), and George Q. Cannon (*Deseret News*, June 30, 1883).

28. George Q. Cannon, Diary, under November 6, 1885; see Edward Leo Lyman, "The Mormon Quest for Utah Statehood," Ph.D. dissertation, University of California at Riverside, 1981, 57–60. Lyman's work is an incredibly in-depth presentation of the political climate, events, and intrigue that led to the 1890 Manifesto.

29. Wilford Woodruff. Quoted in Van Wagoner, 111.

30. Orson Pratt, September 26, 1875, printed October 2, 1875, *Deseret Evening News*, vol. 8, no. 265. Quoted in N.B. Lundwall, comp., *Inspired Prophetic Warnings* (Salt Lake City: author, 1940), 26 .

31. Wilford Woodruff, October 8, 1875, *JOD* (Liverpool: Joseph F. Smith, 1877; lithographed reprint of original edition, 1966), vol. 18, 127. Woodruff stated: "There is another word of the Lord unto me . . . that is, to call upon all the inhabitants of these mountains as far as I have an opportunity, to go to and lay up their grain that they may have bread. For the last three months I have not felt as if I could answer my own feelings unless, at every meeting I have attended, I call upon the farmers to lay up their grain. . . . Know ye, Latter-day Saints, that the Lord will not disappoint you or this generation with regard to the fulfillment of his promises."

32. Wilford Woodruff, *MS*, April 21, 1879, vol. 41, 242–243. Quoted in Jerald Tanner and Sandra Tanner, *The Changing World of Mormonism* (Chicago: Moody, 1981), 267, online at http://www.xmission.com/~country/chngwrld/chap9c.htm. Also see Internet article "The Prophecy of Joseph Smith on the United States and the Constitution Hanging by a Thread," online at http://members.tripod.com/~tamago000/const.html.

33. Wilford Woodruff, excerpt from Epistle of Wilford Woodruff, April 21, 1879, *MS* vol. 41, 241, online at http://www.kingdomofzion.org/doctrines/library/aub/TM_Vol1.txt. In 1880 Woodruff said he knew America would soon be destroyed because God had revealed it to him. He explained: "I know it by the administrations of angels, and I know it by the inspiration of heaven, that is given to all men who seek the Lord; and the hand of God will not stay these things. We have no time to lose." Also see Wilford Woodruff, August 1, 1880, *JOD* (Liverpool: Albert Carrington, 1881; lithographed reprint of original edition, 1966), vol. 21, 301.

34. Orson Pratt, March 9, 1879, *JOD* (Liverpool: William Budge, 1880; lithographed reprint of original edition, 1966), vol. 20, 152. Pratt declared:

> "It will be very different from the war between the North and the South. . . . It will be a war of neighborhood against neighborhood, city against city, town against town, county against county, state against state, and they will go forth destroying and being destroyed and manufacturing will, in a great measure, cease, for a time among the American nation. . . . [Farmers] will leave their farms and they will flee before the ravaging armies from place to place, and thus will they go forth burning and pillaging the whole country; and that great and powerful nation, now consisting of some forty millions, of people, will be wasted away, unless they repent. Now these are predictions you may record. You may let them sink down into your hearts. And if the Lord your God shall permit you to live, you

will see my words fulfilled to the very letter. They are not my words, but the words of inspiration, the words of the everlasting God who has sent forth his servants with this message to warn the nations of the earth. . . . [T]he Lord also made a similar decree . . . in regard to the present great populous nation called the people of the United States. They must perish, unless they repent. . . . . A time is coming when the great and populous city of New York, the greatest city of the American Republic, will be left without inhabitants."

35. Joseph Smith, *HC* (Salt Lake City: Deseret Book Company, 1976/1980), vol. 2, 182.

36. Joseph Smith, *HC* (Salt Lake City: Deseret Book Company, 1976/1980), vol. 5, 324, 336.

37. Peter L. Crawley, *The Essential Parley P. Pratt* (Salt Lake City: Signature Books, 1990), 142.

38. Russell R. Rich, *Ensign to the Nations: A History of the LDS Church from 1846 to 1972* (Salt Lake City: Brigham Young University Publications, 1972), 383. This is a highly biased pro-Mormon volume by a devout Mormon and should be researched with a discerning eye.

39. Samuel Taylor, 17.

40. Samuel Taylor, 19.

41. Nels Anderson, *Desert Saints: The Mormon Frontier in Utah* (Chicago: University of Chicago Press, 1942; paperback edition, 1966), 335.

42. Samuel Taylor, 20–21, footnote #15.

43. Edwin Brown Firmage and Richard Collin Mangrum, *Zion in the Courts* (Urbana: University of Illinois Press, 1988), 230.

44. Rich, 383.

45. Roberts, vol. 6, 211. For an excellent look at the "cohab" arrests, see Ken Driggs, "The Prosecutions Begin: Defining Cohabitation in 1885," *Dialogue: A Journal of Mormon Thought*, vol. 21, no. 1, 109–125. For an interesting look at the prison conditions endured by jailed polygamists, see Van Wagoner, 120–122.

46. Wilford Woodruff, 1836–1837 Diary, under April 4 11, 1837, reprinted in Dean Jessee, "The Kirtland Diary of Wilford Woodruff," *BYU Studies* (Summer 1972), vol. 12, 388. Wilford wrote: "[K]ings would tremble upon their thrones at my word. . . . I should become a Counsellor & multitudes should seek counsel at my mouth & I should have great wisdom & power to fly through the midst under heaven . . . I should have power over my enemies & have long life & bring many into the kingdom of God Also that I should have the riches of the earth." This document can be found on the *New Mormon Studies CD ROM: Comprehensive Resource Library* (Salt Lake City: Signature Books, 2000).

47. Woodruff, 1836–1837 Diary, under January 3, 1837, reprinted in Jessee, 380. [M]y enemies may confine me in Prisions & chains & that I would rend the prisions & chains in twain in the name of Jesus Christ & that the Lord would give me great Power, Knowledg[e], & wisdom & faith so that I should heal the sick caus[e] the Blind to see the lame to leap . . . [the] Deaf to hear stop the mouths of Lions & ra[i]se the dead to life. . . . [T]that I should stand before Kings & Princes & that they would send for me to receieve wisdom knowledge & instruction at my mouth because they considered me wiser than themselves in like manner as the Egyptians sought wisdom at the hand of Joseph. . . . [T]hat I should then return & stand upon Mount Zion in the flesh even in Jackson County Missouri at the cumming [sic] of Christ & that I should be cought up to meet him in the Clouds of heaven for he said this was the word of God unto me & Also that I should visit COLUB [Kolob]." This document can be found on the *New Mormon Studies CD ROM: Comprehensive Resource Library* (Salt Lake City: Signature Books, 2000).

48. Wilford Woodruff, from *Wilford Woodruff Journal*, as copied by Joseph W. Musser, online at http://www.kingdomofzion.org/doctrines/library/tlc/GospelDiscussionsFolder/ PluralMarriage/PM4HiddenRev.htm. This revelation went on to state: "Let my servants who officiate as your counselors before the courts make their pleadings as they are moved upon by the Holy Spirit, without any further pledges from the Priesthood, and

they will be justified. I, the Lord, will hold the courts, with the officers of government and the nation responsible for their acts towards the inhabitants of Zion. I, Jesus Christ, the Saviour of the world, am in your midst. I am your advocate with the Father. Fear not, little flock, it is your Father's good pleasure to give you the Kingdom. Fear not the wicked and ungodly. . . . I the Lord will deliver my Saints from the dominion of the wicked in mine own due time and way. I cannot deny my Word, neither in blessings nor judgments. Therefore let mine anointed gird up their loins, watch and be sober, and keep my commandments." This document can be found on the *New Mormon Studies CD ROM: Comprehensive Resource Library* (Salt Lake City: Signature Books, 2000).

49. For a good overview of the political interactions and deal-making that went on behind the scenes with regard to the drafting and adoption of this document, see Van Wagner, 133–142 (Chapter Thirteen, "The Wilford Woodruff Manifesto").

50. This declaration can be found in modern versions of the *Doctrine and Covenants*, and is online at http://deseretbook.com/scriptures/dc/dcod1.html.

51. Joseph F. Smith, letter to Sarah E. Smith, September 24, 1890, Joseph F. Smith Papers (Letterbook). Quoted in Edward Leo Lyman, *Political Deliverance* (Urbana: University of Illinois Press, 1986), 138.

52. George Reynolds, at the Reed Smoot hearings in 1904, said that he "assisted to write it," in collaboration with Charles W. Penrose and John R. Winder who "transcribed the notes and changed the language slightly to adapt it for publication." Moving far beyond that statement, John W. Woolley told his polygamist followers in the 1920s that "Judge Zane [a non–Mormon] had as much to do with it [the Manifesto] as Wilford Woodruff except to sign it," and Lorin C. Woolley told Mormon Fundamentalists that Wilford Woodruff was not the author of the Manifesto but that it was actually written by Charles W. Penrose, Frank J. Cannon, and "John H. White, the butcher," revised by non-Mormon federal officials, and that Woodruff merely signed it. Moreover, Woolley and his Fundamentalist followers have accused George Q. Cannon of pressuring Presidents Taylor and Woodruff to write a manifesto abandoning plural marriage, and at least one Fundamentalist called him "The Great Mormon Judas." The authorship of the Manifesto remains controversial. Frank Cannon says, "He told me he had written it himself, and it certainly appeared to me to be in his handwriting. Its authorship has since been variously attributed. Some of the present-day polygamists say that it was I who wrote it. Chas. W. Penrose and George Reynolds have claimed they edited it. Thomas J. Rosser stated that, when a missionary to Wales in 1908, he asked the mission president, Charles W. Penrose, during a missionary conference, if the Manifesto was a revelation from God. "Brethren, I will answer that question, if you will keep it under your hats," Penrose said. "I, Charles W. Penrose, wrote the Manifesto with the assistance of Frank J. Cannon and John White. . . . Wilford Woodruff signed it to beat the devil at his own game" (D. Michael Quinn, "LDS Church Authority and New Plural Marriages, 1890–1904," *Dialogue: A Journal of Mormon Thought*, vol. 18, no. 1, 11–12, online at http://website.lineone.net/~mahonri/Quinn_Post_Manifesto_Dialogue.txt; *Proceedings Before The Committee On Privileges And Elections Of The United States Senate In The Matter Of The Protests Against The Right Of Hon. Reed Smoot, A Senator From Utah, To Hold His Seat* (Washington, D.C.: Government Printing Office, 1904), vol. 2, 51, 52; and Thomas J. Rosser, letter dated August 4, 1956, missionary to England and Wales during 1907 and 1908, online at http://website.lineone.net/~mahonri/cpmr.htm.

53. See B. Carmon Hardy, *Solemn Covenant: The Mormon Polygamous Passage* (Urbana: University of Illinois Press, 1992), 394ff. This reference actually lists by name the more than 200 Mormon polygamous marriages, which took place after Woodruff's 1890 Manifesto.

54. Brigham Young, August 1, 1852, *JOD* (Liverpool: F.D. Richards, 1855; lithographed reprint of original edition, 1966), vol. 1, 361).

55. In a 1911 telegram to Reed Smoot, LDS president Joseph F. Smith told Smoot that plural

marriages had been solemnized in both Canada and Mexico (Joseph F. Smith, letter to Reed Smoot, April 1, 1911, Reed Smoot Correspondence, LDSCA). However, in another letter written to Smoot by George Gibbs, it is communicated that Smith's inclusion of Canada in the telegram was a mistake (George Gibbs, letter to Reed Smoot, April 12, 1911, Reed Smoot Correspondence, LDSCA). Although the certainty of this claim is questionable since no record exists of Smith correcting himself.

56. J. Reuben Clark, *Messages of the First Presidency* (Salt Lake City, UT: Bookcraft, 1965–1975), vol. 3, 230–231.

57. Wilford Woodruff testimony. Quoted in Van Wagoner, 149–150. Consider the following extract from his testimony:

U.S.:	State whether or not it would be contrary to the law of the church, for any member of the church to enter into or contract a plural marriage.
WOODRUFF:	It would be contrary to the laws of the church.
U.S.:	What would be the penalty?
WOODRUFF:	Any person entering into plural marriage after that date, would be liable to become excommunicated from the church.
U.S.:	Do you understand that that language was to be expanded and to include the further statement of living or associating in plural marriage by those already in the status?
WOODRUFF:	Yes, sir; I intended the proclamation to cover the ground, to keep the laws -to obey the law myself, and expected the people to obey the law. . . .
U.S.:	Was the manifesto intended to apply to the church everywhere?
WOODRUFF:	Yes, sir.
U.S.:	In every nation and every country?
WOODRUFF:	Yes, sir; as far as I had a knowledge in the matter.
U.S.:	In places outside of the United States as well as within the United States?
WOODRUFF:	Yes, sir; we are given no liberties for entering into that anywhere. . . .
U.S.:	Unlawful cohabitation, as it is named, and spoken of, should also stop, as well as future polygamous marriages?
WOODRUFF:	Yes sir, that has been the intention.
U.S.:	And that has been your views and explanation of it?
WOODRUFF:	Yes, sir, that has been my view.

58. Matthias F. Cowley, minutes of Council of the Council of the Twelve, May 10, 1911. Quoted in Van Wagoner, 151.

59. Abraham H. Cannon. Quoted in Van Wagoner, 150; also see D. Michael Quinn, "LDS Church Authority and New Plural Marraiges, 1890–1904," *Dialogue: A Journal of Mormon Thought*, vol. 18, no. 1, 61, online at http://website.lineone.net/~mahonri/Quinn_Post_Manifesto_Dialogue.txt.

60. Joseph F. Smith. Quoted in William Edward Biederwolf, *Mormonism Under the Searchlight* (Chicago: Glad Tidings Publishing Co., 1915), 65.

61. Lorenzo Snow, April 10, 1898, *Conference Report*, 14, 64. Quoted in Marvin W. Cowan, *Mormon Claims Answered* (Salt Lake City: Utah Christian Publications, 1997), online at http://www.utlm.org/onlinebooks/mclaims5.htm. Cowen's entire volume is online at http://www.utlm.org/onlinebooks/mclaimscontents.htm.

62. During Snow's trial a particularly interesting exchange occurred between him and Mr. Bierbower, the prosecuting attorney. Bierbower predicted that one day because of legal pressure "a new revelation would soon follow, changing the divine law of celestial marriage." To this comment, Snow replied: "Whatever fame Mr. Bierbower may have secured as a lawyer, he certainly will fail as a prophet. The severest prosecutions have

never been followed by revelations changing a divine law, obedience to which brought imprisonment or martyrdom. Though I go to prison, God will not change his law of celestial marriage. But the man, the people, the nation that oppose and fight against this doctrine and the Church of God, will be overthrown" (Andrew Jenson, "Lorenzo Snow," *HR*, February 1887, vol. 6, no. 2, 144). Bierbower's prediction came true. Snow, on the other hand, was as surprised by the 1890 Manifesto as every other Mormon.

63. Quoted in Samuel Taylor, 8.

64. Quoted in Samuel Taylor, 9–10.

65. Quoted in Samuel Taylor, 10.

66. Van Wagoner, 159. Anthony W. Ivins performed 29 of these marriages, which according to a March 7, 1911 letter he wrote to his son, were done with the approval of the LDS church hierarchy. He stated: "You may depend upon. I have never performed a marriage ceremony without proper authority."

67. Hardy, 389–425. D. Michael Quinn, summarized the statistics during a lecture he delivered in 1991: "All First Presidency members either allowed or authorized new plural marriages from 1890 to 1904, and a few as late as 1906 and 1907. One Church President married a plural wife, and three Counselors in the First Presidency performed marriages for men who had living wives already. A Presidency's secretary proposed polygamous marriage in 1903, and another Presidency's secretary performed a polygamous marriage in 1907. Of the sixteen men who served only as Apostles . . . eight of these sixteen men married post-Manifesto plural wives. Three of them who did not do so, performed plural marriages. Two of them who did not do either of the above, arranged for plural marriages. . . . Now, looking at the men individually. Wilford Woodruff . . . personally approved 7 new plural marriages, to be performed in Mexico. He also approved polygamous ceremonies for a couple of Mexican residents as early as 1891. He delegated George Q. Cannon, his first counselor, to give approval for plural marriages from 1892 to 1898. That approval was in the form of written letters. . . . Woodruff himself married a new Plural Wife in 1897. . . . [Lorenzo Snow] cohabited with his youngest plural wife who went to Canada briefly, in 1896, to bear his last child. And in so doing, he violated the testimony that he had given publicly in 1891, that the Manifesto prohibited cohabitation with plural wives. . . . [Joseph F. Smith] In 1896 as a counselor, he performed in the Salt Lake Temple a "proxy plural marriage" for Abraham Cannon, which had been approved earlier by the First Presidency. . . . Smith instructed Seymour B. Young of the First council of seventy, to perform two plural marriages in Mexico. And later that same year, second counselor Smith authorized Patriarch Alexander F. MacDonald to perform new plural marriages in Mexico for any Mexican residents who requested them. . . . George Q. Cannon was Presidency counselor and next in line to be Church President from 1899 to 1901. He personally authorized new plural marriages performed in Mexico, Canada, and the United States, from 1892 until his death in 1901. This included plural marriages performed for 3 of his sons and 3 of his nephews" (D. Michael Quinn, "Plural Marriages After The 1890 Manifesto," lecture delivered August 1991 at Bluffdale, Utah, online at http://www.ldshistory.net/pc/postman.htm).

CHAPTER FIFTEEN: MAKING THE TRANSITION

1. M.R. Werner, "Since Brigham Young," *Readers Digest*, May 1940. Quoted in Joseph W. Musser, "Is the Church Changing?" *Truth*, June, 1940, vol. 6, no. 1, online at http://www.kingdomofzion.org/doctrines/library/aub/TM_Vol6.txt.

2. Kenneth L. Cannon II, "After the Manifesto: Mormon Polygamy 1890–1906," in D. Michael Quinn, ed., *The New Mormon History* (Salt Lake City: Signature Books, 1992), 203–204.

3. Reed Smoot. Quoted in Thomas G. Alexander, *Mormonism in Transition: A History of the Latter–day Saints, 1890–1930* (Urbana: University of Illinois Press, 1986), 24.

4. Alexander, 20–21.

5. Alexander, 18.

6. B. Carmon Hardy, *Solemn Covenant: The Mormon Polygamous Passage* (Urbana: University of Illinois Press, 1992), 251.

7. *Arguments Before the Committee On Privileges and Elections of the United States Senate In the Matter of the Protests Against the Right of Hon. Reed Smoot, A Senator from the State of Utah, to Hold His Seat* (Washington: Government Printing Office, 1905), 231, contained in *Proceedings Before the Committee On Privileges and Elections of the Unites States Senate In the Matter of the Protests Against the Right of Hon. Reed Smoot, A Senator from the State of Utah, to Hold His Seat* (Washington: Government Printing Office, 1904; 4 volumes), vol. 4.

8. John D. Lee, *Mormonism Unveiled; Including The Remarkable Life And Confessions Of The Late Mormon Bishop. John D. Lee* (St. Louis: N.D. Thompson and Company, 1877), 160, online at http://www.helpingmormons.org/Rare_Books.htm.

9. William Dame, commander of the Mormon militia unit involved the massacre had received an 1854 Patriarchal blessing that stated:"[T]hou shalt be called to act at the head of a portion of thy Brethren and of the Lamanites in the redemption of Zion and the avenging of the blood of the prophets upon them that dwell on the earth." In mid–1857 Philip Klingensmith, another key participant in the tragedy at Mountain Meadows, received a similar patriarchal blessing from Patriarch Isaac Morley (a member of the Council of Fifty): "Thou shalt yet be numbered with the sons of Zion in avenging the blood of Brother Joseph for thy heart and thy spirit can never be satisfied until the wicked are subdued" (for documentation of both blessings, see D. Michael Quinn, *The Mormon Hierarchy: Extensions of Power* [Salt Lake City: Signature Books, 1997], 248).

10. *Sacred Hymns and Spiritual Songs* (1871). Quoted in Quinn, *The Mormon Hierarchy: Extensions of Power*, 250.

11. D. Michael Quinn, *The Mormon Hierarchy: Origins of Power* (Salt Lake City: Signature Books, 1994), 179.

12. In 1987, *Dialogue: A Journal of Mormon Thought* carried an outstanding article on the development of the Mormon temple ceremony and the oath of vengeance (see David John Buerger, "The Development of the Mormon Temple Endowment Ceremony," *Dialogue: A Journal of Mormon Thought* [Winter 1987], vol. 20, no. 4, 34–76, quote on p. 55).

13. Jerald Tanner and Sandra Tanner, *The Changing World of Mormonism* (Chicago: Moody, 1981), 533, online at http://www.utlm.org/onlinebooks/changech22b.htm#533.

14. *Proceedings*, vol. 2, 78–79, 148–149. The testimony verifying the existence of the oath reads as follows:

MR. TAYLER:	What other vow?
MR. WALLIS:	. . . and another vow was what we used to call the "oath of vengeance" . . . .
MR. TAYLER:	Stand up, if it will help you, and give us the words, if you can.
MR. WALLIS: (standing up)	"That you and each of you do promise and vow that you will never cease to importune high heaven to avenge the blood of the prophets upon the nations of the earth or the inhabitants of the earth"

[TESTIMONY OF NEXT DAY]

MR. WALLIS:	In repeating the obligation of vengeance I find I made a mistake; I was wrong. It should have been "upon this nation." I had it "upon the inhabitants of the earth." It was a mistake on my part.

15. *Proceedings*, vol. 4, 496,497; cf. Jerry Benson and Dianna Benson, "The Mormon Temple," Internet article online at http://www.challengemin.org/temple.html and Jerry Benson and Dianna Benson, *How to Witness to Mormons* (El Cajon, CA: Challenge Ministries, 1993), 59, online at http:www.challengemin.org/WITNESS.PDF.

16. For an excellent treatment on Mormon polygamy and LDS efforts to cover-up its history, see Jerald Tanner and Sandra Tanner, "Polygamy And Truth: From Its Inception To A United States Senate Investigation," *Salt Lake City Messenger* (#66), January 1988, online at http://www.utlm.org/newsletters/no66.htm#AN%20INVESTIGATION.

17. *Proceedings*, vol. 1, 129.

18. Cannon II, 217, endnote #38. The tradition in the Cannon family is that Smith performed the Abraham H. Cannon-Lillian Hamlin marriage on a pleasure cruise from Los Angeles to Catalina Island (see Hardy, 216–222). Edna Smith—one of Joseph F. Smith's wife—stated that "Orson Smith," a local church leader in northern Utah, performed the ceremony (Carl A. Badger journal, December 9, 1905). However, D. Michael Quinn has convincingly argued that that "Orson Smith" was a code name for Joseph F. Smith and that Joseph F. Smith, when Second Counselor to the First Presidency in 1896, did indeed perform the wedding (D. Michael Quinn, "LDS Church Authority and New Plural Marriages, 1890–1904," *Dialogue: A Journal of Mormon Thought*, vol. 18, no. 1, 84, also see Quinn's endnotes #301–#303 from this same article, online at http://website.lineone.net/~mahonri/Quinn_Post_Manifesto_Dialogue.txt).

19. Cannon II, 207.

20. Cannon II, 207.

21. Rulon C. Allred, *The Most Holy Principle* (Murray, UT: Gems Publishing Company, 1970–75), vol. 4, 86.

22. Brigham Young, Jr., Journal, under June 5, 1902, New York Public Library.

23. *Journal History*, under November 19, 1903; cf. "John Henry Smith Diary," November 19, 1903.

24. *Proceedings*, vol. 1, 129.

25. *Proceedings*, vol. 1, 177.

26. For example , Smith could not remember making a speech at a Weber Stake Reunion in Ogden in 1903 (*Proceedings*, vol. 1, 192–193). During this particular speech he advocated polygamy and illegal cohabitation, even though earlier in his testimony he stated that he had never made any such statements.

27. *Proceedings*, vol. 1, 145–147.

28. *Proceedings*, vol. 1, 127.

29. *Proceedings*, vol. 1, 27.

30. *Proceedings*, vol. 1, 128, 335.

31. *Proceedings*, vol. 1, 192–193.

32. *Proceedings*, vol. 1, 334–335. Smith's testimony on this point reads as follows:

MR. TAYLER:	You say there is a State law forbidding unlawful cohabitation?
MR. SMITH:	That is my understanding.
MR. TAYLER:	And ever since that law was passed you have been violating it?
MR. SMITH:	I think likely I have been practicing the same thing even before the law was passed." (Ibid., p. 130)
THE CHAIRMAN:	. . . you are violating the law?
MR. SMITH:	The law of my State?
THE CHAIRMAN:	Yes.
MR. SMITH:	Yes, sir.
SEN. OVERMAN:	Is there not a revelation published in the Book of Cov-enants here that you shall abide by the law of the State?
MR. SMITH:	It includes both unlawful cohabitation and polygamy.

SEN. OVERMAN: Is there not a revelation that you shall abide by the laws of the State and of the land?

MR. SMITH: Yes, sir.

SEN. OVERMAN: If that is a revelation, are you not violating the laws of God?

MR. SMITH: I have admitted that, Mr. Senator, a great many times here.

33. Stanley S. Ivins, Journal, under November 19, 1944. Quoted in Cannon II, 211. Ivins noted in his journal, under November 29, 1934, the concerns of one post-Manifesto plural wife regarding Smith's testimony: "I met K.K. Steffenson at lunch [about a month ago] and we got to talking about post-manifesto polygamy. His sister was a post-man wife of one of the—He said that she had refused to be married by anyone but Pres. Smith and he had married her in the Salt Lake Temple. When he later testified at the Smoot investigation that there had been no authorized post-manifesto plural marriages, she was upset and had her brother, K. K., go to see Pres. Smith about it. He told K.K. to tell his sister that her marriage was O.K., but he had had to say what he did in Washington to protect the Church" (see Richard S. Van Wagoner, *Mormon Polygamy: A History* [Salt Lake City: Signature Books, 1989],174).

34. *Proceedings*, vol. 3, 442–443.

35. *Proceedings*, vol. 1, 510–511.

36. *Proceedings*, vol. 2, 37–39.

37. *Proceedings*, vol. 2, 44; cf. 45.

38. *Proceedings*, vol. 2, 284–285.

39. *Proceedings*, vol. 2, 2, 285. John Henry Smith was born on September 18, 1848.

40. *Proceedings*, vol. 2, 2, 105.

41. See "Scope and Content" of the David Eccles Papers, online at http://library.weber.edu/libabout/sandc.htm, located at Weber State University, Ogden, Utah.

42. Matthias Cowley, testimony before Quorum of the Twelve, 1911. Quoted in Samuel W. Taylor, *Rocky Mountain Empire* (Macmillan Publishing Co., Inc., 1978), 131.

43. *Proceedings*, vol. 1, 456.

44. *Proceedings*, vol. 1, 457.

45. *Proceedings*, vol. 1, 455.

46. *Proceedings*, vol. 4, 13.

47. *Proceedings*, vol. 4, 14.

48. *Proceedings*, vol. 3, 204.

49. D. Michael Quinn, "Plural Marriages After The 1890 Manifesto," lecture delivered August 1991 at Bluffdale, Utah, online at http://www.ldshistory.net/pc/postman.htm.

50. Quinn, "Plural Marriages."

51. Raymond Clapper, May 1932. Quoted in Milton R. Merrill, "Reed Smoot: Apostle in Politics," Ph.D. dissertation, Columbia University, 1950; also see Milton R. Merrill, "Reed Smoot, Apostle-Senator," *Utah Historical Quarterly*, October 1960. Quoted in Taylor, 98–99.

52. Robert Gottlieb, Peter Wiley, *American Saints: The Rise of Mormon Power* (New York: G.P. Putnam's Sons, 1984), 68–69. "When apostle Reed Smoot finally took his seat in the Senate, he formalized the emerging ties between certain prominent Mormons and the Republican party. . . . Smoot dominated state politics for more than two decades and established the first church presence in Washington. Under Smoot, more and more young Mormons followed the church's counsel that political activity was an important civic responsibility and flocked to Washington to join his circle."

53. Reed Smoot, letter to E.H. Callister, March 22, 1904. Quoted in Van Wagoner, 167.

54. Joseph F. Smith, The Church of Jesus Christ of Latter-day Saints, *Conference Report*, April 6, 1904, 74, 75, online at http://www.polygamyinfo.com/manfesto.htm.

55. Smith (see previous endnote).

56. B.H. Roberts, *CHC* (Salt Lake City: Deseret News Press, 1930], vol. 6, 401.

57. John Henry Smith noted that he and others "favored Taylor and Cowley doing something

to ease public sentiment both at home and abroad" (Merlo J. Pusey, *Builders of the Kingdom—George A. Smith, John Henry Smith, George Albert Smith* [Provo, Utah: Brigham Young University Press,1982], 192). According to Taylor's wife Nellie, Cowley and Taylor agreed to tender their resignations in an altruistic gesture designed to help both Smoot and the church. "It was better to smooth things over with the Government," she said, "keep Smoot in the Senate . . . [by] deposing Cowley and Taylor. Then, when conditions were more favorable, the two could be reinstated." This motion was voted unanimously by the Quorum of the Twelve according to her testimony (Samuel W. Taylor, under January 8, 1936, interview with Nellie E. Taylor, Taylor Collection (see Van Wagoner, 169–172).

58. Smoot Collection. Quoted in Van Wagoner, 171.

59. Francis M. Lyman, letter to Reed Smoot, December 15, 1904.

60. *Salt Lake Tribune*, October 5, 1910.

61. Heber J. Grant was the son of the fire and brimstone Mormon preacher Jedediah Grant, whose fanatical devotion to his faith kicked off Brigham Young's bloody reformation in the mid-1800s.

62. Quinn, "Plural Marriages."

63. George D. Smith, "Mormon Plural Marriage," *Free Inquiry* (Summer 1992), vol. 12, no. 3, 36.

64. *Proceedings*, vol. 2, 401–402. Grant's departure was precipitated by a rather foolish comment he made during a lecture for about 1,000 university students. He lamented the fact that only $50 could be given per person to the alumni association, but that he would give $150 anyway—$50 for himself, and $50 for each of his two wives. He added that he would take a third wife if he could, but that the law forbade it. This was enough of an admission of bigamy/polygamy/cohabitation for the county attorney to issue a warrant for his arrest, which in turn prompted Grant to flee America.

65. In 1939, for instance, well–respected Mormon Joseph T. Jones wrote to the General Authorities of the church, saying: "I confess that I have defended the principle involved in the Mormon marriage system, which you, dear brother, not only believe in but have acted upon, and was the first person to suffer imprisonment for your convictions, if I remember right. For me to stand idly by while spurious Mormons scandalize and vilify a system of marriage that gave me parentage and birth and cost the best blood of this generation to establish, without raising my voice in protest and defense would make me feel that I was but a craven coward. Three of my grandparents were driven out of Nauvoo and the fourth lost her all—father, mother, and husband, in the snows of Wyoming with the belated Martin handcart company. All were true to their convictions and steadfast in their belief in the purity and sacredness of the marriage system that cost the Prophet his life to establish. That heritage has been passed on to me, and I refuse to repudiate a principle that gave me parentage and birth, or to listen to foul mouths that trample it in the dust of the earth" (Joseph T. Jones, letter to General Authorities, December 24, 1939. Quoted in "Know the Truth and the Truth Shall Make You Free," *Truth*, October, 1940, vol. 6, no. 5).

66. E. Cecil McGavin and Willard Bean, "Leaves From An Old Scrapbook," *Deseret News*, June 1, 1940.

67. Wilford Woodruff, 1890 Manifesto, available in modern editions of *Doctrine and Covenants* and online at http://deseretbook.com/scriptures/dc/dcod1.html. The 1890 Manifesto was added to the *D&C* in 1908.

68. *Proceedings*, vol. 4, 480.

69. July 27, 1953. Quoted in Taylor, 102.

70. John J. Stewart, *Brigham Young and His Wives and The True Story of Plural Marriage* (Salt Lake City: Mercury Publishing Company, Inc.,1961), 41.

71. Joseph Fielding Smith, *Doctrines of Salvation* (Salt Lake City: Bookcraft, 1955), vol. 2, 67.

72. *Deseret News 1974 Church Almanac* (Salt Lake City: Deseret News, 1974), 17.

73. Maxine Hanks, "Polygamous Wives Need Help to Escape," *Deseret News*, June 7, 1998, online at http://www.polygamyinfo.com/deseret_news2.htm. Numerous articles on the many different polygamous groups in America is available online at http://www.rickross.com/groups/polygamy.html.

74. See "Green Requests New Trial," *Salt Lake Tribune*, August 22, 2001. online at http://www.sltrib.com (archives).; Kevin Cantera, "Green's Family Pleads for Mercy," *Salt Lake Tribune*, August 17, 2001, online at http://www.sltrib.com (archives); Michael Vigh and Kevin Cantera, "Jurors Say No Bias in Green Trial, Polygamist's Behavior Helped to Prove Charges," *Salt Lake Tribune*, May 23, 2001, online at http://www.sltrib.com (archives). For dozens of articles dealing with this case and related issues, see the listing of archived newspaper stories online at http://www.sltrib.com (archives).

75. CBS News.com, "Polygamist Gets 5-Year Sentence," August 24, 2001, online at http://www.cbsnews.com/now/story/0%2C1597%2C308061-2%2C00.shtml.

76. Geoffrey Fattah, "History piqued Green's Interest, He Says Stories of Pioneers Led to His Polygamy," August 22, 2001, *Deseret News*, from the LDS church's publication site, online at http://www.deseretnews.com/dn/view/0,1249,295019468,00.html.

77. Michael Vigh, Stephen Hunt and Kevin Cantera, "Polygamy Offensive Not Likely, Green Case Called An Exception," May 20, 2001, *Salt Lake Tribune*, online at http://www.sltrib.com (archives).

78. Vigh, Hunt and Cantera.

79. Paul Avery, "One Happy Family with Four Wives," November 8, 1987, *San Francisco Examiner and Chronicle*, A-14.

80. Ray Rivera, "Kingston Gets Maximum Term, Lecture on Incest," July 10, 1999, *Salt Lake Tribune*, online at http://www.rickross.com/reference/polygamy/polygamy23.html. The girl, known as M.K. in court documents, testified she was pulled from junior high school and was forced to marry her uncle on Nov. 15, 1997. The newlyweds spent their wedding night at a Park City hotel, the girl said, but they did not have sex. She said she had sexual intercourse with her uncle on four occasions between January and May 1998. Kingston would show up carrying a suitcase, they would have perfunctory sex, and he would leave the next day, she said.

81. Rivera, http://www.rickross.com/reference/polygamy/polygamy23.html.

82. For interesting and important information on polygamy from former plural wives, see Internet site by Tapestry Against Polygamy at http://www.polygamy.org/.

83. Quoted in Van Wagoner, 198.

84. Dan Harrie, "House Nixes Bill To Fight Crimes By Polygamists," *Salt Lake Tribune*, January 28, 2000, online at http://www.rickross.com/reference/polygamy/polygamy27.html

85. CNN, "End of the world? Sect Withdraws Kids from Utah Schools," September 12, 2000, online at http://www.cnn.com/2000/US/09/12/polygamists.schools.ap/.

86. Greg Burton, "Political Polygamists Coming Out of the Closet," December 11, 2000, *Salt Lake Tribune*, online at http://www.rickross.com/reference/polygamy/polygamy49.html.

87. The conviction of Green has made polygamists throughout Utah and other states extremely nervous. Polygamist Raymond Carlson, for instance, has stated: "If prosecutors in the state of Utah continue on the path they are on in seeking us out, I hate to tell you what might happen. To put it bluntly—the mountains could come down upon them. I think they are going to get shook up. I think we are in store for a lot of things if we don't repent and return to the way of God" (see Julie Cart, "Polygamy Verdict Set Precedent Law: Utah Is Likely to Go After Others," May 20, 2001, *Los Angeles Times*, online at http://www.rickross.com/reference/polygamy/polygamy62.html).

88. Michael Vigh, "Green's Prosecutor Is Arming Himself After Death Threats," June 27, 2001, *Salt Lake Tribune*, online at http://www.sltrib.com (archives).

89. Vigh, "Green's Prosecutor Is Arming."

90. Greg Burton, "Descended From Proud Polygamists," June 18, 2001, *Salt Lake Tribune*, online at http://www.sltrib.com (archives).

91. McConkie, *Mormon Doctrine* (Salt Lake City: Bookcraft, 1958; second edition, 1966), 578.

92. Ronald W. Walker and Richard W. Sadler, "Church History c. 1898–1945, Transitions: Early-Twentieth-Century Period," *Encyclopedia of Mormonism* (New York: Macmillan Publishing Company, 1992), vol. 2, 632–638.

93. Walker and Sadler, 633.

94. Walker and Sadler, 633–634. A great dispersion of Saints took place between 1919 and 1927 when the number of Latter-day Saints in California increased from fewer than 2,000 to more than 20,000.

95. Walker and Sadler, 634.

CHAPTER SIXTEEN: MORMON RACISM:BLACK IS NOT BEAUTIFUL

1. Joseph Smith, January 2, 1843, *HC* (Salt Lake City: Deseret Book Company, 1976/1980), vol. 5, 217-218.

2. *Deseret News 2001–2002 Church Almanac* (Salt Lake City: Deseret News, 2000), 149.

3. *Church Almanac*, 534.

4. Wallace Turner, *The Mormon Establishment* (Boston: Houghton Mifflin Company, 1966), 113, 119, 135.

5. Racism is resoundingly condemned in the Bible. Several passages, for example, plainly say that "God is no respecter of persons; but in every nation he that feareth him, and worketh righteousness, is accepted with him" (Acts 10:34–35, KJV). The Bible additionally says that there should be absolutely no race distinctions (Gal. 3:28).

6. *PGP, BOA* 3:22.

7. Mark E. Petersen, "Race Problems As They Affect The Church," Address At the Convention of Teachers of Religion On the College Level, delivered at Brigham Young University, Provo, Utah, August 27, 1954, on file at BYU Library, Special Collections.

8. Orson Hyde, *Speech of Orson Hyde, Delivered Before the High Priests' Quorum, in Nauvoo, April 27th, 1845, Upon the Course and Conduct of Mr. Sidney Rigdon* (Liverpool: James and Woodburn, 1845), 309.

9. John J. Stewart, *The Glory of Mormonism* (Salt Lake City: Mercury Publishing Co., Inc., 1963), inside front flap book cover and 144.

10. Stewart, 145.

11. Joseph Fielding Smith, *Doctrines of Salvation* (Salt Lake City: Bookcraft, 1954), vol. 1, 61.

12. Stewart, 152.

13. Concerning this "rebellion in heaven," Mormon historian B.H. Roberts made the following statement: "Only those, however, who wickedly rebelled against God were adjudged to deserve banishment from heaven, and become the devil and his angels. Others there were, who may not have rebelled against God, and yet were so indifferent in their support of the righteous cause of our Redeemer, that they forfeited certain privileges and powers granted to those who were more valiant for God and correct principles. We have, I think, a demonstration of this in the seed of Ham. . . . I believe that race is the one through which it is ordained those spirits that were not valiant in the great rebellion in heaven should come; who through their indifference or lack of integrity to righteousness, rendered themselves unworthy of the Priesthood and its powers, and hence it is withheld from them to this day" (B.H. Roberts, "To the Youth of Israel," *The Contributor* [Salt Lake City: Junius F. Wells, 1885], vol. 6, 296–297). According to apostle Bruce McConkie: "Those who were less valiant in pre-existence and who thereby had certain spiritual restrictions imposed upon them during mortality are known to us as the *negroes*" (Bruce McConkie, *Mormon Doctrine* [Salt Lake City: Bookcraft, 1958; second edition, 1966], 527).

14. McConkie, 109; cf. *PGP, BMO* 7:8 and *PGP, BOA* 1:21–26.

15. Brigham Young, October 9, 1859, *JOD* (Liverpool: Amasa Lyman, 1860; lithographed reprint of original edition, 1966), vol. 7, 290.

16. George F. Richards, *Conference Report*, April 1939, 58.

17. Joseph Fielding Smith, *The Way to Perfection* (Salt Lake City: Genealogical Society of Utah, 1931), 101. Interestingly Smith contradicted himself on this point by also writing: "The Latter-day Saints . . . have no animosity towards the Negro. Neither have they described him as belonging to an 'inferior race'" (Joseph Fielding Smith, *Answers to Gospel Questions* [Salt Lake City: Deseret Book Company, 1979], vol. 4, 170).

18. Fielding Smith, *Way to Perfection*, 101–102.

19. Fielding Smith, *Way to Perfection*, 101–102.

20. Peterson, on file at BYU Library, Special Collections (see this chapter, endnote #7).

21. Wallace Turner gives the following account of what happened when Petersen found out his speech was being circulated: "This speech was delivered in a closed meeting. A copy of it came into the hands of James D. Wardle, the Salt Lake City barber who is a member of the Reorganized LDS church. Wardle has enjoyed many years of baiting his Utah Mormon townsmen, and made his copy available to Jerald Tanner, the LDS apostate who specializes in circulating anti-LDS materials. Tanner went to the LDS library, found a copy of the speech and assured himself that it was the same speech he had received from Wardle. But the church would not give him a copy he could take away with him. Using the Wardle copy as his source, Tanner began to circulate the address. At that time Apostle Petersen was in England leading the mission there. In early 1965 he wrote to Tanner threatening to sue him if he did not stop publication and recall the previously issued copies of the speech. Tanner gleefully reproduced and circulated the letter. Since then Petersen has returned to Salt Lake City and no suit has been filed" (Turner, 253–254).

22. Alvin R. Dyer, "For What Purpose?," Missionary Conference in Oslo, Norway, March 18, 1961, printed in *The Negro in Mormon Theology*, 48–58. Quoted by Jerald Tanner and Sandra Tanner, *Mormonism: Shadow or Reality?* (Salt Lake City: ULM, 1987), 264–265.

23. McConkie, 527.

24. Joseph Fielding Smith, mimeographed letter, July 9, 1963. Quoted in Stewart, 154.

25. Lowery Nelson, letter to First Presidency, October 8, 1947. Quoted in Stewart, 146.

26. LDS First Presidency, letter to Lowery Nelson, July 17, 1947. Quoted in Stewart, 153.

27. Thelma Geer, *Mormonism, Mama & Me* (Chicago: Moody, 1986), 24–25.

28. *Juvenile Instructor*, vol. 3, 165. Quoted in Tanner and Tanner, 266.

29. Peterson (see this chapter, endnote #7).

30. Stewart, 155.

31. Brigham Young, *JOD* (Liverpool: Daniel H. Wells, 1865; lithographed reprint of original edition), vol. 10, 110.

32. LDS First Presidency, letter to Lowery Nelson, July 17, 1947. Quoted in Stewart, 153–154.

33. Petersen; cf. Turner, 252. Both Ezra Taft Benson and Mark E. Petersen were sent on an extended mission to Europe. It is believed that they were sent abroad because of their outspoken ways and extremely conservative political views.

34. "I think Hawaiians should marry Hawaiians," said Peterson. "[T]he Japanese ought to marry the Japanese, and the Chinese ought to marry Chinese, and the Caucasians should marry Caucasians" (see Turner, 253).

35. LDS First Presidency, letter to Virgil H. Sponberg, May 5, 1947. Quoted in Lester E. Bush, *Mormonism's Negro Doctrine: An Historical Overview* (Arlington, VA: Dialogue: A Journal of Mormon Thought, 1973), 42. This short booklet originally appeared as an article by the same title in the periodical *Dialogue: A Journal of Mormon Thought* (Spring 1973), vol. 8.

36. "From Caucasian to Negro," *Juvenile Instructor* (1868), vol. 3, 142. Quoted in Bush, 57–58, endnote #99).

37. "From Caucasian to Negro." Quoted in Quoted in Bush, 57–58, endnote #99.

38. Turner, 218.

39. Turner, 228.

40. Turner, 229.

41. Robert Gottlieb and Peter Wiley, *American Saints: The Rise of Mormon Power* (New York: G.P. Putnam's Sons,1984), 179.

42. Gottlieb and Wiley, 179.

43. Gottlieb and Wiley, 240–241.

44. Gottlieb and Wiley, 179–180.

45. Gottlieb and Wiley, 180.

46. D. Michael Quinn, *The Mormon Hierarchy: Extensions of Power* (Salt Lake City: Signature Books, 1997), 81.

47. Ezra Taft Benson. Quoted in Turner, 255.

48. Ezra Taft Benson. Quoted in Quinn, 79.

49. "Reed Benson Says Welch Was Correct in Calling Eisenhower Communist," *Provo Daily Herald*, April 22, 1965, 2 (also see Quinn, 83).

50. Quinn, 83.

51. Reed A. Benson, "Memo to the Utah Chapters," September 2, 1965, on letterhead of the Birch Society, photocopy in Williams Papers; Quinn G. McKay to J.D. Williams, May 20, 1966, Williams Papers. Quoted in Quinn, 84.

52. "NAACP Says 'Too Fantastic' Rumors of Demonstrations," *Ogden Standard-Examiner*, September 27, 1965, 20; and "Race Riots in Utah," *Daily Utah Chronicle*, September 28, 1965; "NAACP Chapter Claims Riot Report 'Malicious,'" *Ogden Standard-Examiner*, September 28, 1965, A-6; "Rumors of Riot Hit By Area NAACP," *Deseret News*, September 28, 1965, B-1; NAACP Assails Rumors of Protest at LDS Meet," *Salt Lake Tribune*, September 29, 1965, 18.

53. Gottlieb and Wiley, 181.

54. See this chapter, endnote #52.

55. LeGrand Richards. Quoted in Gottlieb and Wiley, 181.

56. Quinn, 96; for additional information and research sources, also see Quinn, 461, endnote #248.

57. Gottlieb and Wiley, 184.

58. Declaration 2, released to *Deseret News*, June 9, 1978, page 1A. Printed in *D&C*, modern editions. For a highly detailed look at the events that led up to this so-called revelation, see Sandra Tanner and Jerald Tanner, "Blacks Receive LDS Priesthood Pressure Forces Mormon President To Issue New 'Revelation,'" *Salt Lake City Messenger* (#39), July 1978, online at http://www.utlm.org/newsletters/no39.htm.

59. Brigham Young, December 3, 1854, *JOD* (Liverpool: F.D. Richard, 1855; lithographed reprint of original edition), vol. 2, 143; cf. Young, in *JOD*, vol. 7, 290–291: "[T]he Lord put a mark upon him, which is the flat nose and black skin. Trace mankind down to after the flood, and then another curse is pronounced upon the same race—that they should be the 'servant of servants;' and they will be, until that curse is removed. . . How long is that race to endure the dreadful curse that is upon them? That curse will remain upon them, and they never can hold the Priesthood or share in it until all the other descendants of Adam have received the promises and enjoyed the blessings of the Priesthood and the keys thereof. Until the last ones of the residue of Adam's children are brought up to that favourable position, the children of Cain cannot receive the first ordinances of the Priesthood. They were the first that were cursed, and they will be the last from whom the curse will be removed. When the residue of the family of Adam come up and receive their blessings, then the curse will be removed from the seed of Cain, and they will receive blessings in like proportion."

60. Joseph Fielding Smith, *Way to Perfection*, 101, 106.

61. John Lewis Lund, *The Church and the Negro: A Discussion of Mormons, Negroes, and the Priesthood* (Salt Lake City: John Lewis Lund, 1967), 45.

62. Lund, 46.

63. "If the prophet of God were to receive a revelation tomorrow giving the Negroes the

Priesthood it would certainly be accepted regardless of what Brigham Young or any previous prophet has said. This is because the words of the living oracles relate more
specifically to the era in which we live." (Lund, 45).

64. Declaration 2 (D&C).

65. Larry B. Stammer, "Mormons May Disavow Old View on Blacks," *Los Angeles Times*, May
18, 1998, online at http://www.lds-mormon.com/t0000467.shtml.

66. Tanner and Tanner, 293-E.

67. Tanner and Tanner, 293-E. According to a 2001 *Newsweek* exposé on Mormonism, the
religion of the Latter-day Saints primarily is still a white man's religion because "almost
every member of the Salt Lake hierarchy is a successful, politically conservative businessman—and white." The article also observes that even though the priesthood is now
open to Blacks, "the appeal of Mormonism to people of color is mainly among the less
well-off" (Ken Woodward, "The Mormon Way," *Newsweek*, September 10, 2001, 51).

CHAPTER SEVENTEEN: IS MORMONISM CHRISTIAN?

1. Gordon B. Hinckley, April 1998 General Conference, "We Bear Witness of Him," reprinted
in Ensign, May 1998, 4, online at http://www.lds.org/conference/talk/display/0,5232,23-
1-26-1,00.html; cf. Peggy Fletcher Stack and Bob Mims, "Mainstream Christianity Drive
Doesn't Go Smoothly for LDS Church," *Salt Lake Tribune*, March 31, 2001, online at
http://www.sltrib.com (archives).

2. Kenneth L. Woodward, "The Mormon Way," *Newsweek*, September 10, 2001, 48.

3. Joseph Fielding Smith, *Doctrines of Salvation* (Salt Lake City: Bookcraft, 1954), vol. 1,
236.

4. A prime example of the church's emphasis on traditional values would be the 1995
"Family Proclamation." It states "that marriage between a man and a woman is ordained
of God and that the family is central to the Creator's plan for the eternal destiny of His
children." These sentiments and other moral/social positions in the document appeal to
many persons in the conservative segment of society. However, what many persons
seem to overlook in the document is its proclamation that everyone is a child of God
from a "premortal realm" possessing a "divine nature and destiny," and can progress to
"perfection" through Mormon temple rites. In other words, the whole "family" emphasis is little more than a proselytizing tool (text online at http://www.ldsetc.com/
proclamation.html).

5. "Faith in Transition: Road to Salvation," *Online Newshour* (PBS), July 18, 1997, online at
http://www.pbs.org/newshour/bb/religion/july-dec97/mormons_7-18.html.

6. "Faith in Transition," online at http://www.pbs.org/newshour/bb/religion/july-
dec97/mormons_7-18.html.

7. Lutheran Church Missouri Synod, "Are Mormons generally regarded as Christians, and
how do their beliefs differ from those of the Missouri Synod?," Q & A Internet site, online
at http://www.lcms.org/cic/mormon.html.

8. Joseph Smith, *PGP*, Joseph Smith—History 1:19.

9. *BOM*, 1 Nephi 13:6.

10. *BOM*, 1 Nephi 14:10.

11. Brigham Young, October 6, 1863, *JOD* (Liverpool: Daniel H. Wells, 1865; lithographed
reprint of original edition, 1966), vol. 10, 265.

12. Heber C. Kimball, July 26, 1857, *JOD* (Liverpool: Asa Calking, 1858; lithographed reprint
of original edition, 1966), vol. 5, 89.

13. Orson Pratt, *The Kingdom of God—Part I*, no. 2, October 31, 1848, 3. Reprinted in Orson
Pratt, *Orson Pratt's Works*, vol. 2 (Orem, UT: Grandin Book Co., 1990).

14. Kent P. Jackson, "Early Signs of the Apostasy," *Ensign*, December 1984, 9.

15. Bruce McConkie, *Mormon Doctrine* (Salt Lake City: Bookcraft, 1958; second edition,
1966), 136 and Jackson, 9.

16. McConkie, 269, 374–375.

17. Bernard P. Brockbank, "The Living Christ," *Ensign*, May 1977, 26.

18. Joseph Fielding Smith, vol. 1, 130 and Ezra Taft Benson, *Teachings of Ezra Taft Benson* (Salt Lake City: Bookcraft, 1988), 14. Quoted in "Gethsemane Was Site of "Greatest Single Act,'" *Church News*, June 1, 1991, 14.

19. Joseph Fielding Smith, vol. 1, 188.

20. This Christian view is found in the Bible (1 Peter 2:24; Col. 1:20).

21. Rom. 5:8–9; 2 Cor. 5:17–20; Heb. 10: 12.

22. Gordon B. Hinckley. Quoted in "'Crown of Gospel is Upon Our Heads,'" *LDS Church News*, June 20, 1998, 7, online at http://www.desnews.com/cgi-bin/libstory_church?dn98&9806210091; cf. Bill McKeever, "Who is the 'Living Christ' of Mormonism?," Internet article online at http://www.mrm.org/articles/the-savior.html and "President Gordon B. Hinckley Says Mormons Believe In A Different Jesus," online at http://www.helpingmormons.org/different.htm.

23. Bruce McConkie, "Our Relationship with the Lord," BYU Speech, March 2 1982, entire speech online at http://www.ricks.edu/Ricks/employee/MARROTTR/RelationshipWithGod.htm.

24. James E. Talmage, *A Study of the Articles of Faith* (Salt Lake City: The Church of Jesus Christ of Latter-day Saints, 1948), 430.

25. Brigham Young, April 9, 1852, *JOD* (Liverpool: F.D. Richards, 1855; lithographed reprint of original edition, 1966), vol. 1, 50.

26. George Q. Cannon, *Gospel Truth*, ed. Jerreld Newquist (Salt Lake City: Zion's Book Store, 1957; Deseret Book Company edition, 1974), vol. 1, 9.

27. Robert L. Millet, "What We Believe," devotional address at BYU, February 3, 1998, online at http://www.cometozarahemla.org/believe/rlmwhatwebel.html, Millet stated: "Occasionally we hear certain Latter-day Saint teachings described as unbiblical or of a particular doctrine being contradictory to the Bible. Let us be clear on this matter. The Bible is one of the books within our standard works, and thus our doctrines and practices are in harmony with the Bible. There are times, of course, when latter-day revelation provides clarification or enhancement of the intended meaning in the Bible."

28. McConkie, *Mormon Doctrine*, 765.

29. McConkie, *Mormon Doctrine*, 764.

30. McConkie, *Mormon Doctrine*, 383.

31. Orson Pratt, "The Bible and Tradition, without Further Revelation, an Insufficient Guide," Divine Authenticity of the Book of Mormon—No. 3," December 1, 1850, 47. Reprinted in Orson Pratt, *Orson Pratt's Works*, vol. 2 (Orem, UT: Grandin Book Co., 1990).

32. Woodward, 44.

33. Greg Burton, "LDS Church Takes Issue With Article," *Salt Lake Tribune*, September 3, 2001, N1.

34. O. Kendall White, *Mormon Neo-Orthodoxy: A Crisis Theology* (Salt Lake City: Signature Books, 1987). Quoted in Richard Ostling and Joan K. Ostling, *Mormon America: The Power and the Promise* (San Francisco: Harper San Francisco, 1999), 324.

35. *Gospel Principles*, (Salt Lake City: The Church of Jesus Christ of Latter-day Saints, 1978), 9, 236, 290, 293.

36. *Gospel Principles*, (Salt Lake City: The Church of Jesus Christ of Latter-day Saints, 1997), 11, Chapter 38 (online at http://www.lds.org/library/display/0,4945,11-1-13-48,00.html), 302, Chapter 47 (online at http://www.lds.org/library/display/0%2C4945%2C11-1-13-59%2C00.html).

37. T. LaMar Sleight, letter to Michael Barrett. Quoted in Bill McKeever, "Excommunicated for Publicly Discussing Mormon Doctrine?," *Mormonism Researched* (Summer 1994), 3.

38. Quoted in McKeever, 3.

39. McKeever, 3.

40. Ostling and Ostling, 148.
41. Don Lattin, "Musings of the Main Mormon," *San Francisco Chronicle*, 13 April 1997, online at http://www.sfgate.com/cgi-bin/article.cgi?file=/chronicle/archive/1997/04/13/SC36289.DTL; cf. Dave Combe, "Truth-Telling and Shifting Theologies: An Analytical Look At How Wide The Divide?," Internet article online at http://www.lds-mormon.com/hwtd.shtml#hinck.
42. *NewsHour with Jim Lehrer*, "Faith in Transition: Road to Salvation," July 18, 1997, http://www.pbs.org/newshour/bb/religion/july-dec97/mormons_7-18.html.
43. Interview transcript online at http://www.irr.org/mit/hinckley.html; cf. David Van Biema, "Kingdom Come," *Time*, August 4, 1997, 56, online at http://www.lds-mormon.com/time.shtml.
44. *Larry King Live*, September 8, 1998, transcript online at http://www.lds-mormon.com/lkl_00.shtml.
45. Gordon B. Hinckley, October 1997 General Conference Address. Quoted in Internet Thread article on Hinckley, online at http://www.lds-mormon.com/gbh.shtml. In an attempt to cover-up Hinckley's disingenuous answer to *Time*, the Mormon church is officially stating that Hinckley was taken out of context. However, a follow-up investigation and information obtained from both *Time* magazine and Richard Ostling (the journalist who conducted Hinckley's interview), reveal that the LDS church president was not taken out of context at all. For the text of several letters dealing with this issue, see documents reproduced in the Internet article "Dodging and Dissembling Prophet?," published by the Institute for Religious Research, online at http://www.irr.org/mit/hinckley.html.
46. Dallin Oaks. Quoted in Gustav Niebuhr, "Adapting 'Mormon' to Emphasize Christianity," *New York Times*, February 19, 2001, online at http://www.nytimes.com/2001/02/19/national/19MORM.html (also online at http://www.nytimes.com/2001/02/19/national/19MORM.html?searchpv=site10).
47. Jan Shipps. Quoted in Niebuhr, online at http://www.nytimes.com/2001/02/19/national/19MORM.html.
48. Kathleen Flake. Quoted in Peggy Fletcher Stack and Bob Mims, "Mainstream Christianity Drive Doesn't Go Smoothly for LDS Church," *Salt Lake Tribune*, March 31, 2001, online at http://www.sltrib.com (archives).
49. Harvey Cox. Quoted in Stack and Mims, online at http://www.sltrib.com (archives).
50. Carolyn Tanner Irish. Quoted in Stack and Mims, online at http://www.sltrib.com (archives).
51. Deacon Owen Cummings. Quoted in Stack and Mims, online at http://www.sltrib.com (archives).
52. Ostling and Ostling, 318; cf. R. Scott Lloyd, "A Conduit for Spirit, Hymns Amply Show Christianity of LDS," *LDS Church News*, August 29, 1998, online at http://www.desnews.com/cgi-bin/libstory_church?dn98&9808300095.
53. Rick Branch, "Mormon Church Infiltrates Christianity," *Watchman Expositor* (1992), vol. 9, no. 3, 7.
54. Branch, 7.
55. Will Schmidt, "Mormons Teach in a Baptist Church," *Watchman Expositor* (1990), vol. 7, no. 3, 2.
56. Irvine Hexham, in Walter A Elwell, ed., *Evangelical Dictionary of Theology* (Grand Rapids: Baker Book House, 1984; 1996 reprint), 289.
57. John A. Saliba, *Understanding New Religious Movements* (Grand Rapids: Eerdmans, 1995),144–45. The Local Church, a religious group many persons consider a cult, serves as an excellent example of how some new religious movements use lawsuits to silence critics. Since 1979 the Local Church has either sued or threatened to sue several Christian publishers and authors, including Ronald Enroth, *The Lure of the Cults* (Christian

Herald Books); Jack Sparks, *The Mind Benders* (Thomas Nelson); Jerram Barrs, *Shepherds and Sheep* (InterVarsity Press); Bob Larson, *Larson's Book of Cults* (Tyndale House). In all of the above cases, references to the Local Church were either partially or entirely removed from the book in question. The most visible legal action taken by the Local Church involved the Berkeley, California, Spiritual Counterfeits Project (SCP), which had published Neil T Duddy's *The God-Men*, a book extremely critical of the practices and beliefs of the Local Church. The suit ended in 1985 with an $11 million judgment against SCP. The counter-cult organization pleaded no contest due to lack of funds and was forced to file bankruptcy.

58. Robert T. Miller and Ronald B. Flowers, *Toward Benevolent Neutrality: Church, State, and the Supreme Court*, vol. 2, 5th ed. (Waco: Baylor University, 1996), 722–735.

59. Saliba, 6.

60. Michael D. Langone, *Recovery from cults* (New York: W.W. Norton and Co., 1993), 34.

61. Langone, 34.

62. Langone, 34.

63. Points 1–4 are taken from Langone, 5, 67–68, 76–77, 89–91, 98–99. Point 5 is taken from Joan Carol Ross and Michael D. Langone, *Cults: What Parents Should Know* (New York: Carol Publishing Group, 1988), 122 (cf. Ronald Enroth, *Churches That Abuse* [Grand Rapids: Zondervan, 1992], 157–79). Points 6–8 are taken from James and Marcia Rudin, *Prison or Paradise: The New Religious Cults* (Philadelphia: Westminster Press, 1980), 26ff, as cited in J. Gordon Melton, *Encyclopedic Handbook of Cults in America*, 6. Points 9–16 are taken from Ronald Enroth, "Voices from the Fringe," *Moody Monthly*, October 1989, 94–104; Ronald Enroth, "Voices on the Fringe," *Eternity*, October 1986, 17–22; and Enroth, *Churches That Abuse*, quoted in Dr. Paul Martin, *Cult-Proofing Your Kids* (Grand Rapids: Zondervan, 1993), 31–32.

64. C.C. and D.F., "A Cult or Not a Cult," *Modern Maturity*, June 1994, 30.

65. This is not to say that all Christian denominations agree on every doctrinal point. Within the Christian community there are many doctrinal areas where honest differences of opinion are acceptable. These beliefs relate to "non-essentials" of the faith. They are peripheral issues that include, but are certainly not limited to, views on baptism, church government, and styles of church-appropriate music. Theological cults, of course, tend to distort these issues as well, often going far beyond the various Christian positions that are biblically feasible, especially concerning sensational issues such as the timing of the world's end. More significant, though, are the positions that cults take on the "essentials" of the Christian faith. These doctrines would include any beliefs that directly relate to one's identification of and relationship to God (the Trinity, the deity of Christ, salvation by grace alone through faith, the virgin birth, the physical resurrection of Christ, etc.). Divergence from these foundational doctrines of Christianity is a sure sign that a particular group is a cult, theologically speaking.

66. Walter Martin, *The Kingdom of the Cults* (Minneapolis: Bethany, 1985 edition), 11.

67. Gordon Lewis, *Confronting the Cults* (Grand Rapids: Baker Book House, 1975), 4.

68. Walter Martin, *The Rise of the Cults* (Grand Rapids: Zondervan, 1955), 11–12. Quoted in Irvine Robertson, *What the Cults Believe* (Chicago: Moody, 1966; 1991 reprint),13.

69. Josh McDowell and Don Stewart, *Handbook of Today's Religions* (San Bernardino, CA: Here's Life Publishers, 1983), 17.

70. Alan W. Gomes, *Unmasking the Cults* (Grand Rapids: Zondervan, 1995), 7.

71. Christian Research Institute, "Cults and Aberrational Groups," Statement DC-920. The Christian Research Institute, founded by Dr. Walter Martin, isa counter-cult organization that stores a vast amount of information oncults. They may be contacted at 949-858-6100 in Rancho Santa Margarita, California.

72. A 2001 survey by Mormon scholars revealed that Protestant clergy in California and Utah found that "only 6 percent characterized Latter-day Saints as Christian, while 78

percent said they are non-Christian and 15 percent believe some members are Christian and some are not" (*Deseret News*, August 4, 2001). In a similar development, the Vat-
ican released a directive that Mormons must be re-baptized before converting to
Catholicism. Catholic officials said the directive "makes clear that the church regards
Mormonism as varying in its essential beliefs from traditional Christianity. Members of
Protestant and Orthodox churches may convert to Catholicism without being re-bap-
tized." (Gustav Niebuhr, "Vatican Decides to Rebaptize Mormons Who Are Converting,"
New York Times, July 24, 2001, online at www.nytimes.com; cf. "Why Mormon Baptism
Is Invalid," *Catholic News*, July 17, 2001, online at http://moff.org/e3news/index.
asp?article_id=131675; cf. *New York Times*, July 24, 2001).

73. Boyd K. Packer, "The Peaceable Followers of Christ," February 1, 1998, lecture delivered
to BYU. Quoted in Gerry Avant, "Be 'Peaceable Followers of Christ,'" *LDS Church News*,
February 7, 1998, online at http://www.desnews.com/cgi-bin/libstory_church?
dn98&9802080064). Packer also made two more interesting comments: 1) "'It is one thing
to say that we are not their kind of Christian. It is quite another to characterize us as not
being Christians at all;" and 2) "There is more to it than simply writing a definition of
what a Christian is and then rejecting anyone who does not conform to it." The absurdity of Packer's remarks can be seen when they are transferred to another religious
group—e.g., Nation of Islam (NOI), under Louis Farrakhan. The media, mainstream
Muslims, and world religious leaders all reject the NOI as being part of Islam because it
diverges significantly from Islamic beliefs. According to Ibrahim Hooper of the Council
on American-Islamic Relations, the NOI is definitely "outside mainstream Muslim beliefs
because of Farrakhan's racist views" (Quoted in Herbert Toler, "Marching to A Different
Drum," *Charisma*, May 1996, 31). The NOI has "always been regarded by serious Muslim
organizations as a fringe group of heretics" (Anthony M. Platt, "Born in the USA," *Los
Angeles Times Book Review*, March 2, 1997, 8). Imagine if Farrakhan were ever were to
say something like: "It is one thing to say that we are not their kind of Muslims. It is quite
another to characterize us as not being Muslims at all" or "There is more to it than simply writing a definition of what a Muslim is and then rejecting anyone who does not conform to it"—his arguments would be no more legitimate than Boyd K. Packer's.

74. Quoted in Eric Johnson, "The Battle Over 'Christian,'" *Mormonism Researched*, 1998
(second quarter), 8.

CHAPTER EIGHTEEN: COVER-UPS, CONSPIRACIES, AND CONTROVERSIES

1. Bill Clinton, July 26, 1997, letter to The Church of Jesus Christ of Latter-day Saints.
Reprinted in "Pres. Clinton Sends Greetings," *LDS Church News*, July 26, 1997, online at
http://www.desnews.com/cgi-bin/libstory_church?dn97&9707270096.

2. Kenneth L. Woodward, "The Mormon Way," *Newsweek*, September 10, 2001, 46; Richard
N. Ostling and Joan K. Ostling, Mormon America: The Power and the Promise (San Francisco, 1999), 115.

3. *LDS Church News*, April 22, 1984, 3. Quoted in "The Finger of Scorn," *LDS Church News*,
March 24, 2001, online at http://www.desnews.com/cgi-bin/libstory_church?
dn01&0103260018.

4. Peggy Fletcher Stack, "A Free Spirit? Collin's Call," *Salt Lake Tribune*, January 20, 2001,
online at http://www.sltrib.com (archives).

5. Celia R. Baker, "Tabernacle Choir to Sing At Inaugural," *Salt Lake Tribune*, December
27, 2000, online at http://www.sltrib.com (archives).

6. Baker (http://www.sltrib.com [archives]). In addition to performing at George Bush's
inauguration in 1989, the Tabernacle Choir performed for the inaugurations of Lyndon
Johnson in 1965, Richard Nixon in 1969 and 1973, and Ronald Reagan in 1981. Regarding their appearance at Bush's inauguration, Heather Barney of Hatch's Salt Lake City

office said that "the senator made a suggestion on behalf of the choir, thinking it would be a wonderful thing for the choir to be part of the inauguration festivities."

7. For an excellent introduction to these issues and related topics, see Richard Packham, "To Those Who Are Investigating Mormonism," Internet article online at http://www.exmormon.org/tract2.htm.

8. This phrase is used by a variety of Mormon-watchers: e.g., Bill McKeever, Mormonism Research Ministries, online at http://www.mrm.org/.

9. Helen Radkey, "The Mormon Church Attempts to Conceal Temple Records for Adolf Hitler," Internet article online at http://www.utlm.org/onlineresources/hitlertemplework.htm.

10. Bob Mims, "LDS Try to End Unauthorized Work for Jews," *Salt Lake Tribune*, May 2, 2001, http://www.sltrib.com (archives).

11. "Baptizing Dead People For Salvation," Internet article online at http://www.letusreason.org/LDS5.htm. For a Christian refutation of the Mormon practice of baptizing the dead, see "Did Jesus Establish Baptism For The Dead?" (online at http://www.irr.org/mit/baptdead.html) and "Does the Bible Teach Salvation for the Dead?" (online at http://www.irr.org/mit/sdead.html), both of which are Internet articles published by the Institute for Religious Research.

12. Erik Davis, "Databases of the Dead," *Wired*, July 1999, online at http://www.wired.com/wired/archive/7.07/mormons_pr.html.

13. Kahlile B. Mehr, "I Have A Question—How much of the human family has had its temple work done?," *Ensign*, March 1997, 73. This LDS article estimated that as of 1997, 140 million had been baptized.

14. Mims, http://www.sltrib.com (archives).

15. Mims, http://www.sltrib.com (archives).

16. Leonard J. Arrington, "The Search for Truth and Meaning in Mormon History," in D. Michael Quinn, ed., *The New Mormon History* (Salt Lake City: Signature Books, 1992), 1.

17. Francis Nelson Henderson, "Exit Statement of Francis Nelson Henderson," 1999, online at http://www.exmormon.org/whylft131.htm.

18. Fawn Brodie. Quoted by Newell G. Bringhurst, "Fawn McKay Brodie: Dissident Historian and Quintessential Critic of Mormondom," in Roger Launius, Linda Thatcher, Leonard J. Arrington, eds., *Differing Visions: Dissenters in Mormon History* (Urbana: University of Illinois Press, 1994), 290.

19. B. Carmon Hardy, "Truth and Mistruth in Mormon History," in Lavina Fielding Anderson and Janice Merrill Allred, eds., *Case Reports of the Mormon Alliance* (Salt Lake City: Mormon Alliance, 1997), vol. 3, 279. This volume, as well as volumes 1 and 2, are available for purchase online from ULM:
    - Volume 1, http://www.utlm.org/booklist/titles/xb059_casereportsmormon alliancevol1.htm
    - Volume 2, http://www.utlm.org/booklist/titles/xb060_casereportsmormon alliancevol2.htm
    - Volume 3, http://www.utlm.org/booklist/titles/xb061_casereportsmormon alliancevol3.htm

20. Ostling and Ostling, 247.

21. Ostling and Ostling, 249, summarizing the views of Mark P. Leone, *Roots of Modern Mormonism* (Cambridge: Harvard University Press: 1979), 204, 211.

22. In 1971 Dean C. Jessee, who at that time worked in the LDS church's Historian's Office, admitted that Smith came no where near to completing his history. At the time of Smith's death, the narrative was only written up to August 5, 1838. "By February 4, 1846, the day the books were packed for the journey west, the History had been completed to March 1, 1843. . . . [R]esumption of work on the History occurred on 'Dec. 1, 1853 [when] Dr. Willard Richards wrote one line of History being sick at the time—and was never able to do any more.' . . . The remainder of Joseph Smith's History of the Church from March 1,

1843 to August 8, 1844, was completed under the direction of George A. Smith. . . . The Joseph Smith History was finished in August 1856, seventeen years after it was begun" (Dean C. Jessee, "The Writing of Joseph Smith's History," *Brigham Young University Studies* [Summer 1971], vol. 11, 469, 470, 472). For in-depth examinations of the many changes to Mormonism's official *History of the Church* can be found in Jerald Tanner and Sandra Tanner, *Mormonism: Shadow or Reality?* (Salt Lake City: ULM, 1987), 126–162D, as well as in Jerald Tanner and Sandra Tanner, *The Changing World of Mormonism* (Chicago: Moody, 1981), 398–416, online at http://www.utlm.org/onlinebooks/changech13.htm. An extremely detailed look at the issue can be found in Jerald Tanner and Sandra Tanner, *Changes in Joseph Smith's History* (Salt Lake City: ULM, 1965), available for purchase online at http://www.utlm.org/booklist/titles/ub035_changesinjosephsmithshistory.htm; also see Jerald Tanner and Sandra Tanner, *Major Problems of Mormonism* (Salt Lake City: ULM, 1989), available for purchase online at http://utlm.org/booklist/titles/ub004_majorproblemsofmormonism.htm. The Internet versions of this entire volume is online at http://www.utlm.org/onlinebooks/changecontents.htm.

23. *HC*, vol. 5, 85, 393–394, 398.

24. *The Wasp*, August 13, 1842. The 126 words that immediately follow the quoted portion also have copied nearly verbatim into the *History of the Church* volume, as if Joseph Smith himself composed the text. For a complete citation of the text, see Tanner and Tanner, *Shadow or Reality?*, 132.

25. *HC*, vol. 5, 86–87.

26. Mormon leaders additionally claim that their official history is not only "an unusually accurate historical document," but is "the most accurate history in all the world" (John Widtsoe, *Joseph Smith-Seeker After Truth* [Salt Lake City: Deseret News Press, 1951], 297 and Joseph Fielding Smith, *Doctrines of Salvation* [Salt Lake City: Bookcraft, 1955], vol. 2, 199). Wiidtsoe further stated: "There is in them [i.e., the *HC* volumes] no attempt to 'cover up' any act of his life. . . . Mormon history and doctrine have been carefully preserved in the published records of the Church—and all has been published" (256–257). The *HC* itself asserts that "no historical or doctrinal statement has been changed" in the Joseph Smith history (*HC*, vol. 1, vi). But as the documentation provided shows, this history of the LDS church has been significantly altered over the years in an effort to: 1) conceal negative aspects of Smith's personal life; 2) delete crude language and profanity he used; and 3) cover-up doctrinal changes and false prophecies that Smith presented to his followers. Moreover, most of the history was not even written by Smith (see this chapter, endnote #22).

27. Samuel W. Taylor, *Nightfall in Nauvoo* (New York: Macmillan, 1971), 383.

28. Hugh Nibley, letter to Morris L, Reynolds, May 12, 1966. Quoted in Jerald Tanner and Sandra Tanner, *Case Against Mormonism* (Salt Lake City: ULM, 1967), vol. 1, 132, online at http://www.xmission.com/~country/reason/changes.htm. This three volume work is available for purchase online from ULM:

- Volume 1, http://www.utlm.org/booklist/titles/ub026_caseagainstmormonism vol1.htm
- Volume 2, http://www.utlm.org/booklist/titles/ub027_caseagainstmormonism vol2.htm
- Volume 3, http://www.utlm.org/booklist/titles/ub028_caseagainstmormonism vol3.htm

29. Hugh B. Brown, letter to Morris Reynolds, May 13, 1966. Reprint in Tanner and Tanner, *Major Problems of Mormonism*, 133, online at http://www.xmission.com/~country/reason/changes.htm (see endnote #22).

30. Widtsoe, 119, 122.

31. Joseph Fielding Smith, *Doctrines of Salvation* (Salt Lake City: Bookcraft, 1954), vol. 1,

170. Smith was not yet LDS president when he made this statement. He was the church historian.

32. John J. Stewart, *Joseph Smith the Mormon Prophet* (Salt Lake City: Mercury Publishing, 1966), 57.

33. Tanner and Tanner, *Major Problems of Mormonism*, 135.

34. "Ward Teachers Message," *Deseret News* (Church Section), May 26, 1945, 5. This statement subsequently appeared in the *Improvement Era*, June 1945, 354 (the official church magazine before the *Ensign*). The declaration was sent out to the church membership as the official ward teaching message and printed in two publications of the church (one being the official church publication). The message has never been rescinded in any official way.

35. Brigham Young, February 23, 1862, *JOD* (Liverpool: George Q. Cannon, 1862; lithographed reprint of original edition, 1966), vol. 9, 289.

36. Bruce McConkie, *Conference Report*, October 1984, 104.

37. Marion G. Romney, quoting LDS president Heber J. Grant, *Conference Report*, October 1960, 78. Similar statements from high-ranking Mormon leaders followed Romney in subsequent years. In 1972, Joseph Fielding Smith stated: "[T]here is one thing which we should have exceedingly clear in our minds. Neither the President of the Church, nor the First Presidency, or the united voice of the First Presidency and the Twelve will ever lead the Saints astray or send forth counsel to the world that is contrary to the mind and will of the Lord" (*Ensign*, July 1972, 88). Smith's statement was re-reprinted by the *Ensign* in an article by L. Aldin Porter (see *Ensign*, November 1994, 63). Apostle N. Eldon Tanner, in 1979, reiterated: "When the Prophet speaks the debate is over" (*Ensign*, August 1979, 2–3).

38. Boyd K. Packer, *Conference Report*, October 1992, re-printed in *Ensign*, Nov. 1992.

39. Ezra Taft Benson, "Fourteen Fundamentals In Following The Prophet," February 26, 1980, online at http://www.xmission.com/~country/authority/14_fund1.htm. Excerpts from this speech:

> "To help you pass the crucial tests which lie ahead I am going to give you today several facets of a grand key which, if you will honor, will crown you with God's glory and bring you out victorious in spite of Satan's fury. . . . Here then is the grand key: follow the prophet. And here now are fourteen fundamentals in following the prophet, the President of The Church of Jesus Christ of Latter-day Saints. . . . First: The prophet is the only man who speaks for the Lord in everything. . . . Second: The living prophet is more vital to us than the standard works [i.e., the Bible, *Book of Mormon*, *Doctrine and Covenants*, and *Pearl of Great Price*]. . . . Third: The living prophet is more important to us than a dead prophet. . . . [T]he most important prophet so far as you and I are concerned is the one living in our day and age to whom the Lord is currently revealing His will for us. Therefore, the most important reading we can do is any of the words of the prophet contained each week in the Church Section of the Deseret News, and any words of the prophet contained each month in our Church magazines. . . . Beware of those who would pit the dead prophets against the living prophets, for the living prophets always take precedence. . . . Fourth: The prophet will never lead the Church astray. . . . Sixth: The prophet does not have to say "Thus saith the Lord" to give us scripture. . . . Said Brigham Young, "I have never yet preached a sermon and sent it out to the children of men, that they may not call scripture" [*JOD*, vol. 13, 95]. . . . Ninth: The prophet can receive revelation on any matter—temporal or spiritual. . . . Fourteenth: The prophet and the presidency—the living prophet and the First Presidency—follow them and be blessed; reject them and suffer." Benson's lecture also included this remarkable anecdote: "Brother Joseph turned to Brother Brigham Young and said, 'Brother Brigham, I want you to take the stand and tell

us your views with regard to the living oracles and the written word of God.'
Brother Brigham took the stand, and he took the Bible, and laid it down; he took
the Book of Mormon, and laid it down; and he took the Book of Doctrine and
Covenants, and laid it down before him, and he said: 'There is the written word of
God to us, concerning the work of God from the beginning of the world, almost,
to our day. And now,' said he, 'when compared with the living oracles those books
are nothing to me; those books do not convey the word of God direct to us now, as
do the words of a Prophet or a man bearing the Holy Priesthood in our day and
generation. I would rather have the living oracles than all the writing in the
books.' That was the course he pursued. When he was through, Brother Joseph
said to the congregation: 'Brother Brigham has told you the word of the Lord, and
he has told you the truth'" [see *Conference Report*, October 1897, 18–19]. For an in-
depth analysis of the lecture, see http://www.utlm.org/onlinebooks/following
thebrethren.htm.

40. An excellent, scholarly paper addressing the issue of intellectual stifling within Mormonism was prepared by Jason J. Baker, "Who is the Representative Mormon Intellectual? Assessing Mormon Apologetics," online at http://www.orthodoxstudies.org/cults/
ldspaper.htm. This paper was given at the Annual Meeting of the Southwest Region of
the Evangelical Theological Society, New Orleans, LA, March 26, 1999.

41. *Larry King Live*, September 8, 1998, transcript online at http://www.lds-
mormon.com/lkl_00.shtml.

42. Steven Benson, *60 Minutes*, April 7, 1996, transcript online at http://www.lds-
mormon.com/60min.shtml.

43. For an in-depth treatment of the expulsion of prominent Mormon intellectuals from the
church, see Jerald Tanner and Sandra Tanner, *The Mormon Purge* (Salt Lake City: ULM,
1993), 1, available for purchase online at http://www.utlm.org/booklist/titles
/ub044_mormonpurge.htm.

44. Jerald Tanner and Sandra Tanner, "Mormon Inquisition?: LDS Leaders Move to Repress
Rebellion," *Salt Lake City Messenger* (#85), November 1993, online at http://
www.utlm.org/newsletters/no85.htm.

45. Tanner and Tanner, "Mormon Inquisition?," http://www.utlm.org/newsletters/no85.
htm.

46. Lavina Fielding Anderson, "The LDS Intellectual Community and Church Leadership: A
Contemporary Chronology," *Dialogue: A Journal of Mormon Thought* (Spring 1993), vol. 26.

47. It remains unclear as to exactly why Gileadi's book—*The Last Days: Types and Shadows
from the Bible and the Book of Mormon*— caused his excommunication. The volume
actually was vetted and issued by the LDS church-owned Deseret Book Company. Journalist Richard Ostling has theorized that the decision was made by church leaders, who
did not want millennial/doomsday expectations to be accentuated now that Mormons
have been able to distance themselves from their public image as a group of end-time
hopefuls. Gileadi gained rebaptism and renewed full membership in 1996.

48. Toscano had for many years been a church leadership critic, but the final straw was a
Sunstone Symposium lecture he delivered—"All Is Not Well in Zion: False Teachings of
the True Church" (1993)—about the church's General Authorities.

49. In addition to Hanks' public statements in support of a more feminist approach to LDS
theology, she edited *Women and Authority: Re-emerging Mormon Feminism* (Salt Lake
City: Signature Books, 1992).

50. D. Michael Quinn, "On Being a Mormon Historian (and Its Aftermath)," in George D.
Smith, ed., *Faithful History: Essays On Writing Mormon History* (Salt Lake City: Signature Books, 1992), 76 (footnote #22 in Quinn). The LDS church's attitude toward history
was perhaps best communicated by Apostle Boyd K. Packer in a 1981 speech ("The Mantle Is Far, Far Greater Than the Intellect") he delivered to the Fifth Annual Church Edu-
cational System Religious Educators' Symposium, on August, 22, 1981: "There is a temp-

tation for the writer or the teacher of Church history to want to tell everything, whether it is worthy or faith promoting or not. Some things that are true are not very useful. Historians seem to take great pride in publishing something new, particularly if it illustrates a weakness or mistake of a prominent historical figure. . . . The writer or the teacher who has an exaggerated loyalty to the theory that everything must be told is laying a foundation for his own judgment. . . . That historian or scholar who delights in pointing out the weaknesses and frailties of present or past leaders destroys faith. A destroyer of faith . . . places himself in great spiritual jeopardy. He is serving the wrong master, and unless he repents, he will not be among the faithful in the eternities. . . . In the Church we are not neutral. We are one-sided. There is a war going on and we are engaged in it" (Boyd K. Packer, *Let Not Your Heart Be Troubled* [Salt Lake City: Bookcraft, 1991], 106).

51. Boyd. K. Packer. Quoted in *Salt Lake Tribune*, September 20, 1993 (see Tanner and Tanner, "Mormon Inquisition?" [http://www.utlm.org/newsletters/no85.htm]).

52. *Private Eye Weekly*, Oct. 20, 1993. Quoted in Tanner and Tanner, "Mormon Inquisition?," 9, online at http://www.utlm.org/newsletters/no85.htm.

53. See Bryan Waterman and Brian Kagel, *The Lord's University: Freedom and Authority at BYU* (Salt Lake City: Signature Books, 1998).

54. Quoted in Tanner and Tanner, "Mormon Inquisition? ," 6, http://www.utlm.org/newsletters/no85.htm.

55. Quoted in Tanner and Tanner, "Mormon Inquisition? ," 6, http://www.utlm.org/newsletters/no85.htm.

56. Quoted in Tanner and Tanner, "Mormon Inquisition?," 6, http://www.utlm.org/newsletters/no85.htm.

57. David P. Wright, "'In Plain Terms that We May Understand'": Joseph Smith's Transformation of Hebrews in Alma 12-13," in Brent Metcalfe, ed., *New Approaches to the Book of Mormon* (Salt Lake City: Signature Books, 1993), 207.

58. Gordon B. Hinckley, "Prophet Pre-eminently Grateful for Testimony," *LDS Church News*, April 8, 2000, online at http://www.desnews.com/cgi-bin/libstory_church?dn 00&0004100007.

59. Ostling and Ostling, 354. For more information on issues involving actual Mormon spy rings at BYU, the CIA, Howard Hughes, Watergate, and ties to the Mormon church, see the fascinating *Mormon Spies, Hughes, and the C.I.A.* (Salt Lake City: ULM, 1976) by Jerald Tanner and Sandra Tanner.

60. Peggy Fletcher Stack, "Feminist BYU Professor Fired, but Not Discredited," *Salt Lake Tribune*, June 8, 1996, online at http://bioag.byu.edu/botany/Rushforth/WWW/AAUP/aaupga2.htm.

61. Hardy (see this chapter, endnote #19, vol. 3, 279).

62. *Deseret News 2001–2002 Church Almanac* (Salt Lake City: Deseret News, 2000), 54–56.

63. Hinckley has on numerous occasions demonstrated his willingness to downplay, almost to the point of lying outright, any issues that might be construed as controversial. In addition to the many instances cited in this chapter, another particularly interesting exchange with Hinckley took place during an interview on December, 18 1998, with KUED Public Television Station in Salt Lake City, Utah. During the interview, conducted by KUED TV "Civic Dialogue" host Ted Capener, Hinckley was asked: "Are we living in the last days?" Hinckley's astonishing answer was "I don't know." This answer is most perplexing because as the church's "Prophet, Seer, and Revelator," one would think Hinckley would know about such an important belief. All of his predecessors and other Mormon leaders seemed to know about it. Consider the following:

- Ezra Taft Benson: "We should not be lulled away into a false security as Nephi said many would be in the last days" (*Conference Report*, September 1950).
- Harold B. Lee: "From this lineage a chosen people was to be prepared to set up the kingdom of God in these last days, and it was over this kingdom which the

> Christ was to reign when he came on earth for the second time" (*Conference Report*, October 1956).

- Joseph Fielding Smith: "Let me call your attention to this fact which you, of course, all know that we are living in the last days, the days of trouble, days of wickedness, spoken of as days of wickedness several hundred years before the coming of Christ by Nephi, as it is recorded in the twenty-seventh chapter of Second Nephi" (*Conference Report*, April 1952). "I feel to say, O our Eternal Father, pour out thy Spirit more abundantly upon these thy saints, upon this remnant of scattered Israel which has gathered to thy gospel in these last days" (*Conference Report*, October 1970).

- Spencer W. Kimball: "The Prophet Nephi looked forward to these last days and made some remarkable predictions: 'For behold, at that day shall he [Satan] rage in the hearts of the children of men, and stir them up to anger against that which is good. . . . and thus the devil cheateth their souls, and leadeth them away carefully down to hell.' (2 Nephi 28:20–21.) Then, he warns: '[W]o unto all those who tremble, and are angry because of the truth of God!'" (*Conference Report*, April 1965).

64. *Larry King Live* (http://www.lds-mormon.com/lkl_00.shtml).
65. *60 Minutes*, http://www.lds-mormon.com/60min.shtml or http://www.watchman.org/lds/hstintro.htm.
66. Larry Stammer, "Mormons May Disavow Old View On Blacks," *Los Angeles Times*, May 18, 1998, online at http://lds-mormon.com/t0000467.shtml.
67. *BOM*, 2 Nephi 30:6 (pre–1981 edition).
68. *BOM*, 2 Nephi 5:21, which reads: "[T]hey had hardened their hearts against him, that they had become like unto a flint; wherefore, as they were white, and exceedingly fair and delightsome, that they might not be enticing unto my people the Lord God did cause a skin of blackness to come upon them."
69. Brigham Young, October 8, 1859, *JOD* (Liverpool: Amasa Lyman, 1860; lithographed reprint of original edition, 1966), vol. 7, 336.
70. Kimball, *Improvement Era*, December 1960, 922–923. Quoted in Bill McKeever and Eric Johnson, "Pure and Delightsome," *Mormonism Researched*, Spring 1994, 5.
71. Kimball. Quoted in McKeever and Johnson, 5.
72. George Edward Clark. Quoted in McKeever and Johnson, 5.
73. An incredibly detailed and fascinating account of the Mark Hofmann tragedy is Jerald Tanner's *Tracking the White Salamander* (Salt Lake City: ULM, 1987), online at http://www.utlm.org/onlinebooks/trackingcontents.htm.
74. Ostling and Ostling, 252.
75. Jerald Tanner and Sandra Tanner, "Hofmann Talks," *Salt Lake City Messenger* (#64), January 1987, 7, online at http://www.utlm.org/newsletters/no64.htm.
76. Jim Bell. Quoted in Robert Lindsey, *A Gathering of Saints* (New York: Simon & Schuster, 1988), 236. A good review of this book is online at http://www.irr.org/mit/GATHERING.HTML.
77. Jerald Tanner and Sandra Tanner, Mormon Leaders Suppress "Key" Item in Murder Case," *Salt Lake City Messenger* (#83), November 1992, 3–4, online at http://www.utlm.org/newsletters/no83.htm.
78. Bruce McConkie, *Mormon Doctrine* (Salt Lake City: Bookcraft, 1958; second edition, 1966), 197. McConkie was merely repeating what Mormons believe God himself said in a revelation recorded in the *D&C* 46:27.
79. The bogus revelation stated: "Verily thus Saith the Lord unto Hyram Smith if he will come strate away to Far West and inquire of his brother it shall be shown him how that he may be freed from de[b]t and obtain a grate treasure in the earth even so Amen" (misspellings in original).
80. According to Hofmann, Hinckley said that the Stowell letter, for an indefinite period of

time, would be revealed only to select high-ranking LDS officials (e.g., the First Presidency and the Quorum of the Twelve). The church acquired the letter in 1983, but did not reveal it to the public until 1985, and then only after Hofmann had leaked information about the letter to various persons. A *Salt Lake Tribune* article also was published about the letter, which practically forced the church to make its existence known (see http://www.utlm.org/newsletters/no64.htm). The following material is taken from "Hoffman Talks!" by Jerald and Sandra Tanner (p. 13):

> *"Time* magazine for May 20, 1985, reported that 'The church offered no explanation for withholding news of the earliest extant document written by Smith, . . . 'John Dart commented: 'As it became clear during this week that photocopies of the letter would soon be circulated by sources outside the official church, Cahill announced that the church would discuss the contents and release a photocopy of the letter.' (*Los Angeles Times*, May 11, 1985) It seems obvious that if the letter had upheld the image of Joseph Smith that church leaders wish to portray to the public, it would have been published immediately in the *Deseret News* with a large headline announcing its discovery. When Mark Hofmann "discovered" Joseph Smith's mother's 1829 letter, Mormon officials proclaimed it to be 'the earliest known dated document' relating to the church, and it was hailed as a vindication of Joseph Smith's work. Since the letter to Stowell was supposed to have been written by the Prophet himself some four years earlier, we would expect it to receive even greater publicity. Instead, the Mormon leaders buried it and engaged in a cover-up. In the *Salt Lake Tribune*, Oct. 20, 1985, Dawn Tracy revealed that even top Mormon historians, including the Church Archivist, were kept in the dark concerning the purchase of the 1825 letter: 'Don Schmidt, retired LDS Church archivist, said members of the First Presidency didn't tell him or church historians about the 1825 letter. Nor did they ask him or anyone in his department to authenticate the letter.' While Apostle Oaks is correct in stating that the letter was released before the bombings, he "conveniently omitted" (to use his own words) the fact that the letter was suppressed for 28 months and was only released after the press had been furnished with a copy!"

81. Richard Robertson, *Arizona Republic*, February 16, 1991, B9. One of Paul Dunn's most stirring tales, a story about the death of his good friend Harold Brown, is found in Mr. Dunn's tape-recorded message, "World War II Experiences." Dunn claimed that on the night of May 11, 1945, Brown, who was "50 to 75 yards" away, was wounded by a shell which landed in his foxhole: "Well, it commenced to get daylight about 5:30 . . . I scampered over to the hole where he was, and it had almost filled up from the rain and. . . it's all he could do to hold his head out of the water to stay alive. . . . Well, I pulled him out of that muddy hole and got him up on seemingly dry ground, and took off his helmet, loosened the bandoleers around his neck . . . to give him what comfort you can under those conditions and I took a clean canteen of water and washed his face. It was caked with mud and blood. How in the world he lived that night I don't know. I counted, after his death, 67 shrapnel wounds in him, some large enough to where you could put your whole hand in. And yet, somehow, he had held on, but I found out why. As he lay there, his head limp back in my lap, he said, 'Paul, I know this is the end,' and I'd say, 'Harold, it isn't. Just hold on. I'll get you out of this.' 'No, this is the end.' . . . He said, 'I've held on as long as I could, cause I want you to do two things for me if, you would.' Why, I says, you just name it. It'll be done.' He said, 'If you ever live through this terrible ordeal, will you somehow get word to my mother. . . . Will you assure her that I was faithful to the end in the principles she taught me. . . . Will you do it, Paul?' Gosh, would I do it! How thrilled I am to report to you that the very day I got back in this country, before going to my own home, I took a plane back to Missouri and reported to that dedicated family. . . . And he said . . . 'If you ever have an opportunity . . . to talk to the young people of America, will you tell them for me that it's a privilege to lay down my life for

them.' Now, with that testimony on his lips, he died, as did thousands like him in order that we could come and be like we are tonight. And do you know what we placed over the 77th division cemetery on Okinawa . . . This is the inscription we put for the Harold Brown's and the thousands like him: 'We Gave Our . . . Todays In Order That You Might Have Your Tomorrows.' And he did" (Paul H. Dunn, "World War II Experience").

82. Robertson, B9. In the Mormon church's *New Era*, August 1975, page 7, Dunn related some of his experiences, such as the following: "[T]here were 1,000 of us in my combat team who left San Francisco on that fateful journey, and there were six of us who came back 2 1/2 years later. How do you like that for odds! And of the six of us, five had been severely wounded two or more times and had been sent back into the line as replacements. There had been literally thousands of incidents where I should have been taken from the earth by the enemy and for some reason was not." Dunn went on to say that on one occasion his squad was caught behind enemy lines and were forced to flee through enemy fire. His companions asked him to "lead them in prayer" before they made their attempt to escape. The following appears on page 8 of the *New Era* article:

> [T]he zero minute came, and we shook hands, and you never saw 11 men scamper like that before. . . . Three or four of the others didn't get above the surface of the ground; they were cut down with machine guns. One of my good friends was almost cut in two with a burst. . . . I could tell I had a sniper with a machine gun right on me because the dirt and the mud behind me would just kick right up, move right around me and then I'd move this way and then he'd pick me up again and move back. I was going with all I had. By then it was everybody for himself, and as I scampered within 50 yards of our hole, the sniper got a direct beam on me, and the first burst caught me in the right heel. It took my combat boot right off, just made me barefooted that quick without touching me physically, and it spun me around, and I went down on my knee. As I went down another machine gun burst came across my back and ripped the belt and the canteen and the ammunition pouch right off my back without touching me. As I got up to run, another burst hit me right in the back of the helmet, and it hit in the steel part, ricocheted enough to where it came up over my head, and spilt the helmet in two, but it didn't touch me. Then I lunged forward again, and another burst caught me in the loose part of the shoulders where I could take off both my shirt sleeves without removing my coat, and then one more lunge and I fell over the line . . . I was the only one of the 11 who had even made it the first 100 yards . . . . A thousand such incidents happened to me in two years of combat experience."

83. In his tape, "World War II Experiences," Dunn boasted: "I used to play with [the] Saint Louis Cardinals. That's true." In his book, *You and Your World*, page 128, he declared: "I used to play baseball with the St. Louis Cardinals. Now, it takes a lot of preparation to become a big league ballplayer." In 1973, the church's Deseret Book Company published Paul Dunn's *Discovering the Quality of Success*. On page 33 Dunn wrote that he went back to school "after five years of professional baseball." The Deseret News *1977 Church Almanac* likewise says Dunn "played professional baseball for four years" (p. 74).

84. Jerald Tanner and Sandra Tanner, "Dunn in the Name of God," *Salt Lake City Messenger* (#78), June 1991, online at http://www.utlm.org/newsletters/no78.htm.

85. Robertson, B9.

86. Dunn's belief that "the end justifies the means," of course, falls far short of the biblical standard. Colossians 3:9 admonishes: "Lie not one to another, seeing that ye have put off the old man with his deeds;" and James 3:14 affirms that we should "lie not against the truth."

87. Robertson, B9.

88. Vern Anderson, "Pursuit of Dunn Story Proves Costly for Veteran Journalist," *Salt Lake Tribune*, February 21, 1991, B3.

89. Anderson, B3.
90. Anderson, B3.
91. Robertson, B9.
92. Quoted in Tanner and Tanner, "Dunn in the Name" (http://www.utlm.org/newsletters/no78.htm).
93. "Official Apologizes for Embellishing Stories," *Washington Times*, October 28, 1991, online at washingtontimes.com.
94. "Popular LDS Speaker Admits Telling Tales About War, Baseball," *Salt Lake Tribune*, February 16, 1991, 2B.
95. Merrill Osmond, "In Memory of Paul Dunn," online at http://www.osmond.com/merrill/merrill-inmemory.html.
96. Robertson, B6: Baseball records also show that Dunn signed a professional player contract in 1947 with the Ontario Orioles, in California's 'Class C' Sunset League. "But he practiced only a few weeks, played only in the first regular game and then was released."
97. Lisa Carricaburu, "LDS Church See Olympics As PR Dream," *Salt Lake Tribune*, August 23, 1997, online at http://www.sltrib.com (archives).
98. Carricaburu, http://www.sltrib.com (archives).
99. Carricaburu, http://www.sltrib.com (archives).
100. Carricaburu, http://www.sltrib.com (archives).
101. Peggy Fletcher Stack, "LDS Visitor-Center Upgrades To Stress International Flavor," *Salt Lake Tribune*, January 13, 2001, online at http://www.sltrib.com (archives).
102. Stack, http://www.sltrib.com (archives).
103. When the Olympic scandal broke, Mormons became the target of comedians around the globe. Jay Leno said: "The rumor is, the Bulls were going to pay Michael Jordan $37.5 million this year. Where else in sports can you make that kind of money? Other than being an Olympic official in Salt Lake?" The Olympic Games, usually wrapped in language of sports heroics and community and national pride, have suddenly become a subject of mirth. During another "Tonight Show," Leno jokingly suggested a new promotional slogan for the state should be "Seven Bribes for Seven Brothers." Then, on a third night, he staged a parody of a familiar credit card advertisement: "On the screen flashed images of skiers, the Olympic flame, suit-and-tie types and a flush of credit cards, backed by the Games' familiar fanfare: 'Salt Lake City, Utah, where the world's greatest athletes will test their skill at the 2002 Winter Olympics,' boomed the announcer, Edd Hall. 'But if you plan on catching Olympic fever, don't bring your Visa, American Express or Discover card, because the International Olympic Committee accepts only cash—lots and lots of cash. Bribe money. It's everywhere you want to be." Leno was not alone in lampooning Salt Lake City. Randy Youngman of the Orange County Register wrote: "The Wall Street Journal says the mascot for the 2002 Winter Games in Salt Lake City will be 'Tickle-My-Palm Elmo.'" Salt Lake radio station KKAT came up with an "unofficial bribery mascot" of its own—a man slathered with shaving cream upon which dollar bills were stuck. "Then we had him right in front of SLOC headquarters," said Jon Cloward, the station's promotions director. Editorial cartoonists also had a heyday. Clay Bennett (*Christian Science Monitor*) turned the fifth of the Olympics' interlocked rings into a dollar sign, while Kevin Siers of the Charlotte Observer put a gigantic diamond on the same ring, along with the inscription, "Bribes." In one cartoon, an Olympic torchbearer turned toward a path littered with cash; in another, a stogie-smoking back-roomer passed a bundle of bucks to another man instead of the Olympic torch; and in a third comic strip, a maitre d' objected to a restaurant customer waving a financial inducement, saying, "Sir! This is not the Olympics." (This material paraphrased with many direct quotations from "Comedians Laugh Up Salt Lake's Troubles," *Salt Lake Tribune*, January 18, 1999, online at http://www.nonmormon.com/newsstatic/comediansOlympic.htm)
104. "The Scandal: A 5-Year Chronology," *Salt Lake Tribune*, July 21, 2000, online at http://www.sltrib.com (archives).

105. "The Scandal," http://www.sltrib.com (archives).

106. These and other issues are covered in numerous *Salt Lake Tribune* articles located online at http://utlm.org/onlineresources/sltribarticles/sltribarticles_olympicsandlds.htm.

107. Hatch, however, claimed that he was unaware of the help and that his office did nothing out of the ordinary (see Jim Woolf, "Hatch Denies Trying to Interfere in Bribe Case," *Salt Lake Tribune*, August 16, 2001), online at http://www.sltrib.com (archives)

108. "Delay Sought in Olympic Bribery Trial," August 31, 2000, CNN online at http://sports illustrated.cnn.com/wintersports/news/2000/08/31/saltlake_delay_ap/.

109. Linda Fantin, "Olympic Dismissals May Be Appealed," *Salt Lake Tribune*, August 14, 2001, online at http://www.sltrib.com (archives).

110. "Delay Sought" (http://sportsillustrated.cnn.com/wintersports/news/2000/08/31/saltlake_delay_ap/).

111. Lynne Cropper. Quoted in "Media-Savvy Mormons Welcome Olympics," March 10, 2001, *The Daily Camera*, online at http://www.bouldernews.com/livingarts/religion/10pmorm.html.

112. Gary Shepherd. Quoted in "Media-Savvy," http://www.bouldernews.com/livingarts/religion/10pmorm.html.

113. Mark Crispin. Quoted in Susan Greene, "Games Being Used As Pulpit?," *Denver Post*, July 1, 2001, online at http://www.denverpost.com/Stories/0,1002,118%257E55341,00.html.

114. Jan Shipps. Quoted in Greene (http://www.denverpost.com/Stories/0,1002,118%257E55341,00.html).

115. Mitt Romney. Quoted in Greene (http://www.denverpost.com/Stories/0,1002,118%257E55341,00.html).

116. Greene (http://www.denverpost.com/Stories/0,1002,118%257E55341,00.html).

117. Joseph F. Smith, *Conference Report*, October 1912, 11.

118. Melvin J. Ballard, *Conference Report*, October 1928, 108. In 1933, Ballard also stated: "I believe that it is the destiny of the Latter-day Saints to support the Constitution of the United States. The Prophet Joseph Smith is alleged to have said—and I believe he did say it—that the day would come when the Constitution would hang as by a thread. But he saw that the thread did not break, thank the Lord, and that the Latter-day Saints would become a balance of power, with others, to preserve that Constitution. If there is—and there is one part of the Constitution hanging as by a thread today—where do the Latter-day Saints belong? Their place is to rally to the support of that Constitution, and maintain it and defend it and support it by their lives and by their vote. Let us not disappoint God nor his prophet. Our place is fixed (*Conference Report*, April 1933, 127).

119. Mark E. Petersen, *Conference Report*, April 1946, 171.

120. Joseph Fielding Smith, *Conference Report*, April 1950, p. 159

121. Harold B. Lee, *Conference Report*, October 1952, p. 18

122. Senator Wallace F. Bennett, *BYU Speeches*, February 15, 1961, 13.

123. Dr. Ernest L. Wilkinson, *BYU Speeches*, April 21, 1966, 7.

124. Ezra Taft Benson, "Jesus Christ-Gifts and Expectations, "*New Era*, May 1975, 19.

125. Ezra Taft Benson, *Teachings of Ezra Taft Benson* (Salt Lake City: Bookcraft, 1988), 619. Benson quoted the White Horse prophecy in numerous lectures and publications (see Introduction, endnote #18). Many examples are online at http://www.utlm.org/online resources/whitehorseprophecy.htm.

126. Daniel H. Ludlow, ed., *Selections from Encyclopedia of Mormonism* (Salt Lake City: Deseret Book Company, 1995), "The Church and Society," 122.

127. "Weatherman's politics cloud his role on TV," *Seattle Times*, November 24, 2000, 2, online at http://archives.seattletimes.nwsource.com:80/cgi–bin/texis/web/vortex/display?slug=thom25m&date=20001124, also online at *Mormon News*, http://www.mormonstoday.com/001124/P2TSpencer01.shtml.

APPENDIX C: ABRAHAM'S BOOK?

1. All quotations taken from F.S. Spalding, *Joseph Smith, Jr., As A Translator* (1912), 23, 24, 26-27, 29. Quoted in Jerald Tanner and Sandra Tanner, *Mormonism: Shadow or Reality?* (Salt Lake City: ULM, 1987), 299–300.

2. For more in-depth information on the problematic nature of Smith's *Book of Abraham*, see: Charles M. Larson, *By His Own Hand Upon Papyrus: A New Look At the Joseph Smith Papyri* (Grand Rapids: Institute for Religious Research, 1985; revised 1992 edition); H. Michael Marquardt, *The Book of Abraham Papyrus Found* (Salt Lake City: ULM, 1981); H. Michael Marquardt, *The Book of Abraham Revisited* (Salt Lake City: ULM, 1983); Jerald Tanner and Sandra Tanner, *Joseph Smith's Egyptian Alphabet & Grammar* (Salt Lake City: ULM, 1966); Jerald Tanner and Sandra Tanner, *Flaws in the Pearl of Great Price* (Salt Lake City: ULM, 1991); David Persuitte, *Joseph Smith and the Origins of the Book of Mormon* (Jefferson, NC: McFarland & Co., 2000) All of these books are available from Utah Lighthouse Mission and can be ordered online at http://www.utlm.org/booklist/ordergroup.htm#Historical%20Issues.

3. Tanner and Tanner, *Shadow or Reality?*, 369.

APPENDIX D: FAILED JOSEPH SMITH PROPHECIES

1. Hyrum Smith. Quoted by Abraham O. Smoot, 1868, Provo School of the Prophets (see D. Michael Quinn, *The Mormon Hierarchy: Origins of Power* [Salt Lake City: Signature Books, 1994], 639.

2. *PGP*, Joseph Smith—History 1:40

3. B.H. Roberts, *CHC* (Salt Lake City: Deseret News Press, 1930), vol. 1, 165; cf. David Whitmer, *An Address to All Believers in Christ* (Richmond, MO: author, 1887), 30–31.

4. *D&C* 29:8.

5. *D&C* 29:9–11.

6. *D&C* 45:64–74.

7. *D&C* 57:1–5.

8. *D&C* 84:2–5 (cf. v. 31).

9. *D&C* 84:114–115.

10. *HC* (Salt Lake City: Deseret Book Company, 1976/1980), vol. 1, 315–316.

11. *D&C* 97:18–20.

12. *HC*, vol. 1, 455.

13. Reed Peck, *Reed Peck Manuscript*, 3, online at http://www.connect-a.net/users/drshades/reedpeck.htm.

14. *D&C* 104:1, 2–6.

15. *D&C* 105:13–15.

16. *HC*, vol. 2, 145.

17. *HC*, vol. 2, 182

18. Nephi Lowell Morris, *Prophecies of Joseph Smith and their Fulfillment* (Salt Lake City: Deseret Books, 1926), 261.

19. *D&C* 111:4.

20. *D&C* 112:3–4, 7–8, 11.

21. *D&C* 114:1.

22. *D&C* 121:11–15

23. Quinn, 634.

24. Joseph Smith, *Manuscript Diary*, under January 20, 1843, in Scott H. Faulring, ed., *An American Prophet's Record: The Diaries and Journals of Joseph Smith* (Salt Lake City: Signature Books,1987), 294.

25. *HC*, vol. 5, 336.

26. *HC*, vol. 5, 336.

27. *HC*, vol. 5, 336.

28. *HC*, vol. 5, 394.

29. Joseph Smith, *MS*, vol. 22, 455; cf. Faulring, under December 16, 1843, 432. Mormons have attempted to excuse this false prophecy by stating that: "This prediction doubtless has reference to the party in power; to the 'government' considered as the administration;" (see footnote in *HC*, vol. 6, 116). In other words, according to this footnote in *HC*, Smith was referring to the Democratic Party, which was in control at the time. But the prediction says "*Congress* shall be broken up as a government" and Congress is made up of representatives from both parties. Moreover, the Latter-day Saints in Smith's day were making an appeal to the U.S. government in general, not just the Democratic Party—a fact confirmed by the summary statement in the left margin beside this prophecy, as recorded in the *HC* ("Comment on Appeal to the General Government for Protection").

30. Joseph Smith, *Manuscript Diary*, February 6, 1844, omitted from the *HC*. Cited in Quinn, 642; cf. Faulring, 445.

31. Quinn, 644.

Select Bibliography

Abanes, Richard. *American Militias: Rebellion, Racism, and Religio*n. Downers Grove: InterVarsity Press, 1996.

_____ . *Cults, New Religious Movements and Your Family*. Wheaton, IL: Crossway, 1998.

_____ . *End Time Visions: The Road to Armageddon?* New York: Four Walls Eight Windows, 1998; paperback edition, 1999, published as *End-Time Visions: The Doomsday Obsession*. Nashville: Broadman & Holman, 1999.

Alexander, Thomas G. *Mormonism in Transition: A History of the Latter-day Saints, 1890-1930*. Urbana and Chicago: University of Illinois Press, 1986.

_____ . *Things in Heaven and Earth: The Life and Times of Wilford Woodruff, A Mormon Prophet*. Salt Lake City: Signature Books, 1991.

Allen, James B. *Trials of Discipleship: The Story of William Clayton, A Mormon*. Urbana: University of Illinois Press, 1987.

Allen, James B., and Glen M. Leonard. *The Story of the Latter-day Saint*s. Salt Lake City: Deseret Book Co., 1976.

Anderson, Nels. *Desert Saints: The Mormon Frontier in Utah*. Chicago: University of Chicago Press, 1942; paperback edition, 1966.

Anderson, Robert D. *Inside the Mind of Joseph Smith: Psychobiography and the Book of Mormon*. Salt Lake City: Signature Books, 1999.

Anderson, Rodger I. *Joseph Smith's New York Reputation Reexamined*. Salt Lake City: Signature Books, 1990.

Arrington, Leonard J. and David Bitton, *The Mormon Experience*. Champaign, IL: University of Illinois Press, 1992.

Arrington, Leonard J. *Brigham Young: American Moses*. New York: Alfred A. Knopf, 1985.

_____ . *Adventures of a Church Historian*. Urbana: University of Illinois Press, 1998.

Bancroft, Hubert Howe. *History of Utah. 1540-1887*. San Francisco: The History Company Publishers, 1890.

Benson, Ezra Taft. *Teachings of Ezra Taft Benson*. Salt Lake City: Bookcraft, 1988.

Berrett, William Edwin. *The Restored Church*. Salt Lake City: Deseret Book Company, 1949.

Bigler, David L. *Forgotten Kingdom: The Mormon Theocracy in the American West, 1847-1896*. Logan, Utah: Utah State University Press, 1998.

Bitton, Davis and Leonard J. Arrington, *Mormons and Their Historians*. Salt Lake City: University of Utah Press, 1988.

Blackman, Jr., Milton V. *Joseph Smith's First Vision*. Salt Lake City: Bookcraft, 1971; second edition, 1980.

Blomberg, Craig L., and Stephen E. Robinson. *How Wide the Divide?: A Mormon and An Evangelical In Conversation*. Downers Grove: InterVarsity Press, 1997.

Brodie, Fawn M. *No Man Knows My History: The Life of Joseph Smith, the Mormon Prophet*. New York: Vintage Books, 1995; original edition by Alfred A. Knopf, 1945.

Bromiley, G.W., ed. *The International Standard Bible Encyclopedia*. 4 vols. Grand Rapids: Eerdmans, 1979.

Brooke, John L. *The Refiner's Fire: The Making of Mormon Cosmology, 1644-1844*. New York: Cambridge University Press, 1994; paperback edition, 1996.

Brooks, Juanita. *The Mountain Meadows Massacre*. Norman, OK: University of Oklahoma Press, 1962, 1970.

Buerger, David John. *The Mysteries of Godliness: A History of Mormon Temple Worship*. San Francisco: Smith Research Associates, 1994.

Bush, Lester E., Jr., and Armand L. Mauss, eds. *Neither White nor Black: Mormon Scholars Confront the Race Issue in a Universal Church*. Midvale, Utah: Signature Books, 1984.

Bushman, Richard L. *Joseph Smith and the Beginnings of Mormonism*. Urbana: University of Illinois Press, 1984.

Campbell, Eugene E. *Establishing Zion: The Mormon Church in the American West, 1847-1869*. Salt Lake City: Signature Books, 1988.

Cannon, Frank J. and Harvey J. O'Higgins. *Under the Prophet in Utah; the National Menace of a Political Priestcraft*. Boston: The C. M. Clark Publishing Co., 1911.

Chamberlain, Solomon. *A Short Sketch of the Life of Solomon Chamberlain*. [n.p. n.d.]

Chandler, Russell. *Doomsday*. Ann Arbor, MI: Servant Publications, 1993.

Church of Jesus Christ of Latter-day Saints, *Family Home Evening Manual*. Salt Lake City: The Church of Jesus Christ of Latter-day Saints, 1972.

_____. *Achieving a Celestial Marriage*. Salt Lake City: The Church of Jesus Christ of Latter-day Saints, 1976.

_____. *Deseret News 1974 Church Almanac*. Salt Lake City: Deseret News, 1974.

_____. *Deseret News 2001-2002 Church Almanac* (Salt Lake City: Deseret News, 2000.

Compton, Todd. *In Sacred Loneliness: The Plural Wives of Joseph Smith*. Salt Lake City: Signature Books, 1997.

Conkling, Christopher. *A Joseph Smith Chronology*. Salt Lake City: Deseret Books, 1979.

Corrill, John. *A Brief History of the Church of Jesus Christ of Latter Day Saints*. St. Louis: author, 1839.

Cowen, Marvin. *Mormon Claims Answered*. Salt Lake City: Utah Christian Publications. 1997.

Crawley, Peter L. *The Essential Parley P. Pratt*. Salt Lake City: Signature Books, 1990.

Crowther, Duane S. *Prophetic Warnings to Modern America*. Bountiful, UT: Horizon Publishers, 1977; second edition, 1979.

Davidson, James West. *The Logic of Millennial Thought: Eighteenth-Century New England*. New Haven, CT: Yale University Press, 1977.

Douglas, J.D. rev. ed., and Merrill C. Tenney, gen. ed., *The New International Dictionary of the Bible*. Grand Rapids: Zondervan Publishing House, 1987.

Durham, Reed C., Jr. *Is There No Help for the Widow's Son?* Nauvoo, Ill.: Martin Publishing, 1980.

Ehat, Andrew F., and Lyndon W. Cook. *The Words of Joseph Smith*. Orem, Utah: Grandin Book Co., 1993.

Elwell, Walter A., ed. *Baker Encyclopedia of the Bible*. 2 vols. Grand Rapids: Baker Book House, 1988; 1995 edition.

_____ . *Evangelical Dictionary of Theology*. Grand Rapids: Baker, 1984.

Embry, Jesse. *Mormon Polygamous Families: Life in the Principle*. Salt Lake City: University of Utah Press, 1987.

Enroth, Ronald. *Churches That Abuse*. Grand Rapids: Zondervan, 1992.

Erickson, Dan. *As A Thief in the Night*. Salt Lake City: Signature Books, 1998.

Faulring, Scott H. ed., *An American Prophet's Record: The Diaries and Journals of Joseph Smith*. Salt Lake City: Signature Books,1987.

Firmage, Edwin B., and Richard Collin Mangrum. *Zion in the Courts: A Legal History of the Church of Jesus Christ of Latter-day Saints, 1830-1900*. Urbana: University of Illinois Press, 1988.

Flanders, Robert. *Nauvoo: Kingdom on the Mississippi*. Urbana: University of Illinois Press, 1965.

Geer, Thelma. *Mormonism, Mama & Me*. Chicago: Moody, 1986.

Gomes, Alan W. *Unmasking the Cults*. Grand Rapids: Zondervan, 1995.

Gottlieb, Robert and Peter Wiley. *American Saints: The Rise of Mormon Power*. New York: G.P. Putnam's Sons, 1984.

Gregg, Thomas. *The Prophet of Palmyra*. New York: John B. Aldeen, 1890.

Gunnison, John W. *The Mormons or the Latter-day Saints, in the Valley of the Great Salt Lake*. London: Sampson, Low, Son, & Co., 1852.

Hallwas, John E. and Roger D. Launius. *Cultures in Conflict: A Documentary History of the Mormon War in Illinois*. Logan, UT: Utah State University Press, 1995.

Hanks, Maxine, ed. *Women and Authority: Re-emerging Mormon Feminism*. Salt Lake City: Signature Books, 1992.

Hansen, Klaus J. *Mormonism and the American Experience*. Chicago: University of Chicago Press, 1981.

_____ . *Quest for Empire: The Political Kingdom of God and the Council of Fifty in Mormon History*. East Lansing, MI: Michigan State University Press, 1967.

Hardy, B. Carmon. *Solemn Covenant: The Mormon Polygamous Passage*. Urbana: University of Illinois Press, 1992.

Heinerman, John and Anson Shupe. *The Mormon Corporate Empire*. Boston: Beacon Press, 1985.

Hickman, Bill. *Brigham's Destroying Angel: Being the Life, Confession, and Startling Disclosures of the Notorious Bill Hickman*. Salt Lake City: Shepard Publishing Company, 1904; lithographed reprint of original edition, 1964.

Hill, Donna. *Joseph Smith: The First Mormon*. Midvale, UT: Signature Books, 1977.

Hill, Marvin S. *Quest for Refuge: The Mormon Flight from American Pluralism*. Salt Lake City: Signature Books, 1989.

Hilton, Hope A. *"Wild Bill" Hickman and the Mormon Frontier*. Salt Lake City: Signature Books, 1988.

Hine, Edward. *Forty-Seven Identifications of the British Nation*. London: S.W. Partridge & Co., 1871.

Hirshon, Stanley P. *The Lion of the Lord: A Biography of the Mormon Leader, Brigham Young*. New York: Alfred A. Knopf, Publisher, 1969.

Howe, E.D. *Mormonism Unvailed*. Painesville, OH: E.D. Howe, 1834.

Hunter, Milton R. *The Gospel through the Ages*. Salt Lake City: Stevens and Wallis, 1945.

Hyde, Orson. *Speech of Orson Hyde, Delivered Before the High Priests' Quorum, in Nauvoo, April 27th, 1845, Upon the Course and Conduct of Mr. Sidney Rigdon.* Liverpool: James and Woodburn, 1845.

Jarman, William. *USA—Uncle Sam's Abscess or Hell Upon Earth for U.S.* Exeter, England: H. Leduc's Steam Printing Works, 1884.

Jenson, Andrew. *Church Chronology*. Salt Lake City: Deseret News, 1899.

_____. *Historical Record*. 9 vols. Salt Lake City: Andrew Jenson, 1886-1890; bound volumes, only vols. 5-9 in English.

Jessee, Dean C., ed. *The Papers of Joseph Smith*. 2 vols. Salt Lake City: Deseret Book Company, 1989/1992.

Journal of Discourses. Liverpool: Miscellaneous, 1855-1886.

Keil, C.F. and F. Delitzsch. *Commentary on the Old Testament*. Peabody, MA: Hendrickson Publishers, 1996 edition.

Kenney, Scott G., ed. *Wilford Woodruff's Journal: 1833-1898*. 9 volumes. Midvale, UT: Signature Books, 1983.

Kimball, Stanley B. *Heber C. Kimball: Mormon Patriarch and Pioneer*. Urbana: University of Illinois Press, 1981.

Kirkham, Francis. *A New Witness for Christ in the America*. Salt Lake City: Utah Printing Co., 1942; 1960 edition.

Laake, Deborah. *Secret Ceremonies: A Mormon Woman's Intimate Diary of Marriage and Beyond*. New York: William Morrow & Co., 1993.

Langone, Michael D. *Cults: What Parents Should Know*. New York: Carol Publishing Group, 1988.

Larson, Charles M. *By His Own Hand Upon Papyrus*. Grand Rapids: Institute for Religious Research, 1985; 1992 revised edition.

Larson, Stan. *Quest for the Gold Plates: Thomas Stuart Ferguson's Archaeological Search for The Book of Mormon*. Salt Lake City: Freethinker Press in association with Smith Research Associates, 1996.

Launius, Roger D. *Joseph Smith III. Pragmatic Prophet*. Urbana: University of Illinois Press, 1988.

Launius, Roger, Linda Thatcher, and Leonard J. Arrington, eds. *Differing Visions: Dissenters in Mormon History* (Urbana: University of Illinois Press, 1994.

Launius. Roger D. and John E. Hallwas, eds., *Kingdom on the Mississippi Revisited*. Urbana: University of Illinois Press, 1996.

Lee, John D. *A Mormon Chronicle: The Diaries of John D. Lee, 1848-1876*, Robert Glass Cleland and Juanita Brooks, eds. San Marino, CA: Arthur H. Clark, 1955.

Lee, John D. *Mormonism Unveiled; Including The Remarkable Life And Confessions Of The Late Mormon Bishop. John D. Lee*. St. Louis: N.D. Thompson and Company, 1880.

Lee, Rex E. *What Do Mormons Believe?* Salt Lake City: Deseret Book Co., 1992.

Leone, Mark P. *Roots of Modern Mormonism*. Cambridge: Harvard University Press: 1979.

LeSueur, Stephen C. *The 1838 Mormon War in Missouri*. Colombia, Mo.: University of Missouri Press, 1987.

Lewis, Gordon. *Confronting the Cults*. Grand Rapids: Baker Book House, 1975.

Linn, William A. *Story of the Mormons*. New York: The MacMillan Company, 1902.

Ludlow, Daniel H., ed. *Encyclopedia of Mormonism*. 4 vols. New York: Macmillan, 1992.

Lund, John Lewis. *The Church and the Negro: A Discussion of Mormons, Negroes and the Priesthood*. Paramount Publishers, 1967.

Lundwall, N.B., comp. *Inspired Prophetic Warnings*. Salt Lake City: author, 1940.

_____ . *Temples of the Most High*. Salt Lake City: Bookcraft, 1954.

Lyman, Edward Leo. *Political Deliverance. The Mormon Quest for Utah Statehood*. Urbana: University of Illinois Press, 1986.

Malone, Michael P., ed. *Historians and the American West*. Lincoln: University of Nebraska Press, 1983.

Marquardt, H. Michael, and Wesley P. Walters. *Inventing Mormonism: Tradition and Historical Record*. San Francisco: Smith Research Associates, 1994.

Marquardt, H. Michael. *The Joseph Smith Revelations: Text and Commentary*. Salt Lake City: Signature Books, 1999.

Martin, Paul. *Cult-Proofing Your Kids*. Grand Rapids: Zondervan, 1993.

Martin, Walter. *The Kingdom of the Cults*. Minneapolis: Bethany, 1985 edition.

_____ . *The Rise of the Cults*. Grand Rapids: Zondervan, 1955.

Mauss, Armand L. *The Angel and the Beehive: The Mormon Struggle with Assimilation*. Urbana: University of Illinois Press, 1994.

McConkie, Bruce. *Mormon Doctrine*. Salt Lake City: Bookcraft, 1958; second edition, 1966.

McDowell, Josh and Don Stewart. *Handbook of Today's Religions*. San Bernardino, CA: Here's Life Publishers, 1983.

McGavin, E. Cecil. *Mormonism and Masonry*. Salt Lake City: Bookcraft, 1956.

McKay, David O. *Gospel Ideals*. Comp. G. Homer Durham. Salt Lake City: Improvement Era, 1953.

McKeever, Bill. *Answering Mormons' Questions*. Minneapolis: Bethany, 1991.

McKeever, Bill, and Eric Johnson. *Mormonism 101*. Grand Rapids: Baker Books, 2000.

_____ . *Questions to Ask Your Mormon Friend*. Minneapolis: Bethany, 1994.

Metcalfe, Brent Lee, ed. *New Approaches to the Book of Mormon: Explorations in Critical Methodology*. Salt Lake City: Signature Books, 1993.

Morgan, William. *Illustrations of Masonry, by One of the Fraternity, Who Has Devoted Thirty Years to the Subject. With an Account of the Kidnapping of the Author*. Second Edition. New York: William Morgan, 1827.

Morris, Nephi Lowell. *Prophecies of Joseph Smith and their Fulfillment*. Salt Lake City: Deseret Books, 1926.

Newell, Linda King, and Valeen Tippetts Avery. *Mormon Enigma: Emma Hale Smith* (Urbana: University of Illinois Press, 1994).

Newton, Joseph Fort. *The Religion of Masonry: An Interpretation*. Richmond: Macoy, 1969.

Nibley, Hugh. *The Myth Makers*. Salt Lake City: Bookcraft, 1967.

O'Dea, Thomas F. *The Mormons*. Chicago: University of Chicago Press, 1957.

Persuitte, David. *Joseph Smith and the Origins of the Book of Mormon*. Jefferson, N.C.: McFarland and Co., Inc., 1991.

Petersen, LaMar. *Hearts Made Glad: The Charges of Intemperance Against Joseph Smith the Mormon Prophet*. Salt Lake City: author, 1975.

Pratt, Orson. *Divine Authenticity of the Book of Mormon. From a series of pamphlets*. Liverpool, England: n.p., 1851.

_____ . *Interesting Account of Several Remarkable Visions, and of the Late Discovery of Ancient American Record.* Edinburgh: Ballantyne and Hughes, 1840.

_____ . *The Seer.* Photo reprint of newspapers published between January 1853 through August 1854. Republished in 1990 by Eborn Books (Salt Lake City).

_____ . *A Proclamation of the Twelve Apostles of the Church of Jesus Christ of Latter-day Saints. To All the Kings for the World, to the President of the United States of America; to the Governors of the Several States, and to the Rulers and People of All Nations.* Liverpool: Wilford Woodruff, James and Woodburn, 1845.

_____ . *A Voice of Warning and Instruction to All People.* New York: W. Sanford, 1837.

_____ . *Autobiography of Parley P. Pratt,* Parley P. Pratt, Jr., ed. New York: Russell Brothers, 1874; modern reprint in Salt Lake City: Deseret Book Company, 1979.

_____ . *Key to the Science of Theology: A Voice of Warning.* Salt Lake City: Deseret Book Co., 1978.

_____ . *Mormonism Unveiled; Zion's Watchman Unmasked and its Editor, Mr. LaRoy Sunderland, Exposed: Truth Vindicated, The Devil Mad, and Priestcraft in Danger!!!* New York: Joseph W. Harrison, 1842.

Proceedings Before the Committee On Privileges and Elections of the Unites States Senate In the Matter of the Protests Against the Right of Hon. Reed Smoot, A Senator from the State of Utah, to Hold His Seat. 4 vols. Washington: Government Printing Office, 1904-1906.

Quinn, D. Michael. ed. *The New Mormon History: Revisionist Essays on the Past.* Salt Lake City: Signature Books, 1992.

Quinn, D. Michael. *Early Mormonism and the Magic World View.* Revised and enlarged edition. Salt Lake City: Signature Books, 1998.

_____ . *The Mormon Hierarchy: Extensions of Power.* Salt Lake City: Signature Books/Smith Research Associates, 1997.

_____ . *The Mormon Hierarchy: Origins of Power.* Salt Lake City: Signature Books/Smith Research Associates, 1994.

Reid, Daniel G. cord. ed., *Dictionary of Christianity in America.* Downers Grove, IL: InterVarsity Press, 1990.

Reynolds, George. *The Story of the Book of Mormon.* 3rd edition. Chicago: Henry C. Etten and Co., 1888.

Rich, Russell R. *Ensign to the Nations: A History of the LDS Church from 1846 to 1972.* Salt Lake City: Brigham Young University Publications, 1972.

Richards, Franklin D. and James A. Little. *A Compendium of the Doctrines of the Gospel.* Salt Lake City: Deseret News, 1882.

Richards, LeGrand. *A Marvelous Work and A Wonder.* Salt Lake City: Deseret Book Co., 1976.

Ricketts, Norma Baldwin. *The Mormon Battalion: U.S. Army of the West, 1846-1848.* Logan, UT: Utah State University Press, 1996.

Robert Lindsey, *A Gathering of Saints.* New York: Simon & Schuster, 1988.

Roberts, B. H., comp. *Comprehensive History of the Church of Jesus Christ of Latter-day Saints.* 6 vols. 1930.

Roberts, B.H. *New Witnesses for God.* 3 vols. Salt Lake City: Deseret News, 1909-1911, 1950 edition.

_____ . *Studies of the Book of Mormon.* Salt Lake City: Signature Books, 1992.

_____ . *The Life of John Taylor, Third President of the Church of Jesus Christ of Latter-day Saints*. Salt Lake City: G. Q. Cannon & Sons Co., 1892.

_____ . *The Rise and Fall of Nauvoo*. Salt Lake City: Deseret News, 1900.

Robertson, Irvine. *What the Cults Believe*. Chicago: Moody, 1966; 1991 reprint.

Robinson, Stephen. *Are Mormons Christian?* Salt Lake City: Bookcraft 1991.

Rostling, Richard N., and Joan K. Ostling. *Mormon America: The Power and Promise*. San Francisco: Harper San Francisco, 1999.

Rudin, James and Marcia Rudin. *Prison or Paradise: The New Religious Cults*. Philadelphia: Westminster Press, 1980.

Schindler, Harold. *Orrin Porter Rockwell, Man of God, Son of Thunder*. Salt Lake City: University of Utah Press, 1966.

Shipps, Jan. *Mormonism: The Story of a New Religious Tradition*. Urbana: University of Illinois Press, 1985.

Sillitoe, Linda, and Allen Roberts. *Salamander: The Story of the Mormon Forgery Murders*. Salt Lake City: Signature Books, 1989.

Skousen, Cleon. *The First 2,000 Years*. Salt Lake City: Bookcraft, 1979.

Smith, Ethan. *View of the Hebrews; or the Tribes of Israel in America*. Second Edition. Poultney, VT: Smith and Shute, 1825.

Smith, George D., ed. *An Intimate Chronicle: The Journals of William Clayton*. Salt Lake City: Signature Books/Smith Research Associates, 1995.

_____ . *Faithful History. Essays on Writing Mormon History*. Salt Lake City: Signature Books, 1992.

Smith, Joseph F. *Gospel Doctrine: Selections from the Sermons and Writings of Joseph F. Smith, Sixth President of the Church of Jesus Christ of Latter-day Saints*. Salt Lake City: Deseret News, 1919.

Smith, Joseph Fielding, ed. *Teachings of the Prophet Joseph Smith*. Salt Lake City: Deseret Book Co., 1938.

Smith, Joseph Fielding. *Answers to Gospel Questions*. 4 vols. Salt Lake City: Deseret Book Co., 1957-63.

_____ . *Doctrines of Salvation: Sermons and Writings of Joseph Fielding Smith*. 3 vols. Ed. Bruce R. McConkie. Salt Lake City: Bookcraft, 1954-56.

_____ . *The Way to Perfection*. Salt Lake City: Deseret Book Co., 1975.

Smith, Joseph, Jr. *Book of Commandments*. Zion: W.W. Phelps, 1833.

_____ . *History of the Church of Jesus Christ of Latter-Day Saints*. An introduction and notes by B. H. Roberts. Published by the Church. 7 Volumes. Salt Lake City: Deseret News, 1902-1912, 1932.

_____ . *The Book of Mormon*. Third Edition, Carefully Revised by the Translator. Nauvoo, IL: Robinson and Smith, 1840.

_____ . *The Book of Mormon: An Account Written by the Hand of Mormon, Upon Plates Taken from the Plates of Nephi*. Palmyra: E. B. Grandin, 1830.

Smith, Lucy Mack. *Biographical Sketches of Joseph Smith the Prophet, and his Progenitors for Many Generations*. Liverpool: Published for O. Pratt by S. W. Richards; London: Latter-day Saints Book Depot, 1853.

Sproul, R. C. *Essential Truths of the Christian Faith*. Wheaton, Ill.: Tyndale House, 1992.

Stenhouse, T.B.H. *The Rocky Mountain Saints*. Salt Lake City: Shepard Book Company, 1873; 1904 edition.

Stewart, John J. *Brigham Young and His Wives and The True Story of Plural Marriage.* Salt Lake City: Mercury Publishing Company, Inc.,1961.

_____ . *The Glory of Mormonism.* Salt Lake City: Mercury Publishing Co., Inc., 1963.

_____ . *Mormonism and the Negro.* Orem, Utah: Bookmark, 1960.

Stout, Hosea. *On the Mormon Frontier: The Diary of Hosea Stout.* 2 vols. Juanita Brooks, ed. Salt Lake City: University of Utah Press, 1964.

Talmage, James E. *Jesus the Christ.* Salt Lake City: The Deseret News, 1915.

_____ . *The Articles of Faith.* Salt Lake City: The Deseret News, 1899.

Tanner, Jerald, and Sandra Tanner. *Case Against Mormonism.* Salt Lake City: ULM, 1967.

_____ . *Changes in Joseph Smith's History.* Salt Lake City: ULM, 1965.

_____ . *Major Problems of Mormonism.* Salt Lake City: ULM, 1989.

_____ . *Mormonism, Magic and Masonry.* Salt Lake City: ULM, 1988.

_____ . *Mormon Spies, Hughes, and the C.I.A.* Salt Lake City: ULM, 1976.

_____ . *The Mormon Church and the McLellin Collection.* Salt Lake City: ULM, 1993.

_____ . *3,913 Changes in the Book of Mormon.* Salt Lake City: ULM, 1996.

_____ . *The Changing World of Mormonism.* Chicago: Moody, 1981.

_____ . *Mormonism: Shadow or Reality?* Salt Lake City: ULM, 1982.

Taves, Ernest H. *This is the Place: Brigham Young and the New Zion.* Buffalo: Prometheus Books, 1991.

Taylor, Samuel W. *Rocky Mountain Empire.* Macmillan Publishing Co., Inc., 1978.

Tucker, Pomeroy. *Origin, Rise and Progress of Mormonism.* New York: D. Appleton and Co., 1867.

Turner, Wallace. *The Mormon Establishment.* Boston: Houghton Mifflin Company, 1966.

Underwood, Grant. *The Millenarian World of Early Mormonism.* Urbana: University of Illinois Press, 1993.

Ure, James W. *Leaving the Fold: Candid Conversations with Inactive Mormons.* Salt Lake City: Signature Books, 1999.

Van Wagoner, Richard S. and Steven C. Walker. *A Book of Mormons.* Salt Lake City: Signature Books, 1982.

Van Wagoner, Richard S. *Mormon Polygamy: A History.* Salt Lake City: Signature Books, 1989.

_____ . *Sidney Rigdon: A Portrait of Religious Excess.* Salt Lake City: Signature Books, 1994.

Vetterli, Richard. *The Constitution By A Thread.* Salt Lake City: Paramount Publishers, 1967.

Vogel, Dan, ed. *Early Mormon Documents.* 3 vols. Salt Lake City: Signature Books, 1996-2000.

Vogel, Dan. *Indian Origins and the Book of Mormon: Religious Solutions from Columbus to Joseph Smith.* Salt Lake City: Signature Books, 1986.

_____ . *Religious Seekers and the Advent of Mormonism.* Salt Lake City: Signature Books, 1988.

Walters, Wesley P. *The Use of the Old Testament in the Book of Mormon.* Salt Lake City: ULM, 1990.

Waterman, Bryan, and Brian Kagel. *The Lord's University: Freedom and Authority at BYU*. Salt Lake City: Signature Books, 1998.

White, James R. *Is the Mormon My Brother?: Discerning the Differences Between Mormonism and Christianity*. Minneapolis: Bethany House Publishers, 1997.

_____ . *Letters to a Mormon Elder*. Southbridge, MA: Crowne Publication, 1990.

Whitmer, David. *An Address to All Believers in Christ*. Richmond, MO: author, 1887.

Whitney, Orson F. *Life of Heber C. Kimball, An Apostle; The Father and Founder of the British Mission*. Salt Lake City: Juvenile Instructor Office, 1888.

_____ . *The Strength of the "Mormon" Position*. Independence, MO: Zion's Printing and Publishing Co., 1917.

Widtsoe, John A., and Franklin S. Harris, Jr. *Seven Claims of The Book of Mormon: A Collection of Evidences*. Independence, MO: Zion's Printing and Publishing Co., 1937.

_____ . *Joseph Smith As Scientist*. Salt Lake City: The General Board Young Men's Mutual Improvement Associations, 1908.

_____ . *Joseph Smith-Seeker After Truth*. Salt Lake City: Bookcraft, 1951.

Wilkinson, Ernest L. and W Cleon Skousen. *Brigham Young University: A School Of Destiny*. Provo, Utah: BYU Press, 1976.

Wilson Coil, Henry. *A Comprehensive View of Freemasonry*. Richmond: Macoy, 1973.

Wilson, John. *Our Israelitish Origin*. London: James Nisbet & Co., 1840; 1843 edition.

Winn, Kenneth H. *Exiles In A Land of Liberty*. Chapel Hill: University of North Carolina Press, 1989.

Wyl, W. *Mormon Portraits*. Salt Lake City: Tribune Printing & Publishing Company, 1886.

Young, Ann Eliza. *Wife No. 19, or the Story of A Life In Bondage, Being A Complete Exposé of Mormonism, and Revealing the Sorrows, Sacrifices and Sufferings of Women in Polygamy*. Hartford, Ct: Dustin, Gilman & Co., 1875.

Index